Midwest Studies in Philosophy
Volume XIV

MIDWEST STUDIES IN PHILOSOPHY

EDITED BY PETER A. FRENCH, THEODORE E. UEHLING, JR., HOWARD K. WETTSTEIN

EDITORIAL ADVISORY BOARD
  ROBERT AUDI (UNIVERSITY OF NEBRASKA)
  JONATHAN BENNETT (SYRACUSE UNIVERSITY)
  PANAYOT BUTCHVAROV (UNIVERSITY OF IOWA)
  RODERICK CHISHOLM (BROWN UNIVERSITY)
  DONALD DAVIDSON (UNIVERSITY OF CALIFORNIA, BERKELEY)
  KEITH DONNELLAN (UNIVERSITY OF CALIFORNIA,
    LOS ANGELES)
  FRED I. DRETSKE (UNIVERSITY OF WISCONSIN, MADISON)
  GILBERT HARMAN (PRINCETON UNIVERSITY)
  MICHAEL J. LOUX (UNIVERSITY OF NOTRE DAME)
  ALASDAIR MACINTYRE (UNIVERSITY OF NOTRE DAME)
  RUTH BARCAN MARCUS (YALE UNIVERSITY)
  JOHN R. PERRY (STANFORD UNIVERSITY)
  ALVIN PLANTINGA (UNIVERSITY OF NOTRE DAME)
  DAVID ROSENTHAL (CITY UNIVERSITY OF NEW YORK
    GRADUATE CENTER)
  STEPHEN SCHIFFER (UNIVERSITY OF ARIZONA)
  MARGARET WILSON (PRINCETON UNIVERSITY)

Many papers in MIDWEST STUDIES IN PHILOSOPHY are invited and all are previously unpublished. The editors will consider unsolicited manuscripts that are received by January of the year preceding the appearance of a volume. All manuscripts must be pertinent to the topic area of the volume for which they are submitted. Address manuscripts to MIDWEST STUDIES IN PHILOSOPHY, Box 601, Notre Dame, IN 46556.

The articles in MIDWEST STUDIES IN PHILOSOPHY are indexed in THE PHILOSOPHER'S INDEX.

Forthcoming Volumes.

Volume XV 1990 Philosophy of the Human Sciences
Volume XVI 1991 Philosophy and Art

Available Previously Published Volumes

Volume III   1978 Studies in Ethical Theory
Volume IV   1979 Studies in Metaphysics
Volume V   1980 Studies in Epistemology
Volume VI   1981 Foundations of Analytic Philosophy
Volume VII   1982 Social and Political Philosophy
Volume VIII   1983 Contemporary Perspectives on the History of Philosophy
Volume IX   1984 Causation and Casual Theories
Volume X   1985 Studies in the Philosophy of Mind
Volume XI   1986 Studies in Essentialism
Volume XII   1987 Realism and Anti-Realism
Volume XIII   1988 Ethical Theory: Character and Virtue

Midwest Studies in Philosophy Volume XIV

Contemporary Perspectives in the Philosophy of Language II

Editors

Peter A. French
Trinity University

Theodore E. Uehling, Jr.
University of Minnesota, Morris

Howard K. Wettstein
University of California, Riverside

University of Notre Dame Press - Notre Dame, Indiana

Copyright © 1989 by the University of Notre Dame Press.
All rights reserved. No part of this publication may be reproduced, stored in a retrieval system, or transmitted, in any form or by any means, electronic, mechanical, photocopying, recording, or otherwise, without the prior written permission of the publisher.

Published by the University of Notre Dame Press
Notre Dame, IN 46556
Printed in the United States of America

Library of Congress Cataloging-in-Publication Data

Contemporary perspectives in the philosophy of language II / editors, Peter A. French, Theodore E. Uehling, Jr., Howard K. Wettstein.
   p.   cm. — (Midwest studies in philosophy ; v. 14)
  ISBN 0-268-01374-8   — ISBN 0-268-01375-6 (pbk.)
  1. Analysis (Philosophy)   I. French, Peter A.   II. Uehling, Theodore Edward.   III. Wettstein, Howard K.   IV. Series.
B808.5.C565   1989
149'.94—dc20   89-16514

The University of Notre Dame
is an equal-opportunity
educator and employer.

Midwest Studies in Philosophy
Volume XIV
Contemporary Perspectives in the Philosophy of Language II

What Are Concepts?................................Christopher Peacocke	1
Manifesting Realism..Simon Blackburn	29
Misconstruals Made Manifest:	
A Response to Simon Blackburn ....Crispin Wright	48
Between Reference and Meaning....................Julius M. Moravcsik	68
Cognitive Architecture and	
the Semantics of Belief....................................Graeme Forbes	84
Semantic Holism Without Semantic Socialism:	
Twin Earths, Thinking, Language, Bodies,	
and the World ....Hector-Neri Castañeda	101
Aboutness and Substitutivity..............................Genoveva Marti	127
Divided Reference ....Igal Kvart	140
A Theory of Reference Transmission and	
Reference Change ....Alan Berger	180
On Synonymy and Ontic Modalities..............Andrzej Zabludowski	199
Against Direct Reference..Michael Devitt	206
Intrinsic Reference and the New Theory ....Laird Addis	241
What Water Is or Back to Thales ....Avrum Stroll	258
Belief and the Identity of Reference ....Keith S. Donnellan	275
Contradictory Belief and	
Cognitive Access ....Joseph I. Owens	289
How I Say What You Think.................................Mark Richard	317
You Can Say *That* Again..............Ernest LePore and Barry Loewer	338
Might...Jonathan Wilwerding	357
Quantified Modal Logic and	
the Plural *De Re* ....Philip Bricker	372
A Vagueness Paradox and Its Solution ....Felicia Ackerman	395
Geometrical Semantics for	
Spatial Prepositions ....Colleen Crangle and Patrick Suppes	399

Midwest Studies in Philosophy
Volume XIV

What Are Concepts?[1]

CHRISTOPHER PEACOCKE

Talk of concepts is often, and understandably, regarded with great suspicion. The word "concept" so often seems to be implicated in spurious explanations. A skeptic could be forgiven for thinking that the word "concept" is the one Goethe had in mind when he wrote sarcastically that " . . . just when ideas fail, a *word* comes in to save the situation."[2] I hope to show that things need not be quite so bad.

The concepts which are my intended subject-matter are very roughly indicated by saying that they can be taken as Fregean senses. They may be of any category—singular, predicative, or of higher level. Within any one category, they may be of various types: descriptive or demonstrative in the singular case; relatively observational or highly theoretical in the predicative case. Occasionally I will slip into using the word "sense" as a stylistic variant for "concept."

This really is only a rough indication of a subject-matter. Even the most ardent neo-Fregean is unlikely to accept everything Frege said about senses. The strand in Frege's conception of sense which matters to me here is that in which distinctions between senses are tied to differences in potential informativeness. One sense or concept is distinct from a second if substitution of the first for the second in a Thought can yield a Thought with a different cognitive significance. I formulate this at the level of thought, in order to emphasize that you can still have an interest in the concepts which are my subject-matter even if you are quite unhappy with Frege's use of the notion of sense in the semantics of natural language. Several theorists who reject any neo-Fregean treatment of atomic singular terms still use a notion of a "way of taking" an object, and they individuate these ways by considerations of potential informativeness. What I have to say about concepts can be seen as relevant to the nature of these "ways of taking" recognized by such theorists.

Many crucial general questions arise about concepts so understood. What is it to grasp a concept? Can the notion of grasping a concept be squared with a correct account of rule-following? What is the nature of the normative dimension of concepts? Can it be reconciled with a naturalistic worldview? What are we to make of the ontology of concepts?

None of these questions can be addressed properly, however, until we have at least a provisional answer to a more basic question, viz.: What form should be taken by a theory of a particular concept? The issues involved in answering this question will be my concern in this paper. From the standpoint of those who have worked hard on particular concepts, some of what I say may seem like trying to draw up a map of a small town from a position out in orbit. My reply is that there are some patterns which can be seen only from afar.

CONCEPTS, POSSESSION, AND REFERENCE

In this material, I will try to respect the following Principle of Dependence: the principle that there can be nothing more to the nature of a concept than is determined by a correct account of the capacity to have propositional attitudes to contents containing that concept (a correct account of "grasping the concept"). Suppose someone suggests that there are concepts which do not conform to this principle. Then the respects in which these alleged concepts slice more finely than concepts which do conform to it must be as nothing to us. The extra properties of these alleged concepts will play no role in propositional attitude psychology. The Principle of Dependence is the concept-theoretic analogue of what is right about a Dummettian principle about language: that a theory of meaning must be a theory of understanding.[3]

Accepting the Principle of Dependence opens up a possibility. This is the possibility that we can in a single account simultaneously say what individuates a particular concept, and also say what it is to grasp that concept. A maximally oversimplified general form which could be taken by such an account is this (where 'F' is a schematic letter and 'C' a genuine variable over concepts):

The concept F is that concept C to possess which a thinker must meet the condition $A(C)$.

One simple example of this form is the following treatment of conjunction:

Conjunction is that concept C to possess which a thinker must, for arbitrary thoughts p, q he grasps, find the following primitively compelling: that pCq given the set of suppositions $\{p,q\}$; that p given the supposition pCq; and that q given the supposition pCq.

To say that the thinker finds such transitions primitively compelling is to say that he finds them compelling and that, for possession of the concept of conjunction, he does not need to take them as answerable to anything else. The details of this treatment of conjunction could be improved: all that matters at present is that there is nothing immediately illegitimate or circular about its form. Another example would be this explicit statement based on the treatment in *Sense and Concept* of the secondary quality concept *red*:

> The concept *red* is that concept C to possess which a thinker must: (i) be disposed to judge that a perceptually given object falls under C when it is presented in a 'red' region of his visual field in conditions he takes to be normal and when he takes his perceptual mechanisms to be working properly, and to make the judgment for the reason that it is so presented; and (ii) the thinker must be disposed to judge of an object not so presented perceptually that it falls under C when he takes it to have the primary quality ground (if any) of the disposition of objects to cause experiences of the sort mentioned in (i).[4]

Again, this is hardly uncontroversial; but it is not circular—it does not presume that the thinker already possesses the concept *red*. This possession condition uses 'red' in specifying a property of the thinker's visual field. This is a sensational property in the terms of *Sense and Concept*, and one which can be possessed without the subject's possessing the concept *red*. What is important for illustrative purposes is that this possession condition does not use 'red' within the 'that . . . ' clauses attributing propositional attitudes to the thinker. Since my intent is purely illustrative at this point, I should emphasize that even if there were no sensational properties, we could still use techniques similar to those used in these possession conditions in order to avoid circularity in the account of possession of the concept *red*.

In an account of a particular concept which meets the general form of interest to us, the condition $A(\ )$ on C may itself use the concept F outside the scope of the thinker's psychological attitudes. But it must not ineliminably mention that concept as the concept F within the scope of psychological attitudes of the thinker, on pain of not having fully eludicated what it sets out to elucidate. Any ineliminable use of an expression for the concept F inside the scope of a psychological attitude context will just take for granted what we wanted to explain—possession of the concept. We should also require, to avoid various kinds of trivialization, that it be a substantive claim in the theory of content that a concept C meeting the condition $A(C)$ can only be the concept F. This identity must not follow simply by logic, or by considerations independent of the theory of content.[5] When an account $A(C)$ of this form for a given concept F is correct, I will say that $A(C)$ gives the *possession condition* for the concept F. Sometimes acceptance of certain patterns of reasons for judging a given content, or for judging other contents on the basis of that content, are internal to the identity of a content. In such cases, the possession condition will mention them. We can call the general form here outlined "the $A(C)$ form."

A relaxation and some observations may make the general $A(C)$ form more plausible. The relaxation is motivated by the fact that, in a wide range of cases, a concept is a member of a set of concepts such that one can give an account of possession of any one of the members only by mentioning what is involved in possession of the others. This is the case in which we have a local holism. It is in the spirit of the $A(C)$ form to allow it to deal with several concepts simultaneously:

> concepts $F_1...F_n$ are those concepts $C_1....C_n$ to possess which a thinker must meet the condition $A(C_1....C_n)$.

It is equally within the spirit of the $A(C)$ form to allow the individuation of a type of concept by the condition which has to be met by a thinker possessing an instance of that type. Suppose we are concerned with perceptual demonstratives such as "that cup," "that apple," of the sort made available in thought by the thinker's perceiving a cup or an apple. Here we should give a general account of the individuation of concepts of the type "that F," where some F is apparently perceived in a given way (W, say). Someone who accepts Evans's account of such perceptual-demonstrative concepts and wants to exhibit the account as of the $A(C)$ form applied to types could then say this:

> $[W, F( )]$ is that type T of singular concept such that for any thinker p and time t, if x is the F perceived by p at t in way W, then for the thinker to be grasping a concept m of that type T is for the thinker's evaluation of thoughts containing m to be controlled as thoughts about an F by nonconceptual information about x, acquired by his perceiving x at t in way W.

Here "nonconceptual information" and "control" are Evans's terms of art.[6]

The first of the observations which may make the $A(C)$ form more plausible starts from the point that there may be a well-ordering of the "occurrences" of a given concept. When there is, it does not matter if the account of higher-level occurrences can be given in terms which presuppose the thinker's possession of the concept, provided what is presupposed involves only occurrences earlier in the well-ordering. Allowing this is implicit even in admitting so humble a case as that of conjunction. The treatment displayed above individuates the concept of conjunction as it occurs in $p\&q$, which contains n "occurrences" of conjunction, in terms of the contents p and q, which will both contain fewer than n occurrences of conjunction.

The other observation which may lend plausibility to the account is that offering an account which instantiates the $A(C)$ form is consistent with acknowledging a major insight of the later Wittgenstein. This is the insight that an account of what is involved in employing one concept rather than another—following one rule rather than another—has to mention what thinkers employing the concept find it natural to do. The consistency of accepting both this and the $A(C)$ form is again illustrated by the above possession condition for conjunction. Its mention of what is found primitively compelling respects the

Wittgensteinian insight. A thinker who meets the possession condition for conjunction does not need examples which by themselves impossibly determine a unique correct application in a new case. Nor does he need to have surveyed in advance all the correct applications.[7]

The possession conditions for *red* and for conjunction plausibly specify intrinsic properties of the thinker.[8] There is, however, nothing in these constraints to exclude the possibility that the possession condition for a given concept makes reference to the thinker's social and physical environment, nor to exclude the possibility that it requires him to have a language. On the present approach, whether these possibilities are realized must depend upon further argument, and perhaps upon particular features of the concept in question. We can consider the case of a possession condition for a relatively observational concept. It is plausible that such a possession condition will link mastery of the concept in question to the nonconceptual representational contents of the thinker's perceptual experience. Anyone who holds that the nonconceptual representational contents of experience are not intrinsic to the thinker will then equally be committed to saying that such a possession condition for an observational concept does not specify an intrinsic property of the thinker either.

The possession condition for a concept provides a point of contact between philosophical and psychological accounts. One task of a subpersonal psychology is to say how it is possible for human beings to meet a correctly formulated possession condition. But in the order of discovery, neither the philosophical nor the psychological account has priority. A philosophical account meeting the $A(C)$ form must be rejected if, for instance, it requires computational capacities humans empirically lack. A subpersonal psychological theory must be inadequate if it fails to ground a compelling possession condition.

Neither the Principle of Dependence nor the $A(C)$ form leads to an elimination or a reduction of the ontology of concepts or senses. We no more eliminate or reduce a concept by saying that it is determined by its possession condition than we eliminate or reduce a number by saying that *it* is determined by the condition for it to number the things having a given property. Ontological issues about concepts are of great interest, both in themselves, and for the theory of abstract objects more generally. But I will not pursue those issues here, because it is not possible to discuss them fruitfully until the theory of concepts itself is better understood.

The concepts I am discussing occur as constituents of complete propositional contents which are potentially evaluable as true or false. The truth value of a complete propositional content depends on properties of the semantic values of its constituent concepts. A concept, together with the world, determines a semantic value. In the present context, these platitudes impose an obligation on us. If a concept is individuated by its possession condition, and a concept (together with the world) determines a semantic value, then we had better be able to establish the following: that a possession condition, together with the world, determines a semantic value. If we cannot, then the claim that concepts are individuated by their possession conditions will not have been substantiated.

We need, then, for each concept, a theory of how the semantic value of the concept is determined from its possession conditions (together with the world). We can call this part of the theory of content *Determination Theory*. Often we take a particular sense and its determination of a semantic value for granted, and ask how grasp of that sense is manifested. Theories of manifestation aim to address that question. Sometimes by contrast it is better understood what possession of a sense or concept consists in; what is less clear is how it can fix an appropriate semantic value. In that case we need a determination theory. A determination theory takes for granted what a manifestation theory tries to elucidate; a manifestation theory takes for granted what a determination theory tries to elucidate. The construction of theories of both kinds should be on our agenda because it is in some cases one part, and in other cases another part, of the system of relations between sense, possession, and reference which are obscure to us.

A simple example of a determination theory can be given for the proposed possession condition for conjunction displayed above. The theory would state that the truth function which is the semantic value of conjunction is that function which makes the primitively compelling principles mentioned in the possession condition truth-preserving under all assignments of truth values to the components p and q. That function is the classical truth function for conjunction.[9]

Determination theory can also play a regulative role, and it may do so in one of two ways. One type of case is that in which we know what semantic value a concept should receive, and some proposed possession condition for the concept fails to give it that semantic value. A relatively uncontroversial example would be the proposed possession condition for *red* which results from that displayed above by omitting the second clause, labeled "(ii)." Such an account would fail to explain how unperceived objects fall under the concept *red*. This is a special case of a more general kind of case: that in which we know that the semantic value of a certain concept has a property, and we use this fact to rule out all accounts on which the semantic value fixed in accordance with determination theory does not have this property.

A second, more radical, regulative use of determination theory is that in which an alleged sense is declared spurious because no account is possible of what has to be the case for something to be its semantic value. This is of course to be distinguished from ruling out partially defined senses. A singular sense, for instance, is partial if, together with the world, it does not always determine a referent. But a partial sense is still a genuine sense because there is an account to be given of how the world has to be for it to have a referent: it is just that, for one reason or another, no object fulfills the requirements of that account. For a spurious sense, by contrast, there is no such account to be given: it has not been settled how the world has to be for something to be its semantic value. Corresponding remarks apply *pari passu* for other categories of senses.

Spurious cases commonly result from the following combination of circumstances: the spurious sense purports to be of a general kind for which there *does* exist a uniform determination theory for members of that kind. But applying that uniform account to the particular features of the alleged sense, no semantic value is determined. Prior's famous non-connective *tonk* arguably falls in this category.[10] The rules given for *tonk* are that from A, it can be inferred that $A\,tonk\,B$; and from $A\,tonk\,B$ it can be inferred that B. It is impossible to assign a binary truth-function to *tonk* which makes these rules truth-preserving under every valuation. In the case in which A is true but B is false, the first rule requires $A\,tonk\,B$ to be true, while the second rule requires it to be false. It would be wrong to assimilate the failure of an (alleged) thought of the form '$A\,tonk\,B$' to have a truth value to the failure of a complex term such as "the greatest prime number" to have a referent. In the latter case, the term has components with determinate senses and references: we know that for arithmetical reasons nothing can meet the condition for being the referent of the whole phrase. In the case of *tonk*, we have not, by contrast, settled *what* function of the truth values of A and B '$A\,tonk\,B$' is to take.

Some conceptions of absolute space and of subjective experience also arguably permit this kind of radical regulative use of determination theory. On these conceptions, no account of possession of concepts of them can be given which determines semantic values of the sorts they ought, on those conceptions, to possess.[11] Where *tonk* suffers from a surfeit of conditions on something to be its semantic value — a combination of conditions which are mutually inconsistent — these alleged concepts of space and experience suffer from insufficiency. No amount of material in the account of possession suffices to determine the desired reference.

In the present framework, it is a condition of adequacy on proposed possession conditions for a pair of concepts that they be in *concord* with Frege's intuitive identity condition as applied to those concepts. Frege's identity condition is, to speak in a multiply unFregean way, this: that concept F is identical with concept F' if and only if propositional contents differing only in that one has F' where the other has F do not differ in informativeness. What I mean by being "in concord" is this. Suppose we have proposed possession conditions $A(C)$ for F and $A'(C')$ for F'. Concord with Frege's condition then requires two things. First, if a content $\Sigma(C)$ containing a concept individuated by the possession condition $A(\ )$ can be informative when a counterpart content $\Sigma(C')$ containing the concept individuated by $A'(\ )$ is not, then $\Sigma(F)$ really can be informative when $\Sigma(F')$ is not. This requirement bites when, for example, F and F' are logical concepts, individuated by different sets of introduction rules. If instances of the premises of one of F's introduction rules may rationally be accepted when no instances of the rules for F' are accepted, the thinker may be in a position rationally to move to a conclusion containing F, but not to the corresponding conclusion containing F'. The other requirement for concord is that if the possession conditions $A(\ )$ and $A'(\ )$ are actually identical, then there are no circumstances in which a thought $\Sigma(F)$ is informative while a thought $\Sigma(F')$ is not. (No "bare truths" about differences in informativeness.) To fail on that requirement would be to allow that a concept's possession condition does not uniquely individuate it.

Meeting the possession condition for a concept can be identified with knowing what it is for something to be the concept's semantic value (its reference). Dummett has forcefully argued that grasping a sense should be identified with knowing the condition for something to be its semantic value.[12] The apparatus introduced so far helps to underwrite these identifications. For these identifications can be sustained only if the possession condition for a concept determines its reference. Without this, it would be unjustifiable to describe meeting the possession condition as knowing what it is for something to be the concept's reference. The required justification is provided once we give, for any possession condition, the appropriate determination theory.

The form "knowing what it is for something to be the semantic value of a concept" does not presuppose that someone can first grasp a concept, and then go on to raise the question of what it is for something to be its semantic value. On the present theory, since grasp consists in knowing the answer to that question, such a state of ignorance is not possible. It is important then that in the form "knows what it is for something to be the semantic value of m," the concept referred to by m is either not thought of by the subject under a mode of presentation at all, or else it is thought of under a mode of presentation available only to those who already possess the concept.

One can conceive of a theorist who holds that while meeting the possession condition is part of knowing what it is for something to be the reference of a concept, it is not the whole story. That is not my position. If meeting the possession condition were not enough, then there would have to be something insufficient for the required knowledge in the case of the earlier possession condition for conjunction. But it is hard to see what the extra could be: it seems that meeting that possession condition is enough for grasping conjunction. If it is enough, then any stronger notion should not be made a requirement for concept possession.

The notion of knowing what it is for something to be the reference of a concept has application far beyond the case of unstructured concepts. It applies to arbitrarily complex concepts, and in particular to complete propositional concepts — the case of knowing what it is for a complete thought to be true. Knowledge of what it is for something to be the semantic value of a complex content rests upon knowledge of the conditions for entities of the appropriate categories to be the semantic values of its constituents. Take a complex content $[s_1,...,s_n]$, where the s_i are concepts and [.........] is a particular mode of combining them. To grasp this complex content is to know the condition for something to be its semantic value solely as a result of applying one piece of knowledge to certain other pieces of knowledge. The piece of knowledge applied is knowledge of the way the semantic values of a content of the form [........] is determined from those of its constituents; it is applied to one's knowledge, for each component sense s_i, of what it is for something to be the semantic value of s_i. In all cases, whether complex or not, I will refer to the identification of possession of a sense with knowledge of what it is for something to be its semantic value as simply "the Identification."

We have not so far addressed the question "With what in the present framework are we to identify knowledge of the semantical significance of a mode of combination, and, derivatively, with what are we to identify knowledge of what it is for something to be the semantic value of a complex content?" It seems that an implicit semantical role for predicational combination in the thinker's thoughts has already been assumed throughout. When we said that the truth-function referred to by "&" is that which makes the transitions in the possession condition for conjunction always truth-preserving, we were assuming this: that the function in question takes as arguments the semantical values of the thoughts p, q on which conjunction operates, and has as its value the truth value of the complete thought $p\&q$. Without this assumption, the question "What assignment to "&" makes the transitions always truth-preserving?" has no determinate meaning. But with the assumption, we are taking for granted an implicit semantical role for predication in a thinker's thoughts.

Suppose, then, that we have a possession condition for a monadic concept F and a possession condition for a singular concept b, and that these conditions determine references for their respective concepts. I conjecture that these possession conditions together implicitly determine the conditions under which the complete thought Fb is true. By parity of reasoning with the case of unstructured concepts, this determination allows us to say that a thinker who possesses F and b knows what it is for the thought Fb to be true—and does so on the basis of his knowledge of what it is for its components to have particular references. On such a treatment, the role of a concept in predicational combination is essential to it, and given automatically in its individuating possession condition. This is only to be expected if, as is plausible, there is no such thing as possessing a concept while failing to grasp its significance in predicational combination.

THE $A(C)$ FORM AND SOME CURRENT ISSUES

Before putting the framework introduced so far to some work, I want to consider its relation to three topics at the center of recent philosophical discussions of concept-possession.

(i) The $A(C)$ form points to a middle way between two more extreme positions. The two more extreme positions are those of John McDowell and a possible philosopher I will call "Michael Dummett*."[13] Whether Michael Dummett* is identical with any real philosopher—for instance, Michael Dummett—is a question I defer for a few paragraphs. In any case, Dummett* agrees with the real Dummett when the real Dummett offers this sketch of grasp of the concept *square*:

> At the very least, [to grasp the concept] is to be able to discriminate between things that are square and those that are not. Such an ability can be ascribed only to one who will, on occasion, treat square things differently from things that are not square; one way, among many other possible ways, of doing this is to apply the word "square" to square things and not to others.[14]

This sketch of an account uses the concept *square* as applied to things in the world; the legitimacy of using the concept in such an account is not in question. What the sketch does not do is use the word "square" within attributions of propositional attitudes to the subject. Furthermore, the sketch does not quantify over or mention the concept *square*—as opposed to using it. It is definitive of the hypothetical Michael Dummett*'s position that these negative features of the account are mandatory: that is, an account of possession must not, according to him, quantify over or mention (as opposed to making use of) that concept. *A fortiori* then such an account does not make any requirements on the role of the concept in question within complete propositional contents the thinker may judge.

John McDowell very reasonably objected to any such account, saying that no account can be correct which purports to say what it is to possess a concept without mentioning its role in complete propositional contents.[15] McDowell concluded that theories of meaning should be modest—that is, they should not aim to give accounts of the primitive concepts of a language. Indeed he holds that "the possibility of avoiding both behaviourism and psychologism depends precisely on the embracing of modesty."[16]

Both parties to this dispute—that is, McDowell and Dummett*—seem to me to overlook the possibility of the $A(C)$ form of account. As a result, each party overshoots in moving to a position which avoids the bad features of his opponent's position. Consider an account of a concept which is of the $A(C)$ form. This account need not attempt to characterize possession of the concept "as from outside" its role as a determinant of complete propositional contents, in McDowell's phrase.[17] On the contrary, we would, for a given concept C, expect its possession condition $A(\ )$ to concern in part the conditions under which the thinker judges or rejects certain complete propositional contents containing C. The above accounts of possession of conjunction and of *red* both do so.

Yet equally there is nothing in the general $A(C)$ form to suggest that we can go any further in Dummett*'s direction; there is nothing to suggest that some account of possession of a concept is possible which does not explicitly mention its role in contents to which the thinker has propositional attitudes. Accounts of the $A(C)$ form need not be free of intentional notions. The instances of the $A(C)$ form we just gave for *red* and for conjunction contain intentional notions. So do Gareth Evans's accounts of particular kinds of singular modes of presentation, which can be cast in the $A(C)$ form. Indeed, endorsing the $A(C)$ form is consistent with holding McDowell's views on the relations between language and thought. The desire for a noncircular account should not motivate a nonintentional, and certainly not a behaviorist, requirement. We already avoided circularity in requiring that, if $A(C)$ is the possession condition for a concept F, then F must not be mentioned *as* F within the scope of the thinker's propositional attitudes within the condition $A(C)$. To demand more cannot be forced by a noncircularity requirement.

On the present suggestion, then, the possibility of avoiding both behaviorism and psychologism does not depend on embracing modesty. We have a form of account which explicitly concerns a concept's role in the determination of complete contents of propositional attitudes, but which is also consistent with the knowability of another's propositional attitudes. We need not lower our sights as far as modesty to preserve these crucial properties. [18]

If the positions of Dummett* and McDowell were the only options, we would indeed have a painful choice. Theories are developing in the literature of what it is to possess certain specific concepts: the first person, logical notions, and many others. While there is much that is still not understood, and not all of what has been said is right, it is hard to accept that the goal of this work is completely misconceived. On the contrary, there are often phenomena specific to the concept treated which are explained by these accounts. McDowell would not let us say that these accounts are theories of what it is to possess these concepts. But I cannot see what else they can be; and we can hardly just dismiss them. If Dummett* were right, on the other hand, we can accept these theories at face value only if they are taken as waystations on the road to accounts which do not mention the role of these concepts in propositional attitudes at all; and we have no reason to believe this destination exists. If we endorse the $A(C)$ form, though, we can take the accounts at face value without prejudice as to the existence of that destination.

It is not easy to determine from the published literature whether Michael Dummett* is the real Michael Dummett. The feature of possession conditions which Michael Dummett* says is mandatory is found in some of the real Michael Dummett's examples; but it does not follow that the real Dummett would endorse only possession conditions which have it. On the other hand, the real Michael Dummett does not consider the $A(C)$ form in his reply to John McDowell, even though doing so would provide a strong response. It is perhaps worth noting explicitly that the $A(C)$ form is available both to realists and to antirealists.

(ii) What is the relation between the present conception and the view of a theorist like Donald Davidson whom we would expect to emphasize the role of radical interpretation procedures in an account of the possession of concepts? Such a theorist is likely to say that to possess the concept F is to be credited with propositional attitudes containing F in their content by an adequate radical interpretation (or more generally radical ascription) procedure. It seems that this proposal cannot be cast in the $A(C)$ form. However that is not what I want to concentrate on here. Even if this proposal is not of the $A(C)$ form, and so in a sense is not individuating, it may nevertheless be *true*. Let us grant its truth, *pro tem*. Why is it true, and is it in competition with accounts cast in the $A(C)$ form?

A radical ascription procedure must rely in part upon constraints derived from the possession conditions for particular concepts. Suppose, say, we have a candidate assignment of content-involving mental states to a subject which has him enjoying an experience of an object as red, but also has him refusing to judge that it is red, though he takes all relevant conditions to be normal and his perceptual mechanisms to be in order (and he is not in the grip of a philosophical theory). This would be an assignment of mental states we should reject, *ceteris paribus*, and the possession condition for the concept *red* makes it clear why we should reject it. When we generalize this reflection, it begins to seem that there could not be any competition between a theory of possession conditions in the $A(C)$ form and the claim that every case of possessing a concept is one in which an adequate radical ascription procedure ascribes it to the subject. This impression of harmony between the two approaches will certainly be correct if the constraints on intelligibility in the ascription procedure are precisely those given by the possession conditions for concepts.

The impression of harmony will be correct more precisely if two conditions are met: (a) all constraints deriving from possession conditions are incorporated into the radical ascription procedure; and (b) there are no other constraints in that procedure. (a) will presumably hold of any acceptable radical ascription procedure. Does (b) also hold? It is not to the point to mention constraints we apply in attributing attitudes to humans which evidently derive from a species-specific psychology (such as limitations on memory or perceptual powers). We surely do use such constraints all the time, and they will not be reflected in the possession conditions for the concepts ascribed. Nor should they be if possession conditions aim to be an account of what it *is* to have the concepts. An objection to (b) would rather have to be a case of an example of ascriptions of attitudes which result in unintelligibility of the ascribee, but in which this unintelligibility could not be accounted for by appeal to accounts of what it is to have the concepts in the contents of the attitudes in question. It is not easy to think of examples of this. It may be in the nature of unintelligibility that there can be none: perhaps an assignment of attitudes makes the subject unintelligible only if there are facts about the component concepts in question which make the assignment unintelligible. If this should prove to be so, then those approaching these matters from an interpretational angle and those using the present apparatus may be studying the same system of constraints from different perspectives.

(iii) In what sense can possession conditions contribute to explanations? Here there is a broad division of cases: those in which a thinker's fulfillment of the possession condition is explanatory, and those in which features of the possession condition itself are explanatory. On the present account, explanations of both sorts are possible.

A thinker's meeting a possession condition for a particular concept can causally explain his judging a content containing the concept. This can be so even in circumstances which, as a matter of what is involved in possessing the concept, are sufficient for being prepared to judge the content. Take *red* again. A person can experience an object as having a particular shade which is clearly within the range of the spectrum covered by *red*; and he may believe too that he is not misperceiving in any way. This is not enough for him to be prepared to judge that the presented object is red, since these facts are jointly consistent with his not possessing the concept *red*, which picks out a particular, fuzzily bounded, segment of the color spectrum. When a thinker is prepared to judge the object to be red, his possession of the concept *red* is an additional causal factor contributing to his readiness to do so.

Why should anyone deny this? One reason may be that it is *a priori* that if a thinker has the concept *red*, enjoys an experience of an object as falling under a shade which is a shade of red, and does not take there to be any misperception (etc.), he is prepared to judge that the perceptually presented object is red. This is not a good reason. Before it was known which chromosomal abnormality is responsible for Down's syndrome, we might refer to the abnormal property as "the D-property." It would then have been *a priori* that if Down's syndrome is caused by a chromosomal abnormality, someone with Down's syndrome has chromosomes with the D-property. It can hardly follow that having the D-property does not cause Down's syndrome. No doubt it follows that there must be some other characterization possible of the D-property. But there will be other characterizations of a particular person's state of possessing a given concept: it is one of the aims of a subpersonal psychology to supply precisely this.

A different reason that might be canvassed for saying that possession of a concept cannot be explanatory is an *a priori* conditional in the reverse direction. As the notions are used here, it is *a priori* that if someone can judge a content containing a given concept, then he possesses that concept. However, quite generally in the philosophy of mind and language there are capacities which can exist only if their existence has a causal explanation of a certain kind. Consider, for instance, the ability to hear the sentence "London is noisy" as meaning that London is noisy—hearing the occurrence of "London" as meaning London, and so forth. This ability can exist only if some states implicated in the perception of utterances contain the information that "London" means London, and so forth. These states are causally explanatory of the person's hearing the utterance as meaning that London is noisy. But I doubt that we can conceive of precisely this capacity existing without its having an explanation of this sort.

Possession conditions themselves, as opposed to thinkers' meeting them, may be explanatory at several levels. At the most specific level, a possession condition for a particular concept may contribute to the explanation of truths about thoughts involving that concept. These truths may be normative, epistemological, or of any other sort with which the identity of a concept has special links. (The apparent infallibility of certain first-person present-tense psychological ascriptions may fall in this case.) A case of a less specific sort is that in which something is explained for all concepts of a certain kind, for instance all demonstrative modes of presentation. At the most general level, it may be that all possession conditions have to conform to certain requirements. If they do, then their doing so may explain certain principles which hold for all concepts without restriction. I will be developing some examples of this in the next section.

GENERALITY AND PRODUCTIVITY: AN EXPLANATION AND ITS RIVALS

There are some data about concept possession which I will try to explain by this theory of concepts. Though as far as I know no one in the published literature has questioned the correctness of these data, a variety of views have been held as to why they are correct.

The datum I will consider is essentially what Evans called the Generality Constraint.[19] For the special case of a first-level, monadic predication, the Generality Constraint states this:

> If a thinker has the resources for entertaining the thought Fa, and also possesses the singular mode of presentation b, which refers to something in the range of objects of which the concept F is true or false, then the thinker has the conceptual capacity for propositional attitudes containing the content Fb.

So it follows from the Generality Constraint that, for instance, if a thinker can entertain the thought that *Mrs. Thatcher is blonde*, and possesses the singular mode of presentation *the greatest living soprano*, he has the conceptual capacity for attitudes to the thought *the greatest living soprano is blonde*. It will be convenient to label the range of objects of which a given concept is true or false its "range of significance." The Generality Constraint also holds for concepts vis-à-vis singular modes of presentation. If a thinker is capable of entertaining the thought Fa, and possesses a concept G with the same significance range as F, then he is capable of attitudes to the thought Ga. The Constraint applies to relational concepts too.

The Constraint also applies at every level in the Fregean hierarchy. If, for example, a thinker can have attitudes to the thought *Every F is G*, and possesses the concept H with the same significance range as that of G, then he has the conceptual capacity for attitudes to the thought *Every F is H*.

By speaking of a "conceptual capacity" for attitudes with the content Fb, I do not mean merely that the thinker possesses the conceptual constituents of Fb. That would make the consequent of the Generality Constraint follow trivially from its antecedent. Understood in that way, the Constraint would not need the argument I will be giving for it. Nor by "conceptual capacity" do I mean that the thinker will easily entertain the thought that Fb.

For certain contents, self-deception, repression, and the like may prevent the thought from being so much as entertained. There may also be preventing factors at the level of hardware. A thinker might really have a language of thought; and it might be that attempts to concatenate his Mentalese symbols for the concepts F and b produce strange chemical reactions which prevent him from entertaining the thought Fb. What I do mean by a conceptual capacity for attitudes with the content Fb is rather this: the thinker is in a position to know what it is for the thought Fb to be true. That is, if there is some block to the thinker's attaining states with the content Fb, what is missing is not any knowledge about concepts, or any conceptual capacity.

I will be endorsing what I will label "the Referential Explanation" of the Generality Constraint, so understood. The Referential Explanation relies upon two premises. The first premise is implicit in the whole framework so far: it is that attitudes are relations to complex senses, composed in a distinctive way from other senses possessed by the thinker. The second premise is the Identification — the identification we made earlier of possessing a sense with knowing the condition for something to be its semantic value.

We are given, then, that a thinker is capable of entertaining the thought Fa, and possesses the singular sense b. What we are required to prove is that he is in a position to know what it is for the thought Fb to be true. We consider the case in which F is an atomic, monadic, first-level predicative concept. I shall also be taking it that a thinker is in a position to know what it is for a given thought to be true just in case these two conditions are met: (i) for each constituent of the thought, he knows what it is for something to be its semantic value, and (ii) he grasps the semantic significance of the mode of combination of the thought's constituents. From the Identification and the thinker's possession of F, we conclude that the thinker knows what it is for an arbitrary object to fall under F.[20] Similarly, from the Identification and the thinker's possession of b, we conclude that the thinker knows what it is for an arbitrary object to be the referent of b. The thinker's grasp of the semantic significance of predicational combination is already presupposed in his fulfillment of the possession conditions for F and b. There could not be a thinker who (say) knows what it is for an arbitrary object to fall under the concept F, but who does not implicitly grasp the semantic significance of the predicational combination of F with an appropriate first-level sense. Possession of any concept requires the capacity to make judgments whose contents contain it. Judgment necessarily aims at truth; and aiming at truth in judging a content presupposes implicit grasp of the semantic significance of the modes of combination in the content. If this is correct, then when the antecedents of the Generality Constraint are met, then the thinker has all that is required to be in a position to know what it is for the thought Fb to be true.[21]

It may be tempting to derive the Constraint slightly differently. The temptation is to characterize a thinker's grasp of the semantic significance of predicational combination by attributing to him a piece of propositional knowledge, thus:

The thinker knows that an arbitrary thought of the form ϕt is true just in case the referent of t falls under the concept ϕ (or perhaps: is mapped to *true* by the semantic value of ϕ).

I was myself tempted by such a characterization in previous efforts. The characterization would certainly allow the derivation of the Generality Constraint. But it also seems to lead to insuperable problems. First, any attribution of propositional knowledge, including that just displayed, will presuppose the thinker's grasp of the semantic significance of predicational combination. So the attribution of any piece of propositional knowledge can never fully elucidate that grasp of predicational combination. Second, the particular piece of propositional knowledge displayed seems to require excessive conceptual sophistication of the thinker. Third, the proposal makes it highly problematic whether a possession condition for the concept of reference itself could ever be written. Propositional knowledge of the sort displayed requires possession of the concept of reference. Perhaps, in some dimly glimpsed state of greater philosophical insight than we now have, we could one day write a possession condition, in the $A(C)$ form, for the concept of reference itself. But if grasping thoughts containing the concept of reference involves knowing what it is for them to be true; and if this in turn involves the displayed propositional knowledge which presupposes possession of the concept of reference; then we will have a circle in our explanation of possession of the concept of reference. It is not tempting to exempt the concept of reference from the demands of the $A(C)$ form.

The derivation of the Generality Constraint which I have endorsed can be reapplied recursively to treat the case in which F is first-level but not atomic. It can also be generalized to other levels.

The Referential Explanation of the Constraint prompts two observations. The first observation concerns the interplay of the levels of sense and reference in the Referential Explanation. The Constraint is an *explanandum* concerning grasp of sense. But if the Referential Explanation is correct, one cannot properly explain this datum without mentioning the role of reference in an account of sense and its grasp. The explanation turns, for instance in the first-level case, on the implicit generality in grasp of a predicative sense. This generality explicitly concerns the level of reference; it is knowledge of what it is for an arbitrary object, at the level of reference, to fall under the concept which allows the derivation to go through.

Second, the Referential Explanation is independent of the kind of object referred to by the senses quantified over in the Constraint. It is of equal application to thoughts about material objects, numbers, sets, mental events, or anything else. As far as the explanation of the Constraint is concerned, no subject matter has any explanatory priority. As soon as we have a domain of reference and senses presenting members of the domain, the holding of the Constraint is guaranteed by the nature of the relations between sense, possession, and reference.[22]

For any particular concept, its fulfillment of the Generality Constraint may well be trivially establishable, given the concept's possession condition. The earlier possession condition for conjunction illustrates the point. That possession condition leaves no room for the possibility that a thinker has the resources for entertaining the thought *p&q*, and for entertaining the thought *r*, but lacks the conceptual capacity for attitudes to the content *p&r*. The interest of the Referential Explanation lies not in such particular instances, but in the fact that it shows the Constraint to hold for an arbitrary concept. The Referential Explanation is not, of course, a causal explanation. It rather aims to derive a property of all concepts — fulfillment of the Constraint — from the Identification; and so ultimately from the requirement that for any possession condition, there exist a Determination Theory for it.

The Generality Constraint is not the only principle which results from facts about an arbitrary concept, its relation to the level of reference and its possession condition. Suppose a thinker possesses the predicative concept *spherical*, and continues to possess it after acquiring a new singular concept, say *the physical particle meeting condition C*. Such a thinker knows what it is for the thought *the physical particle meeting condition R is spherical*, without the need for any further stipulations or determinations about the concept *spherical*. This holds even if the object picked out by the description *the particle meeting condition R* is one which was not, prior to his acquiring the new concepts in *R*, in his ontology. The principle illustrated here we can call the *Productivity Principle*, by analogy with the phenomenon linguists pick out by that name. A more general statement of the Productivity Principle is this:

> Suppose a thinker possesses the first-level concept F, and acquires a new singular concept m, which denotes something in the significance range of F. If in these circumstances the thinker continues to possess F, then he is in a position to know what it is for the thought Fm to be true, without the need for any further stipulations or determinations about the concept F.

The Productivity Principle also holds at all levels of the Fregean hierarchy. It is not strictly entailed by the Generality Constraint, since the Principle speaks of new concepts; and the Constraint is silent on the thinker's capacities in relation to new concepts. We could, though, formulate a SuperPrinciple, which has both the Constraint and the Productivity Principle as logical consequences. The SuperPrinciple states, for the case of a monadic concept F, that:

> If a thinker possesses the concept F, then necessarily: for any concept c of suitably lower level and which refers to something in the significance range of F, if the thinker continues to possess F and possesses (or comes to possess) c, then he is in a position to know what it is for the thought Fc to be true, without any further information or stipulation.

In considering potential explanations of the Generality Constraint, one should always check to see whether they carry over to give an explanation of the Productivity Principle too. The Referential Explanation does. Suppose the antecedents of the Productivity Principle are fulfilled. In possessing the concept F, the thinker, we can infer from the Identification, knows what it is for an arbitrary object within its significance range to fall under it. The thinker also grasps the predicational mode of combination; and he knows what it is for an object to be the reference of m. So he is in a position to know what it is for the thought Fm to be true.

The Referential Explanation takes it for granted that possession conditions have a modal dimension. We can bring this out as follows, in connection with the example of conjunction. We would not accept this as a good objection to what has been said so far: "The possession condition for conjunction speaks only of what inferences a thinker finds compelling involving the actual range of contents he grasps; it cannot commit us to anything about what he would find compelling in relation to any enlarged range of contents he may come to grasp, and which may feature as conjuncts in his thoughts." On the contrary, the possession condition is put forward as having such modal or counterfactual commitments. As always with a possession condition, we can consider the matter either from the aspect of requirements on grasp of a concept, or from the aspect of concept individuation.

From the aspect of grasp, a concept C is not, intuitively, conjunction if a thinker does not find, in relation to some newly acquired content s, inferences from a premise of the form pCs to s primitively compelling (and similarly for the other forms). From the aspect of concept individuation, we can make the corresponding point about the modal dimension as follows. A possession condition is meant to *individuate* a concept. Even if a possession condition is stated entirely nonmodally, when it is put forward as a possession condition, it should be understood as incurring this commitment: that in worlds other than the actual world, there is nothing more to being the concept in question than having the same possession condition as has been stated for the actual world. This is an instance of a general point about the individuation of abstract objects. We can pursue the parallel with the individuation of a natural number by the condition for it to number the instances of some property. We may say, nonmodally, that the number 3 is individuated by the conditon for it to be the number of Fs, a condition familiarly formulable in a first-order schema. If we say that that is all there is to being the number 3, then we will endorse this consequence: that in other possible worlds too, the condition for 3 to be the number of Fs is the same condition as is required for it to number them in the actual world.

I have been offering the Referential Explanation as correct for both the Generality Constraint and the Productivity Principle. My stance contrasts with that of a position which also holds that the Constraint and the Principle are indeed both necessary, but which offers a different reason for their necessity. According to this rival account, the Constraint (to concentrate on it) is a trivial definitional truth: this account states that, as a stipulative matter, we will not count anything as thought, or as exercise of concepts, unless it meets the Constraint. On this view, the Constraint has a status like that of "All sloops have only one mast."

A plausible rough account of what is involved in a truth being stipulatively restrictive is this. "All sloops have only one mast" is stipulatively restrictive, because (a) sloops are yachts (or more generally vessels) and (b) it is not necessary that all yachts (or vessels) have only one mast. Generalizing, we can say that a necessary and *a priori* truth "All Fs are Gs" is stipulatively restrictive just in case there is some underlying sortal kind such that (a) Fs are objects of that sortal kind and (b) it is not necessary that all members of that sortal kind have the property G.[23] The underlying intuition here is that when a truth of the relevant form is stipulatively restrictive, being an F amounts to falling under some more general sortal concept, together with some further restriction which requires the property of being G.

When a necessary, *a priori* truth of the form "All Fs are Gs" is not stipulatively restrictive, we would expect there to be some explanation of its truth, an explanation which appeals to what is involved in falling under the fundamental sortal kind which has Fs as members. The case differs from that in which the truth is stipulatively restrictive, where the idea of a deeper explanation seems out of place. When a necessary, *a priori* truth of the form "All Fs are Gs" is not stipulatively restrictive, let us say that it is *inextricable*. If the Referential Explanation of the Constraint and the Principle is correct, those necessary and *a priori* truths are inextricable, and their explanation traces back to the general nature of concept possession. This is just by way of further characterization of the Referential Explanation.

A theorist who holds that the principles we have been discussing are stipulatively restrictive has to explain how it is possible that thought conforms to them. Let us take the Productivity Principle. How is a thinker able to have the capacity it mentions, a capacity which concerns arbitrary new concepts? It is not plausible that the statement that the thinker has the capacity to grasp a thought Fm of the sort mentioned in the Productivity Principle can be a *barely true* statement, in Dummett's sense.[24] If the statement cannot be barely true, we have to address the question of what actual property of the thinker, one which he has prior to his acquisition of m when m is new, grounds this capacity. If we accept the Identification, then we have an answer to this question — in possessing the concept F, the thinker already knows what it is for an arbitrary object to fall under it. But if he offers this answer to the question, the theorist begins to shift from the stipulatively restrictive view of the Productivity Principle, to the view that it is inextricable.

A defender of the stipulative view of the Constraint and of the Principle is committed to holding that there can be exercises of what are otherwise just like concepts and a faculty of judgment, but which do not conform to the Constraint or to the Principle. At this point, the position of the stipulative defender overlaps with that of a third theorist, one who claims that though the Constraint and the Principle are true, they are simply contingent. The positions overlap because both are committed to the real possibility of cases in which there is exercise of an ability which is in all other respects just like judgment involving thoughts and concepts, but whose contents differ from those of actual thought solely in failing to conform to the Constraint and the Principle. I want lastly in this section to consider the view that the Constraint and the Principle are simply contingent.

It is no easy matter to spell out in detail a hypothetical counterexample to the necessity of the Generality Constraint of the sort which must exist if it is contingent. Attempts to do so all seem to founder on the same general dilemma. Suppose it is suggested that we have a description of a possible case in which a thinker is, for instance, capable of judging something of the form *Rab* but does not have the conceptual capacity to judge that *Rba*. Does the thinker know what it is for an arbitrary ordered pair of objects to fall under R, or not? If he does, he has the capacity to judge that *Rba* after all. If he does not, how are we to justify the claim that he is capable of judging *Rab*? There is no such state as knowing what it is for the pair $<a,b>$ to stand in the relation R while not knowing what it is for the pair $<b,a>$ to stand in that same relation. In ascribing to a thinker the use of a concept R, we are ascribing use of something which has an ineliminable element of generality. The ascription is undermined if the thinker is not capable of doing what, in context, he ought to have the capacity to do given the generality involved in grasp of a concept.[25]

These difficulties in spelling out the details of a counterexample to the Generality Constraint are not just an appeal to the definitional of the sort to which we would be reduced if it were queried whether sloops have to have only one mast. They are difficulties in reconciling requirements on grasp of concepts with failure of the Generality Constraint. The problem is only more pressing when the issue is not formulated schematically, but instead we fix on particular concepts. Can we make sense of the possibility that someone grasps the thought that 17 is a prime number, but is not capable of grasping the thought that 31 is a prime number, even though he is capable of thinking of the number 31? It seems that if he knows what it is for a number to be prime, he cannot fail to have the capacity for grasping 31 is prime; and if he does not have that knowledge, he will not have the capacity to judge that 17 is prime either. At one point, Fodor notes that on certain "inferential role" theories of the logical constants, as a matter of what is constitutive of grasping the concept, certain sorts of systematicity are guaranteed.[26] Though I am not defending an inferential role semantics for all concepts, my position is indeed that what is constitutive of grasping an arbitrary sense ensures the form of systematicity stated in the Generality Constraint.[27]

To clarify my position, I should emphasize that I am not denying that, for instance, it is an empirical and contingent matter that if a creature is making a selective discriminative response to situations in which the cup is to the left of the box, it is also capable of making the same selective response to situations in which the box is to the left of the cup. The necessity of the Generality Constraint does not contradict the fact that such conditionals are contingent. The Constraint says nothing about such conditionals, since they do not concern the exercise of concepts by the creature, but only kinds of situation to which the creature responds. What I am committed to claiming is noncontingent is this: if a creature is capable of forming the conditional intention to do so-and-so when the cup is to the left of the box, then there is no conceptual bar to its forming the intention to do so-and-so when the box is to the left of the cup.[28]

4. TRACTARIAN ISSUES

In the *Tractatus*, Wittgenstein did not operate with a notion of sense as distinct from that of reference. But he was clearly concerned with abstract, general requirements on the meaningfulness of sentences. Many of these general requirements continue to stand after a sense-reference distinction is introduced, and after the formulations are reapplied at the level of thought. There are complex interrelations between the present framework and the *Tractatus*. Some of the connections consist in compelling conditions of adequacy formulated in the *Tractatus*, conditions of adequacy which proposers of other theories must show their own efforts to fulfill. There are also connections resulting from the bearing of the present framework on issues and problems in the *Tractatus*. Let me give three illustrations.

(a) Wittgenstein complained that one of Russell's theories of judgment does not meet the following requirement: that one can only judge what makes sense. As Wittgenstein formulated it, " . . . from the proposition 'A judges that (say) a is in relation R to b', if correctly analyzed, the propositions 'aRb v ~ aRb' must follow directly *without the use of any other premiss*."[29] The present theory meets the condition. A thinker can judge only contents which he grasps; grasp consists in knowing the condition for the content to be true (on the basis of his grasp of its components and its mode of composition); and if there is such a condition, any sentence expressing the content will make sense. In a neo-Fregean theory, Wittgenstein's requirement is met in a very direct way: grasp of the content consists in knowledge of the very condition the grasped content imposes on the world.

(b) In his penetrating study of the development of Wittgenstein's philosophy, Pears notes a tension between separatist and holistic elements of Wittgenstein's early thought.[30] The holistic aspects are found in Wittgenstein's comparison of a proposition with a set of coordinates fixing a point in space.[31] As Pears emphasizes, one can appreciate a set of coordinates only if one has grasped a system of reference to points by coordinates. The separatist element is to the fore in such passages as this: "The reality that corresponds to the sense of the proposition can surely be nothing but its component parts, since we are surely *ignorant* of *everything* else."[32] With a sense-reference distinction and in the context of the present theory, we can resolve this tension. Separatism holds at the level of reference. The reality relevant to the truth of a proposition consists of the semantic values of its component senses; the truth or falsity of the proposition depends only on the relations of these semantic values to one another, and not on anything else. But holism (in the sense with which Pears is concerned) is correct at the level of sense. If the considerations of the earlier sections above are correct, what is involved in possessing the concept F necessarily puts someone who grasps it in a position to grasp the contents $Fa, Fb, Fc,...$ for suitable lower-level senses $a, b, c, ...$ in the repertoire of the thinker; and similarly for a suitable lower-level sense vis-à-vis a range of concepts $F, G, H, ...$.

(c) The $A(C)$ form also bears on one reading of the elusive doctrine that some things can only be shown, and not said. Pears, with some hesitation, expounds part of this doctrine thus: "There is certainly something here which we cannot do: we cannot give a complete account of the sense of any factual sentence" (144). More particularly, "[if the doctrine of showing is right], we cannot give a complete account of the sense of a factual sentence without reusing that sentence's method of correlation with the possibility presented by it" (148). Pears notes that this means that an explanation of the method of correlation of sentences with the world would be no use to someone who does not already understand it or something equivalent to it (144–45, 148). This will certainly be true of what Pears would label, in the literary rather than the truth-functional sense, the "tautological" account that "George is bald" means that George is bald. In reply to someone who says that we know what the sentence means, and what we want is an explanation of it having the meaning it does, Pear writes: "the tautological account manifests another deficiency: it cannot explain a fact of this kind, because it has no way of getting past it and finding any further independently specifiable fact to support it" (148).[33]

We need here to distinguish two readings of "independently specifiable." For if the $A(C)$ form is correct, things are not so bleak. If the Principle of Dependence we stated at the outset is right, then a full account of grasp of a given sense can be an account of the nature of that sense itself too. One respect in which that account may not be independently specifiable is that it may ineliminably use the sense grasp of which, and so the nature of which, is being elucidated. This certainly prevents the account from being understood by one who does not possess the sense in question. But this does not prevent the account from being substantive and nontautologous provided that in it, the sense in question is not mentioned as such within the scope of the thinker's propositional attitude (as opposed to being quantified over). If an account is not independently specifiable in that it violates *this* proviso, then there is indeed a circularity. But we have already in earlier sections given accounts of individual senses which do not violate independent specifiability in this sense. In brief, we can distinguish an extreme demand for independent specifiability, which on the present theory is in some cases not to be had, from a moderate demand which is fulfillable. The unmeetability of the extreme demand shows only that in some cases a complete account of a sense must use that sense. It does not show that complete accounts of a sense are impossible.[34]

5. KNOWING-WHAT-IT-IS-FOR AND THE EXPLANATIONS

I now turn to consider the notion of knowing-what-it-is-for, and its role in the above explanations. I have leaned heavily on the notion in the Referential Explanation of the Generality Constraint. The notion has an intuitive appeal. It is highly intuitive that one cannot have any propositional attitude (of the sort in question in this paper) to the content that p unless one knows what it is for it to be true that p. It is equally intuitive that knowledge of what it is for it to be true that p results from knowledge of what it is for things to be the semantic values of its constituent concepts. But what is the status of the notion of knowing-what-it-is-for — or in other words, of a possession condition — and how does it contribute to explanations? These issues need much more discussion than I can give here. What I aim to do is to indicate which regions of logical space are available for theoretical developments involving the notion.

Knowing-what-it-is-for seems to be distinct both from knowing that and from knowing how. It is not reducible to knowing that, if the present account is correct, on pain of infinite regress. If what I have said is right, then any case of knowing that so-and-so rests upon several cases of knowing-what-it-is-for, viz., knowing what it is for something to be the values of the various conceptual components of the content that so-and-so. If these latter pieces of knowledge were in turn reducible to knowledge that, we would be launched on an infinite regress.[35]

Nor is there any obvious reduction of knowing-what-it-is-for to knowing how. I am trying to give a theory acceptable to a realist, so knowing how to verify or how to falsify a thought are unavailable as reductions to knowing how. It is true that some instances of knowing how — for instance knowing how to speak a particular language — suffice for the possession of knowledge of what it is for things to be the semantic values of the various concepts expressed in the language. But it would be a non sequitur to infer that knowing-what-it-is-for must therefore be a form of knowing how. Many cases of knowing how involve knowledge-that: knowing how to prove Pythagoras' Theorem would be an example. Knowing how to speak a language is plausibly another. If it is, then by the regress argument, this route offers no reduction either.

Is knowing what it is for something to be the semantic value of a concept identifiable with knowing when to judge certain contents containing that concept? The problem with this is that a set of contents does not in general determine whether it should be accepted in the presence of given evidence. Two thinkers with the same conceptual repertoire and in the same evidential position may differ in which contents they are disposed to accept, because one is bolder, more imaginative, or more ingenious than the other. Can we then at least identify knowing-what-it-is-for with knowing what are the constraints on the acceptance of contents? If this means knowing *that* the constraints are such-and-such, it attributes unnecessary philosophical sophistication to the ordinary thinker. It is also vulnerable to the regress argument. The suggestion could be made more plausible by taking it to mean that there is some kind of knowledge of what the constraints are which is reflected in the thinker's willingness to make certain judgments for certain reasons. But in this sense, to say that someone knows what the constraints are on a given concept seems to be not much more than a stylistic variant on saying that he knows what it is for something to be its reference: it does not offer an illuminating reduction.

To say that someone possesses a particular concept is to make commitments about the kind of contents to which he is capable of having propositional attitudes. Propositional attitudes are at what Dennett distinguishes as the personal level, rather than his subpersonal level.[36] So if we accept the identification of possessing a concept with knowing what it is for something to be its semantic value, knowing-what-it-is-for is at the personal, not the subpersonal, level (at least in the cases which concern us). All the specific possession conditions we gave above were in fact at the personal level. They mention a person's reasons for judgments.

Contents which may in some individuals feature only as contents of subpersonal states, such as those involved in the computations underlying the earlier stages of vision, need not conform to suitable analogues of the Generality Constraint. But even if they did happen to conform to such analogues, that would not make these subpersonal contents conceptual contents. For they would still not have possession conditions which state requirements formulated at the personal level.

There are many skeptical positions which compete with the stand I have been taking. Some such skeptical positions are defined by their claim that the notion of knowing-what-it-is-for is philosophically epiphenomenal. According to skeptical positions in this class, it is our practice to say that a thinker knows what it is for something to be the semantic value of a sense when we are prepared to attribute to him attitudes to contents containing that sense; and that is also the order of explanation, according to these skeptics. Talk of possession conditions or of knowing-what-it-is-for is, for them, nothing but redescription of certain facts about the legitimate attribution of propositional attitudes. Such redescriptions cannot be explanatory, they will insist, and certainly not causally explanatory.

Here we can consider a partial parallel with another case. In other work, I argued that certain facts about a speaker's relation to his language—for instance the fact that by any sentence containing the word "London" he means something about London—can be explained by the speaker's subpersonal possession of semantic information about the word "London."[37] The present explanation of the Generality Constraint is similar to those explanations in three respects. (i) If someone no longer (subpersonally) possesses semantic information about the word "London," then *ceteris paribus* he no longer understands sentences containing it; equally if someone no longer knows what it is for something to be the semantic value of a given sense, then *ceteris paribus* he loses the capacity to have propositional attitudes to contents containing that sense. (ii) Both the subpersonally possessed semantic information and the knowledge of what it is for something to be the semantic value of a sense operate recursively. (iii) Both states are explanatory of knowledge—respectively, of knowledge of certain features of the meaning of certain sentences, and of knowledge of what it is for certain contents to be true.

There are also two disanalogies, of course. The subpersonally possessed semantic information is information *that* so-and-so; I have been arguing that knowing-what-it-is-for cannot be knowledge of that kind. Second, I have claimed that knowing-what-it-is-for is at the personal, not the subpersonal level.

How can a skeptic who takes possession conditions to be epiphenomenal explain the truth of the Generality Constraint? The Constraint cannot be explained as a trivial consequence of what is involved in a concept's having a certain significance range. If the object which is the referent of the singular mode of presentation b is in the significance range of the concept F, it does indeed seem to follow that the content Fb is intelligible, that it *could* be grasped by some thinker or other. But the Generality Constraint's consequent speaks not of what could be grasped by some thinker or other, but of what a thinker who satisfies the antecedent is actually in a position to know. It is hard to see how to derive that consequent without relying on the Identification.

Alternatively, the skeptic may say that conformity to the Constraint is simply an additional requirement on the acceptability of a set of attitudes putatively attributed to a thinker by a radical ascription procedure. If he says this, the skeptic need not reject the Identification, nor need he deny that we can write possession conditions for concepts of the sort I have been discussing. His view is just that they have no explanatory power. I close with a query for this kind of skeptic.

The query is whether we should not try to explain any universal constraint on radical ascription in a way which relates it to what is fundamental to propositional attitude psychology. Just saying that we attribute attitudes in such a way as to make the Constraint and other principles come out true leaves their status unexplained. The Referential Explanation, by contrast, grounds them in facts about making another thinker intelligible to us. A subject's thought and action has to be intelligible given the way he represents the world to be; and representing the world to be a certain way involves knowledge of what it is for things to fall under the representing concepts. On the explanation I am suggesting, systematicity is found wherever there is *Verstehen*.

Notes

1. My thanks to Simon Blackburn, Martin Davies, Michael Dummett, Dorothy Edgington, and Graeme Forbes for helpful comments in 1987-8. I also benefited from the discussion of this material at the April 1988 meetings of the Anglo-French project on Concepts and Categorization.

2. *Faust* I, Studierzimmer (iii); my emphasis. Actually the speech is Mephistopheles', and he is speaking of the language of lawyers.
3. "What is a Theory of Meaning? (I)" in *Mind and Language* edited by S. Guttenplan (Oxford, 1975), 99.
4. For 'red', see my *Sense and Content* (Oxford, 1983), chaps. 1 and 2.
5. This rules out accounts in which $A(\ )$ contains "judges that . . . C . . .; and in fact C is the concept F."
6. The material which I have here transposed into the $A(C)$ form for types is drawn particularly from pp.121-22 of Evans's *The Varieties of Reference* (Oxford, 1982).
7. For an illuminating discussion of Wittgenstein's insight, see D. Pears, *The False Prison*, vol. II (Oxford, 1988).
8. For a discussion of intrinsic properties, see D. Lewis, *On the Plurality of Worlds* (Oxford, 1986).
9. For some necessary refinements here, see my paper "Understanding Logical Constants: A Realist's Account" in *Proceedings of the British Academy* 73 (1987): 153-200.
10. A. Prior, "The Runabout Inference Ticket," reprinted in *Philosophical Logic*, edited by P. Strawson (Oxford, 1967). Elsewhere I have argued that only verificationists can object to *tonk* on the grounds that it nonconservatively extends a deducibility relation. See further "Understanding Logical Constants."
11. This is one way of reading the argument of my paper "The Limits of Intelligibility: A Post-Verificationist Proposal," *Philosophical Review* 97 (October 1988). The Discrimination Principle of that paper is a consequence of the Principle of Dependence, which provides the ultimate rationale for the Determination Principle.
12. *The Interpretation of Frege's Philosophy* (London, 1981), especially chap. 3. The conception is also in his earlier writings: see *Frege: Philosophy of Language* (London, 1973), 229-40.
13. M. Dummett, "What is a Theory of Meaning? (I)," and J. McDowell, "In Defense of Modesty," in *Michael Dummett: Contributions to Philosophy*, edited by B. Taylor (Dordrecht, 1987), together with Dummett's reply to this paper.
14. "What Do I Know When I Know a Language?" (Stockholm, 1978), 7: quoted by McDowell, "In Defense of Modesty," 62.
15. "In Defense of Modesty," 68ff.
16. Ibid., 69.
17. Ibid., 61.
18. I do not pretend that the $A(C)$ form gives us an adequate theory of our knowledge of what others mean by their words and of their propositional attitudes; and part of McDowell's objection to Dummett concerns the epistemology of meaning. The $A(C)$ form, and particular possession conditions, are intended to address questions of the type "What is it to mean this rather than that?" rather than those of the form "How is it possible to know what another person means?" Certainly, answers to questions of the first sort must not make impossible answers to those of the second, epistemological, sort. But it does not seem plausible that the correct epistemology of meaning would undermine the possession condition for conjunction displayed earlier, or the 'commitment' account of universal quantification over natural numbers outlined in my *Thoughts: An Essay on Content* (Oxford, 1986). As far as I know, no one at present has a satisfactory epistemology of meaning.
19. *The Varieties of Reference*, section 4.4.
20. For conciseness I drop the qualification about significance ranges. The derivations go through *pari passu* if the qualifications are inserted throughout.
21. Enthusiasts will want to compare this derivation of the Generality Constraint with that given by Evans in *The Varieties of Reference*. The differences demand an extended discussion, which I have had to exclude from a paper which is already long enough.

22. At this point, the Referential Explanation constrasts with that offered by J. Campbell in his paper "Conceptual Structure," in *Meaning and Interpretation*, edited by C. Travis (Oxford, 1986).

23. For sortals, see D. Wiggins, *Sameness and Substance* (Oxford, 1980). The restriction to sortals is necessary; otherwise the concept *object* would trivialize the criterion.

24. See Dummett's "What is a Theory of Meaning? (II)" in *Truth and Meaning*, edited by G. Evans and J. McDowell (Oxford, 1976), 94: "a statement is barely true if it is true but there is no class of statements, not containing it or trivial variants of it, to which any class containing it can be reduced." The notion of reduction used here by Dummett is defined on the same page.

25. This is arguably yet another application of the Tightness Constraint of *Sense and Content*, chap. 3.

26. Fodor, *Psychosemantics* (Cambridge, Mass., 1987), 152.

27. Fodor's view is that "it's about as empirical as anything can be whether [the minds of animals] are systematic" (p. 153). But it is worth noting that elsewhere in *Psychosemantics* Fodor endorses views that nudge one in the direction of the necessity of the Generality Constraint. He insists that to grasp a content one must possess its conceptual constituents (p. 92, in discussion of Stich's views); and he also links understanding a proposition with "having some idea of what it would be" for it to be true (p. 55). It seems unlikely that this idea of "what it would be like" could be elucidated without relying on the element of generality in the concepts from which the content is built up.

28. If the Generality Constraint is necessary, that in no way preempts arguments that concept possession can be realized only in a creature which possesses a language of thought.

29. Wittgenstein, *Notebooks, 1914–1916*, translated by G. E. M. Anscombe (Oxford, 1961).

30. *The False Prison*, vol. 1 (Oxford, 1987), 132–33.

31. *Tractatus* 3.032, 3.41, 3.411, 3.42.

32. *Notebooks*, 20 November, 1914.

33. This passage need not be taken as Pears speaking *in propria persona*: it could be a statement of the Wittgensteinian position.

34. And if they are, then what is wrong with the above accounts for conjunction, *red* and perceptual demonstratives?

It is fair to note, though, that there is a special problem in the early Wittgenstein's thought which makes the present resolution unavailable. Since he recognizes no level of sense, there is for him nothing for a theory of grasp to be a theory *of*. One cannot plausibly say it is a theory of the nature of the objects referred to: though Wittgenstein shows signs of slipping into this, the issues clearly concern grasp, rather than objects on the level of reference. If Wittgenstein were to introduce different relations to the objects at the level of reference, he would be introducing senses by the rear door: different senses would correspond to different relations to a given object.

35. After reading a draft of the present paper, Martin Davies drew my attention to John Fisher's pioneering and unduly neglected "Knowledge of Rules" *Review of Metaphysics* 28 (1974): 237–60. Fisher's main concern is knowledge of the rules of language. He develops the theory that knowing a rule of language is not propositional knowledge — by which he means that it does not consist in knowing any proposition about the rule. But he goes on to suggest more generally that such nonpropositional knowledge "seems to be essentially involved...in what it is to have a concept" (254); and to suggest that this rule knowledge must be nonpropositional, on pain of infinite regress (254–55). The present paper, if along the right lines at all, can be regarded as a vindication and theoretical elaboration of these points, with satisfaction of a possession condition playing the role of Fisher's "non-propositional rule knowledge."

36. See his *Brainstorms* (Cambridge, Mass., 1978).
37. "Explanation in Computational Psychology: Language, Perception and Level 1.5," *Mind and Language* 1 (1986): 101–23.

Manifesting Realism

SIMON BLACKBURN

This paper returns to a familiar theme in modern philosophy: the arguments concerning the "manifestation of understanding" that are propounded by Professors Michael Dummett and Crispin Wright. The issue is well known, and some would say, well worn. My excuse for returning to it is twofold. First, the appearance of Crispin Wright's collected papers gives us a sustained view of the antirealist polemic or "challenge," including replies to one kind of criticism that I and others had made. Second, and more importantly to me, it is not easy to see how any antirealism generated by their considerations stands in relation to an antirealist project of my own, motivated differently and in origin at least centered on quite different areas. Should my character—the quasi-realist—ally himself to Dummett and Wright? Is he at heart opposed to truth-conditional accounts of meaning in a way parallel to theirs? Or is there little or nothing in common to the two philosophies?

The paper proceeds as follows. In the first three sections I shall discuss some doubts about the case presented by Dummett and Wright and try to assess where they leave the issues raised. The focus of this discussion is the difficulty of actually characterizing the "realist" who is allegedly vulnerable to their charges. I then turn to alternative characterizations, and consider whether a debate may be better formulated in rather more traditional ways.

I

A fairly typical exposition of the many arguments that Wright and Dummett have given is this:

> Knowledge of use is not essentially verbalizable knowledge. So if knowledge of declarative sentence meaning is to be knowledge of truth-conditions, we should not construe the latter as essentially articulate.

Rather it must be a recognitional capacity: the ability to recognize, if appropriately placed, circumstances which do, or do not, fulfill the truth-conditions of a sentence and to be prepared accordingly to assent to, or withhold assent to, its assertion. . . . What is contentious is the converse connection: is it acceptable that if someone understands a declarative sentence, he must possess a recognitional grasp of the circumstances under which it would be true? The difficulty is immediate: what if our standard conception of the truth-conditions of the sentence is such that if actualized, they would not, or need not, be recognizably so? Multifarious types of sentence are in this situation: unrestricted spatial or temporal generalizations, many subjunctive conditionals, descriptions of the remote past, hypotheses about the mental life of others or of animals. If it is to be insisted that knowledge of truth-conditions has to be a recognitional capacity, then in cases like these there is not, or need not, be anything in which this alleged knowledge can consist.

Wright considers that this prompts a dilemma:

we can retain in such cases the connection between understanding and knowledge of truth-conditions only at the cost of attributing to ourselves a capacity to know what certain circumstances would be like which reduces to no capacity of recognition; what, in that case, of the connection between understanding and knowledge of use? *Or* we can reject the suggestion that the concept of truth plays the central role in our knowledge of the meanings of sentences of these sorts.

And the latter is the antirealist course:

Grasp of the sense of a sentence cannot be displayed in response to unrecognizable conditions; nor, if we take seriously the connection between meaning and use, can such grasp go any further than its capacity to be displayed. But it cannot be supposed a mere illusion that we understand sentences of this kind. For there is a communal capacity of discrimination between correct and incorrect assertoric uses of them. So the right account is rather that our understanding of sentences whose truth-conditions we picture to ourselves as (possibly) verification transcendent — because their 'verification' would require an infinitistic extension of capacities we possess, or possession of capacities which we altogether lack — is to be dislocated from such pictures of the 'circumstances' under which they would be true; instead it must have to do with more mundane circumstances which we can actually (or at least in principle) recognize to obtain.[1]

 Similar statements can be found in many places in Dummett. He too contrasts decidable statements, for which "we have no difficulty in stating what constitutes a speaker's knowledge of the condition for the truth of a sentence," since "the condition in question is one which he can be credited with recognizing whenever it obtains" and undecidable ones for which understanding cannot be equated with such an ability. And he too draws the conclusion that the realist is guilty of crediting us with an unattainable capacity of recognition.[2]

The passage makes plain one point that needs emphasis. The argument is about statements that we do understand. It is because we understand them that realism is threatened, since it supposedly stands committed to an account of what this understanding consists in that is unacceptable. We shall see in the course of this paper why this initially clear point is apt to blur a bit, but for the moment it is firmly and uncontroversially in place.

There is one incontrovertible point that one might read these passages as making. Suppose some would-be realist suggests that to understand a sentence is to be able to tell whether it is true or whether it is false. Call this the realist as *teller*. She is refuted once it is conceded that there are statements which we do understand, but for which we cannot tell this. Let us agree with Wright and Dummett that there are such statements, typically including many from the list Wright gives us. Then we have to admit that since we can understand a statement without being able to tell whether it is true or false, understanding does not imply or consist in being able to tell this. This refutes the realist as teller.

But this reading of 'realism' trivializes the issue: it is impossible to see why anyone should play upon such a cracked instrument. Yet it is, at first sight, the one that Dummett and Wright seem to be offering their opponent. For what is the 'recognitional capacity' or 'recognitional grasp of circumstances' (in which a sentence is either true or false) that is handed to the realist in these passages, except an ability to tell that a sentence is true when it is, or that it is false when it is?

In Dummett we can see a line of thought leading to characterizing the realist as teller. Dummett is satisfied with one account of understanding of *decidable* mathematical sentences. It is the capacity to recognize a proof, which in turn is the mastery of the decision procedure: "that is, his ability, under suitable prompting, to carry out the procedure and display, at the end of it, his recognition that the condition does, or does not obtain."[3] With this firmly in place as the account of understanding decidable sentences, it is possible to imagine someone attempting a parallel verificationist account for undecidable ones. This would mean keeping *recognition* in place as the central ability, without noticing the looming contradiction. But the contradiction is immediate, and it is hard to imagine self-respecting realists or truth-conditional theorists staying with it very long.

Although I am not in this paper centrally concerned with doubts about any particular account of understanding decidable sentences, this may be a good place to pause and consider whether Dummett's should go by blank assertion, especially in the strong form here offered. *Prima facie* there are many decidable mathematical statements of which I could by no ordinary standards be thought capable of recognizing as a proof, far less of constructing one (even with "suitable prompting"), yet which I might reasonably be credited with understanding. Many people apparently understand the proposition that four colors are sufficient to color any map on a Euclidean plane without a boundary separating two areas of the same color: the four color theorem. It will be suggested that in principle we (with our lay understandings) are capable of checking each step of the proof, so there is no harmful idealization involved in imagining us stringing together the necessary steps, and saying that in a harmlessly extended sense we have the capacity to recognize the proof. But it is neither plain that the idealization is appropriate, nor in any case why it is harmless. To take the first point, the proof proceeds by dividing up the possible cases; it is not at all obvious why the division is exhaustive—it might take a highly advanced course in analytical geometry to learn why it is. Such processes would naturally be thought of as *increasing* mathematical understanding. Learning to recognize the proof as a proof is therefore much harder than learning to understand the theorem, and implies a capacity beyond any possessed by persons who can do this.[4] And if one can understand the theorem, but cannot recognize any construction as a proof of it, the two capacities are not the same.

The second point is that the logical paradigm of stringing together individually obvious steps, so that there *should* be no more to understanding a whole proof than is involved in understanding the steps individually, is by no means an accurate model of our actual abilities. A person may typically become confused, incapable of keeping track, subject to faulty remembrance of where the proof has got to, in which case once more he lacks any 'recognitional capacity' for the proof. It is no good sidestepping this problem by talking of idealizations of our actual ability: that is like pretending that I can recognize the number of stars in the sky because no more is involved than an idealization of something I can do—recognize the number of eggs on my plate. It is actual abilities that are needed if understanding, which is actual, implies their existence. So there is at best an indirect connection between any actual understanding of the end point, and the limited things people can actually do, such as recognize elements of the proof, in isolation, as truth preserving steps.

Not that one should write as if proof forms the only assertion procedure in mathematics. Mathematical creativity leads to new postulates and new procedures which are not themselves proved, but whose worth leads to their eventual acceptance and assertion. At present there is a rough division between set theorists over forty who accept that the continuum hypothesis is useful, and those under, who simply think it is true—not because they have a proof of it, but because it yields better mathematics. And this attitude has to be coherent, for there is the related question of the truth of whatever we start our proofs from.

These considerations only serve to sharpen the question: Why do Dummett and Wright find it so easy to associate realism with an ability to do something that we cannot do? Whence the 'recognitional capacity' account of understanding?[5]

II

Since the realist as teller proves an uninteresting opponent, the next suggestion must be that the recognitional capacities in question are not quite as strong as I have taken them to be. I have taken them to imply a capacity to tell truth values which we cannot tell. Perhaps they are intended as less — something more like a capacity to imagine what it would be for the sentence to be true or false. This introduces my next persona, the realist as *surveyor*. Perhaps the idea is that the realist account of our understanding needs to credit us with an imaginative capacity which cannot really play the desired role. Imagining ourselves "surveying" an infinite totality or confronting the whole of time from a vantage point outside it would be examples. Now it is undoubted that philosophers can fall into mistakes here. They picture possession of understanding in an inappropriate way, notably through misguided reliance on visual images. And there is some evidence that it is false accounts of the genesis of our understandings that particularly trouble Dummett and Wright. Consider again the passages I quoted at the beginning of the paper, with their stress on "recognitional grasp" of circumstances, and consider too the diagnosis that Dummett offers of a propensity to bivalence, which is that people credit themselves with magical powers of survey of infinite totalities, survey of the past laid out like the present, and so on.[6] Here the enemy is a particular imagining of what it would be to tell the truth about some matter — one that takes something like a visual display or confrontation with circumstance as its paradigm.

Consider the case of someone insisting that either a sentence or its negation must be true, even if the issue is potentially undecidable. He may claim for himself an understanding of something that serves to make just one of the propositions in question true. He is asked what this is, and what it is to exercise this understanding, and supposedly can do nothing to satisfy the request. In his embarrassment such a person might go on to claim the things that rightly offend Dummett and Wright: that he can just "see" what the extra fact is, that he can imagine himself conducting some kind of survey of this extra fact, or coming into some sensory confrontation with it. He might say that he understands it because of some acquaintance with an image in his own mind, and so on.

We can certainly retort that these imaginings afford no proper route to the understanding he is claiming for himself. For we have all learned from Wittgenstein (or perhaps Kant) that imagination, when conceived of as a kind of visual or sensory representing of a perceptible aspect of the world, is never an explanation of understanding in any case. So this realist is being given a very primitive account of our ability to see how past facts outstrip possible detection, or how more is involved in the truth of an unrestricted empirical generalization than anything provided by finite evidence.[7]

Can the realist be forced to damage himself with these poor accounts of the origin of his understanding? I think not. It is not apparent why reliance on such imagining should be her only candidate for the necessary abilities. A brief remembrance of the classical debate in the philosophy of science may here be in order: in that forum it is typically the theoretical antirealist (the instrumentalist or old-fashioned reductionist) who is nervous about our understanding of states of affairs of which we have no imaginative or phenomenal conception; by contrast the realist is happy to admit an understanding created by an indirect, theoretical, description of the features or things involved. The realist as surveyor is being handed a typically empiricist equation between a conception of a fact and a conception of a sensory access to the fact, and this is an equation realists typically avoid.

The realist as surveyor cites the imaginative abilities as his answer to a challenge: What is it to exercise the abilities that make up understanding? Anyone worth calling a realist must be allowed to trawl for other abilities, as Dummett and Wright know. *Prima facie* he can fish up many: the ability to construct explanations dependent upon the truth or falsity of the putatively undecidable sentence, the ability to tell why attempts at verification are blocked, the ability to tell things of related sorts, even if not this one, the ability to work out what else would be so if the sentence in question were undetectably true, the ability to embed the sentence in complex contexts, and so on.

Dummett associates such suggestions with what he calls "holism," but the charge has not impressed many.[8] It is not that on this holism we need to understand everything else to understand anything, but only that we need to understand some other things to understand anything, and this "neighborhood realism" seems highly plausible. Furthermore, and I think this is less often noticed, Dummett cannot properly oppose it. For consider his own positive account of understanding. So far we have been given the ability to recognize decision procedures as the essential capacity when decidable sentences are in play, and have seen no positive account when putatively undecidable ones are. But a little pressure reveals the problem. For in the mathematical case there may apparently *be* no assertibility conditions: nothing might be much like a proof or much like a disproof of the sentence. So what can the right sensitivity to assertibility conditions be if a sentence is actually undecidable? Not the ability to recognize a proof when one is presented, for no such thing ever could be presented. It is not just that these sentences have lost 'truth-conditions' (thought of as things we recognize). They have also lost 'assertibility conditions', a defect which leaves the antirealist as badly lost when he tries to identify the abilities needed to understand them as his rival was said to be.

In this predicament the antirealist must point to the same neighboring abilities. Consider the typical case of a putatively undecidable universal quantification over an infinite domain: every even number is the sum of two primes.

Then someone can exercise a capacity to understand the predicates involved, notably by recognizing what counts as a proof that a number is even, and a proof that it is the sum of two primes. It might be that his understanding of the generalization is to be identified with an ability to churn out this verification procedure for *any* submitted instance, and this is an ability he might have although the quantification itself remains undecidable. However, as a positive account of the abilities involved in understanding a universal quantification this is surely insufficient: one might have this ability without apparently understanding the quantifier. A creature might have the disposition to react in such and such a way to any presented instance of a generalization without thereby being credited with a belief about the totality, nor the capacity to form such a belief.[9] So anyone admitting the sentence to be intelligible needs to add a further account of understanding of quantification in general, and then see the understanding of the sentence as something certified by the existence of these other capacities—the very ones the neighborhood realist cited.

I suspect that the problem of keeping the positive account in focus has alienated much sympathy from Dummett and Wright. It is as if they come to undecidable sentences apparently set to undermine them with the familiar verificationist bomb. Instead they place this weapon under an apparently uninvolved bystander, the truth-conditional theorist, to whom in any case they are standing uncomfortably close. Thus in a typical passage Dummett concludes that "any behaviour which displays a capacity for acknowledging the sentence as being true in all cases in which the condition for its truth can be recognised as obtaining will fall short of being a full manifestation of the knowledge of the condition for its truth . . . "[10] But he might just as well have said that this behavior will fall short of being a full manifestation of knowledge of its *meaning*. For the sentence has to be understood in such a way that its meaning possibly outruns its connection with proof or disproof—that is why it is putatively undecidable.

As I have said Dummett's only way out of this problem is to cast around for neighboring abilities that exercise our understanding of the components and neighbors of the sentence. On the other hand if reliance on neighboring abilities is not a move Dummett allows because of the threat of "holism" then he is clearly hoist with his own petard. This partly explains the temptation to see him as "really" denying intelligibility to undecidable sentences.

We are left, then, with a realist who gladly cites ancillary abilities, and with an antirealist who does well not to oppose them. But when these ancillary abilities are brought in, there is a last possibility. This is that everyone is now joining hands with the antirealist. For suppose it goes this way. Suppose we have some putatively undecidable sentence S. And we turn our backs on the suicidal suggestion that our understanding consists in being able to tell whether S is true or false. Suppose we agree that it is sufficient that we recognize some circumstances not as ones in which S is true or false, but as ones which provide evidence or special kinds of evidence for or against S; we may or may not add ancillary abilities, as I suggested above we would need to do, regardless of which corner we are fighting. Then, while this kind of proposal might help locate the needed abilities, it only does so by conceding the argument. For *this* kind of recognition is the very kind that 'assertibility-condition' theorists like: it is the very kind of sensitivity to evidential pressures which, in their view, is the key ability involved in understanding.

Wright and Dummett might reasonably claim this as a victory: the only remaining account of the capacities that constitute understanding a putatively undecidable sentence are ones consisting in sensitivity to appropriate evidential pressures (or ancillary abilities). No role in the account of understanding remains for a different thing—a grasp of their truth-conditions.

A victory, but for whom? A friend of truth-conditions will well protest that he never wanted grasp of them to play an explanatory role (especially via the poisoned pawn "recognition") in an account of understanding. He may have been content with an equation between understanding and grasp of truth-conditions, each equally to be explained further, if possible, by identifying the capacities that count as exercise of the understanding. So we are still left with the feeling that only a straw man has been vanquished.

III

Dummett and Wright can put some stuffing into the straw man by making him say further, vulnerable, things about truth-conditions and understanding. Or they can tighten up what is required by way of manifesting abilities until some real men start to demur. It seemed to some of us in previous discussion that the second course had been taken, by limiting the kind of "manifestation" of abilities that was to count. Critics wondered how the extraordinary conclusion that 'an individual cannot communicate what he cannot be observed to communicate' emerged from Dummett's thoughts, and diagnosed it as depending on the demand that an individual must be able to manifest his understanding—but manifest it to an audience itself restricted to making observations.[11] This rules out the realist as theorist, and would explain why realists, in a sense the term has traditionally taken in debates in the philosophy of science, are threatened. They allow our understanding to encompass theoretical terms and relations; their opponents try to confine it to observation, and give either a reductionist or a 'black box' (formalist) account of the use of theory. It seemed at that time as though Dummett might be intending to contribute to that debate by insisting that understanding be manifested to those capable of making observation. But taken as such, the proposal did not seem very helpful: enlarge the powers of understanding of the audience, so the counter went, and this restriction vanishes. Communication about the distant, the theoretical, the exotic, or even the unknowable, is restored.

Wright reacts strongly to this counter, saying that it "should carry no conviction at all." For although the audience-dependence of what can be manifested is correct: "we are, precisely, *not* getting any detailed account of what this (i.e., realist) understanding consists in, or of how that very species of understanding might enable one to recognize it in others. The proposal is, so far, just so much hand-waving. . . . "[12] In a sense this is so, but the point was to wave at something that needed saying: the purpose was not to give a positive account of understanding, but to remove an implausible restriction on any such account, namely one that at a stroke confines understanding to observation.

The suspicion was that the realist as theorist was being made to play to a deaf audience. The general caveat was to beware of words like 'manifest' (reveal, display, "make plain to the eye or to the mind"). The right demand is that understanding, conceived of as a capacity, should be capable of being *exercised*. It is quite a different thing even to insist that the exercise should be communication of it to an audience, and still another thing to insist that it should be communication to a deaf audience. It might be reasonable to insist that understanding should be capable of being shared, and in that sense communicated, but that would be so if the exercise is capable of being transmitted, and we still do not know why a realist should find special problems with that.

If this is not the way it goes, we need some more stuffing in the straw man. This introduces the realist as *antireductionist*. He holds the 'dangerous error' of thinking of grasping the truth-conditions of a putatively undecidable statement as

> something ulterior, the formation of a conception of something inaccessible, a conception which informs and governs both exercise of the relevant skill and all other aspects of the use of the sentence, e.g. in inferences.

The contrast here is with an antirealism which

> differs from realism in holding that a reductive account *is* possible, in terms of the practical skills regarded by (A) as constitutive of an understanding of that sentence, of what it is to possess a conception of what those truth-conditions are.[13]

The practical skills in question being those of operating with the assertibility conditions in appropriate ways.

The issue here is reductionism: one side, the realist, believes that we form a conception of a state of affairs that 'informs and governs' all our practical skills which make up our use of a sentence; the antirealist says that possession of such a conception reduces to possession of the practical skills: there is no separate informing and governing fact about us. The issue is now of a familiar shape: Do we have an extra fact, or merely a new way of putting the other facts; inference or logical construction?

It is slightly surprising to find a philosophy as Wittgensteinian in spirit as Wright's espousing a reductionist claim. The Wittgenstein who holds out for a middle way between Cartesian ghosts and reductive behaviorism might also hold out for a middle way between an equally ghostly 'informing and governing' fact of understanding and an account that reduces it to the practical skills it supposedly informs and governs. If Wittgenstein can protect our right to say, for instance, that I behave as I do *because* I am in pain, can he not also protect our right to say that I regard evidence in some matter as I do because I have a conception of what it is evidence for? Wright considers one charge of reductionism.[14] But he dismisses it by replying, quite rightly, that he is not proposing a reduction of understanding to *behavior*: only to the abilities in question, which may be subject to open-ended varieties of behavioral manifestation. However this need not be the burden of the complaint. One can well admit that if understanding is a capacity, it is yet one which can be exercised in a variety of ways. The issue is whether it is right to say that understanding informs and governs use, or whether it is reducible to it. And the truth is that Wittgenstein seems to be more on the side of a properly sanitized antireductionism. When I find method and intelligence in someone's researches, when I can represent his aims to myself, and appreciate his attempts—good, bad, partial, quixotic—to fulfil them, don't I deem him to be guided and informed by some conception or other? Isn't this, as it were, part of the human vocabulary making up the *Lebenswelt*?

What is distinctive of someone who denies the reduction? That he should just *say* that understanding informs and governs use? Where is the harm in that? I say: I have a conception of what it would have been for Jones to have been brave (say) which informs and governs my assertoric practice. It leads me to say things like: We have no evidence either way, but perhaps something might provide some; we could check his school record, genetic make-up, trials with the dentist, and so on without end. It leads me to understand what someone else is doing and why when I find her checking Jones's army record or asking his dentist how he stood up to fillings. One might say: This conception shapes the investigations it is appropriate to make, even when they are doomed to failure through an actual evidential vacuum. The opponent says: There is nothing informing and governing such practices: there are only the practices themselves. But why should we say this (having read Wittgenstein)? Surely I will deem myself and others to be informed and guided by the right idea when I see intelligence and good aim in their investigations and mine.

Of course, Wittgenstein may take credit for weaning us away from some accounts of understanding—those attributed to the realist as surveyor. But I doubt whether Wittgenstein would have taken credit for making us think that the phenomenon itself—being rule guided, or having a conception of a state of affairs that informs and guides assertoric practice—is chimerical, or reduces to something that is apparently different. A different kind of dangerous error might be to think that we are informed and guided into logical practices that are to be criticized on other grounds—the unrestricted confidence in bivalence, for example—and this might well be Dummett's answer. But the issue seems orthogonal to the present suggestion: one might be antireductionist at this point, but also dislike bivalence, or reductionist and like it, for there is no telling yet whether blithe assent to bivalence amounts to a capacity or an incapacity.

I am not sure then that Wright was well advised to make the issue of reduction central. It seems not to help the issue with which we left section I — the question of who was vanquished by the demise of a 'realistic' conception of our understanding of putatively undecidable sentences. For someone who believes that his conception of the truth or falsity of one of these really informs and governs a proper reason-seeking practice need not also say that the conception enables him to recognize something that he clearly cannot, or to misconstrue observational contact with facts; nor need it lead him to suppose that understanding can exist without abilities: its informing and governing role may reasonably be regarded as essential to it.

IV

The position so far is that the realist as teller or as surveyor was offered uninterestingly unplayable hands, whereas the realist as theorist or antireductionist is not under effective threat. I think I can offer a fifth way that Wright and Dummett may be thinking of their realistic opponents. This brings in what is commonly called "verification transcendence," although to discuss it properly we may do well to avoid the term, which covers too much. To introduce the issues we need a distinction. Let us call the sentences mentioned in the argument — the ones formed by unrestricted generalization, talk of the remote past, some subjunctive conditionals, and so on — 'putatively verification transcendent', or PVT for short. The putative part comes in because typically there is no proof that any particular sentence is indeed verification transcendent; indeed in the mathematical case this is never so, since it is never assertible that some particular sentence is undecidable, even if some unidentifiable sentences may be. It can apparently be contingent whether a statement is PVT — contingent upon the actual absence of observations, or of traces, travel, and experiment. The distinction we need to observe arises because being PVT does not imply having a stronger property that I shall call insulation from reason. By this I mean complete absence of any possible relation to procedures of confirmation or disconfirmation. This is the property of pure isolation from procedures of reason that the positivists believed to belong to the theses of metaphysics. By contrast, untried Jone's bravery, unrestricted generalizations and statements about the remote past are not on the face of it in this category. They are not isolated from procedures of investigation and reason: we know perfectly well what might be done to amass reason for believing such things. They are not *a priori* insulated from reason in the way that, arguably, the theses of metaphysics are. Indeed it was a fatal weakness in positivism that it tended to find them in the same camp.

As Wright himself remarks, insulation from procedures of verification is a rare property: "old campaigners like 'Everything is uniformly increasing in size' and the inverted spectrum suggest themselves for consideration, but perhaps not many more."[15] And he concedes that a good number of people might be uncomfortable about a 'realist' interpretation of villains such as these, without feeling much sympathy with a more extensive antirealist program.

Now there are philosophical positions (or pressures) which would have us warp other statements into the same category as the old campaigners, by giving mistaken theories about how we understand them, or what their truth may consist in. Cartesian theories of the self, Russellian theories of the past, perhaps Lewisian theories of possibilia, all give rise to the charge that according to them statements which we do manage to assess and confirm ought to be completely insulated from any such process. For want of a better word I shall call any philosophy which (rightly or wrongly) construes the truth of some statements in such a way that they become insulated from reason *insulationist* about those statements. Naturally the most obvious symptom of insulationism is skepticism: since there is no good reasoning for or against a thesis so construed it is hard to see how there can be any knowledge of it. Equally naturally, the next episode is likely to be skepticism about whether, on the same insulationist construal, the thesis actually has any meaning at all.

In some sections of their work Wright and Dummett say things that suggest very strongly that it is just insulationism that they have in mind. For example, at one point Wright introduces a theoretical notion of 'super-assertibility'—a property going beyond assertibility as provability goes beyond production of actual proof. Squaring up to the challenge that we may not be able to tell whether a statement has this property, which therefore ought to be suspicious from an antirealist point of view, Wright replies that nevertheless it can serve as an 'intelligible objective' for a practice:

> It is a common misunderstanding of the thrust of the antirealist's criticisms of the role assigned to truth in classical semantics that he believes that the central notion in the theory of meaning should be an effectively decidable one. But there is, so far as I can see, no good motive for asking for so much. I can *try* to steer a certain course if, but only if, I know what will be a reason to think that I have gone off course and what a reason to think I am continuing on it. The reasons don't have to be conclusive, but they do have to be such that I can actually recognizably have them. . . . [16]

And in the Introduction, along with the 'acquisition' argument and the 'manifestation' argument he places a normativity argument: realistic truth cannot *be* aimed at, cannot serve as a target or regulative ideal:

> Why should anyone value it? How can a rational subject have beliefs about how to secure it? How can the satisfactions and frustrations of the subject disclose that it was indeed his aim?[17]

These passages put forward a constraint: We have to be able to try to gain truth, and that requires that we know what will be a reason for thinking that we are nearer or further from it. What kind of theorist infringes the constraint? Evidently one who allows truth or falsity to the old campaigners — propositions genuinely insulated from reason, and also the insulator who has a conception of various matters (such as the past of the pains of others) which puts them beyond the bounds of confirmation.[18] Wright's present argument is that on such philosophies the "truth" of these statements becomes incapable of serving as a norm governing any activity, so that there could be no such thing as trying to get at their truth, and only an illusion of reasoning concerning them.

Naturally, in the case of the old campaigners, or of statements construed in a insulationist way, it is not just that they have no "truth-conditions." They have no "assertibility conditions" either: there is no disciplined process of reasoning connected with them at all. So by Dummett and Wright's own lights this means that there are no capacities connected with their understanding, and therefore there is no understanding them. This means that the whole story could have been more easily told. The claim would be that for some sentences, on some philosophical construal, meaning lapses because nothing counts as understanding them, because in turn nothing could count as possessing an ability to reason for or against them. This is clearly a small variation on traditional positivism, differing by stressing the need for abilities rather than concentrating immediately on verification. But since the abilities in question are those of operating criteria and assertibility conditions, the difference is not so very great. Once more we see some excuse for those who have seen the whole issue as a restatement of verificationism.

Like its positivist parent, this anti-insulationist argument meets opposition from anyone who is confident in their grasp of skeptical possibilities, and is then either unimpressed by the equation between understanding and ability, or thinks that other abilities than deployment of evidence can manifest the required understanding. Truth may indeed be a norm governing assertoric discourse, but, the opponent will complain, this may not be its only role. The concept appears to figure in thoughts like "there may be truths about which we shall never be able to reason" or "there may be truths accessible only to minds alien to ours," and a proponent of the normativity argument will need to wrestle with the stubborn appearance of intelligibility in such thoughts.[19]

The insulator comes on the scene to put stuffing in the straw man, the realist. But why tar the realist with the insulationist brush? Well, we could stipulate: Construing the truth of a statement realistically is construing it in such a way that nothing could give us reason for thinking we are nearer to or further from the truth about it. But few philosophers who think of themselves as realists would accept this description. Most want to conform to the ordinary evidential practices according to which there are, or could be, better or worse reasons for believing these things. It is one thing to accept bivalence for the past, and another to accept Russellian skepticism about the evidential value of traces and memory.

I do not deny that insulationism is tempting and worth fighting against. I also think that there is an argument against it that uses Wittgensteinian materials. This argument goes: The insulator takes an ordinary sentence, and urges that it is insulated from reason. But what gives her an understanding of this sentence in the first place? Only its use. But its use embeds it in an assertoric practice of reasoning. She must therefore be misunderstanding or changing our understanding of the sentence. I am not here concerned with the strength of this argument: an opening remark is that it bears affinity to tainted forebears like the paradigm case argument and the 'ordinary language' dissolution of the problems of skepticism.

Quite apart from his supposed vulnerability to the normativity argument, I think it is easy to find passages in which the realist is more or less surreptitiously damned by association with insulationism. For example, Dummett conceded that on a Wittgensteinian account of other minds, there is a trivial (homophonic) truth-condition for the statement 'John is in pain', and asks whether such an account vindicates realism. It does not, according to Dummett, because "we think that an understanding of such a statement must consist in a grasp of what would make it true; and further that a grasp of that must in turn consist in a knowledge of how we could recognise that condition as obtaining. Thinking that only actually having the pain could constitute direct and conclusive recognition that the condition obtained we fall victim [to the private language illusion]."[20]

The conjuring trick is, or course, associating what comes before the words "and further" with what comes after them. In part this is handing the realist the familiar cracked instrument, turning him into a champion of direct, conclusive, recognitional conceptions of our awareness of the reality he is claiming. But his vice here is even more one of making the layer of reality he wants into something cognitively inert, on which reasoning cannot get a foothold, according to the private language argument. In such passages the opponent is only the insulator.

Wright thinks that the straw man need not be stuffed quite so full, so that there is a more interesting target, and this gives us a penultimate characterization of realism. He allows that antirealism ought not to deny that truth is an appropriate notion to play the central role in a philosophical theory of meaning:

> It all depends on how the notion is understood, on whether the proviso —that we have the sort of practical criteria described—is guaranteed. The crux is that the classical realist conception of truth can in general offer no such guarantee. The distinctively realist thesis is precisely that our language affords the means for depicting no end of states of affairs whose obtaining connects only contingently, at best, with our capacity to accumulate grounds for claiming that they obtain. Among the various strands in the antirealist polemic, none is more central than the reproach that as soon as this connection becomes one of contingency, the belief

that truth is suitable to play the regulative role essential to the central notion of a theory of meaning is itself reduced to contingency.[21]

Here the target is not, apparently, a philosophy of some statements that insulates them from reason and breeds skepticism (and eventually skepticism about their meaning). It is a philosophy which cannot "guarantee," because of contingency, that our ways of reasoning are indeed connected with the likely truth of the things we are reasoning about. Perhaps the difference between something approaching a guarantee that ways of reasoning are disconnected (the insulationist predicament) and the weaker lack of guarantee that they are (on this suggestion, the realist predicament) gives Wright exactly the wider scope for his argument than any we have so far discovered. The opponent is now the realist as nonguarantor.

But what exactly is the reproach? Consider the familiar case of untried Jones. As we cast around trying to uncover evidence bearing on his bravery, we can offer no guarantee that the grounds we can accumulate for thinking him brave will connect other than contingently with whether he was. But what of it? For all we know we might on the contrary find grounds that are suggestive, or even conclusive, one way or the other, and the possibility (not guarantee) of success would normally be thought to give our activities their point and aim. The lack of guarantee simply does not put us in the position of those in a sham game, "aiming" at invisible targets and in which success is undetectable and has no consequences. Even if circumstances are, contingently, such that the seeker will not succeed, how can it be that because of the dearth of facts she is deluded about what she is trying to do—indeed, about whether she is trying to do anything? How could the *ontological* fact, that there is no evidence, prevent someone genuinely attempting to find some, and hence to determine whether Jones was brave? Notice how normally we have no hesitation in allowing that genuine attempts are possible in the face of contingent absences of conditions that are in fact necessary for success. Such is the stuff of tragedy: the captain scans the horizon for the extinguished beacon, the sailor waves his shirt in vain for the rescue that never comes. We do not say "they didn't even try!"[22]

Now in such cases success is possible, but more than that, detectable. The real target of Wright's suggestion may be better located as someone thinking not only that it is contingent whether our evidential practices tend to yield truth, but that *this contingency is itself insulated from reason*. The idea becomes one of an insulated space between best evidence and truth, and it is the realist as guardian of this space who is supposedly objectionable. It remains, however, very unclear just who is the guardian of such a space. Think of the original mathematical example: surely one may want classical mathematics and bivalence without thinking that 'we shall never know' whether in general proof in mathematics conduces to truth, and even without thinking that this question makes much sense. Again, the realist as guardian of this space is an insulator—he thinks he has identified a proposition that is immune to reason, namely that best evidence does tend to yield truth. But guarding such a space is, once more, an open route to skepticism, to placing the propositions in question in the same bracket as the old campaigners, and we have already complained that few realists would happily see themselves in such a light.

V

We have tried, without much success, to identify the realist. Whether as teller, surveyor, theorist, antireductionist, insulator, or nonguarantor, in each case his position is either unattractive, but trivially so, or attractive and apparently immune to the antirealist polemic. Is this, then, a reverse fairytale, in which there is a voluminous display of pomp, but no emperor?

In some of Dummett's writings there is a simple, different, and more attractive point. It is occasionally clearly visible, but just as often camouflaged. It is not a point which Dummett can acknowledge as fundamental, for it has nothing essential to do with the assets with which the philosophy of language is supposed to take over traditional metaphysics: manifestation, communication, and understanding. These enter only tangentially, as diagnostic aids. It goes like this.

(1) If something is true then there is something that makes it true.
(2) We should allow that in some cases (potentially undecidable mathematical statements, some kinds of counterfactual, perhaps the past) there may be nothing to make a sentence true, and nothing to make its negation true.
(3) This allowance should be reflected by adopting a nonclassical logic.

This argument generalizes what we should all naturally say about fictional discourse. If Conan Doyle never got up to saying anything that bears on it, then we might not allow it as true that Sherlock Holmes's waistcoat had an odd number of buttons, nor that it did not. There is a gap in the fictional world, and no truthmaker for either proposition. If proof stands to truth in mathematics in an analogous way to that in which author's say-so stands to truth in fiction, there may be a gap in mathematical truth; similarly with actual happenings and counterfactuals.

In this argument, there is no need to deny that a person can show that he has a realist understanding of a matter. He might show this in the first instance by accepting unrestricted bivalence, and when it is complained that he may only do this because he is dominated by some false picture, he may defend himself by trying to say how in this area truth outstrips the proposed basis — writings, proof, or actual events. The complaint is not that he cannot show that this is how he understands the area. The complaint is that he ought not to understand it like that, for that is to misunderstand it. The misunderstanding can be indulged, exercised, and communicated, but it is a misunderstanding for all that. This is what we would naturally say if we found someone insisting that Holmes's waistcoat had just some number of buttons, in spite of Doyle's silence.

The arguments about understanding only come in as a diagnosis of one kind of opposition to (2), namely those arising from the realist as surveyor. But this is not the interesting opposition, which comes instead from anyone (any *radical* antirealist) who insists on a policy of disallowing cracks in bivalent practice, for any of a variety of reasons. Thus, although in mathematics it is arguable that the distinctively realist practice is permission to use classical logic, and that the antirealist cannot legitimately issue this permission, even here there will be the possibility that the law is thought of not as a piece of mere optimism, but as a legitimate regulative principle. For Kant it is *because* mathematics, as opposed to empirical science, is concerned solely with the nature of our own representations, that "every question arising within [the] domain should be completely answerable".[23]

VI

I do not doubt that a starting point for many debates is the understanding a realist claims for himself (just knowing what objective moral facts would be, or a causal nexus, or space of possible worlds). And Dummett was right to be suspicious that unless this understanding is genuine, we may not be being offered anything discussable.[24] The question will be how any distinctively realistic understanding or misunderstanding shows itself in practice. For some it shows itself just as soon as there is real commitment to the practice; as soon as the existential quantifications (there are such things as rights, possible worlds, electrons, past events) are issued without reduction. But according to the view I maintain, that is unhelpful. It confuses two different possibilities, the one that there is no philosophical standpoint from which to conduct a metaphysical debate, and the other that there is, and that reference to a genuine order of objective facts is necessary to explain some aspect of our practice.[25]

It is in opposition to this last explanatory stance that I see a proper role for assertibility conditions. This opposition will take the conduct of some assertoric practice (or perhaps its success) as an explanandum. But it will conduct the explanation without seeing the practice as answering to some layer of fact that it is its business to describe. This is surely the territory for antirealist theorizing to inhabit. It is the territory occupied by projectivists, instrumentalists, intentional stance theorists, probabilistic theorists of conditionals, and so on. The symptoms that an area is suitable for such a treatment may be many and various, and one cannot expect swift agreement about the merits of rival explanations.

The moral of the story is quickly drawn. The right conclusion is not that there are no debates to be had. It is that there are many, although they each require their own geography, for the shoe may pinch in different places, in the theory of morals, of possibility, probability, cause, or mind. The only real casuality of the matter is the belief that the philosophy of language, the imperial "taking with full seriousness the view of language as an instrument of social communication," [26] affords us a new overarching view of the issues, or even a set of arguments playing any useful role in their solution.[27]

Notes

1. Crispin Wright, *Realism, Meaning and Truth* (Oxford, 1987), 53-54.
2. "What is a Theory of Meaning (II)," in *Truth and Meaning*, edited by G. Evans & J. McDowell (Oxford, 1976) 81-82.
3. Ibid., 81.
4. There is also the threat of a regress at this point. Understanding that "these are all the cases" will be involved in understanding that the original construction is a proof, but *proving* that these are all the cases may involve further abilities again. Barry Taylor pointed out to me that perhaps not just any proof but a special sort of proof — a "canonical" proof — needs to be recognized for true understanding. This makes things worse, for if the recognitional capacity is yet more restricted, then it is more likely that one can have understanding without having it.
5. The oddity of imputing to the realist an empiricist stress on recognition, as opposed to inference or other theoretical identifications, is raised by Colin McGinn, "Truth and Use," in *Reference, Truth and Reality,* edited by M. Platts (London, 1980). The same question is posed in Anthony Appiah, *For Truth in Semantics* (Oxford, 1986), 22. As far as I know it has met no response from Dummett.
6. E.g., "What is a Theory of Meaning (II)," 98.
7. Barry Taylor, in "The Truth in Realism," *Revue Internationale de Philosophie* 160 (1987), 55, makes the reliance on an 'alien sense' definitive of a typical Platonist, and also makes an interesting comparison between this figure and the real Plato.
8. See for instance "The Philosophical Basis of Intuitionistic Logic" in *Truth and Other Enigmas* (London, 1978), 218-20: Dummett wants to assign each sentence a determinate content, and his molecular theory of language seems to insist that to each there is also its own determinate ability. In which case an 'assertibility-condition' account of our understanding of sentences which lack any content is going to be hard to provide.
9. Jonathan Bennett, *Rationality* (London, 1964), chap. 9, makes this point especially clear.
10. "The Philosophical Basis of Intuitionistic Logic," 225.
11. Simon Blackburn, *Spreading the Word* (Oxford, 1984), 65. Edward Craig, "Meaning, Use, and Privacy," *Mind* (1982). The quotation is from Dummett, "The Philosophical Basis of Intuitionistic Logic." McDowell, "On 'The Reality of the Past' " in *Action and Interpretation*, edited by C. Hookway & P. Pettit (Cambridge, 1978), notices the relativity of manifestation to audience, but responds by expanding the areas of reality that are manifest to audiences to include parts of the past, other persons' psychology and so on. This cannot be an appropriate move: as Dummett remarks in "What is a Theory of Meaning (II)," the important fact is not how far observation can be stretched, but that it cannot be stretched as far as is needed (98). In other words, once the "manifestation" challenge is accepted in its own terms, it does not matter where we locate the chasm, once we deny ourselves the apparatus for crossing it.
12. *Realism, Meaning and Truth*, 21.
13. "Strawson on Anti-Realism," *Realism, Meaning and Truth*, 76.
14. Ibid., 23.
15. Ibid., 13.

16. Wright, "Davidsonian Meaning-theory and Assertibility," *Realism, Meaning and Truth*, 307.
17. This argument is fully displayed in Wright's Introduction, 23-27.
18. It is because he interprets Dummett as inveighing against insulationist philosophies that Putnam finds him an ally in his opposition to "metaphysical realism." See *Reason, Truth and History* (Cambridge, 1981), 56-57.
19. See for example Edward Craig, *The Mind of God and the Works of Man* (Oxford, 1987), 282-90.
20. *Truth and Other Enigmas*, preface, xxxv.
21. Wright, in *Truth and Other Enigmas*, 307.
22. Could this charity stem from incipient Cartesianism according to which thought is independent of context and a mind is peculiarly transparent to its own self-understanding? Of course not. For we can fill in enough ordinary context, and we can make the question as third-person as we wish: there is a noncollusive practice of agreeing about what persons are trying to do which survives the unveiling of its actual futility.
23. Kant, *Critique of Pure Reason*, A 476/B 504. For an excellent discussion, see Carl J. Posy, "Kant's Mathematical Realism," *Monist* 67 (1984).
24. "The Philosophical Basis of Intuitionistic Logic," 228ff. This is also a prime text for the take-over bid of metaphysics by the theory of meaning, referred to above.
25. By the former of these positions I mean 'quietism', or the 'Natural Ontological Attitude' of Arthur Fine, "Unnatural Attitudes: Realist and Instrumentalist Attachments to Science," *Mind* 95 (April 1986).
26. "The Philosophical Basis of Intuitionistic Logic," 226.
27. I am indebted to many people for discussion and comment, including audiences at the Universities of Ohio State, Michigan, and North Carolina, where I was able to present ancestors of this paper. I am particularly indebted to Robert Kraut, Larry Sklar, Marianne Talbot, Barry Taylor, and Crispin Wright.

Misconstruals Made Manifest: A Response to Simon Blackburn
CRISPIN WRIGHT

Blackburn's interesting paper makes three principal claims. First, he argues that the semantical antirealist ideas explored in Dummett's and my writings suffer for want of an opponent who is both vulnerable to the arguments developed and interesting. Second, he asserts that Dummett's overarching ambition, to use (the resolution of) issues in the theory of meaning to illuminate traditional metaphysical controversies concerning realism, is misconceived — both in the assumption that an underlying unity in such controversies is to be expected across different subject matters and in the cardinal role assigned to the philosophy of language. Rather the issues between realists and antirealists vary with the regions of discourse — science, mathematics, modality, probability theory, morals, etc. — about which they are in dispute. There is no overriding debate in the philosophy of language, and no talisman is provided thereby for use in the debates which there are, nor "even a set of arguments playing any useful role in their solution."[1] The debates " . . . are many, although they each require their own geography, for the shoe may pinch in different places, in the theory of morals, of possibility, probability, cause, or mind."[2] Third — and somewhat surprising in company with the second claim — Blackburn does wish to commend a certain overview of these debates: it is one in which the realist is someone who believes that " . . . reference to a genuine order of objective facts is necessary to explain some aspect of our practice,"[3] and thus stands opposed to a character, Blackburn's *quasi-realist*, who holds that all aspects of the discourse in question can be conservatively explained without invocation of the idea of such a "genuine order of objective facts" to which we should think of the assertions within it as owing truth-conditional allegiance.

I have some qualified sympathy with Blackburn's second claim. In the Preface to *Realism, Meaning and Truth*,[4] I counseled caution both about Dummett's global identification of realism with belief in the appropriateness of a certain sort of truth-conditional theory of meaning and about the weaker thesis that these traditional metaphysical issues are generally amenable to relocation in a meaning-theoretic setting. But, as urged in the Introduction to that book, it is unquestionable—or seems so to me—that, in an important class of cases, the metaphysical realist must offer up hostages to be redeemed by meaning-theoretic fortune. Not every realist, about whatever subject matter, is happily identified with Dummett's realist; but many kinds of realist that there actually are, about discourses as various as mathematics, science, history, and intentional psychology, should have the keenest interest in the debate about Dummett's realist—for their philosophical survival may depend on its outcome.

In saying that, I am presupposing, of course, that there *is* a debate about Dummett's realist, whose outcome is still uncertain—Blackburn's parade of notional strawmen and putative hardmen notwithstanding. Setting out its main lines will be the primary business of this essay,[5] and I have little space to attempt anything further. There is much in Blackburn's paper which I will not be able to engage. But I cannot resist a few, very general questions and comments about the "quasi-realist" alternative which Blackburn champions. So I will begin with those.

I: QUEASY-REALISM

What exactly is the recommended format for a demonstration that it *is* possible to explain the functioning of a discourse without invoking the idea of a "genuine order of objective facts" to which its apparent assertions (mis)correspond? In particular, is it necessary to provide an account of the discourse by whose lights its apparent assertions are portrayed as *only* apparent? This seemed to be so in *Spreading the Word*. There, the quasi-realist program for moral discourse explicitly undertakes an expressive, *ergo* nonassertoric construal of moral 'assertions' in general, including forms of construction, such as the conditional, which are regarded as problematical precisely because they seem to demand that (some of) their constituents be apt for assertion. But if this is the way that matters are supposed to go, then Blackburn's confident advocacy would seem to prejudge the satisfactory resolution, from his point of view, of a clutch of difficulties to which he has, so far as I am aware, no published effective response. To date, for instance, he has produced no satisfactory account of the validity of moral *modus ponens*, patterns of inference, like

> Stealing is wrong;
> If stealing is wrong, so is encouraging others to steal;
> ---
> Encouraging others to steal is wrong.

The *Spreading the Word* proposal has the effect that someone who accepts the premises but rejects the conclusion of such an inference is guilty only of a *moral* shortcoming,[6] while the modified account in "Attitudes and Contents"[7] implicitly surrenders, as Hale has demonstrated,[8] the expressive construal of moral 'assertions'. But in the absence of any account of so simple an inference pattern, there is simply not the slightest reason to believe that the quasi-realist has the resources for a satisfactory construal of moral argument.

There is, in any case, a very familiar kind of methodological peculiarity about this particular version of the quasi-realist proposal. Success could only consist, it seems, in establishing rules of transformation between ordinary, apparently assertoric moral discourse—to stay with this particular battleground—and a discourse in which no genuine assertions were made. But now a simple dilemma arises: Are the rules of transformation somehow guaranteed to be content-preserving? If not, nothing has been shown. If so, how is it supposed to be clear that no genuine assertions are made in the *reductive* discourse? If apparently assertoric syntax can mislead, so can apparently non-assertoric syntax. So in which direction does the significance of the transformations run? The question could only be answered in the light of an *independent* account of genuine assertoric function. But if we had one, why couldn't we apply it directly to moral discourse—what possible purpose is served by laboring for a putatively expressive reconstrual, no matter how ingeniously, if its significance must remain in doubt until an independent demonstration is to hand that moral discourse has no genuinely assertoric function?

This is only an adaptation of a difficulty which a large class of reductionist proposals have to meet. It is most familiar, of course, in the context of ontological reduction.[9] So far as I am aware, Blackburn nowhere explicitly addresses it. I do not present it as insoluble. But at least it is clear that a response which conserved the *Spreading the Word* conception of the quasi-realist program would have to establish a robust distinction between assertoric syntax—sentences' susceptibility to embedding within negation, the conditional construction, and operators of propositional attitude—and genuine assertibility. I see no cause to believe that any such distinction can be drawn which is suitable for Blackburn's purpose.[10]

The broad alternative is to drop the *Spreading the Word* conception, and to allow that any discourse which possesses the right kind of overt syntax and whose use exhibits sufficient discipline—minimally, there have to be recognized standards of proper and improper use of its ingredient sentences—is genuinely assertoric, and hence truth-value bearing[11] (*alethic*). This is not to surrender all vestige of quasi-realist *motif*—the program remains of making out a distinction between alethic discourses in accounting for which we need to invoke the idea of "a genuine order of objective facts" and alethic discourses for which that is not so. Blackburn himself has recently shown some sympathy for this redirection[12] and it is one to which I myself am sympathetic. But now it needs to be recognized that the major part of the work is to supply definite content for the type of phrase, like that just quoted, which too often passes for a formulation of what is in dispute in particular cases but is evidently incapable of discharging that role. Until that is done, it is utterly unclear what is really at issue about morals, or any of the other problematical discourses, or how it might competently be debated. One great merit of Dummett's overall interpretation of realist-antirealist disputes is its very clear response to this need. One may question whether Dummett's proposal is appropriate in every such dispute. But it is no easy matter to do better, or to elicit from Blackburn's paper any proposal approaching the same degree of clarity.

One distinction which Blackburn's phrase might conjure, and which I believe is at least part of his meaning, is that between discourses which respectively pass and fail the Best Explanation constraint.[13] A discourse passes the Best Explanation constraint if mention of states of affairs of the sort which it putatively describes features ineliminably in the best explanations of our forming the beliefs attested to by our assertions within it. This idea has, of course, been extensively discussed, particularly in the context of its apparent bearing on science and morals.[14] My own view, which I cannot attempt to substantiate here, is that it is doubtful whether the requisite notion of *best* explanation can easily be clarified—at least if the target comparison is to be to the disadvantage of morals—and that the important consideration in the vicinity is not whether e.g., moral facts need to be adverted to in the best explanation of moral belief but whether they enjoy a sufficiently *wide cosmological role*— whether they have enough of a part to play in the explanation of things *besides* our moral beliefs—to give substance to the idea that our moral beliefs *respond* to them.[15] However that may be, the fact is that if such are to be the issues between the realist and the quasi-realist, Blackburn ought not to write as though he is offering a new perspective. That there is a crux, on this point, for our intuitions about objectivity is already widely believed.

The suggestion that alethicity need not be at stake in such cruces, if that is indeed the direction in which Blackburn is now moving, seems to me to be important and correct. So too does the emphasis on the diversity of issues at stake in realist-antirealist debates. But Blackburn errs, in my opinion, when he writes—dubiously consistently, as noted—as if this diversity precluded any useful overall perspective. The right picture, it seems to me, is rather along the following lines. Sometimes alethicity is at stake, and antirealism takes the form of irrealism. When that is so, the issue concerns whether the discourse in question can be established in such a way as to conform to the somewhat minimal constraints of syntax and discipline which the applicability of a truth predicate calls for. This is, to give a single instance, precisely what is at issue over 'private language'. More often, however, alethicity is not—or ought not to be—at stake. It is not the issue, in particular, in any of the cases which Blackburn cites as prospective material for quasi-realist treatment (whatever exactly such a treatment would now consist in). What has been or may be at issue in such cases is indeed diverse: the prospects for convergence of opinion, the question whether divergence of opinion has to be attributable to something worth describing as cognitive shortcoming,[16] the questions to do with Best Explanation and Wide Cosmological Role, issues concerning whether the relation between *best* opinion—opinion formed by cognitively ideal subjects in cognitively ideal circumstances—and truth is, broadly, a relation of *consti-*

tution or of *tracking*, and indeed the question whether truth for the discourse in question is correctly taken to be evidentially unconstrained — any of these five issues and, no doubt, others can provide a *relevant* focus of debate. But they provide a relevant focus because, in each case, should the decision go in favor of the realist, the truth predicate takes on characteristics which go beyond anything demanded merely by its role in alethic discourse, and which are related in germane ways to the basic realist intuition of truth as a matter of a substantial correspondence between our thought and a domain of independent truth-conferring states of affairs.

It is clear enough, for instance, that we are committed so to regarding the truth-conferrers in the case of any discourse which, we suppose, satisfies the Best Explanation constraint; if states of affairs feature in the best explanation of our having certain beliefs, there is no question of regarding them merely as a *reflection* of the truth of those beliefs — something to which we are committed only and purely by holding the beliefs in question. Similarly, should best opinion in a particular discourse turn out to stand in a tracking relation to the truth, rather than in a constitutive relation, we are forced to think of truth for that discourse in a way which contrasts it with ideal assertibility, and of our most refined standards of acceptability as means of *access* to truth, which is constituted independently. By contrast, there is nothing in the alethicity of a discourse as such — before any of these matters are investigated — to frustrate the construal of its truth predicate in terms of assertibility.[17]

Inevitably, these remarks are very compressed. I am under no illusion that they provide an argument for the overview I am recommending. But maybe they serve to suggest a strategy of some promise. What is very immediate is that the issue of the evidence-transcendence of truth fits in perfectly. There is no clearer way of giving content to the realist image of thought in confrontation with an independent world: that *has* to be the way to conceive of the truth-conferrers if truth can clash with, or float free from the deliverance of all accessible evidence. To demonstrate that our understanding of a particular discourse is informed by such a conception of truth is not, of course, to show that what, in so understanding it, we take to be possible really is possible. Thus Dummett's realist cannot *win* by meeting his opponent's 'manifestation challenge' — he merely deflects an assault. But a demonstration that the challenge cannot be met is another matter. For it is surely absurd to suppose that the world might undetectably confer truth and falsity upon certain of our beliefs if nothing in our understanding of them involved any conception of how that might be so. Take it, then, that any such conception must be manifestable, and the dialectical point of the 'manifestation challenge' is evident enough.

To be sure, the overall picture I have outlined would not allow us immediately to write off realism about a discourse for which the manifestation challenge proved unanswerable. The possibility may remain of giving substance to and justifying a realist view of it in one of the other ways briefly canvassed. Equally, it may not — evidence-transcendent truth may be too central a commitment of the realism in question to allow of retrenchment to a view which dispenses with it yet remains realist in the same spirit. That is the situation of the kind of mathematical Platonism which stands opposed to mathematical Intuitionism as Dummett has interpreted it. And it is also, I would surmise, the situation of scientific realism if some appropriately nontrivial version of the Underdetermination thesis does indeed hold globally. In any case, the rightful place in the overall agenda belonging to the issue between Dummett's realist and his antirealist is, *pace* Blackburn, incontrovertible.

II: THE MANIFESTATION CHALLENGE

A head-on response to Blackburn's paper would identify one of his characters — the Teller, Surveyor, Theorist, Anti-reductionist, Insulationist, or Non-Guarantor — with the Real Realist, and proceed to explain why that character was indeed vulnerable to antirealist criticism. But there is, of course, absolutely no reason why such a response should be appropriate. To think otherwise is to mistake the point of calling the various antirealist lines of thought "challenges." A philosophical challenge consists in an argument that a number of beliefs, which are held individually to be attractive, are, if not outright inconsistent, at any rate in tension with each other. In the cases with which we are concerned, 'antirealism' is the label associated with certain specific responses to such a putative tension. But the ingredients in the tension are multiple, and it is therefore to be expected that someone to whom the recommended responses are unattractive will have options; at the least, there will be the option of trying to make out that there is in reality no tension. The character whom the antirealist is 'anti' can thus be anyone who, for whatever reason, either disputes the reality of the tension, or favors a nonrecommended response to it. It is, actually, easier to characterize the realist — for the purposes of this debate — than Blackburn manages to make it seem, and I will do so below. But the substantive questions are whether the tensions felt by the antirealist are genuine, and whether, if so, there are defensible responses besides those 'recommended'.

What in these terms are the beliefs which combine to set up the 'manifestation challenge'? Essentially, they are three. The first is the broadly Wittgensteinian conception of meaning and understanding according to which understanding an expression is knowing its proper use, and such knowledge consists in a complex of practical abilities. The Wittgensteinian idea is familiar (and vague) enough to strike most people now as a harmless platitude. But it has implications of importance. One is its repudiation of the idea of understanding as a kind of *interior informational state*, the source and explanation of competent use. Another is that *practical* abilities, in the spirit of the Wittgensteinian conception, are essentially abilities to perform appropriately in public: to perform in ways which may be publicly appraised as coming up to scratch, in the prevailing circumstances, or not. Now, possession of a publicly appraisable ability need not, in the general case, imply any capacity of self-appraisal, nor any capacity to recognize if or how prevailing circumstances are apt for its exercise. It is possible to be a performer without having the concepts of the critic—indeed, without having any concept of the circumstances to which the performance is a response. But it is different with understanding: the ability to appraise one's own and others' uses is here an essential ingredient in the original ability. The performance abilities that constitute an understanding of an expression do not count unless associated with the ability to *evaluate* one's own and others' performance with that expression. So understanding, if it is to be viewed as a practical ability at all, has to be seen as a complex of *discriminatory* capacities: an overall ability intentionally to suit one's use of the expression to the obtaining of factors which can be appreciated by oneself and others to render one's use apt.

A normal understanding of a declarative sentence, in particular, will involve a wide range of performance abilities: the ability to discriminate, *modulo* other germane beliefs, between what constitutes favorable, unfavorable, and neutral evidence with respect to it; the ability to recognize its inferential ancestry and progeny; the ability to construct explanations which use it, or bear on why it might be true or false; the ability appropriately to deploy ascriptions of propositional attitude which embed it; and so on. But each of these is essentially an appreciable—that is, manifestable—ability, which is also—since such appreciation is part of understanding—a *recognitional* ability, an ability to recognize whether and, if so, what in a prevailing context renders a particular use of the sentence appropriate. Thus the slogan: knowing the content of a statement is a complex of manifestable, recognitional skills.

Call this first Wittgensteinian ingredient the Manifestability Principle. The second ingredient is the thesis that what constitutes an understanding of any declarative sentence is a knowledge of its truth-conditions, a knowledge of how matters have to stand in order for it to be, respectively, either true or false. The Manifestability Principle and the Truth-Conditional Conception are not in overt tension exactly, although someone who wishes to endorse both at least has some explaining to do. The Manifestability Principle bids us view the understanding of a declarative sentence as a complex of abilities, and the Truth-Conditional Conception seems to superimpose a unifying frame, to postulate a thread which runs through the evidence-sifting, inferential, and other abilities involved in understanding the sentence and somehow binds them together. Knowing the truth-conditions of the sentence has to be a state which somehow guarantees possession of these various abilities, and the question must therefore arise how the guarantee is sustained.

It is when the third ingredient—the thesis that truth is unconstrained by the availability of evidence (Evidence Transcendence)—is introduced that a real tension is generated. For if truth in general is evidentially unconstrained, then—depending on its subject matter—knowing the truth-conditions of a sentence may require an understanding of how it could be undetectably true. And how could that knowledge consist—as the Manifestability Principle requires it must — in any ability whose proper exercise is tied to *appreciable* situations? How can knowing what it is for an unappreciable situation to obtain be constituted by capacities of discrimination exercised in response to appreciable ones?

I take it as obvious only that this is a good question, not that it does not have a good answer. But suppose it does not have a good answer. Then we ought to reject one or more of the ingredients. What is characteristic of any antirealist response to the manifestation challenge is that it will hold the first ingredient to be inviolable. There is, in the antirealist view, simply nothing for understanding to *be* if it is not conceived as by the Manifestability Principle. Now, there is, of course, logical space for a denial of that — Blackburn's Surveyor, for instance, occupies this space. But occupancy of the space is not the adversarial target of the challenge. On the contrary, the whole argument *presupposes* that nobody ought to want to be there.[18] In any case, Blackburn never suggests that this is a space which he personally would favor occupying, or that it is a response to the challenge worth taking seriously.

The antirealist, then, at least as far as the Manifestation Challenge is concerned, is someone who suspects that there is an irreconcilable tension between the three ingredients, and maintains that no satisfactory response to it can proceed via rejection of the Manifestability Principle. His or her options are therefore two: rejection of the Truth-Conditional Conception of statement understanding, or its retention subject to the constraint that the 'truth' in 'truth-conditions' denote an evidentially constrained notion. Many of Dummett's and my own earlier discussions of these matters proceeded on the assumption that truth is nothing if not classical (evidence-transcendent) and hence that the Truth-Conditional Conception has to be supplanted by something in which warranted assertion, or perhaps verification, plays the central role. It is therefore understandable that Blackburn's discussion should proceed on the same assumption — more specifically, on the assumption that antirealist semantics has to be assertibility-conditional.[19] But, if understandable, it is an assumption which he should nevertheless have avoided. For the bifurcation in the antirealist's options is explicit in the Introduction to *Realism, Meaning and Truth*[20] (henceforward, "the Introduction") and the prospects for a truth-conditional version of antirealist semantics are the center of attention in chapter 9, in which the play is made with the notion of superassertibility to which Blackburn refers.[21]

When the issue is set up in the way I have been describing, it is clear that Blackburn has heavy-weathered the question, Who is the realist? Realism about a given discourse, for the purposes of the manifestation challenge, is simply the combination of views (a) that the proper account of our understanding of its statements is evidence-unconstrained truth-conditional, and (b) that the world on occasion exploits, so to speak, this understanding — does on occasion deliver up undetectable truth-conferrers for those statements.[22] And, to repeat, it is worth describing such a view as "realism" because of the sharp separation which it imposes between the statements' being true on the one hand and their meeting our most refined criteria of acceptability on the other. None of the characters in Blackburn's parade is described as holding exactly this realism, though—if (b) is assumed—the Insulationist and the Non-guarantor will presumably do so.

Blackburn's claim, to be fair, was that it is difficult to find a *vulnerable* target for the manifestation challenge. Since there simply is no challenge if the Manifestability Principle is rejected, and since Blackburn himself shows no inclination to reject it, his thought has accordingly to be that there is no real tension: that it is consistent with accepting the Manifestability Principle to hold (a). So one real target is the realist as *Compatibilist*: a realist who aspires to a portfolio which contains (a), (b), and the Manifestability Principle. Is this a vulnerable target, or can such a combination be made coherent?

III: COMPATIBILISM

I have no general, conclusive proof that it cannot. But Blackburn, for his part, simply fails to confront the issue squarely. In order to see what confronting it squarely would involve, consider the example discussed in the Introduction,[23] of applications of simple predicates of taste—"sweet," "salty," "bitter," "sour," "spicy," and so on. What is it to understand statements of the form, "This is F," in which 'F' is one of these adjectives of taste and the demonstrated object is one of a number of food and drink samples placed in easy reach? What abilities are associated with such understanding? Well, there will typically be a number of "neighborhood abilities," in Blackburn's useful phrase: the abilities, for instance, to reason to and from such statements on the basis of collateral information, and to handle successfully more complex sentences, for instance, ascriptions of propositional attitude, in which descriptions of taste occur as embedded clauses. But in this instance, at least, there is an ingredient ability which is plausibly regarded as fundamental: the ability to recognize the tastes of the various samples by tasting them, and to report such recognition by using the statements in question.

That "This is salty" expresses a truth is a state of affairs which, in appropriate circumstances, may be verified to obtain by tasting the demonstrated substance. So much is uncontentious, and quite neutral on matters like the defeasibility of simple descriptions of taste or the question whether they somehow typify a class of judgments which might play a foundational role in some semantic or epistemological project. Simply: there is such a thing as the ability to discriminate tastes by tasting, and it is an appreciable, recognitional ability. Since to exercise it is to recognize whether or not the truth-conditions of sentences of the sort in question are satisfied, it is perfectly appropriate to regard it as amounting to a knowledge of their truth-conditions.

This ability unquestionably constitutes one aspect of our understanding of the sentences in question. Is it just one aspect, though? It is tempting to say more: *viz*. that this recognitional grasp of the truth-conditions of such judgments constitutes the core of understanding them, so that if someone does indeed have this grasp, but apparently lacks some of the neighborhood abilities, we are obliged to locate the deficiency in understanding—if that is what it is—elsewhere. Conversely, we are strongly inclined to say that someone who proved unable to acquire the core recognitional abilities could have no real understanding of the content of such statements, even if that person was rather successful at acquiring the neighborhood abilities—rather as someone whose vision was monochromatic might acquire grasp of a good stock of proxy-grounds for claims about color.

If these ideas are defensible, then, in the case of such judgments, the Manifestability Principle and the Truth-Conditional Conception can be made to cohere perfectly. Grasp of such judgments' truth-conditions will be a manifestable, recognitional skill, and there will be a case for regarding it as constitutive of an understanding of them. But what is here conspicuously lacking, of course, is any place for the third ingredient in the original tension: the Evidence-Transcendence of truth. It is possible—if it is possible—to bring the Manifestability Principle and the Truth-Conditional Conception together in the fashion sketched only because 'grasp of truth-conditions' can here be *identified* with a recognitional ability; and it can be so only because we conceive of the states of affairs which confer truth and falsity on these judgments as, by their very nature, detectable. It would be different if we were concerned with a type of judgment whose truth-conferrers we conceived as merely sometimes detectable, but on other occasions inaccessible to us. For to grasp the truth-conditions of such judgments could not be identified merely with the ability to recognize that they were satisfied in the favorable kind of case; it would be necessary, in addition, to understand what it would be for them to be satisfied unrecognizably. And the problem would then be to construe that understanding as the Manifestability Principle requires.

Blackburn's patter about "men of straw" and "cracked instruments" notwithstanding, I believe that most people would be instinctually drawn to the idea that the role played by grasp of truth-conditions in the taste example is in no way special—that what is special is only that here we can find a distinctive practical ability for grasp of truth-conditions to be. That is: when, as in the examples, statements about the remote past, counterfactual conditionals, putative general laws, and so on, on which the debate has tended to concentrate, the 'neighborhood abilities' are all the practical abilities that there are, our instinct is to think that there is something more: precisely, the old 'interior informational state', serving to inform the exercise of the neighborhood abilities and to bind them together. The thought is that understanding a statement is *always* like that in essentials; what distinguishes the taste example is just that, quite unusually, the core of understanding here steps forward to show itself on the surface. As I say, I believe that this is our instinctual view. But it does occasionally surface in professional philosophy. A very clear contemporary expression is due not to a strawman but to Strawson:

> A rational speaker's grasp of this language is *manifested* in, *inter alia*, his responding in certain ways to the recognizable situations with which he is and has been confronted. . . . Wright seems to take it as evident that the rational speaker's response to such situations can in *no* case be *governed* by a certain kind of conception—a conception of a state of affairs, of a condition of truth, which, for one reason or another, in fact or in principle, is not, or is no longer, or is not for the speaker, accessible to direct observation or memory . . . [But] this question—whether the rational speaker's response can be so governed—is just the question at issue.[24]

How can we interpret the emphasis on "governed" if it is not that Strawson intends that the understanding should be thought of as something detached from the neighborhood abilities from which they flow?

However that may be, Blackburn is, as noted, agreed that this noncompatibilist direction is not the way to go. But then, what is the way to go? So far as I can see, there is only one: the compatibilist line has to be that the connection between understanding and grasp of truth-conditions is *platitudinous*.[25] And such is, in effect, Blackburn's proposal. One could spell the thought out like this. To understand a statement is to know what it says, which will be that a certain state of affairs obtains. But it is *a priori* and common knowledge, that when S says that P, it follows that S is true if and only if P. So the obtaining of the relevant state of affairs has to be conceived, by one who understands the statement, as necessary and sufficient for its truth. Hence, whatever abilities constitute the understanding of a statement, we cannot but acquiesce in its description as "grasp of truth-conditions." In particular, if only 'neighborhood abilities' are available, then *they* constitute a knowledge of the statement's truth-conditions.

The antirealist who favors responding to the manifestation challenge by "dethroning truth and falsity from their central place in . . . the theory of meaning"[26] presumably has some work to do in response to this line of thought. Not so, though, the antirealist who favors retention of the Truth-Conditional Conception, *modulo* an evidentially constrained conception of truth. And the staring fact is that the line of thought does absolutely nothing to dissipate the tension to which this antirealist is responding. *Identifying* grasp of a statement's truth-conditions with possession of a network of practical, discriminatory abilities—the 'neighborhood abilities'—simply makes it the more puzzling how, in grasping those truth-conditions, we are somehow guaranteed to understand the possibility, in the case of a suitable example, that those conditions be satisfied undetectably. There is absolutely no progress. The question remains: how, specifically, is the idea that statements of a certain kind can be unrecognizably true or false on display in our ordinary evidential, inferential, explanatory, and other practices with them? The 'neighborhood abilities' are all appreciable, recognitional abilities. Let it be a platitude, or a consequence of platitudes, that they compose a knowledge of truth-conditions; the question is, how do they compose a knowledge of (potentially) *evidence-transcendent* truth-conditions—how would they differ if, for whatever reason, we thought of truth as essentially evidence-constrained?

Blackburn resurrects the charge, first made in *Spreading the Word*,[27] that the demand for manifestability is ill-conceived until we have specified the powers of the intended audience. I discussed this charge in the Introduction, but although Blackburn refers to that discussion, I do not seem to have succeeded in making its point clear. Summarily: there is no problem at all about specifying the powers of the intended audience—to manifest my understanding of a statement, I need an audience who *understand* that statement. This whole debate is taking place with respect to regions of discourse which all the protagonists are presumed fully to understand. The question is: what can someone do, in using a particular statement, to rightly convince an audience, who understand that statement, that the proper description of his or her understanding combines all three elements in the original tension? Blackburn's reply then comes to this: maybe nothing can be done unless the *audience's* understanding already combines those elements. But this offers no assurance whatever in a context in which their combinability is already *sub judice*. Besides, if Blackburn is right, the chances are that his antirealist opponent provides a 'suitable audience', *malgre soi*. So why not just answer the question? Let us have a description—appreciable by anyone who understands whatever kind of statement is giving rise to the problem—of what specifically, in the exercise of an understanding of such statements, manifests the fact that it consists in grasping a potentially evidence-transcendent truth-condition.

It is important not to mistake what is being requested. The question is not—at least in the first instance—how one might manifest the *belief* that one's own understanding was realist. Presumably it would be allowable to *say* that it was. The issue rather concerns what in one's use of the relevant class of statements would manifest the fact that this belief was *true*.[28] In the nature of the case, then, one is looking for evidence in linguistic practice apart from the mere protestation of realism. Someone could *profess* a conception, for instance, which allowed that the comic quality of a situation could be evidence-transcendent. "For the humor of a situation to be inaccessible to us," they might claim, "is only and purely for the situation relevantly to resemble situations whose comic quality is apparent to us, but without the resemblance being apparent." Compare: for someone to be unbreakably stoically in pain —a Putnam X-worlder[29]—is just for it to be with them as it is with others who are in pain and, one way or another, can be brought to show it; it is just that this subject cannot be brought to show it. Such a possibility strikes us (doesn't it?) as an absurd misrepresentation of our understanding of discourse about the comic; we have no conception, surely, of what comic quality could consist in if it is allowed to transcend any elicitable human response. But *showing* that is so would require, precisely, a demonstration that the best account of our understanding of statements about the comic, as manifested in our use of them, left no space for the alleged possibility.

So too for any philosophy of mind which would allow inscrutable stoicism to be a possibility: the prior question is whether we actually understand ascriptions of sensation, and of mental states in general, in such a way that evidence-transcendent truth-conferral makes sense. And that is a question which can be settled only by reference to the verdict on the matter of the best account of our use of discourse concerning the mental. Making good the compatibilist response, when understanding is regarded as platitudinously truth-conditional, has to consist in finding something in the overt nature of the 'neighborhood abilities'—apart from mere professions of realism—which is best explained by viewing the 'truth' that is thereby platitudinously linked with understanding as (potentially) evidence-transcendent. The story could concern, perhaps, our acceptance of a particular kind of evidence, or inference pattern; or it might be that the use of certain embedding contexts was hard to explain otherwise.[30] I am far less confident than I was ten years ago that such a story can never be told. But to meet the manifestation challenge is to tell such a story, and Blackburn's paper contains no clear response to this simple and utterly legitimate demand. Indeed, except in his discussion of what he perceives as the shortcomings of the assertibility-conditions approach to our understanding of undecided mathematical statements, he never so much as gets down to cases.

Let me stress again that the manifestation question only concerns the character of our understanding. The question is: Have we assigned meaning to the statements in a certain discourse in such a way that there is space for the world to deliver up evidence-transcendent truth-conferrers for them? So an affirmative answer is not yet a commitment to realism.[31] Someone might give an affirmative answer and hold that, for independent reasons, there is no reality to which the discourse answers at all. What we are exploring, in the issue about manifestation, is whether a *necessary* condition is satisfied for the appropriateness of a certain kind of realist view: the view that holds that, in the discourse in question, truth and optimal justification extensionally diverge, and hence that we have to think of the domain of states of affairs in which the truth-conferrers are to be found as constituted independently of our cognitive activity.

IV: REVISIONISM AND HOLISM

If the whole antirealist polemic were provided by the manifestation challenge, as described, it might seem very unclear how there could be any support for the revisionist philosophy of logic which Dummett has famously advocated. For surely one cannot sensibly urge both that it is moot whether anything in one's practice of a discourse of a certain kind manifests understanding of a certain character and, in the same breath, urge revision of aspects of the practice which, it is claimed, would only be appropriate *if* the understanding were of that character. Either, it seems, the case for revision must be inconclusive

— because the relevant aspects of the practice could as well be sanctioned in other ways — or else it is ill-founded, those very aspects providing the requisite distinctive manifestation that one's understanding of the discourse has the character in question.

One answer would be that no difficulty need arise if the Dummettian revisionist can provide an *independent* argument that understanding cannot be evidence-transcendent truth-conditional — perhaps from considerations to do with concept-acquisition. But in that case there would be no purpose to the argument about manifestation. The ground for saying that the problematical understanding could not be manifest in practice would be that it could not in any case be *possessed*; and that would directly provide motive enough for revision of aspects of practice which seemed to depend upon it. So the question remains: How can the manifestation challenge contribute, as Dummett evidently intends that it should, to a revisionary philosophy of logic?

The answer is that revisionism, if it is to be based on the manifestation challenge, needs *molecularism*: it needs the claim that the dubious kind of understanding, if it were not to be dubious, would have to be manifest in our practice within a *fragment* of the discourse where it is, at least *prima facie*, not manifest. Only then can it coherently be argued that aspects of the discourse outside that fragment, in whose practice the dubious conception *is* reflected, involve malpractice.[32] Dummett, I hasten to say, has never been under any illusions about this, and has always taken an explicitly molecular view, believing that anything else will lead to an incoherent form of holism.

I myself am far from persuaded whether that is so; and somewhat skeptical also about the possibility of making good the presupposition that our understanding of the statements in a discourse may be fully on display in advance of any consideration of the way we use certain contexts which embed them.[33] But the point I want to emphasize here is that it is in this context that the issues to do with holism arise. Blackburn represents Dummett as invoking the specter of meaning-holism in response to the extension of 'grasp of truth-conditions' to cover all the 'neighborhood abilities'.[34] I suspect that Dummett would, rightly in my view, offer no objection to so using 'grasp of truth-conditions'. In any case, the issues to do with holism are properly located elsewhere on the map.

V: THE ARGUMENT FROM NORMATIVITY

I have here concentrated on considerations to do with the manifestation of understanding, because Blackburn concentrates on them. Understandably, since the suggestion was not developed in *Realism, Meaning, and Truth*, he makes nothing of the fourth antirealist argument which I briefly canvassed in the Introduction — that which ties the issues concerning evidence-transcendent truth-conditions to what have come to be known as 'the rule-following considerations'. The key thought here is that, since the relation which obtains between a statement and its truth-conferrer is an *internal* relation—it being an essential characteristic of that statement to be rendered true by that state of affairs and an essential characteristic of that state of affairs to render true any statement with that content—belief in evidence-transcendent truths is a commitment to belief in unratifiable internal relations. And that belief can be sustained only on the picture of rules and rule-following which embodies the "myth of super-rigid machinery" on which Wittgenstein targets his discussions. My own belief is that this is probably the most powerful of the weapons in the antirealist's armory, although I cannot of course go into its details here. But note that it bites in a rather different place to the manifestation challenge. The target of the latter is whether anything in our understanding of a discourse prepares for the possibility that the world might confer truth-values upon its statements undetectably; but the conclusion of the argument from rule-following is to the effect that, even if our understanding of a discourse is so prepared, the world cannot ever actually *bring about* a determinate undetectable truth. For a statement's being undetectably true could only consist, to repeat, in the obtaining of an unratifiable internal relation.

Blackburn does, however, have some things to say about what, in the Introduction, I called the Argument from Normativity. In rough outline, the argument runs like this. Only sentences with assertoric content are apt to be true. And, trivially, for a sentence to have assertoric content is for its content to equip it for use in accordance with whatever constraints assertions distinctively have to conform to. Accordingly, since truth is normative of proper assertion—is that at which assertion is, properly, essentially aimed—it is a condition of a sentence's having assertoric content that it may in certain circumstances be used as an *attempt* at the truth. But, for reasons to do with the nature of intention which were outlined in the Introduction,[35] there is no aiming at the truth by the use of a sentence whose truth, it is known—if it could be true—would transcend all possible evidence.

As Blackburn in effect argues, the argument bears directly only on his realist as Insulationist—a realist who believes that, in the nature of the case, the truth-values of the statements in a certain region of discourse are beyond human ken. For in that case, whatever is regulating proper practice in the discourse in question, it cannot be the aim of truth so conceived; and the 'grasp of truth-conditions' which platitudinously constitutes understanding of those statements cannot be grasp of conditions of insulated truth. Blackburn does not quarrel with the point about intention, and acknowledges that "insulationism is tempting and worth fighting against." Nevertheless, he finds the argument unconvincing:

> Truth may indeed be a norm governing assertoric discourse, but . . . this may not be its only role. The concept appears to figure in thoughts like "there may be truths about which we shall never be able to reason", or "there may be truths accessible only to minds alien to ours" and a

proponent of the normativity argument will need to wrestle with the stubborn appearance of intelligibility in such thoughts.[36]

Well, but are the allegedly possible truths to which these putatively intelligible thoughts advert at least to be expressible in our language? They had better be: it would be a stupendous *ignoratio elenchi* to reproach an argument which—like all the arguments for semantic antirealism—is concerned with the proper account of truth and truth-conditions for assertoric discourses which we understand for its failure to foreclose on realist sentiment which takes refuge in the ineffable. Assume, therefore, that Blackburn is not doing that, and that the 'stubbornly intelligible-seeming' thoughts refer to possible truths which we would have the means to convey by intelligible assertion. In that case, the argument was that it is a constraint on the means of conveyance that it be possible to use the relevant sentences to aim at the truth. So can we so aim in the putative cases in question? Not, according to the considerations about intention, if we *know* that the sentences in question, if they express truths at all, express truths which we cannot reason about and which cannot be accessible to minds like ours. But if our knowing that is not part of the scenario, then the supporter of the intelligibility of the thoughts in question cannot be Blackburn's Insulationist. The position calls, rather, for the realist as Non-Guarantor.

The Non-Guarantor holds not that truth and falsity within a given discourse are *a priori* inaccessible to us, but only that they may be. Is this position engaged by the argument from normativity? Blackburn fails to see that it can be, arguing that if truth for the statements of the discourse is merely potentially evidence-transcendent, then we can surely try for it, even if, *de facto*, we cannot actually succeed. But if I seemed to suggest to the contrary, I shouldn't have. The argument, as against the Non-Guarantor, is not that we cannot aim at truth in regions of discourse where we are prone to conceive of truth as potentially inaccessible, but rather that it is not that notion of truth at which we should be regarded as aiming. One case for saying so, sketched in "Truth-conditions and Criteria,"[37] is to the effect that there is simply no difference between aiming at a potentially evidence-transcendent objective and aiming at the realization of a situation in which there is evidence that the objective has after all been attained. This argument brings the issue back into the area of manifestability: the claim is that, as far as the pattern assumed by my linguistic practice is concerned, it is all the same whether I am aiming at a species of truth which may be associated with favorable evidence but may also be inaccessible in any particular case, or at a species of truth which, I conceive, must issue in the availability of favorable evidence whenever it applies. Either way, the constraints on proper assertion will be the same.

In the Introduction, however, I tried to tackle the Non-Guarantor somewhat differently.[38] To understand a statement as associated with potentially evidence-transcendent truth-conditions would have to be—assuming sufficient expressive resources in the language—to understand what it would be for a statement which averred that the former *was* undetectably true to be itself true, *a fortiori* undetectably so. But the possible truth of such a statement requires its possession of assertoric content, and therefore, it was supposed, its serviceability under certain circumstances for an *attempt* to speak the truth. And, so it was argued, there is no attempting anything if one has no beliefs about how to succeed, no intelligible motive for success, and if success will have no discernible consequences. So we cannot attempt the truth by the use of any statement which, like '*S* is undetectably true' can only be true by being so undetectably. The consequence would be that such a statement lacks genuine assertoric content, and hence is not itself in the market for truth, so that our understanding of the original *S* was misrepresented when portrayed as involving its association with potentially evidence-transcendent truth-conditions.

One difference between this argument against the Non-Guarantor and the original directed against the Insulationist is that the point about intention may seem slightly less secure in the former case, where failure at least—in the form of *S*'s turning out *detectably* true or false—can have discernible consequences. But I do not think that this is an important difference. At most, it can reinstate the *avoidance of detectable failure* as an attemptable objective; and avoiding detectable failure is not, in the examples we are concerned with, the same thing as success. In any case, the obligations of an opponent of these arguments are quite clear: reason must be found to reject either the proposed constraint on assertoric content, or the considerations about intention. Again, there is obviously much more to say, and I am by no means confident that it will go the antirealist's way. For instance: Can statements of, by the lights of the argument, dubious assertoric content ('*S* is undetectably true') sustain determinate logical relations with statements ('*S* is detectably true') for which the argument occasions no difficulty? But this is not an occasion when I can pursue these issues. My purpose in this section has been only to clarify the normativity argument somewhat and to scotch the impression given by Blackburn that I had made no distinction between the Insulationist and Non-Guarantor as far as the bearing of the argument was concerned, believing that the *de facto* unavailability of evidence for the truth of a statement would be as much an obstacle to the possibility of using it with the aim of truth as would the knowledge *a priori* that no such evidence could be available.[39]

Notes

1. See p. 46 of Blackburn's "Manifesting Realism" in this volume.
2. See p. 45 in this volume.
3. See p. 45 in this volume.
4. Wright, *Realism, Meaning, and Truth* (Oxford, 1987), ix.
5. It is, in a way, disappointing to have occasion to do so. I had hoped that the Introduction, in particular, to *Realism, Meaning, and Truth* might have set the issues in a somewhat clearer light than Blackburn's discussion reflects. But there are no

canonical formulations of these matters, and none, I am sure, in *Realism, Meaning, and Truth* that cannot be improved.

6. See p. 33 and note 19 of my "Realism, Anti-realism, Irrealism, Quasi-realism," in *Midwest Studies in Philosophy* 12 (1988):25-49. Other problems besetting the *Spreading the Word* proposals for an expressive construal of moral discourse are raised by Bob Hale in "The Compleat Projectivist," *Philosophical Quarterly* 36 (1986): 65-84, and G. F. Schueler, "Modus Ponens and Moral Realism," *Ethics* 98 (1988): 492-500.

7. Simon Blackburn, "Attitudes and Contents," *Ethics* 98 (1988): 501-17.

8. Bob Hale, "Can There Be a Logic of Attitudes?" in *Reality: Representation and Projection*, edited by John Haldane and Crispin Wright (Oxford, 1990).

9. See W. P. Alston, "Ontological Commitments," *Philosophical Studies* 9 (1958): 8-17, and my *Frege's Conception of Numbers as Objects* (Atlantic Highlands, N.J., 1983), chap. 1, section v.

10. One such possible but, for Blackburn's purposes, unsuitable distinction is proposed in the concluding section of the present essay—unsuitable because it engages only 'assertions' which are apparently apt for undetectable truth and so has no bearing, presumably, on moral assertions. For further misgivings about the kind of distinction Blackburn needs, see "Realism, Anti-realism, Irrealism, Quasi-realism," and also my "Anti-realism: The Contemporary Debate—Whither Now?" in *Reality: Representation and Projection*, edited by John Haldane and Crispin Wright (Oxford, 1990), and the Introduction to my *Realism, Rules, and Objectivity* (London, forthcoming).

11. Since it is by way of a platitude that to assert a sentence is to present it as true.

12. In the Nelson Lectures at the University of Michigan, September 1988.

13. Cf. "Realism, Anti-realism, Irrealism, Quasi-realism," 40-42, and "Anti-realism: The Contemporary Debate—Whither Now?" section IV.

14. See, for instance, Gilbert Harman, *The Nature of Morality: An Introduction to Ethics* (Oxford, 1977), chap. 1; David Wiggins, *Needs, Values, Truth* (London, 1987), essay IV, "Truth as Predicated of Moral Judgments," sections 9 and 10; Nicholas Sturgeon, "Moral Explanations," in *Morality, Reason, and Truth*, edited by David Copp and David Zimmerman (Totowa, N.J., 1985), 49-78.

15. For more on this see, again, "Anti-realism: The Contemporary Debate—Whither Now?" section IV, and *Realism, Rules, and Objectivity*.

16. The question of *Rational Command* as it is styled in "Realism, Anti-realism, Irrealism, Quasi-realism."

17. Or, more specifically, in terms of *superassertibility*. See *Realism, Meaning, and Truth*, chap. 9, and "Anti-realism: The Contemporary Debate—Whither Now?" section II.

18. That is not to say that only men of straw—or their progeny—are to be found there. Cf. the passage from Sir Peter quoted below. If it seems to us obvious nowadays that there is nothing to be made of understanding if it is conceived contrary to the Manifestability Principle—for instance, as an interior representation of correct use—it is largely owing to the assimilation into the general philosophical consciousness of the critique of such ideas in the *Philosophical Investigations*. And the target of this critique was not the views of some imaginary Aunt Sally, but an extremely natural and influential lay-philosophical misconception.

19. It is still, of course, an egregious error to attempt to make capital out of the supposed consequence of such a semantical approach that statements—like the "old campaigners"—which are *a priori* insulated from all rational assessment, and hence have no conditions of warranted assertion, are therefore meaningless. Meaningless sentences to be sure, do not have conditions of warranted assertion. But Blackburn argues as if the converse were evident (p. 41). And the fact is that the antirealist has as much

title as anyone else to treat it as a criterion for understanding one of the old campaigners—for instance, if it indeed comes into that category, "Everything is uniformly increasing in size"—that someone be able e.g., to explain why, in view of the meanings of its constituent expressions and their manner of combination, nothing could count as evidence for its truth.

20. *Realism, Meaning and Truth*, 36.

21. P. 40 in this volume.

22. Strictly, it might be enough if, even if the world never actually so delivered, its failure to do so was merely contingent. Note that Dummett's original formulations of realism, in which the view is characterized as essentially the endorsement of a bivalent truth-conditional semantics, thereby involve, for suitable discourses, a rolled-into-one version of the semantic and worldly aspects which I have separated as (a) and (b).

23. *Realism, Meaning, and Truth*, 17f.

24. P. F. Strawson, "Scruton and Wright on Anti-realism Etc.," *Proceedings of the Aristotelian Society* 77 (1977): 15-21, esp. 16.

25. This is the line pursued by John McDowell in "Anti-realism and the Epistemology of Understanding," in *Meaning and Understanding*, edited by H. Parret and J. Bouveresse (Berlin, 1981), 225-48, see especially pages 229-31. For further references and discussion, see the Introduction, 18 f.

26. Dummett, concluding pragraph of "Truth," in *Proceedings of the Aristotelian Society* 59 (1959): 141-62.

27. *Spreading the Word*, 65-66.

28. The situation is dialectically somewhat subtle, however. Suppose we recoil from the idea that a subject's possession of a belief could be manifest only in its avowal; then it might be a condition of so much as believing—genuinely believing—that one's understanding of a class of statements was realist that one behave in ways which would supply the materials for a direct response to the manifestation challenge, and thereby establish the belief as true.

29. Hilary Putnam, "Brains and Behavior," in his *Language, Mind and Reality: Philosophical Papers*, vol. 2 (Cambridge, 1975): 325-41.

30. Relevant problems here are posed by the so-called Paradox of Knowability; see the Appendix, "Could Thatcher be a Master Criminal?" to chap. 9 of *Realism, Meaning, and Truth* for discussion and references. More recent references include a series of discussion notes by Timothy Williamson, including "On Knowledge of the Unknowable," *Analysis* 47 (1987): 154-58; "On the Paradox of Knowability," *Mind* 96 (1987): 256-61; and "Knowability and Constructivism," *Philosophical Quarterly* 38 (1988): 422-32.

31. This distinction is well emphasized in Michael Luntley's *Language, Logic, and Experience* (San Pablo, Calif., 1987).

32. For detailed discussion of the issues here, see Neil Tennant's *Anti-realism and Logic* (Oxford, 1987), sections 6-10.

33. See *Realism, Meaning, and Truth*, chap. 10, "Anti-realism and Revisionism," for elaboration of these misgivings.

34. P. 35 in this volume.

35. *Realism, Meaning, and Truth*, 24-26.

36. P. 41 in this volume.

37. Section IV; *Realism, Meaning, and Truth*, 58-61.

38. *Realism, Meaning, and Truth*, 24.

39. Simon Blackburn presented an ancestor of "Manifesting Realism" as a Nelson Lecture at the University of Michigan in September 1988. When I learned that it was destined for the present volume, I was very keen that something by way of reply should

appear alongside it. I am extremely grateful to Howard Wettstein for being willing to publish the present, inevitably very hastily drafted effort, and to Bob Hale and Stephen Yablo for very helpful criticism at short notice.

Between Reference and Meaning*

JULIUS M. MORAVCSIK

In the tradition of Frege and Carnap meanings of lexical items like words or phrases are construed as sets of qualitative conditions of application, necessary and jointly sufficient. The elements to which the given word or phrase applies constitute the denotation or reference of the word. This dichotomy has been used successfully to explain many semantic phenomena. In recent decades this framework has come under attack from various quarters. In the case of indexical expressions, in particular demonstratives, we need a more elaborate conceptual scheme; the meaning—denotation distinction will not suffice—a fact anticipated to some extent by the originators of the theory. Evidence has been presented also to show that the "standard theory," as we will call it, is not adequate for the analysis of proper names in natural languages, and that some of the inadequacies uncovered in this connection might affect also the analysis the standard theory would give of natural kind terms. Still other attacks have centered on claims that, in the case of analyzing certain expressions, the semantics has to take into consideration the speaker's knowledge of the world and possibly his perceptual context, or in some cases the shared knowledge of reality possessed at any given time by a linguistic community.

I mention all of this only to lay it aside. The claim I shall develop in this paper is independent of whatever position one might take on the issues surveyed above. I am considering the meanings of certain words under the assumption that these meanings are constituted by qualitative conditions that are necessary and are *prima facie* candidates for being jointly sufficient. My claim is that apart from indexicality and other kinds of speaker-hearer relative context-sensitivity, even in the case of the qualitative meaning specifications, there is a need to posit a level of semantics between meaning and reference or denotation. Meanings, in the intuitive sense of this word, do not by themselves determine reference in many cases. Thus I wish to substitute for many words a three-level analysis to replace the traditional two-level analysis. The meanings that a dictionary would give us provide only necessary conditions of a certain kind. Reflection on these necessary conditions enables us to see that linked with these meanings we find many distinct ranges of denotation. These ranges constitute the second level. We move from these to the third level which is constituted by the set of elements to which the word truly applies. I shall offer some thoughts about how we are able to move from the necessary conditions provided by the meanings to the necessary and sufficient conditions which jointly determine the denotation, i.e., the third level. I shall also attempt to delineate, roughly, the extent to which this phenomenon affects a language like English, and draw some tentative conclusion of what all of this shows about the semantics of lexical items in general.

I. A STORY AND A PROPOSAL

Let us suppose that a certain Professor Jones is the chairperson of a philosophy department, and that he is going on a six-month leave to Europe. Before he departs he has a discussion with his secretary about how to manage things while he is away. In the course of this discussion he says to her: "Don't phone me except in case of an emergency." She agrees. I take it that at this point on the one hand it is true that both the professor and the secretary understand the meaning of 'emergency', and they have no difficulty fitting this word into the sentence quoted. Nevertheless, it seems that further discussion is called for. The situation is not analogous to contexts like the one in which a wife says to her husband: "Please get my red dress from the other room." In that case, understanding what is being said and being able to locate "the other room" is all that is needed in order for the appropriate action to ensue, at least as far as semantics is concerned. And sure enough, Professor Jones continues the conversation by saying: "By 'emergency' I mean here things like an earthquake, injury to my children, the university going bankrupt, etc." Even if both secretary and professor understand English perfectly, it is informative for Professor Jones to add this. Furthermore, his proposal is subject to critical assessment. One can imagine the secretary simply nodding, or raising questions of clarification, or of a critical nature. In short, there is conceptual room for negotiation, and in such negotiations norms of a public and social nature may be invoked.

Let us suppose now that Professor Jones returned from abroad, but after having cleared away the administrative work that has piled up, he feels that it is appropriate for him to take half a day off here and there so that he can get his research done. On a day before such an event, he discusses with his secretary the fact that he will work at home the next day, and in the course of the discussion says to her once more: "Don't phone me except in case of an emergency." Again the secretary nods, but again we feel that there is a need for further discussion. And Professor Jones being a good administrator does indeed go on to say: "By 'emergency' I mean here the students staging a protest march, one of my colleagues rushing in hysterically, or a memo from the Dean announcing that he intends to cut the budget of every department for next year by 20 percent and giving each department twenty-four hours to raise objections." As in the previous case, there is room for further discussion and even negotiation. The nature of the discussion, reasons put forward, and negotiation is roughly the same as in the other case.

I hope that it would be agreed generally that such things can and do happen in departments all the time. We observe, first, the professor is using 'emergency' in the two cases with the same meaning. It would make no sense to say that in these cases 'emergency' is being used ambiguously. It seems also clear that meaning by itself in these cases does not determine denotation. We have two use occasions with the same meaning evoked and different denotations. Thus we need to figure out how the denotations in the two cases are eventually determined. But there is a prior question. Brief reflection on the two cases should convince us that there are in fact many denotation-determining contexts for a conversation involving the linguistic units mentioned. There is a father talking to his family as he prepares for going outside the house to clean the gutters, the physician leaving his office for lunch, and the lawyer ducking out early to get in a round of golf, etc. And yet we feel that these denotation-determining circumstances are not arbitrarily generable. They have something intuitively important in common which we need to conceptualize.

The different applications considered in the story generate genuine contradictions. That is to say, even though the circumstances mentioned under which it is legitimate to phone the professor abroad are also legitimate circumstances when he just stays at home for a morning, this does not hold the other way around. Thus a colleague running around hysterically both is and is not an emergency. It is not an emergency when the professor is abroad, but it is when he is just at home for a few hours.[1]

In summary, there seem to be three levels for the semantics. First, there is the meaning of the word 'emergency'. Second, there are the many circumstances that determine denotation ranges. Third, there is the matter of fixing within each one of these ranges what the denotation really is. The last sentence requires a qualification. Intuitively it might sound better if one said " . . . what the denotation is, or should be." This suggests that there is something normative about some of the factors determining denotation, and this will have to be accounted for.

Let us now consider the meaning of 'emergency'. The following rough definition will do for our purposes: 'emergency' = 'a state of an impending or already occurring harmful event, requiring immediate response'. It is easy to show that the conditions embodied in this definition are necessary. An emergency is clearly a state and that is how we individuate it. It is not an activity or a material object or an abstract entity like the number 2. In a universe in which there are not states, there are no emergencies. The event has to be impending or already occurring. If it is still far in the future, then things look tough but we do not have, yet, an emergency. That the event has to be harmful needs hardly a mention; 'emergency' has negative connotations. The emergency room in the hospital is not called that for nothing. The condition that there is a "requirement" here brings up interesting issues with which we shall deal later. Here it suffices to point out that without some "requirement" in a relevant sense, there is only a disaster, not an emergency. Similar considerations hold for the last condition involving immediate response. It is because of the immediacy that we want a good person, who is capable of quickly surveying situations, at the helm when emergencies arise.

Having seen that the conditions are necessary, we shall review the evidence showing that they are not sufficient. We need not bother with the notions of event and state, since it is obvious that these only place the emergency and one of its constituents in the appropriate categories. But 'impending' already poses problems. Clearly, an event can be impending in some minimal sense and still not be in the right proximity so as to evoke a state of emergency. For example, an impending disaster can be two or twenty or two hundred years away, depending on whether we are talking about floods, earthquakes, or environmental catastrophe. What counts as "about to happen" depends on the social, economic, or physical context and their interpretations. Thus one would have to add: "sufficiently or appropriately impending" in order to get at the condition one wants in a given set of circumstances. There are even greater problems with 'harmful'. An event can be harmful in a minimal sense and still not count as the kind of event that will evoke an emergency. But there is no way to specify an intensive quantity of harmfulness "across the board" that will serve as the right threshold. We have to see whether we are considering lawyers, professors, physicians, etc. and leaves of absence or visits to a mother-in-law. Thus merely being harmful is not enough. Similar considerations affect the conditions of immediacy and of being a response. How immediate is the response that is required? For a declaration of war it might be weeks, for a firefighter it might be minutes, for a surgeon in O.R. it might be seconds. Merely being immediate in some minimal sense is not enough. Finally, we encounter the same difficulties when considering the notion of a response. What counts as a response? For example shrugging your shoulders? Scratching your back? Again, we need to look at the public roles of the agents involved, the nature of the impending event, etc. Furthermore, the factors mentioned are not unrelated.

On any literal reading, then, the proposed definition provides necessary but not sufficient conditions. But someone might try to remedy the situation by inserting the words 'sufficiently' or 'appropriately' in the right places as modifiers for the phrases which we found wanting. But this move seems to be just a case of playing with words, a roundabout way of saying that when we want to find the denotation we need to look at factors other than the ones mentioned in the definition. Furthermore, adding these words as modifiers still does not take us away from the fact that for fixing denotation we are not looking at every individual case, but at types of cases, and the types form a nonarbitrary class, linked in some conceptual way to the ingredients of the meaning of 'emergency'.

This last consideration shows also why it is a mistake to assimilate the semantic phenomena considered to the more general phenomenon of vagueness or indeterminateness. My claim does not deny that a word like 'emergency' may have an indeterminate meaning, i.e., without a sharply delineated set of boundaries. It may or may not; as we saw, once circumstances are set determining denotation, we may end up with a fairly precise range of entities to which the term under those circumstances applies. But what has been shown about the need for a level intermediate between meaning and reference is independent of or additional to whatever we might decide about indeterminateness.

On the basis of these reflections on our example, the following proposal is submitted. In the case of some words their lexical semantic structure is comprised of three levels. The first level is that of meaning in the ordinary pretheoretical sense. This is the one captured typically by dictionary definitions. On closer inspection this turns out to be a set of qualitative necessary conditions. (Not any kind of necessary condition will do; further specification of their nature will be given below.) The second level is a set of circumstances that determines ranges of denotation. The elements of this set have certain intuitively salient features in common. Furthermore, they have a conceptual link to the meaning of the word. Both the common denominator between the members of the set, and the conceptual link these have to the meaning of the word will be described below. Finally, on the third level we have for each circumstance determining denotation range a set of entities, be these states, events, objects, etc., to which the word truly applies. Our task will include the further specification and clarification of this claim, and the exploring of how much of the vocabulary of descriptive words is affected by this phenomenon.

II. FURTHER OBSERVATIONS

Let us compare the phenomenon unearthed to some of those mentioned at the outset which we layed aside. First, there is indexicality, as in the case of 'current', 'here', 'I', 'you', etc. Here too we distinguish three layers of semantic structure. There is the meaning of an expression like a personal pronoun or a temporal indexical. This gives us information about criteria of application. The second level gives the relevant times, places, and persons in connection with which or whom the criteria of application have to be invoked. Finally, we have the denotations, demarcated from the point of view of the context of use. But note that we arrive at the second level in a way very different from what we have seen in the case of 'emergency'. All we need to understand in the case of indexicals is the articulation of space and time into their parts, and the fact that the universe is made up of distinct persons, events, and objects that can be singled out by having speakers and intended audience located in various spatio-temporal regions of the world. This is clearly not enough for understanding what the denotation determining circumstances are for 'emergency', nor is the additional information gained on the second level in the case of indexicals comparable to that gained on the second level in the case of 'emergency'. In the latter case we gain more purely qualitative phenomena that specify the nature of the situations in which we apply the word. In the case of the indexicals we are sent "out into the world" to find the appropriate person or point at which the evaluation and application is to be made.

The phenomenon we explored differs also from what some people since J. S. Mill have claimed about proper names. In the case of proper names the claim is that there is no purely qualitative sets of necessary and sufficient conditions that determine application for each name. Thus there must be some nonqualitative factors determining reference. The nature of these nonqualitative factors has been a matter of dispute and we need not enter upon this issue. What is relevant for our purposes is that the three-level phenomenon discovered in the case of 'emergency' is not related to nonqualitative conditions. It is, rather, a case of requiring a splitting up of the denotation range in certain predictable ways, and then adding further qualitative conditions to the determination of denotation.

There are other cases in which the speaker's social context is relevant to the way in which appropriate reference can be executed. Thus only certain people can address a certain woman as "mother!" or describe a certain man as "the manager." But this is once more not a matter of deriving circumstances for denotation ranges, but rather a matter of taking into consideration the individual context of a speaker in a given situation. We can handle the matter of indexicals and the phenomenon discussed in this paragraph when it comes to evaluating what the sentence under consideration says by adding indices. We can evaluate an utterance in terms of its content at a given time, place, point of view of a speaker, his or her social circumstances, etc. But the phenomenon I pointed to cannot be handled in a semantics by just adding another index to the evaluation points. Among other things, that would not bring out the element of negotiation and normative reflection that we saw going into denotation range determination in the case of a word like 'emergency'.

Finally, I want to keep our phenomenon distinct from what has been labeled at times "open-endedness." This can be illustrated by a word like 'vehicle'. What is a vehicle? What counts as a vehicle? Given that technology changes, and new types of products are produced, there is no way for us to decide now for all times, what does and will count as a vehicle. That would be like trying to legislate for all eternity what does and will count as theft when we cannot envisage all of the changes that will take place in the evolution of the notion of property and property rights. Today we are witnessing the evolution of a new specialty in law which deals with the stealing of ideas in the electronics industry. It is absurd to suggest that an all-wise judge should have provided legislation for all such possible cases fifty years ago. Now in all such cases of "open-endedness" the key point is that a part of the range over which denotation has to be determined is not in existence yet, and that the nature of future species cannot be envisaged by us. It may be that terms like 'emergency' are affected by this too. But in any case, the phenomenon I pointed to is not the same as this. What I showed about emergencies would remain true if the "evidence" were to "close" today; i.e., somehow a powerful spirit would intervene and arrange the future of the world so that no new types of emergency would ever arise again. The intermediate level is already needed to explain the ordinary cases, not the future and conceptually remote cases.

Let us now begin the examination of how denotation is determined in the case I presented. There seem to be three main elements. First, the considerations bearing on the matter are social and not matters of individual taste and intention. If someone says in the context of Jones going to Europe for six months that emergencies will include the secretary cutting her hand or a graduate student breaking up with his girl friend, then we can say that the person is misusing the word 'emergency'. There may be "grey" areas in which individual taste and intention may enter, but it would be quite wrong to say that in this type of reference fixing "anything goes." Reactions like: "he considers *this* an emergency?" or "she should not call *that* an emergency," or simply "this is not an emergency" are common, and require justification. The social norms may not be sharply defined, but for every circumstance determining denotation, they are there, just the same.[2] And yet, in such cases the distinction between saying "it is not true that this is an emergency," "it is odd to call this an emergency," and "you should not call this an emergency" is not as sharp as in cases in which the three levels need not be invoked.

This reservation leads us naturally to the second factor entering into this type of reference fixing, namely negotiation.[3] In order to appreciate the flavor of what is taking place in these cases, let us contrast it with two other types. First, let us take a case in which we deal with a science that has a fixed abstract domain of entities as its subject, namely mathematics. Some positive integers are even while others are not, and we define 'even' as 'divisible by 2'. Applying this criterion is a simple mechanical task. It neither requires nor leaves room for negotiation. Nor do we need an intermediate level between meaning and denotation. Let us now consider a case in which the applications are empirical and there is vagueness. This holds for color terms. The point of bringing this up is to show that mere vagueness is not the same as the phenomenon we are considering. The borders among colors like red, pink, and orange are not sharply fixed. For restricted purposes we can introduce temporary sharp demarcations, but this does not change the state of nature in which colors remain imprecisely determined. One cannot really negotiate about vagueness the way one can and does negotiate about fixing a denotation range for 'emergency' in a certain set of circumstances.

The negotiation in the story involves a number of factors, such as Professor Jones's view of how work can go on, the secretary's view of the same question, certain institutional expectations, and to some extent matters of personal taste and convenience. But it is important to stress that the last item is rather marginal, and that the other items are subject to public standards and critical assessment. Thus in viewing this process as a negotiation of some sort we should not assimilate it to such paradigmatic cases of negotiation as labor disputes or the settling of international disputes. The aspect of maximizing utility for the affected parties in the semantic case plays much less of a central role than in the political or economic cases. Still, it would be misleading to think of the denotation as already there, waiting for us to discover it. To some extent, though not arbitrarily, the negotiations contribute to creating the denotation for that set of circumstances.

The third important element entering into the denotation determination in these cases is the normative factor. We saw already that the relevant question is not only: "What is the denotation of 'emergency' in these sets of circumstances?" but also "What should the denotation be?" And that assessments are not just in terms of true or false, but also in terms of what the professor and the secretary should or should not have agreed to call this or that item. The negotiations terminate not only with what has been decided to be the case, but with what is a good and appropriate semantics for these circumstances. In view of what has been stressed all along, we should realize that the normative element is heavily constrained, is not arbitrary, and the objectivity it carries is not solely ethical or prudential. That is to say, someone might try to explain the use of 'should' exemplified above in terms of what is morally required or practically useful. But many of the considerations entering into the "successful" denotation fixing are not of either a moral or a prudential nature. The demands of the semantics of 'emergency' and the nature of the ingredients of the meaning components have to be considered. To settle on a use that is best for the professor and the secretary is not necessarily to settle on a use that will be as consistent as possible with the requirements of the semantics of English.

In summary, we see these three factors entering into denotation determination. As a first approximation people would come to consider our phenomena with questions like: "Is there a denotation out there, in the world, for the word to have?" and "Do we just decide on or create a denotation?" and "Do we discover or legislate a denotation for this circumstance?" On the basis of what we saw in connection with the three factors I answer all three of these questions with: "yes and no," and when pressed for further clarification simply refer the inquirer to a detailed consideration of the three-level proposal and the three factors entering into denotation fixing.

III. THE NATURE AND RANGE OF THE PHENOMENON

We mentioned above the fact that the way the circumstances determining denotation ranges are specified has some conceptual link to the meaning ingredients of 'emergency'. It is time to look at this matter in some detail. It seems clear that the ingredients entering into the delineation of the set of denotation-determining circumstances are roughly the same as the ones whose consideration enabled us to see that the "definition" one would standardly provide yields only necessary and not sufficient conditions of application. That is to say, the meanings of 'impending', 'harmful', 'requiring', 'immediate', and 'response' combine to delineate the set of denotation-determining circumstances. With regard to each of these items we can raise not only the question: "How much?" but also the question: "How much is enough or appropriate?" and that the second question will be answered in different ways depending on the circumstances. Putting this the other way around, when the answers to these questions are different, we know that we have separate denotation-determining circumstances. This will become clearer by a consideration of each of the items.

What is impending cannot be specified in terms of a purely quantitative measurement of time. An impending environmental crisis can have a timespan of twenty to a hundred years, while an impending crisis in a philosophy department is likely to mean something within the next month or year. An impending crisis in surgery can mean seconds or at most minutes. The same consideration applies to harmfulness. The harm of a person being injured can constitute an emergency for a hospital but might not be an emergency for the city government. The question is not: How much harm results in an emergency, but rather, given that you are a physician, administrator, father, social worker, etc., How much harm and harm of what nature leads to emergencies? The question has to be answered from the points of view of these different roles. Again, as we saw, what is "required" may be a not very precise notion. But quite independently of that, it is also a role-relative notion. That is to say, we need to specify what the denotation of 'required' is for persons with different social roles in different socially determined situations. The same applies to 'response'. What is a response from the mayor's office need not count as a response from your mother, or the other way around. Thus we see that the denotation-determining circumstances are delineated with the help of a combination of concepts each of which stands for something quantitative, i.e., we can ask: "How much?" and in the case of each of which we can raise the question: "How much is enough, or appropriate?" Before we shall make this more precise, we will have to see how what we said applies to other examples, and how it fits with what we said about meaning.

All we said about meaning was that it was constituted by necessary conditions. There are, however, many different kinds of necessary conditions. My proposal is that the necessary conditions listed for 'emergency' above are those that would be invoked when we try to explain to someone, roughly, what counts as an emergency. The conditions listed account for why we can answer certain questions truly and informatively by saying: " . . . because it is an emergency."[4] For example, take the questions, from different contexts, such as: "Why run?" "Why call a meeting?" "Why press for immediate action?" We can answer these questions in the appropriate contexts by saying "because this is an emergency," and that the necessary conditions listed account for why such a reply is satisfactory. Running is an appropriate reaction to an emergency because running is a way of moving fast, and this is needed since emergencies in the right context involve this kind of immediacy. Calling meetings, etc., are appropriate reactions because they are parts of dealing, in certain contexts, with harmful things affecting a community.

We should note that explanations of what counts as a so-and-so vary greatly in nature, depending on the kind of word whose meaning we analyze. In the case of a word like 'emergency' the explanation centers on what to do and why. In the case of other kinds of words, e.g., color terms, or other terms introducing secondary qualities like sound or taste, the explanation would center on recognitional qualities. Still other kinds of words like 'love' or 'friendship' require as the meaning components conditions that figure in explaining human interactions.

Having given, then, a rough characterization of the meanings of the words to which the three-level theory is meant to apply, let us consider various kinds of examples of the phenomenon. Let us first consider as a group the meanings of 'sand', 'hexagonal', 'picture', and 'ill', a grammatically heterogeneous group that nevertheless exhibits some interesting semantic similarities. Our key questions with regard to each of these are: "What constitutes a . . . " and "What counts as a . . . . " If the answer has to be of the form: "for an agent or agents in such-and-such a social, biological, or institutional role, it is this, but for agents or other elements of reality with other roles it is that," then the word falls into the range of those to which the three-level theory applies.

The meaning of 'sand' is roughly 'small grain of crushed rock'. This invites immediately the question: How small? And that, in turn, is answered in terms of the different ways in which we use sand. What counts as sand for purposes of construction does not count as sand for purposes of filling in a beach or of the bottom part of a glass container for tropical fish. One might try to get around this by saying that there are different kinds of sand, and we use at times this and at times that. But this is just playing with words once more. One can also say that there are different kinds of emergencies, but the point remains that we have to fix denotation for the different circumstances. In the case of 'sand' the circumstances have to do with the fact that smallness admits of degrees, that we can say in the right context: "this is small enough," and that we make use of sand. Obviously the semantics could be different in a "possible world" in which the inhabitants have no practical applications for sand.

The example of hexagonality is taken from informal instructions I heard from John L. Austin. His example was the sentence: 'France is hexagonal', which he claimed was true when part of a geography textbook but false when part of a geometry text. He used this to show that there are various ways of assessing a sentence "from the point of view of the dimension of veracity." We can see this case as one of those falling within the range exemplifying our phenomenon. Hexagonality, and other terms denoting shape in terms of angles and other such salient features, invites the question: "How exactly hexagonal, etc., must the specimen be?" In cases in which descriptions in terms of shapes interact with important human activities, e.g., navigation by shapes of rocks, reading maps by identifying shapes, doing crystallography, etc., we will have to specify the appropriate degree or kind of exactness with reference to the activity or institutional setting in which the description is assessed. In this case, even more so than in the previous one, it is clear that we cannot sweep the issue under the conceptual rug by saying that there are "many kinds of hexagonalities."

A picture is a painting or drawing that counts as some sort of an achievement, possibly though not necessarily as a work of art. But achievements are graded according to biological and cultural levels. Thus what counts as a picture when produced by a five-year-old might not count as a picture when produced by an artist. It is important to realize that this can be true also the other way around. A painting of a very abstract non-representational sort might count as a picture when produced by an artist, but not when produced during play by a child. Thus this example introduces a new element. In the previous examples the elements were use or interaction and quantities that need be specified as sufficient or appropriate for certain role-determined circumstances. This example introduces the kind of achievement that we grade depending on biological and professional differences in qualification.

Finally, 'to be ill' exemplifies our phenomenon in yet another way. For the meaning is, roughly, 'to be in bad or less than satisfactory health'. But in our society levels of health are associated with kinds of fitness that relate to social roles such as being a farmer, an office worker, a professor, etc. For different professions we have different standards as to what counts as an excuse for less than acceptable performance. A relevant illness or injury in the context of the life of a factory worker will not count as such in the case of a college professor, and also the other way around. A condition of a certain sort can render a factory worker unfit to perform his job and thus gives him sick leave, while the same condition will not count as an illness in the case of a college professor, for example, some condition that affects only the use of one's fingers. We would say in one case "something is wrong with his body, look at his fingers" but we would not count it as an illness, while in the case of the worker we would say "he is ill, and unfit to work."

Next we shall consider a number of words whose meanings include a component signifying achievement. The assessment of these achievements is graded in our culture relative to biological or social roles, hence the meanings of these words exhibit the phenomenon we are illustrating. Consider the meaning of 'walk'. The meaning of this word is captured roughly by 'activity of movement, placing each foot in front of the other, keeping one foot on the ground at any time'. We see immediately that some of the ingredients invite the questions: "How much?" and "What is enough or sufficient?" and that our answers will depend on factors like age or health. What counts as a walk for an infant taking her first steps is different from what counts as a walk for a healthy adult under normal circumstances, and there is still a different range for a recovering sick person. This can be seen when considering a sentence like: "She took her first walk today." There are certain minimal criteria for the infant, then others for the recovering patient, and many instances that count as walking in those two contexts would not count as walking for the healthy adult. The related noun 'walk' exhibits the same fact. I cannot invite a colleague of mine to go from my office to the neighboring coffee house by saying "Let us go for a walk," but I can invite a young child to traverse the same distance by saying, "Let us go for a walk."

What is true of a verb like 'walk' is also true of the verbs 'push', 'pull', or 'read', verbs whose meanings in other ways exhibit interesting heterogeneity. Pushing and pulling involve the use of force to move things away or toward or after oneself, and thus the questions will arise: how much force, how much movement, and what are levels of appropriateness for different age levels and states of health? The meaning of 'read' is captured by 'to traverse with one's eye sets of symbols, with understanding'. Again, the question arises how much traversing one needs to do as a minimum, and—above all—how much understanding. Thus what counts as knowing how to read is once more relative to age and health.

So far we considered cases involving either interaction with external features of the world via use, and qualifications for use, or cases involving what one might call "graded achievement." Both of these types of cases differ from the original example of 'emergency'. Thus someone might wonder whether that word and the complexities of its meaning may be an idiosyncrasy, rather than an indication of what many words share. Thus in concluding the presentation of examples let us consider words that seem semantically very much like 'emergency'. Such words are: 'help', 'interfere', 'contribute', and 'inadequate'.

To help is to do someone else's work, or to contribute to something happening. For example, we say that Jones helped Bill in writing that book, or that the economic conditions helped to bring about war. Once more, the ingredients indicate conceptual room for asking how much of someone else's work was done and what kind of work and in what way and to what extent did something contribute to something else coming into being. This creates circumstances in which we must ask what counts as help. The extent and ways of cooperation involved in helping with a book or article are quite different from the extent and ways in which physicians help each other in operations or medical treatment. Furthermore, in these cases everything we said about negotiation, social and normative factors, etc. in connection with 'emergency' applies here too. Surgeons and anesthesiologists have to work out what will count as help in their cooperation, but once again "not anything goes." 'Interfere' means 'to keep something from happening, or to obstruct the plans or activities of others'. Again, this gives us necessary conditions that explain what sort of things count as interference. But we need now to look at sets of circumstances and see in any one of these how much and what kind of activity counts as interference. How much obstruction and what kinds count as interference, for example, when children complain that parents interfere with their activities, or noise interferes with one's work, or the research of a physician interferes with his clinical practice. For each of these circumstances we need to go through a process of denotation determination similar to the one we described in the case of 'emergency'.

By now it should be obvious how this analysis applies to an adjective like 'inadequate', since its meaning components include reference to standards of acceptable state or performance, and these need to be fixed for different activities and different levels of ability. Likewise, 'contribute' means roughly 'to add something of significance to a project or state explicitly or contextually specified'. The qualifications of adding something and of it being of some significance brings with them the key questions we stated already, and with these the circumstances that determine ranges of denotation. To reflect on, negotiate, determine, etc., a range of denotation for 'contribute' is very similar to the process that involves 'emergency'. We must specify what counts as a contribution, what are minimal levels of significance, etc.

In all of these cases the meanings of the words include components standing for use, achievement, or interaction with humans or other important elements of reality, such that these admit of quantitative specifications and questions of appropriate quantities are determined not just on an individual basis but on the basis of the point of view of social, institutional, or biological roles of the participants.

This does not include the whole vocabulary of a natural language like English. It does not include words or phrases like 'positive integer', 'even', 'financial contribution', 'river', 'rose', etc. – in short, words and phrases to which the above given characterization does not apply.

It is notoriously difficult to convince philosophers of a semantic point by the use of examples. Thus I will get at the phenomenon also by pointing to differences between the semantic tasks of understanding the meanings in the relevant cases, and determining denotation in any given relevant circumstance. Understanding the meaning of 'emergency' or 'interfere' as I sketched it, involves the understanding of necessary conditions which play two roles. First they constitute salient factors in explanations of what counts as an item falling under the word. Second, from some of them we can see how the denotation-determining circumstances are derivable. But the second task involves more than merely "knowing meanings" in any intuitive sense. Understanding the meaning of 'emergency' tells me that the denotation-determining circumstances will have to do with how harmful, how immediate, etc., the situation is, but I need knowledge of the world and my culture in order to know that some of these circumstances will involve professors and administrators, physicians, naval officers, etc. I am not informed about the nature and existence of these institutions by the mere knowledge of the meanings of words like 'emergency'.

Furthermore, the skills and information required to determine successfully denotation for any given set of circumstances such as between physician and nurse, or captain and gunnery officer, are quite different from those needed to perform the first task, namely, understanding the meaning. Someone can be good at the first without being good at the second, and again the other way around. Thus mere reflection on the cognitive tasks involved already supports my claim that for a certain class of words we need the three-level analysis proposed. Let us keep in mind that the three levels are all within that part of language whose constituents admit of purely qualitative specification, thus the "Fregean Core," as one can call this. Considerations of indexicality and other individual-relative context-sensitivities are material for additional semantic structure.

So far we have been talking about word or lexical meaning. But the account would not be complete if we were not able to indicate how the items scrutinized contribute to the truth of the sentences in which they occur. Brief reflection should show us that since propositions are generated at the third level, this is also where truth and falsity arise. If we have only the sentence 'this notice constitutes an emergency' without specifications of the sort we reviewed, we do not have as yet a proposition assignable to the sentence. On the next level we have this sentence paired with sets of circumstances. On the third level we have the sentence within one of the denotation-determining circumstances, and this makes the application of 'emergency' in this context a matter of necessary and sufficient conditions. Hence something true or false emerges.

Having said this, a couple of qualifications are needed. First, the additional material that joins to the necessary conditions — material that makes the complex sufficient — is a rather loose, disjunctive set of elements, and though the resulting denotation range may be sharply delineated in certain practical circumstances, it may remain vague, with "shadowy border-lines." Second, as I presented the meanings of the words reviewed, much room was left for very general presuppositions required for the words to have meanings at all. The necessary conditions cited for 'help' or 'emergency' are hardly definable across "all logically possible worlds." Thus for some projected possibilities the meanings of the words remain undefined. Therefore, the propositions emerging from this semantic analysis are indeterminate in certain predictable ways. This does not prevent them from doing the jobs one can reasonably expect of propositions introduced by the relevant parts of a natural language.

IV. FINAL OBSERVATIONS

One of the important sources for the phenomenon demonstrated is the fact that we use language in interactions with each other and with other parts of reality, and that such interactions are subject to standards of appropriateness which are fixed differently for skill levels, biological age, state of health, and institutional roles. But we should not jump from this to the conclusion that the three-level phenomenon does not apply to the "language of the sciences," whatever that may mean. Words like 'experiment', 'prediction', etc., are likely to be exemplifying the same semantic structure as what we explored, and as soon as science interacts with use, as in the case of technology, its contents too will have similar semantics. For example, different things count in different contexts as a bridge or a road.

We should separate the two key conceptual parts of the "three-level" analysis. One of these is that we need in the case of some words and phrases a semantic level between the standardly recognized levels of meaning and reference. The other was that we need a certain set of procedures involving social, normative, and interactive or negotiative factors in the fixing of a range of denotation. The second may hold also for many words and phrases for which the first one does not. For example, maybe words like 'factory' or 'university' do not call for a three-level analysis. But in these cases too, there is room, indeed demand, for the kind of negotiation involved in denotation fixing that we illustrated above. We need to come to a consensus about what counts as a factory or university, even if we do not do this in installments. The same applies to many other words such as 'red', 'blue', etc., or artifact terms like 'table'. Thus we can look at what is presented in this essay as a "special thesis" about a part of the lexicon, which is presumably to be placed within the framework of a "general thesis" that deals with and demonstrates the complex denotation determining processes over a large part of the lexicon. But carrying out this task is beyond the scope of this paper.[5]

We should not look at the phenomena presented as imperfections of some sort, to be ignored when we consider semantics under idealization. In this treatment already we ignored many intervening factors. These include the epistemological question of how do we know the denotation of a given term. The semantic structures we uncovered are very useful for natural languages. They enable us to articulate thought in ways that render such thought employable in our interactions with the world. This is not the only use of language, but it is one of the uses, and an idealization that ignores it, would miss an important part of the structure of natural languages.

Wittgenstein thought that natural language was all right as it is. By this, I take it, he meant — among other things — that important features of use should not be viewed as imperfections from some "higher" point of view. This essay is meant to support this stance. At the same time it is meant to suggest also that this does not exclude the systematic study — possibly in part quite precise — of the structure of natural languages, and above all it is not meant to deny that natural languages have such tractable structure.

Notes

* This essay was prepared at the Sackler Institute of Advanced Studies of Tel Aviv University. I am grateful for the support of the institution and also for help from Asa Kasher.

1. In another case, an officer's secretary is told by higher command that all leaves for enlisted men are canceled for the next forty-eight hours. If the officer is on base, she will phone him; if he is in Washington for a month, she will not. I am indebted to Asa Kasher for this case.

2. This was suggested to me by some remarks of Howard Wettstein, in a different context.
3. This was suggested to me by conversations with Terry Winograd.
4. For more on this sort of theory, see my "How Do Words Get Their Meanings?" *Journal of Philosophy* 78 (1981): 5–24.
5. This will be argued in my *Thought and Language*, forthcoming.

Cognitive Architecture and the Semantics of Belief
GRAEME FORBES

In this paper I argue that some familiar objections to Fregean semantics for oblique contexts can be solved by appeal to a theory of mental or cognitive organization. By 'Fregean semantics for oblique contexts' I mean a semantics which ascribes both a customary reference and a customary sense to all semantically significant units; in which customary sense is conceived of as a way of thinking of customary reference which *determines* reference; and which holds that within the scope of the 'that' which takes sentences to form names of propositions, semantic primitives refer to their customary senses. The motivation for the ascription of a sense as well as a reference to a semantic primitive is that it nicely explains apparent differences in informativeness of certain sentence-pairs which have coreferential primitives at corresponding points in their common structure (Frege 1892). The motivation for the reference-shift thesis about 'that' is that it nicely explains apparent failure of substitution of primitives with the same customary reference when they are within the semantic scope of an oblique context such as 'believes that'.

In the other pan on the balance, there is the main objection to Fregean accounts that there are simply no plausible candidates for the role of senses of such semantic primitives as indexicals, proper names, and names of kinds of thing (Kripke 1980; Schiffer 1987, chap. 3). It is this problem which my account of cognitive organization addresses. But before introducing it, I should say something about the complementizer 'that' of oblique contexts, which I take to be elliptical for the term-forming operator 'the proposition that', as in 'the proposition that snow is white'. These terms for propositions are no ordinary definite descriptions. An ordinary description, like 'the first man on the moon', specifies a condition, being a man and being first on the moon, which can be read off the description. But 'being a proposition and being that snow is white' makes little sense. The role of 'the proposition' is rather to be understood by comparison with *'Santa Claus*: the movie' and 'the philosopher

Aristotle'. That is, 'the proposition' is a disambiguator (the movie *Santa Claus*, not the book or person, Aristotle the philosopher, not the shipping magnate) which fixes a reference of a specific kind for "that snow is white." The reference is to be a proposition rather than, say, a fact. It is really 'the proposition' which induces reference shift to customary sense, these words being implicit in attitude ascriptions. One does not need to say 'John believes *that snow is white*, the proposition', since it is only propositions, not facts or states of affairs, to which thinkers stand in the belief relation.[1]

In a world of spatio-temporal particulars, cognizers are constantly bombarded with information about a vast range of individual things. When we take ourselves to be receiving information about a thing with which we take ourselves to have had no previous cognitive encounter, this information is stored in a way that depends on the kind of encounter involved. If the encounter is perceptual, the various pieces of information derived from it may be grouped together by mutual association with a demonstrative way of thinking of an object, such as is expressed by e.g., 'that F over there'. This way of thinking is subject to *realignment* as time passes and as the thinker moves, becoming e.g., 'that F here' or 'that F which I saw there yesterday' (Evans 1982, 192–96).

On the other hand, a cognitive encounter, whether perceptual or by report (I regard being told or being misled about a thing as a way of encountering it cognitively), may involve an object for which we are given a name, or for which we invent one on the spot. The neo-Fregean theory I develop in this paper is based on the hypothesis that names play the following rather special role in cognitive architecture. When a name is given, our "mental operating systems" create a *dossier* and put the information derived from the encounter into it, while *labeling* the dossier with the name just introduced. On any future occasion when we take ourselves to be receiving information about the same thing, either because the name in question is used or because some feature of the cognitive environment activates the dossier in virtue of its contents, we file the new information in that dossier.[2] In an ideal situation, there would be a one-one correspondence between a thinker's dossiers and the objects with which he has had cognitive encounters (abstracting from forgetfulness, encounters that are too fleeting, etc.). Specifically, in an ideal situation there would be no dossiers which lack a corresponding object, and no object would be the subject of two or more dossiers. But the actual situation is hardly ever ideal.[3]

The dossier hypothesis is relevant to semantics because it furnishes a candidate for the sense of a name. I claim that the sense of a name 'NN' for a thinker S can be articulated as 'the subject of *this* dossier', where the demonstrative refers to the dossier which in S's cognitive system is labeled by 'NN'. My view is that if 'NN' refers to x, then 'the subject of *this* dossier' captures the way of thinking of x that S associates with the name 'NN'. What *makes it the case* that 'NN' refers to x will then be that the information in the dossier is predominantly information about x.[4] Although the notion of 'information about' is complicated, it seems to be a quite coherent notion and I know of nothing in a Fregean philosophy of language to preclude the use of causal concepts in its analysis. It is certainly *not* the case that 'the subject of *this* dossier' may be construed as 'the individual of whom (a weighted most of) this information is true'.

I should enter two further caveats here. When I say that the sense of '*NN*' can be articulated as 'the subject of *this* dossier', I speak loosely. First, by '"the subject of *this* dossier"' I mean to denote the sense of a token of the description for an agent in a context of which he is the subject, and in which '*this* dossier' refers to the appropriate dossier of that agent. Moreover, the sense of the description varies with the dossier denoted by the demonstrative. Thus in a very broad sense of 'type', we might say that everyone attaches the same *type* of sense to every name; at the same time, on the finest discrimination of senses, no two thinkers can attach the same sense to different names, since distinct thinkers cannot share numerically the same dossier. Of course, there are intermediate senses of 'type' on which all thinkers who employ a name attach the same type of sense to that name, and different types to other names. But the fundamental notion is the most finely discriminated one, since it is senses so discriminated which constitute the propositions to which thinkers stand in attitude relations.[5]

The second caveat is that it is not really my view that the sense of a name '*NN*' is *identical* to the sense of any description 'the subject of *this* dossier'. Rather, I regard senses as things with cognitive significance, and the descriptions one uses to explain a sense, such as 'the subject of *this* dossier' for a name or 'where I am now located' for 'here', as expressions not of the senses themselves, but only of their cognitive significance. However, since the problems for which this distinction is germane will not arise here, I shall continue to speak of the sense itself as being given by the description, so long as it is understood that this is a *façon de parler* (see further, Forbes 1989, chap. 5).

It is a constraint on any account of the sense of a name '*NN*' for a subject S that if ϕ embodies the account, '*NN* is ϕ' should be *a priori* for S. As is well known, 'famous deeds' sense theories (Lewis's phrase) fail to satisfy this requirement. But I think that the account of the senses of names just sketched satisfies it: if '*this* dossier' refers to the dossier labeled '*NN*' in S's cognitive system, then '*NN* is the subject of *this* dossier' is *a priori* for S. But talk of labeling dossiers is clearly metaphorical. If it is correct that '*NN* is the subject of *this* dossier' is *a priori*, what underlies that fact? After all, '*this* dossier' is itself a demonstrative with a sense. How does this sense preempt the question 'Is *NN* the subject of *this* dossier?' or more colloquially, 'Is *NN* the person when all the information I have grouped here is about?'

One possibility is that when a name '*NN*' is entertained in thought, certain pieces of information automatically come to mind, and the automatic nature of this process bestows on those pieces of information the character of *presenting themselves as* information about *NN*. But that cannot be quite right, otherwise sentences of the form '*NN* is ϕ', where ϕ is some *a posteriori* condition which *NN* may or may not satisfy, would be *a priori*. Instead, we should conceive of the process whereby some pieces of information automatically come to mind when a name is thought as bestowing on that information the character of presenting itself as *information from* the '*NN*'-dossier.[6] Indeed, automaticity does not seem to be necessary, although it is common: even if a thinker has to concentrate quite hard to access his '*NN*'-dossier, the fact that the piece of information which eventually results was produced by a process which began by *trying* to associate information with '*NN*' is sufficient for that information to present itself as being from the '*NN*'-dossier.

A plausible candidate for the sense of '*this* dossier' as it occurs in '*NN* is the subject of *this* dossier' is 'the dossier in which this information is stored'. Here 'this information', relative to a context, refers to some piece of information produced in the context as a result of accessing the dossier by thinking the name '*NN*'. Putting this account together with the story of the previous paragraph, it follows that there is no epistemic possibility of the subject of this dossier being anyone other than *NN*.

This may seem to be too strong a conclusion. For example, it is possible to get the names of two people mixed up. We say about a person who does this: "When he says 'Jones' he means 'Smith', and vice-versa," so it looks as if Smith is the subject of the confused person's 'Jones'-dossier. But there is a spectrum of cases here. At one end, the thinker in question, call him *A*, does not have mastery of the names 'Smith' and 'Jones'. Perhaps he met the two individuals the previous evening and has only the haziest recollection of which was which—he began by associating the names correctly, but later they switched. An implication of this is that the process of dossier-formation and labeling has been imperfectly executed, and there is no obligation to suppose that *A* even expresses determinate propositions when he uses the names.

Alternatively, *A* may for some time have had the practice of using the names wrongly, though otherwise his information about the individuals, derived, say, from surveillance, is substantive and accurate. This means that his dossier labeled 'Smith' has Jones as its subject and vice-versa. It follows that when *A* makes statements of the form 'Smith is *F*' he expresses thoughts which are *de re* with respect to Jones, *mutatis mutandis* for statements involving 'Jones'. So when he asserts 'Smith is the subject of *this* dossier', referring to the dossier labeled 'Smith' whose subject is Jones, his thought correctly attributes to Jones the property of being the subject of that dossier. Indeed, if someone remarked that *A*'s belief that Smith if *F* is clearly false, it would be natural to correct this judgment by providing the information that *A* uses 'Smith' for Jones. The gist of the correction seems to be that the thought which *A* is expressing with 'Smith is *F*' is right, even if what *A* said is wrong. And my claim is merely that '*NN* is the subject of *this* dossier' always *expresses* an *a priori* truth for an agent in a context who can use it to express a complete proposition.[7]

Two names for the same object may have the same sense or different senses. The apparatus I have just sketched is suggestive of the following account of sameness of sense for names. The prominent feature of cases where two names '*NN*' and '*MM*', both of which refer to a certain object x, have different senses, is that the names are acquired on different occasions of cognitive encounter with x, and the thinker, who does not realize that they stand for the same object, creates a new dossier for the second name. Whether failure to realize that the names stand for the same object is necessary for the creation of the second dossier is open to dispute. But the fact that the names are attached to different dossiers by itself accounts for their difference in sense: 'the subject of *this* dossier' and 'the subject of *that* one' are different ways of thinking of the things in question, even if those things are one and the same, and even, I think, if the dossiers contain precisely the same pieces of information.[8]

Correspondingly, sameness of sense should be associated with sameness of dossier. If you met Marilyn Monroe and she told you that she has two names, 'Marilyn' for professional purposes and 'Norma Jean' for her friends, you would form just one dossier, with two labels, on that occasion. Again, talk of dossiers is figurative, and one wants to know what phenomena underlie the sameness of sense and consequent uninformativeness of the identity 'Marilyn = Norma Jean'. After all, a double-labeled physical dossier could have its names on opposite sides, so that the fact of the names labeling the same dossier is not transparent.[9] First, what makes the identity 'Marilyn = Marilyn' uninformative? It cannot just be that the same name is repeated, since 'Paderewski = Paderewski', in one sense, is clearly informative for Kripke's Peter (Kripke 1979). The underlying phenomenon, I think, is that when a subject judges 'Marilyn = Marilyn' it is transparent to him that thinking the second occurrence of 'Marilyn' does not occasion opening a store of information for access. Instead, whatever store is opened in thinking the first occurrence of the name is simply made available in the second. The same is true, I suggest, for a subject for whom 'Marilyn' and 'Norma Jean' have the same sense. It is not as if when such a subject judges 'Marilyn = Norma Jean', the same dossier is opened twice (uninformativeness would then require that we explain how it is transparent to the subject that it *is* the same dossier which is reopened). There is rather a single opening of a dossier establishing a single path for outputting information which is shared by the two names. And that this arrangement is in play is something which, I think, is transparent to the thinker.[10]

II

How does this account of the senses of names help with the semantics of belief sentences? There is a technical difficulty for any semantics that posits reference shift in oblique contexts if it also abandons Frege's simplifying assumption that speakers of the same public language attach the same sense to any particular name, or indeed, any particular word at all.[11] For it we say that S in 'B believes that S' refers to its customary sense, and the sense of S differs for the ascriber A and believer B, then the question arises of *whose* customary sense it is to which S refers in 'B believes that S'. Presumably the two candidates are A's sense and B's sense, but neither seems right, as the following example brings out.

Suppose that for Ralph, 'Superman' and 'Clark Kent' have the same sense, while for Lois Lane they have different senses. Suppose Ralph asserts

(1) Lois believes that Clark Kent is not Superman.

Then on the view that indirect reference is to the *ascriber's* customary sense, Ralph has accused Lois of believing an obvious *a priori* falsehood. But it seems intuitively clear that he has not. So perhaps indirect reference is to the *believer's* customary sense. But in that case, if Lois laughingly reports

(2) Ralph believes Clark Kent is Superman

she is ridiculing him for believing an obvious *a priori* truth. Again, it seems intuitively clear that this is the wrong verdict.

One resolution of the difficulty is as follows (Forbes 1988): take the gist of Ralph's (1) to be that Lois believes a nonidentity involving ways of thinking of Clark Kent which are 'derivatively' labeled, respectively, 'Clark Kent' and 'Superman', and the gist of Lois's (2) to be that Ralph believes an identity involving ways of thinking of Clark Kent which are derivatively labeled, respectively, 'Clark Kent' and 'Superman' (note that the ways of thinking may be, but do not have to be, distinct). A way of thinking of Clark Kent is derivatively labeled 'Clark Kent' iff Clark Kent is thought of in that way as the subject of *this* dossier, where '*this* dossier' refers to a dossier labeled 'Clark Kent'. We can then introduce the idea of a way of thinking being 'so-labeled' (a locution which works like 'so-called') where the back-reference is to some name previously used in the discourse. Thus for

(3) Lois believes that Superman can fly

we have the analysis

(4) Superman is such that for some so-labeled way of thinking of him α, Lois believes $\alpha \wedge \ulcorner$can fly$\urcorner$.

Here 'α' is a variable over sense, $\ulcorner$can fly$\urcorner$ is the sense of 'can fly', and '$\wedge$' constructs complex senses from less complex ones. (4) is true, since we can assign Lois's way of thinking of Clark Kent labeled 'Superman' to 'α'. Note that although 'Superman' occurs outside the scope of 'believes' in (4), substitution is blocked by the effect of 'so-labeled'. (3) and (4) may be contrasted with

(5) Superman is someone whom Lois believes can fly

and its analysis

(6) Superman is such that for some way of thinking of him α, Lois believes α ∧ ⌜can fly⌝.

(5) and (6) both correctly permit substitution of 'Clark Kent' for 'Superman'.

(3) and (5) are sometimes classified as *'de dicto'* and *'de re'* respectively, but this seems to me to be unfortunate usage. A *de re* belief is a belief which is *about an object*, and both (3) and (5) are surely to be understood as ascribing beliefs about Superman, that is, beliefs which are *de re* with respect to Superman. The difference between them is just that by giving the proper name *internal* occurrence in (3), we characterize the content of Lois's belief more fully. A genuine example of a *de dicto* belief would be one which contains no *de re* senses, that is, no ways of thinking about objects. An example is the belief that the shortest spy is a spy, if held on the purely general grounds that there are finitely many spies and no two are the same height. In a quite intuitive sense, this is not a belief *about*, say, Arthur Walker, even if it is he who is the shortest spy.[12]

III

The semantics of belief ascriptions sketched in the previous section needs further elaboration if it is to be applicable to all cases, but the present simplified version suffices for the applications I wish to make here.[13] I said at the outset that the motivation for the reference-shift thesis is that it nicely explains why substitution of expressions with the same customary reference within oblique contexts seems invalid: it *is* invalid, since the expressions being substituted may not have the same reference *within the context*. The mechanics of belief ascriptions using names according to section II above is essentially similar: substitution is invalid because such ascriptions characterize a particular component of the thought which the believer believes, and the characterization changes to one the thought may not satisfy if substitution is made merely on the basis of sameness of customary reference. So the theory of section II retains this advantage of the Fregean approach.

According to Nathan Salmon, the advantage is illusory: there are examples where the Fregean approach does permit substitution, but where the results are as awkward as substitution on the basis of sameness of customary reference. Hence Frege's semantic diagnosis of why customary reference substitution seems invalid must be missing the real point (Salmon 1989a, 1989b). Here is one of Salmon's cases. We are to suppose that a certain foreign-born individual, Sasha, learns 'ketchup' and 'catsup' not by being taught that they are synonyms, but by consuming the condiment and reading the labels on the bottles. However, Sasha only sees bottles labeled 'catsup' being shaken over eggs and hash browns in the morning, and only bottles labeled 'ketchup' being shaken over hamburgers at midday. He concludes that ketchup and catsup are different condiments, and that it would be a glaring *faux pas* to call for catsup at lunchtime. For Sasha, 'ketchup is ketchup' is uninformative while 'ketchup is catsup' is informative, and it seems wrong to infer from 'Sasha believes ketchup is ketchup' that Sasha believes ketchup is catsup. Yet since the words are synonyms in English, we should be able to make the substitution. But if we *do* make it, the non-Fregean is entitled to wonder why we insist that it is invalid to substitute on the basis of sameness of customary reference as grounds for outlawing it, for the results of such substitution seem no worse than the result of substituting synonyms in this example.

Evidently, this objection to the Fregean approach depends on the assumption that if two words are synonymous in English then they have the same sense for a generally competent English-speaker who can use them to express his beliefs. And there is no doubt that on many versions of Frege's approach, this assumption is correct. But on the theory I have developed here, it is incorrect, as we shall see.

The example also presupposes that 'ketchup' and 'catsup' are synonyms, yet it is unclear how applicable the notion of linguistic synonymy is to these terms. We can draw a broad distinction between words which stand for particular things, or kinds of thing, on the one hand, and words which express classifications of things according to their function or role, on the other. Roughly speaking, what I shall call a 'kind' word is one whose applicability as a predicate to an object or quantity of stuff depends on the intrinsic nature of that object or quantity; some well-known examples include 'water', 'gold', 'tiger', and color terms (Kripke 1980; Putnam 1975; Burge 1979). Function and role terms, by contrast, apply to things according to what those things are for or what they do; examples include 'glue', 'paint-stripper', and 'barrister'.[14]

The notion of linguistic synonymy applies clearly enough to function and role terms. For example, two function terms are synonymous if any account of what a thing must do for one of the terms to apply to it is an equally good or bad account for the other term. Such terms easily lend themselves to dictionary definitions. But on the likeliest reading of Salmon's case, 'ketchup' and 'catsup' are kind terms, not function terms, and kind terms are less easily dictionary-defined. Certainly, knowledge of the intrinsic feature of a thing which guarantees inclusion in the kind which the term stands for is not a condition of competent use of the term.

In the respect of resisting definition, kind terms are more like names, so I propose to apply my account of the senses of names to them. Learning a term for a sort of thing or stuff occasions the opening of a dossier with that term as its label. The sense of the term will be 'the subject of *this* dossier', where the subject is not a spatio-temporal particular, as is the case with most proper names, but something more abstract, a natural kind or sort. Again as with proper names, a thinker may have two dossiers with the same subject, and the labels for those dossiers will be no more intersubstitutable in ascriptions of beliefs to him than 'Clark Kent' and 'Superman' are intersubstitutable for Lois Lane. To be specific, for

(7) Sasha believes ketchup goes well with lunch

we have the analysis

(8) Ketchup is such that for some so-labeled way of thinking of it α, Sasha believes $\alpha \wedge \ulcorner$goes well with lunch$\urcorner$.

If this account is correct, then the notion of linguistic synonymy is irrelevant to the question of substitution of kind terms in oblique contexts, either because that notion has no application to such terms, or else, supposing for the sake of argument that it does have some kind of application, because linguistic synonymy is not a sufficient condition for sameness of sense relative to a thinker. Granted (8), the theory of section II provides a complete explanation of what is going on in Sasha's case (and in other comparable ones, such as Kripke's 'furze'/'gorse' example [1979, 269]). As a result of the manner in which Sasha learnt 'ketchup' and 'catsup', he has two dossiers, one labeled 'ketchup', the other 'catsup', and substitution of one word for the other in specifications of his beliefs is blocked by the occurrence of 'so-labeled' in the analysis of belief-ascriptions. The dossier description of Sasha's situation strikes me as rather plausible, and if it is correct, the version of the Fregean approach based on it retains the advantage, even in these cases, of licensing just those belief attributions which are in accord with pretheoretic intuition.

IV

On an alternative reading of Salmon's case, 'ketchup' and 'catsup' are function terms, like 'glue'. Function and role terms are among the best candidates for traditional 'descriptive' accounts of the (reference-fixing) sense of a word, since speakers can usually articulate explicit criteria which guide them in applying such terms. I do not think we could use 'glue' in internal position in correctly specifying the beliefs of a subject who is completely incapable of saying what glue is for (idiosyncracy in his account is another matter, discussed below). On this reading of the example, Sasha has two different functional conceptions of condiment: one conception is expressed by his term 'ketchup', and has 'appropriate only for lunches' as a component, the other by 'catsup', with 'appropriate only at breakfast' as a component. Since the conceptions are different, the words by which Sasha expresses them cannot be interchanged in describing his beliefs.

The functional reading of 'catsup' and 'ketchup' is somewhat unnatural, so to pursue the discussion I shall change the example by saddling Sasha with a further confusion, this time about social roles. Suppose that Sasha thinks that doctors in general are underpaid, but that physicians are a certain elite kind of doctor who earn absurdly high salaries. Then in classical Fregean terms, the proposition Sasha would express with

(9) Doctors are underpaid

(a proposition he believes) is a different proposition from the one he would express with

(10) Physicians are underpaid

(a proposition he does not believe) because those thoughts of his differ in their component senses. In that case, substitution of the synonymous 'physician' for 'doctor' in specifications of Sasha's beliefs is invalid, again for a perfectly understandable Fregean reason. There appears to be a complete absence of mystery here.

But with function and role terms, matters may be more complex than they are with names and kind terms, and I am disinclined to give the 'doctor'/'physician' case a treatment parallel to that of the 'catsup'/'ketchup' case.[15] In part, this is because the idea that such words label dossiers that contain information about a certain kind of 'thing' strikes me as unrealistic. But more interestingly, the argument against substitution is weaker. Refusal to substitute a synonymous role term in the true belief-ascription

(11) Sasha believes doctors are underpaid

is motivated primarily by the thought that

(12) Sasha believes physicians are overpaid

is also true, and we do not wish to ascribe obviously incompatible beliefs to Sasha. But (12) is questionable. Returning to belief-ascriptions using names and kind words, according to my analysis such ascriptions involve a *use* of the term in question outside the semantic scope of the attitude context. Hence if the believer uses the term with the wrong reference—clearly Sasha had the right *reference* for 'catsup' and 'ketchup', *via* his perceptual encounters with that substance—it would be at best a coincidence if an ascription of a belief to him with the term in internal position were correct. This feature of the analysis is one of its advantages, since there is an intuition that in making such ascriptions as (3) or 'Sasha believes ketchup is tasty' there is a use of the obliquely occurring referring term with its *customary* reference, whatever else may be going on with it. And though I have no semantic analysis of it to offer at this juncture, I think (12) has a similar feature: the standard conception of what a physician is has a salience that may block use of this word in characterizing the contents of Sasha's beliefs. The problem seems to be that Sasha has the wrong *property* for 'physician', whereas he did not have the wrong object for 'ketchup' and 'catsup'.

The thought which these points prompt is that perhaps synonymous social role terms *can* be intersubstituted without ascribing an unlikely combination of beliefs to a subject, since ascriptions which echo what the subject says using role terms he misunderstands may be incorrect (similarly for function terms etc.). Is this idea really defensible? To defend it, one must engage Tyler Burge's forceful arguments that a believer's misunderstanding of a term does not exclude its use in characterizing the contents of his beliefs (Burge 1978, 1979), and it is to this which I now turn.

Burge's most persuasive cases are of two specific kinds. First, there is the case of a subject Bertrand who misunderstands what arthritis is, in that he thinks it can afflict muscles as well as joints. But this does not prevent our saying of him that he believes, e.g., that the older you get, the more susceptible you are to arthritis. My response to this example is that the analysis of the 'catsup'/'ketchup' case is applicable to it, since 'arthritis' is a kind term, albeit it of a special sort: one whose reference, a particular disease, is a definitionally circumscribed object, the definition using a kind term of a standard sort ('rheumatism').[16] It seems reasonable to say of Bertrand that he has a dossier labeled 'arthritis', and that, given his linguistic context, it is features of arthritis that have given rise to the bulk of the information in that dossier. This means that analyses of belief-ascriptions to him in the style of (4) and (8) can be correct even when they employ 'arthritis' in oblique position, and despite Bertrand's misunderstanding: arthritis *is* such that for some so-labeled way of thinking α, Bertrand stands in the belief-relation to propositions with α as a constituent. But consequently, the case does not show that misunderstood *functional* and *role* terms can be used similarly.[17]

The other kind of belief-ascription where it seems *prima facie* unobjectionable to use a word in oblique position—apparently no matter *how* huge the believer's misconceptions about what it means—are ascriptions which spell out that very misconception. Burge gives a simple autobiographical example (1978, 126):

(13) I used to believe a fortnight is a period of ten days.

It does not seem that the first-person nature of the example is significant, so if that is what Burge used to believe, then *we* can say

(14) Burge used to believe that a fortnight is a period of ten days.

(13) and (14) are examples of what we can call *conception-explaining* ascriptions. Note that (14) could not be understood as explaining Burge's conception if we treated 'a fortnight' as implicitly having external position, as in 'A fortnight is something Burge believed to be a period of ten days'.

I regard conception-explaining ascriptions as another special case. Burge emphasizes the naturalness of ascriptions like (13) and (14), but notes that pretheoretic intuition tends to resist such an ascription as

(15) Burge believed Jones would be gone a fortnight

even though Jones told Burge he would be gone ten days and Burge *said* to many people *that* Jones would be gone a fortnight.[18] But if Burge believed that a fortnight is a period of ten days, and believed Jones would be gone ten days, and thought the words 'he will be gone a fortnight' to himself with inward assent, it almost seems to *follow* that he believed Jones would be gone a fortnight. Reluctance to accept this last step, *if* we accept that he believed a fortnight is a period of ten days, is certainly in need of explanation. And one possible explanation is that there is something unusual about conception-explaining ascriptions.

The first account to come to mind of what sets conception-explaining ascriptions off from others is that they are implicitly quotational. According to this view, what (14) really says, or what it should be charitably interpreted as saying, is that Burge used to believe that 'fortnight' means 'a period of ten days'. Burge rejects various possible arguments for this proposal (1978, 126-30; 1979, 96-103), and I agree that there is not much that is *intrinsically* compelling about the quotational account. But how else are we to explain the difference in intuitive reaction to (14) and (15)? The source of resistance to (15), it seems, is that the correct understanding of 'fortnight' has a certain salience, however it is to be brought out in logical form. If (14) encounters little resistance, that suggests that in conception-explaining ascriptions, the correct understanding of the problematic word has no salience, or at least does not have salience in the same way, and the quotational analysis is certainly a decent explanation of how that could come about.[19]

But it is not the only possible explanation. An alternative view is that in conception-explaining ascriptions, words with oblique occurrence refer to the customary sense which they express in the believer's mouth. There is no puzzle about how the ascriber can make such a reference, since in the nature of the case he knows what the believer's customary sense is (or was). However, this proposal is inconsistent with the fact that if Burge used to believe a fortnight is a period of ten days, he used to believe something false, since it implies that the embedded sentence in (14) refers to a true proposition.

We can come up with a better alternative by considering not conception-explaining ascriptions, but rather the embedded conception explanations themselves. Suppose a Briton and an American are in conversation and the Briton uses the word 'fortnight'. The American asks "What's a fortnight?" and receives the answer

(16) A fortnight is a period of fourteen days.

In comprehending (16), the American's sequential processing procedure cannot assign 'fortnight' a standard interpretation, since *ex hypothesi* he does not know what the proper interpretation of 'fortnight' is. Again, we could suppose that he takes (16) quotationally, interpreting it as " 'fortnight' means 'a period of fourteen days'," but it seems to me that someone could understand explanations like (16) without mastery of quotation, which after all is a rather special way of talking about written and spoken symbols. But mastery of some way of thinking or talking about words does seem to be required, and is surely guaranteed by the ability to identify the component of the utterance which is not understood and to raise a question about it. A *demonstrative* way of thinking or talking about words would suffice for this.

In addition, I think that other conception-explanations which proffer the same explanation about a different word do not differ in meaning in the way one would expect if the word being explained is functioning normally. We can imagine an example in which the problem word is 'furlough', and the learner is incorrectly instructed that

(17) A furlough is a period of fourteen days.

Though (16) and (17) differ in meaning, the difference is not the difference in meaning between 'fortnight' and 'furlough'. To my ear, the difference between (16) and (17) does not go much beyond the difference in *identity* of the word being explained.

Putting these points together, I suggest that in the sequential processing of a conception-explanation, the learner assigns to the new word the sense (a sense with the cognitive significance of) 'what this word stands for', in which 'stands for' is being used in a loose, intuitive way not meant to be assimilated to the notion of Fregean reference. The learner's complete interpretation of (16) will then be a true proposition, while the corresponding interpretation of (17) will be a false one. And these two interpretations will differ only in containing distinct token demonstrative modes of presentation, modes of presentation which are plausibly of the same type (see Peacocke 1981 for the type-token distinction I am using here).[20]

Returning now to conception-explanation *ascriptions*, it appears that the special features of such examples as (13) and (14) can be accounted for by taking the reference of the embedded sentence, in these cases 'a fortnight is a period of ten days', to be the interpretation of the sentence the learner gives it when that conception-explanation is advanced as such in isolation. Specifically, the internally occurring 'a fortnight' refers to the sense 'what this word stands for', in which the token demonstrative constituent itself refers to the very occurrence of 'fortnight' in the conception-explanation ascription in question. Thus (13) and (14) do attribute belief in a falsehood to Burge. And the proposed analysis does not make any of the assumptions Burge justly criticizes in connection with the strategy of quotational reconstrual. Certainly, whatever we take the indirect sense of 'a fortnight' in (14) to be, nothing suggests that it would involve quotation.

This account of conception-explanation ascription need not be restricted to ascriptions involving role or function words. It would apply to kind terms as well, so long as we agree that conception explanations can be given for them too. We can then use the theory of this section together with the earlier analysis of Salmon's case not merely to agree with, but to *explain*, Burge's intuitions about his memorable case of a man who thinks 'orangutan' applies to a kind of fruit (1979, 90). Burge agrees that it seems wrong to say that such a man believes he ate some orangutans for breakfast this morning, but thinks that we can say that he believes that an orangutan is a kind of fruit. On my view, the latter ascription is of the conception-explaining kind, and is literally true for the same reason that (14) is literally true: the embedded occurrence of 'an orangutan is a kind of fruit' refers to the special interpretation it would be given by a sufficiently susceptible learner who asked "What's an orangutan?"

and was told it is something like a tangerine. On the other hand, we cannot say that our man believes he ate orangutans for breakfast, since 'orangutan' is a name for a species of ape, that is, a *kind* term. Ordinary belief-ascriptions to this subject would therefore take the same form as (8). So for such an ascription to be true, the subject would require some way of thinking *of orangutans* labeled 'orangutans'. But Burge emphasizes the radical nature of the misunderstanding which his example involves, and the theoretical significance of its radical nature, I suggest, is that it prevents us from plausibly maintaining that the subject does have some way of thinking of orangutans, one which just happens to figure in some spectacularly false beliefs. As the case is described, the misunderstanding is of a sort to make the conclusion that the subject has no way of thinking of orangutans irresistible. So no ordinary belief-ascription to him which has 'orangutan' in internal position could be correct.

The upshot of my discussion is that, conception explanations aside, we are not inclined to use function and role words a thinker misunderstands to characterize the contents of the thinker's beliefs. This in turn leaves it open that we may interchange function and role synonyms in belief ascriptions without generating ascriptions which unjustifiably make the believer seem foolish. I end therefore by considering a specific example of such a substitution. *Contra* Salmon, it will not lead to consequences as objectionable as substitution on the basis of sameness of customary reference, but we should check that it can stand on its own merits.

Recall that Sasha thinks that doctors in general are underpaid, and that 'physician' applies to a certain kind of doctor who is invariably found at the top end of the salary scale. From (11), 'Sasha believes doctors are underpaid', I am suggesting that it is unobjectionable to infer

(18) Sasha believes physicians are underpaid

even though Sasha will assertively utter 'Physicians are overpaid' and vigorously dissent from 'Physicians are underpaid'. How is inferring (18) any less objectionable than inferring 'Lois Lane believes Clark Kent can fly' from (3)? The crucial difference is that there is a clear sense in which Sasha misunderstands the social role term 'physician' and there is no way for him to somehow latch onto the property it expresses independently of the role conception he associates with it. On the other hand, with cases of ordinary names or kind terms to which the believer attaches the right reference, the notion of misunderstanding has no application, and even when the reference of a name is definitionally circumscribed, as with the disease name 'arthritis', someone who does not know the correct definition can still attach the right reference to the name, since that reference is something with which he has had cognitive encounters and is the source of the information in his dossier labeled with the name.[21]

Notes

1. This account of 'that' is quite different from the paratactic account of Davidson 1969. There is an interesting discussion of the paratactic analysis in Segal and Speas 1986.
2. I take no position about whether or not the information has to be represented propositionally, as opposed to, say, being sometimes in the form of images. For discussion of this issue, see Pylyshyn 1984, chap. 8.
3. I do not regard it as part of the specification of an ideal situation that a single name (syntactically individuated) never labels two or more dossiers, since multiple labeling is not indicative of a mismatch between the subject's belief-world and the real world. For application of the apparatus of this paragraph to Kripke's 'Paderewski' puzzle (Kripke 1979), see Forbes 1988.
4. This is just an account of speaker's reference. I am assuming that some Gricean story can be built on it to yield an account of reference in a public language.
5. Fodor has recently argued that fine discrimination of senses, which he calls 'relational' individuation, is no more respectable than relational individuation of brain states or fundamental particles (1987, chap. 2). But relational individuation is not the engine which drives fine discrimination: it is rather the question of what belongs to the intrinsic nature of a thing. No one supposes that facts about which side up Fodor's dime lies determine the intrinsic nature of fundamental particles on the other side of the universe. But to say that an artifact A realizes a design D is to say something about A's intrinsic nature, despite the fact that realization is a relation. I think the same is true of the relation between a mode of presentation and what it is of.
6. It is not *a priori* that information from the '*NN*'-dossier is accurate information about *NN*.
7. See Forbes 1988 for discussion of other problem cases.
8. This could happen after a period of time, when various pieces of information have been forgotten. Such dossiers could even have the same label, as in the 'Paderewski' case (cf. Kripke 1979, 260). Their separateness derives from how they were created in the first place, and from their having been maintained as distinct—metaphorically, at distinct locations—since then; they are distinct as *stores*.
9. Timothy Williamson pointed this out to me.
10. Clearly, on this account it will be rather unusual for different names to have the same sense. For discussion of the impact on dossier-structure of coming to believe an identity or nonidentity which alters some previously held identity beliefs, see Forbes 1988.
11. Frege thought this assumption correct for 'the theoretical structure of a demonstrative science' (Frege 1892, 58 n.).
12. There is a fuller discussion of the *de re/de dicto* distinction and internal versus external occurrence in Forbes 1987a, section 1. 'Lois believes the shortest spy is a spy' would get the analysis '*B*(Lois, the shortest spy is a spy)', in which 'the shortest spy' is analyzed as a binary restrictive quantifier phrase, and not, as the historical Frege would have had it, a singular term. Of course, 'the shortest spy' still has a customary reference which helps determine the customary reference of 'the shortest spy is a spy' (a state of affairs, in my view), but the reference of 'the shortest spy' is no more a particular individual than is that of 'at least one short spy'. My complete theory of customary reference is in chap. 5 of Forbes 1989.
13. The main qualification has to do with what it is for a dossier to be so-labeled with respect to a name used in a belief-ascription. We need the notion of a linguistic counterpart relation to allow the use of names in ascriptions of beliefs to foreigners who have a different name for the object in question in their language. This relation will be person-relative; for example, 'Londres' will not be a linguistic counterpart of 'London' for Kripke's Pierre. See Forbes 1988, section 3, 4.

14. The classification of this paragraph is not meant to be exhaustive. In particular, there is a class of terms semantically akin to kind terms in applying to things by virtue of intrinsic nature, but much more amenable to dictionary definition, since there is some canonical account of their meaning which itself uses a kind term; 'arthritis' is the most famous example (Burge 1979).

15. One problem with a parallel treatment is that the quandary of whether the term with oblique occurrence stands for the ascriber's or the believer's sense arises again. Refusal to substitute suggests that terms with oblique occurrence refer to the believer's sense, but then it is hard to construe Sasha's criticism of a normal speaker that he does not distinguish physicians from ordinary doctors: recall the discussion of Ralph and Lois Lane at the beginning of section II.

16. For more on definitional circumscription of objects, see Forbes 1987b, section 3.

17. In Forbes 1987b, I justified ascribing beliefs about arthritis to Bertrand because of the *similarity* of the sense he expresses with 'arthritis' and the sense expressed by a knowledgeable speaker. However, my change of view about why Bertrand in fact has beliefs whose subject-matter is arthritis does not affect the main argument of that paper.

18. Burge suggests that he can remain neutral on the issue of whether or not (15) is an allowable ascription (1978, 133-34). But Takashi Yagisawa has argued that Burge's views about belief-ascription are subject to a *reductio* (Yagisawa 1984), and it seems to me that only by disallowing belief-ascriptions other than conception-explaining ones where a misunderstood term occurs in oblique position can Yagisawa's argument be blocked. Yagisawa imagines a speaker A who believes that an object can satisfy a linguistic expression containing a numeral without satisfying the same expression with the numeral replaced by the English words for that numeral, and then argues that by Burge's principles it would follow that in written belief-ascriptions, numerals and words for numbers are not intersubstitutable (p. 411). It appears that the only way for Burge to block the conclusion is to deny all instances of 'A believes x satisfies . . .', on the grounds that these are not conception-explaining ascriptions and A's misapprehension about satisfaction precludes use of 'satisfies' in characterizing his beliefs.

19. Thus *contra* Burge 1978, 132, there is at least this theoretical reason for reconstruing the likes of (14).

20. A different situation arises when one is listening in to a conversation in which there is frequent occurrence of a word one does not understand. In this case I would say that the listener only partially interprets the utterances he hears, and inserts a 'marker' in the blank spots of his interpretation. If he succeeds in deducing what is meant by the new word from what the speakers say, he can then make a second pass through as many of the marked interpretations which have been retained in memory, substituting the deduced interpretation for the markers.

21. Research for this paper was supported by a grant from Tulane University's Committee on Research, for which I express my sincere appreciation. The paper benefited form discussions with John Campbell and correspondence with Nathan Salmon and Takashi Yagisawa.

References

Burge, T. 1978. "Belief and synonymy." *Journal of Philosophy* 75: 119-38.
Burge, T. 1979. "Individualism and the mental." In *Midwest Studies in Philosophy: Studies in Metaphysics*, 4: 73-121.
Davidson, D. 1969. "On saying that." In *Words and Objections*, edited by D. Davidson and J. Hintikka, Dordrecht, 158-74.
Evans, G. 1982. *The Varieties of Reference*. Oxford.
Fodor, J. 1987. *Psychosemantics*. Cambridge, Mass.

Forbes, G. 1987a. "Indexicals and intensionality." *Philosophical Review* 96: 3–33.
Forbes, G. 1987b. "A dichotomy sustained." *Philosophical Studies* 51: 187–211.
Forbes, G. 1988. "The indispensability of *Sinn*." Forthcoming.
Forbes, G. 1989. *Languages of Possibility*. Oxford.
Frege, G. 1892. "On sense and reference." In *Translations From the Philosophical Writings*, translated by P. Geach and M. Black. Oxford.
Kripke, S. 1979. "A puzzle about belief." In *Meaning and Use*, edited by A. Margalit. Dordrecht.
Kripke, S. 1980. *Naming and Necessity*. Cambridge, Mass.
McDowell, J. 1984. "*De re* senses." In *Frege, Tradition and Influence*, edited by C. Wright. Oxford.
Peacocke, C. 1981. "Demonstrative thought and psychological explanation." *Synthese* 49: 187–217.
Putnam, H. 1975. "The meaning of 'meaning'," in *Mind, Language and Reality: Philosophical Papers Volume 2*. New York.
Pylyshyn, Z. 1984. *Computation and Cognition*. Cambridge, Mass.
Salmon, N. 1989a. "Illogical belief." In *Philosophical Perspectives Volume 3*, edited by J. Tomberlin. Atascadero, Calif.
Salmon, N. 1989b. "How to become a millionaire." Forthcoming in *Noûs* 23 (1989).
Schiffer, S. 1987. *The Remnants of Meaning*. Cambridge, Mass.
Segal, G. and M. Speas. 1986. "On saying ðat," *Mind and Language* 1: 124–32.
Yagisawa, T. 1984. "The pseudo-Mates argument." *Philosophical Review* 93: 407–18.

Semantic Holism Without Semantic Socialism: Twin Earths, Thinking, Language, Bodies, and the World

HECTOR-NERI CASTAÑEDA

During the last decade, under the leadership of Hilary Putnam[1] and Tyler Burge,[2] a family of arguments pivoting on Twin Earths and Doppelgängers has been growing. Their conclusions are fundamental and varied, with repercussions in all the main branches of philosophy. Their distinctive impetus is strongly anti-individualist: *What* one believes or *what* one's words mean does not depend solely on oneself, but also on one's own community of speakers. They are the heirs of Wittgenstein's attacks against private language. Some arguments of Burge's pivot on Wittgenstein's question: How can a speaker's use of an expression be in error? The answer: by diverging from the standing use in the relevant community of speakers.

Here we investigate the significance of some of those arguments for our understanding of the role of language in thinking. The investigation includes a partial defense of what may be called *emergentist genetic super-functionalism* and of *methodological epistemological physicalism*.

I. THE IMPORTANCE AND PERSPECTIVES OF TWIN-EARTH ARGUMENTS

(A) Some Twin-Earth arguments make claims in the Philosophy of Mind and Cognitive Psychology. Some are aimed at rebutting dominant versions of functionalism. This is the view that mental states and events are functional properties of the states or events in a system. A functional property is a higher-order property consisting of a state of, or event in, a system being causally related in certain systematic ways to the other states (or events) of the system, to the inputs and outputs of the system, and to objects in the system's environment. This functionalism equates mental states and events with *causal profiles*. This seems to be immediately correct concerning mental states that, in contrast with episodes of consciousness, are dispositional.

To a mind-body property dualist who believes in the causal unity of the world, equating mental states or events with causal profiles is congenial. He objects only to the word 'consisting'. He claims that every event has a unique causal position and every realizable state has a characteristic causal pattern. He adduces, however, that the causal pattern of second-order properties just described is so general that it can — indeed, must — be found in properties that are clearly not mental, for instance, the property of being a carburetor, being a water faucet design, being a triangular hole that lets triangles pass through while intercepting other shapes. He urges that the distinctiveness and peculiarity of psychological states and events needs accounting for. At this point this dualism forks. One branch posits some irreducible mental events as outputs, or as inputs (say, episodes of consciousness). Another branch posits outputs, or inputs (e.g., pains, or presented secondary qualities) that are neither mental nor physical. Mental states with causal patterns involving such outputs or inputs would not be physical in the standard sense. To be sure such outputs may be called "physical" in an extended sense. After all, felt pains do have spatial positions and relations, have volume and shape, and some move. Of course, the two branches may converge. Both of these dualisms can be mounted on the thesis that the nonphysical properties emerge from certain complex physical systems. Since they have at their disposal certain irreducible nonphysical properties, they need not restrict mentality to biological systems. Hence, these dualists, as well as classical mind-body parallelists, may accept that mental states and events supervene on, or are codetermined by, physico-chemical states (hereafter *total internal physical state*), whether neurophysiological or not.

The dominant versions of functionalism are physicalistic. The individuals, the events, and the first-order properties of minded systems are all taken to be physical. These versions of functionalism need not, however, be materialistic or reductionist. A mental state is a complex causal pattern that can in principle be instantiated in many different types of physical systems with different electric, chemical, or biological natures. It may be an emergent state, it being an empirical matter whether and how it emerges.

Twin-Earth arguments have been devised to show that a person and her Doppelgänger can be in the same total internal physical state, and yet be in different states of belief, or refer to different things. Hence, a person's state of belief, it is claimed, does not supervene on the person's total internal physical state. This result may be acceptable to a traditional dualist. To prevent this move, some arguments attack an internal mental state, regardless of its dependence on the physical state of the corresponding body. To such arguments the typical physicalist reacts by moves within the physical realm.

Putnam and Burge have been promoting the view that a person's state of belief is determined, or individuated, with reference to the community of speakers. This role of the community need not be understood in terms of classical dualism, say, of a community spirit. On the contrary, this move to the community is, presumably, to be elucidated in terms of the co-speakers' total internal physical states and their environment.

These arguments thus leave fundamental ontological questions unanswered. Its issue is of course ontological, namely: the sufficiency of internal physical (or internal mental) state for mentality.

Now, a functionalist (whether dualist or physicalist) may accept that mentality emerges only in members of communities. She may invoke the existence of a community of systems as a supersystem *genetically* required for the emergence of mentality *in* the individual systems, not in the supersystem — without accepting it as a requirement for the supervenience of each mental event or state. Once mentality has emerged it can continue operating in the individual independently of the community. This is *genetic super-functionalism and synchronic functionalism*.

The main issue is: Is this mixed functionalism really viable? According to some Twin-Earth arguments the answer is "No!"

(B) Some Twin-Earth arguments pertain to the philosophy of language: The Theory of Semantics. They support the claim that the *meanings* of a person's expressions do not supervene on the person's total internal physical state. The personal meanings are again theorized to be determined by the way language is used by the community of speakers.

(C) Other Twin-Earth arguments belong in The Theory of Speech Acts. They claim that what a speaker *refers* to is not determined by her total internal physical state. The community of speakers intervenes to determine the speaker's reference. These arguments, by dealing with mental events, seem to be more directly connected to the Main Issue distilled above.

There are other applications of Twin Earth arguments, e.g., to scientific holism and to epistemology. These applications rest on the three basic types (A)–(C).

Applications (A)–(C) are, though distinct, closely connected. The meanings of one's words and sentences are a part of what one thinks when one uses a token T of a sentence containing those words as a means of thinking, or as an expression of what one thinks.[3] Then one uses the word tokens in T to refer to individuals, properties, and relations that conform to the meanings of their constitutive word types. Hence, the basic arguments are those aimed at establishing that current total internal physical state does not by itself determine reference, or meaning as this is used in speech acts.

II. BACKGROUND AND MAJOR ISSUES

1. Language and thinking

The Twin-Earth arguments lie at the intersection of thinking, reality, and the use of language. They are meant to contribute to our understanding of how language functions in experience. Thus, a partial deployment of elementary data about how language actually works is a needed foil for any evaluation of those arguments.

In recent discussions language is typically seen from the vantage point of a sophisticated hearer who knows what the real world consists of. The speaker is considered as a source of discourses to be interpreted. This is certainly fine. To understand how language functions we must certainly understand how it works in dialogue. We have learned language in communicational situations and use it to live our lives, which are inextricably woven with the members of our communities. Natural languages are originally means of communication and remain so. As the Wittgensteinian antiprivate arguments have established, in certain senses of 'private' a system of symbols cannot be just a means of thinking, but must also be a means of communication. Here, however, we are not at all concerned with private languages.[4]

Here we focus on some crucial complementary trivialities, which are also fundamental data for any attempt at understanding how language functions in our lives, in our culture, in the development of technology, in the growth of civilization.

First, to be heard and interpreted *language must be spoken*. Second, it is the destiny of language to be used by mature, autonomous speakers capable of using it on occasion as a mere means of thinking. A mature speaker of a natural language L is one who has developed a system of speech habits to use expressions of L correctly as a matter of course, has acquired the ability to identify some misapplications of those expressions, and possesses metamonitorial habits of self-correction, often automatic. That is, a mature speaker has internalized the rules of the languages she speaks as speech propensities to use language as a thinking speaker, not merely as an interpreter of others' speeches. She is able to produce linguistic outputs, even if she is alone and cannot enjoy her co-speakers' guidance and correction. These abilities become her basic possession of the language. When she interprets others' utterances she thinks *herself* what they say — rather, what she *thinks* or takes them to be saying. In brief, a language exists primarily in the speech habits and propensities of its speakers. It exists in hearer's capacities and propensities to interpret its tokens only to the extent that these hearers are language users.

2. Speaker's autonomy: control of criteria for word usage

There is a serious circularity in supposing that every word one uses one uses from the conception, or representation, of a rule governing the use of the word.[5] We have to take it for granted that normally speakers perform speech acts in a habitual manner, automatically conforming to the rules governing the expressions they use. In general, to account for speaking, as contrasted with interpreting speech tokens, we must hold on to serial causal-semantic schemata. (Here we use implicitly Quine's corners around variables referring to expressions.) The first clauses of a schema for an expression F pertain to situations containing external, perceptual outputs originating in inputs containing something F-like that cause the perceiving speaker to think (even express verbally) a content of the form "That is an F," or "That F is G."

Other clauses present the tokening of sentences containing the term F as outputs of sequences of events in which nothing F-like occurs. That thinking of F-things does not require the presence in the vicinity, or the existence anywhere, of F-things is of central importance for biographical living. We certainly plan to bring about not yet existing objects or states, and often we fail and they continue to be nonexisting.

In sum, a speaker must normally apply his linguistic rules correctly. This implies that the criteria for the application of the expressions in a person's idiolect are in some degree built into his propensities to use those expressions.

Within a background of correctly used expressions a speaker can ask whether a particular use of an expression is correct (appropriate, proper, or whatever, given the relevant normative terminology), or not. He may be able to ask the question metalinguistically: "Is this use of '. . .' correct?" Yet he need *not* have a metalinguistic consciousness. He must, at any rate, be able to ask the question in an *object-language* form: "Is this (an) F?" This presupposes that the expression F (for which 'F' stands) is somehow within his linguistic resources and within his reach. In the primary cases, he supposes the noise or mark F to lie in his idiolect, or in the general language to which his idiolect belongs. Yet these presuppositions need not be beliefs the speaker can rehearse. He may lack metalinguistic awareness; the presuppositions may simply be for him a nonthinkable *taken-for-granted*.

The object-linguistic level of semantic manipulation is the basic stage in language learning. As a first step in his internalization of linguistic rules the speaker must acquire propensities to use words correctly. His linguistic autonomy requires that he internalize the normative aspect of the rules by acquiring propensities to correct himself, or others, object-linguistically by means of *negation*: "That is not (really) F." Furthermore, in the early stages of his development a speaker may possess the ability to recognize noninstances without yet having the matching ability to verbalize a reason for his rejection of F.

Once again, the developing speaker acquires those abilities under the prodding and guidance of mature speakers, in a community of speakers. Nevertheless, these abilities *she* must acquire.

3. Meanings and the natural semantics of thinking

The criteria for correctly applying, as well as the criteria for correctly refusing to apply, an expression E built into the speech propensities of a person P at a given time t determine the *meaning(s) of E for P at t*. E can have several meanings for P at t. In such a case P's propensities to apply E and propensities to refuse to apply E fall into unified bundles corresponding to a meaning, an operational meaning. This unity comes from the use of E as an element of a sentence complex as a means of thinking. It arises from what P thinks and expresses with tokens of E.

Putnam and other philosophers find, with reason, the notion of meaning unclear, except when the meaning of an expression E is equated with an *extension* of *E*. Thus, the class of cats is said to be the best candidate for equation with the meaning of 'cat', and the class of oceans, seas, lakes, rivers, and pools of water the only decent thing to be considered as the meaning of 'water'.

Undoubtedly, expressions have extensions, and to understand how language functions in life we have to take extensions into account. For instance, certain structural relationships between language and reality can be studied by means of set-theoretical models, conceived as systems of extensions. This is sometimes called *formal semantics*. Moreover, the criteria for the application of an expression *E* to an entity *X* are tantamount, or equivalent, to criteria for determining whether *X* is in the extension of *E*.

Nonetheless, there is more to language than formal semantics. To understand the role of language using in life we must consider the thinking of extensions as derivative. The basic relationship between thought content and reality pertains to a *natural semantics*. Our basic thinking is of properties as instantiated or exemplified by objects.

Let us consider class membership. To ascertain whether *X* goes into the extension *E** of *E* we have to identify both *X* and the class *E**. *X* we identify by its properties. *E** we can identify by itself through its members (of course) if it is a very small and fully defined set. However, most extensions are indefinite, and are large classes. They cannot be present in experience. We identify an extension by means of a property that determines it. Consider the extension of Putnam's example: 'water'. The pieces of water on earth are too many for us to confront the set of them, so to speak, *in propria persona*. We need a criterion for membership in the extension of 'water'. The criterion may be incomplete and vague, but it must be capable of presenting itself in (finite) experience. Here again there is a full analogy with the contrast drawn above between thinking metalinguistically whether something is called "water" and thinking object-linguistically whether something *is* water. Simply to think *X is water* is different from, and basic to, thinking that *X* is in the extension of 'water'. In fact, the idea of an extension of 'water' requires a more complex concept than the mere concept of extension. This has to do with 'water' being a mass term, that is, a term that does not include in its rules for use an automatic principle of individuation, the way, in which, for example, 'cat' includes one.[6]

The meanings of a predicate, which are thinkable contents, are not extensions, but *intensions*: unified bundles of properties, which in their turn unify the manifolds of speech propensities to use the predicate in question. Doubtless, predicates have extensions, and it is true, as noted above, that *this is F* is Tantamount, or Equivalent, to *this is in the extension of 'F'* and to *this satisfies the criteria for membership in the extension of 'F'*. However, equivalence is not identify.[7] And, as we well know, thinking is not closed under logical equivalence. The constructive and finitist nature of thinking hinges crucially on that lack of closure. Succinctly put:

(Th.Int) Thinking intensions is the fundamental form of thinking, and thinking of extensions is built on it and includes it.

This inclusion depends on an ontological principle stressed by Frege:

(Int.Ext) Intensions [and reality] determine extensions.

To the extent that thinking is representational and symbolic, a language exists in its speakers' speech propensities. More generally, and basically, the thinking activity underlying speech is bodily (in the human case, brain) activity. This suggests the following postulate:

(Th.B) An episode of thinking an intension by X is determined by X's total internal physical state.

With the proper interpretation of 'determined' the mind-body dualist, whether emergentist or parallelist, may accept (Th.B).

It is important to understand what enters in the notion of total internal physical state. The core of this state is the network of the thinker's capacities to discriminate and think, together with her speech propensities. The thinker's discriminations are not necessarily ones she can articulate. In the same vein, she does not need to be aware that she *is* discriminating, let alone discriminating what she is discriminating. Thought contents appear in fused or confused ways, yet their appearance issues in appropriate behavior. Thus, one *feels tired* (without articulating this, or being aware that *one* feels tired). This causes one's looking for a place to sit; one sees a seat, and estimating its height, proceeds to sit on it. Most of the time that is the end of the story: one's brain has computed the height correctly and has coordinated the calculation and the action of sitting. The total internal physical state includes, then, capacities to react to distinctions in the environment that are much more fine grained than those entering conceptualized consciousness. On the other hand, it includes capacities that have developed up to the point of certain thresholds of unconscious discrimination, determined by the limits of confrontation of the properties and objects in the environment. Thus, things with the same internal chemical structure may be visually indiscriminable; yet perceptually indiscriminable objects may be digestively discriminable. Of course, at any time objects indiscriminable to both experience and theory may later on become discriminable to both. New propensities to think and speak develop, some unified under new meanings.

Language is a fundamental tool for living. One has to live his or her own life in his or her own time, and use the language one has. One must use the meanings currently at one's disposal.

4. *Natural language: Semantic holism*

To know the meaning of an expression is to know how to use the expression, that is, to use it as the means of, or expression of, thinking thoughts pertaining to what the expression means. Palpably this allows of degrees. Externally, the manifold of propensities to use a word as a means of thinking may be acquired piecemeal—in social interaction to be sure. Internally, this implies that one's thoughts pertaining to a property belong in increasing domains.

There is, however, a profound reason for our knowledge of meanings having degrees. Let us focus on descriptive, rather than imperative or emotive meanings. Language is in this sense a system of devices to think what the world is like. The world is one and language captures that oneness by its own semantic unity. The unity of the world imposes semantic holism as an epistemological and psychological foundation. Thus the properties of the world belong in families, and these families relate to one another by certain structural relationships. These are relationships of implication, of coherence, of incompatibility, of probabilistic overlap, or divergence. *A consistent property is at once: (i) an exemplifiable and thinkable content and (ii) an intersection of implication, incompatibility, and probability coordinates in the logico-ontological space of properties*. The propositions formulating those structural relationships as they intersect at a property P are postulates in the logic *of P*. They are, obversely, semantic postulates constituting the meaning of an expression E that denotes P, as well as of the other expressions occurring in the formulation.

Consequently, a speaker masters the meaning of an expression E denoting a property P only partially, until she knows how to think object-linguistically, using E, of all the semantic structural relationships linking P to all families of properties.[8] Whenever a person comes to know of a new family of properties she has to undergo *semantic growth*. Her knowledge of the new properties includes her mastering of some explicit structural coordinates linking the new properties to old ones in her idiolects. Semantic growth is at the center of the scientific discovery of new properties. New meanings (whether attached to old marks or to newly minted signs) have to be linked to the meanings of the old expressions. This is the background operation of building our map of the ontology of properties within which the new scientific discoveries are located.

5. Natural semantics: its pragmatic anchor

The preceding semantic holism is static, synchronic. The living use of language requires a dynamic application of its semantics. Every expression E has a static semantics built into a speaker's propensities to use it. This static semantics is characteristically a schema which is filled in in an actual speech-thinking act. In some cases this is obvious because the schema is very broad. This breadth is a part (but only one part) of the vagueness of ordinary expressions. For instance, the pair of expressions 'long'/'short' is at the purely semantic, dispositional level a schema of a family of relations of height. On occasions of use it gains specificity.

The general concept of quantification is the schema: all—— [where the blank stands for a semantic slot to be filled in pragmatically as a specification of the appropriate universe of discourse]. The predicate 'is red' is also a semantic schema with specifications on speech occasions.

6. De Dicto *reference vs.* Hearer's De Re *reference*

Thinking intensions is (more or less) what is often referred to as *de dicto* thinking. Clearly, the same considerations hold for acts of referring. A person who thinks of an entity as such, say, the president of West Germany in 1987, or water, refers to it *from inside* her experience of thinking. This is *de dicto reference*. She may believe that what she is referring to, internally, exists, externally, in the world. That is, she may intend *de re* reference, but she discharges her intention through *de dicto* reference. To understand, then, how language functions as a means of thinking we must provide an account of *de dicto* reference, whether what is internally referred to (or, if you wish, purportedly referred to) exists, that is, is a *res* or not.

The expression '*de re* reference' has another use, which needs careful segregation. An attribution of reference is said to be *de re* when the person making the attribution posits an external referent. That is, *de re* reference is *speaker's reference*. Consider for example Jones's stating "Columbus believed that Castro's island was China." Jones means to refer herself to Fidel Castro, without meaning to attribute to Columbus any idea about this man. The reference to Castro's island is really external to Columbus: it is just the speaker's. Evidently, a speaker's (purported) referent may fail to exist, thus failing to be *de re* in the above sense. Speaker's reference here is a report about something heard or read, or something hypothesized as something that can be heard or read. It is within the hearer's purview. We call this *de re* attribution of reference, *speaking hearer's de re reference*. It plays a major role in Twin-Earth arguments.

7. *Summary of major data*

There is much more that we already know about how language functions as a means of thinking. For our purpose here perhaps the preceding trivialities suffice. The crucial points can be summarized.

The linguistic autonomy of a speaker is a fundamental feature of language in its function as a means of thinking. It is the destiny of language to rise, from its social origins and its constant communitarian nature as a means of communication, to functioning as a means of thinking.

Before it can be heard language must be spoken. And it is spoken from the current speech propensities of the speaker. Other speakers and their speech propensities can certainly be taken into account. Nevertheless, this is feasible only to the extent that they are conjectured and internalized in the speaker's speech repertory. If one needs to rely on linguistic experts to speak, one must have some access to those experts. Long-dead experts or long-distant future experts one knows nothing about are of no use to one's speaking now what one has in mind now.

This central role of the speaker is, as so far described, compatible with the speaker using meanings given to her by her community of speakers. Likewise, the speaker may so far refer to what the community determines her referents to be. Similarly, the speaker may have and express nothing but the belief contents determined by her community of speakers.

We must now attend to Putnam's and Burge's arguments for the Social-Dependence Thesis about what one's words mean, what one refers to, and what one believes.

III. PUTNAM'S ORIGINAL TWIN-EARTH ARGUMENT; SOME OF ITS LESSONS

1. Two assumptions under fire

Putnam started the Twin-Earth arguments with his highly celebrated paper mentioned above. His goal was to show a tension between the following widely held assumptions in the theories of language and mind (134f):

(I) Knowing the meaning of a term is just a matter of being in a certain psychological state (in the sense of "psychological state" in which states of memory and psychological dispositions are such).

(II) The meaning of a term (in the sense of "intension") determines its extension (in the sense that sameness of intension entails sameness of extension).

Assumption (I) is a tenet about the chief disposition of (linguistic) thinking. Thus, it is included in (Th.Int) and (Th.B) above. Assumption (II) is (Int.Ext) above.

Putnam's underlying motive was to show that the meanings of (at least many) words are determined by the linguistic usage of the community of speakers. As a support *for* this view the argument is circular. However, the argument might be seen as creating a problem and then the view as a *proposal* of a solution to that problem. Of course, the view is then not a consequence of the argument; although it may very well be the best view for the problem.

As we shall see below, Putnam has, correctly, given up his original Twin-Earth Twin-Water argument. He has also modified the formulation of the original problem in terms of assumptions (I)-(II).

2. The first Twin Earth and its Twin Water

Putnam's first Twin-Earth thought experiment is as follows (139–141, mostly in his own words, the capitals expressing my own added emphasis):

> Somewhere in the galaxy there is a planet we shall call Twin-Earth ... very much like Earth; in fact, people of Twin Earth even speak *English*. [Each person in Earth] has a *Doppelgänger*—an identical copy—on Twin Earth. One of the peculiarities of Twin Earth is that the liquid called "water" is not H_2O but a different liquid whose chemical formula is very

long and complicated ... XYZ. XYZ is indistinguishable from water at normal temperatures and pressures, ... it tastes like water and it quenches thirst like water. ... The oceans and lakes on Twin Earth contain XYZ [and] it rains XYZ.

If a spaceship from Earth ever visits Twin Earth, then the supposition at first will be that "WATER" HAS THE SAME MEANING ON EARTH AND ON TWIN EARTH. This supposition will be CORRECTED WHEN IT IS DISCOVERED that "water" on Twin Earth is XYZ, and the Earthian spaceship will report as follows:

(1) On Twin Earth the word 'water' means XYZ. [Of course]
(2) On Earth the word 'water' means H_2O.

The word simply has two meanings (as we say). ... The extension of "water" in the sense of water$_E$ is the set of all wholes consisting of H_2O molecules, or something like that; the extension of "water" in the sense of water$_{TE}$ is the set of wholes consisting of XYZ molecules, or something like that.

[In] 1750 chemistry was not developed on either Earth or Twin Earth. Let Oscar$_1$ be a typical Earthian English speaker, and let Oscar$_2$ be his counterpart. ... Suppose that Oscar$_1$ and Oscar$_2$ are exact duplicates in appearance, feelings, beliefs, thoughts, interior monologue, etc. [that are molecule for molecule counterparts]. Yet the extension of the "water" was just as much H_2O on Earth in 1750 as in 1950; and ... XYZ on Twin Earth in 1750 as in 1950. OSCAR$_1$ AND OSCAR$_2$ UNDERSTOOD the term "water" DIFFERENTLY IN 1750 although they were in the same psychological state, and although, given the state of science at the time, it would have taken the scientific communities fifty years to discover that they UNDERSTOOD THE TERM "water" DIFFERENTLY. Thus THE EXTENSION OF THE TERM "WATER" (AND, IN FACT, ITS "MEANING" IN THE INTUITIVE PREANALYTICAL USAGE OF THAT TERM) IS NOT A FUNCTION OF THE PSYCHOLOGICAL SPEAKER BY ITSELF.

3. Speaker's de dicto *references and hearer's* de re *references*

The immediately striking feature of Putnam's argument is its pervasive exclusive hearer's perspective. Even that most internalist word 'understood' is used by Putnam with a speaking hearer's *de re* sense. A 1950 hearer interprets the 1750 statements made by Oscar$_1$ and by Oscar$_2$. They know nothing about chemistry; their 1950 posthumous hearer knows. They use their word 'water' to think about items in their respective environments and in the world beyond; their later hearer provides a chemical analysis of the items they are thinking of. Presumably on Twin Earth, as on Earth, nobody has lived from 1750 through 1950. Those Oscars and their predecessors were able to use the term 'water' successfully all their lives without the guidance of chemistry. They taught their children how to use the term, and corrected its misuses. Given the discussion above, we may certainly suppose that there were not many misuses of 'water' and that all misuses were corrected successfully. The uses and the corrections involved the application of the internal criteria built into their speech propensities to think and communicate their thoughts about pieces of water. Their ignorance of chemistry hindered some technological developments. It certainly precluded them from internalizing further criteria for the use of 'water', i.e., from acquiring further meaning postulates in the logic of water. Yet it did not prevent their *using language* effectively to live their lives. By the central hypothesis of Putnam's example the chemical composition of their waters play no role at all in their psychological or physiological development. For their plans about drinking, preparing different concoctions, swimming, cleaning, etc., the chemistry they do not know is irrelevant. And so it is, too, when they carry out their plans, and when they criticize their friends for not using the right amounts or kinds of water. As they understood (*de dicto*) their words, they used them in exactly the same way, in accordance with the same rules and criteria, on qualitatively identical instances.

To sum up, the Oscars did not refer *de dicto* to chemical composition. The posthumous hearer's *de re* reference is irrelevant to our understanding of how they *spoke*, one English, the other Twin English.

4. Meanings

If the hypothesis of total lack of discrimination applies to $Oscar_1$ and $Oscar_2$, then they have exactly the same pattern of propensities to think and speak. Their words have the very same meaning. By hypothesis, besides, their exercises of their respective propensities are fully parallel. They use parallel tokens of the same words to make parallel references to items in their environment and beyond. Of course the items are different individuals. This is clearly so when, for instance, they say in parallel:

(3) This water is too hot for me to take a bath.

Yet nothing in the story necessitates that there be any *de dicto* indexical component as a part of their meaning of 'water'. The individuality of the different pools of water is wholly expressed by the indicator 'This'.

Any difference in meaning will have to appear in universal statements. Suppose they exclaim:

(4) Water is 60 percent of our bodies!

What are they thinking of? According to Putnam's story they are *not* thinking of chemical composition. They know nothing about it. They are obviously thinking of the different roles water plays in their lives. There is nothing here that restricts the meaning of 'water' (not the speaking hearer's *de re* reference) to the planet where the word is uttered.

Putnam reports that the first Earthians visiting Twin Earth may think that 'water' has the same meaning on both planets. He forgot to mention that some of those travelers brought to Earth a huge tankload of Twin-Earth water. This was distributed among many people before anybody realized that their chemical composition was different. Thus Earthians were drinking the foreign water and bathing in it without any linguistic confusion. Then somebody raised a question:

(5) I wonder whether there is water on other planets, and whether it has the same chemical composition as on this planet?

The questioner is perfectly consistent.

Doubtlessly, once chemistry is developed new terminology with new semantic rules are needed and are introduced. The old terms are linked to the new ones. *This is required by semantic holism.* English gains then new mixed semantic postulates linking the old term 'water' to the new term 'H_2O'. Among them are: (i) water is not necessarily H_2O; (ii) a typical piece of water may be largely composed of H_2O molecules; (iii) a compound of nothing but H_2O molecules is a pool of water.

5. *Putnam's Thesis I, chemistry, biology, quarks, and SnQ's*

Putnam's result that reference is not determined by psychological state is, nevertheless, utterly correct. Except for a bit of ambiguity because of its compactness, it should *Not* be at all controversial. It is the thesis that neither psychological nor physical state determines speaking Hearer's *de re* reference. In fact we must endorse more precisely:

Putnam's Thesis I Generalized. Neither a speaker's total psychological state, nor her total internal physical state, at the time she makes a (surely) *de dicto* reference (including this *de dicto* referring) determines a speaking hearer's *de re* reference, which the hearer may construe in different ways.

It is important to fasten to the fact that Putnam's notion of reference, i.e., speaking hearer's *de re* reference, is not only relative to the hearer but also to the hearer's stipulation. In Putnam's example the 1950 hearer is just a proxy for Putnam himself. This relativity to himself is for the most part expressed by Putnam indexically, autobiographically. In the case of his original Twin-Earth Twin-water example, he has chosen as *de re* referent the chemical composition of the items to which his Oscars apply the word 'water'. In other examples, for instance, about animals and trees, he has chosen biological structure. Some of his followers equivocate. Sometimes they stipulate (speaking hearer's *de re*) reference to be to genetic structures, sometimes to genetic structures as these have been determined by evolution on Earth. As far as I can see, those stipulations lie within Putnam's theoretical prerogatives. The diversity of stipulation is perfectly reasonable. It pivots on the different theoretical or practical interests one may have. Sometimes we want to deal with whales as wholes; sometimes we must consider them as patterns of molecular systems; and sometimes in some other way. Clearly, for irrigation projects, for industrial development, for sanitary policies in Nepal it is important to ascertain the chemical composition of waters in the rivers and the lakes of Nepal. Palpably, this ascertainment presupposes postulate (i) above.

Obviously, there is *no* fixed metaphysical level at which one must pitch one's explanations. For certain deep theoretical purposes one may want to uniform everything at the level of patterns of patterns of patterns of . . . of the basic particulars of physics. Thus, some theoretical hearers of Putnam's Oscars may want to fix their useful hearer's *de re* reference at the level of quarkic physico-chemical analysis. Of course, there are at present no experts on such analyses. Hence, nobody knows what we actually refer to, i.e., refer *de auditoris re* to. Putnam's thesis still holds true. The quarkic structures of the objects we talk about are not determined by our conceptions of such objects. Such conceptions guide our *de dicto* references to them, but neither these references nor our total psychological states determine uniquely any quarkic structure.

6. *Extensions*

We have already explained that extensions are not the basic contents of thought. In fact Putnam's proposal that extensions be taken as the meanings of predicates amounts to a *proposal* to take a thought content as a hearer's *de re* referent. This proposal does not help understand how language functions in experience as a means of thinking. In fact it obscures the problem of understanding language.

Putnam also attacks (Int.Ext). His argument for this is not as perspicuous as we would like it to be. It is not clear how to construe his conclusion. Perhaps we can put his contention as follows:

> *Putnam's Thesis II.* A speaker's using a word W with a *de dicto* meaning M does not determine the extension of W.

This cries out for a characterization of the meaning of 'extension'. Obviously this does not mean the extension of 'extension'. What we need is a *criterion* for determining the extension of a word. Patently, we cannot simply say that the extension of 'water' is the class of objects to which the term 'water' has been applied. This does not provide for ambiguity. Given that by hypothesis the two Oscars use the word 'water' with the same meaning, then their uses determine the same extension of 'water'. This is not quite the union of the extensions Putnam proposes, namely: the pools of H_2O and the pools of XYZ. Putnam's extensions include weak teas and weak coffees, which are excluded by the Oscars' extension of 'water'. Putnam's extensions, as he declares in a text cited below, excludes items that are in the Oscars' extension of 'water'.

Putnam has simply made a stipulation of the speaking hearer's type. So interpreted his Thesis II is just as true as his Thesis I. And so is:

SEMANTIC HOLISM WITHOUT SEMANTIC SOCIALISM

Putnam's Thesis III. The total internal physical state of a speaker who uses a word W with some *de dicto* meaning does not determine the speaking Hearer's stipulated extension of W.

7. *Putnam's view of rigidly fixed meanings*

The chemical diversity of waters runs against Putnam's view about meanings and their teaching. He claims (148f) that the meaning of 'water' is taught as what is the *same* liquid as some paradigmatic samples. On his view the sameness in question is chemical composition and the paradigms fix it firmly:

[the] term 'water' is *rigid* [in Kripke's sense[9]] . . . when I give the ostensive definition '*this* (liquid) is water', the demonstrative 'this' is rigid.

That is, we stipulate a referent for the term and from then on that referent, as thus stipulated, is denoted by the term in all possible worlds, *a fortiori* in all situations within our galaxy. Any change in the stipulated referent is a change in the meaning of the term. Putnam claims we fix rigidly the reference of 'water' as the chemical composition H_2O through the paradigm samples.

Obviously, this is not an entirely accurate description of the nature of the procedures by which we have been teaching the meaning of 'water'. It is most doubtful that the samples that have been used in the teaching of the meaning of 'water' during the last year — let alone the previous three hundred years — have really had the same chemical composition. Perhaps the samples are meant to remain rigid, i.e., fixed as samples. However, that in furnishing the samples we intend to refer, whether *de dicto* or *de re* being immaterial, to the chemical composition of the samples is not true in my experience or in the experience of my acquaintances. In fact, benefiting from Putnam's thought experiment, samples of imported twin water can be used to teach the meaning of 'water' on Earth. We may suppose that chemically ignorant janitors drank cupfuls of it and brought differing amounts of it to their homes. Some of their children and grandchildren learned the meaning of 'water' from samples of twin water, others learned it from both kinds of sample. I suspect that some mixtures were also used.

Putnam's view of the use of the indicator 'this' to fix the chemical composition of the paradigm goes beyond the normal roles of the indicator. On his view the samples are rigid. But could $Oscar_1$ and $Oscar_2$ in 1750 have kept the paradigms intended in Putnam's way fixed rigidly, without knowing any chemistry?

Some of us know chemistry well enough to tell whether a certain liquid volume is H_2O or not. But liquids can have different chemical composition. Suppose, contrary to fact, that the Oscars decide to keep rigidly fixed certain samples as paradigms. How can they act on that decision? Suppose they wish to determine whether a certain liquid encountered later is really water or merely twin water, or something else. Must they, to be semantically responsible, carry along with themselves a chemical analyzer? The rigidity of the chemistry of the samples of terms denoting natural kinds would require a laboratory to be carried by each mature speaker.

The waters on Earth do not have the same chemical composition. For example, the brown dirty waters of mountain rivers filled with mountain-eroding rains are different chemically from well waters, from the water in the Canal Grande in Venice, from the tap water in New York City. Putnam has appreciated this and has given up his Twin Water argument.

IV. PUTNAM'S NEW ARGUMENT AGAINST CONTENT: TWIN RURITANIA

1. Self-criticism concerning the old Twin-Earth Twin-Water Argument

In a new study Putnam has given up the original Twin-Earth Twin-Water argument.[10] His discussion is somewhat disingenuous. He quickly summarizes an immediate criticism the argument prompted in some if its readers (MHEH, 256, the capitals represent my added emphasis):

> (A) I thought that the layman's "water" is chemically pure H_2O give or take some impurities. But this is *too* simple. A glass of coffee is more than 99% H_2O but the layman won't class it as a "glass of water"—even if he knows that it is more than 99% chemically pure WATER. He will say that the "coffee consists mostly of water," not that it *is* a glass of water. On the other hand, he will probably say that a glass of H_2O with 2% dirt floating in it is a "glass of muddy water."

The capitalized 'WATER' occurs with internal construal in the scope of 'He knows'. It has referential cumulation. It expresses Putnam's use of 'water' to refer to H_2O as chemically pure water, and it represents his hypothetical attribution of knowledge of this equation to the layman. Five pages later Putnam explains why neither he nor the layman could ever know that. With a gesture at precision Putnam, in a footnote, as a casual afterthought, throws away the crux of his water examples (MHEH, 261 n11):

> (B) I say, "at the level of high-school chemistry" because the actual molecular structure of water is extremely complicated. For example, in addition to H_2O (and D_2O), there are such forms as H_4O_2, H_6O_3, ... and quantum mechanical superpositions of all of these states.

Why couldn't XYZ, allegedly composing pure twin water, be one more molecular variety of water?

Putnam still clings to the tenet that the meaning of 'water' includes chemical composition. He argues as follows (MHEH, 255, the capitals expressing my added emphasis):

> Suppose there is . . . a liquid, say, "oxyhydroblahblah," such that it has all the "obvious" properties of water except supporting life; . . . maybe

there is a slight peculiarity about taste or feel . . . A mixture of H_2O and oxyhydroblahblah will, however, pass as water (no worse than Philadelphia water). Suppose you give a layman a glass of *fifty percent* H_2O and *fifty percent* oxyhydroblahblah. If you TELL a layman that it is a glass of 99% H_2O and one percent of harmless something else, he will perhaps still be willing to call it "water." But if you TELL him the TRUTH, he won't say it is "water" (although he will say it is *fifty percent* "water"). The fact that what he is given consists of as much as half of a substance which does not occur as a constituent of "normal" water at all certainly debars it from being classed as water. IN SHORT, EVEN THE LAYMAN INCLUDES in his concept of water some notion of HAVING A STANDARD OR NORMAL "COMPOSITION."

This is a difficult argument. Putnam himself rebuts the claim about the 99 percent mixture being water on the next page, in the above passage (A). Given his experiences of rain water, summer river waters, weak coffees, etc., it is not clear what the layman's notion of standard water composition may be. Putnam himself establishes, in passage (B) above, that the *non-layman*'s notion of standard composition is muddy. It turns out to be an indefinite disjunctive conception that allows of many different chemical compositions. Furthermore, the conclusion, announced by 'In short', a performative inferential expression, is extremely weak. It can hardly support the claim that twin water is not water.

In any case, the layman's refusal to call "water" the mixture you present him with does not show anything about normal chemical composition of water. If you *Tell* him the truth as described and he believes you, then he believes, as Putnam remarks, that it is a fifty-fifty percent mixture. The layman will probably believe this even if you lie to him. The problem lies on the reported mixture ratio. Suppose the layman divides an amount of water, oil, a mixture of whatever you like, into two containers A and B. Then you offer him a glass and tell him (lying or not) persuasively that the glass contains fifty percent from container A and fifty percent from container B. I am confident that he will refuse to say that the glass is full of the liquid from container A. He will repeat what you tell him: fifty percent A and fifty percent B. And this has nothing to do with the normal composition of liquids in those containers. It has to do with the mixture and the mixture ratio.

2. *The major assumption of Putnam's new reductio*

Putnam marshals new variants of Twin-Earth arguments against the thesis that psychological state determines reference, or extension. His argument is offered in support of meaning holism. His declared opponent is Jerry Fodor, who is represented as challenging "the step *from* holism with respect to belief fixation *to* holism with respect to meaning" (MHEH, 259). This is fascinating, at least for me, who has for decades adopted a version of semantic holism.

(See Note 9.) Yet it is not clear what Putnam's issue is. He offers no precise characterization of meaning holism. He declares (260, emphasis added):

> Since Quine, *we have come to see* the whole language as the 'unit of empirical significance'.

Quine's slogan is difficult. One aspect of it is relevant here.

How is it that Greta, a three-year old girl in Dortmund, who makes excellent empirical sense of her little world in German employs the whole of language as her unit of empirical significance? The whole of the German language? Or the whole of her own German *idiolect*?

Here we can see that Quine's slogan can be adduced as implicitly promoting the Social-Dependence Thesis. Clearly, if the child's speech acts mobilize meanings that involve the whole of the adult language, then every statement she makes gains empirical significance from the adults' standpoint. Patently, as an argument for the Social-Dependence Thesis this would be a flagrant *petitio* – unless we have both a clear notion of how the whole (adult) language is semantically involved in Greta's saying anything, and a wholly independent way of establishing the reality of that involvement. This reality should not of course be a mere empirical reality, but appropriately necessary.

As things seem to be nowadays, were Greta to be left alone in the world, she would gain the linguistic and psychological equipment to continue and even improve her making empirical sense of the world around her. Again, the original social dependence on others can be cut off at the moment Greta becomes a mature speaker of her German idiolect.

The situation now is reminiscent of Putnam's 1950 hearer explaining the referents of $Oscar_1$'s and $Oscar_2$'s 1750 uses of 'water'. This *ex post facto* external assessment was entirely irrelevant to those 1750 speakers. Now we have contemporary speakers who can intervene in Greta's speech acts. But why restrict the *whole* language to the language used by a population at a given time? Why not be wholly holistic and take the *whole* language from beginning to end? Why not have Greta's utterances gain meaning that involves the speakers of German in the year 3000 – with their as yet unforeseeable language and unimaginable scientific knowledge?

Social origin of language is fine. In the end, however, a speaker cannot help but speak from his resources and his meanings as these are built into his speech propensities. Hence, because of the unity of the world and the unity of the person's experience, we must at least endorse an Idiolectal Hierarchical Semantic Holism. We have endorsed it above.

Putnam has, however, a more specific goal: to rebut Fodor's "sophisticated mentalism." This he characterizes as a view composed of three components (MHEH, 261, the capitals signal my added emphasis):

> (1) Postulate "meanings" as psychological entities. (But do not postulate that they need to be, at most times, available to consciousness . . .)

(2) Postulate that these entities are, in some way, associated with individual words, morphemes and sentences.
(3) Postulate that the step *from* the meaning of a sentence to its assertibility conditions involves the use of general intelligence and background knowledge — which is WHERE THE "HOLISM" WILL COME IN.

Presumably the meanings postulated in (1) are universals and propositions, though it is not clear why Putnam calls them "psychological entities." Are they fictional entities supposed to contrast with *social entities*, which the argument will establish as the crux of the holism of meaning? We still need a characterization of meaning holism.

Immediately after formulating postulation (3) Putnam declares, punningly, that the "task of [his] essay is to show that this option [sophisticated mentalism] has, in a sense, no content." This task he pursues by arguing that three essential "constraints on any theory of contents" (MHEH, 263) conflict. Hence, he claims, the threefold postulation (1)–(3) is empty: "*There are no entities which are plausible candidates for the role of "contents" associated with our [. . .] linguistic expressions*" (167, original emphasis). His argument is, therefore, a *reductio ad absurdum*.

Postulation (3) announces where the *reductio* will creep in. In the mist of the assumed holism of belief (and knowledge) holism of meaning will appear. That is, he claims (*de re*) that doxastic cooperation implies semantic socialism.

The three essential constraints in conflict are:

I. Different contents must, in general, be associated with sentences which we preanalytically suppose to differ in meaning, and the same or closely similar contents must be associated with sentences which we preanalytically suppose to be the same in meaning. In short, "contents" must have the correct powers of *disambiguation*. (263)
II. Contents must remain invariant under normal processes of belief fixation. (265)
III. Contents must be "associated" with the relevant words and sentences by each speaker who counts as fully competent in the use of the words and sentences. (267)

Thus, Putnam's specific assumption for his *reductio* is the conjunction I&II&III. The argument of course involves other premises besides this and (1)–(3). Clearly, a dissenter may conceivably seize upon one of these other premises to cling to his content. In the end the real issue is about the construction of a theory that can account for *all* the known data about how language functions in *all* types of experience.

3. Putnam's Twin Ruritanias

Putnam's argument is as follows (268f, where again the added capitals express my own emphasis):

One of the differences between the dialect of Ruritanian which is spoken in the north and the dialect spoken in the south is that in north Ruritanian *grug* MEANS "silver," while in south Ruritanian this word MEANS "aluminum." . . . Silver is so common in north Ruritania that in the north the pots and pans are made of silver. One might imagine that in the Middle Ages 'grug' MEANT 'POT METAL' in Ruritanian, and that it is the FACT that north Ruritanian pots are made of silver AND south Ruritanian pots of aluminum that accounts for the MEANING SHIFTS that have taken place. In any case, northern children grow up KNOWING that pots and pans are normally made of "grug" and southern children grow up KNOWING that pots and pans are normally made up of "grug."

In the example, Oscar [a south Ruritanian boy] and Elmer [his north Ruritanian counterpart] are supposed to be in the same psychological condition (in Fodor's "solipsistic" sense of 'psychological condition'), i.e., the same with respect to all "mentalistic" parameters relevant to language at t_0.

So, although in the ADULT COMMUNITIES to which they belong, 'grug' has TWO DIFFERENT MEANINGS, it has the same content, for *Oscar* and for *Elmer* at t_0. At t_1 (when they have become adults) the words MUST DIFFER IN CONTENT IN THE TWO IDIOLECTS as much as 'silver' and 'aluminum' for the speakers of English. Hence the word must *change content* between t_0 and t_1 (for at least one of the children, and presumably for both). . . .

However, all that happened between t_0 and t_1 was normal belief fixation. . . . At t_0 both children know that "grug" is a metal, that is shiny-gray in color, that it tarnishes, that Mother has grug pots and pans, etc. By t_1 Oscar knows that grug is called 'aluminum' in American English and . . . in north Ruritania, where silver (called 'zilber' in south Ruritanian) is used for pots and pans . . . and Elmer knows that "grug" is called 'silver' in English. . . . Moreover, any place we decide to stipulate that the difference in "content" has taken place will be QUITE ARBITRARY, AND UNRELATED TO ACTUAL PRACTICES OF PARAPHRASE AND INTERPRETATION (will violate constraint I).

4. *Perplexing reductio*

This is a very tantalizing argument. *First*, we were promised a *reductio*. Instead we are given an outline where presumably a *reductio* could be developed by the reader. Putnam challenges the reader to specify the semantic learning accrued to Oscar or Elmer between times t_0 and t_1. He claims that any such specification will be "arbitrary" and will violate constraint I. Is this so?

Second, in accordance with his plan of attack Putnam mentions a good deal of beliefs the two boys acquired between t_0 and t_1. He contends that this belief acquisition does not constitute a change in the meanings of their word 'grug'. Yet some of those beliefs are clearly semantic. For instance, Oscar has learned that 'grug' is *called* "aluminum" in American English and in North Ruritanian, and that North Ruritanian 'grug' is called (i.e., means the same as) 'zilber' in South Ruritanian. At what time did they acquire these pieces of semantic information?

Third, the target of the argument is a "psychological entity," which seems to be like a property to which the speaker has access. Given Putnam's predilection for chemical composition, presumably the properties of having atomic weight 107.88 and having atomic weight 26.97 can certainly function as *the* meanings of South Ruritanian 'grug' and of North Ruritanian 'grug', respectively. Thus, we can determine the time at which the children undergo the fundamental change in meaning as the time they learn these chemical facts. The children move, cumulatively, from an experiential, behavioral meaning of 'grug' to a chemical one. Their homophonic words 'grug' acquire an important ambiguity. This ambiguity can be specified, and conforms to "actual practices of paraphrase and interpretation" without violating constraint I.

Fourth, seizing upon atomic weights as the meanings of words denoting chemical elements is to cleave the Social-Dependence Thesis from Semantic Holism. Atomic weights can be associated with chemical words on a one-one basis, without the meanings of these words needing (it seems) connections to the meanings of other words. This would be Semantic Non-holism. On the other hand, those speakers who lack knowledge of those associations would not know the meanings of the chemical words they use. Their use would then be supported by the chemists, the relevant semantic experts.

Patently, the word 'meaning' has changed meaning. We began with a *de dicto* meaning: as those criteria that determine what the person using the word means, and the properties meant being internal to the thought content. Now what a speaker thinks *de dicto* does not include the meaning of the words with which he thinks: this is a *de re* meaning of 'meaning'. The shift parallels the shift we encountered in the early Twin-Earth arguments. There we saw a shift from *de dicto* reference to speaking hearer's *de re* reference.

Similar comments are valid for the shift in meaning of 'meaning'. For instance, why take chemistry as the level of semantic expertise, and not particle physics? From a deeper ontological "understanding" the ultimate particles of physics are the genuine stuff. We can claim not just that nobody knows what her words mean, but that it is unlikely (or impossible) that anybody will ever know. This clearly establishes that there are no meanings satisfying Putnam's constraints I-III.

This shows the high ideality of *de re* meanings. Fortunately, we do not need them. Just as the 1750 Oscars managed very well to use 'water' efficiently, Elmer and Oscar in Ruritania can manage to live with grug pots. The problem of explaining how language is spoken remains. We want an account of how reference is made from *inside* experience.[11] We need an elucidation of the connections between a person's idiolect and the dialects and language of the speaking community.

5. *Total internal physical state and comparative discriminations*

Putnam's target is Fodor's mentalism, a physicalistic reductionism. Mental states are for Fodor just functional states of physical systems. To attain his chief desideratum Putnam proposes to show that two persons can be in exactly the same internal state and use tokens of the same sentence type within different meanings. Presumably, by an argument like the one at the end of section I.2, those two persons have different thought contents. In other words, mental acts or states do not supervene on total internal physical state. As recorded above, a traditional mind-body dualist welcomes this result. However, Putnam is not (yet) jumping on this platform.

The refutation of Fodor's (and early Putnam's) functionalism is the very same task for which the original Twin-Earth argument was designed. One problem, we saw, is that our water is indistinguishable from twin water. Hence, it was difficult to believe that 'water' has different meanings in English and in Twin English. The difficulty becomes a near-impossibility when one reflects on the chemical diversity of waters. As registered above, Putnam has conceded this much.

The Twin-Ruritanian example is meant to alleviate those difficulties. The word 'grug' denotes clearly distinct metals in the two countries. The difference of the denotations is built in openly and within reach of the subjects' discriminatory powers. It is almost a *de dicto* difference. It is not a *de dicto* difference because neither Oscar nor Elmer can compare aluminum with silver before time t_0. Thus, we are ready to accept that they think different thought contents. The exercise reduces simply to securing that they instantiate the very same internal state. This seems easy. Elmer and Oscar grow up in twin environments within twin families and households. They are physiological twins. They have twin perceptual stimuli and respond with twin perceptions. Their physiological systems and their environments undergo twin developments. Thus, one evening they say in parallel:

(11) That grug pot is hot.

We are prone to believe that they have different thought contents. But do they? We cannot really say. It all depends on how they are using the noise 'grug'. Which propensities are mobilized in their production of their tokens of sentence (11)?

There are two cases to consider. *Case A*: Elmer and Oscar are still early in their development and they mobilize the very same propensities. *Case B*: Elmer and Oscar have developed enough understanding of their environment to have acquired within their twin development some asymmetrical discriminatory abilities. These abilities need not yet be matched by expressive speech propensities. Nevertheless, their physiological systems have by then broken their twin parallelism. Case B is allegedly ruled out by the construction of the example. Perhaps. But then we must appreciate fully the meagerness of Case A.

By hypothesis Elmer and Oscar live in twin houses, with twin objects, in twin arrangements — except that wherever Elmer's house has a silver pot Oscar's has one twin pot made of aluminum. Let us ponder this. Consider Elmer's pot $E(s)$; its twin counterpart is Oscar's pot $O(a)$. How much twinness encompasses $E(s)$ and $O(a)$? They must look alike in shape and size and in relative position to other objects. Only if this is so can Elmer and Oscar have the same retinal images and the same trains of nervous activity in the same patterns. To secure twin physiological developments the pots must also feel the same and *weigh* the same. This is important.

One cannot adduce that Elmer's house is simply the house you obtain by replacing aluminum with silver everywhere in Oscar's house. You must decide what sort of twinness you wish to maintain. If you choose visual geometric twinness, then you must exclude tactual and motor twinness. If the two pots $E(s)$ and $O(a)$ are of the same size and shape, then $E(s)$ is heavier than $O(a)$. This neither Elmer nor Oscar can experience (*de dicto*). Yet these boys can have experiences of twin objects with different chemical composition that are of the same shape and size, or of the same weight, as either $E(s)$ or $O(a)$. With these they can compare their grug pots.

Perhaps Elmer has not reached the stage of comparing $E(s)$ with pots lighter than $E(s)$ but heavier than $O(a)$. That is, perhaps Elmer has never carried these pots at the same time or for several minutes in close succession. He has never investigated the weights of the pots or the objects in his house. Evidently, after some lifting experiences Oscar and Elmer acquire an asymmetric physiology pertaining to those objects with a weight between those of $E(s)$ and $O(a)$. Likewise, in the case of tactually twin objects $E(s^*)$ and $O(a^*)$ that have the same weight, Elmer and Oscar will soon develop different optic physiology. Comparative judgments about texture, scratchability, oxidation, etc. will soon ensue in different internal physical states in them.

By the considerations made above about propensities (recall the action of sitting) there need not be in the twin boys any discrepant verbal ability. Their capacities to discriminate are more basic.

In brief, with surprisingly small diversity of experiences Elmer and Oscar can develop asymmetrical physiologies. Hence, the Elmer and the Oscar Putnam needs have very limited experience, e.g., they may have seen pots but not lifted them. They have internalized propensities to use 'grug' in a wholly primitive way, without being able to discriminate between different metals. This is Case A. Then they use 'grug' with the same (*de dicto*) meaning. As before, mere speaking hearer's *de re* reference or meaning just does not help us to understand how Elmer and Oscar use their language.

Children and people learn words with certain meanings to talk about the things surrounding them. Some of those words become more general, as when 'salt' is moved from applying to kitchen salt (mostly sodium chloride) to other salts and eventually to chemical compounds arising from acids. Other words become specialized. One outstanding example is small babies' use of 'da-da' or 'ta-ta' to refer to any adult male in their little world.

The crucial question is: At what time did Elmer and Oscar undergo the semantic growth that left them with different meanings of 'grug'? The answer is clear. When they have developed enough asymmetric discriminatory powers so that different counterfactual conditionals are true of them. That is, when they reach Case B described above. Some of the relevant counterfactuals are obvious. For example: "Would Elmer say that his pot $E(s)$ is heavier than a weight-alike of Oscar's pot $O(a)$?" "Would Oscar, were he carried to North Ruritania, find that humidity makes grug pots there black?" "Would Elmer, if he received a load of grug pots from South Ruritania, say that Southern grug is very different from Northern grug?" Patently they need no special laboratory tests to decide that different metals are called by them "grug."

Oscar and Elmer may come to find an ambiguity they can signal by standard practices of paraphrase and interpretation. In the absence of other words each boy may use 'grug' as a generic term to cover both silver and aluminum as well as a specific term denoting one of these. By this time Oscar and Elmer will have acquired some relevant conceptual differences, some meaning postulates, which differentiate aluminum from silver. Later on they will learn some meaning postulates that relate North Ruritanian 'grug' to the chemists' symbol 'AG', and some meaning postulates that relate South Ruritanian 'grug' to the chemical term 'AL'.

V. CONCLUSION

Putnam did the right thing in abandoning his original Twin-Earth argument. The argument turns on an example that does not get off the ground. Its strategy consists of shifting the discussion from speaker's *de dicto* reference to speaking hearer's *de re* reference. The argument cannot support the Social-Dependence Thesis.

Putnam's Twin-Ruritania argument aims at defending "holism of meaning." Although it is not very clear what this holism amounts to, the aim is correct.

In my opinion we must adopt Idiolectal Hierarchical Semantic Holism. Lurking behind Putnam's argument is an equation of meaning holism and the Social-Dependence Thesis. Yet they seem to be independent of each other. The Social-Dependence Thesis is fine if it is understood in a genetic sense. Putnam's Twin-Ruritania argument does not appear to be successful either as a defense of meaning holism or as an attack against Fodor's "sophisticated mentalism." It involves, surprisingly, the assumption of a sort of *atomistic physicalism*. One metal is throughout substituted for another as if there were no discriminable differences between the comparative differences between each of the metals and other substances. The human body is a very sophisticated discriminatory system.

I have always been opposed to atomisms and reductionisms,[12] and I am fond of unity and holisms. Thus, I am deeply attracted to nonreductionist *methodological epistemological physicalism*. This is the hypothesis, for the purpose of guiding research, that every mental state or episode has some distinctive physical manifestation. The rationale is simple: however subjective mental states and episodes may be, they are part of the one total causal order of reality; for us to consider them they should manifest their presence in that order; moreover, the subjective mental states or acts we can attribute to others must have an attribution basis in the one shared common world of physical objects and events. Methodological epistemological physicalism is daring only in the methodological positing of a distinctive physical sign for each mental state or episode within the causal order.

The conclusions spearheaded by Putnam's Twin-Earth arguments are not in themselves reductionist. Nevertheless, it is reassuring that the arguments do not succeed in defeating methodological epistemological holistic physicalism.

Notes

1. Hilary Putnam, "The Meaning of 'Meaning'," in *Language, Mind, and Knowledge*, edited by Keith Gunderson (Minneapolis, 1975). Page references to this essay are given by page number only.

2. Tyler Burge, "Individualism and the Mental," *Midwest Studies in Philosophy: Metaphysics* 12 (1979): 73-121.

3. For a detailed discussion of how properties, rather than classes, are the primary cognitive content, see Hector-Neri Castañeda's "Appendix: Characters: Meanings vs. Functions from Contexts to Contents" at the end of "Direct Reference, the Semantics of Thinking, and Guise Theory (Constructive Reflections on David Kaplan's Theory of Indexical Reference)," in *Themes of Kaplan*, edited by Joseph Almog, John Perry, and Howard Wettstein (Oxford, 1989).

4. On private languages, see Ludwig Wittgenstein, *Philosophical Investigations*, translated by G. E. M. Anscombe (Oxford, 1952). For an intriguing interpretation, see Saul Kripke, *Wittgenstein on Rules and Private Language* (Cambridge, Mass. 1982). For a reply to Kripke, see G. P. Baker and P. M. S. Hacker, *Scepticism, Rules and Language* (Oxford, 1984). See also Brian Loar, "Review of *Wittgenstein on Rules and Private Language*," *Noûs* 19 (1985): 273-80, and Paolo Leonardi's "Review of *Scepticism, Rules and Language*," *Noûs* 22 (1988): 618-24. My own interpretation is criticized by Carl Ginet, "Castañeda on Private Language," in *Agent, Language, and the Structure of the World*, edited by James E. Tomberlin (Indianapolis, 1983). My position on the topic is essentially the same as the one adopted by Vladislav A. Lektorsky, *Subject Object Cognition* (Moscow, 1984), as follows:

> Three kinds of activity are linked together at the outset of the formation of consciousness: external practical activity, the process of cognition, and communication. (150) Later, at the stage when consciousness has been formed, the direct links between practical activity, cognition, and communication, are broken. (151)

5. This has been remarked many times, and according to some this is the main point of Wittgenstein's discussion of what it is to follow a rule. See Baker and Hacker mentioned in note 4. In this section and later on I am adopting the discussion in "Private Language Problem" in *The Encyclopedia of Philosophy*, vol. 6, edited by Paul Edwards (New York, 1967).

6. See Helen Morris Cartwright "Heracleitus and the Bath Water," *Philosophical Review* 74 (1965): 466-85, and "Quantities," *Philosophical Review* 79 (1970): 25-42.

7. The simplest proof that equivalence between propositions is not identity is this: (*Px*) being blue is most strongly equivalent to (*Qx*) being blue (and) round or blue. These properties are entirely different. They have different logical form. They have different extensions. The extension of *Px* is the set of blue things; the extension of *Qx* is the set of triples of the form < *b, a, b* >, where *b* is a blue thing and *a* is any object whatever of the domain of discourse. On this and related issues, see Hector-Neri Castañeda "Ontology and Grammar: I. Russell's Paradox and the General Theory of Properties in Natural Language," *Theoria* 42 (1976): 44-92.

8. My first statement of semantic holism appears in *Thinking and Doing* (Dordrecht, 1977), chap. 13. See also Hector-Neri Castañeda, *On Philosophical Method* (Bloomington, Ind., 1980).

9. Saul Kripke, "Naming and Necessity," in *Semantics of Natural Language* edited by Donald Davidson and Gilbert Harman (Dordrecht, 1972).

10. Hilary Putnam, "Meaning Holism and Epistemic Holism," in *Theorie der Subjektivität*, edited by Konrad Cramer, Hans Friedrich Fulda, Rolf-Peter Horstmann, and Ulrich Pothast (Frankfurt am Mein, 1987): 251-77. This will be cited as *MHEP*.

11. The problem of *de dicto* reference, of reference from the inside of experience is a classical one found in Kant's *Critique of Pure Reason*. It is at the heart of Frege's Sense/Referent View. See his "The Thought: A Logical Enquiry," translated by A. and M. Quinton, *Mind* 65 (1956): 289-311. That problem is the one that guided the development of Guise Theory. See the papers by Romane Clark and Alvin Plantinga and Castañeda's replies to them and to John Perry in the Tomberlin volume mentioned in note 4. See also Hector-Neri Castañeda, *Sprache und Erfahrung*, translated by Helmut Pape (Frankfurt, 1982) and *Thinking, Language, and Experience* (Minneapolis, 1989), and the papers by Ray Rosenberg, David Smith, and Jeffrey Sicha in *Hector-Neri Castañeda*, edited by James E. Tomberlin, (Dordrecht, 1986). See further the essays by Guido Küng, Klaus Jacobi, Hans Burkhardt and Carlos Dufour, Tomis Kapitan, Heinz-Dieter Heckmann, Friedrich Rapp, and Wolfgang Künne, and Castañeda's replies in *Das Denken und die Struktur der Welt*, edited by Klaus Jacobi and Helmut Pape (Berlin, 1989). Other relevant studies are: James E. Tomberlin, "Identity, Intensionality, and Intentionality," *Synthese* 46 (1984); Jig-Chuen Lee, "Guise Theory," *Philosophical Studies* 46 (1984): 403-15; William Rapaport, "Meinongian Theories and a Russellian Paradox," *Noûs* 12 (1978): 153-80, and his "Non-existing Objects and Epistemological Ontology," *Grazer Philosophische Studien* vol. 25/26 (1984/1986): 61-95.

12. For some of my reasons for not endorsing mind-body reductionism, see "Supervenient Properties, Emergency, and the Hierachy of Concrete Individuals," *Proceedings of the 1987 Meetings of the German Semiotic Society* (forthcoming). For a different approach, see Jaegwon Kim, "Concepts of Supervenience," *Philosophy and Phenomenological Research* 45 (1984): 153-76.

Aboutness and Substitutivity

GENOVEVA MARTI

1. THE "PUZZLE" AND THE DOCTRINE

The philosophy of language has been dominated by an *extensionalist ideal*: truth value ought to remain constant when codesignative singular terms (or coextensional general terms) are interchanged. More explicitly, sentences that behave according to the following Principle of Substitutivity are supposed to be paradigmatic:

[PS] The truth value of the proposition expressed by a sentence that contains an occurrence of t_1 remains constant when t_2 is substituted for t_1, provided that t_1 and t_2 are codesignative or coextensional terms.[1]

Since it is obvious that not all sentences fit this picture, the extensionalist tendency is to regard the recalcitrant contexts, so-called *intensional contexts*, as deviant. Such contexts are puzzling. They need to be *explained* by an adequate theory of meaning. It is assumed, however, that so-called *extensional contexts* need no special explanation.[2] There is no reason to ask for an explanation of why the substitution of 'the number of planets' for 'nine' in 'nine is greater than seven' preserves truth value, in spite of the fact that the subject matter of that sentence and the subject matter of 'the number of planets is greater than seven' are, from an intuitive point of view, very different. The former expresses a claim about numbers and their relationships, whereas the latter makes an assertion about our solar system.

Even philosophers whose general views about language are essentially opposed tend to agree on the issue of substitutivity. Frege and Quine, as different as their respective approaches to semantics are, agree in regarding extensional contexts as paradigmatic. As for intensional contexts, Frege follows a reductionist strategy, beating them into submission to show that, contrary to appearance, substitutivity reigns. Quine, on the other hand, ostracizes intensional contexts by banning them from the realm of respectable sentences. On Quine's view, intensional contexts are sealed packages: trying to apply our theory about the semantics of 'nine' to an occurrence of that expression in an intensional context makes as much sense as expecting the theory to apply to the occurrence of 'nine' in 'canine'. The approach to intensionality inspired by

Frege thus differs radically from Quine's approach. Nevertheless, for both philosophers, whether intensionality is or is not problematic depends on whether the principle of substitutivity that holds for extensional clauses can be extended to intensional contexts.³

The extensionalist approach to substitutivity has the status of a doctrine tacitly taken for granted and the lack of explicit arguments in its favor is often overlooked. At most, we find scattered remarks in the philosophical literature to the effect that PS is a fundamental principle that follows directly from other well-established principles of the theory of meaning, and that is supported even by indisputable laws outside the domain of semantics, like the Principle of Indiscernibility of Identicals and Leibniz's Law.⁴ I think however that the reason why the extensionalist approach to substitutivity is so powerful is not just because PS seems to follow from this or that fundamental principle, but rather because we have been misled into thinking that extensionalism captures some very natural pretheoretical intuitions, that PS itself is supported by a straightforward account of the semantic contribution of expressions, singular terms in particular, to the determination of the truth or falsity of assertions.

I believe, on the contrary, that none of our pretheoretical beliefs about the semantic role of singular terms supports the extensionalist ideal. Those pretheoretical beliefs, the same ones that the champions of extensionalism rely on to justify PS, in fact provide reasons to reject the extensionalist approach to substitutivity. Extensionalists are not entitled to request a *solution* to the problems posed by failures of PS, because they have failed to show that the breakdown of PS should be regarded as a problem.

2. ABOUTNESS

Consider an utterance of the sentence 'Cicero was an orator'. If we ask ourselves what the truth value of the assertion expressed should depend upon, a straightforward answer could proceed as follows: that utterance asserts something about Cicero and it attributes to him a certain property. Because the world is such that Cicero happened to be an orator, the claim expressed is true. Had that state of affairs failed to obtain, the claim in question would have been false. The truth or falsity of the assertion depends on Cicero and on whether he was as we claim him to be. That is all.

Of course, if the truth of the assertion depends only on whether an individual has a certain property, it does not depend on what expression was used to designate him, for no one would think that the way in which the individual in question is designated alters the properties he happens to have. I think that this intuition is essentially correct and that the extensionalist relies on it, assuming that it supports PS. For instance, this is how a champion of extensionalism justifies PS:

the basis of the principle of substitutivity appears quite solid; whatever can be said about the person Cicero . . . should be equally true of the person Tully . . . , this being the same person.[5]

Let us add a few remarks along these lines: what is truly said about the number nine should be equally true when said about the number of planets. If we have succeeded in expressing a true claim about the morning star, we have also succeeded in saying something true about the evening star. After all, the number of planets is nine and the morning star is the evening star.

The conclusion that the extensionalist wants to draw from these remarks is that the *expressions* 'nine' and 'the number of planets' ('the morning star' and 'the evening star', 'Cicero' and 'Tully') should be interchangeable without altering the truth value of the propositions expressed by sentences in which they occur; that if something is truly said using the expression 'nine', something equally true should be said when 'the number of planets' is substituted for 'nine'. However, there is a missing link in the step between the intuitive considerations on the aboutness of claims and PS. The latter is a thesis about expressions and the conditions under which they should be intersubstitutable. The remarks on aboutness emphasized by the extensionalist himself, on the other hand, appeal to considerations involving the person Cicero (Tully) and what should hold true of him. Nothing is said about what should hold true of the expressions 'Cicero' and 'Tully'. Yet, the extensionalist feels entitled to move from comments concerning objects and their properties to principles concerning the expressions that designate those objects. Underlying that move is the assumption that the intersubstitution of codesignative singular terms preserves the aboutness of the assertion: that what is said, for instance, by an utterance of 'nine is odd' and what is said after replacing 'nine' with 'the number of planets' is *the same thing about the same object*.[6] If such an assumption were correct, then the extensionalist's puzzlement in the face of failures of PS would be justified. We will see that it is not. But before discussing why the extensionalist is wrong I will try to point out what I think his mistake consists in.

The pretheoretical remarks on aboutness give rise to the following picture: a given use of a declarative sentence asserts, correctly or incorrectly, that a certain state of affairs obtains, and it does so because expressions in the language are connected to things in the world. It is because of this connection that by uttering sentences we manage to express propositions *about* things; assertions whose truth value depends on whether the things we are talking about are as we claim them to be. The subject matter of an assertion, i.e., what the assertion is about, plays a central role in determining which facts must obtain for that assertion to be true. In other words, the *truth conditions* of a proposition depend on the proposition's aboutness.[7] So, for instance, the assertions expressed by 'Cicero was an orator' and by 'Demosthenes was an orator' clearly differ in subject matter; the facts that must obtain in order for the claims in question to be true are different too, but this is no surprise given the difference in subject matter.[8]

We can try to capture the intuitions underlying these considerations on assertions and what makes them true or false by appeal to an intuitive Principle of Aboutness [PA], according to which *the subject matter of the proposition expressed by an utterance of a sentence is the contribution of the expressions occurring in the sentence to the determination of the state(s) of affairs whose occurrence would make that proposition true.*[9]

The statement of PA is not meant to be an analysis of the notion of aboutness, nor a clear-cut criterion to determine which propositions are about which things. For instance, PA does not even tell us whether 'Cicero was an orator' expresses a claim about Cicero. In spite of the lack of precision, some predictions concerning which substitutions will preserve truth value follow quite directly from PA. Suppose that an utterance of a sentence that contains an occurrence of t_1, $\ulcorner t_1$ is $P \urcorner$, expresses a claim about a, the designatum of t_1. Now, if the substitution of t_2 for t_1 does not alter the subject matter of the claims expressed—namely if the assertions are about a and what is attributed to a is the same in both cases—we should expect their truth value to be the same.[10] The outlines of a principle of substitutivity are thus suggested: if the substitution of t_2 for t_1 in a given sentence preserves the aboutness of the claim originally expressed, then the resulting assertions will coincide in truth value. In other words, substitutions that fully preserve subject matter preserve truth value.

The extensionalist approach to substitutivity relies on the assumption that PS is just a more precise formulation of the remarks on substitutivity that follow from PA. On the extensionalist's view PS becomes the criterion for aboutness: the preservation of truth value when codesignative terms are interchanged in a sentence shows that the claims expressed are about the object designated. In Quine's words:

> failure of substitutivity merely reveals that the occurrence to be supplanted is not purely referential, that is, *that the statement depends not only on the object* but on the form of the name. For it is clear that whatever can be affirmed about the object remains true when we refer to the object by any other name.[11]

On the other hand, the assertions expressed by sentences that do not behave according to PS are not about objects, or at least not about the customary designata of singular terms.[12] The extensionalist is wrong in assuming that codesignativeness of expressions should guarantee co-aboutness of claims. I think that the discussion that follows will show that there are simple sentences, sentences of the form $\ulcorner t$ is $P \urcorner$ which behave according to PS and that do not express assertions about the designata of the singular terms they contain, in the sense of aboutness that underlies the intuitive remarks leading to PA, a sense of "being about" that requires the designatum to figure essentially in the determination of truth conditions, a sense of "being about" that requires the singular term in question to act as a *surrogate* for the object it designates.

If I am right, in these cases we cannot maintain that the claims expressed by the original sentence and the one that results after substituting codesignative terms attribute the same thing to the same object. Consequently, we cannot say that the reason why PS holds for some sentences is *because* these sentences express propositions about the designata of the singular terms occurring in them. In general, we cannot appeal to aboutness to explain why PS holds or why it fails, because the class of sentences that express claims about the things designated by singular terms does not coincide with the class of sentences that behave according to PS.

3. SURROGATES AND TRUTH MAKERS

Let us resort to some familiar illustrations. Consider the following sentences:

(1) Cicero was an orator
(2) The man who denounced Catiline was an orator
(3) The author of *De Amicitia* was an orator.

The extensionalist thinks that the claims expressed by (1), (2), and (3) have the same subject matter, that in each case the same thing is truly said of Cicero. The reason is the following: ultimately it is the same fact that makes the claims expressed by these three sentences true. Cicero was an orator, and that makes the claim expressed by (1) true; but since Cicero happened to be also the man who denounced Catiline and who was the author of *De Amicitia* — namely since 'Cicero', 'the man who denounced Catiline' and 'the author of *De Amicitia*' are codesignative terms — in the end it is his being an orator that makes the propositions expressed by (2) and (3) true. Thus, given the previous considerations on aboutness, it seems quite sensible to conclude that the intersubstitution of the three singular terms in question preserves truth value because it preserves subject matter.

I think that this line of reasoning is flawed because if confuses two types of facts or conditions that should be kept apart: the facts that determine what is expressed by an utterance of a sentence and the facts that determine the truth or falsity of what is expressed by an utterance of a sentence. A simple illustration may help explain why that confusion is so crucial. Suppose that I point to my mug and I utter 'this is yellow'. We do have some clear, although maybe not too precise, intuitions concerning what makes the assertion expressed true or false. Its truth or falsity clearly depends on whether a certain fact involving my mug obtains. We have also some ideas concerning what the truth or falsity of the assertion does not depend on. For instance, it does not depend on the color of the book sitting next to the mug, since facts about the book are irrelevant when it comes to fixing the way the world must be if the claim expressed by my utterance is to be true. The mug plays a role in determining what must hold in order for the claim to be true, the book does not.

The mug is a *truth maker* of that claim because the assertion is about the mug. Truth makers constitute the subject matter of assertions, so they determine the states of affairs that must hold for a given assertion to be true.

It is easy to be misled and include the wrong things as the truth makers of assertions. For instance, it might seem that whether I said something true or false when I uttered 'this is yellow' depends on which language I was using and also on a series of facts that accompany the utterance. Had I been using a language in which 'this is yellow' meant that Russell was a violinist, or had I been pointing at the book instead of the mug, we would have a completely different set of truth conditions. But this is wrong; the fact that I was speaking English or the fact that I was pointing to the mug do not determine the states of affairs that must hold in order for the claim that I did express to be true. Facts about language, meaning, and the conditions under which the utterance is produced make it possible to express a claim that attributes a property, being yellow, to a certain object, the mug, by uttering a certain sequence of words. They are *accessory* facts or conditions because their occurrence makes it possible to *access*, to express, a certain proposition by using a certain sentence. Accessory conditions are the pillars we rely on in order to succeed in asserting what we want to assert. They provide the truth makers, the subject matter of propositions, leading from the physical production of the utterance to the assertion that the utterance expresses. And they leave us exactly there.

Accessory facts do not affect the truth conditions of the claims they help express. A certain proposition has been "accessed" by uttering 'this is yellow'; that my mug be yellow is the state of affairs that must obtain, the *decisive* condition the world must fulfill, for that assertion to be true. The occurrence or non-occurrence of that condition *decides* the truth or falsity of my claim.[13]

It is important to keep the accessory and the decisive apart, for the substitutions which preserve subject matter are the ones that preserve truth makers and decisive facts. The intuitive remarks on substitutivity that follow from PA tell us that the claims expressed by ⌜t_1 is P⌝ and by ⌜t_2 is P⌝ will have the same truth value if they both have the same subject matter. To preserve subject matter, it is a necessary condition that t_1 and t_2 be surrogates for the same object, for then accessory conditions will provide the same object as a truth maker of both assertions.[14] But the mere presence of a singular term in a sentence does not guarantee that the claim expressed by an utterance of that sentence has the object as a truth maker, for the singular term may not apply to its designatum only by virtue of accessory facts. Consequently, the fact that ⌜t_1 is P⌝ and ⌜t_2 is P⌝ contain two singular terms that designate the same individual a, does not guarantee that either of the two sentences is about a.

This is exactly the problem with sentences (1), (2) and (3). If the extensionalist is justified in appealing to aboutness in order to support PS, the singular terms in subject position in (1), (2), and (3) should all designate Cicero just by virtue of accessory facts, for then they would all provide the same object as a truth maker and the three claims would have the same individual as part of their subject matter. I think that (1) contains a singular term that designates Cicero just by virtue of accessory facts and therefore it does express a claim about Cicero. But (2) does not and neither does (3). For instance, 'the man who denounced Catiline' does not designate Cicero just by virtue of the meanings that the component expressions have in English nor by virtue of facts that accompany the utterance of (2). All these factors determine that the designatum of 'the man who denounced Catiline' is the person who denounced Catiline, if any; they do not suffice to determine that Cicero is that person. It is a fact about the world, not a fact about meaning, that Cicero denounced Catiline or that he wrote *De Amicitia*.[15] My use of the expressions 'the man who denounced Catiline' or 'the author of *De Amicitia*' does not provide access to propositions about Cicero, propositions in which Cicero himself is a truth maker determining which states of affairs are decisive for truth or falsity.

The contributions of 'Cicero', 'the man who denounced Catiline', and 'the author of *De Amicitia*' to the subject matter of the assertions expressed by (1), (2), and (3) are different because different things are determining the truth conditions of each of the assertions. The first case is the only one in which it seems quite obvious that Cicero is involved in fixing which facts must obtain in order for the claim to be true. In the latter two cases, properties, like having denounced someone or having written a certain piece, figure essentially in shaping the states of affairs whose occurrence would make the assertions true. The sense of aboutness that the extensionalist is relying on when trying to justify PS applies naturally only to the proposition expressed by (1). (1), unlike (2) and (3), expresses a claim about Cicero, because Cicero is a truth maker contributed by an expression that functions as a surrogate for its designatum. The claims expressed by (2) and (3) clearly are not about Cicero in that sense. We could appropriate Russell's terminology and say that the claims expressed by (2) and (3) are not subject-predicate.[16] Accessory facts are insufficient to determine that the designatum of 'the man who denounced Catiline' and 'the author of *De Amicitia*' is the same individual, hence the contributions of these singular terms to the subject matter of claims are different.[17] The assertions expressed by (1), (2), and (3) do not have the same subject matter, they are not about the same things, even though they contain codesignative terms whose intersubstitution does not alter truth value.[18]

Not all singular terms are surrogates for the objects they designate. Some utterances of sentences contain singular terms that do not contribute their designata to the determination of the facts whose occurrence makes or would make the assertion expressed true. In some cases the attributes used to specify the designatum play a role in determining truth conditions. Those are the cases in which the claim is not about the individual designated by a given singular term. And those are precisely the cases in which we cannot appeal to intuitions concerning the aboutness of propositions to explain why the intersubstitution of codesignative terms happens to preserve truth value.

4. WHAT ABOUTNESS IS NOT ABOUT

Substitutions that preserve subject matter preserve truth value. This approach to substitutivity differs from the extensionalist approach, according to which substitutions of codesignative terms should preserve truth value. It differs, because codesignativeness of terms does not guarantee sameness of truth maker and therefore it does not guarantee sameness of subject matter.

Now, from the claim that preservation of subject matter preserves truth value, it seems to follow that surrogates for the same object should be intersubstitutable in every context. If t_1 and t_2 are surrogates for the same object then the substitution of the latter for the former in ⌜t_1 is P⌝ leaves us with the same truth maker. If that substitution does not alter the truth maker contributed by t_1, the subject matter of the claim expressed by the original sentence is not altered. Therefore, truth value should remain unchanged.

Were we to run into a context in which these two singular terms did not seem intersubstitutable *salva veritate* we would have one of the following two alternatives: either we should claim that our intuitions are wrong and that, in spite of the appearances, the substitution of t_2 for t_1 preserves truth value, or we should claim that t_1 and t_2 provide different truth makers in the context in question, because the context of occurrence may alter the semantic contribution of a term.

I do not think, however, that a choice between these two alternatives is forced upon us. The reason is the following: from the claim that t_2 and t_1 are surrogates and that their intersubstitution in ⌜t_1 is P⌝ preserves the subject matter, or truth maker, contributed by t_1 *it does not follow* that the whole subject matter of the assertion expressed by ⌜t_1 is P⌝ has been preserved when t_2 is substituted for t_1. The predicate ⌜is P⌝ makes also a contribution to the subject matter of the claim expressed and the substitution of t_2 for t_1 may alter the property that is attributed by the words ⌜is P⌝, even if that substitution does not change the individual which is the subject of the attribution.

I will try to clarify this point with another familiar example. Let us suppose that the names 'Giorgione' and 'Barbarelli' are surrogates for the same individual. We should say that the substitution of one for the other in 'Barbarelli was a chess player' preserves truth value because it does not change the subject matter of the original claim, i.e., the property attributed and the individual to whom the property is attributed. Consider now the sentence (4) 'Giorgione was so-called because of his size'. The substitution of 'Barbarelli' here fails to preserve truth value. The extensionalist explanation is that the claim expressed by that sentence is not about, or not *just* about, Giorgione. Since the extensionalist has turned PS into a criterion for aboutness, he has to say that the above sentence, as it stands, does not express a claim about Giorgione, since "whatever can be affirmed about the object remains true when we refer to the object by any other name."[19] The name allegedly performs a "double function," standing for the individual designated and for itself, as if there actually were two occurrences of 'Giorgione'. This, supposedly, becomes obvious when we paraphrase the above sentence into 'Giorgione was called 'Giorgione' because of his size'.

I think that there is another story to be told about these cases, a story that presupposes neither that the original sentence needs to be rephrased nor that the name is not functioning purely as a surrogate. I think that the claim expressed by (4) is about Giorgione, without qualifications, and so is the claim expressed by (5) 'Barbarelli was so-called because of his size' because both terms contribute the same truth maker to the determination of truth conditions. However, the property attributed to that very same individual is different in each case. In the first case it is the property of being called 'Giorgione', in the latter it is the property of being called 'Barbarelli'. There is no property that the expression 'is so-called because of his size' stands for; it is part of the semantics of 'is so-called because of his size' that this predicate comes to attribute a definite property when combined with other expressions.

This way of interpreting sentences like (4) is not equivalent, in disguise, to an explanation which presupposes that the name 'Giorgione' in (4) has a double function, namely an explanation according to which the contribution of 'Giorgione' to the subject matter is not just the usual truth maker—the individual named—but also a new truth maker—the name itself. Just to provide one reason: it is very misleading to say that the name itself is a truth maker for it seems quite clear to me that the claim expressed by (4) is not about the name 'Giorgione'; it is about the property of being called 'Giorgione'— as well as about Giorgione himself—and those are different things.

The subject matter of the claims expressed by (4) and (5) is not the same. The reason, however, is not because the singular terms provide different truth makers, but rather because the intersubstitution of the singular terms in question alters the property being attributed to that truth maker. This is one clear case, I think, in which the substitution of two surrogates for the same individual provides the same truth maker, as we should expect, but fails to preserve the subject matter of the whole claim. Consequently, it is not a surprise that the substitution in question fails to preserve truth value.[20]

The above considerations should not be taken to provide a general theory of why expressions that contribute the same truth maker may fail to be intersubstitutable in some contexts. In particular, these remarks are not meant to provide a positive theory of the way in which belief reports function. It seems to me that expressions that behave as surrogates, like 'Cicero' and 'Tully', fail to be intersubstitutable *salva veritate* in belief reports. I do not know if we can provide for those cases the same explanation that, I think, is natural in the "Giorgione cases." I am not sure that a sentence like 'John believes that Cicero was a historian' is, or is *always*, about Cicero. But, at any rate, I think that we can learn a lesson from the "Giorgione cases": if we were to conclude that the claim expressed by that belief report is not about Cicero, I do not think that such a conclusion should be motivated by the fact that 'Cicero' and 'Tully', which clearly seem to function as surrogates in simple sentences, fail to be intersubstitutable *salva veritate* in that context. And such a conclusion should be even less motivated by the observation that the substitution of other codesignative singular terms, like 'the man who denounced Catiline', for 'Cicero' does not preserve truth value.

The considerations about the "Giorgione cases" help establish a point about logical dependence. The claim that intersubstitution of co-surrogates t_1 and t_2 preserves the truth maker they contribute to the determination of truth conditions does not entail t_1 and t_2's interchangeability across the board. This is partly why the discussion concerning the aboutness of assertions does not hinge upon the behavior of sentences embedded in larger contexts. Whether the truth value of a complex sentence ϕS is determined exclusively by the subject matter of the assertion expressed by S depends on the semantic properties of ϕ, not just on the semantics of S. Hence, no conclusion concerning the aboutness of the claim expressed by S follows directly from the truth value of assertions expressed by complex sentences which contain S, and vice versa.[21] The discussion does not hinge upon questions of cognitive value either. Utterances of ⌜t_1 is P⌝ and ⌜t_2 is P⌝ may express claims about the same individual, and a competent speaker's intuitions may strongly suggest that t_1 and t_2 function as surrogates for their respective designatum. But intuitions alone fall short from providing the knowledge required to establish that the object involved in both cases is the same.[22] The only considerations that have played a role in the discussion appeal directly to intuitions concerning how the truth conditions of assertions expressed by simple sentences of the form ⌜t is P⌝ are determined.

Finally it should be stressed that the conclusion that PA is not a source of support for PS does not depend on the acceptance of theories of meaning grouped under the label of *Direct Reference*. Direct reference has brought dramatically to the surface the contrast between assertions about individual objects and other types of assertions. However, the argument here does not depend on accepting that some expressions are surrogates for their designata, but rather on the fact that there are singular terms that are *not* surrogates. For if a singular term in a given use of a sentence does not function as a surrogate, there is no reason to expect the replacement of that term by a codesignative one to preserve the aboutness of the claim. Once we see this, it is difficult to understand why Frege and Quine defend the extensionalist approach to substitutivity, since on their respective views there are no terms whose contribution to the determination of the truth conditions of an assertion is just the object the term designates.

The extensionalist views on the topic of substitutivity rely on the assumption that codesignative singular terms are intersubstitutable in some sentences because such substitutions preserve the aboutness of the assertions expressed. But the intuitions regarding aboutness that the extensionalist appeals to are intuitions concerning what determines the states of affairs that must hold for a given claim to be true; in other words, they are intuitions concerning how expressions contribute with truth makers to the determination of decisive facts. Sameness of designatum does not guarantee sameness of truth maker;

codesignativeness of terms does not guarantee co-aboutness of claims. If there is any reason why we should expect codesignativeness to preserve truth value, which I think is doubtful, it is not because it preserves subject matter. If there are any grounds to espouse extensionalism, which I think is doubtful too, the reasons are *not* connected to our intuitive beliefs regarding the aboutness of language.[23]

Notes

1. Two remarks about PS may be in order: first, I assume that what is true or false is not a sentence nor an utterance, but rather the *assertion—claim* or *proposition—* that an utterance of a sentence expresses. Second, the philosophical discussion concerning PS and its connection to other principles has usually focused only on singular terms. Here I will concentrate primarily on this type of expression.

2. I am adopting the letter, but not the spirit, of Carnap's classification of contexts. On Carnap's view, the categories *extensional* and *intensional* are not exhaustive.

3. Both for Frege and Quine the failure of PS in a given context shows that the expressions in the context in question do not have their customary semantic value. It is interesting to notice that their respective approaches contrast sharply with Carnap's views in *Meaning and Necessity* (2nd edition. Chicago, 1956). According to Carnap, the semantically relevant properties of an expression (intension and extension) are uniform across all types of contexts. Different types of contexts are *sensitive* to different semantic values; thus, the truth value of sentences may depend on the extension of its component expressions, or on their intension, or even on more complicated features, like for instance, on the way in which the intensions of complex components are determined by the intensions of simpler components. But, at any rate, for Carnap the context does not *cause* alterations in the semantic values of expressions.

4. Whenever the connections between the latter principles and PS have been discussed, however, the conclusions do not favor the extensionalist approach. Richard Cartwright in "Identity and Substitutivity," in *Identity and Individuation*, edited by M. Munitz (New York, 1971), 119-33, argued against the connection between PS and the Principle of Indiscernibility of Identicals. Hidé Ishiguro in *Leibniz's Philosophy of Logic and Language* (Ithaca, N.Y., 1972) focused on the lack of connection between PS and Leibniz's Law. Still the advocates of extensionalism feel entitled to demand an explanation of the reasons why some sentences do not behave according to the standard set by PS. For instance, Anthony Appiah in "Why Componentiality Fails: A Case Study," *Philosophical Topics* 15 (1987): 23-45, reviews some of the classical illustrations of failures of PS and he concludes: "I rehearse all this familiar story because it seems to me that the fact that this is a problem, that there is something here to explain, gets lost from time to time in recent semantic theorizing."

5. W. V. O. Quine, "Reference and Modality," in *From a Logical Point of View* (Cambridge, Mass., 1961), 139-59 at 139.

6. This is not to say that the propositions expressed by utterances of 'the number of planets is odd' and 'nine is odd' are, from the extensionalist's point of view, identical.

7. I am applying the notion of *truth conditions* to propositional content. The truth conditions of the proposition expressed by an utterance of S are the facts that must hold, the way the world must be, for that proposition to be true.

8. Similarly, I think that the assertions expressed by 'Cicero was an orator' and by 'Cicero was bald' differ in their subject matter. Assertions are about properties and relations as well as about objects. It may be objected that it is not natural to extend the notion of aboutness or subject matter to properties or relations. Nothing in the argu-

ment that follows depends on accepting my terminology. The important point is just the obvious fact that 'was an orator' and 'was bald' attribute different properties.

9. It would not be correct to say that the subject matter of a claim determines entirely the claim's truth conditions. For instance, the propositions expressed by (a) 'the Empire State building is taller than the Eiffel Tower' and (b) the 'Eiffel Tower is taller than the Empire State building' have the same subject matter, but incompatible truth conditions. There is a difference between the two claims, over and above what they are about. I will not explore here what that difference consists in, since the issue is not relevant for the discussion. However, it should be noted that the difference between the claims expressed by (a) and (b) is not there because the contributions of the expressions in these two sentences differ.

10. Two temptations that, I think, should be resisted: first, it is tempting to say that the reason why we should not expect an alteration in truth value is because both sentences will express the same proposition. This would amount to espousing a certain view of how propositions are individuated, and PA is quite independent of our views on that topic. PA may give us some positive ideas concerning what determines the truth conditions of propositions, but it does not tell us how propositions are constituted. Second, it may seem obvious that the same property is attributed by $\ulcorner t_1$ is $P\urcorner$ and by $\ulcorner t_2$ is $P\urcorner$, since the expression in predicate position is the same. Although this is a safe rule of thumb for most cases, I think that the preservation of the *expressions* that constitute the predicate does not guarantee sameness of attributed property (sometimes we have to change the words to express the same things, as Frege taught us). This point will be important for the rest of the argument, although I will not try to clarify it until section four. For the time being I will just state it: the subject matter of the claims expressed by $\ulcorner t_1$ is $P\urcorner$ and by $\ulcorner t_2$ is $P\urcorner$ can be different, even if the subject matter contributed by the two singular terms is the same.

11. "Reference and Modality," 140; emphasis added. Similar considerations underlie Quine's explanation of why contexts in which PS fails do not allow the application of the rule of existential generalization.

12. The latter conclusion is where the Fregean and the Quinean brands of extensionalism depart. On Frege's view expressions in non-extensional contexts designate entities of a different type. For Quine they fail to designate altogether.

13. The distinction between accessory and accidental conditions goes back to Joseph Almog's distinction between the generation stage and the evaluation stage for propositions. See "Naming without Necessity," *Journal of Philosophy* 83 (1986): 210-42.

14. Also, the property being attributed by P must be the same in both cases. I would not hesitate to say that the property in question is a truth maker of the assertion provided by accessory conditions.

15. What is at issue here is whether the semantic function of a singular term is just to be a surrogate of its designatum. This point is independent of whether the singular term would designate or fail to designate the same individual, had the world been different. In other words: codesignativeness is not a sufficient condition for co-aboutness and neither is necessary codesignativeness.

16. This is only partly an appropriation of Russell's terminology, since on Russell's view it is linguistic entities that are or are not subject-predicate. The distinction here does not rely on the structure of (1), (2), and (3) nor on the structure of other sentences associated to those as their respective logical forms. But I think that the reasons that led Russell to classify some sentences as not being "really" subject-predicate, although not always explicit, are closely connected to the issue of aboutness.

17. It is important to stress that the point of the argument does not depend on accepting that 'Cicero' is a surrogate or that Cicero himself is a truth maker of the claim expressed by (1). The important issue here is that the other two singular terms

clearly are *not* surrogates for Cicero and that Cicero himself clearly is not a truth maker of the claims expressed by (2) and (3).

18. Keith Donnellan's distinction between referential and attributive uses of definite descriptions ("Reference and Definite Descriptions," *Philosophical Review* 75 (1966): 281-304) gave rise to a discussion regarding whether definite descriptions can be used to contribute just their designata to the determination of the states of affairs whose occurrence makes assertions true (see David Kaplan, "Dthat," in *Syntax and Semantics* 9 [1978]: 221-43, and Howard Wettstein, "Demonstrative Reference and Definite Descriptions," *Philosophical Studies* 40 [1981]: 241-57). That discussion can be interpreted as a discussion regarding whether the condition that an object a must satisfy in order to be the designatum of ⌜the F⌝—being the F—can be taken as an accessory condition, i.e., as a condition whose occurrence provides access to a proposition in which a is a truth maker.

19. W. V. O. Quine, "Reference and Modality," 18. See also *Word and Object* (Cambridge, Mass., 1960), § 32.

20. Curiously, this explanation of the "Giorgione cases" does not violate one of the basic tenets of extensionalism, namely, that truth value is determined only by the extensions of a sentence's parts. The substitution of 'Barbarelli' for 'Giorgione' in (4) alters the property being attributed to Giorgione; and the new property has altogether a different extension. So, there is a perfectly extensional explanation of why there is a change in truth value. Nevertheless, the extensionalist cannot accept that the intersubstitution of expressions with the same relevant semantic value, like 'Giorgione' and 'Barbarelli', may alter the semantic contribution of other expressions in the same sentence. The reason for this attitude has to do, I think, with certain misconceptions concerning compositionality, but the discussion of this point will not be undertaken here.

21. See Joseph Almog's discussion of this issue in "Form and Content," *Noûs* 19 (1985): 603-16.

22. See Howard Wettstein's discussion in "Cognitive Significance without Cognitive Content," *Mind* 97 (1988): 1-28 and "Turning the Tables on Frege," forthcoming (1989) in *Philosophical Perspectives: The Philosophy of Mind*, edited by J. Tomberlin.

23. I wish to thank Joseph Almog, Carl Hoefer, Leora Weitzman, and Howard Wettstein for their helpful comments on a previous draft.

Divided Reference

IGAL KVART

In this paper I illustrate the phenomenon of divided reference (for singular terms); defend it; suggest a theoretical framework which enhances our grasp and comprehension of it; and explore the mechanisms which govern the dynamics of this phenomenon.

I. INTRODUCTION

On various occasions speakers refer to objects via singular terms. Thus, for example, at the Democratic National Convention in 1988, when Senator Edward Kennedy said, "Where was George?" he referred to George Bush. This phenomenon is known as *speaker reference*, explored mostly by Donnellan (1966) and followed up by Kripke (1979). The phenomenon of speaker reference, however, need not be conceived as confined to speech acts alone, the terminology (*speaker* reference) notwithstanding.[1] The very same phenomenon occurs with silent occurrent thoughts. Someone hearing Kennedy's speech might have said, "Bush will have a rough time confronting this slogan," thereby referring to George Bush. But that person might have just thought it out silently, while refraining from making any such assertion. There is no question that he would still be referring to George Bush. The mere addition of the vocal utterance does not affect the basic referential features of the occurrent (verbal) thought: rather, the assertion *borrows* its referential features from those of the occurrent thought it expresses. Moreover, this phenomenon need not occur just in assertive thoughts: people may by the same token have one object or another in mind when they entertain thoughts or ponder questions (Kennedy might have wondered: "Is George going to win this election?" thereby referring to Bush), and even when they have nonoccurrent thoughts. Someone may be said to have an ongoing conviction which he would express as 'my father is devoted to me', and (in normal circumstances) this conviction is surely about his father even when nonoccurrent. The term 'speaker reference' is thus misleading: it specifies a phenomenon which, despite the term employed, is not limited to speech acts.[2]

What are our speech acts, thoughts, and nonoccurrent beliefs *of*, and in virtue of *what* are they *of* what they are *of*? This is a fundamental question of the theory of reference. Intuitions are not uniform on such questions; yet there is a vast range of cases which are uncontroversial. On the whole, the mainstream in the philosophical community today has acknowledged the Donnellan-Kaplan-Kripke intuitions that causal connections (of the appropriate type) are necessary for a particular assertion or thought to be *of* (that is, in the strong sense of 'about') an object. That such an *of*ness relation holds is required for the warranted ascription of *de re* beliefs, and accordingly, in cases in which it does not hold, no such ascriptions are warranted, despite an occasional loose colloquial tendency to admit aboutness.[3] My concern here will be with this strong sense of aboutness that warrants ascriptions of *de re* attitudes: the ascription to a subject of, e.g., a belief *of* a particular object, or the characterization of a particular object as such that the believer believes *of* it that it is such-and-so. I will accordingly proceed within this mainstream conception in holding that a causal connection is necessary for *de re* attitudinal ascriptions.[4]

However, a number of philosophers hold a view, which to many, myself included, seems entirely counterintuitive; they refuse to acknowledge the pertinence to *de re* ascriptions of the gulf between those cases in which the appropriate causal connection exists and those cases in which it does not. Thus, various proponents of the so-called latitudinarian conception allow the linguistic forms of *de re* ascriptions (e.g.: *b* is believed by *a* to be *F*; or: *b* is such that *a* believes him to be *F*) across the board: they require that there be linguistic denotation, but do not require the existence of a causal interaction between the cognizer under consideration and the object in question (and thus put no constraints on the character of such a causal relation).[5] On my view these intuitions are off-base.[6] They rest on a refusal to acknowledge the central importance of the requisite causal connection for the establishment of the special type of link between the cognizer and an object that warrants *de re* ascriptions, and consequently on a failure to acknowledge the importance of the requisite type of causal link for the functioning of proper names. Such a conception amounts to doing away with many of the important phenomena in this area. I will not, however, enter into a polemical discussion about this conception here. Rather, I take the range of cases where the appropriate causal connection occurs to reveal a very important phenomenon on which I will concentrate: the phenomenon that underlies *de re* ascriptions (and the use of proper names[7]).

Elsewhere I have elaborated on the general framework in which such a phenomenon ought to be couched, and on the mechanism whereby reference is acquired (1989). Here I would like to explore an intriguing class of cases which pose a substantial theoretical challenge — the cases in which more than one object seems to qualify as an appropriate referent of a cognizer in a given assertion or thought. These cases involve the phenomenon of the conflation of two individuals by the speaker. The questions that arise are how the referential mechanism works in such cases; whether we should recognize the intuition that there is more than one referent in such cases; how to account for this intuition; and whether we can account for the variety of intuitions as to which referent is more prominent than another. If (as I shall argue) more than one referent is indeed involved in such cases, the phenomenon encountered here is the phenomenon of *Divided Reference*. It will perhaps be best to begin with a few examples.[8]

II. EXAMPLES

First case: A few years ago, when Senator Henry Jackson from the state of Washington was alive, our believer r, who had a substantial interest in politics, saw him many times on television, read news items about him and numerous statements by him in the newspaper,[9] believed that he was a senator from the state of Washington, and was familiar with how he looked, but had little knowledge of his personal habits or interests. This was more than enough, of course, for him to speaker-refer to Senator Jackson by his use of the term 'Senator Jackson'. On one occasion, however, at a party attended by some important politicians, he saw a man who looked to him just like Senator Jackson looked on television. Furthermore, he was introduced to this person, and the host presented him as Mr. Jackson from Washington. This was enough to convince our believer that the person he was talking to was none other than Senator Jackson himself. During the conversation, this Mr. Jackson recounted his great interest in fishing in the ponds and rivers of Washington, and went on at some length about other aspects of his life. The conversation, however, for reasons of etiquette, never touched on the subjects of politics or occupations. On the way out, our believer r said to his wife, "What extensive knowledge about fishing Mr. Jackson possesses, and how he enjoys it!"

Of course, as our story has already suggested, our believer r was misled: the Jackson at the party was not Senator Jackson, r's beliefs notwithstanding. The question is: To whom did r refer when he marvelled, upon leaving the party, about the extensive knowledge Mr. Jackson possessed about fishing: to the Jackson at the party or to Senator Jackson, whom he had never, in fact, seen in person? The answer, I believe, should be that, at the very least, our intuitions point in the direction of the Jackson at the party. This I take as data concerning our intuitions.

However, a short time later, while watching television, r saw an extract of a political statement made by Senator Jackson. Still not realizing that he was not the Jackson of that party, he commented thereafter to his wife, "Senator Jackson has just made a very hawkish political statement." To whom was he referring: Senator Jackson or the Jackson at the party? I take it that, on this occasion, the scales point in the direction of Senator Jackson.

Let us move on to a second case. Take a variation of Donnellan's famous example of the person standing in the corner holding a martini glass at some party, that is, a man who in fact drinks water but is believed by our believer to be drinking a martini. There is, however, in fact one (and just one) martini drinker elsewhere at the party, in another room, unnoticed by our believer. When our believer says, noticing the conversational vocabulary of the man in the corner, whom he takes (erroneously) to be drinking a martini, "The martini drinker is a philosopher," there is no question, I take it (in agreement with Donnellan), that he is referring to the man in the corner, and not to the martini drinker whom he never saw or was aware of. This, I take it, is by now part and parcel of our shared philosophical wisdom. Furthermore, suppose our believer holds a certain preconception to the effect that martini drinkers either come from or aspire to belong to a certain social milieu. Given this, and observing the man in the corner with the martini glass in his hand, he comments, "The martini drinker reveals quite clearly his social origins or aspirations." Again, I take it, he is referring to the man in the corner with the water-filled martini glass in his hand.

A third example: Since parties seem to be the favorite setup for the conflation of individuals, let us move on to a party held in New York City under the auspices of the U.N., which our believer attended. His host, in whom he had considerable confidence, told him (correctly), while pointing to a distant figure, who could only be seen from the back, that that was the Prime Minister of the Fiji Islands, who was in town for the ongoing session of the U.N. General Assembly. Our believer, however, knew very little about the Fiji Islands, other than that they constituted a state in the southwestern Pacific. Moments later, however, after moving around, he was introduced to a person who looked and behaved like a distinguished statesman, and who, during the ensuing conversation, mentioned a few things relating to Fiji Islands' concerns. This, plus sparse physical resemblance, sufficed for our believer to conclude that his interlocutor was the Prime Minister of the Fiji Islands. In fact he was not — he had just heard the General Assembly speech by the Fiji Islands' Prime Minister, hence his references to the Fiji Islands in the conversation. During that conversation, our believer learned quite a bit about his interlocutor, and in particular was impressed with his engaging conversational style. Upon leaving the party he said to his companion, "The Prime Minister of the Fiji Islands is quite a charming person." To whom was he referring? The intuitive answer, I believe, is that the scales point to his interlocutor at that party.

As our last example, let us consider another variation on the party case. The most important owners of gold mines in South Africa attended a gathering where some economic decisions of substance were to be made. Suppose that on the basis of general considerations, our believer r had reason to believe, correctly, that the richest man in South Africa was a gold mine owner and, again, correctly, that like other major figures in the South African gold mining industry, he was present on that occasion. When r's interlocutor at that gathering talked at length about himself, it was easy for r to realize how wealthy he was. It was obvious that he was both a mine-owner and a resident of South Africa, and he spoke vehemently against apartheid. In view of some remarks he made, r concluded, incorrectly, that he was the richest man in South Africa. Thus r formed the belief: the richest man in South Africa opposes apartheid. There is little doubt here that this belief of his was formed *of* his interlocutor at that gathering.

III. THEORETICAL UNDERPINNINGS

It is time to try to fit these examples into some theoretical framework and, in particular, to search for an explanatory framework that can throw light on and account for our intuitions regarding the question of where reference goes in such cases. Some, notably Kripke, Donnellan, and Kaplan, believe that matters regarding reference depend on features of the causal chains involved plus the intentions of the speakers which play a role in various conversational maxims. Grice serves as the *locus classicus* for the elaboration of the latter (Kripke 1979). My convictions, as I will now briefly sketch them, lie elsewhere. Intentions, I believe, are not *constituents* of the phenomenon of reference: they may be merely present at the time, or merely epiphenomenal to referential features: they may themselves have referential features, or even, in certain cases, be causal antecedents of referential features.[10] Furthermore, conversational maxims, so favored by Kripke and Donnellan, have no *constitutive* role to play in reference either: they too are not constituents of the reference phenomenon. This becomes quite clear when one realizes, as we noted above, that the reference phenomenon, contrary to Donnellan's paradigm, is not restricted to speech acts: it is also present in occurrent thoughts, and even in nonoccurrent ones. No speech act needs to occur when reference takes place, no audience needs to be present, and in particular no audience needs to be assumed by the speaker for him to refer successfully. Conversational maxims and the Gricean machinery are, Kripke notwithstanding, the wrong building blocks here, since the very same phenomenon, with all its myriad features, occurs when no conversation takes place.

A crucial dimension has been neglected by these writers who focus on conversational components, and its absence in their treatment may partly account for their resorting to conversational components: this is the dimension of the concurrent cognitive phenomena. Here, of course, some theoretical resistance sneaks in. For those whose orientation is akin to Kaplan's, semantics is best pursued in isolation: the requisite cognitive models seem to require too wild speculation or command too meager empirical support. Semantics ought, on such an outlook, to stand on its own two feet. These are not, however, important substantive arguments against recognizing the cognitive dimensions of the reference phenomenon; and as methodological arguments in favor of relinquishing the exploration of these dimensions, they are at best dubious.[11] Lack of the apparatus and technology to observe, or effectively theorize about, the internal structure and composition of matter, would provide no grounds for a substantive argument in favor of construing heat as a macroscopic phenomenon. Whether the attempt to incorporate relevant cognitive parameters is methodologically barren or too far out of reach remains to be seen. What I thus want to bring to bear on the discussion of these issues is the impact of cognitive phenomena related to the epistemic frame of the believer. Cognitive phenomena constitute, as I will argue, major components of the reference phenomenon, and to ignore them is to miss much of it. No viable account of reference can, I claim, proceed in the absence of considerations that lie at the cognitive level.

However, in order to engage in cognitive considerations, some modeling must be resorted to. In the absence of better tools, I shall attempt to sketch a simulatory representational model of how cognizers might represent individuals. This model will, of course, constitute an idealization, and consequently some of its features will be mere approximations of actual phenomena. It will, however, offer enough tools to provide us with the capacity to understand the phenomena in question from a sharper and more insightful perspective. I shall thus outline what a representational model for individuals might look like.

But first some terminological points must be attended to. The notion of *speaker-reference* must be clearly distinguished from that of *denotation*: the denotation of a definite description (in a context) is the sole object (individual) which the definite description descriptively specifies (in that context). If there is no one such object, the definite description (in that context) has no denotation. Thus, the denotative function of a definite description (in a context) relates it to an object exclusively in virtue of its descriptive features. In this respect the notion of denotation differs fundamentally from the notion of speaker-reference.[12]

However, in view of the fact that the notion of speaker-reference has been used in the philosophical jargon exclusively for speech acts, whereas my concerns are with instances of reference which *overlap* but also *transcend* these boundaries, it seems appropriate to coin another phrase instead of 'speaker-reference', such as 'thinker-reference'. The phenomenon of thinker-reference, therefore, as I view it, is indeed present in what have been standardly taken to be speaker-reference cases, but extends also to cases of unexpressed thoughts, occurrent and nonoccurrent. Part of the reason that motivates this conception of the cases which have been standardly taken to be cases of speaker-reference as instances of a phenomenon that applies to a broader range of cases is that, on my view, elements such as communicative (and other) intentions of the speaker, conversational topics, and interests of speakers and audience are not constituents of this thinker-reference phenomenon, whether in its instances that involve utterances or in its instances which do not. Thus, on my view, thinker-reference is rooted at the level of the cognitive framework and its formational history, whereas thinker-reference of speech acts (i.e., in the standard jargon, speaker-reference) is derivative upon thinker-referential features of thoughts which they reflect. Consequently, various features of communicative contexts, considered necessary for fixing such a relation, are, as I briefly elaborated above, dispensable.[13]

From a perspective such as mine, it might seem best to argue that Donnellan speaker-referred by his use of 'speaker-reference' to a phenomenon more prevalent than he anticipated[14] (since his conception of the underpinnings of this phenomenon was incorrect and in part too restrictive). Yet, as in cases of reference shifts,[15] he nevertheless successfully specified (fixed) the phenomenon. From such a perspective, there is no stronger motivation to rename the phenomenon 'thinker-reference' than there is to rename the Holy Roman Empire (as in Kripke's example). But in order to allow a broad enough basis for dialogue, it may be best to sidestep the controversial philosophical issues underlying this contention at this stage and resort to the new nomenclature of thinker-reference.[16]

IV. A REPRESENTATIONAL MODEL

Let us consider, then, the representational framework of a cognizer insofar as his representation of individuals is concerned. When an individual is represented, considerable information can be stored and associated together: perceptual information (visual, auditory, etc.); linguistically representable information (concerning, e.g., his profession, place of residence, etc.); and symbolic information of sundry sorts (certain character features, aspects of his demeanor, etc.). As our first approximation, we shall assume that the pertinent information is *linguistically represented*. (This, of course, amounts to resorting to a somewhat ideal cognizer, or, alternatively, to a somewhat restricted range of cases.) Furthermore, to abstract from more complex but less central features of the representational framework, we shall restrict ourselves to information representable by one-place predicates (thereby excluding relational features). Consider, then, all this information, framed along such lines, and thus consisting of linguistic items — predicative expressions and singular terms such as definite descriptions and proper names. Such information, so stored according to our model, and associated by our believer as pertaining to one individual, can be considered as constituting a *cluster* in his framework of individual representations.[17] A cluster, then, in that framework, is an aggregate of linguistic items of the aforementioned sorts that the believer takes to hold for one individual. Different clusters will thus purportedly represent different individuals. We can accordingly consider the representational framework of a cognizer insofar as individual representations are concerned as consisting of such a *system of clusters* — each cluster purportedly representing some individual. Of course, the same predicative expressions can occur in different clusters: one may consider two different people to be, e.g., handsome.[18]

Information stored in a given cluster can be taken to model our cognizer's beliefs as well.[19] Thus, suppose that he entertains thoughts concerning, as he would express it, the man in the corner, and in particular has a belief to the effect (as he would put it) that the man in the corner is a philosopher. On our model, then, there would be a cluster in his representational system which would include two items: the definite description 'the man in the corner' and the predicate 'a philosopher'. That these two items belong to one cluster—a fact that we will express by calling them *co-clusteral*—will represent significant information that he possesses: it will reflect his acceptance of the sentence, 'the man in the corner is a philosopher'. Co-clusterality, then, within our model, mirrors the cognizer's acceptance of the sentences in question, and thus reflects beliefs of his which are couched in that cluster. The co-clusterality of two items—say, a singular term 'a' and a predicative expression 'F'—reflects his taking them both to apply to the same individual, and, within the framework of our model, amounts to his having a (verbal) belief to that effect, i.e., a is F.

On this model, a cluster consists of linguistic expressions—predicative expressions and singular terms. However, as remarked earlier, the referential features of the representational framework of a cognizer need not be limited to occurrent beliefs, let alone to utterances and speech acts. On the sentential (symbolic) conception of beliefs which I favor (1986c), as long as a singular term and a predicative expression belong to a cluster, the belief they form (when properly conjoined) is one the believer holds—occurrent or not. One can reasonably expect, however, that this model can be naturally extended beyond the sentential boundaries in a way that might suit some other conceptions of beliefs as well.[20] In any event, I will try *not* to ground the thrust of this paper in this particular conception of beliefs.[21]

V. CLUSTERAL REPRESENTATION

Thus far we have considered our cognizer's representational system 'from within', that is, from his own perspective. We have not touched on the question of how it relates to the world: which clusters represent which individuals. This is the fundamental issue regarding reference to individuals and intentionality. But the crux of this question is: In virtue of what does a particular cluster, a particular individual representation, constitute a representation *of* a certain individual (where the '*of*' reflects the strong sense of representation with which we are exclusively concerned throughout our discussion here)?

That a cognizer can represent certain individuals and ascribe to them features correctly or incorrectly is quite obvious. We often possess mistaken information regarding a particular individual, stored (together with accurate information regarding him) in a certain cluster in our representational framework. While this cluster will then contain some false information about that individual, it may nevertheless constitute a *bona fide* representation *of* that individual. Furthermore, mistakes we sometimes make often reveal significant phenomena. Thus, we may possess individual representations of no one at all. Someone can, simply by mistake, e.g., by hallucination, believe on a dark night that a burglar is at work in the basement, when in fact there is no one there at all—not even a mouse (and even without any squeaking piece of wood): just pure imagination. Yet he may thereby form a substantial cluster, the items in which he would *take* to apply to one individual — he would firmly believe, albeit mistakenly, that there is a burglar in the basement at the time. A cluster, then, may be an individual representation without representing anybody or anything at all.

In virtue of what, then, does a cluster of this sort represent no one, while other clusters represent particular individuals? Surely, again, not in virtue of fit alone: it is not in virtue of the information in the cluster fitting a particular individual that that cluster constitutes a representation *of* that individual. Perfect match mistakes are cases in point. One may, due to the impact of drugs, have a nightly hallucination to the effect that there is a burglar in the basement, taking it to be the case that there are different burglars on different nights. Suppose that, by sheer coincidence, on one particular night a burglar was indeed at work in the basement, yet neither heard nor seen by our drugged cognizer, but still fitting, again by sheer coincidence, the information in the cluster our cognizer formed that night. We could still not say that that cluster constituted a representation *of* that burglar, in the strong sense of representation that sanctions the attribution of *de re* beliefs that concerns us here. Our cognizer does not possess any *de re* beliefs *of* that burglar: there was no causal connection whatsoever between that burglar and the formation of the pertinent cluster by our cognizer or the inclusion in it of particular items. Mere descriptively accurate information or mere fit do not suffice, then, for the strong relation of representation we are after.

Nor, as we observed above, would incorrect information bar a cluster from being a representation of a particular individual: we may be, and often are, mistaken vis-à-vis various features of individuals we represent and have *de re* beliefs about. Descriptive accuracy is thus neither necessary nor sufficient for representation.

VI. CONFLATION OF INDIVIDUALS

Another notorious and common sort of mistake is of course the conflation of two individuals. We have considered such mistakes earlier in the Jackson example. Our cognizer in that case formed a single cluster that included such items as 'the senior Senator from the state of Washington' and 'the Jackson that attended the party'. Each item, however, descriptively specified a different individual. Yet it would be a distortion to consider the cluster as a representation of only one of these two Jacksons, with some mistaken information applying to the other. The cluster *as a whole* reflects a genuine conflation of two individuals, representing each and exclusive to neither. How, then, does one sort out the cognizer's beliefs manifested in such a cluster? Which belief is about which of the two Jacksons? Is there a definite answer to a question of this sort? What we need is a theory of representation to account for such issues.

The relation of representation (via singular terms) in the strong sense we are concerned with is no other, I argue, than the relation of thinker-reference. Thus, once the reference relation is acknowledged as applying not just to speech acts but also to one's beliefs and representations, whether expressed or not, whether occurrent or not, it should become clear that the reference relation resides at the level of the clusteral framework of one's representational system, its internal structure and its formational history.[22] The referential aspects of speech acts expressing beliefs are *mere manifestations* of the referential features of the representational system: a speaker refers to a particular individual when he expresses his thought via a particular sentence just in case the cluster containing the singular term occurring in that sentence has that particular individual as a referent. But the reference relation would obtain for that singular term at that time regardless of whether that sentence was uttered or not, and regardless of whether the thought it expressed was occurrent or not.[23]

Thus, the formational history of the representational system provides two major constituents of reference—the causal component and the epistemic component (see the next section for the roles of the notion of knowledge and of the causal factor in the definition of 'strict anchor'). The structure of the representational system involves its clusteral constitution as well as its subclusteral constitution—the internal structure of clusters, on which we will expand below. (This structure governs the manner in which reference dissipates from strict anchors to other singular terms). These three—the causal element, the epistemic component, and the structural factor—are key constituents in the genesis of the reference relation.

VII. STRICT ANCHORS AND UNIFORM CLUSTERS

How, then, is thinker-reference determined? Consider the Donnellan example concerning the water-drinker in the corner holding a martini glass in his hand, but believed erroneously by our cognizer to be drinking a martini (while there is no martini drinker at that party). Surely the referent of the believer in this case, when he says (or thinks), 'the martini drinker is a philosopher', is the man in the corner—the one with the martini glass in his hand: it is of him that our believer believes (erroneously) that he drinks a martini. So surely thinker-reference cannot be determined simply by the denotation of the definite description used: in this case the definite description has no denotation, yet there is reference. And even if we were to modify the example and have one martini drinker elsewhere at the party, entirely out of contact with our believer, he would not be the referent in this case. Yet there is in this case another definite description in our believer's representational system, co-clusteral with the definite description he used—'the martini drinker'—which does denote the actual referent: 'the man in the corner'. So in the same cluster we have two definite descriptions, which, we can assume, as in the above variation, denote (i.e., apply correctly to just one individual in the context in question). Yet both thoughts, 'the martini drinker is a philosopher' and 'the man in the corner is a philosopher', have the man in the corner, *not* the martini drinker, as their referent (for our believer). It is easy to verify that in this particular case,[24] any other (verbal) thought with a singular term belonging to that cluster would intuitively have the man in the corner as its referent. What is it then about one definite description in the cluster — such as 'the man in the corner' in this example — in virtue of which its denotation constitutes the referent not only of thoughts expressed via it but also of thoughts expressed via *other* definite descriptions co-clusteral with it, even if not co-denotational with it?

There are, I have argued (1989), for a given believer, *privileged* definite descriptions in his representational framework that are unique in that they serve as his referential links to objects in the world: it is *through them* that he acquires thinker-reference. They are unique in that they must fulfill special causal and epistemic constraints, in virtue of which not only their own occurrences in the believer's verbal thoughts (and utterances) possess reference, but in virtue of which they also confer reference on the occurrences (in the believer's verbal thoughts) of *other* singular terms co-clusteral with them. They therefore constitute, so to speak, the believer's referential *anchors* to objects in the world. Furthermore, they are such that their thinker-referent *coincides* with their denotation. I will not go into the motivation for this story here, since I have elaborated on it elsewhere (1989), but will merely indicate the criterion for being such privileged definite descriptions, which I call strict anchors:

> A definite description '$ixHx$'[25] is a *strict anchor* for a believer r iff, for some predicative expression 'F', r knows (*de dicto*): $ixHx$ being $H\#$ (for some predicate '$H\#$' subsumed by 'H') is a cause of r's believing '$FixHx$'.[26]

(One predicative expression 'F' is subsumed by another 'G' when being F is a logical consequence of being G.)

In our example, then, the definite description 'the man in the corner' is a strict anchor, satisfying the above condition. The definite description 'the martini drinker' is *not* a strict anchor in this example, even in the variation in which it denotes, since the above condition does not obtain: That martini drinker drinking a martini has no causal impact, in this variation, on our believer's believing anything of the form, 'the martini drinker is F'. It is not hard to verify that in the above example, with no further mistakes added, any other strict anchor would be co-denotational with 'the man in the corner'. The cluster therefore has only one thinker-referent: all of its strict anchors are co-denotational. In such a case, as illustrated in this example, all (verbal) beliefs couched in the cluster have just one thinker-referent — regardless of the denotation of their singular terms: the only thinker-referent that the cluster has. In this way other definite descriptions which appear in (verbal) beliefs couched in that cluster[27] obtain thinker-reference *vicariously* via strict anchors co-clusteral with them. We can call such clusters which have just one referent uniform clusters.

The above notion of strict anchor plays a major role in a more general outlook regarding reference and the relation between the *de dicto* and the *de re* levels that I advocate.[28] The general outlook within which the views presented here are grounded is one where reference is ultimately rooted in such strict anchors.[29] Strict anchors are the vehicles through which reference *emerges* — couched in descriptive accuracy, appropriate causal roots, and epistemic constraints.

However, cognizers refer via singular terms other than strict anchors, and there the crucial function of the clusteral framework comes in. For singular terms other than strict anchors, reference is conferred *vicariously* via the co-clusterality relation. In uniform clusters (where all the strict anchors are co-denotational), singular terms other than strict anchors acquire their reference via that of the strict anchors in the cluster. The referent of such singular terms is thus (the cluster being uniform) the referent of the cluster. This holds not only for definite descriptions which do not denote their referents (as was the case with 'the martini drinker' in the example above), but also with definite descriptions which do but which lack the requisite causal and epistemic features to be strict anchors and function as reference generators, even when they do have a referent which they denote. Thus, one may believe, with no grounds whatsoever, but nevertheless correctly, that the man in the corner is the most accomplished man in the room. In this case, he would refer via 'the most accomplished man in the room' to the man in the corner, *not* because the latter singular term is a strict anchor (it is not here, as we constructed the case), but because it is co-clusteral with a strict anchor, 'the man in the corner'. This is how the co-clusterality relation serves to channel reference from its roots — the strict anchors — to other singular terms, such as definite descriptions and proper names.[30]

Contextual aspects are involved in fixing the *denotation* of definite descriptions (which are normally context dependent). But it is easy to mistakenly view aspects of the conversational situation as contributing to the determination of reference via a particular utterance. Thus, "what the conversation is about" is not an independent feature out there in the conversational context, which helps secure the speaker reference of utterances made in that context. Rather, each speaker refers via the singular terms he uses in his utterances (as well as via singular terms in other [verbal] occurrent thoughts he may have but not express). It is these that determine what the conversation is about: if many singular terms are co-referential (have the same referents for their respective employers), the conversation is likely to be about that common referent. Thus, the relation of "what the conversation is about" *supervenes* on what each participant refers to,[31] and *not* the other way around.

Similarly, (sincere) assertive utterances by speakers take on as their referents the referents of the beliefs they express.[32] In general, nonmisleading utterances assume as their referents the referents of the clusters to which their singular terms belong (for the same speaker-cognizer, of course). In that respect, the referential features of utterances are *derivative* upon those of the speaker's clusteral system, and in particular upon the referential features of the clusters to which the singular terms he uses belong.[33]

VIII. NONREFERENTIAL CLUSTERS AND CONFLATION OF INDIVIDUALS

Some clusters, of course, have no strict anchors at all. This would be typical of cases in which one believes correctly that there is a person fulfilling a certain definite description, but in which one does not have any *de re* beliefs about him, and hence no thinker-reference for him. Quine's famous example concerning the shortest spy would be a case in point: under certain assumptions one can believe correctly that there is just one shortest spy (in the U.S.). But it is generally agreed that one has no *de re* beliefs about the shortest spy, nor does one refer via the definite description 'the shortest spy'. Thus, one's cluster containing this definite description would, in such a case, have no strict anchor and hence no reference. Another kind of cluster of this sort would be found in cases of illusions, such as in the above example concerning the burglar in the basement: the relevant cluster in this case has no strict anchors even in a case in which there was one burglar in the basement (but was unnoticed by our believer). In the case in which in fact there was no burglar, the definite descriptions in the cluster even fail to denote.

There is no special problem relevant to our present discussion with cases where one sees the same individual on different occasions and does not recognize him as one and the same. In such cases, the cognizer forms two separate clusters, in both of which he may have strict anchors, and thus through both he may have reference via definite descriptions, and these referents would be one and the same person. That two clusters share the same referent just indicates a certain informational gap or error on the cognizer's part; but from the point of view of the characterization of his representational system and its referential features, this case presents no special difficulty.[34]

The situation becomes far more complicated, however, when conflation of two individuals is involved, that is, when the cognizer takes two different individuals to be one and the same. Then the relevant cluster may involve different strict anchors which are not co-denotational; that is, in such cases the cluster will have more than one referent. The determination of the referents for various singular terms in beliefs couched in the cluster (and thus in utterances expressing them) — *of* whom, via them, the believer is having a belief (or making a statement) — becomes a complex problem. A case in point is our first example concerning Senator Jackson and the Jackson at the party. In that case, the believer conflated these two different individuals, taking them to be one and the same. His cluster, then, would include such strict anchors as 'the person I had a long conversation with at the party' as well as 'the guest on yesterday's television program "Nightline".'[35] What, then, are his referents when he expresses various beliefs couched in this cluster, via these strict anchors, other strict anchors, or other singular terms in it? Would they be *of* one referent or the other? *Of* neither, or *of* both? Before we attend to these issues, however, another phenomenon must be observed.

IX. MISTAKEN PARASITIC POSITIONS

The key to these questions lies, I believe, in the internal structural features of the relevant clusters. Let us first go back to our Donnellan-type example in the variation where there was in fact no martini drinker. We observed that, although 'the man in the corner' is a strict anchor, 'the martini drinker' is not. We also observed that in this case thoughts formulated with these two definite descriptions have the man in the corner as their referent. The definite description 'the martini drinker' thus occupies a peculiar position in the cluster: its denotative[36] function does not bear at all on the referential features of the cluster or the beliefs couched in it. The reference of all the thoughts formulated via this definite description is channeled via the strict anchors of the cluster, which are co-denotational (the cluster being, as we called it, uniform). The referential status of this definite description is thus somewhat like that of a free rider: its content—as manifested in its denotative function—serves no referential function in the cluster. We can thus say that this definite description occupies a mistaken parasitic position in the cluster, in that its referential features are parasitic on the strict anchors in the cluster, and in that, although the believer takes it to be co-denotational with those strict anchors (otherwise it would not have been co-clusteral with them), he is mistaken: in fact it is not. The referent of thoughts formulated via a singular term that occupies a mistaken parasitic position in such a uniform cluster is the referent of the cluster, not the person (or object) that constitutes the denotation of that singular term.[37]

X. CLUSTERAL SPLIT

The special status of a singular term that occupies a mistaken parasitic position comes to light when one explores the internal cohesiveness of the cluster: how tightly, or how loosely, epistemically speaking, the various constituents are bound together. A helpful metaphor in this context is that of atoms or nuclei composed of various particles: bombarded by certain particles, nuclei often split. A lot can be learned about the internal structure of nuclei from the way they split under circumstances of one sort or another by certain bombardments. In our type of cases, the clusters consist of various constituents— singular terms and predicative expressions. They can be 'bombarded', so to speak, by giving the believer *authoritative inputs* of certain sorts. Thus, suppose the believer is given an authoritative input of the form '$a \neq b$', for two singular terms 'a' and 'b' in the cluster. What would he do? How will this cluster evolve? This is a case in which the cluster is 'bombarded' by a nonidentity input. If our believer is to remain consistent, the cluster cannot remain intact. Since the input was authoritative, i.e., of greater weight than the pertinent information he previously possessed, the input should prevail. The internal structure of the cluster will thus have to change.

How a cluster will change in view of such a nonidentity input illuminates various features relating to the cohesiveness of the cluster. Thus, the cluster could simply *vanish* altogether from the representational framework of the believer: he might withdraw his belief that any of the definite descriptions in the cluster denotes. Alternatively, only some elements in the cluster may evaporate: one or more singular terms may be excised to restore consistency. This will indicate that the believer, though continuing to hold that there is an individual with the features described by the remaining elements in the cluster, no longer takes the features expressed by the items dropped to apply to such an individual, nor does he believe that there is another individual uniquely specified by items that were dropped. Another possibility is that the cluster might *split*, resulting in two distinct clusters, each being a *subcluster* of the original one, with each member of the original cluster belonging either to one of the evolving ones, or perhaps evaporating altogether. This development reflects that the believer restored consistency by assessing that he had previously, i.e., prior to the nonidentity input, conflated two individuals.

Of course, what a given believer will do with a given nonidentity input depends largely on how rational his epistemic data processing is. In order for such clusteral development to be of interest, we should thus limit ourselves to a somewhat idealized cognizer whose data processing in this particular respect is sufficiently rational.[38] The representational system of a cognizer is in one particular state or another at any given point in time, and (normally) moves from one state to another upon the introduction of external informational inputs, such as the nonidentity inputs we considered. (It can, of course, also move from one state to another due to internal processing alone, without external inputs.) It is thus comparable to a sort of state machine.

After a clusteral split, the new clusters will contain items that were present in the original clusters. As aggregates of items, the resulting clusters are therefore included in the original cluster, and thus can be considered subclusters of the original cluster. A cluster (relative to a given nonidentity input) can be viewed as containing subclusters — aggregates of items that would form new clusters upon the introduction of the nonidentity input.

Consider, then, our Donnellan-type example in the variation where there is a martini drinker elsewhere at the party. Suppose our cognizer is given the input, 'the man in the corner is not the martini drinker'. How will this input affect the cluster in question? In this example the answer is clear (given, again, our sufficiently rational believer, and the various features, spelled out or implied, of that episode):[39] He has had, given our example, no grounds for believing there was a martini drinker at that party other than his perception of the martini glass in the hand of the man in the corner. He would therefore realize, upon the introduction of that input, that the man in the corner drinks no martini.[40] He would then drop the item 'the martini drinker' from the cluster containing 'the man in the corner'; but the dropped item would no longer belong to any cluster at all. His representational system will thus evolve by contracting the cluster in question — by one (or more) elements of it simply vanishing. This is a fundamental characteristic of a singular term that occupies a mistaken parasitic position: the singular term cannot stand on its own. Once the umbilical cord—the identity belief—is severed, the singular term will not form a cluster of its own, but will simply be deleted.[41] Its presence in the representational system is entirely dependent upon the mistaken identity belief, in virtue of which its position is a mistaken parasitic position.[42] It is thus not surprising that the referential features of such a singular term are also entirely parasitic on those of the strict anchors in the cluster to which it belongs, and that therefore (verbal) thoughts in which it figures have, as their referents, the referent of the cluster, which is different than the denotation of that singular term.

XI. SPLITTING REFERENTIAL CLUSTERS

Let us move now to the example concerning the South African gold mine owner. In this case, there is no question that all the (verbal) thoughts couched in the cluster have just one thinker-referent—the interlocutor at the party. This is so because this cluster has the interlocutor as its sole referent. Since the believer *r* has no appropriate causal connection, directly or via a source, with the richest South African, he has no thinker-reference to him at all, via the definite description 'the richest man in South Africa' or via any other definite description.

However, the clusteral structure in this case is different than in the example we just considered, since the definite description 'the richest South African' does not occupy a mistaken parasitic position. Thus, if *r* is given the nonidentity input, 'your interlocutor is not the richest South African', his pertinent cluster will indeed undergo a transformation. But this transformation will not amount to the excision of the singular term in question from the clusteral system altogether: *r* will still continue to believe, on the same independent grounds, that the richest South African exists, and perhaps that he is at that party, although not that he is his interlocutor. Thus, the result of the nonidentity input will be a clusteral split into two distinct clusters: one will contain 'my interlocutor', 'rich', 'owns gold mines', 'South African', 'opposes apartheid', etc., and the second resulting cluster will contain 'the richest South African', 'owns gold mines', 'now at the party', and perhaps some others. Thus, constituents of the original cluster will gravitate to one or another of the resulting clusters. Some predicates will presumably be present in both (though no definite descriptions, if *r* is minimally consistent). Some items, which were inferred on the basis of other items in the original cluster which parted ways during the split (some ending up in one resulting cluster while others ending up in the other), might vanish altogether.

There is a noteworthy point about the resulting clusters: the one containing 'my interlocutor at the party' will have various strict anchors, and thus thinker-reference, and furthermore, given our story, just one referent for all the strict anchors of the cluster. Yet the other cluster, the one containing 'the richest South African', will have no strict anchors whatsoever: r just no longer has any thinker-reference via this definite description to the richest South African. Although he has various (verbal) thoughts involving that singular term, those thoughts are not anymore *de re* thoughts *of* that individual. The status of 'the richest South African' for r (after the clusteral split) is similar to that of 'the shortest spy' in Quine's famous example: although most of us are aware that one exists, only few of us have *de re* beliefs about him and thinker-reference to him. This is, then, a nonreferential cluster. Thus, while prior to the input r believed (erroneously) that the richest South African was his interlocutor, and thereby had (vicariously) thinker-reference via 'the richest South African' to his interlocutor, he lost that thinker-reference, and was thereby left with no thinker-reference at all for that definite description once the nonidentity input was processed. This case thus illustrates how thinker-reference is channeled from a strict anchor to a definite description via their co-clusterality relation, and how, once that co-clusterality is no longer there, the definite description *loses* its thinker-reference.

Clusteral splits upon the introduction of nonidentity inputs occur as well in the two other examples we considered at the beginning of this paper, although they are of quite a different sort. Consider first the example of Senator Jackson and the Jackson at the party. Upon the introduction of the veridical input 'the Jackson at the party is not Senator Jackson', r's cluster containing both singular terms will surely split. Neither of those singular terms will disappear from his representational framework, since he will not stop believing either that he met someone named 'Jackson' at the party (according to the way we told the story), or that Senator Jackson from the state of Washington exists. Each cluster will be quite rich: r had a visual and auditory acquaintance of a direct nature with the Jackson at the party—a "close encounter"—and thus, as is typical of perceptual encounters, acquired a variety of strict anchors for that person: 'my interlocutor at the party', 'the person who said this and that', 'the person at the party who looked thus and so', etc. Similarly, he had a considerable amount of information concerning Senator Jackson, including a variety of strict anchors garnered from his watching him on television. The resulting clusters after the split due to the nonidentity input will thus both be referential clusters (i.e., with thinker-reference), each including a variety of strict anchors and fairly rich information, and each having uniform thinker-reference. Furthermore, they will both have comparable strict-anchoral 'weight'—comparable 'amounts' of strict-anchoral information. There is no question that, after the split, (verbal) beliefs involved in one resulting cluster will have as their referent Senator Jackson, and (verbal) beliefs in the other resulting cluster will have as their referent the Jackson at the party.

In view of this, what can we say of (verbal) beliefs involved in the original, unified cluster prior to the introduction of the input? After all, an input of this sort need not take place: such inputs may serve us as a mere hypothetical testing device. The original cluster had two distinct thinker-referents, one denoted by the members of one set of strict anchors in it, the other by the members of the other set of strict anchors. How did that affect the reference of (verbal) thoughts couched in that cluster?

XII. DIVIDED REFERENCE

The answer, I believe, is that in such a case there is no escape from the conclusion that singular terms in (verbal) thoughts of this sort have *divided reference*. The singular terms in them do not have reference exclusively and purely to just one of the referents of the cluster, but to both. Whom did the speaker refer to when he said that Senator Jackson was very charming at the party? Well, to Senator Jackson, but also to the Jackson at the party. Whom did the speaker refer to when he said that Mr. Jackson is a hawkish politician who is also socially amiable? Well, to Senator Jackson, but also to the Jackson at the party. He in fact believed *of* Senator Jackson that he liked fishing, and he in fact believed *of* the Jackson at the party that he espoused a tough foreign policy line. Thus, each (verbal) belief couched in the cluster is *of* both people, and each predicate in the cluster is taken, by our believer, to apply to each of the clusteral referents. (Note, however, that one can say that in the [verbal] belief, 'Senator Jackson is a political hawk', the reference is clearly predominantly to Senator Jackson, though much less so to in the [verbal] belief, 'Senator Jackson likes fishing'.) This is a distinct complication of our theoretical outlook, but there is no escape from the phenomena: we must recognize the phenomenon of divided reference, and incorporate it into our account.

My claim here, in the light of the preceding considerations, that we should recognize the phenomenon of divided reference, might be resisted in two ways. On both of these lines of response, the basic reaction would be that reference cannot be shared (and is not subject to predominance characterizations): either there is reference to one particular individual (or object), or else there is no reference at all. Yet these two lines of response differ, and I shall consider each in turn.

On the first kind of response, one might argue that in a cluster resulting from the conflation of two individuals, there is just no reference whatsoever, and in particular no divided reference. That two individuals—say, Senator Jackson and the Jackson at the party—played a certain role in the production of the cluster indicates that there is no one candidate *alone* that did so properly, and our reaction then ought to be that there simply is no referent.

This line of thought, I believe, is untenable. First, notice that to claim that there is no referent at all is to assimilate this cluster to the cluster of the man who believes there is a burglar in the basement, when in fact there happens to be one, although he has no auditory (or other) causal effect on our believer at the time.[43] In both cases some definite descriptions in the cluster denote, but there is clearly an enormous difference between these two clusters. The difference is that in the Jackson-Jackson case, the cognizer possesses strict anchors in the cluster for both individuals. Strict anchors are the ultimate conferers of reference. They are the referential links of one's representational system to individuals in the world. In the case of the man with the burglar in the basement, the cluster has no strict anchors whatsoever. To consider him and our believer (in the Jackson-Jackson case) in the same category as having no referents for their respective utterances or beliefs is to miss the crucial phenomenon in this area: the emergence of reference via strict anchors.

Thus, the above response stands in sharp contrast to the fundamental elements of the theoretical framework we elaborated on: once strict anchors appear, reference emerges, and there can be no retreat to the denotation-but-no-reference stance. Our subject has strict anchors for each of the two Jacksons, and thus, via each strict anchor, has descriptive accuracy for one of them or the other. It is the *cluster* that lacks uniformity of strict-anchoral denotation (not just descriptive accuracy). Mere failure of descriptive accuracy in clusters happens in many, perhaps in most, cases, where reference is unproblematic and no conflation of individuals occurs. The strict anchors in the cluster are not uniform in that different ones pick out (descriptively, and thus—being strict anchors—referentially) different individuals.

Furthermore, to adopt the response of no referent is to put, on the same footing, when it comes to the matching of the cluster and the world, Senator Jackson, the Jackson at the party, and, for that matter, President Reagan: none of these is, on that line of thought, a referent of the cluster in question. But this is absurd. There is an obvious sense in which the cluster and (verbal) beliefs couched in it are *of* Senator Jackson and the Jackson at the party in a way in which they are not *of* Reagan. To adopt the no-reference line is to ignore this obvious differential phenomenon. That one cannot simply decide between the two Jacksons by eliminating one as a referent is still a far cry from putting them both vis-à-vis this cluster on the same referential footing with Reagan—or anybody else, for that matter. On the no-reference line of thought, not just Reagan but every individual—including the tree in front of my house and the first stone to have been thrown in Tanzania—is on a par with the two Jacksons when it comes to the issue of whether they are referents of the cluster in question: none of them are, on this line of thought. This conclusion is, I believe, untenable. The proper way of recognizing the major referential role that the two Jacksons play via-à-vis this cluster, a role that no other individual or object plays, is to consider them both as referents: to acknowledge divided reference.

A second consideration which tells against the no-reference approach to such clusters has to do with the gradual nature of shifts of balance in the referential phenomenon in divided clusters. It will be addressed at the end of section XVI.

A third weighty consideration against the no-reference line relates to the possibility of belief attribution. The position taken here is motivated by an approach to attitudinal ascriptions according to which *de re* attitudinal ascriptions require thinker-reference: this is the heart of the conception according to which the exportation inference also unveils a necessary condition for *de re* attribution (Kvart 1984). Exportation, when construed narrowly, merely as an inference, provides a sufficient condition for the ascription of *de re* attitudes, namely, that the appropriate *de dicto* ones be present, and that the right sort of reference relation obtain. But on a stronger construal it reveals a more fundamental aspect: correct *de re* attributions must be accompanied by (and, in fact, rest upon) an appropriate reference relation between the cognizer and the object. One cannot be said to believe anything *of* Reagan unless he possesses reference to Reagan (not necessarily, of course, via the term 'Reagan').[44] It is precisely the presence of the reference phenomenon which brings in the causal element (among others) that makes possible the sanctioning of *de re* ascriptions about Reagan, but not about the shortest spy.

It would be highly counterintuitive, I believe, to deny that the subject in our Jackson-Jackson case believes *of* Senator Jackson that he is a hawk. Nor can one deny that he believes *of* the Jackson at the party that he likes fishing. So *de re* attitudinal ascriptions are appropriate in cases of divided reference clusters. But to allow for them, while denying that there is reference involved, is to forsake the crucial and indispensable connection between *de re* ascriptions and reference. A line of thought that would sanction *de re* attributions without admitting thinker-reference would lead straight into the latitudinarian position, and thus to the conflation of cases where an appropriate causal connection obtains and cases in which it does not, vis-à-vis the viability of *de re* attitudinal ascriptions. For those of us who reject this position, the above option is thus not available. *De re* attributions require reference; *de re* attributions are patently legitimate in divided reference cases; hence reference must be recognized in such cases, and with it the conception of divided reference.

The second line that opposes divided reference takes an opposite view. On this line, there would be an acknowledgment of reference in clusters we considered divided reference clusters. But that recognition of reference would attempt to vindicate *un*divided reference. On that line of thought, reference is carried *exclusively* by the predicate in question. Thus, in the case of the belief formulated as 'Senator Jackson likes fishing', the referent of the subcluster containing 'likes fishing' (which is the subcluster containing 'the Jackson at the party') prevails, and that Jackson is the *sole* referent of that belief. There is reference, then, but no divided reference.

A serious objection to this approach would again arise out of the gradual nature of shifts of referential prominence that will be elaborated at the end of section XVI. But notice that even as it stands this line of thought will not work: the reference of a singular term in a given (verbal) belief cannot be determined strictly by the subcluster to which the predicative expression belongs, since there need not be one such subcluster. Thus, consider the assertion, 'Senator Jackson is a politician who likes fishing'. The predicative expression 'is a politician who likes fishing' belongs to neither of the two subclusters. Rather, it is epistemically grounded in both: it is grounded in the predicate 'is a politician' which belongs to one subcluster, and in the predicate 'likes fishing' which belongs to the other. If one insists that (verbal) beliefs couched in this cluster do have reference, but that reference is determined by the subcluster to which the predicate belongs, this kind of example constitutes an obstacle to that route.

One may then modify one's position and say: In cases where the predicative expression belongs exclusively to one subcluster, then, as before, the utterance (or verbal belief) has as its exclusive referent the referent of that subcluster. But when it does not, there is no reference at all.

This line of thought would still run into the obstacles mentioned above. First, the gradual nature of shifts of referential prominence (see section XVI) would have to be ignored and left unaccommodated. Secondly, in cases of (verbal) beliefs containing a predicate which does not belong to a single subcluster, there again would be no differentiation between the referential status of the referents of the cluster and that of any other individual. Thirdly, ascriptions of beliefs in cases where the predicative expression does not belong to a single subcluster would be blocked again, in an entirely counterintuitive way, in view of the considerations mentioned above. Thus, it seems clear that our subject believes *of* the Jackson at the party that he is a politician who likes fishing. But the predicate belongs to neither subcluster, and in an utterance or a (verbal) belief to this effect there would be no referent on this line of thought. This hybrid option is, therefore, not viable either.

Furthermore, on the second line above, as well as on its modification now under consideration, reference is viewed as being carried *exclusively* by the predicative expression. But there are strong reasons to reject this view. Thus, suppose that in one class there are twins: one of whom is the best student in the class, the other is one of the worst. Our subject has become acquainted with the bright twin, is aware that he is very bright, but is unaware that he has a twin brother. Upon the release of the grades for a given exam, he sees the not-so-bright twin glance at the grades and walk away looking depressed. Our subject mistakes him for his twin brother, the bright one, and says, "Look, the brightest student received a low grade." Now to consider this utterance as being *exclusively of* the less-bright student twin, on the grounds that the predicative expression belongs exclusively to the subcluster which has the bad student as its referent (the subcluster to which 'the student walking away from the bulletin board' belongs), is a clear distortion of the point of this utterance.[45]

XIII. SOME THEORETICAL REPERCUSSIONS

The incorporation of the phenomenon of divided reference into our theoretical apparatus requires care. If, as on my view (which I have tried as much as possible to leave on the sideline in this paper), beliefs are sentential or symbolic representations, all that has to be recognized, when a (verbal) belief of the above sort is considered, is that it has divided reference—two distinct referents—and that it is *of* each of them. The same, of course, holds with respect to asserted utterances. Furthermore, the reporting device would sanction a report, regarding every feature expressed by some predicate in the cluster, to the effect that the believer believes of *each* of the two referents that he (it) has such a feature. If, however, one's theoretical apparatus regarding beliefs is that of singular propositions on the one hand and of conceptual propositions on the other, the situation is trickier. In the case of the South African, one might say that, upon asserting 'the richest South African abhors apartheid', the believer expressed a conceptual proposition, with an individual concept expressed by 'the richest South African', and *at the same time*, via the *same sentence*, another belief as well — a singular proposition, the individual component of which was his interlocutor. A certain uneasiness might be involved in ascribing to the believer two such beliefs expressed by the same sentence.[46]

The situation, on that theoretical line, becomes trickier when the Jackson case is considered, once the phenomenon of divided reference is acknowledged. Then, upon the assertion, 'the Jackson at the party is a political hawk' (or, perhaps, 'Senator Jackson is a politician who likes fishing'), three distinct beliefs are being expressed: the conceptual one, but also (and this is the salient point) *two singular beliefs*, one with Senator Jackson as a constituent, the other with the Jackson-at-the-party as a constituent. Those who conceive beliefs as conceptual or singular propositions must then in principle recognize *any number* of *distinct* beliefs expressed by a single assertion, since clusters can, and often do, have many distinct referents, not just two as we have so far considered (see section XVI). This inflational aspect is quite a consequence to swallow for holders of this conception: that upon the assertion of a given sentence, a multitude of beliefs have been expressed. On the conception I advocate (1986c), the belief is still one and the same, but the referents can be various, and the believer may be reported to have said something (*de re*) of more than one individual via that one assertion. The problem for the theoretical line which construes beliefs as singular or conceptual propositions is that it seems quite unappealing to consider a singular proposition with, say, an ordered pair of individuals as a constituent. Similarly, the conception of the referential use of a singular term on this line as one in which something is being said about a certain individual in such a way that the manner in which he is picked out is entirely incidental (which calls for the proposition expressed thereby to be singular), is stretched when the speaker is taken to have in mind two individuals whom he conflates.

So far I have tried to avoid discussion of how truth fits into the picture (since it requires allusion to the sentential theory I espouse), but a brief comment may be in order. If, via a given assertive utterance (or verbal thought), a subject refers to an individual (exclusively or not), he can be correctly reported to have said something true (or false) of that individual (as the case may be). Thus, if he said in the early 1970s, 'the senior Senator from the state of Washington likes fishing', he might have asserted something false of Senator Jackson, as well as something true of the Jackson-at-the-party. The *sentence itself*, though, in the context in question, is true or false in accordance with whether whoever the senior Senator from Washington at the time is (it happened to be Senator Jackson) does or does not like fishing. Thus, in addition to truth value assignment to sentences in a context, an adverbial ascription of truth values may be appended to attitudinal ascriptions: a subject believes truly (falsely) or a certain person that he is such-and-so. This will hold[47] in cases in which he indeed believes of that person that he is such-and-so, and that person is in fact such-and-so. (For some more elaboration on this issue, see Kvart 1986c.[48])

XIV. REPRESENTATIONAL STRENGTH

Having recognized the phenomenon of divided reference, we must face the ensuing question: If, via a given utterance (or verbal thought), more than one individual can be referred to, is it the case that one referent can be the predominant one, but not the other? Can one referent be more prominent than the other? And if so, are there any general principles ranking the prominence of the various referents of a particular utterance (or verbal thought)? In order to have a better grip on this issue, consider our example concerning the Fiji Islands.

In that example, upon the introduction of the nonidentity input, 'the Prime Minister of the Fiji Islands is not the interlocutor at the party', there will occur a clusteral split. One new cluster will include, 'my interlocutor at the party' and a variety of other strict anchors and predicates that were acquired during the acquaintance at the party. The other new cluster will include 'the Prime Minister of the Fiji Islands',[49] and perhaps a few other bits of information r may have. Both clusters will be referential: the first will include a variety of strict anchors due to the perceptual acquaintance situation, and the second will include at least one strict anchor due to r's brief glimpse of the Fijian Prime Minister from the back during the exchange with his host. But there will be consequently a considerable difference between the two clusters: one will be rich in strict anchors, the other extremely poor. Let us call such a feature of a cluster, its richness in strict-anchoral information, its *representational strength*. The richer it is in strict anchoral information, the more representational strength it possesses. Our first new cluster will thus have considerable representational strength, whereas the second will have scant representational strength.

Our intuitions regarding this example will reveal a new feature. As before in the Jackson case, it will be hard to deny that utterances (by the believer) reflecting beliefs couched in the original cluster are *of* the interlocutor as well as *of* the Fijian Prime Minister. But it is also evident that there is a clear asymmetry as to how prominently these two figure as referents of the appropriate singular terms in such (verbal) beliefs: such beliefs are predominantly about the interlocutor. Thus, in saying 'the Fijian Prime Minister is a charming politician', the reference was predominantly to the interlocutor at the party, and only peripherally to the Fijian Prime Minister (though our believer indeed believed *of* the Fijian Prime Minister as well that he was charming). Whereas in the verbal expression of the beliefs relating to the Jackson case there was a much greater intuitive balance between the two referents as to which was the referent of particular beliefs,[50] there is a glaring intuitive imbalance in this example in favor of the interlocutor as referent:[51] he is the prominent referent of the (verbal) beliefs couched in the original cluster.[52]

The explanation for this phenomenon lies, I believe, in the phenomenon of representational strength. When there is a major imbalance in the representational strengths of the two clusters that emerge from the split after the appropriate nonidentity input, the by-and-large prominent referent of (verbal) beliefs in the original cluster tends to be the one belonging to the resulting cluster with the greater representational strength. In the Jackson-Jackson case, the new clusters had comparable representational strength, and consequently, in the beliefs couched in the original cluster, there was a relative balance between the two referents as referents of the pertinent beliefs.[53] Thus, differences in representational strengths of new referential clusters confer differences as to which referent is more prominent in the original cluster. (This phenomenon, of course, is not relevant in our other two examples – the ones dealing with the martini drinker and the gold mine owners – since they had only one referent in the original cluster.) Representational strength is thus a major factor determining prominence of one clusteral referent over another.[54]

XV. PARASITIC BELIEFS

Representational strength, however, is not the only factor affecting the balance of prominence of referents. There can be variation in the prominence of two referents in split clusters in which the representational strength of the two resulting clusters is balanced. Such variations of prominence cannot of course be explained in terms of representational strength. Rather, another factor is at work, interweaving with the phenomenon of representational strength: this is the phenomenon of *parasitic beliefs*.

Consider again the Jackson case. When our believer says, 'Senator Jackson holds tough foreign policy views', our intuitions clearly suggest that the predominant referent by far is Senator Jackson. But when our believer says, 'Senator Jackson enjoys fishing' (recall his lengthy conversation on this subject with his interlocutor at the party), our intuitions suggest that there is a shift in referential prominence (in comparison with the previous case) toward the Jackson at the party. Yet the singular term used in these two sentences is one and the same: 'Senator Jackson'.

However, upon the introduction of the nonidentity input 'Senator Jackson is not the Jackson-at-the-party', the predicative expression 'holds tough foreign policy views' will land exclusively in one resulting cluster – the one with the singular term 'Senator Jackson' – whereas the other predicative expression, 'enjoys fishing', will land exclusively at the other resulting cluster – the one including 'the Jackson at the party'. The belief formulated as 'Senator

Jackson enjoys fishing' is, therefore, a parasitic belief. It will not survive the nonidentity input: its predicative expression and singular term will, after the split, belong exclusively to distinct clusters (with distinct referents), and the belief in question will not be sustained. The belief is thus parasitic on the mistaken-identity belief in the sense that its being held is contingent upon adherence to the mistaken-identity belief that holds the cluster together. It will be abandoned once the mistaken identity is corrected. When a cluster receives a nonidentity input which results in one (or more) clusters which survive the input, such clusters will be included, as aggregates of items, to the original cluster, and can thus be considered (and consequently called) subclusters of it. A belief formed by properly conjoining a predicative expression and a singular term which belong exclusively to distinct subclusters (in a cluster held together by a mistaken-identity belief) is thus a paradigmatic case of a parasitic belief.

Whether a belief is parasitic in the sense described is of importance to the prominence of one referent or the other with respect to the singular term that figures in its formulation. Thus, in the absence of a representational strength imbalance, and if both the singular term and the predicative expression belong exclusively to the same subcluster (in which case the belief is not a parasitic belief), the predominant referent is the referent of the subcluster to which they both belong. However, if the belief is a parasitic one, where its predicative expression belongs exclusively to a different subcluster than the one to which the singular term in it exclusively belongs, then, when both subclusters have referents, the respective weights of the two referents will be different than (and not as lopsided as) in the previous case. Hence, in the belief formulated as 'Senator Jackson holds tough foreign policy views', which is *not* parasitic, the by-far predominant referent is Senator Jackson. But in the belief formulated as 'Senator Jackson likes fishing', which is parasitic, the prominence of the two referents is clearly more balanced.[55]

These two phenomena affecting referential prominence in cases of divided reference — the phenomenon of imbalance of representational strength and the phenomenon of mistaken parasitic beliefs — interface. In cases where the difference in representational strength is very substantial, this phenomenon will tend to overshadow the effect of parasitic beliefs. Where the representational strength is more or less balanced, the phenomenon of parasitic beliefs will tend to loom large.

XVI. PREVALENCE OF DIVIDED REFERENCE

Far from being an esoteric phenomenon, divided reference is, on the contrary, quite prevalent. We often confuse two individuals. We routinely mistake ephemeral figures in our lives for people we know well: we erroneously believe that the person at the back of the theatre hall we attended yesterday is a relative whom we have not seen in a while; that the person who drove the red Corolla in front of the supermarket is our next-door neighbor; and that the person who left a message but no name on the answering machine is a high-school friend. Such conflations result in short-lived intrusions into the histories of established clusters representing a well-known acquaintance, and thus result in relatively tiny, though nonetheless referential, subclusters of such established clusters. The result is divided reference. (Conflations of this sort exhibit, of course, substantial imbalance of representational strength.) This phenomenon will be manifested also in the behavior of proper names (when they belong to clusters with divided reference). Conflations of individuals which result in divided reference clusters with more balanced representational strength are not as common, but still prevalent. We often confuse two students, public figures, or acquaintances with similar appearances, names, demeanor or whatever—not to mention cases of impostors, successfully disguised acquaintances, or conflation (e.g., of twins) with substantial time intervals separating the two encounters.

In section XII we argued against attempts to deny the phenomenon of divided reference. One of the arguments we mentioned but postponed discussing had to do with the gradual nature of shifts of referential prominence. This is an aspect we shall take up now.

As we saw, prominence of reference can shift with the two factors considered above. Variations in differences of representational strength correspond to variations of referential prominence, and so do transitions from parasitic to nonparasitic beliefs. The latter, however, are limiting cases of differences in the 'degree of affinity' of a predicative expression to a particular subcluster, which are correlated with variations in referential prominence as well. We shall now elaborate on these points.

First, we saw that in cases where there is a very substantial imbalance of representational strength, there is a shift of referential prominence towards the referent of the subcluster with the weightier representational strength.[56] When we considered cases of relative balance of the representational strengths of two subclusters, the relative weights of the two referents were more on a par.[57] But the relative representational strength of two subclusters can assume many intermediate degrees. The relative prominence of reference will vary accordingly with changes in the relative imbalance of representational strength (as consideration of pertinent examples will confirm).

A similar phenomenon is manifested in the effect that parasitic beliefs (and their cognates) have on referential prominence. Consider, for that matter, cases of balanced representational strength. When the predicative expression belongs exclusively to one subcluster, it exercises considerably more pull towards the referent of that subcluster as the referent of the (verbal) belief or utterance involved than would a predicative expression (with the same singular term) that belongs to *both* subclusters, or a predicative expression which belongs to neither, but is grounded (in terms of its epistemic roots) in both subclusters more or less to the same degree. An example of the first kind would be 'Senator Jackson likes fishing'. An example of the second would be 'Senator Jackson is human'. An example of the third kind would be 'Senator

Jackson is a politician who likes fishing'. The affinity of a predicative expression to the respective subclusters is, then, a matter of degree. The predicative expression can belong to one subcluster exclusively; to the other subcluster exclusively; or to both; or it can be rooted, epistemically speaking, in components within each of the two subclusters. Such differences in turn correspond to differences in relative referential prominence (as they correspond to differences in the relative pull that the two referents of the cluster exercise). [In the latter case, in which the predicate is rooted in components in both subclusters, but belongs to neither, one can perhaps even argue that various relative levels of epistemic prominence, or weight, can be assigned to the components in which it is rooted in one subcluster as opposed to the components in which it is rooted in the other. Such differences in the relative epistemic weights or levels of prominence of components from one of the two subclusters versus components from the other subcluster vis-à-vis the predicate in question would arguably correspond to a difference in the relative weight that the referents of the two subclusters would carry (concerning beliefs formulated via that predicate). Thus, even the phenomenon of the affinity of the predicative expression to one subcluster or the other arguably comes in gradations (more finely tuned than depicted above), which in turn correspond to gradations in referential prominence.]

The phenomenon of gradations or levels of referential prominence fits naturally and smoothly into our conception of divided reference. This phenomenon exists, and cannot be simply dismissed along the lines we argued against above—the lines which reject divided reference.[58] To deny reference in cases which we considered to be cases of divided reference clusters as above is to deny the phenomenon of gradations or levels of referential prominence. The same holds if one maintains that there is undivided reference in cases where the predicate belongs exclusively to one subcluster, and no reference otherwise. Thus, the recognition of the phenomenon of referential prominence and the variations and gradations in which it appears flies in the face of those lines of thought. But this phenomenon, I claim (and have tried to make plausible), is real. It can neither be ignored nor thrown into the philosophical wastebasket bearing the title of vagueness. (Another aspect of the gradual nature of shifts of referential prominence in split clusters emerges out of the character of internal focusing, and will be discussed at the end of section XVIII.)

This is not the whole story concerning the phenomenon of divided reference. This account has ramifications for the issues of reference to natural kinds, which will not, however, be pursued here.[59] Hopefully, the phenomenon of divided reference has been displayed, and some of the mechanisms at work have been brought to light. But the internal structure of clusters is still more complicated than what has been depicted here. In particular, the mechanism of clusteral split via nonidentity inputs requires more care and elaboration. What requires further attention before we end, however, is the fact that the two factors dwelled upon here—representational strength and parasitic beliefs—are not always the only ones affecting referential prominence. These two factors dominate the scene particularly when the pertinent thoughts are nonoccurrent. In those cases, only features of the formational history of the representational system and its internal clusteral and subclusteral structure are involved, and they decide the issue of referential prominence along the lines spelled out above. But these two factors—representational strength and parasitic beliefs—are often accompanied by a third, and sometimes highly potent, factor, when the pertinent thoughts involved are occurrent. This is the phenomenon of *internal focusing*.

XVII. INTERNAL FOCUSING

It is customary to talk about focusing attention on an object, or attending to an object. This, however, is not a building block available to us in the present project for the following reason. First, such expressions are *de re*, whereas our analysis of divided reference is designed to fit into the general analysis of thinker-reference I advocate, while the notion of thinker-reference is in turn conceived as playing a central role in the reduction of the *de re* to the *de dicto* level of reporting via the thinker-reference relation (Kvart 1984, 1989). Moreover, focusing, as will become clearer shortly, can occur even when there is no external referent, and thus when there is no attending to an object.

Instead, the notion we are after here is that of internal focusing. That focusing attention need not be on any external object (though normally it is) is quite clear. An American soldier taken prisoner in Vietnam might have developed an unjustified confidence in his captors, who in turn fed him a wholly fabricated story about political developments back home since he was taken prisoner. For the purpose of this fabricated story, new political figures were invented. Our soldier, who had an intense interest in the political situation back home, might have obviously focused his attention now on this figure, now on another, though there was no real individual he was focusing his attention on. Rather, the phenomenon of his attention being focused must be understood in terms of his own representational framework, i.e., his clusteral system. He formed various clusters, corresponding to the figures in the fabricated history, and his focusing attention on those figures must then be understood in terms of features of those clusters. Yet, such features cannot be structural features of his representational system. The reason for this is that in general the representational system may be stable (so long as no new information comes in, and no structural changes ensue via internal processing) while focus shifts. Focusing and (shifts in focusing) need not (though they may) be accompanied by (or be a part of) any internal processing that results in changes in the informational makeup or the structural aspects of the clusteral system.

However, our soldier's focusing on one fabricated political figure rather than another must be related to some sort of attention-prominence that one cluster rather than another enjoyed at that time. Thus the question is: What does internal focusing amount to? What does focusing on one cluster rather than another at any given time amount to?

The answer resides in the *pattern of occurrent thoughts* that the cognizer has at the time. Consider a cognizer in a normal situation. If the bulk of his (occurrent) verbal thoughts involve the singular terms 'Ronald Reagan' and 'the present President of the U.S.' and hardly any, or relatively very few, involve 'Jimmy Carter' or 'the former President of the U.S.', then we can say that he is focusing on the cluster including 'Ronald Reagan', not on the cluster including 'Jimmy Carter'. The resort to occurrent thoughts here should be construed in a very liberal way: such thoughts need not be assertive thoughts: they may well be, for instance, interrogative thoughts. Thus, one may focus on a cluster including 'my daughter', while having predominantly interrogative rather than assertive occurrent thoughts (e.g., 'Where is my daughter now?', 'What is my daughter doing now?' etc.).

What holds for internal focusing regarding different clusters, holds as well for internal focusing regarding different subclusters in a divided cluster. Thus, suppose one is watching a television show on which Senator Jackson is giving a speech. One's (verbal) occurrent thoughts on that occasion may well involve mostly predicative expressions belonging to the subcluster to which 'Senator Jackson' belongs, and a sizable portion of those predicative expressions may belong to that subcluster exclusively, while perhaps only a very small fraction of one's (verbal) occurrent thoughts at that time would involve predicates belonging exclusively to the subcluster to which 'the Jackson-at-the-party' belongs. The reverse may be the case right after the party (recall our first example of section II). In the first case, then, there would be internal focusing on the subcluster to which 'Senator Jackson' belongs, whereas in the second the focusing would be on the subcluster to which 'the Jackson at the party' belongs. Different external circumstances may be conducive to the emergence of occurrent thoughts of one kind or the other, and thus to the subject's focusing on one particular subcluster or another.[60]

Focusing can vary in its intensity, exclusivity, and sharpness. Where focusing on a cluster (rather than a subcluster) is at issue, the aggregate of thoughts, in a given time interval, involving linguistic items belonging exclusively to that cluster may be relatively large or small,[61] and in particular in comparison with the general flow of occurrent thoughts during that time interval. Focusing on that cluster during that time interval will have high or low intensity. Thoughts involving linguistic items belonging exclusively to another specific cluster may also be occurrent during the same time interval: the more numerous they are, the less exclusive the focusing on the first cluster will be. And the same holds with respect to subclusters: the intensity of focusing on a subcluster is quite analogous to the intensity of focusing on a cluster, and so is the exclusivity of focusing on a subcluster (vis-à-vis some other cluster or clusters). Focusing on a subcluster can, furthermore, be more or less acute depending on how large the aggregate of thoughts containing the predicative expressions and singular terms which belong exclusively to that subcluster is in comparison with some other aggregate of thoughts containing the predicative expressions and singular terms which belong exclusively to another subcluster (in the same cluster).

External focusing — the common and often-mentioned phenomenon of focusing attention on an object — is indeed just the product of internal focusing and thinker-reference. Thus, if there is internal focusing on a given cluster, which possesses a single referent, the subject *thereby* focuses attention on the object which is the referent of that cluster. Elsewhere I have argued in favor of viewing the exportation inference as reflecting the reducibility of *de re* ascriptions to *de dicto* ones via the thinker-reference relation, when sentential attitudes are involved (Kvart 1982, 1984). In this case, we see the reference relation as being the extra building block which, when conjoined with internal focusing, results in (external) focusing of attention on an object, which is the thinker-referent in question. The mediating (and reductive) role that thinker-reference plays in the case of nonsentential attitudinal states (and ascriptions) is analogous to the role it plays in the case of sentential attitudinal states (and ascriptions). Recall again the example of the man convinced there is a burglar in the basement. Consider it first in a case in which there is no one there (he is just hallucinating), and then in a case in which his beliefs (as he would report them), despite being the same, are caused in the regular (auditory) way by a burglar in the basement. In both cases he is preoccupied with what he takes to be going on in his basement. But whereas in the first case his attention is focused on a cluster (including 'the burglar') for which he has no reference, in the second the analogous cluster does have a referent. It is in virtue of this that in the second case (but not in the first) he is attentive to the actual burglar. If we allow for there to be a burglar in the basement in the first case, but one who has no causal impact on our believer (thus in fact unnoticed by him), he still would not be attentive *to the burglar* despite his attention being focused on a cluster which may match his features closely.

Focusing can shift as a result of external stimuli, emotional factors, or will. External stimuli can, and often do, bring about focusing on an object,[62] but they interact, as causal antecedents of focusing, with the other factors as well. Internal focusing is thus a different sort of component of referential phenomena from those we have dealt with so far. Unlike the other components involved in the determination of thinker-reference, it is not part of the causal-formational history of any cluster, nor is it a constitutive feature of the representational system and its structure.[63] Rather, it is a transient feature than can appear, disappear, and change in various ways while the other components remain unchanged. Thus, the representational system (and of course its formational history) can remain fixed while the subject focuses first on one cluster, then on another, with varying degrees of intensity. However, whether the subject is internally focused at a given time, and if so, on which representations, and with what intensity, is a matter of psychological-cognitive fact about him.[64] (Whether he thereby also is externally focused depends also on epistemic and historical dimensions.)

XVIII. INTERNAL FOCUSING AND DIVIDED REFERENCE

When only pertinent nonoccurrent beliefs are involved, or the pertinent clusters barely figure in the current occurrent thoughts, there is no pertinent focusing.[65] In that case, the referential mechanism is as elaborated throughout most of this paper. But when pertinent focusing is present (via pertinent occurrent beliefs, of course), it can affect, and can often dominate, the referential dimensions of the case. Whether focusing is present or not is immaterial for reference via a term in a referential cluster that is not a divided reference cluster (i.e., a cluster with just one referent). Focusing becomes relevant when divided reference is involved. In such cases, focusing can tip the scales and overshadow other features. The factors which bear upon referential prominence that we considered were the following. First, there was the clusteral system, the cluster in question, its subclusters, and their referents. Then there were the two features associated with the subclusters involved: representational strength and parasitic beliefs. The story told above must now be considered as strictly applicable only in cases where pertinent focusing is not involved.[66] In such cases, representational strength is a dominant factor; but when there was a sufficient balance between the representational strengths of the two subclusters involved, the question of whether the belief in question is parasitic carries considerable weight.

Now consider divided reference cases where there is (sufficiently intense and acute) focusing on a particular subcluster. The predominance of reference involved in such cases will be governed by the focusing phenomenon. If there is such focusing on a subcluster, then the referent of that subcluster will dominate via-à-vis the singular terms in (verbal) thoughts couched in the cluster in question (or utterances of such thoughts).[67]

Thus, consider again the Jackson-Jackson case. It was a case with balanced representational strength. We considered (verbal) beliefs of the sort 'Senator Jackson holds hawkish political views', which was not a parasitic belief, as well as beliefs such as 'Senator Jackson was charming at the party', which was. Now suppose the case involves (sufficiently intense and acute) focusing. Suppose the believer focuses on the subcluster containing 'Senator Jackson'. To make this plausible, consider external circumstances that will be conducive to such focusing, e.g., when our subject watches Senator Jackson making a television appearance. He consequently has occurrent (verbal) thoughts involving 'Senator Jackson' and concerning his present demeanor, message, motivations, etc. Once such focusing takes place, I submit, the prominent referent of the two beliefs considered above (and not just of the first one), will be Senator Jackson. But now consider circumstances conducive to the believer's focusing on the subcluster containing 'the Jackson-at-the-party'; e.g., suppose he has just had a conversation with the Jackson at the party, and reports his impressions to his companion. Assume he now focuses (with sufficient intensity and sharpness) on the subcluster associated with 'the-Jackson-at-the-party' (and thus has numerous [verbal] occurrent thoughts involving 'the Jackson at the party' and concerning information obtained during that conversation). In this case, I submit, the prominent referent of not just the second belief but even the first[68] will be the Jackson at the party. Thus, if this is indeed the case, focusing, when present, distinct, and sufficiently intense and acute, governs referential prominence over and above the question of whether the belief involved is parasitic or not. Thus, in particular, focusing dominates parasiticality.

But focusing also dominates representational strength. Thus, consider again the Fiji Islands example. In that example, one subcluster, the one including 'the Fijian Prime Minister', was overwhelmingly weaker in terms of representational strength than the other subcluster, the one including 'my interlocutor'. We have seen that, in the absence of pertinent focusing, representational strength governs referential prominence in this kind of case. But now consider again the belief 'The Fijian Prime Minister is a concerned politician', and suppose that the believer focuses on the subcluster containing 'the Fijian Prime Minister'. (Thus, assume that he has finished his conversation, moved about some more, and then again caught a glimpse of the real Fijian Prime Minister from the back, recognizing him as the Fijian Prime Minister, and is focusing now on features associated with the subcluster containing 'the Fijian Prime Minister'—what it takes to be a Prime Minister in such remote islands, etc.) Now it seems that intuitively the Fijian Prime Minister would have referential prominence in the belief in question, and not the interlocutor. Therefore, if this is correct, focusing dominates representational strength.

As we noticed, however, focusing need not be a clear-cut, present-or-not-present, phenomenon. We saw that focusing need not be present at all (in the absence of occurrent beliefs), or need not be pertinent to the beliefs under consideration.[69] But even when present and pertinent, focusing can vary in degrees of pertinence, intensity and sharpness,[70] and thus in the extent to which it dominates the other factors that underlie referential prominence in cases of divided reference. Thus, focusing need not be acute, and may involve more than one subcluster. In such a case, the impact of the focusing factor vis-à-vis referential prominence may be weakened or neutralized, and the field may be left open to the other two factors (i.e., representational strength and parasiticality). And, of course, this kind of case can come in various forms and gradations, thus yielding different extents of efficacy of the focusing factor. Furthermore, the degree of intensity of the focusing factor is correlated with the degree to which focusing dominates the other two factors. When focusing is present, and is exclusively on one subcluster (and thus pertinent and very sharp), and has sufficient intensity, it dominates. But when it is diluted in one of the above ways, its efficacy will diminish correspondingly.

We have seen that focusing on one subcluster rather than another is a matter of degree.[71] Since, as we have just argued, focusing is a major ingredient in the determination of referential prominence in divided reference clusters, we have an additional reason to uphold the gradual nature of shifts of balance in the referential prominence phenomenon, and thus an additional reason to reject the lines of thought which oppose the acknowledgment of the divided reference phenomenon that were discussed in section XII.

There is more that needs to be explored about the workings of the internal focusing mechanism and the extent to which it overshadows the other factors that interact with it in yielding referential prominence in divided reference clusters (e.g., the correspondence between the extent to which the internal focusing is sharp or diluted, to the point of dissipation, and the extent to which the other factors surface). Hopefully, the exploration of the various cases and their different facets and the elaboration on the arguments presented have been pursued to a sufficient degree to warrant recognition of the phenomenon of divided reference and acknowledgment of the viability of the conceptual apparatus which is required to characterize it and display its features.[72]

Notes

1. Compare Kvart 1989, section 2. But see below, end of section III, for a terminological adjustment concerning the notion of speaker reference.

2. I shall pursue this point below in section III.

3. For an elaboration of the scope of the speaker-reference relation and *de re* attributions, see Kvart 1989, section 1. For the relation of speaker-reference as underlying the ascriptions of *de re* attitudes, see Kvart 1982, 1984.

4. Some diverging intuitions are to be found as to how meager the causal connection might be and still warrant *de re* ascriptions (although they pertain to fairly marginal cases): I have strong intuitions to the effect that a whole range of cases with even meager cognitive content concomitant with the requisite causal connection and epistemic aspects allows for such *de re* ascriptions; see my forthcoming article "The Objective Dimension of Believing *de re*."

5. That is, they are willing to acknowledge such ascriptions as true even in cases in which the appropriate causal connection is absent.

6. For my position on the *de dicto–de re* distinction, see Kvart 1982, 1984, and especially 1986c.

7. In this paper, however, I sidestep the issue of proper names. The many implications of the position presented here for proper names will have to be brought out elsewhere.

8. Issues concerning partial reference have been discussed by Field 1973 and Devitt 1981, chap. 5.

9. In order to facilitate the example, I have resorted in part to mediated reference, despite my wish to confine the discussion in this paper to *un*mediated reference as much as possible (e.g., by relying *solely* on strict anchoral information in the notion of representational strength—see below, section XIV).

10. Intentions with referential features would be *de re* intentions (e.g., intentions to draw attention to certain individuals), which in turn consist of *de dicto* intentions and thinker-reference. A *de dicto* intention may well be a causal antecedent of a speech act, and the referential features of the belief expressed thereby would then be determinants of the referential features of the speech act. But the *de dicto* intention is not a constituent of the belief expressed or its referential features. *De dicto* intentions may even have some common causal roots with referential features of the cluster in which the belief in question is couched, thereby being epiphenomenal to them. *De dicto*

intentions can also serve as causal antecedents affecting referential predominance; see the last section.

11. Though they can be very well respected as personal motivations for one's research direction, reflecting individual taste, style, and heuristic speculation.

12. Accordingly, my use of the notion of representation above, which I employ throughout only in its strong sense (the one that requires an appropriate causal connection and sanctions ascriptions *de re*), is aligned with the notion of reference (speaker-reference, thinker-reference — see below), and *not* with the notion of denotation.

13. See also below, section VII, and Kvart 1989, and the forthcoming "The Objective Dimension of Believing *de re*."

Since the thinker-reference relation need not be accompanied by any speech act, I will use, instead of the locution '*r* refers [*by* '*a*', in a particular utterance, to *b*]', the locution, '*r* has thinker-reference (or just reference, or even speaker-reference) [*by* '*a*', in a particular (verbal) belief, to *b*]'.

14. In this paper I discuss only speaker-reference to *individuals* and *objects*. So my use here of speaker-reference to *phenomena* extends beyond the theoretical treatment I engage in this paper.

15. That is, cases in which a speaker uses a definite description to refer to an object not accurately (or uniquely) described by that definite description (in that context).

16. However, since I believe that the phenomenon of thinker-reference has been successfully speaker-referred to by Donnellan, I consider the above introduction of the notion of thinker-reference to be a mere terminological concession, designed to facilitate understanding. Yet I do *not* consider this change necessary on substantive grounds.

17. Discussion of representational frameworks henceforth will be limited to frameworks for *individual* representations (i.e., which serve to represent individuals, rather than, e.g., events or phenomena). I shall often allow myself to drop the qualifier 'individual'.

18. I will not attempt to carve the discussion below to fit cases of singular terms which occur in more than one pertinent cluster. Their incorporation requires amplification of the conceptual resources so far employed (mostly by resorting to the internal focusing phenomenon; see below, section XVII).

19. My use of the term 'belief' in this paper requires some comments. Elsewhere (1986c) I have elaborated and defended a conception of beliefs as sentential (symbolic) representations. However, my concerns and claims in this paper are largely *independent* of that conception of what beliefs are. It is important that the reader keep in mind that my claims about divided reference do *not*, by and large, require adherence to the above conception of beliefs. Since my concern here will be with reference via singular terms, the discussion will be virtually limited to cases where linguistic formulation is present or can be assigned in relatively unproblematic ways. Assertions or utterances will thus be focal cases, as well as unexpressed thoughts formulated verbally. (They need not be *accepted* thoughts: they may well be just *entertained* thoughts.) My discussion below will apply so long as one can consider them as formulated in linguistic terms, or as readily amenable to linguistic formulation. Then the question arises as to the subject's reference via the pertinent singular terms. The thrust of the discussion in this paper can be molded to fit conceptions of beliefs or thoughts as consisting of concepts as well. Then, however, one would need to complicate one's machinery by considering reference by singular concepts and the like, and incorporate proper names in some way as well (see note 20). But apart from that, a natural way of making the discussion in this paper accessible and pertinent to such conceptions is perhaps to consider the thrust of this paper as limited to sufficiently ideal cognizers who possess the linguistic expressions for their relevant concepts.

Given this clarification, I will attempt, whenever possible, to use the notion of belief *without* assuming commitments to a sentential (symbolic) theory of beliefs. Accordingly, I will attempt to talk about thoughts or about beliefs as the subject would express them, and often invoke the parenthetical qualifier '(verbal)'. If a reader with a different orientation than mine on this issue feels on occasion puzzled by my use of the notion 'belief', he can try to substitute the notion 'accepted sentence' in its stead.

20. Thus, one perhaps might take a cluster to consist of *concepts* (or other symbolic representations, e.g., visual images) rather than linguistic expressions. Co-clusterality of suitable concepts would then amount to a belief being held (occurrent or not). In this way recourse to linguistic expressions is avoided. I consider this line to be substantially contiguous with (rather than opposed to) the sentential (symbolic) view that I advanced (1986c). However, on this view, one would have to consider the thinker-reference relation as pertaining to individual concepts rather than singular terms. Proper names pose the obvious difficulties, which are in general (as mentioned above) beyond our present scope. But only may well opt for a hybrid model of a representational system, consisting of concepts (for which the cognizer might have no linguistic items) *and* linguistic expressions as well. Then a cluster could include both linguistic items (such as proper names) as well as concepts. But again, one may confine one's concerns at this stage of inquiry, when issues of reference are at stake, to *sufficiently idealized* cognizers who possess the requisite linguistic items for the formulation of their relevant thoughts, and then proceed on the working hypothesis that not much of substance is affected by taking the linguistic items (rather than their conceptual correlates) as elements in such a model of the representational framework.

21. See note 19.

22. But it is also affected by the occurrent beliefs the subject has in cases of conflation of individuals; see section XVIII. I may occasionally omit this qualification.

23. For more on this point, see the end of section VII.

24. Without any further complications added.

25. My usage of scare quotes, here and elsewhere, is lax and extends to cases where, strictly speaking, corner quotes should be used.

26. The knowledge here must be unmediated (not acquired via a source); it is also in general latent knowledge (see section 14 in Kvart 1989). The condition is formulated here so as to apply to an English speaker *r*. Note too that this condition must further require that the definite description in question be referentially pure and not too 'inflated' informationally vis-à-vis what it takes for it to fulfill its denotative function; see note 30 and Kvart 1989.

27. That is, verbal beliefs formed by properly conjoining a definite description and a predicative expression which belong to that cluster. See above, end of section IV.

28. My comment here on this issue is all too brief, since I am trying to keep this paper as self-contained as possible. For further elaboration, see Kvart 1989. This outlook is further developed in my (unpublished) manuscript *Reference and Knowledge*.

29. Where mediated reference (i.e., reference acquired via a source) is present, other phenomena and mechanisms play a role (although they bear important analogies to the case of unmediated reference). But even then, reference ultimately boils down to strict anchors—even if they are the strict anchors of one's source (or of the source of one's source). In this paper I attempt to stay away from mediated reference as much as possible.

30. The reader should note that a variety of aspects pertinent to the *de dicto–de re* reduction and the role that strict anchors play in it have not been touched upon here (see Kvart 1982, 1984, 1986c, 1989). Thus, a major requirement concerning strict anchors is that they be *referentially pure*—i.e., containing no predicative expression which involves referential locutions or *de re* locutions. On my view, the thinker-reference relation serves as the reductive element for the grounding of *de re* ascriptions in *de dicto* ones.

31. As well as by what he takes, rightly or wrongly, others there to refer to.

32. That is, for singular terms which occur in those utterances (and verbal beliefs). Since I take this to be obvious by now, I may not repeat such qualifications.

33. But in divided reference clusters, the referential features also depend on what other occurrent beliefs he has at the time, due to the impact of focusing. See below, section XVIII.

34. It does, however, present a serious difficulty as to how to *report* his beliefs via the usual ascriptional constructions (e.g.: he believes that . . .). For my proposal concerning this issue, see Kvart 1984 and 1985.

35. I avoid here (and below, in examples in section XI) commentary on qualifications concerning tense.

36. Recall that I take the denotation of a definite description (in a context) to be that individual (object) to which it uniquely descriptively specifies (in that context).

37. This characterization of the notion of a mistaken parasitic position is, however, not complete: see the next section (and note 42) for another crucial feature characteristic of this type of position.

38. The idealized element of the rationality of the believer can be abstracted from when, instead of relying on his rational processing, one considers the evidential base for the relevant bits of information he has, and then determines how such an input, given such an evidential base, *ought* to be processed. Despite the greater generality achieved thereby, this leaves us still somewhat short of full generality, since certain epistemic systems may be so irrational and chaotic that there may be no telling how they should process certain inputs. Yet it becomes questionable, in such frameworks, what the facts of the matter are regarding the speaker-reference of such a confused believer via particular definite descriptions.

39. For the idealized element involved in such a conception of authoritative inputs and how it can be generalized via certain counterfactual conditions, see my forthcoming "Seeing that and Seeing as," section IX.

40. I assume that in this example his conviction that he is facing one man in that corner is stronger than other pertinent beliefs of his. The input therefore does not make him doubt that there is one man in that corner. I may also assume that he believes that no other person at that party drinks a martini, and that this conviction of his is sufficiently more robust than his belief that the man in the corner drinks a martini.

41. Thus, the subject's belief, that the definite description in question denotes, hinges crucially on the mistaken-identity belief: the latter constitutes indispensable grounds for his holding that belief.

42. This feature is an essential constituent of the notion of a singular term occupying a mistaken parasitic position.

43. A more accurate analogy would be a case where the believer wrongly takes (on grounds of psychological speculation) the first man to have arrived at the party to be the person most anxious to be there, whereas he (the believer) refers by neither definite description. But the point I am making here does not really require such an improvement of the analogy.

44. A limitation of scope is invoked here through a resort to sufficiently competent cognizers; cf. the last part of note 20.

45. This conception is also highly implausible with respect to cases where the predicative expression belongs to both subclusters. It seems odd to say that although the assertion 'the Jackson at the party is a hawk' does have Senator Jackson as its referent, the assertion 'Senator Jackson is human' does not at all have Senator Jackson as a referent. On such a line of thought, one might proceed to suggest that when the predicative expression belongs to both clusters, the referent is the referent of the subcluster to which the singular term belongs. But then the presumed exclusive primacy of the predicative expression as determining the referent (via the subcluster to

which it belongs exclusively, when it does) is undermined: Why not have the singular term carry some weight in those cases too? And, furthermore, some of the above problems will recur when neither the predicate nor the singular term belong exclusively to one subcluster.

46. In this example, I suspect, this move might be resisted. Thus, someone (say, Kripke) might insist that the use of the definite description in question was either referential or attributive. In the first case, according to such a response, the belief expressed would be a singular proposition; in the second, a conceptual proposition. However, the view according to which the attributive-referential distinction (on its standard conception) is exclusive in character seems forced in some cases, and thus of questionable tenability: something seems to be lost if the individual in question (to whom the cognizer has speaker reference via the definite description he employs) does not enter the picture (insofar as the proposition expressed is concerned), which would be the case if the proposition expressed is taken to be a conceptual proposition, following a construal of the use of the definite description as attributive. And elements regarding the content of the definite description would be lost if the use of the definite description is taken to be referential, and the proposition expressed is accordingly construed as singular. This seems to apply to the example used at the end of section XII about the twins. To regard the assertion by our subject, 'the brightest student received a low grade' as expressing *only* a conceptual proposition (with the use of the definite description construed as attributive) would seem to neglect the fact that he is, *thereby*, speaker-referring to the bad student twin. But to regard this assertion as expressing *only* a singular proposition (with the use construed as referential) would miss the point of the assertion. Either way, quite a bit of the communicational-referential situation would be missed. (In order to press further the point that something important would be lost on the attributive reading, modify the sentence as follows: '*this* brightest student here received a low grade'.) The more appropriate response, in cases of this sort, would be to say that the speaker expressed one proposition as well as the other. The position seems available to Donnellan, but not to Kripke. (See Donnellan's 1979 and Kripke's 1979.)

47. With the 'truly' modifier, of course.

48. A sentential theory of belief will obviously fit naturally into this mold. However, if one acknowledges accepted sentences as beliefs, then, on this approach, such beliefs are true or false in accordance with whether the sentences that embody them are true or false in the context in question: thinker-reference does not enter into this picture. But, at the same time, if such beliefs are *of* a particular individual (and, for simplicity, have a subject-predicate structure), the cognizer believes truly or falsely of that individual that he is such-and-so, depending on whether that individual satisfies the predicative expression in that sentential belief.

49. Here I again rely on the requisite epistemic features assumed in this example. Compare the corresponding qualifications stated in note 40 concerning the martini case.

50. That is, when there is symmetry concerning the parasiticality aspect; see section XV.

51. Despite the fact that the predicate belongs exclusively to neither subcluster, while the singular term belongs to the subcluster that has the Fijian Prime Minister as its referent; see section XV.

52. The reader puzzled about my allusion to (verbal) beliefs in association with singular terms and *of*ness throughout this discussion may be advised to consult note 19 above. (Recall also Wilfrid Sellars's conception of speech as thinking-out-loud.) The reader should be reminded that much of what is said here can be recast in terms of the referents of utterances and assertions (of the corresponding sentences), of accepted sentences (see also Perry 1980) and of verbal occurrent thoughts. Much the same

points about divided reference can be made this way as well. Thus, in order to avoid bringing in my own bias toward a sentential (symbolic) theory of beliefs, my use of 'beliefs couched in a cluster' can be simply recast as: accepted sentences of a subject-predicate form which consist of singular terms and predicative expressions belonging to the cluster in question.

53. Again, when parasiticality is factored out.

54. The exact scope of strict anchoral information obviously depends on the fine tuning of the notion of strict anchor. For a more detailed treatment of the latter, see Kvart 1989.

Notice also that by limiting the notion of representational strength to strict anchoral information, information acquired via channels which generate mediated reference has been neglected. This artificial distortion is in line with the general confinement of most of this paper to cases and aspects of unmediated reference, though it is quite obvious that its themes extend to cases of mediated reference as well.

55. I have not dwelled on a very closely related case: one where the singular term belongs exclusively, as before, to one subcluster but the predicative expression is hybrid— belonging to neither subcluster. (A predicative expression will be of this sort when it is epistemically grounded in ingredients in both subclusters.) In such a case, the level of prominence of the referent of the subcluster to which the singular term belongs will be in between the corresponding ones in these two examples.

56. Notice that figurative talk about such 'transitions', 'variations', 'pulls', and 'shifts' here and below should be taken as amounting to comparison of referential prominence in two situations, involving very similar parameters, where one parameter—say, representational strength imbalance—varies to a certain (say small) degree between the two situations.

57. In making such comparisons, we keep the aspect of parasitic beliefs fixed, while considering changes in representational strength.

58. Thus, even one who is skeptical about whether there is a certain correlation between relative degrees in which a predicate is epistemically rooted in two subclusters and degrees of referential prominence, should recognize a correlation between variations in referential prominence and features such as the inclusion of the predicate in one subcluster only, the other subcluster only, both, or neither. Thus, one should be aware that my case for the correlation between variations in referential prominence and differences regarding the parasiticality of the beliefs involved does not *hinge* on a claim about the impact on referential prominence of differences in degrees of epistemic rooting of the predicate in one subcluster versus the other. See also note 60 below.

59. See Field (1973) on a related issue concerning theoretical terms.

60. This example illustrates the gradual nature of shifts of balance in the phenomenon of internal focusing: relative differences as to how large or small the aggregate of linguistic items (in one's [verbal] occurrent thoughts) which belong only to one subcluster is in comparison with the aggregate of those which belong only to another subcluster may determine whether one focuses more on the one subcluster or on the other. Consequently, the phenomenon of shifts in referential prominence in divided reference clusters must have a gradual nature as well: see the end of section XVIII below.

61. In comparison, e.g., with the aggregate of thoughts involving linguistic items belonging exclusively to another cluster, or the same cluster on a different occasion. The notions of large (small) aggregates of thoughts (here and below) must also reflect how enduring those thoughts are during the time interval in question.

62. But beware: external circumstances do not *determine* focusing: they may merely serve as causal antecedents conducive to focusing on a particular cluster or subcluster. Yet despite such conducive external circumstances, one's focusing *may* go any other way.

63. That is, the clusteral system, its composition of subclusters, and the epistemo-

logical underpinnings that underlie it (see the knowledge component of the strict-anchor concept).

64. The approach taken here to focusing thus avoids concerns about internal homunculi; see Lycan 1981.

65. Beliefs and focusing are pertinent if they are related to the clusters (and thereby their referents) under consideration. We thus entirely ignore unrelated occurrent thoughts that may be present (and thus yield some unrelated focusing).

66. That is, not just when there is no focusing at all, but also when focusing involves clusters other than the one(s) under consideration.

67. The referent of a subcluster (or a cluster), if there is one, is the unique object denoted by the strict anchors in that subcluster (or cluster).

When assertions (or utterances) are discussed, the discussion often applies only to assertions which reflect the cognizer's beliefs.

68. Even if less prominent.

69. That is, when focusing (and thus the concurrent occurrent thoughts) involves clusters other than the one under consideration.

70. One can focus on matters entirely unrelated to the referential aspects of the particular occurrent belief which concerns us (as ascribers), and to an overwhelming degree. While being fully engaged in putting out a fire, the cognizer may be asked, "Incidentally, is Senator Jackson charming?" A response to a question of this sort, a question entirely unrelated to what he is focusing on at the time (despite the corresponding belief being very briefly occurrent) leaves focusing pretty much irrelevant to the referential aspect of that occurrent belief: this belief's being occurrent is entirely overshadowed by the stream of occurrent thoughts involving the fire. A case like this is akin to cases of nonoccurrent beliefs, where focusing plays no role. Thus, the referential features of nonoccurrent beliefs are manifested in their temporary occurrent phases when focusing (and thus the bulk of the subject's occurrent beliefs) have to do with unrelated concerns (or when focusing is hardly present at all).

71. Those degrees vary with sharpness and intensity. (Recall too the discussion of the Jackson-Jackson example in the previous section.)

72. I would like to acknowledge with gratitude conversations on this subject with Keith Donnellan and David Kaplan. I am also grateful to William Lycan and Eddy Zemach for numerous helpful comments on an earlier draft of this paper. I would like to thank Ariele Lazar and Sergio Tenenbaum for their stimulating comments.

References

Devitt, Michael. 1981. *Designations*. New York.
Donnellan, Keith. 1966. "Reference and Definite Descriptions." *Philosophical Review* 75: 281-304.
Donnellan, Keith. 1979. "Speaker Reference Descriptions and Anaphora." In *Contemporary Perspectives in Philosophy of Language*, edited by P. French et al., 28-41. Minneapolis, Minn.
Field, Hartry. 1973. "Theory Change and the Indeterminacy of Reference." *Journal of Philosophy* 70: 462-81.
Kaplan, David. 1969. "Quantifying in." In *Words and Objections*, edited by D. Davidson and J. Hintikka, 206-42. Dordrecht.
Kripke, Saul. 1979. "Speaker's Reference and Semantic Reference." In *Contemporary Perspectives in Philosophy of Language*, edited by P. French et al., 206-42. Minneapolis, Minn.
Kvart, Igal. 1982. "Quine and Modalities *de re*: A Way Out?" *Journal of Philosophy* 79: 295-328.
Kvart, Igal. 1984. "The Hesperus-Phosphorus Case." *Theoria* 50 (1): 1-35.

Kvart, Igal. 1986a. "Kripke's Belief Puzzle." *Midwest Studies in Philosophy* 10: 287–325.
Kvart, Igal. 1986b. *A Theory of Counterfactuals*. Indianapolis, Ind.
Kvart, Igal. 1986c. "Beliefs and Believing." *Theoria* 52 (3): 129–45.
Kvart, Igal. 1988. "Seeing That." In *Philosophy of Law, Politics, and Society*, edited by Ota Weinberger et al., 314–20. Wien.
Kvart, Igal. 1989. "A Theory of Speaker Reference." *Journal of Philosophy* (forthcoming).
Kvart, Igal. "Seeing that and Seeing as." Forthcoming.
Kvart, Igal. "The Objective Dimension of Believing *de re*." Forthcoming.
Kvart, Igal. "Kripke's Belief Puzzle, Part II." Manuscript.
Kvart, Igal. "Reference and Knowledge." Manuscript.
Lycan, William. 1981. "Form, Function, and Feel." *Journal of Philosophy* 78 (1): 24–50.
Perry, John. 1980. "Belief and Acceptance." *Midwest Studies in Philosophy* 5: 533–42.

A Theory of Reference Transmission and Reference Change[1]
ALAN BERGER

Contemporary philosophers, such as Kripke, Putnam, and others, defend a "new theory of direct reference" for proper names and certain sorts of scientific and natural-kind terms. They reject the view that these terms have senses or (in some cases) that the senses they do have suffice to determine their referents. In their view, the referents of names and certain other sorts of terms are determined directly without the mediation of a "sense." Kripke, in his well-known *Naming And Necessity*, includes such terms among those he calls 'rigid designators', that is, terms that denote the same object in every possible world, or else fail to denote. For, proper names and certain sorts of scientific and natural-kind terms may be said to "rigidly" pick out the same objects as their referents in every possible world in which the objects exist.

A central problem for any theory of reference is how we determine what the referent of a term is. According to the Frege-Russell theory of descriptions, the answer for ordinary proper names is clear: such a name is an abbreviated definite description, and thus the referent of a name is the object that satisfies the description associated with the name. However, if there is no such descriptive content associated with names, then how do we use names to refer to things?

Kripke and Putnam have raised several basic objections to the definite description account of how names and certain other kinds of terms refer. In its place, they sketch what they call a "causal picture" of reference determination. According to that account, names (and certain other kinds of terms) simply refer to what they initially referred to at the time the terms were introduced.

The "causal" view, following Kripke, breaks down the process of reference determination into this initial baptism or "dubbing," which provides the term with a reference, and the subsequent transmission of that reference. Transmission takes place by means of a historical chain of speakers' intentions to use a term to refer to what some previous speaker in the chain referred to by using that term. If we trace back the reference of a term, we arrive eventually at the baptismal step, where the rigid designator term first came to be used to refer to the particular object. The object baptized, or dubbed, at this initial step is the referent of the term.

This account, however, does not include a theory of reference change. As a result, it seems to be vulnerable to certain supposed counterexamples, all of which involve instances of unintended changes in the references of terms.

In this paper, I begin by suggesting a distinction between two ways in which referents of rigid designator terms are determined: the first rests on an intentional notion that I call 'focusing'; the second rests on the semantic notion of 'satisfying-a-given-condition'. With the aid of this distinction, I then develop what I call an *anaphoric* theory of reference transmission and reference change.

In my account of reference transmission, I shall introduce the notion of mode of transmission. I shall argue that certain modes can take precedence over the historical chain in determining a term's reference. In particular, I shall argue that in order for an unintended change of reference to take place, the mode of transmission must be a certain one of the two that rest on the notion of focusing.

My aim here is to preserve the historical chain view of reference determination without, however, requiring that rigid designator terms must in all cases refer to what they referred to at the initial baptismal step. In particular, I seek to show that the historical chain view of reference determination, when supplemented with my theory of reference change, is immune to the purported counterexamples.

A word of caution. For convenience, when we talk of a term undergoing a reference change, we are not talking about the term merely as a *syntactic item*. Rather, what we have in mind is a term individuated by a historical chain of intentions to corefer, going all the way back to and including the initial baptismal step.[2]

I. STYLES OF RIGID DESIGNATION

In *Naming and Necessity*, Kripke mentions two ways in which an object may be initially baptized: "The object may be named by ostension, or the reference of the name may be fixed by a description" (p. 96). Kripke adds (in a footnote): "usually a baptizer is *acquainted* in some sense with the object he names and is able to name it ostensively" (emphasis added).

Let us consider the case in which the referent of the name is initially fixed by ostension. For example, we may name an object by pointing to the heavens and uttering "Let that star be called 'Hesperus'" or by pointing to a baby and uttering "Let this baby be called 'Cicero'."[3]

Now in my view, ostension itself typically involves two aspects. First, the baptizer attends to or, as I say, 'focuses' on a particular thing (or things).

Second, the baptizer generally at the same time employs a description — but a description used ascriptively — not attributively. That is, the baptizer ascribes a certain property to that object, or takes the object to have that property.

This is not to say that the act of baptizing an object by means of focusing necessarily requires perceptual access during the act of dubbing or informational linkage.[4] It is compatible with my notion of dubbing an object by means of focusing that a speaker may do so — even in the absence of the object — provided the speaker had previously focused on the object and is now offering a description (used ascriptively) of the object. In the case of general terms, the speaker may ascriptively describe the term's ostension, "typical" members of which the speaker has focused on previously. What is central about this means of fixing the reference of a term is that its referent (or members of its extension) is in one way or another being determined by perceptual encounters with it.

It should also be noted that in using a description ascriptively, the baptizer may of course be mistaken. Nevertheless, the name whose reference becomes fixed by ostension refers to the particular thing (or things) that is taken to have that property. Thus when we say "There is a very bright star out tonight. Let that star be called 'Hesperus'," the term 'Hesperus' refers to the thing taken to be a star whether the thing in question is or is not a star.

Now it is the *focusing* on an object, as distinguished from *taking some thing as having a certain property*, that generally plays the principal role in fixing reference by ostension. The ascribing of some property to the thing usually serves only to indicate or draw attention to the thing the speaker wishes to focus on.[5]

A speaker may be aware of several descriptions that are taken to apply to the thing focused on, any one of which may serve to draw attention to the thing. Later speakers may never be aware of what properties were previously ascribed to the referent; yet as long as they know what object was focused on in using the term, they can determine the reference of the term. They may not know whether, at the time the planet Venus was baptized with the name 'Hesperus', the property ascribed to it was the property 'the star first seen in the evening' or 'the star that can be seen at the latest time of the morning' or, whether what occurred was merely a pointing to a certain region of the sky and the uttering of "that star." As long as they know what object (e.g., Venus) the community focused on in using the term, they know the reference of the term.

According to the historical chain view, then, for any term whose referent was focused on when the object was dubbed with the term, we can determine the reference by means of a historical chain. The chain goes back to the initial dubbing of the referent focused on. And the links in the chain are speakers' intentions, when using the term, to corefer, that is, to use the term with the same reference as the person from whom the speaker acquired the term.[6] It is not required that a speaker, when transmitting the reference of a term, focus on or could ever have focused on the referent of the term. Thus reference determination for this sort of term requires only that the referent of the term was focused on previously.

Any term whose reference for a given linguistic community is obtained by focusing on a thing taken as having one or another property, I shall call an *F-type term*. The process of determining reference in this manner, I shall call *F-style rigid designation*.

This notion of '*F*-type term' does not require, however, that the reference of an *F*-type term must have been initially fixed by means of focusing. Later, we shall see that certain terms, initially fixed by description, may later have their reference fixed for a linguistic community by means of focusing. These terms are thus *F*-type terms, even though initially they were not.

Every *F*-type term is linked to one or more background statements by a historical chain of intentions to corefer. These background statements play a central role in initially determining the term's reference. In the example above, such statements are, "There is (something taken to be) a very bright star out tonight" and "Let that star be called 'Hesperus' ". Statements of this sort we shall call *anaphoric background statements*, and the anaphoric background statements of an *F*-type term we shall call the *A-B-F* statements of that term. So much for F-style rigid designation.

The second style, which we shall call *S-style rigid designation*, employs descriptions used attributively — Kripke's second way to fix the referent of a name.

When a description is used attributively to fix the reference, the referent of the description is whatever object actually satisfies that description. For example, the expression 'the actual murderer, whoever that person may be, of the shortest Soviet spy' refers to whoever actually murdered the shortest Soviet spy. Now in such a case we may have no knowledge, not even a clue, as to who this murderer is. Still we may give a name to the murderer as follows: "Let us call the (actual) murderer of the shortest Soviet spy 'John Doe.'" If we assume that the context of this utterance is the actual world, 'John Doe' rigidly denotes whoever actually satisfies that description. For even if we say counterfactually "Had John Doe been bought off by the Soviet Union, he would not have murdered the shortest Soviet spy," still 'John Doe' refers to the actual murderer if there is one.

Kripke uses the case of 'Neptune' to illustrate how the reference of a name may be fixed by an attributive use of a definite description. Neptune was hypothesized as the planet that caused such and such discrepancies in the orbits of certain other planets. To quote Kripke, "If Leverrier indeed gave the name 'Neptune' to the planet before it was ever seen, then he fixed the reference of 'Neptune' by means of the description just mentioned."[7] For at that time, there was no heavenly body that could be seen (even with a telescope) or taken to satisfy the description. In other words, *F*-style rigid designation would not have been possible at that time.

Thus it is necessary to recognize that there are cases in which the fixing of a term's reference is based on what in fact satisfies the given description rather than on any ostension, or focusing. In these cases, the reference of the term is not grounded on focusing on a particular object, or on "ostending" that object. We are not focusing on some thing as the referent of a description and then naming it (while taking it to satisfy the description regardless of whether it does in fact satisfy the description).

What is important about fixing the reference of rigid designators by the attributive use of definite descriptions is that the terms so introduced rigidly denote whatever objects actually turn out to satisfy the decriptions (in a given context of use). Such terms may be thought of as designating or referring to a satisfier of the open sentence formed by removing a quantifier from a bound variable sentence.[8] For example, suppose a speaker says that some woman (or other) will be the forty-first president of the United States, and continues with "She will be a Democrat. Let that woman—whoever she may be—be called 'Alice'." The pronoun 'she' in this context does not refer to any particular person being focused on or taken under consideration. Yet the pronoun does act as a rigid designator referring to the satisfier of the matrix of the following bound variable sentence:

$(\exists!x)A(x$ is a woman & $x = $ 41st president of the United States & (x is a Democrat)), where 'A' stands for the actuality operator (to be read 'it is actually the case that').[9]

In the case of terms of this sort, a speaker may never be aware of what actual description, attributively used, was initially employed to fix the reference. A speaker may not know, for example, what description was initially given in fixing the reference of 'Neptune'. Nonetheless, if the reference of the term is fixed by the original description, its reference is grounded in, or rests on, a description used attributively.

Any term whose reference is obtained by letting the referent be whatever actually satisfies a given description, we shall call an *S-type term*. This manner of determining the reference of a term, we shall call *S-style of rigid designation*. The anaphoric background statements that play a central role in initially determining the reference of *S*-type terms, we shall call their *A-B-S* statements. In the above example, the pair, "Some woman will be the forty-first president of the United States" and "Let that woman—whoever she may be—be called 'Alice' " are the *A-B-S* statements.

II. A THEORY OF REFERENCE TRANSMISSION AND REFERENCE CHANGE

Our aim in the remainder of this paper is to use the distinction between *F*-style and *S*-style rigid designation to develop what we shall call an *anaphoric* theory of reference transmission and reference change for rigid designator terms. We shall formulate a necessary condition for a rigid designator term to undergo an unintended reference change, that is, for the term to acquire a different referent at a given stage in its reference transmission from the one it had initially or previously. We shall also suggest the sort of conditions that, in conjunction with the necessary condition, would provide for a variety of situations, the desired necessary and sufficient conditions for reference change.

In addition to the notion of anaphoric background statement, we shall also make use of the notion of an *anaphoric chain* and the notion of a chain being *grounded* in an object. An anaphoric chain is a chain of communication where each link consists of speakers' intentions to corefer. A term is passed on from link to link by means of a mode of transmission going back to the object, if any, to which the term refers or to the relevant anaphoric background statements otherwise. If the anaphoric chain ultimately goes back to an object initially baptized with that term, we say that the chain is *grounded* in that object.[10]

§ I. Reference transmission for F-type terms

First, let us examine how we transmit the reference of an *F*-type term. This takes place in two ways. To illustrate them, let us consider two cases, one in which we cannot currently focus on the referent of the term, the other in which we can.

Take, for example, the *F*-type term 'Aristotle'. Obviously since Aristotle has long been dead, there is no object that we can *now focus* on and call 'Aristotle'. There is no entity that any member of the community can point to and refer to by direct ostension or by a demonstrative (excluding, of course, deferred ostension). Moreover, no one around today was once acquainted with Aristotle or was once able to refer to him by direct ostension. So even though the term 'Aristotle' may have been introduced at the initial baptism stage by an ordinary focusing on the object, the current transmission of its reference cannot take place by focusing on the term's referent.

Instead, when we transmit the reference of the name 'Aristotle', we do so by giving a definite or indefinite description. We may say something like "Aristotle was a famous Greek philosopher who wrote the *Nicomachean Ethics*." But for reasons now well known,[11] this description does not give the meaning of the term 'Aristotle'. In fact, it does not even fix the reference of the term 'Aristotle'. We do not say "Let the famous Greek philosopher, whoever that person is, who wrote the Nicomachean Ethics, be called 'Aristotle'." For we agree that we may discover that Aristotle did not write the *Nicomachean Ethics*, or that he was not a philosopher or even that he was not Greek. Similar remarks apply, or course, to any description that a speaker might use when intending to corefer with other members of the linguistic community when they use the term 'Aristotle'.

How, then, is a description used to transmit the reference of 'Aristotle'? The description is used to indicate something the speaker or the linguistic community, by and large, believes is true of the referent of the term. By the use of a description, then, a speaker helps indicate which historical chain (of intentions to corefer) he is on when he uses a given occurrence of the term 'Aristotle'. The historical chain enables us to determine the referent of the name 'Aristotle'. But the use of a *definite* description helps indicate whom the speaker or the linguistic community believes is the referent of the term. Thus in transmitting the reference of the *F*-type term, 'Aristotle', we may use a definite description as follows: 'Aristotle' denotes whomever the historical chain of intentions to corefer ultimately goes back to, whoever that may be, and we *take* it that that person is the famous Greek philosopher who wrote the *Nicomachean Ethics*.

Perhaps a person can succeed in referring even if there is no description, definite or indefinite, that the speaker takes or knows his community takes to be true of the referent of the term, 'Aristotle'. But to say the least, the speaker would have a very limited ability to use the name. If asked, "To whom do you refer when you use the term 'Aristotle'?" the speaker may simply reply, "To whomever the speaker from whom I acquired the name intended to refer to with that name." The speaker would not even be able to distinguish the use of certain phonetic sounds to refer to the philosopher from the use of those same sounds to refer to the shipping magnate. Supposed a speaker (or a linguistic community) has knowledge of an indefinite description taken to be true of the referent determined by one historical chain but not by the other. This would at least suffice to determine, for a given occasion of use, along which chain the term passed.[12]

This account describes the way in which the reference of an *F*-type rigid designator term is commonly transmitted. We use the term 'Aristotle' to refer to the individual who was initially baptized with this term. But a linguistic community is not often in an epistemic situation in which it can focus on the referent of a term. Where this is the case, community members can usually help indicate what it is that they are referring to by using ascriptively one or more descriptions that they currently *take* the referent to satisfy. By using these descriptions, the speaker who is passing on the term directs attention to the specific historical chain (of speakers' intentions to corefer) along which the term is being passed. The specific chain, in turn, enables us to determine the referent of the given term.

This mode of transmitting reference, we shall call 'mock-focusing'. It is a process by which community members pass a given *F*-type term, say 'Aristotle', along a historical chain of speakers' intentions to corefer; and they do so by ascribing to Aristotle what may not in fact be true of him. This ascriptive use of descriptions, in passing the term along the chain, plays a central role in determining the particular historical chain along which the term is being passed. By means of this process, the community passes the term 'Aristotle' from link to link along an anaphoric chain that is grounded in the object focused on at the baptismal step. Thus reference determination for terms whose reference is transmitted by "mock-focusing" rests ultimately on an actual focusing.

Consider next the case in which we can focus on the referent of an *F*-type term, say, 'Alan Berger'. How does a community transmit the reference of this term? Here the referent is still alive. People can, and do, focus on the referent. They focus on him by pointing to him and referring to him by direct ostension or by a demonstrative. In that sense we may say that various members of the community are acquainted with him.

To be sure, not all focusings by community members will count as correct focusings on the referent of this or any other term. There are many focusings that the community will not accept as reliable. But various members of the community count as experts in focusing on the referent of a term. In the case of 'Alan Berger', they would include the referent's immediate family, close personal friends, and so on. When in doubt, it is usually focusings by these experts to which the community defers.

Furthermore, a description, definite or indefinite, may accompany a focusing on an object in transmitting the reference of a term. An example might be "Alan Berger is the guy in the room pounding away at the typewriter." A description used in transmitting reference by focusing serves merely to help convey which object is being focused on. It does not matter whether or not the description is true of the object, as long as it helps indicate which object is being focused on. The desription is used merely ascriptively.

Of course, members of a community do not always focus on the referent of the *F*-type term, 'Alan Berger', when they currently transmit its reference. Usually they rely on descriptions, such as 'the author of this manuscript'. This does not mean, however, that the transmission of the reference of the term 'Alan Berger' occurs in a mock-focusing way, as it does in the case of the transmission of the term 'Aristotle'. One important difference is that whereas no one around today is or has been acquainted with Aristotle, people living today are and have been acquainted with Alan Berger. Hence, for the term 'Aristotle', the community can rely only on a description used ascriptively to transmit the term's referent. On the other hand, a linguistic community is not forced to rely only on the mock-focusing mode when transmitting the reference of the term 'Alan Berger'. For, both the referent and the experts on focusing on the referent are available to the community. Hence it may transmit the term's reference by focusing on the referent.

This mode of transmitting reference, we shall call 'genuine focusing'. It is a process through which a linguistic community passes an *F*-type term along a historical chain (of speakers' intentions to corefer) by means of currently focusing on an object — an object that the community takes to be the referent of the term. Through this process, the community passes the *F*-type term from link to link along an anaphoric chain that is grounded in the object focused on at the baptismal step.

Now when both genuine and mock-focusing modes of transmission are available to a linguistic community, the object taken to satisfy a description used in transmitting the reference of a term by means of a mock-focusing may differ from the object currently focused on when transmitting the reference of the term by means of a genuine focusing. For example, suppose we use the description 'the author of this manuscript' in transmitting the reference of the term 'Alan Berger' by means of a mock-focusing. Then, the object taken to satisfy this description may not be the person focused on when we transmit the reference by means of a genuine focusing. In that case, the mode of transmission used by the linguistic community is either *genuine focusing* or *mock-focusing*, depending upon which of the two the community relies on during a given period of time in transmitting the term's reference (i.e., counts during that time as determining the correct referent of the term).

Furthermore, where both modes are available, and the objects determined by the mock-focusing and the genuine focusing differ, the community as a rule does not rely on mock-focusing. Usually the community defers to the focusings carried out by those who are "focusing experts" with respect to the referent of that term. Recall that the use of descriptions with F-type terms is always merely ascriptive: to communicate what we currently take to be the referent of the term. That is, these descriptions help indicate which object we are focusing on in the case of a genuine focusing or to indicate which historical chain the term is passed along in the case of a mock-focusing. Thus the genuine focusing mode of transmission takes precedence over the mock-focusing mode in determining the term's referent for a linguistic community. When an F-type term can be transmitted by both modes, and thus the possibility arises of disagreement concerning the referent, we shall assume that the community will rely on genuine focusing as determinative and thus that the mode of transmission for the community is a genuine focusing.

§ II. *Reference change for* F-*type terms*

We shall now formulate and apply a necessary condition for reference change of F-type rigid designator terms: An F-type term can undergo an unintended change in reference at a particular stage in the transmission of its reference only if at that stage the term's reference is transmitted by a genuine focusing on a new referent. Here, current or later focusings can dominate over previous or even initial focusings in determining the term's referent. This condition holds regardless of whether the F-type term is a singular or a general term. Later, we shall suggest the sort of conditions that, taken with this necessary condition, provide necessary and sufficient conditions for a change in reference of an F-type term.

Before we do so, however, let us note and discard two kinds of situations in which we loosely speak of reference change. First, there is the situation in which we incorrectly introduce a term from one language into another. In such a case, there are no rules governing the kind of mistakes that we can make. F-type terms can become S-type terms, singular terms can become general, etc. The anaphoric chain of the term is broken when it is mistranslated; when it is introduced into another language, a new anaphoric background statement is introduced for the term.[13]

REFERENCE TRANSMISSION AND REFERENCE CHANGE 189

Second, an *F*-type term may at some point come to acquire a mythic or fictional character as its referent, as for example the term 'Santa Claus'. Such cases involve what I would call domain shifts from the actual world to a fictional world.

Let us begin our discussion by considering three examples of (unintended) reference change. Since the historical account of reference determination lacks a theory of reference change, these examples can be cited as counterexamples to that account.

First, I want to show that all three examples of reference change satisfy the necessary condition stated above for an *F*-type term to undergo a change in reference. Second, I want to suggest the kinds of things that, in conjunction with this necessary condition, would supply sufficient conditions as well. Finally, I conclude that the historical chain view of reference determination, when supplemented with my theory of reference change, is immune to these three purported counterexamples.

First, there is Gareth Evans's well-known 'Madagascar case'.[14] According to him, 'Madagascar' was a native name for a part of the continent of Africa. Marco Polo erroneously took the natives to be using that name to refer to an island off the coast of Africa. Today the term is so widely used as a name for the island that this usage has overriden the earlier historical connection to the referent assigned to 'Madagascar' at the initial baptism.

In this case, we have an *F*-type singular term. At a certain stage in the transmission of its reference there is a genuine focusing not on its original (or previous) referent, but on an island off the coast of Africa. Subsequently, the mode of transmission of the reference of 'Madagascar' continued to be a genuine focusing — but we focus on the island now taken to be the referent of the term 'Madagascar'. Thus the necessary condition for reference change formulated above is fulfilled.

It is true that most of us have never seen the island of Madagascar and can pick it out and transmit the term only by description — at best, we can find the place on a map and then describe its location at such and such a longitude and latitude. But the community at large does not in general rely on these descriptions to determine the referent of this term. Hence the current mode of transmission of the term is not a mock-focusing as in the case of 'Aristotle'. There, the term refers to the thing focused on initially. Here, if an individual who has never seen Madagascar transmits the reference in what seems to be a mock-focusing manner, this mode is not what the community relies on in transmitting the reference of 'Madagascar'. On the contrary, the community relies on its focusing experts — the geographers and the travellers — for the correct transmission of the term's reference. And these experts, in turn, rely ultimately on their focusings when they transmit the reference of the term. In transmitting the reference of 'Madagascar', they focus on a place that they take as having, say, a certain latitude and longitude. The experts may, of course, be mistaken in what they ascribe to Madagascar. For example, geological shifts may take place; the position of a whole continent may change.

This may affect the latitude and longitude of Madagascar. Nonetheless, for the lingustic community the current stage in the transmission of the term's reference, as determined by experts, rests on a genuine focusing.

So much for the necessary condition in the Madagascar case. We suggest that conditions that, together with the necessary condition, would give us necessary and sufficient conditions, should be sought in various social and legal conventions (for example, those governing the selection and status of names), special interests that attach to certain kinds of referents, the time period during which a community focuses (genuinely) on the new referent and the like.

As a second example, let us imagine that at the initial baptism of the word 'water' all the lakes, rivers, oceans, and so on were filled with the substance xyz and the clear liquid that people drank and bathed in was xyz, and so on, instead of H_2O, where xyz is the name for a substance whose molecular structure is not identical with H_2O, but which has all the phenomenal qualities of H_2O (as described in Putnam's famous twin earth example.)[15] In the course of natural change, xyz was replaced everywhere on earth by H_2O. But the community continued to use the term 'water' to refer to the present stuff in the lakes and the present clear liquid that we drink and so on. Thus this use of the term 'water' came to override the original use of the term 'water'.

This example is better than the 'Madagascar case' since it does not depend upon adopting a term into our language. The introduction by adoption of the term into our language could be considered a second baptism, and would thus be counted as a new term rather than as a change of reference.

Note that not only is the term 'water' an F-type term, but, the current mode of transmission of 'water' is a genuine focusing. Even now when we currently transmit the term, we still focus on samplings of water when we point to a certain clear, odorless liquid that we drink or to the lakes, rivers, and oceans around us.

As in the case of the singular term 'Alan Berger', so, too, with the natural-kind term 'water', we do not always focus on the referent when we currently transmit the reference of the term 'water'. Sometimes we rely on descriptions, such as those above ("clear, odorless, liquid"), to transmit the reference of the term. This does not, however, make the current mode of transmission a mock-focusing, as is the case with the term 'Aristotle'. Again, a basic difference is that while no one around today is or has been acquainted with Aristotle, the same cannot be said of water. Again, should the samplings taken to satisfy the description used in transmitting the term 'water' by means of a mock-focusing differ from samplings currently focused on by community experts in transmitting this term, it is the focusing by experts to which the community would defer.

Now in the "initially xyz" case, what happens is that the thing taken to have these properties (i.e., the thing initially taken to have the properties of being a clear, odorless liquid filling the lakes, rivers, etc.) is no longer the thing that we currently take to have these properties. The thing that we now take to have these properties is phenomenally indentical with the thing we initially took to have these properties. But the thing that we currently focus on has a different structure and therefore is not the same thing that we initially focused on.

Note that our necessary condition stated above for a term changing its referent has been met: the term 'water' is F-type and its current mode of transmission is a genuine focusing. Our community interest in focusing on the thing that we currently take to have these properties overrides the fact that initially the term had a different referent. Our social interests, such as our interests in the thing we currently take to be a clear liquid, etc., together with the long lapse of time since the initial baptism, give us a sufficient condition for the term having a change in reference from the initial baptismal step.

Finally, as a third example, we draw on Putnam's case of imaginary twin earth. Let us imagine that while on earth originally all the lakes, etc., were filled with H_2O and the clear liquid that we drank and bathed in was H_2O, on twin earth the lakes, rivers, etc., were originally filled with xyz and our twin-earthian counterparts bathed in and drank the clear liquid xyz. Suppose further that although our science of space travel has advanced immensely, and we have had interplanetary travel with twin-earthians, no one has yet discovered the molecular structure of the stuff that was originally in the lakes, etc., on earth or the stuff originally on twin earth. Now also imagine that it has become a common practice for earthians and twin-earthians to trade back and forth in "water." (There is a snooty part of twin-earth, for example, that bottles its water for only $1.50 a bottle. They call it 'Perrier'.) Later, after a *widespread* mixing of the two liquids had occurred, it was discovered that what we call 'water' has two molecular structures, H_2O and xyz. In such a situation, since both molecular structures are present in abundance and since we referred to both as 'water' prior to the discovery that there are two structures, it is natural to think that our term 'water' would still continue to refer to both H_2O and xyz despite the initial baptism of the term 'water' on earth. (The case can be made more emphatically if we imagine that on earth there were plentiful quantities of several chemically different liquids all phenomenally like water.)

Perhaps we might distinguish the two molecular structures for water as we presently distinguish between "heavy" water, or deuterium (which has an extra neutron in its hydrogen atoms) and regular water. But, nevertheless, we still refer to both structures by the generic name 'water', and I surmise that we would do the same in the situation described above.

Once again, we have an F-type term, 'water', transmitted by a community through a genuine focusing. Here, again, our necessary condition is met for a change in reference from that of the initial baptismal step. The word 'water', which initially referred by genuine focusing to H_2O now refers by genuine focusing to either or both H_2O and xyz. And once the necessary condition has been met, social factors would seem to provide sufficient conditions for the change in reference from the initial baptismal step. We are unable to distinguish which microstructure was initially dubbed with the term 'water'.

There is an abundance of the stuff around us that we currently focus on, and our interest is in this stuff, whether it has one microstructure or two. Finally, there is a long-term history in our linguistic community of referring to both H_2O and xyz as 'water'.

§ III. Reference transmission for S-type terms

Thus far, we have discussed F-type terms with a genuine focusing mode of transmission and have formulated a necessary condition for reference change for such terms. We now examine whether the same necessary condition can be extended to S-type terms as well.

We begin by discussing briefly the transmission of reference for S-type terms. Recall that an S-type term is a rigid designator term whose referent is the satisfier of the open sentence formed by removing an existential quantifier from the term's A-B-S sentence. In part I, we gave as an example of A-B-S sentences the following pair.

> Some woman — or other — will be the forty-first president of the United States.

> Let that woman — whoever she may be — be called 'Alice'.

Here 'Alice' is an S-type singular term whose referent is the satisfier of the above existential statement.

Now one obvious, indeed, usual way in which the reference of an S-type term gets transmitted is by the attributive use of a description. Often we take the description used in the existential A-B-S sentence itself as the description used in transmitting the reference of the S-type term.[16] In answering the question, "Who is Alice?" we may say "She is whichever woman will be the forty-first president of the United States." That is to say,

(1) $(\exists x)$ (x is a woman & x = the forty-first president of the United States & (x = Alice))

Note that in this case, unlike reference transmission by genuine focusing or mock-focusing, the description itself is used attributively, its context of use is extensional. Thus the referent of an S-type term (here, 'Alice') must satisfy the description used in its A-B-S sentence.[17] For Alice is simply whoever satisfies that sentence.

This mode of transmitting S-type terms we shall call purely descriptive. It is in sharp contrast with the two modes of transmission — genuine focusing and mock-focusing — discussed above. For example, when we transmit the reference of the F-type term 'Aristotle' in a mock-focusing manner, the description is embedded in a nonextensional context. Letting Jones be the speaker, we have in contrast with (1) above:

(2) Jones takes it that: $(\exists x)$ (x = Aristotle & x = the famous Greek philosopher who wrote the *Nicomachean Ethics*).

In (2), we may discover that we are wrong in ascribing one or all of these properties to Aristotle.

It should be noted that the distinction between an *F*-type term and an *S*-type term is a distinction between two ways of determining the reference of a term: if the reference of a term is determined by an epistemic condition, the term is *F*-type; if by a satisfaction condition, the term is *S*-type.

Further, when a term initially introduced as an *S*-type term (say, 'Neptune') is later transmitted by the linguistic community through a genuine focusing, the referent is no longer determined by the initial satisfaction condition. The community will now determine the referent of the term by the epistemic condition of focusing on the object. Thus what is initially an *S*-type term may cease to be an *S*-type term if at a given stage in the transmission of its reference, the reference is transmitted by means of a genuine focusing. Regardless of how the term was initially introduced, we shall then say that at that stage in the transmission of the term, the term is *F*-type.

§ *IV. Reference change for* S-*type terms: Singular terms*

We turn now to the question of reference change for *S*-type terms. Our thesis is that an *S*-type term may undergo a reference change only if it changes in reference when transmitted by means of a genuine focusing, as described above for *F*-type terms.

It should also be pointed out that apart from changes in status and changes in reference, *S*-type terms often undergo changes in the "terms themselves." That is, different *A-B-S* sentences come to be associated with the same syntactic item. (An *S*-type term may undergo such a change when it is transmitted in a mode where the description relied on in that transmission is used ascriptively, that is, the description need not necessarily be true of the referent. Such a mode, I call 'mock-satisfying'.[18]) Thus, the only way a term can undergo a change in reference (as distinguished from a change in the term itself) is when it is transmitted by means of a genuine focusing.

We wish to illustrate how an *S*-type singular term may change its status to an *F*-type term and undergo a reference change. Let us consider the introduction of the name 'Neptune'. Recall that Neptune was hypothesized as the planet that caused such and such discrepancies in the orbits of certain other planets. At that time, there was no object that both satisfied the description and could be focused on with the aid of existing telescopes. Thus the term 'Neptune' was introduced at the baptismal step as an *S*-type term. Although there is no focusing on an object at this initial stage, the term is a rigid designator denoting whatever actually satisfies the description.

Later on, however, after the development of more sophisticated telescopes, it becomes possible to focus on a heavenly body that we take to satisfy the above description. That heavenly body we call 'Neptune'. The reference of the term 'Neptune' then becomes transmitted by focusing on the object that we take to satisfy the above description. After a while, the community, when transmitting the reference of the term 'Neptune' begins to rely more on the *focusings* on the object rather than on the original description used when the term 'Neptune' was introduced. At this stage, the transmission for the community of the reference of the term 'Neptune' occurs through a genuine focusing. Thus far, what has changed is the term's status from a *S*-type to *F*-type and the mode of transmission, not necessarily the reference. (In fact, that is pretty much our current situation.)

Now suppose that we discover that, in point of fact, we were wrong in thinking that the heavenly body focused on is the planet that caused such and such discrepancies in the orbits of certain other planets, and that some other planet satisfies this description. It does not seem likely to me that our newspapers and television would then report this new discovery as the "true" discovery of the planet Neptune (that is, they would not say that Neptune is the planet that caused such and such discrepancies in the orbits of certain other planets and that we have now discovered Neptune to be a different planet than the one we focus on and take to satisfy the above description). Rather, it seems to me that we would still call the original planet focused on 'Neptune', despite the fact that it fails to satisfy the above definite description; and the planet that does satisfy the above description we would call something else. Newspapers and television would more likely report this new discovery as the true discovery of the planet that causes such and such discrepancies in the orbits of certain other planets and would report the discovery that our long-held belief about Neptune being the cause of these discrepancies is erroneous.

The reason why we would have a change in the reference of the term 'Neptune' from its original reference (i.e., to the satisfier of the *A-B-S* sentence) is twofold: first, in the current stage in transmission, the reference of the term is transmitted through a genuine focusing; thus the necessary condition for reference change is fulfilled. Second, the long period of time in which reference transmission for 'Neptune' is through a genuine focusing along with various other social factors supply additional conditions which together with the necessary conditions provide the sufficient conditions as well.

§ *V. Reference change of* S-*type terms: General terms*

We turn next to a discussion of reference change in the case of *S*-type general terms. Take, for example, the term 'mass'. We first describe how the term is used in Newtonian Mechanics. We then consider a hypothetical situation in which certain discoveries could have led to a change in the reference of this term.[19]

In his *Lectures In Physics*, the distinguished Nobel Laureate Physicist, Richard Feynman, describes mass as "the quantity (measure) of how hard it is to get something (some physical thing) going."[20] Just how hard it is to get something going, i.e., the property of resisting acceleration (or change in dynamic state) is what we call 'inertia'. Thus mass is a quantitative measure of the inertia of an object. I take these statements to be or to approximate the

A-B-S statements for the terms 'mass' and 'inertia' and to describe their interrelationship as these terms are used in Newtonian Mechanics. I view these terms as *S*-type general terms: mass is whatever quantity satisfies the condition '*x* is the measure of how hard it is to get something going', i.e., '*x* is the measure of resistance to acceleration'; inertia is whatever property satisfies the condition '*x* is the property of a physical thing being more or less hard to get going', i.e., '*x* is the property of resisting acceleration'. The picture presented in Newtonian Mechanics is clear: physical objects have a certain intrinsic resistance to movement or change of movement, i.e., a resistance that is independent both of any forces acting on the object and of its acceleration. Since the force acting on an object can be used to measure how hard it is to get something going, when no other forces are acting on the object and the object is moving at a constant velocity, we can say that the mass of an object is the amount of force needed to overcome its inertia.

Now let us consider a hypothetical situation in order to see how the reference of the *S*-type general term 'mass' can change. Imagine twin-earthians who live in a world governed by the same laws of Newtonian Mechanics that govern our world and who accept Newton's Laws of Motion. They introduce their term 'mass' by the *A-B-S* statement "Mass is the amount of force needed to get an object going," and they are aware that the *A-B-S* sentence holds only when there are no other forces acting on the object and the object is moving at constant velocity. Note that their term 'mass' is an *S*-type general term. Now suppose either that there is no place other than twin earth in the universe, i.e., there are no other heavenly bodies, etc., or that twin-earthians do not postulate universal forces that apply to other regions of the universe. We make this last disjunctive assumption in order to block deriving Newton's Law of Gravitational Forces ($F = {^a}m_1{^m}2/r^2$) using Newton's second law of motion, ($F = ma$). In order to derive Newton's law of Gravitational Forces from his second law of motion, we need to make two additional assumptions: first, we need Kepler's Laws in order to calculate what acceleration and force there must be to hold the planets in their elliptical orbits; second, we need the assumption that there are universal forces. Finally, we shall also assume that twin earth is a perfect sphere so that the same body always receives the same acceleration due to gravity on different parts of twin earth's surface.

Given the hypothetical situation, the above two assumptions would not be available to twin-earthians. Thus they would not be able to distinguish between what we call 'mass' and what we call 'weight'. Hence, they would not be able to determine which of the two, if any, is the satisfier of the twin-earthian's *A-B-S* statement that introduces their term 'mass'.

As a matter of historical fact, Galileo, Descartes, Leibniz, and even Huygens had no clear conception of mass. "*Weight* and *mass* were taken interchangeably; these terms were one and the same thing. The real distinction between the two became evident when it was discovered that the same body may receive different accelerations by gravity on different parts of the earth's surface."[21] Newton, in his extension of the laws of dynamics to heavenly bodies clearly perceived the distinction between 'mass' and 'weight'.[22] Newton's extension of these laws thus delimited the class of satisfiers of the S-type term 'mass'. Future twin-earthian theories or extensions of their theories (say, by accepting the existence of universal forces) might enable twin-earthians to make this distinction and to discover that it is mass and not weight that satisfies their term 'mass'.

Now imagine that at some later stage, the twin-earthians develop operational procedures, such as the use of scales, that enable them to measure easily the quantity they *take* to be the amount of force needed "to get an object going." Although the determinable quantity, weight, may not be something with which we are directly acquainted, the determinate feature that is the particular weight of a given object is epistemically accessible to us. We may take that determinate feature, say, the weight of a given object, to be that amount of force needed "to get *that* object going." The twin-earthians, of course, believe they are measuring the "mass" of the object. Since the new procedure is so easy, it can be quickly and widely adapted, it requires merely focusing on meter readings, etc. Thus the new stage in the transmission of the reference of the term 'mass' for twin-earthians takes place through a genuine focusing. Since the new procedure can be carried out so easily, in the course of time the term 'mass' comes to refer to what we would call an object's 'weight on the twin earth'. Thus our hypothetical example illustrates how an S-type general term can undergo a change in reference, and that when such a change takes place, it does so through a genuine focusing.[23]

We are now in a position to draw several conclusions from the hypothetical twin earth case. First, observe that, as we described the case, initially the twin-earthians' laws are the same as ours, and yet the referent of their term 'mass' is not the same as ours. Their term 'mass' at this stage refers to what we would call 'weight on twin earth'. Indeed, Newton's laws of dynamics would remain the same as they currently are even if he had not postulated the existence of universal forces and even if he had not been aware of a distinction between 'mass' and 'weight'. Newton and many of his predecessors would have had to rely on future theory to learn the referent of their term 'mass'. Here the moral is: Contrary to a current view, we cannot simply look at *just* the laws of a given theory to determine the referents, let alone the meanings, of the terms in that theory. For in the case described above, the laws are the same as ours, and yet the referent of their term 'mass' differs from the referent of our term 'mass'.

Second, observe that even in cases where the laws express identities, and where these identity statements, such as '$p = mv$' (where 'p' denotes momentum) contain terms that seem to have a unique reference, there can still be more than one satisfier for a given term in the identity statement. In the hypothetical case of Newton and in the actual case of many of his predecessors listed above, as well as in the twin earth case prior to the use of procedures to measure how hard it is to get an object going, both quantities, 'weight' and 'mass', satisfy the above identity statement for the term 'm'. Future theories or statements can reduce the class of satisfiers of the term to a unique satisfier. For example, twin-earthians may later come to believe that there are heavenly bodies and that their laws apply to the entire universe. Such a development would prevent the quantity, weight, from satisfying, say, the above equation '$p = mv$'.

Thus the example of mass illustrates how an S-type general term may undergo a reference change if (i) its status is changed to that of an F-type term and (ii) its reference is then transmitted by means of a genuine focusing.

Notes

1. This paper is an adaptation of the first two chapters of my forthcoming book, *Terms And Truth* (Cambridge, Mass.).
2. See Saul Kripke, *Naming And Necessity* (Cambridge, Mass., 1980) 8n. There he suggests adopting the terminology that "uses of phonetically the same sounds to name distinct objects count as distinct names." See also Michael Devitt, *Designation* (New York, 1981).
3. Of course, I am not claiming that the planet Venus was named 'Hesperus' that way or that the person who denounced Cataline was named 'Cicero' that way. These are only meant as illustrations of how demonstrative pronouns are used to help fix the reference of a proper name by ostension.
4. For an interesting discussion on information-linkage, see Gareth Evans, *The Varieties Of Reference* (Oxford, 1982).
5. See chapter 2 of *Terms and Truth* for further refinements concerning fixing the reference of a term by means of focusing.
6. See Kripke, *Naming and Necessity*, 96.
7. Ibid., 79n.
8. In *Terms and Truth*, where we present a formal semantics for these terms we find that this statement about the reference of such terms is accurate only for singly quantified existential sentences.
9. For purposes of the present discussion, I formalize the rigidity of the variable with an actuality operator, but I do not necessarily wish to do so. See *Terms and Truth* for detail.
10. A more precise formal account of an anaphoric chain and grounding is presented in *Terms and Truth*.
11. See Kripke, *Naming and Necessity*.
12. See Edward Erwin, Lowell Kleiman, and Eddy Zemach, "The Historical Theory of Reference," *Australasian Journal of Philosophy* 54 (1976): 50-57, for a problem with viewing these chains as just causal chains. According to them, if such chains are merely causal, we would have no way of distinguishing which causal chain we are on for a given occurrence of a phonetic name.
13. Strictly speaking, given our notion of a term as individuated by a historical chain of intentions to corefer, going all the way back to and including the initial baptismal step, the case described above is not a case of reference change; rather, it is a change in the term.
14. See Evans, "The Causal Theory of Names," *Aristotelian Society* 47 (1973): 187-208.
15. See Putnam, "The Meaning of 'Meaning' " in *Philosophical Papers II: Mind, Language, and Reality* (Cambridge, 1975) 215-71, and "Meaning and Reference" in *Journal of Philosophy* 70 (November 8): 699-711.
16. An S-type term need not be transmitted by means of using the original description used with its A-B-S sentence. Moreover, an S-type term may be transferred by

means of a description that the referent of the term does *not* satisfy. Neither of these points need concern us here. For further details, see *Terms and Truth*.

17. As is pointed out in *Terms and Truth*, we must also allow for what I call a mock-satisfying mode of transmission. There the description occurring with the S-type term's *A-B-S* sentence need not be used attributively.

18. A discussion of this phenomenon, often called "conceptual change," goes beyond the scope of this article. For details, see *Terms and Truth*.

19. In *Terms and Truth*, we compare the term's referent in Newtonian Mechanics and in Relativity Theory and we argue that in both theories the referent is the same.

20. Richard Feynman, *Lectures In Physics* (Reading, Mass., 1963), 9-1, 9-2.

21. Florian Cajori, *A History Of Physics* (New York, 1962), 60.

22. Ernst Mach, "On the Part Played by Accident in Invention and Discovery," *Monist* 6: 166.

23. The determinate weight of a given object may arguably be considered an S-type term since it is a borderline case whether we can focus on a determinate weight. If one takes this line, I would then maintain that we achieved a reference change by mock-satisfying. This would then lead to a change in their concept 'mass' to 'the quantity measured by such and such meter readings and scales'. For details on reference change based upon mock-satisfying, see *Terms and Truth*.

On Synonymy and Ontic Modalities
ANDRZEJ ZABLUDOWSKI

It would seem pretty obvious that two sentences cannot be identical in meaning and yet differ in modal properties (properties such as being necessarily true, being possibly false, being such as to be false if Aristotle had never gone into philosophy, etc.). It would seem at least as obvious[1] that meaning relations between sentences of a language are something that the speakers of the language are able to recognize without any recourse to information about clearly extralinguistic matters. In the exchange that follows, one of the two disputants argues that these two "obvious truths" are at odds with each other.

The dispute was prompted by one of Saul Kripke's well-known arguments against the descriptivist theory of proper names, the argument which runs as follows:[2] let, say, 'the last great philosopher of antiquity' (or something of this sort or some description of the form 'the one who had all or most of the following properties: . . . ', listing a number of properties that we attribute to Aristotle) be the description with which the name 'Aristotle' would on the theory in question be synonymous; now to claim that the two terms are synonymous is to imply that they are, in simple sentences at any rate, interchangeable *salva significatione*, that, e.g., 'Aristotle was fond of dogs' *(S)* and 'The last great philosopher of antiquity was fond of dogs' *(S')* do not differ in meaning. But such two sentences do differ in meaning; for—as 'Aristotle' is a "modally rigid" term (it would be wrong to say that someone other than its actual referent could have been Aristotle), and a description of the sort at issue is not (it is correct to say that someone other than its actual referent could have been the last great philosopher of antiquity, etc.)—*S* and *S'* differ in modal properties: in some counterfactual situations they would fail to match each other in truth value.

The two disputants have promptly agreed that the supporter of the theory under attack, should he accept this particular objection as valid, could meet it by slightly modifying the theory and saying with Alvin Plantinga[3] that names are synonymous not with descriptions of the sort that Frege, Russell, or Searle had in mind, but rather with their "modally rigid" counterparts (or, perhaps, with some still other "modally rigid" descriptions); S differs in modal properties from S', but does not differ in modal properties from the sentence 'The one who *in fact* (as things stand in the actual world) was the last great philosopher of antiquity was fond of dogs'. What is at issue in the exchange below is not the tenability of descriptivist theories of names, but the plausibility of the claim that sameness of meaning implies sameness of modal properties.

X: I have no strong intuitions as to whether names in general can plausibly be held to be synonymous with descriptions—whether, say, 'Aristotle' can plausibly be held to be synonymous with some description of the type 'the ancient Greek philosopher who did (wrote, taught, etc.) so-and-so', or of the type 'the one who has all or most of the following properties: . . . ', or of the type 'the one whose doings are so-and-so causally related to our having the beliefs which we express using the name ≪Aristotle≫' or of some still different type. But the argument that a name is not synonymous with any such description because the substitution of the one for the other in a sentence does not in general preserve the modal properties of the sentence (since, e.g., 'Anyone who met Aristotle met Aristotle' is a necessarily true sentence, but 'Anyone who met Aristotle met the ancient Greek philosopher who wrote . . . and taught . . . ' or the like is not) and hence does not preserve its meaning, does not appear to me convincing. For I am not persuaded that for a pair of sentences to be properly described as identical in meaning, the two must have the same modal properties.

Y: What sense would it make to deny that "whether a sentence expresses a necessary truth or a contingent one depends only on the proposition expressed, and not on the words used to express it"?[4]

X: It is said by some that two sentences have the same "meaning," express the same "proposition," if they don't differ in truth value in any "possible world"—or that they have the same "meaning" if they are transformable into each other by substituting for component terms "synonymous" terms, two predicates or singular terms being "synonymous" if they don't differ in extension in any "possible world"—where the word 'possible' is taken in a non-epistemic sense, in which even a plainly analytic sentence (such as, say, 'Anyone who lives in London lives in what is called ≪London≫' or, in the past, 'The standard meter rod is one meter long') counts as false in some "possible worlds." If this is what you mean by 'meaning', then of course the modal properties of a sentence *are* determined by its "meaning" in your sense of that term. But this is a rather peculiar way of using the word 'meaning'. 'Hesperus' and 'Phosphorus' being "modally rigid," 'Hesperus is Phosphorus' has the same "meaning" in this sense as 'Hesperus is Hesperus'; but it seems weird to call a pair of sentences identical in meaning when the two radically differ in epistemic status.

Y: This is not quite the notion of meaning that I would subscribe to, but let me abstract from the difference for a moment. Consider the pair of sentences mentioned before: 'Anyone who met Aristotle met Aristotle' (S_1) and 'Anyone who met Aristotle met the ancient Greek philosopher who . . . ' (S_2). What S_1 says (that anyone who met Aristotle met Aristotle) is something that would be the case even if Aristotle had never gone into philosophy; what S_2 says doesn't have this property. What S_1 says is something that is necessarily the case; what S_2 says is not. What sense does it make to claim that the two sentences have the same meaning, that they say the same, if what the one sentence says differs in properties from what the other sentence says?

X: If this does not make sense, then, it seems, neither does it make sense to claim, as I presume you would, that what the sentence 'Hesperus is Phosphorus' (S_3) says is identical with what the sentence 'Hesperus is Hesperus' (S_4) says. For, so one might argue, the two things differ in properties: that Hesperus is Hesperus is obvious; that Hesperus is Phosphorus may not be so. But we need not accuse each other of violating Leibniz's Law. Let us say that two sentences describe the same "state of affairs" if they are meaning-identical in your sense of this phrase, and let us say that two sentences express the same "proposition" if they are meaning-identical in my sense of this phrase. The meaning of a sentence, as I understand the word, is, roughly speaking, a matter of its location in a certain network of epistemic connections: evidential connections between observations and sentences and inferential connections between sentences. Now, if you were to assert: "What S_3 says (namely, that Hesperus is Phosphorus) is identical with what S_4 says (namely, that Hesperus is Hesperus)," you would be using the phrases 'what S_3 says', 'that Hesperus is Phosphorus', etc., as referring to "states of affairs." If I were to assert: "What S_1 says (namely, that anyone who met Aristotle met Aristotle) is identical with what S_2 says," I would be using the phrases 'what S_1 says', 'that anyone who met Aristotle met Aristotle', etc., as referring to "propositions." You would not be violating Leibniz's Law, because epistemic properties (being obvious, dubious, etc.) attach to "propositions," not to "states of affairs." I would not be violating Leibniz's Law, because properties such as being necessarily the case, being contingently the case, being such as to not to be the case if Aristotle had died at the age of three, etc., attach to "states of affairs," not to "propositions." But your use of the word 'meaning' strikes me as deviant. Isn't it weird to imply that the speakers of a language may be unable to recognize the "meaning" relations between some sentences of their language without first making suitable discoveries about clearly extralinguistic matters? Granted that 'water', 'H$_2$O', 'heat', 'molecular motion' are "modally rigid" terms,[5] the sentence 'Heat is molecular motion' has the same "meaning" in your sense of the word as the sentence 'Heat is heat', and 'There is water over there' has the same "meaning" as 'There is H$_2$O over there'—"synonymies" which would have gone unnoticed if heat were not discovered to be molecular motion and water had not been discovered to be H$_2$O.

Y: It's time for me to disabuse you: I do *not* equate synonymy with sameness of modal properties. My point was just this: it makes little sense to dissociate the two and deny that sameness of modal properties is a *necessary* condition of sameness of meaning. I am quite ready to accept your requirement of epistemic equivalence as another necessary condition — which is enough to avoid the unwanted results of the sort you have just mentioned.

X: No, this is not enough. Suppose it is decreed: "The term 'meter' is to designate the length which stick *S* had at t_o."[6] (The difference between this definition and the related one which was once actually adopted need not concern us here.) Consider these two sentences: 'Stick *S* was in existence at t_o and one meter < 50 inches' (S_5) and 'Stick *S* was in existence at t_o and the length of stick *S* at t_o < 50 inches' (S_6). Now, since it would make little sense to argue that these two sentences do not satisfy my condition of synonymy, it follows that — unless you have in store some third condition with which to supplement the two now under consideration and which is not clearly satisfied by this pair of sentences — the question whether S_5 and S_6 have the same meaning amounts on your proposal to the question whether they match each other in modal properties. The term 'meter' as we have defined it should be construed as a "modally rigid" designator of a certain length (we don't want to say that if stick *S* had at t_o been longer or shorter than it actually was, then the length of 1 meter would not be the length it actually is; rather, if stick *S* had at t_o been longer or shorter than it actually was, then stick *S* would not have been 1 meter long at that time). Similarly, '50 inches' should be construed as a "modally rigid" designator of a certain length. Thus, the latter question amounts to the question whether S_6 is, like S_5, true in all "possible worlds" in which stick *S* is in existence at t_o, i.e., in brief, to the question whether stick *S* could or could not have then been 50 or more inches long. But this is not a question that one can answer without relying on information about clearly extralinguistic matters, such as the malleability of sticks like *S*.

Y: That stick *S* was made of, say, iron and that an iron stick which is so-and-so long can be made so-and-so longer by being hammered out or exposed to heat is something that you would need to know in order to know *how* it might come about that our stick — suppose it was 1 meter long before t_o as well — would by that time become so-and-so many inches longer. But do you need to know all this to know *that* it could have been so-and-so many inches longer than it was?

X: To say that it could have been so is, I take it, to say that such a state of affairs was not excluded by the causal order of the world. But knowing which among conceptually possible states of affairs are (or are not) compatible with the causal order of the world (whatever this exactly means) is — unlike knowing whether a given sentence means the same as a given other — something that you can't plausibly describe as part of one's linguistic competence.[7] When one observes, as Kripke does, that no one other than Aristotle could have been Aristotle, that no length other than that of 1 meter could be the length of 1 meter, that if this table is wooden then it could not be non-wooden (for if it is wooden then nothing that would not be wooden could count as this very table), that if water is H_2O then it could not be XYZ (for if it is H_2O then nothing that would not be H_2O could count as this very substance), etc., one is engaged in conceptual analysis (exploring certain semantic properties of proper names, indexicals, natural kind terms, our ways of individuating particulars, properties, kinds, and of identifying them in counterfactual situations), not in a factual inquiry into modal properties of things. But, obviously, the assertion that a given stick could have been so-and-so many inches longer than it was is not in that category. Whether some counterfactual situations — e.g., some situations where things are the way they actually are except that in place of a one meter long stick S we have a so-and-so much longer stick because we stretched S or made from the same hunk of matter a longer stick to begin with — can properly be described as situations where it is still the very stick S that is so-and-so much longer, is a semantic matter; that such situations are possible, that things could thus differ from the way they are, is not. And one more point: unless you have in store some third condition of synonymy with which to supplement the two now under consideration and which a pair like S_5 and S_6 does not satisfy, your criterion yields yet another strange result. Since, presumably, it is true that stick S could have been 50 inches long, but false that it could have been, say, 50^{1000} inches long — for, as a matter of physical laws, there can't be sticks that long; if I am wrong, put more zeros in the exponent — S_5 and S_6 do not satisfy the suggested criterion of synonymy, yet the two sentences that result from them when '50 inches' is replaced by '50^{1000} inches' do satisfy it! And, as the term 'meter' is *stipulated* to designate the length of stick S at t_o, it is hard to think of any further condition of synonymy that would be plausible but *not* met by a pair like S_5 and S_6.[8]

Y: One might suggest that for a pair of sentences to count as identical in meaning, the two must also be transformable into each other by substituting synonyms for synonyms, and that a pair of predicates or singular terms are not synonymous if they differ in reference in some possible worlds. The pair of sentences you have just mentioned would then be said to differ in meaning, as much as S_5 and S_6, because of non-synonymy of 'one meter' and 'the length of stick S and t_o'.

X: Yes, but this would not of course eliminate the main trouble. For your belief that stick S could have been longer or shorter than it was is not plausibly described as part of your *linguistic* competence, any more than the belief that it could have been 50 or more inches long. Besides, whatever one's proposed criterion of synonymy of terms, to suggest that if a pair of sentences cannot be transformed into each other by replacing component terms with synonymous terms then the two differ in meaning is to suggest, perversely, that 'Town b is straight to the north of town c and town c straight to the north of town d' differs in meaning from 'Town b is straight to the north of town d and town c is between these two'; that 'France is larger than Spain' differs in meaning from 'Spain is smaller than France'; and that 'John chases Mary' differs in meaning from 'Mary is chased by John'. Nelson Goodman would tell us that 'one meter' and 'the length of stick S at t_o' — and hence S_5 and S_6 — do differ in meaning because the two terms differ in what he calls 'secondary extension': any two distinct terms do.[9] Rudolf Carnap would tell us that S_5 and S_6 differ in meaning because they are not "intensionally isomorphous" in his — rather special — sense,[10] in which no two sentences are intensionally isomorphous if they differ in that the one contains a simple term where the other contains a compound one. But a conception of meaning according to which the meaning of a sentence is never preserved when one predicate or singular term is replaced by another is, I believe, of little interest; so is any conception which, like Carnap's, implies that 'John chases Mary' differs in meaning from 'Mary is chased by John' and that 'Ann has a brother' differs in meaning from 'Ann has a male sibling'.[11]

Notes

1. To anyone who, like the present writer, is not perturbed by Quinean qualms about the distinction between matters of meaning and matters of extralinguistic fact.

2. See his *Naming and Necessity* (Cambridge, Mass., 1980), 6 ff.

3. See his "The Boethian Compromise," *American Philosophical* Quarterly, Vol. 15, No. 2, 1978.

4. Saul Kripke, "A Puzzle About Belief," in *Meaning and Use*, edited by A. Margalit (Dordrecht, 1979), 241. See also *Naming and Necessity*, 6-7.

5. See *Naming and Necessity*, Lecture III.

6. *Ibid.*, 54-57.

7. X is deaf to any talk of "possible worlds" governed by different causal laws, of metaphysical necessities or possibilities in any sense of 'metaphysical' that is to be contrasted with *both* 'conceptual' and 'natural'. If he were not, he would add that knowing which among conceptually possible states of affairs are "metaphysically" possible is not part of one's linguistic competence either, any more than knowing which of them are compatible with the causal order of nature.

8. Here is another implication of Y's position which seems strange. Compare S_6 with the sentence — call it S_6^* — which results from it when we replace 'the length of stick S at t_o' by 'the length stick S *in fact* had at t_o'. Since the latter description, unlike the former, is "modally rigid" (any one of a number of different lengths could have been the length of stick S at t_o; but no length other than that of one meter could have been that very length which stick S in fact had at t_o), S_6 and S_6^* differ in modal properties: if stick S had at the time been hammered out, S_6 would be false, though S_6^* would still be true. Yet to say that because of this difference the one sentence differs in meaning from the other — or, which comes to the same thing, to say that they differ in meaning because they are not interchangeable *salva veritate* in modal sentences ('It could have been the case that . . . ', etc.) or counterfactual conditionals ('If stick S had been hammered out at t_o and stretched by a foot, it would not be true that . . . ', etc.) — would be as weird as to say that 'Anyone can beat S. Bush' does not mean the same as 'Everyone can beat S. Bush' because the two are not interchangeable in 'If . . . then I can'.

9. Two predicates or singular terms have the same "secondary extension" in Goodman's sense if the substitution of the one for the other in a compound expression always preserves the extension of the latter — even when it is an expression like 'triangle-description', where to be a triangle-description is to be a term that not only applies to (some or all) triangles but contains (or is identical with) the word 'triangle'.

See N. Goodman, "On the Likeness of Meaning," *Analysis*, 10 (1949). Since 'triangle-description' in this sense is just a definitional abbreviation for an expression that *mentions* the word 'triangle', Goodman's assertion that 'triangle' is not synonymous with 'equilateral rectangle' because 'triangle-description' differs in extension from 'equilateral-rectangle-description' is just as plausible as the assertion that 'triangle' and 'equilateral rectangle' are not synonymous because, e.g., the term 'the term ≪triangle≫' differs in extension from the term 'the term ≪equilateral rectangle≫'.

10. See R. Carnap, *Meaning and Necessity*, 2nd ed. (Chicago, 1956), 14.

11. Ibid. Carnap did not consider his concepts of intensional structure and intensional isomorphism to be the *only* appropriate analysantia for the concepts of meaning and synonymy. He considered them useful for the analysis of belief-sentences (on his view, believing that p is the same as believing that q if and only if 'p' 'q' are "intensionally isomorphous"; I find this implausible; does it make sense to distinguish between one's believing that John chases Mary and one's believing that Mary is chased by John?) and for the resolution of the so-called paradox of analysis (in my view, his own distinction between the "material mode" and the "formal mode" and his notion of quasi-syntactical sentences provide for a more appropriate comment on that "paradox"; I hope to elaborate on this in another paper).

Against Direct Reference

MICHAEL DEVITT

It is easy nowadays to get caught up in direct-reference mania.
(Salmon 1986: 82)

1. THE THEORIES

The origins of the theory of "direct reference" for proper names are alleged to be found in the works of Saul Kripke, Keith Donnellan, and David Kaplan. Sometimes what may seem to be the same theory of names is called "new"; sometimes, "Millian"; sometimes, "causal"; sometimes, "historical."

Despite appearances, there is not one theory covered by these various names but many. My aim is to distinguish these theories and their origins, and to argue against one of them. My own views have the same sources as the views of direct-reference philosophers but differ sharply in concern and content. The implications of this disagreement stretch way beyond the theory of names. Time and again the disagreement comes back to questions about the nature of semantics.

In this section, I set out the theories and some of the relationships among them. In the next section, I focus on the history, examining particularly the extent to which these theories are correctly attributed to Kripke, Donnellan, and Kaplan. In the following sections, I get on with the argument.

The 'Fido'-Fido theory

The theory that I shall be arguing against is prominent in the discussion of direct reference. It is:

> All there is to the meaning, semantics, information value, or linguistic significance of a name is (standing for)[1] its referent. A name is purely designative or denotative; it is just a tag; it merely labels.

The 'Fido'-Fido theory has problems that have been familiar since Frege and the early Russell:[2] the differing "cognitive values" of '$a = a$' and '$a = b$', which I shall call "the Identity Problem"; the nontriviality of true positive existence statements and the meaningfulness of true negative ones, which I shall call "the Existence Problem"; the meaningfulness of empty names, which I shall call "the Emptiness Problem"; the failure of substitutivity of identicals in thought or propositional attitude ascriptions, which I shall call "the Opacity Problem." These problems seem so massive that it is startling to find the 'Fido'-Fido theory revived by able philosophers who are thoroughly aware of the problems.

The main reasons for the revival come from the other theories appearing under the banner of direct reference and set out below. My first point against the 'Fido'-Fido theory is that these other reasons are insufficient.

The Nondescription theory

One of these other theories, often presented in the same breath as the 'Fido'-Fido theory as if it were the same, is as follows:

> A name is nonconnotative. It does not have a Fregean sense determining its reference. It is nondescriptive.

Although the Nondescription theory is entailed by the 'Fido'-Fido theory, it is not the same as that theory. Why might someone think otherwise? Because of the following semantic presupposition:

> SP: The meaning of a name is either descriptive or else it is the name's referent.

SP presupposes that there are no other possible candidates for a name's meaning. So, if the Nondescription theory is right, the meaning of a name must be the name's bearer: the 'Fido'-Fido theory. I shall argue against SP. I think that a name has a certain sort of nondescriptive, hence nonFregean, sense.

To argue against SP is to take it as a substantive thesis about meaning. However, the discussion of direct reference sometimes proceeds as if SP were true by definition. This would collapse the 'Fido'-Fido theory into the Nondescription theory and leave us without a complete *nontrivial* theory of meaning for names. So, I shall be arguing that 'Fido'-Fido is either false or the result of a trivial addition to Nondescription.

Why do some people behave as if SP were trivial? My diagnosis is that they pay too little attention to what we need a theory of meaning *for*.

The Rigid Designation theory

A third theory associated with direct reference is as follows:

> A name refers to the same object in every possible world.

We can derive the Rigid Designation theory from the Nondescription theory as follows. First, we need an explanation of "reference in a possible world." Consider a singular term, T, in a sentence, S, in a particular context of utterance. The referent of T in a possible world, W, is whatever object T makes relevant to the truth evaluation of S in W.[3] Second, we need an assumption about what makes reference vary from world to world. Suppose that T were a definite description like 'the President of America in 1989'. It seems obvious that T would vary its reference because different objects would be picked out by the description in different circumstances. The needed assumption is that *only if* T is descriptive can its reference vary. So, given the explanation and this plausible assumption, the Nondescription theory implies that a name refers to the same object in every possible world.

Rigid Designation does not entail either Nondescription or 'Fido'-Fido. So far as Rigid Designation is concerned, a name can have any meaning at all provided only that that meaning does not make any object other than the name's actual referent relevant to evaluations in other possible worlds. This proviso will be met if the name's meaning is the referent, as 'Fido'-Fido holds. But we need further argument to show that this is the *only* way to meet the proviso. Indeed, Alvin Plantinga has shown, ingeniously, that a descriptive name could meet it (1978). Even if we use the Nondescription theory to rule out Plantinga's suggestion, we still need to rule out the possibility of other ways of meeting the proviso. Perhaps a term with a nondescriptive sense would meet it. That possibility could be ruled out by the semantic presupposition, SP, but then if we had SP as well as Nondescription, we would not need Rigid Designation to establish 'Fido'-Fido.

There is no fast and clean route from Rigid Designation and Nondescription to 'Fido'-Fido. I shall examine a slow route later (section 3).

I have deliberately presented these three theories without using two terms that are prominent in the discussion of direct reference: 'proposition' and 'content'. These technical terms are open to various interpretations, some of which are appropriate to one of the theories, some to another. The main reason that the discussion is so confusing is that the terms are often inadequately explained and thus tend to blur distinctions between the theories. I will introduce the terms later (section 3).

The Causal theory

The final theory associated with direct reference is as follows:

> A name designates an object solely in virtue of a certain sort of causal or historical chain connecting the name to the object.

The Causal theory clearly entails the Nondescription theory, because it entails that reference is not determined by a Fregean sense. Further, if we accept the earlier explanation of "reference in a possible world," we can derive Rigid Designation from the Causal theory. A name's causal links to an object in the actual world of its utterance—the links that determine its reference—remain fixed however we vary the world of evaluation. Indeed, the Causal theory *explains* why a name has the semantic property of being rigid.

I am enthusiastic about the Causal theory.[4] So I am very concerned to reject the common assumption that it entails the 'Fido'-Fido theory. Clearly, as it stands, it does not, for it says nothing about the meaning, information value, etc., of a name. Indeed, I shall argue that the Causal theory provides the means to reject the 'Fido'-Fido theory, because it provides an explanation of the nondescriptive sense of a name. I have argued this several times before, with no apparent success.[5] In this paper, I hope to do better.

My main aim in this section has been to emphasize that neither the Nondescription theory, the Rigid Designation theory, nor the Causal theory entail the 'Fido'-Fido theory. The most important additional premise to establish that theory is SP. If my argument is good, SP is false.

2. THE HISTORY

Kaplan introduced the term "direct reference" in the mid-1970s in works that were mainly on the semantics of demonstratives and indexicals (1973, 1975, 1979a, 1979b, 1988a).[6] Neither Kripke nor Donnellan used the term. And neither they, nor Kaplan, called their theories "new."

The 'Fido'-Fido theory

Insofar as the theory of direct reference is this theory, it is remarkably inappropriate to call it "new" as some do (e.g., Wettstein 1986):[7] 'Fido'-Fido is the oldest theory in the book, going back at least to Plato. Calling it "Millian" is much more appropriate, though strictly it seems not to be what Mill held. The theory has been unpopular for most of this century, but it was by no means dead when the direct-reference philosophers revived it recently.[8]

Who did revive it? Kripke and Donnellan are often mentioned in discussions of direct reference as if they endorsed the 'Fido'-Fido theory. Yet, interestingly enough, nobody makes a serious attempt to cite convincing evidence that they do.[9] Kripke clearly does not endorse it (1980, 20–21). I have been unable to find any decisive evidence that Donnellan does. In one place, he flirts with a view that might seem to come close (1974), but the view seems more appropriately construed as Rigid Designation. Kaplan does, somewhat tentatively, endorse the theory (1988a, 591), although it is not what he *means* when he says that names are directly referential. And names are not his primary concern.

'Fido'-Fido has flowered in the work of a "new wave" of philosophers who sail under the banner of direct reference: Joseph Almog, Nathan Salmon, Scott Soames, and Howard Wettstein.[10]

The Nondescription theory

This theory is entailed by the 'Fido'-Fido theory and it is just as inappropriate to call it "new." It is, however, appropriate to call it "Millian," because Mill is its most famous exponent. There is no doubt that Kripke (1980), Donnellan (1972), and Kaplan (1988a) do subscribe to this theory. Furthermore, Kripke and Donnellan did something importantly new in relation to it. At a time when its opposite, the Description theory, had been the received view for decades, they produced powerful arguments for the Nondescription theory.[11] The Nondescription theory has been enthusiastically embraced by all the direct-reference philosophers.[12]

The Rigid Designation theory

The Rigid Designation theory has much more claim to be considered "new" though it is, in effect, to be found in Ruth Barcan Marcus (1961).[13] Kripke is famous for urging the theory (1971, 1980). When Kaplan says that names are "directly referential," Rigid Designation is part of what he means.[14] The other part is Nondescription (1988a, 512–16, 521–26). Donnellan did not discuss the Rigid Designation theory in his early articles. However, his idea of a "referential use" of definite descriptions (1966, 1968) was suggestive of the idea, as Kaplan points out (1979a, 383–85). Donnellan did embrace the theory later (1979, 50).

The main interest of the Rigid Designation theory was for logic and formal semantics; in particular, for intensional logic and possible-worlds semantics. The new wave are very interested in this theory.[15]

The Causal theory

This theory is the one that really is "new." It was discovered by Kripke (1980) and Donnellan (1972) in the late 1960s.[16] Kaplan seems always to have been impressed with the theory but, in the end, gives it no semantic significance (1988a, 587–92).

The new wave of direct-reference philosophers typically associate their views with the Causal theory but, of the four theories, it clearly *interests* them least.[17] Their concern with the question 'What determines the reference of a name?' seems to evaporate once they have concluded that the reference is not determined by a Fregean sense.

Consider now the link between the 'Fido'-Fido theory and the Causal theory in the works of the philosophers mentioned. Kaplan and the new wave embrace the 'Fido'-Fido theory but show little interest in the Causal theory. Kripke and Donnellan hold the Causal theory, but the 'Fido'-Fido theory is not to be found in any of their works. So the historical link between the two theories is rather tenuous. It is striking then that the received view seems to be that the Causal theory is a 'Fido'-Fido theory.[18] I am most concerned to break the link between the two theories.

Because of the above history, my term, "the direct-reference theory of names," should be taken as referring to the conjunction of the 'Fido'-Fido theory, the Nondescription theory, and the Rigid Designation theory, but not to the Causal theory. And by "the direct-reference philosophers," I mean Kaplan and the new wave, not Kripke and Donnellan.[19]

In earlier works, I have proposed a theory that developed ideas of Donnellan and Kripke in two ways.[20] First, I drew a distinction at token level, based on Donnellan's distinction at type level, between referential and attributive descriptions,[21] and then I applied this new distinction across the board, covering names, demonstratives, and pronouns, as well as definite descriptions. Second, I gave a causal theory of reference for all the referential tokens.[22] The theory explained their reference in terms of causal chains — I called them "d-chains" — generated by "groundings" in an object[23] and by "reference borrowings" in communication.

In the course of theorizing about the reference of names, I talked also about their meaning. I claimed, in effect,[24] that Frege was right in thinking that a name had a sense which determined its reference — it had a mode of presentation — but wrong in thinking that this sense was descriptive. The sense was a certain type of d-chain (1974, 203-04; 1981a, 153-57). Given the now popular idea that the Causal theory is a 'Fido'-Fido theory, my view about a name's meaning has turned out to be much more radical than I expected. I adopted the view for two reasons. First, a name must have *some* property that determines its reference — it does not refer by magic — and, according to the Causal theory that property is the relational one of being causally linked in a certain way to the referent. In brief, an interest in the *explanation* of reference pointed to a sense of the sort I was proposing. Second, if a name had no sense, it would be impossible to solve the familiar problems that had originally driven people away from the 'Fido'-Fido theory. I took solving those problems to be a requirement on a theory of names (1981a, 6).

The solution to these problems, briefly, is as follows. The Identity Problem: '$a = a$' and '$a = b$' have differing cognitive values because they have different senses; for underlying 'a' and 'b' are different types of d-chain. The d-chains are of different types in virtue of being parts of different "networks" of d-chains. The Existence Problem and the Emptiness Problem: the meaningfulness of a name does not depend on it having a referent; it is meaningful if it has an appropriate network underlying it even if that network is not grounded in a referent. The Opacity Problem: substitutivity does not hold for a name in an opaque thought ascription because the ascription depends for its truth on the sense of the name, not on its referent. I shall return to these solutions in section 7.

It follows from my view that SP is false. Fregean senses and referents are not the only candidates for a name's meaning: its meaning is a nonFregean sense explained in terms of a causal network.

I have already noted the lack of interest of direct-reference philosophers in explaining how names relate to the world. Indeed, though they trace their views back to Russell, they set aside almost without comment the part of Russell that was an attempt to solve this problem: the theory of acquaintance. Their lack of interest in this ultimate question seems to reflect a narrower view than mine of the scope of semantics.[25]

This difference over the nature of semantics is related to another one. My concern is always with language as a natural phenomenon and so the guide for its investigation is empirical science. The direct-reference philosophers tend to be more concerned with language as an abstract system and so the guide for its investigation is formal logic.

3. MOTIVATING THE 'FIDO'-FIDO THEORY

Given the well-known, and apparently overwhelming, problems for the 'Fido'-Fido theory, why has it been revived? The above discussion provides some ideas. In this section I shall develop these ideas in the process of discussing four possible motivations for the theory. Motivations 3 and 4 are certainly influencing the direct-reference philosophers. Motivations 1 and 2 probably are too.

1. Suppose that a person starts with the common assumption:

(1) The meaning of a sentence is the proposition it expresses.

The person adds, perhaps under the influence of some reflections on "ordinary language":

(2) The proposition expressed by a sentence is what the sentence says.
(3) A name's contribution to what a sentence containing it says is simply the name's bearer.

From these three premises, it follows that a name's bearer is its contribution to a sentence's meaning. Add in the uncontroversial,

(4) The meaning of the name is its contribution to the meaning of a sentence containing it,

and the person has arrived at the 'Fido'-Fido theory.

The problem with this argument is its first three premises: (1) and (2) identify the meaning of a sentence with what it says. Suppose we accept that. What *does* a sentence say? Our answer must be guided by the truth conditions of indirect speech reports. But then as Quine and others have shown, these truth conditions are tricky. Consider:

Tom said that Cicero is an orator.

Suppose that the actual words Tom uttered were, "Tully is an orator." Is the report true? According to one popular view, yes and no. It is true if construed transparently. On the basis of that construal, we might feel justified in saying that what is said by "Tully is an orator" is the same as what would have been said by "Cicero is an orator," thus confirming (3). However, if the report is construed opaquely it is false. On the basis of that construal, what is said by the two utterances is not the same, thus falsifying (3). So, for the argument to go through, we have to identify the meaning of a sentence with what is said in the transparent sense. But why should we do that? The traditional problems for the 'Fido'-Fido theory show that this would be a mistake. Perhaps we should identify meaning with what is said in the opaque sense, or with something else altogether. There is no compelling argument here for overlooking the traditional objections.

2. Suppose that a person starts with the popular slogan: "the meaning of a sentence is its truth conditions." This gets interpreted as follows:

(5) The meaning of a sentence is a possible state of affairs: an arrangement of objects, attributes, and so on.

The meaning of a singular term is simply its contribution to this meaning. Applied to names, this yields (4). But what *does* a term contribute? The easy answer is its referent: an object, attribute, or whatever, that partly constitutes the state of affairs. The person rejects this answer as too easy, because some terms are complex, picking out their referent partly in virtue of their structure. This structure and the referents of its parts seem relevant to meaning. Thus the meaning of 'the father of Annette' involves the referent of 'father' and 'Annette', and not simply Harry, who *is* the father of Annette. Nevertheless, the person thinks, the answer is on the right track. It is right for a term that is simple, having no structure:

(6) The meaning of a simple term is its referent.

The Nondescription theory shows that names are simple. The person has reached the 'Fido'-Fido theory.

The traditional problems for the 'Fido'-Fido theory strongly suggest that there is something wrong with truth-referential semantics of the sort reflected in (5) and (6): meaning is not simply a matter of assigning entities to expressions; for example, states of affairs to sentences, and objects to names.[26] Note that this semantics does take *some* account of modes of presentation. *If the term is complex*, then the way in which it presents its referent is important to its meaning. However, if it is simple, only its referent matters. This view could be summed up in a generalization of SP: the meaning of term is either a descriptive structure or else it is the term's referent. The problems suggest, in my view, that modes of presentation are *always* important to meaning; they are important for simple terms as well as complex. The slogan should be understood not as (5) but as: the meaning of a sentence is a *mode of presenting* a possible state of affairs.[27]

3. Kaplan came tentatively to the 'Fido'-Fido theory via an argument in possible-world semantics (1988a, 590-91). Kaplan developed this semantics for indexicals and demonstratives. It yields only three candidates for the meaning of an expression: its referent, its "content," and its "character." Applying this to names,

(7) The meaning of a name is either its referent, its content, or its character.

In Kaplan's semantics the Rigid Designation theory and the Nondescription theory yield,

(8) The content of a name is its referent.

Kaplan argues further that

(9) The character of a name is its content.

The 'Fido'-Fido theory follows. "Because of the collapse of character, content, and referent, it is not unnatural to say of proper names that they have no meaning other than their referent" (1988a, 591). This argument is the slow route from Rigid Designation and Nondescription to 'Fido'-Fido mentioned earlier (section 1).

Before assessing this argument, it is worth mentioning a fast, and very dirty, route from possible-worlds semantics to 'Fido'-Fido. The route establishes (8) one way or another, and then simply identifies content with meaning. The problem with this is that "content" is a technical term in the semantics. We need an argument to show that content, *understood in that way*, is appropriately identified with meaning. To suppose that no further argument is needed is to treat the identification as a matter of definition. This would make the 'Fido'-Fido theory trivial.

What is Kaplan's "content"? Consider a sentence in a particular context of utterance. Its content, or the proposition it expresses, is the aspect of it that is evaluated for truth in each possible world. It can be represented by a function from possible worlds to truth values. The content of a singular term in the sentence is its contribution to what is evaluated; it is the aspect of the term that determines its reference in each possible world. It can be represented by a function from possible worlds to objects. According to the Rigid Designation theory, a name refers to the same object in every possible world. So we can represent its content by a *constant* function; it is "fixed" or "stable." A descriptive name *could be* rigid in this way, as Plantinga showed, but the Nondescription theory rules this out. In these circumstances, rather than represent the name's content as a constant function with the actual referent as its value, Kaplan prefers to follow Russell in thinking of the name's content as the referent itself. Hence (8). The content of the sentence containing the name is then a "singular" proposition (Kaplan 1988a, 529–31).

What is Kaplan's "character"? The character of an expression "is that which determines the content in varying contexts" of utterance (534). "Indexicals have a *context-sensitive* character" (535). Thus the character of 'he' determines different contents, because it determines different referents, as we vary the context of utterance. "Nonindexicals have a *fixed* character" (535). Thus the character of 'cat' determines the same content, cathood, in all contexts. Kaplan goes on to identify the fixed character of a word with its content (536).

All that remains to reach (9) is an argument that names have fixed characters (587-91).

Kaplan's notions of content and character yield an elegant and plausible semantics for indexicals. And there can be no objection to his applying the notions more widely to yield (8) and (9). The controversial move is (7). The traditional objections to 'Fido'-Fido show that the referent of a name is not a plausible candidate for its meaning. Since the content and character of a name, according to Kaplan's semantics, are identified with the referent, they are not plausible candidates either. We need an argument for (7) that Kaplan does not provide; (7) simply "falls out" of Kaplan's semantics. But that semantics was designed for another purpose. It remains to be argued that it is appropriate for names.[28]

One way of modifying Kaplan's semantics so that the 'Fido'-Fido theory can be dropped would be to broaden the notion of character to cover nondescriptive modes of presentation. Thus, even when the character is fixed, determining the same content in all contexts, it is identified not with the content but with the mode of presenting that content. Character in this broad sense could then be identified with meaning. Another way[29] would be to return to the picture that Kaplan discards: the content of a name is not the referent but a function which always has the referent as value. This function is a mode of presentation and can be identified with meaning.

4. What most motivates the direct-reference philosophers to accept the 'Fido'-Fido theory is that they think that there is no viable alternative. The Nondescription theory has ruled out a descriptive meaning for a name. SP is assumed, and so the name's meaning must be its bearer.

I have proposed that a name has a nondescriptive sense, or mode of presentation, which is identified with the type of causal chain that determines the name's referent. What response do the direct-reference philosophers have to this sort of solution to the problems for the 'Fido'-Fido theory?

(i) Wettstein constructs a view along these lines, which he claims to be based on ideas in Perry and Kaplan. He objects to the view because it has the consequence

> that everyone who uses 'Aristotle' to refer to the ancient Greek philosopher must be thinking of him as "the individual who stands in the appropriate historical relation. . . . " Most competent users of that name have never heard of the Donnellan-Kripke account of names and do not think of the referents of names in such terms. (1986, 194)[30]

The objection is beside the point because the view does not have this consequence. The objection assumes that competent speakers must have propositional knowledge of linguistic rules. This assumption is popular, but nonetheless false. Briefly, a competent speaker's behavior is *governed by* linguistic rules without her being (mostly) *aware* of those rules, just as a pocket calculator's behavior is governed by arithmetic rules without its being aware of those rules. I have argued against the propositional view of competence at length elsewhere[31] and will say no more here.

(ii) Another objection to the proposal runs as follows. "The causal chains that constitute a name's meaning, according to the proposal, are external to the mind. So how could differences in such meanings possibly explain the differing cognitive values of '$a = a$' and '$a = b$'?"[32] It is indeed common for people to think that the Causal theory puts meanings entirely outside the head.[33] But this is simply false. A great deal of the network of d-chains for a name consists in mental processing and functioning. Indeed, it is absurd to think otherwise. For subjects to think about an object as a result of its causal action on them, they must first be appropriately stimulated, and second *must process the results of that stimulus appropriately*. The role of the mind in meaning will be discussed more below.

(iii) Almog rejects something close to my proposal in the context of discussing the problem of ambiguous names (1984, 483–84).[34] His rejection is based solely on his argument that historical chains have, in general, the "presemantic" role of preserving the meanings of words. Thus, he claims that we mean by 'you' what we do because our ancestors meant that and there is a causal chain from them to us. In the case of a name, what is preserved by the chains is reference, because its meaning is its referent (479–82). The chains solve the ambiguity problem by determining which meaning, hence which referent, a particular token has.

Aside from the 'Fido'-Fido theory, I agree with these claims.[35] Indeed, as Almog says, they are "compatible with a Fregean semantics" (1984, 486) and "relatively uncontroversial" (487). I claim that the chains *also* explain what it is for a name to mean what it does. They answer the question: In virtue of what do we, our ancestors included, refer to Aristotle by 'Aristotle'? Almog is uninterested in explaining reference. His story of the preservation of meaning takes the meaning preserved for granted.

That the chains feature in some uncontroversial explanations is not, of course, any reason for thinking that they should not feature also in some other, possibly controversial, explanations.

(iv) Salmon makes the most striking response to my proposal. He describes it as "ill conceived if not downright desperate . . . wildly bizarre . . . a confusion, on the order of a category mistake" (1986, 70–71). He says almost nothing in support of this. David Lewis has remarked that an incredulous stare is hard to argue with (1973, 86). So is an incredulous Salmon. However, I hope that what follows is an argument.

Salmon is also motivated by his criticisms of what he calls "the Generalized Frege Strategy," which I shall discuss later (section 7).[36]

4. THE SEMANTIC TASK

In the sections that follow I shall sharpen the objections to the 'Fido'-Fido theory (section 5), assess direct-reference strategies for avoiding the problems that generate the objections (section 6), and develop my own solutions to those problems (section 7). All of these discussions depend, to an extent, on a view of what the task is in semantics. So we need to discuss that matter first.

The need is particularly pressing in assessing the strategies for avoiding the problems. For the main strategies move the problems outside semantics. In considering these export strategies, it is easy to fall into a "merely verbal" disagreement about what we shall *call* "semantics" and "meaning". Thus suppose we ignore empty names (thus ignoring, of course, one of the major problems). Everyone (involved in this debate)[37] will agree that it is semantically significant that 'Cicero' refers to Cicero, 'Reagan' to Reagan, etc. So if 'semantics' is simply *defined* so that everything about a name other than its referent is irrelevant to its meaning or semantics (cf. the fast and dirty argument in section 3), there is no room for substantive disagreement.[38] However, defining away one's problems is clearly too easy an approach to intellectual life. And it has the disadvantage of making the 'Fido'-Fido theory trivial. What the theory needs to avoid this triviality is a justification for export strategies that is based on an independent view of the semantic task. So far as I know, a plausible justification of this sort has not been offered. Indeed, the discussion proceeds with little attention to what semantics is *for*. The view I shall now sketch[39] will be the basis for rejecting the export strategies.

Philosophers do not approach semantics with virgin minds. They already think about language using the familiar notions of folk theory: *meaning, truth, reference*, and so on. Furthermore, they have been educated to use many further notions: *sense, proposition, possible world*, and so on. In thinking about the task in semantics, it is important to set aside as much of this rich theoretical machinery as possible. Otherwise we are in danger of feeding into the description of the task much that is part of an attempted solution and should perhaps be controversial.[40] We need to get back to basics. What are the phenomena that prompted all this theorizing in the first place?

The phenomena are certain sounds and inscriptions which play strikingly important roles in our lives: people produce them in many circumstances and respond to them in a variety of ways. These token linguistic symbols are not abstract entities: they are datable, placeable parts of the physical world. The initial, and fairly theory-neutral, view of the task is: to describe and explain the properties of linguistic symbols that enable them to play the roles we have indicated.

Early on in our theorizing about linguistic symbols, we are likely to start talking about the mind. Indeed, I think that it is obvious that the role of language in people's lives comes from its relation to their minds.[41] I think that we should follow the folk in our theory by ascribing thoughts to people and in seeing linguistic symbols as the expressions of thoughts. And it is because language expresses thought that people are interested in it. Indeed, it is because it expresses thought that it exists at all.

Why then are we interested in thoughts? I think there are two reasons. First, because we are interested in explaining the behavior of the thinker. Second, because thoughts convey information about the way the world is.[42] So people produce and respond to, say, 'It is raining', partly because of what it shows about the likely behavior of the speaker and partly because of what it shows about the weather. We have arrived at a much less vague but more theory-laden way of specifying the roles of linguistic symbols in our lives.

Because of the link between thought and language, we should expect to follow the folk in ascribing many of the same properties to thoughts as to linguistic symbols. I agree with the many philosophers[43] who think that we should ascribe a syntax to thought, thus subscribing to a "language-of-thought" hypothesis. So we can now give a broader, though more theory-laden, description of our semantic task: to describe and explain the properties of linguistic symbols and thoughts that enable them to play their roles in the explanation of behavior and as guides to reality.

It is convenient to use the term 'meaning' as a generic term for the properties of language and thought that are the concern of semantics. The semantic task is then to explain meaning so understood.

5. SHARPENING OBJECTIONS TO THE 'FIDO'-FIDO THEORY

Against this background, the traditional objections to the 'Fido'-Fido theory seem very powerful.

The Identity Problem is that '$a = a$' and '$a = b$' have strikingly different roles whether in language or in thought.[44] People seldom think and seldomer reproduce tokens like the former, and there are few signs of consequences or interest when they do. In contrast, people often think and produce tokens like the latter, and there are lots of signs of consequences and interest when they do.[45] The reason for these differences is that the two tokens differ both as guides to reality and as explainers of behavior. I suggest that the strong conviction of the folk that these two differ in meaning — I have never met a beginning student who did not think that they do differ — is the response of folk semantics to these facts.

The Opacity Problem is even more severe. It arises once *truth* has been introduced into the theory of language. Consider, for example, ascriptions of belief in the above identities. It is hard to resist the claim that though Ralph's utterance, "Flora believes that $a = a$", is certainly true, his utterance, 'Flora believes that $a = b$', may well be false. Yet, according to the 'Fido'-Fido theory, if the two names are coreferential the ascriptions have the same meaning and so must have the same truth value; substitutivity of identicals must hold. We shall see that some direct-reference philosophers have managed to convince themselves, against all intuition, that the two ascriptions do have the same truth value (section 6). Yet still the problem does not go away. The two ascriptions differ radically as sources of information about Flora and as explainers of the behavior of Ralph. So they must differ in meaning. Differences in truth values are sufficient for a difference in meaning here, but they are not necessary.

The Opacity Problem makes the Identity Problem worse. If a name's property of referring to a certain object were the only property that was important to its role in identity beliefs and utterances, then it should be the only property of a name relevant to an *ascription* of an identity belief or utterance. If only the referent matters when we are *confronted* with Flora's belief or utterance, then it should be all that matters when we are *informed about* her belief or utterance. But it is not all that matters when we are informed, as the failure of substitutivity shows in the most dramatic way.

Similarly, if Flora's mode of representing an object often matters when we are informed about her belief or utterance, as I think it does, then that is good evidence that the mode matters when we are confronted with the belief or utterance; it is good evidence that the mode is a property of the name that enables it to play its specified roles.

Ralph's ascriptions of beliefs and utterances to Flora have the same dual roles as his other utterances: explainers of Ralph's behavior and guides to reality. Set aside the first role. What is significant for this debate about Ralph's ascriptions is that the reality to which they are an immediate guide is Flora's beliefs and utterances (which may be about anything from quarks to Quakers). Ralph, like everyone else, is interested in the beliefs and utterances of others as guides to reality and explainers of behavior. So his ascriptions to the likes of Flora show what properties of beliefs and utterances are relevant to those interests. So his ascriptions show what properties go into meaning.

That modes matter to our interest in beliefs and utterances as guides to reality is not initially obvious: we need the traditional problems to bring this home to us. That modes matter to our interest in beliefs and utterances to explain behavior does seem initially obvious.[46] The behavior flowing from a belief involving 'Phosphorus', given a certain stimulus, may well be very different from that flowing from a belief involving 'Hesperus', given the same stimulus. This is particularly striking if the stimulus is a verbal one involving one of the names. I suspect that the stubbornness with which the 'Fido'-Fido theory is maintained is partly the result of an exclusive interest in semantic properties as guides to reality rather than as explainers of behavior.

Finally, there are the Existence Problem and the Emptiness Problem. Empty names in existence statements and elsewhere undoubtedly have roles in our lives just as nonempty ones do. So a theory must not deem them meaningless.

6. AVOIDING PROBLEMS FOR THE 'FIDO'-FIDO THEORY

Direct-reference philosophers have three strategies for avoiding the traditional problems for the 'Fido'-Fido theory. The first is the easiest but has the least to recommend it: ignore the problems. I shall call this "the Ostrich Strategy." The other two are of the export sort already mentioned (section 4): move the problems out of semantics. One, "the Mind Strategy," moves them into the theory of the mind. The other, "the Pragmatics Strategy" moves them into pragmatics.

The Ostrich Strategy

The Ostrich Strategy is bad but underlying it is a sound idea. *All* theories have unsolved problems. Yet it is all right to maintain some theories despite this. Newton's theory is a striking example: it triumphed for more than two centuries despite many unsolved problems. However, what this shows is not that it is all right to *ignore* problems—the Newtonians did not do so—but rather that in appropriate circumstances it is all right to maintain a theory despite *failing to solve* problems. Briefly, when a theory is justified by an inference to the best explanation, it is all right to be a little bit complacent about it in the face of unsolved problems.

Such complacency about the 'Fido'-Fido theory must rest on the strength of the case for it. I have argued that the case is weak (section 3). This argument rests in part on a rival theory which, I claim, solves the problems and is a better explanation of meaning. That theory will be discussed in more detail in the next section.

It would be unfair to accuse a direct-reference philosopher of following the Ostrich Strategy simply because he has not yet confronted a problem; Rome wasn't built in a day; perhaps he is about to confront it. Nevertheless, it is worth noting that none of the direct-reference philosophers have confronted the Existence Problem or the Emptiness Problem, both of which seem catastrophic for a 'Fido'-Fido theorist who is not prepared to adopt a Meinongian or phenomenalist ontology.[47]

The Mind Strategy

The Mind Strategy exports problems from semantics. The interesting and substantive question in assessing export strategies is whether the very same considerations that make us think that the referent of a name is relevant to its meaning in the first place should also make us think that other factors are relevant. Against the background of my earlier sketch of the semantic task (section 4), I think that the answer, overwhelmingly, is that they should.

The Mind Strategy has been popular for dealing with the Identity Problem. Wettstein has been most explicit.[48] According to him, Frege formulated

> a condition of adequacy for a semantic account of singular terms . . . any such account must provide an answer to a crucial question concerning the cognitive significance of language: the question of how identity sentences in which proper names flank the identity sign can both state truths and be informative. (1986, 185)

Wettstein rejects this "epistemic" condition of adequacy, urging a "radically different conception" of semantics (186). On this conception, cognitive matters are not the concern of semantics.

Wettstein sharply distinguishes between singular propositions and the ways in which those propositions are cognized. He prefers to call those propositions "states of affairs" because they are made up of objects and properties "out in the world." In contrast, the cognizing of them is a mental activity (197-99). Semantics should be concerned with the former not the latter; with "the uncovering of the semantic rules that govern our linguistic practices" (200), the "institutionalized conventions" (201), and not "with matters cognitive" (201). In the case of names, we should be concerned to "specify the conditions under which an utterance of a name counts as a reference to an individual" (202) and not with the "ways in which speakers think about their referents" (201), not with their "cognitive perspectives" (202).

(1) I have linked the semantics of language closely to the semantics of thought and given the latter a certain priority (section 4). So if linguistic symbols have such semantic properties as being true or referring, they have them because thoughts do also. On this view there can be no question of divorcing cognitive matters from the semantics of language. Wettstein must reject the view, and he does: he denies that "the first step towards understanding how words refer is to understand how thoughts do so" (1988, 421). What are the alternatives to this view? (a) One might accept that thoughts share those semantic properties with linguistic symbols but deny that this is explanatorily significant. This view seems absurd. (b) More promising, but in my view quite mistaken (Devitt and Sterelny 1987: chap. 10), is the view that the direction of explanation should be reversed: language is prior to thought. (c) One might have a generally eliminativist view of the mind, denying that there are any thoughts or, at least, that there are any with those semantic properties. This faces the problem that all eliminativism faces: explaining behavior without minds. Eliminativism in this case faces an even more difficult problem: explaining language in a thoughtless world *without eliminating reference*. For, if reference goes, so does direct reference. In my view, no eliminativist has offered even sketches of a plausible solution to these problems. Wettstein does not say enough about thoughts[49] to make it clear which alternative he favors, though his appeals to Wittgenstein suggest some version of (c).

(2) According to Wettstein, the semantic task for names is to describe, perhaps explain, the convention or rule that links a name referentially to an object. But *why* is that the task? Why is the reference of a name interesting and why is only its reference interesting? An answer might be: we are interested in reference because of its contribution to the truth conditions of sentences (cf. 2 in section 3). But why are we interested in the truth conditions of sentences and only in those? Our discussion of the phenomena that need explaining show that properties of symbols *other* than their reference or truth conditions, namely their modes of presentation, are important to their specified roles in our lives.

The difference between '$a = a$' and '$a = b$' is not to be set aside as epistemic, cognitive, and unsemantic. We have seen that it is crucial to the role of the two sentences in the explanation of behavior and as guides to reality; it is crucial to what makes us interested in the meanings of the two sentences in the first place.

In the face of this, one can of course insist on applying 'meaning' only to the referential role of a name, but this is an unmotivated verbal maneuver that makes the 'Fido'-Fido theory true by definition and uninteresting. What is needed is some account of the point of semantics that justifies the restriction to reference. Wettstein does not provide this.[50]

(3) Wettstein claims that

> there is no reason to suppose that, in general, if we successfully uncover the institutionalized conventions governing the references of our terms, we will have captured the ways in which speakers think about their referents. (201)

What is involved in uncovering these conventions? Presumably we have not done this for names when we say simply that a name designates an object. Even if we overlook the fact that this is false for some names — the Emptiness Problem — surely semantics should tell us in virtue of what a name refers to a particular referent. That explanation must frequently involve the mind, for there is nothing other than minds and their relations to the external world that *could* establish the conventions of reference. In my view, the mental facts alluded to in this explanation will explain the required difference in cognitive values (section 7).

Wettstein wants to divorce the mind from semantics partly because of his view of the role it would play if it were not divorced. On his view, the meaning of a name would involve the descriptions or concepts that a competent user of the name must associate with it. This association amounts to propositional knowledge of the referent sufficient to discriminate the referent from other objects (1986, 201-204; 1988). But this is to assume that only the Description theory can provide a "cognitive fix" on the referent. In my view, the Causal theory provides that fix: the fix is a network of d-chains generated by conceptual-role links from thoughts to peripheral stimuli and by links from stimuli to the external world. Little if any of this need be conscious knowledge.

The Pragmatic Strategy

The Pragmatic Strategy is another export strategy. It cannot be dismissed out of hand because there clearly are some linguistic phenomena that are rightly treated as matters for pragmatics, not semantics; Gricean conversational implicatures are examples. I suspect that there is not, in general, a theory-neutral way of drawing the line between semantics and pragmatics (1981a, 197-98).

The Pragmatic Strategy has been popular for dealing with the Opacity Problem. Salmon has used it also for the Identity Problem (1986, 77-79).[51]

Salmon's line on the latter is that once we have made the distinction between information that is semantically encoded and information that is pragmatically imparted, it is not obvious that the informativeness of '$a = b$' does not come from what is pragmatically imparted. In the absence of a reason to believe the contrary, Salmon feels justified in putting the Identity Problem aside.

I have argued that when we consider why we ascribe meaning at all—to explain behavior and as a guide to reality—it *is* obvious that the informativeness of '$a = b$' is semantic and not merely pragmatic (section 5). (This is not, of course, to say that the informativeness is not pragmatic at all. Soames demonstrates nicely that it is partly pragmatic; 1988, 104-05.)

Salmon's claims about pragmatics seem to be disastrous for his position that the information semantically encoded by '$a = b$' and by '$a = a$' are equally valuable. He points out that an utterance of S typically pragmatically imparts the information that S is true (1986, 59). Thus the utterance of '$a = b$' imparts the information that that sentence is true and hence, Salmon continues, that the names 'a' and 'b' are coreferential (79). To bring out the disaster, first we express Salmon's view of what is imparted by the identity utterances as follows:

(I1) '$a = b$' is true, hence the referent of 'a' is the same as the referent of 'b'

(I2) '$a = a$' is true, hence the referent of 'a' is the same as the referent of 'a'.

Next, consider what Salmon must similarly claim is imparted by the utterances, "Ben is as tall as Saul," and "Ben is as tall as Ben":

(T1) 'Ben is as tall as Saul' is true, hence the referent of 'Ben' is as tall as the referent of 'Saul'

(T2) 'Ben is as tall as Ben' is true, hence the referent of 'Ben' is as tall as the referent of 'Ben'.

These claims are precisely analogous to (I1) and (I2). What they show first is that, to someone competent with S,[52] the pragmatically imparted information that S is true *matches in value* the information that S semantically encodes. Indeed, it is *because* S has a certain value that 'S is true' has that value. Further, the value of the pragmatically imparted information about the reference of terms in S reflects the value of the information about the truth of S from which it is derived (with the help of some elementary semantic knowledge), and so is also determined by the value of what S semantically encodes. It is *because* it is interesting to know that Ben is as tall as Saul that it is interesting to know that the referent of 'Ben' is as tall as the referent of 'Saul'. It is *because* it is uninteresting to know that Ben is as tall as Ben that it is uninteresting to know that the referent of 'Ben' is as tall as the referent of 'Ben'. So the additional value of (I1) over (I2) is evidence of precisely what 'Fido'-Fido denies: that '$a = b$' has more information value than '$a = a$'.

Salmon takes the Opacity Problem more seriously. He describes it carefully in a way that demonstrates its enormity for the 'Fido'-Fido theory (1986, 80-81, 87-92).[53] He notes that we always entertain a singular proposition under some "guise." Part of this guise is our "mode of acquaintance" with the object the thought is about (107-109).[54] He acknowledges that these modes are "similar in some respects to Fregean senses" (120). So Salmon has provided the motivation and the means to adopt a view like mine. But his faith in direct reference does not waver:

> The ancient astronomer agrees to the proposition about the planet Venus that it is it when he takes it in the way it is presented to him through the logically valid sentence 'Hesperus is Hesperus', but he does not agree to this same proposition when he takes it in the way it is presented to him through the logically contingent sentence 'Hesperus is Phosphorus'. The fact that he agrees to it at all is, strictly speaking, sufficient for the truth of both the sentence 'The astronomer believes that Hesperus is Hesperus' and the sentence 'The astronomer believes that Hesperus is Phosphorus'. (116)

Whatever she says, *Lois Lane really does know that Clark Kent is Superman* (83)![55]

If modes are not relevant to the truth conditions of belief attributions, what is their significance? According to Salmon, they have a "pragmatic function" (1986, 117),[56] which makes

> the first [way of attributing the belief to the astronomer] better than the second, given our normal purpose in attributing belief. Both sentences state the same fact . . . but the first sentence also manages to convey *how* the astronomer agrees to the proposition. Indeed, the second sentence, though true, is in some sense inappropriate; it is positively misleading. . . . (116)

Salmon accepts that the astronomer has his belief under a certain mode of acquaintance and not under others. He accepts that the best belief attribution conveys which mode the belief is under. He accepts that conveying this is important "given our normal purpose in attributing belief."[57] *What better evidence could we have that conveying this is part of the meaning of the attribution*? The apparent difference in meaning between the first and second attribution would remain even if they had the same truth value (section 5). However, if conveying information about a mode is part of an attribution's meaning, what better way is there to explain the apparent difference than to make the modes relevant to truth conditions? This has the happy result that the first attribution is true and the second false, as everyone always thought. Salmon will have none of this:

> it is no part of the semantic content of the sentence to specify the way the astronomer takes the proposition when he agrees to it. The 'that'-clause is there only to specify the proposition believed. (117)

Salmon offers so little support for these claims that we should suspect that the 'Fido'-Fido theory is being made true by stipulation and hence trivial.

Salmon is well aware that his view flies in the face of ordinary intuition (1986, 83-85). However, his problems are much more serious than that. He agrees that we are interested in modes. Why are we? For the same reason that we are interested in thoughts and utterances at all: to explain people's behavior and to gain information about the world. *The very same considerations that motivate meaning motivate modes.* And if we are interested in the modes of thoughts and utterances, we should *expect* to find attributions of thoughts and utterances informing us about modes (sections 4 and 5). Salmon's theory is guided neither by folk opinion nor by scientific methodology.

On my view, an opaque attribution with a name in the content clause conveys information about modes via the mode (= sense) of the name: the mode in the thinker or utterer must be the same as the mode in the attribution. For singular terms in general, I see a systematic relationship between the mode of the term in the content clause and the mode of the term that would make the attribution true. (For example, roughly, one demonstrative requires another, though not usually the same one.) This is one way for the semantics of an attribution to convey information about modes.

Another view has found favor.[58] On this view, attributions have an implicit indexical reference to some feature of the context—for example, the speaker's intention—which determines which mode makes the attribution true. The view gives no special role to the mode of the term in the content clause in determining truth conditions and so is not as strikingly at odds with the 'Fido'-Fido theory as my view. Nevertheless, it is still at odds because it acknowledges the importance of modes to the significance of thoughts and utterances and hence to their meaning.

Soames's approach to the Opacity Problem is similar to Salmon's, as the notes to the above discussion indicate. He has a further argument for treating the problem as nonsemantic.[59] In the course of a lengthy and subtle discussion of thought and utterance attributions (1985, 1987, 1988), drawing on a paper of Mark Richard (1983), Soames offers some reasons for maintaining substitutivity, hence for denying that the attributions are opaque. I have argued that maintaining substitutivity is insufficient to save the 'Fido'-Fido theory (section 5): the evidence will remain that, for example, Salmon's first and second attribution differ in meaning. Nevertheless substitutivity is certainly necessary to save the theory and so I shall consider Soames's reasons.

First, Soames points to some cases where, despite appearances, substitutivity holds, and claims that we can generalize from these (1987, 66-67). However, his discussion overlooks some observations that Quine made long ago.[60] Quine noted that though some thought attributions are opaque, some are transparent; substitutivity holds for them. Transparent attributions can be *obviously* transparent; for example, of the form,

b is such that a believes it to be F.

However, Quine noted further that the most common forms of attribution are ambiguous between an opaque and a transparent reading; for example,

a believes that *b* is *F*

is ambiguous. In the light of these Quinean observations, the response to Soames's argument is simple: substitutivity does indeed hold in his cases because it is appropriate to construe the attributions transparently. But there is no basis here for Soames's generalization that substitutivity *always* holds.

Quine's view that there are both transparent and opaque attributions is not only supported by our intuitive assignments of truth values to attributions, it is also supported by a consideration of the purposes of these attributions. Take Ralph's attribution of a belief to Flora only as a guide to the reality of Flora's beliefs (not as an explainer of *Ralph's* behavior). If our interest in that reality is for the purposes of explaining Flora's behavior, then an opaque attribution will always be appropriate. On the other hand, if our interest in that reality is as a guide to another reality — what the belief is about — then the transparent form will often better suit our purposes.[61]

Second, Soames has a range of cases involving identity where, he claims, certain substitutions are irresistible. Yet the cases yield the same counterintuitive results as does the general substitutivity that is so problematic for the 'Fido'-Fido theory. If we are prepared to put up with the results in these cases, why not do so in general?

Soames's most interesting cases are of attributions involving demonstratives. The truth conditions of these are undoubtedly tricky. Soames also has some cases involving general terms. I think that these cases, particularly the demonstrative ones, do provide some solace to direct reference, but nowhere near enough to save it in the face of the considerations I have adduced. However, I must set their discussion aside until another time.[62] I postpone a discussion of Soames's case involving a name until the next section.

7. SOLVING THE PROBLEMS

In this section I shall expand on my solutions to the Identity Problem and the Opacity Problem. However, the discussion must still be briefer than the problems deserve. And I shall have nothing more to say about my solutions to the Existence Problem and the Emptiness Problem.[63]

I have argued that the strategies adopted by direct-reference philosophers to avoid the traditional problems for the 'Fido'-Fido theory are all mistaken. If my solutions to those problems are along the right lines, the strategies are also unnecessary. The problems can be solved in semantics by abandoning 'Fido'-Fido.

The Identity Problem

I shall start with a paradigm example of an informative identity statement, 'Hesperus = Phosphorus', soon after the discovery of its truth.

My solution begins with the claim that the two names in this statement have different senses in that underlying them are different types of d-chain.[64] Note that the claim concerns types not tokens. If we located the difference between the names in the different token d-chains that make up their networks, we would be driven to the unfortunate conclusion that every name token differs in sense from every other name token.

How do the d-chains differ in type? They involve different types of grounding: in the one case a set of events in the evening, including the sound of 'Hesperus'; in the other, a set of events in the morning, including the sound of 'Phosphorus'. (I talk of sounds, ignoring other media, for convenience.) They involve different types of reference borrowing: in the one case, communications including the sound of 'Hesperus'; in the other case, communications including the sound of 'Phosphorus'. However, these differences cannot be essential.

Consider two look-alikes who are both named 'George'. Clearly the groundings of these names may be indistinguishable aside from the fact that they involve different objects. But now remove that difference: there is one person leading a double life with such success that everyone wrongly thinks that there are two look-alikes. Intuitively, these two uses of 'George', generating two distinct networks, differ in sense as much as 'Hesperus' and 'Phosphorus'. Certainly they can be part of a very informative identity statement: '(This) George = (that) George'. (So in this highly abnormal situation, a statement of the form '$a = a$' is informative.)[65] So different types of grounding cannot be essential to a difference in sense.

This example shows also that different types of reference borrowing cannot be essential to a difference in sense. Indeed, all reference borrowings involving the sound of 'George' are, in the relevant respect, the same.

What is essential to a difference in sense is that members of the speech community process the input involving the names differently and hence keep the networks distinct; the names are associated with different "files." Evidence of this is that the two names are involved in distinct sets of beliefs.

Suppose that Charles already has the ability to use the sound type 'Gail' to designate a certain object, Gail. So he has a "file" consisting of a set of thoughts that include tokens that dispose him to speak the sound type 'Gail' and that have underlying them d-chains that are grounded in Gail. Suppose now that Charles is in the position to borrow reference from Kate. He hears Kate using tokens of 'Gail' which, in fact, have underlying them d-chains grounded in Gail. If he is to take advantage of Kate's utterance, amending that 'Gail' file, he must process Kate's 'Gail' sounds so that they are brought to bear on that file. He must process the input as if he had formed the identity belief, 'Gail (the subject of this conversation) = Gail (the subject of these thoughts)'.[66] This processing task may not be easy because he may know several people named 'Gail'. Similarly, if he is to amend his file in a grounding situation as a result of experience of Gail herself, he must process the input as if he had formed the identity belief, 'That person = Gail'. It is in this way that Charles's thoughts prompted by current experience are unified with pre-existing thoughts involving a name. D-chains are of the same type for Charles if his inner processing links them together in this way.

This is the story of sameness of type *for Charles*; of his *personal* network. It is the story of *speaker* sense. We need also the story of sameness of type period; of the community's network. We need the story of *conventional* sense.

When Charles borrowed from Kate, his processing linked his network to hers. And *everybody's doing it*, not always with Kate, but with other members of the community. The union of all these personal networks is the community's network. For two d-chains to be of the same type, and hence for the names they underlie to have the same (conventional) sense, is for them to be linked together by the inner processing of members of the community into the one network and for them to involve tokens of the sound type conventionally part of the network. (Unions can be imperfect, as we shall briefly see.) D-chains are of different types when they have not been so unified.

D-chains of different types normally arise from groundings in different objects. Where they do not, they will almost always involve differences in sound type and different circumstances of use; the case of 'Hesperus' and 'Phosphorus' is an example.[67] Very rarely, differences in d-chain type may arise despite sameness of object and sound type because of different circumstances of use; the case of 'George' above is an example.

The solution to the Identity Problem falls straight out of this. Because 'a' and 'b' differ in sense, 'a = a' and 'a = b' differ in role and in the "cognitive value" that Frege drew attention to. The difference in sense is a difference of d-chain type brought about by differences in the processing of tokens of 'a' and 'b'. These processing differences affect our understanding of the two identity statements: understanding the first involves accessing the one file twice whereas understanding the second involves accessing two files. Because of these facts about inner processing, and a mastery of identity, a person knows that the first statement must be true and that the second may be true or false.[68]

I solve the Identity Problem by ascribing different meanings to 'a' and 'b' but I do not "give" the meanings. This solution will be a disappointment to those who seek a traditional *a priori* "analysis." In my view, the semantic task does not require such an analysis. The task is to *explain* meaning, not give it. Furthermore, I do not think that the meaning of 'a' can be given in other terms: 'a' gives the meaning of 'a' as well as it can be given.[69]

On my view, what is important about a name token, what enables it to play its specified roles, is that it is part of a certain sort of network that links the token to other tokens of a certain sound type (and of a certain inscription type, etc.). Its meaning (information value, etc.) is its property of being so linked. The referent gets into the picture because, if the name is nonempty, the network will be grounded in an object which is the referent.

We can use this discussion to provide a further argument against the 'Fido'-Fido theory. According to that theory the only thing essential to understanding a name token is assigning it the right referent. The case of 'George' shows that this is not so. In that case the name seems to have two meanings but only one referent. Understanding a token requires assigning it the right meaning—in my terms, linking it to the same network that underlies its production. A person who gets this wrong will have misunderstood the token, which may have important consequences for explaining behavior and gaining information about the world. Yet the person may still have assigned the right referent. So assigning the right referent is insufficient for understanding. So having that referent is insufficient for meaning.

We have seen that the 'Fido'-Fido theory is open to refutation by finding a pair of names that share a referent and yet yield an informative identity statement. Salmon calls this "Frege's Strategy." Salmon thinks that if this strategy is good so also is "the Generalized Frege Strategy." Consider the theory that the meaning of a name is its F. The Generalized Strategy is to find a pair of names that share F and yet yield an informative identity statement. Salmon thinks that if the strategy were good, it would work against any plausible theory. So it cannot be good. So Frege's Strategy is not good. So the 'Fido'-Fido theory can be retained.[70] I claim that my theory is not open to the Generalized Frege Strategy: it is not possible to find two names that share my sort of senses and yet yield an informative identity statement, for any such names will have underlying them the one causal network.

In assessing this claim, two distinctions are important: first, that between *conventional* senses and *speaker* senses; second, that between what is informative *in general* and what is informative to *a particular speaker*. I have been primarily discussing the first half of each distinction. I explain informativeness in general by appealing to the differing conventional senses of the names; for the appeal is to the typing of d-chains in the speech community as a whole. However, some individuals may be partly at odds with the community, with the consequence that a name with one conventional sense has two speaker senses for them. They process tokens of the one name as if they were of two names. Then even a thought of the form '$a = a$' would be informative for them, although the names involved share conventional senses. Consider, for example, Ralph, who does not know that Russell the logician is one and the same as Russell the peace marcher; as a result, he does not unify his input from the two sources into one file. 'Russell (the logician) = Russell (the peace marcher)' is informative for him because the names have two speaker senses (though only one conventional sense).[71]

The Opacity Problem

Sometimes substitutivity holds for ascriptions of thought and utterance and so they are transparent. In such cases, the ascriptions pose no *additional* problem for a theory of names. The additional problem comes from the many cases where substitutivity fails and the ascription is opaque: something other than the name's referent is relevant to the truth of the ascription.

The key to my solution is simple: the truth conditions of the ascription depend on the sense of the name in the content clause.[72] The ascription requires that the subject's thought or utterance uses a name with the same sense as the name in the content clause. This talk of senses is to be understood in the causal way set out above. The solution captures the intuitive idea that the ascription requires the subject to use the same name as the ascriber.

This solution demands that we say more about what counts as sameness of sense, and hence sameness of name.

My convenient restriction to the spoken language encourages a simple view: tokens of the same name must sound the same. So the ascription of an utterance to Flora could not be true unless the name she used sounded the same as the one in the content clause of the ascription. As soon as we remove the convenient restriction, we see that this cannot be true. Flora might have been writing, not talking. Indeed, the ascription might be made true by an utterance in any medium at all. Furthermore, what if the ascription is of a thought not a communication? It can be made true by a mental token.

The name in the content clause of an ascription requires that Flora use a token in the same network but not a token in the same medium. However, if Flora's token is not mental, being in the same network is not alone sufficient for the truth of the ascription, because Flora's token might not be in accord with the conventions that have formed the network; it might be aberrant. The truth behind the simple view is that if Flora's token is a sound, it must be of the same sound type as those in the network; if it is an inscription, it must be of the same inscription type; and so on through all the media of communication.

I have written as if tokens of what is intuitively only one sound type, inscription type, and so on, are conventionally part of a network. This may require modification. Consider Soames's example: the names 'Ruth Barcan' and 'Ruth Marcus' (1987, 67). Suppose that the ascriber used a token that sounded like the former, whereas Flora's utterance contained a token that sounded like the latter. In assessing this ascription, it may seem as if these token have the same sense. Yet, intuitively, they are of different sound types, at least partly. Let us look at the history. For many years, there were sounds of the type 'Ruth Barcan', but none of the type 'Ruth Marcus', in a network grounded in Ruth Barcan Marcus. When there came to be sounds of the latter type referring to her, were they conventionally in the *same* network? To some degree, probably yes: some people probably treated those sounds as if they were tokens of the old name; their processing brought these tokens into the old network. Others almost certainly did not. Doubtless, the same practices go on to this day. So sounds of the two types are partly unified into the one community-wide network and partly not. Unification is always a matter of degree and in this case the degree is well short of what is required for a confident claim that Flora's token and the ascriber's are of the same name type.

So according to the theory, there is some vagueness about sameness of sense. I do not think that this matters to the theory because there is a matching vagueness about the circumstances in which we ordinarily think ascriptions true.

Foreign names pose a similar problem. Tokens of 'London' and *'Londres'* normally count as the same for the purposes of thought ascription. Intuitively, they are of different sound types, inscription types, and so on, though not so very different. At first sight, it may seem as if the networks underlying the two types are not unified at all: one network involves English speakers, the other, French speakers. This is a mistake. It overlooks the many situations where an English speaker processes a French speaker's *'Londres'* to a 'London' file, and vice versa. If a foreign name has not been unified with an English name in this way, then I think that we would not count an English ascription of a thought to a foreigner true on the strength of a thought involving the foreign name. At least we would not count it true *construed opaquely*. Of course, it might well be true construed transparently.

Soames's example enables us to construct a case of the sort that he likes, discussion of which I postponed (section 6):

(a) Flora believes that Ruth Barcan = Ruth Barcan.

(b) Flora believes that Ruth Barcan = Ruth Marcus.

Soames thinks that the substitution of 'Ruth Marcus' for 'Ruth Barcan' is irresistible: they must have the same meaning. Yet, he claims, (b) still seems much more informative than (a). If everyone has to tolerate this counterintuitive result, why not tolerate the similarly counterintuitive results of general substitutivity, thus allowing the 'Fido'-Fido theory to stand?

I bite the bullet here. I think that the substitution is quite resistible. Tokens of 'Ruth Marcus' and 'Ruth Barcan' are not thoroughly unified in the one network. The tendency to favor substitution arises from the partial unification of the networks for the names. Identify of sense is a matter of degree.

8. CONCLUSIONS

The theory of direct reference for names is a combination of three distinct but related theories: the 'Fido'-Fido theory, the Nondescription theory, and the Rigid Designation theory. It does not include the Causal theory. I have argued that the 'Fido'-Fido theory does not follow from the three other named theories, lacks adequate motivation, and is false.

The argument against it is a traditional one: it fails to solve the Identity Problem, the Existence Problem, the Emptiness Problem, and the Opacity Problem. Direct-reference philosophers typically try to avoid this argument by exporting the problems into the theory of the mind or pragmatics. A consideration of our purposes in attributing semantic properties to linguistic symbols — explaining behavior and learning about reality — shows that these export strategies fail. The very same considerations that make us think that the reference of a name is semantically significant, make us think that *more than* reference is significant.

A major reason for thinking that the 'Fido'-Fido theory lacks motivation is that there is an alternative. This alternative ascribes to a name a nondescriptive sense, or mode of presentation, that is explained in terms of the reference-determining causal network for the name. Thus, I argue that the Causal theory not only explains a name's reference, it also points to an explanation of the name's meaning that solves the traditional problems for the 'Fido'-Fido theory. Contrary to popular opinion, the Causal theory supplies not an example of the 'Fido'-Fido theory but a way of replacing it.

In my argument, I take the 'Fido'-Fido theory to be a substantive addition to the Nondescription theory. That is, I take its notion of meaning to be the one we need in an empirical theory attempting to explain linguistic phenomena. However, the discussion often proceeds as if 'Fido'-Fido follows from Nondescription by stipulation: nondescriptive meaning is identified with reference *by definition*. This is not a theoretically useful notion of meaning. The move has the further disadvantage of making 'Fido'-Fido the result of a trivial addition to Nondescription.

Why is the 'Fido'-Fido theory maintained in the face of apparently overwhelming objections? Partly, I think, because far too little attention is paid to the question of what we need semantics *for*. As a result, standard views of the nature of semantics, and of the range of alternative theories, are taken for granted. In my opinion, these standard views are mostly unhelpful, if not mistaken.[73]

Notes

1. The distinction between the theory with the words in parentheses and without them is unimportant for this paper and will be ignored.

2. Though Russell rejected the 'Fido'-Fido theory for ordinary proper names, he did of course hold it for logically proper names.

3. The apparent commitment to possible worlds in this explanation could be removed. Let 'D' abbreviate a total description of W. To say that x is the referent of T in W is to say that, were it the case that D, x would have to have the attribute specified by S for S to be true.

4. Though I think a few qualifications are necessary. One is needed to allow for "attributive" names (Devitt 1974, 196; 1981a, 40-42). Another is needed to allow for the *qua*-problem (Devitt 1981a, 60-64; Devitt and Sterelny 1987, 63-65).

5. Devitt 1980, 271-74; 1981a, 152-57; 1981c, 217-18; 1984a, 388, 403-405; 1985, 222-23. I have also argued a similar line to do with natural-kind terms: 1983, 675-77.

6. Kaplan 1988a, which seems to have made the introduction, circulated widely in an unpublished form from 1977 on. On the semantics of demonstratives and indexicals, see also Perry 1977, 1979.

7. Stephen Schwartz, who seems to have been first to talk of the "new theory of reference," did not include the 'Fido'-Fido theory as a "main feature" of the new theory (1977b, 20-32).

8. See, e.g., Smullyan 1947, 140; Marcus 1961, 309-10; 1981.

9. E.g., Loar 1976 (cf. my 1980); Ackerman 1979a, 58; 1979b, 6; Schiffer 1979 (cf. my 1981c); Marcus 1981, 502; Almog 1984, 482; Baker 1982, 227; Wettstein 1986, 187. So far as I know, Loar was the first to attribute the 'Fido'-Fido theory to Kripke and Donnellan.

10. Salmon 1981, 11; 1986; Almog 1984, 482; 1985, 615-16n; Wettstein 1986, 185, 192-94. I take the theory to be implicit in Soames 1985, 1987, 1988. John Perry is a direct-reference theorist and is often cited as if he subscribed to 'Fido'-Fido, but I can find no clear evidence that he does; but see, e.g., Barwise and Perry 1983, 165. Though the terms 'proposition' and 'content' often make the discussion confusing (section 1), I do not mean to suggest that the new wave is confused.

11. The argument that has had the most attention is a modal one, derived from the Rigid Designation theory, and found in Kripke. The other argument, which strikes me as more powerful, is found in Kripke and Donnellan. It points out that people mostly do not have the knowledge of a name's bearer required by the Description theory. I call it "the argument from ignorance and error."

12. Salmon 1981, 16; 1986, 65-66; Wettstein 1986, 185-86; Almog 1986, 220; Soames 1988, 100.

13. See also Smullyan 1947; Fitch 1949.

14. Kaplan has a subtle discussion of a difference between his formulation of Rigid Designation and Kripke's (1988a, 521-22). I have used Kaplan's formulation.

15. Salmon 1981, chap. 1; 1986, chaps. 1-2; Soames 1985, 1987, 1988; Wettstein 1986, 186; Almog 1986.

16. See also Chastain 1975, an interesting but neglected article.

17. Salmon 1981, xiii, 11; Almog 1984; Wettstein 1986, 192-93; 1988, 420.

18. See references in note 9; also, McGinn 1982, 244; Lycan 1985; Block 1986, 660, 665; Lepore and Loewer 1986, 60; Wagner 1986, 452.

19. I might have included others among the direct-reference philosophers. For example, Lycan subscribes to direct reference and his "paradox of naming" starts from SP (1985). Fodor proposes a "denotational theory" which is, in effect, a direct-reference theory, though he does not mention any of the above literature in his discussion (1987, 72-95). The philosophers I have included are closely related to one another. The detailed discussion of a larger group would have been unmanageable.

20. I became interested in the semantics of singular terms in discussions with Charlie Martin in Sydney in 1966. Martin had a rigidity thesis for names and demonstratives and a view of definite descriptions that was similar to the view that Donnellan was about to publish (1966, 1968). I first heard the causal theory of proper names from Kripke at Harvard in 1967. I proposed my own theory in my PhD thesis (1972). The following later works were largely based on that: 1974, 1976, 1981a.

21. This treatment gives Donnellan's distinction a semantic significance that he may not have intended. Kripke thinks that the distinction does not have semantic significance (1979a). My 1981b is a response to Kripke.

22. Donnellan does not offer a theory of reference for his referential descriptions. In particular, he does not extend his causal theory of names to cover those descriptions (though he does remark in a footnote that such a description is a "close relative" of a proper name; 1972, 378n).

23. It is important to the plausibility of the Causal theory that it allows a name to be *multiply* grounded in its referent, not simply grounded in an initial dubbing (1974, 198-99; 1981a, 56-57).

24. The qualification is necessary because of my caution with the *word* 'sense' (and the *word* 'meaning'). Initially, I was anxious to emphasize the difference between the Causal theory and the Description theory. This led me to use 'sense' as if it applied only to *Fregean* descriptive senses and hence to deny that names had senses (1974). Later I allowed, tentatively, that we might think of causal modes of presentation as

nonFregean senses (1981a, 236). Had I anticipated the rise of direct reference, I would have emphasized the difference between the Causal theory and the 'Fido'-Fido theory by not being at all tentative about this. I am not tentative now (Devitt and Sterelny 1987, 56-58).

25. A lack of interest in this ultimate question has been common among philosophers of language. Consider the long period of rule of the Description theory. Even if the theory had been right, it would not have answered this question. It is essentially incomplete, explaining the reference of one term in terms of the reference of others. But how do *they* refer? Description theories simply pass the referential buck. The buck must stop somewhere with a different sort of theory. This point relates to Putnam's famous arguments for the slogan "Meanings just ain't in the head" (1975, 223-27); see Devitt (in press a).

26. See Wagner 1986 for a sustained criticism of this sort of semantics.

27. I am dissatisfied with the attempt at making this point in Devitt and Sterelny 1987, 33.

28. Perhaps Kaplan would agree, for his approach to names *is* tentative. I think that the semantics, as it stands, is also inappropriate for 'cat'.

29. Which I owe to Georges Rey.

30. Searle makes a similar point in defending the conclusions he draws from his Chinese-room example (1980, 452).

31. 1981a, 95-110; 1983, 674-75; 1984a, 206-11; Devitt and Sterelny 1987, 146-48; in press.

32. Some remarks of Evans suggest this objection (1982, 83). I respond to the remarks in my critical notice (1985, 221-23). I have often heard objections along these lines.

33. See, e.g., Block 1986, 665. Wettstein says that "reference . . . has little to do with the head of the speaker" (1988a, 415).

34. Almog says that an unpublished lecture of Kaplan's in 1971 anticipated the major ideas of his paper (1984, 489n). See also Kaplan 1988a, 587-92.

35. I agree also with Almog's criticisms of Fregean attempts to absorb the Causal theory (1984, 484-86). Searle has recently provided a complicated example (1983, chap. 9) which I have criticized (in press a, sec. 5).

36. Fodor's motive for adopting his denotational semantics is completely different from any of the above (1987). He thinks, rightly in my view, that meaning holism threatens Life As We Know It. He thinks, wrongly in my view, that functional-role semantics leads inevitably to meaning holism. He sees his semantics as the only possible savior.

37. The qualification is necessary because there are many, most notably those in the French structuralist tradition, who think that reference is irrelevant to meaning. On this, see Devitt and Sterelny 1987, chap. 13.

38. An example of such an approach—not taken by the direct-reference philosophers—would be to appeal to an old division of the study of language according to which syntax deals with expressions alone, semantics deals with expressions together with their referents, and pragmatics with the users of expressions and possible contexts of use. Cf. note 59.

39. For more details, and some argument, see Devitt and Sterelny 1987.

40. I doubt the need for abstract entities in semantics, particularly propositions; 1976, 404-405, 414-16; 1984a, 385-86.

41. In emphasizing the relevance of the mind to linguistics, I am emphatically not endorsing the view, found for example in Chomsky and Dummett, that the theory of language is a theory of linguistic competence. I have argued against that view elsewhere (1981a, 92-95; Devitt and Sterelny in press). So has Soames (1984a, 1984b).

42. This is what indicatives do. Interrogatives show what the thinker would like to discover about the way the world is. Imperatives show how the thinker would like the world to be. For convenience, I shall ignore nonindicatives.

43. Including Chastain 1975, 197.

44. Salmon (1986, 12) demonstrates neatly that the problem is not peculiar to identity statements; compare the informativeness of 'Phosphorus is a planet if Phosphorus is' and 'Hesperus is a planet if Phosphorus is'.

45. This picture is too simple; see section 7.

46. See, e.g., Fodor 1980. I think that, for the purpose of explaining behavior, we can abstract from that part of the mode that is outside the skin: only "narrow" meaning matters (in press b). If this is right then, so far as the explanation of behavior is concerned, the referent of a name is not only *not all* of its meaning, it is *not any* of its meaning.

47. Salmon expresses the hope that the Pragmatic Strategy will work for these problems (1986, 127-28).

48. See also Almog 1986, 233-35. Kaplan seems to be tempted; 1988a, 558-69, 591-92. Lycan follows the Mind Strategy in treating the computational roles of thoughts, which are relevant to their role in explaining behavior, as not part of their semantics; 1985.

49. Wettstein is atypical in saying as much as he does. Direct-reference philosophers typically ignore the semantics of thoughts altogether. For example, Salmon's recent book (1986) does not discuss mental representation or functional- (conceptual-) role semantics, nor does it mention any of the many recent works on this topic (including those by Fodor, thus returning the compliment).

50. Nor does Almog, who seems to apply the Mind Strategy to the Opacity Problem as well as the Identity Problem. Certainly, he thinks that failures of substitutivity in "epistemic contexts" are of no concern to the 'Fido'-Fido theory (1985).

51. So have Soames (1988, 104-105) and Fodor (1987, 85-86). Salmon lists many others who have taken this path before; 1986, 167n.

52. Salmon rightly points out that the Identity Problem is properly posed only of speakers competent with the names in question (60).

53. See also Soames 1988, 105-106.

54. See also Soames 1988, 125.

55. See Baker 1982 for a demonstration of the rank implausibility of this view.

56. See also Soames 1987, 67-69; 1988, 104-105, 117-25.

57. Wettstein inclines toward this view also. He accepts that substitutivity often does fail for these attributions. He finds the subject "difficult and messy" but seems to think that a context-relative account of these attributions will leave the 'Fido'-Fido theory unscathed (1986, 204-209). See below.

58. E.g., Schiffer 1979. I criticize the view in 1981c.

59. In a paper defending Tarski and not on direct reference, Soames proposes a division within the study of language between semantics and pragmatics that is reminiscent of the old one mentioned in note 38 (1984c, 425-26). If it were applied here, it would trivialize the disagreement. On Soames's proposal, a language is an abstract object that has its semantic properties essentially; it is a triple consisting of a set of expressions, a domain of objects, and a function assigning objects to expressions. These abstract objects are the concern of semantics. Pragmatics is concerned with the contingent question of which language a person or population speaks. Soames's proposal would make the 'Fido'-Fido theory trivial once the Nondescription theory had been adopted, for on this conception of a language, there would then be nothing that could be a name's meaning except its role of referring to its assigned object. The traditional problems for 'Fido'-Fido would not disappear however. They would become problems for this way of dividing up the subject. Why suppose that the empirically

interesting question posed by linguistic phenomena is: Which of *these abstract objects* does *x* speak? The problems suggest that *x*'s use of a name—part of speaking a language—is *not* adequately explained by relating *x* to a pair consisting of the name and an object—part of the abstract object that is supposed to be the language. If language is to be conceived of as an abstract object, the empirically interesting conception must be richer than Soames'.

60. So does Wettstein's (1986, 205-206) and Salmon's (in press, n.12).
61. For more on this see my 1984a, 394-96; 1984b, 99-101.
62. There is little discussion of them in my 1981a and 1984a either.
63. But see 1981a, chap. 6.
64. For a lot more detail on some aspects of this discussion, see my 1981a, 129-57, 239-40.
65. Cf. Salmon's nice example of Aristotle; 1986, 75.
66. In my 1981a (134-36), I required that the subject actually form the identity belief. I now think that this yields an over-intellectualized account of the processing.
67. Note that in such cases knowledge of the identity does not lead to amalgamation of files. Thus we process some input to our 'Superman' file and not our 'Clark Kent' file, and vice versa. So the names have different modes of presentation; cf. Schiffer 1987, an interesting criticism of Salmon, to which Salmon in press is a reply.
68. The story for demonstratives is different. If '*a*' and '*b*' are such terms, '*a* = *b*' is usually informative. However, this is not to be explained by the differing senses of the terms, for example the differing senses of 'she' and 'you', but rather by what is common to the senses of all such terms: those senses make the reference of a token depend on a d-chain grounded by the speaker in producing that very token (1981a, 42-43). The possibility of tokens of different terms having different referents is intrinsic to the senses of the terms. Indeed, the possibility of tokens of the same term having different referents is intrinsic to the term's sense with the result that '*a* = *a*' can be informative.
69. For more on the place of analysis in semantics, see Devitt and Sterelny 1987, particularly 231-35. I suspect that the "analytical" view of philosophy lies behind motivation 2 in section 3.

Ackerman's view is like mine in that she ascribes different "non-descriptive connotations" to coreferential names (1979a, 1979b). However, she *does* offer analyses of these connotations as a solution to the Identity Problem. I think the solution will not work for similar reasons to those I offered (1983, 676-77) against her similar view of natural-kind terms (1980).

70. Salmon 1986, 73-76. I have adapted the Strategy a little to suit my purposes.
71. If Ralph's situation were general in a community, the case would be like that of 'George': one referent, one sound type, and yet two conventional senses.

Ralph might make a more serious mistake: treating tokens from two names as if they were from one. The earlier mistake is failing to unify where he should; this one is unifying where he should not. This mistake leads to a network grounded in two objects and thus to indeterminacy of speaker reference. I discuss this in 1981a, 138-52.

The Russell case is of the sort that generates Kripke's "Puzzle about Belief" (1979). I have urged a solution making use of the distinction between conventional and speaker senses (1984a, 407-12). I would offer a similar solution to Salmon's case of Elmer (1986, 92-101).

72. For many more details, see my 1981a, chaps. 9 and 10, and 1984a.
73. Shortly after this paper was sent to the publishers, David Kaplan sent me a copy of his "Afterthoughts" (1988b), in which proper names are discussed at some length. He still favors the 'Fido'-Fido theory. However, in contemplating a change in his view of a name's character (similar to those I proposed above on his behalf; section 3, motivation 3), he seems prepared to bring a name's mechanism of reference into its meaning. I am in broad agreement with many of his other remarks about names: on

the relation of thought to language (Devitt 1981a, 83-86; Devitt and Sterelny 1987, 124-28); on being *en rapport* (Devitt 1981a, chap. 9; 1984a); on naming future objects (Devitt 1974, 199-200; 1981a, 59-60).

Earlier versions of this paper were given at the University of Sydney (July 1988), La Trobe University (July 1988), and Princeton University (October 1988). The paper has benefited from the discussions it received on those occasions. I am very grateful to the following for helpful comments on a late draft at very short notice: Fiona Cowie, Norbert Hornstein, Bill Lycan, and Georges Rey. Finally, I must thank Nathan Salmon and Scott Soames for comments that removed some misunderstandings and led to other improvements.

References

Ackerman, Diana. 1979a. "Proper Names, Propositional Attitudes and Non-Descriptive Connotations." *Philosophical Studies* 35: 55-69.
Ackerman, Diana. 1979b. "Proper Names, Essences and Intuitive Beliefs." *Theory and Decision* 11: 5-26.
Ackerman, Diana. 1980. "Natural Kinds, Concepts, and Propositional Attitudes." In French, Uehling and Wettstein 1980, 469-85.
Almog, Joseph. 1984. "Semantic Anthropology." In French, Uehling and Wettstein 1984, 479-89.
Almog, Joseph. 1985. "Form and Content." *Noûs* 19: 603-16.
Almog, Joseph. 1986. "Naming without Necessity." *Journal of Philosophy* 71: 210-42.
Almog, Joseph, John Perry, and Howard Wettstein, eds. 1988. *Themes from Kaplan*. New York.
Baker, Lynne Rudder. 1982. "Underprivileged Access." *Noûs* 16: 227-42.
Barwise, Jon, and John Perry. 1983. *Situations and Attitudes*. Cambridge, Mass.
Block, Ned. 1986. "Advertisement for a Semantics for Psychology." In French, Uehling, and Wettstein 1986, 615-78.
Chastain, Charles. 1975. "Reference and Context." In *Language, Mind, and Knowledge: Minnesota Studies in the Philosophy of Science, Volume VII*, edited by Keith Gunderson. Minneapolis.
Davidson, Donald, and Gilbert Harman, eds. 1972. *Semantics of Natural Language*. Dordrecht.
Devitt, Michael. 1972. *The Semantics of Proper Names: A Causal Theory*, PhD Thesis, Harvard.
Devitt, Michael. 1974. "Singular Terms." *Journal of Philosophy* 71: 183-205.
Devitt, Michael. 1976. "Semantics and the Ambiguity of Proper Names." *Monist* 59: 404-23.
Devitt, Michael. 1980. "Brian Loar on Singular Terms." *Philosophical Studies* 37: 271-80.
Devitt, Michael. 1981a. *Designation*. New York.
Devitt, Michael. 1981b. "Donnellan's Distinction." In French, Uehling and Wettstein 1981, 511-24.
Devitt, Michael. 1981c. Critical Notice of French, Uehling and Wettstein 1979. *Australasian Journal of Philosophy* 59: 211-21.
Devitt, Michael. 1983. "Realism and Semantics," part II of a critical study of French, Uehling and Wettstein 1980. *Noûs* 17: 669-81.
Devitt, Michael. 1984a. "Thoughts and Their Ascription." In French, Uehling and Wettstein 1984, 385-420.
Devitt, Michael. 1984b. *Realism and Truth*. Princeton.
Devitt, Michael. 1985. Critical Notice of Evans 1982. *Australasian Journal of Philosophy* 63: 216-32.

Devitt, Michael. In press a. "Meanings Just Ain't in the Head." In *Method, Reason, and Language: Essays in Honour of Hilary Putnam*, edited by George Boolos, Cambridge.

Devitt, Michael. In press b. "A Narrow Representational Theory of the Mind." In *Representation: Readings in the Philosophy of Mental Representation*, edited by Stuart Silvers, Dordrecht. [Reprinted in *Mind and Cognition: A Reader*, edited by William G. Lycan, Oxford.]

Devitt, Michael, and Kim Sterelny. 1987. *Language and Reality: An Introduction to the Philosophy of Language*. Cambridge, Mass.

Devitt, Michael, and Kim Sterelny. In press. "What's Wrong with 'the Right View'." In Tomberlin in press.

Donnellan, Keith S. 1966. "Reference and Definite Descriptions." *Philosophical Review* 75: 281-304. [Reprinted in Schwartz 1977a.]

Donnellan, Keith S. 1968. "Putting Humpty Dumpty Together Again." *Philosophical Review* 77: 203-15.

Donnellan, Keith S. 1972. "Proper Names and Identifying Descriptions." In Davidson and Harman 1972, 356-79.

Donnellan, Keith S. 1974. "Speaking of Nothing." *Philosophical Review* 83: 3-31. [Reprinted in Schwartz 1977a.]

Donnellan, Keith S. 1979. "The Contingent *A Priori* and Rigid Designation." In French, Uehling and Wettstein 1979: 45-60.

Evans, Gareth. 1982. *The Varieties of Reference*, edited by John McDowell. Oxford.

Fitch, Frederick B. 1949. "The Problem of the Morning Star and the Evening Star." *Philosophy of Science* 16: 137-41.

Fodor, Jerry A. 1980. "Methodological Solipsism Considered as a Research Strategy in Cognitive Psychology." *Behavioral and Brain Sciences* 3: 63-73.

Fodor, Jerry A. 1987. *Psychosemantics: The Problem of Meaning in the Philosophy of Mind*. Cambridge, Mass.

French, Peter A., Theodore E. Uehling Jr., and Howard K. Wettstein, eds. 1979. *Contemporary Perspectives in the Philosophy of Language*. Minneapolis.

French, Peter A., Theodore E. Uehling Jr., and Howard K. Wettstein, eds. 1980. *Midwest Studies in Philosophy, Volume V: Studies in Epistemology*. Minneapolis.

French, Peter A., Theodore E. Uehling Jr., and Howard K. Wettstein, eds. 1981. *Midwest Studies in Philosophy, Volume VI: The Foundations of Analytic Philosophy*. Minneapolis.

French, Peter A., Theodore E. Uehling Jr., and Howard K. Wettstein, eds. 1984. *Midwest Studies in Philosophy, Volume IX: Causation and Causal Theories*. Minneapolis.

French, Peter A., Theodore E. Uehling Jr., and Howard K. Wettstein, eds. 1986. *Midwest Studies in Philosophy, Volume X: Studies in the Philosophy of Mind*. Minneapolis.

Kaplan, David. 1973. "Bob and Carol and Ted and Alice." In *Approaches to Natural Language: Proceedings of the 1970 Stanford Workshop on Grammar and Semantics*, edited by K. J. J. Hintikka, J. M. E. Moravcsik and P. Suppes, 490-518. Dordrecht.

Kaplan, David. 1975. "How to Russell a Frege-Church." *Journal of Philosophy* 72: 716-29.

Kaplan, David. 1979a. "Dthat." In French, Uehling and Wettstein 1979, 383-400.

Kaplan, David. 1979b. "On the Logic of Demonstratives." In French, Uehling and Wettstein 1979, 401-12.

Kaplan, David. 1988a. "Demonstratives: An Essay on the Semantics, Logic, Metaphysics, and Epistemology of Demonstratives and Other Indexicals." In Almog, Perry and Wettstein 1988, 510-92.

Kaplan, David. 1988b. "Afterthoughts." In Almog, Perry and Wettstein 1988.
Kripke, Saul A. 1971. "Identity and Necessity." In *Identity and Individuation*, edited by Milton K. Munitz, 135-64. New York. [Reprinted in Schwartz 1977a.]
Kripke, Saul A. 1979a. "Speaker's Reference and Semantic Reference." In French, Uehling and Wettstein 1979, 6-27.
Kripke, Saul A. 1979b. "A Puzzle about Belief." In *Meaning and Use*, edited by A. Margalit, 239-83. Dordrecht.
Kripke, Saul A. 1980. *Naming and Necessity*. Cambridge, Mass. [A corrected version of an article of the same name (plus an appendix) in Davidson and Harman 1972, together with a new preface.]
LePore, Ernest, and Barry Loewer. 1986. "Solipsistic Semantics." In French, Uehling and Wettstein 1986, 595-614.
Lewis, David. 1973. *Counterfactuals*. Oxford.
Loar, Brian. 1976. "The Semantics of Singular Terms." *Philosophical Studies* 30: 353-77.
Lycan, William G. 1985. "The Paradox of Naming." In *Analytical Philosophy in Comparative Perspective*, edited by B. K. Matilal and J. L. Shaw, 81-102. Dordrecht.
McGinn, Colin. 1982. "The Structure of Content." In *Thought and Object*, edited by Andrew Woodfield, 207-58. Oxford.
Marcus, Ruth Barcan. 1961. "Modalities and Intensional Languages." *Synthese* 13: 303-22.
Marcus, Ruth Barcan. 1981. "A Proposed Solution to a Puzzle about Belief." In French, Uehling and Wettstein 1981, 501-10.
Perry, John. 1977. "Frege on Demonstratives." *Philosophical Review* 86: 474-97.
Perry, John. 1979. "The Problem of the Essential Indexical." *Noûs* 13: 3-21.
Plantinga, Alvin. 1978. "The Boethian Compromise." *American Philosophical Quarterly* 15: 129-38.
Putnam, Hilary. 1975. *Mind, Language and Reality: Philosophical Papers*, vol. 2. Cambridge.
Richard, Mark. 1983. "Direct Reference and Ascriptions of Belief." *Journal of Philosophical Logic* 12: 425-52.
Salmon, Nathan. 1981. *Reference and Essence*. Princeton.
Salmon, Nathan. 1986. *Frege's Puzzle*. Cambridge, Mass.
Salmon, Nathan. In press. "Illogical Belief." In Tomberlin in press.
Schiffer, Stephen. 1979. "Naming and Knowing." In French, Uehling and Wettstein 1979: 61-74.
Schiffer, Stephen. 1987. "The 'Fido'-Fido Theory of Belief." In *Philosophical Perspectives, 1: Metaphysics*, 1987, edited by James E. Tomberlin, 454-80. Atascadero.
Schwartz, Stephen P., ed. 1977a. *Naming, Necessity, and Natural Kinds*. Ithaca.
Schwartz, Stephen P. 1977b. "Introduction" to Schwartz 1977a, 13-41.
Searle, John R. 1980. "Intrinsic Intentionality." *Behavioral and Brain Sciences* 3, 450-56.
Searle, John R. 1983. *Intentionality: An Essay in the Philosophy of Mind*. Cambridge.
Smullyan, Arthur Francis. 1947. Review of W. V. Quine's "The Problem of Interpreting Modal Logic." *Journal of Symbolic Logic* 12: 139-41.
Soames, Scott. 1984a. "Linguistics and Psychology." *Linguistics and Philosophy* 7: 155-79.
Soames, Scott. 1984b. "Semantics and Psychology." In *The Philosophy of Linguistics*, edited by Jerrold J. Katz, 204-26. London.
Soames, Scott. 1984c. "What is a Theory of Truth?" *Journal of Philosophy* 81: 411-29.
Soames, Scott. 1985. "Lost Innocence." *Linguistics and Philosophy* 8: 59-71.

Soames, Scott. 1987. "Direct Reference, Propositional Attitudes, and Semantic Content." *Philosophical Topics* 15: 47–87. [A condensed version, "Direct Reference and Propositional Attitudes," is in Almog, Perry, and Wettstein 1988, 383–409.]

Soames, Scott. 1988. "Substitutivity." In *On Being and Saying: Essays for Richard Cartwright*, edited by J. J. Thomson, 99–132. Cambridge.

Tomberlin, James E., ed. In press. *Philosophical Perspectives, 3: Philosophy of Mind and Action Theory*. Atascadero.

Wagner, Steven J. 1986. "California Semantics Meets the Great Fact." *Notre Dame Journal of Formal Logic* 27: 430–55.

Wettstein, Howard. 1986. "Has Semantics Rested on a Mistake?" *Journal of Philosophy* 83: 185–209.

Wettstein, Howard. 1988. "Cognitive Significance Without Cognitive Content." In Almog, Perry, and Wettstein 1988, 410–43.

Intrinsic Reference and the New Theory
LAIRD ADDIS

The new theory of reference, as Howard Wettstein has called it, while bidding well to become the dominant mode of thought among philosophers of language, contains at the same time, as the work of Wettstein himself reveals, the seeds of its own dissolution, at least within philosophy. This is one point I hope to demonstrate in the pages that follow. And while I refrained from putting 'theory' in double quotes in my title in the context of 'new theory', part of my argument will be that the new "theory" is not really a theory of reference at all; first, because it is not about reference to begin with (to put my thesis rather more strongly than I shall defend it, for the sake of emphasis) and, second, because it is not a theory so much as a *description*, better left to empirical anthropologists, of what external conditions must obtain in order that, as we speak, a person may correctly be said to have referred to something, or else a *prescription* as to how to use the word 'refer'. These points, too, I hope to make plausible. But I shall continue to refrain from putting 'theory' in double quotes, and treat 'the new theory of reference' as a name that is, however, a disguised description for something like 'the account that Howard Wettstein calls "the new theory of reference" '.

In a forthcoming book and an earlier article,[1] I have defended the existence of entities of a sort that, following William of Ockham, I call *natural signs*. The theory of natural signs contains or suggests a theory of reference because, first, it *is* about reference and not the conditions external to it and, second, because it *is* a theory insofar as it defends the existence of entities of a certain kind that other philosophers would say cannot, or at least do not, exist.

It would probably be agreed all around that the key feature of the new theory is that what determines reference cannot (always? ever? usually?) be found in a person's state of consciousness, at least if such states are conceived as "private" to the person who has them in the sense of not being available to public observation. This will be said to be so especially in the case of so-called "singular" reference, and so the philosopher must look "outside" the mind — whether to causal conditions or to context or to something else — in order to specify the, or the remaining, "conditions" of reference. The theory of natural signs, on the other hand, entails or strongly suggests that what, in the analytic sense, determines reference is entirely contained in a person's state of consciousness. Thus the question of whether or not it is possible, and what it means, to refer to a particular person or thing that is not present to one seems to be the locus of the dispute about whether or not "meanings are in the head." I shall argue eventually that in a certain sense there is no real issue here, once one makes a distinction between referring in thought and referring in language.

I shall proceed as follows: first, I shall set out, in sketch only, the theory of natural signs and the theory of reference it contains; second, I shall consider an objection, as formulated by Michael Devitt, to any such theory — an objection that I believe underlies much recent philosophizing about reference; third, I shall develop some general, almost metaphilosophical, ideas about the issue of reference; fourth, I shall examine the writings of one of the new theorists, Howard Wettstein, as an instructive and almost too explicit case of what I believe to be the inevitable direction of the new theorists; and, finally, I shall have some concluding remarks.

THE THEORY OF NATURAL SIGNS

William of Ockham says that a natural sign (*signum naturale*) or what he actually more often calls a conceptual term (*terminus conceptus*) is "a mental content or impression which naturally possesses signification."[2] I prefer to express the idea by saying that a natural sign is an entity that is *intrinsically intentional*, that is, by its very nature as the entity it is, *points to* or is *about* or *of* or *intends* something else. Fregean senses, whatever else they are (or would be, if there were any), would seem to be natural signs; and while the many philosophers who talk about "propositions," especially in the context of what it is that people believe, might seem to be committing themselves to natural signs — that is, propositions as natural signs of the states of affairs that make them true of false — few of them are explicit enough, ontologically, for one to be confident of any such judgment. In Frege's case, however, we may say that he does countenance natural signs, but as entities in a "third" realm, neither mental nor physical, and that exist eternally and independent of particular states of consciousness. Frege appeared to believe (falsely, I think) that if senses were constituents of individual states of consciousness, then truth and falsity would depend in a relativistic way on individual minds in a way that would entail an unacceptable psychologism.

I shall not attempt to argue here, at least not directly, that Frege is wrong. Rather, I shall sketch some of the arguments I made in detail in the aforementioned book and article why it is reasonable to believe that individual states of consciousness contain natural signs. After looking briefly at the ontology of natural signs, we will be in a position to connect the theory of natural signs with matters of reference and meaning.

Apart from the general consideration that the theory of natural signs is better than its alternatives by allowing one to avoid commitment to such "things" as third-realm propositions or false facts or non-existing particulars or possible states of affairs, there are three specific and somewhat overlapping arguments in its favor. One of them, what I call the *scientific argument*, starts from the fact that differences in behavior sometimes stem from (or at least correlate with) differences in what people are thinking about. For example, when I am thinking of the Eiffel Tower and you are thinking of the Great Wall of China, there must be some relevant difference between you and me, and *in* you and me, that would causally explain the different answers we would give to the question of what we are thinking about. Any theory that holds that to think about something is *merely* to be in some relation to it, whether causal relation or uniquely intentional relation, makes such differences in behavior impossible to explain. The argument from the idea that there must be some property of a person that correlates uniquely with what that person is thinking of is not quite, by itself, an argument for natural signs, but it does establish the notion of there being *some kind of property of me* that varies according to what I am thinking about.

A second consideration in favor of natural signs derives from the felt certainty a person may have at the moment of thinking about something as to what it is that he or she is thinking about. If I now imagine that Sirius has ten planets, I have utter certainty *what it is* that I am imagining as well as, not so incidentally, that I am *imagining* and not, say, remembering. And so, again, it would seem that there must be *some property of me* the awareness of whose exemplification, if I care to introspect, allows me to have such certainty. This I call the *phenomenological argument*, but it may be noted that it is not a simple argument as to what is given to us, which "arguments" are rarely convincing, but rather one as to what must be given to us when we consider the nature of a certain phenomenon—the felt certainty as to the object of one's awareness. Further considerations show, I believe, that this property of me must be a *natural* sign of what I am thinking about and not a *conventional* or *learned* sign.

Those further considerations blend into the third argument for natural signs, a partly *a priori* argument to the effect that if there were no *natural* signs, there could not be, as there uncontroversially are, *conventional* signs. The idea of this *dialectical argument* is that if A is a conventional sign of B, there must be a "third" that makes or takes or regards A as a sign of B, ultimately by *thinking* of A as a sign of B. But that presupposes already being able to think of A and B. Thus starts a regress that can be stopped only by supposing that one can just think of something without having a conventional (or learned) sign of it, and that means being able to "represent" it to oneself *naturally*. This argument, especially, takes for granted a certain frame of reference concerning the relation of language and mind that presupposes the primacy of mind to language in all philosophically interesting respects. But I cannot stop to discuss this further here.

These arguments for natural signs, combined with the hint above about one's knowing that one is imagining rather than remembering, suggest that an individual state of consciousness consists minimally of the exemplification of two monadic properties—one a natural sign (or *intentional* property) that specifies what the state of consciousness is a consciousness of, and the other a *mode* property that specifies the kind of awareness it is. The link or relation between a state of consciousness and what it is of, then, is precisely the connection between a natural sign and what it is a sign of; and that connection, unique to the intentional situation but common to all of them, I call simply the *intentional connection*.[3] It is this connection alone that can reasonably be called the relation of reference.

It is common in the literature to make a distinction between *descriptive* properties and relations on the one hand and *logical* properties and relations on the other or, to speak somewhat more ontologically, between the world's *content* and the world's *form*. It is also commonly supposed, and I agree, that whereas descriptive properties and relations are or may be causally efficacious in the sense of appearing as relevant variables in true laws of nature, logical properties and relations are not causally efficacious. So if I now assert that the intentional connection is, or is like, a logical relation while intentional and mode properties are descriptive properties, it will be evident that on this analysis all descriptive features of the intentional situation are properties and none relations. It is this feature of the analysis that preserves the scientific respectability of the theory of natural signs as will become clearer in the next section.

It remains here, however, to say something more about *reference*. As a "neo-Fregean" I hold (1) that reference can be understood only by understanding the nature of thought and its intentionality and that, therefore, anything reasonably called "semantics" whether of thought or language necessarily involves intentionality; (2) that, in the primary sense, reference is "achieved" by a person only when that person has a thought of what is referred to—whether in thought or language—which thought uniquely picks out the referent; (3) that thoughts are, or contain, *natural signs*, that is, entities of a sort that by their nature point to, or are about, something else; (4) that natural signs are *properties* exemplified by people and thus (*contra* Frege) are not "eternal" except in the sense in which, strictly speaking, no property is in time; and (5) that *meaning*, when it cannot be simply identified with what is in the present consciousness of the person who speaks, is nevertheless a function of actual or possible states of mind.

Analytically speaking, it is clearest to characterize the situation with regard to reference and meaning as follows: In the richest sense, to *think of* a particular person or thing that is not present[4] is to exemplify a natural sign of it alone, that is (to speak more commonly), to have in mind a definite description of that person or thing; to the extent that one lacks such a sign or description, one is not thinking of just that person or thing to the exclusion of all others.[5] So too, to *speak of* a particular person or thing that is not present is, in the richest sense, also to exemplify a natural sign of it alone while speaking, that is, to have in mind a definite description of that person or thing.

But now comes the asymmetry between thought and language, for, *as we use the language*, we are indeed prepared to say that a person may *speak of* (that is, *refer to*) a person or thing that is not present even if the speaker does not have in mind a definite description of the person or thing and even if, perhaps, the speaker has little or no thought of the person or thing in mind. In fact, little more seems to be required than that the person be barely conscious and be someone who has some knowledge of the language that he or she is using. But whatever the anthropological details may be, it is obvious that in such cases, we are concerned with the *public* meaning of the words, with what is "asserted" or "communicated" whatever the speaker may have had in mind. It is this kind of situation on which the new theorists focus and which, they believe, somehow presents a challenge to the neo-Fregean.

Nothing seems clearer to me that the fact that, whatever the details, public meaning is a function of the thoughts that people *do* have, *would* have, and *might* have. If we *choose* to say that a person who is drunk or almost asleep or otherwise with little awareness of what he or she is saying nevertheless referred to Socrates when mumbling the words 'Socrates was happy', then granted that this "reference" is not determined by the speaker's possession of a successful definite description of Socrates or even of the speaker's possession of such a description under certain unrealized conditions (although there is, necessarily, *some* condition under which he or she would possess it, for what it matters), it is nevertheless determined by the *possibility* of such a thought and implicit reference to that possibility. By that I mean that if anyone — speaker, listener, or anyone else — is pressed as to what or whom we the linguistic community mean by, say, 'Socrates', it will not suffice, as some seem to imagine, to keep saying 'Socrates' in an increasingly louder voice. We can fully satisfy ourselves only if we come to believe that we *can* produce a definite description that picks out Socrates alone (assuming that in historical fact there was exactly one person who did the things customarily ascribed to Socrates). Definite descriptions, as linguistic items, are usually characterized syntactically, but if they are to serve their semantic function(s), they must necessarily be conceived as the expression of actual or possible *thoughts*. And it is not possible to *think of* Socrates to the exclusion of everyone and everything else except by way of what in thought corresponds to the linguistic notion of a definite description.[6]

AN OBJECTION TO THE THEORY OF NATURAL SIGNS

Opponents of the philosophical theory (and commonsense belief) that what a person is thinking about is determined, to the extent that it is determined, by the contents of that person's state of consciousness sometimes profess to be mystified by the very idea that, as Devitt puts it, "an intrinsic property of an object can determine its relation to a particular object external to it."[7] Devitt goes on to say that "This is no more possible for the relation of reference than it is for the relations of kicking, teaching, being taller than, or being the father of."[8] He links this objection to the theory of intrinsic reference with Putnam's "Twin-Earth" argument which is based on the supposition that under certain conditions, two persons with identical thought contents would be referring to different things and thus follows Putnam in adopting the largely rhetorical device of labeling such theories as "magical" ones.

Putnam's arguments have been effectively attacked elsewhere; here I wish to focus on Devitt's rather general complaint, for, if I am not mistaken, it underlies much of the resistance to the theory of natural signs. That complaint, once again, is that the very idea of a property that intrinsically determines a relation to something else is one of something impossible. It is, to use some ever receding metaphysical language, the idea of an *internal* relation, one that is in some sense determined by the natures of one or more of its terms, as opposed to a purely *external* relation which is one that things just happen to have to each other in the sense that while their being in that relation is, to be sure, causally determined by something or other including, probably, some properties of the things in the relation, in no case can one *deduce* or otherwise figure out that those things are in that relation just from knowing what properties they possess. More precisely, it is, in the case at hand, the idea of an internal relation to some *other* object; and yet more precisely, the idea of an internal relation not only to some other object but, to use Devitt's language again, "to a particular object external to it."

And just why is it impossible that there be natural signs, that is, properties of a sort that *do* determine a relation to particular objects external to them? Devitt gives no reason at all except to list a number of other relations of which it is uncontroversially true that no property of any object so determines their particular exemplifications. But surely the fact that some relations are external relations is no reason at all for supposing that there cannot be a relation that is not an external relation. Nor, to my knowledge, does Devitt or any of the advocates of a causal "theory" of reference give any *argument* against the possibility of such a property; its impossibility is merely asserted (as in Devitt's case) or otherwise presupposed. So we must look behind the scenes.

I strongly suspect that what does lie behind the unargued-for assumption is the belief that for us in the empiricist, analytic tradition from Hume through Mill and Russell and the logical positivists, it is a settled matter that all relations are external. That is something that is imagined to follow from the "atomistic" way of thinking that characterizes our analytic modes of philosophizing and thinking about the world. To believe otherwise, some might say were they to give full voice to their assumption, is to be "unscientific," to revert to "holistic" or "organic," not to say "idealistic" or even "religious" ways of thinking. Now I have no wish, for it would be contrary to my own deeply rooted impulses, to be "religious" rather than "scientific" or "holistic" rather than "analytic." But I do wish to suggest that the idea of a natural sign and thus of a property that, in the disputed way, determines a relation of an object to another particular object is not only coherent in itself but accords fully with a scientific, analytic worldview and philosophical method.

Part of Putnam's reason for calling the theory of natural signs a "magical" theory is his notion that any such theory is linked somehow with those superstitions according to which by intoning certain words or thinking certain thoughts one can manipulate or otherwise affect, either directly or through the gods, those objects and events that those words and thoughts are about.[9] Putting aside all suggestions of any commission of the genetic fallacy, it is nonetheless important to be clear that *act* theory, as embodied in a theory of natural signs, does not in any way presuppose or entail or lend any credence to the proposition that our thoughts have any effect on their objects or, even more important, that anything occurs in this universe that does not admit of a purely physicalistic explanation.[10] Had this requirement, the satisfaction of which goes a long way to demonstrating the compatibility of natural sign theory with the scientific worldview and in particular with scientific psychology, been clearly kept in mind by Devitt, he would have seen at the outset that the relation of reference, the intentional connection, is radically different from the others he lists, all of which are such that being in such a relation to someone or something else does or may involve having a causal effect on it.

The fact that the relation of reference is of a sort that, as such, no causal effects are involved suggests that this relation, whatever it is, is not a *descriptive* relation but instead is, or is very much like, a *logical* relation. This suggests further that the worry about internal relations may be somewhat misplaced insofar as the arguments from the analytic tradition directed against such relations have usually been against *internal, descriptive* relations.[11] If the relation of reference is more like, say, *being-taller-than-by-five* (between numbers) or *being-identical-to* than, say, *being-taller-than* or *being-the-father-of*, then it is much more plausible to say that it, like the first two, is determined in a particular case by the nature of one or more of its terms. Questions about the ontological status of logical relations and about whether or not, in the case of reference, the relation actually holds when the object of thought does not exist are, to be sure, very important ones; but the first task is correctly to have located the ontological category to which that relation belongs.

Is there then any remaining argument against the possibility of natural signs, of properties that by their nature represent something else? I think not. Arguments against such properties based on their evolutionary improbability apply to all properties and those that are based on their causal idleness (which impotence I am prepared to grant, in a sense) only reflect their proponents' commitment to an ontology of the *basic*—the belief that only the properties of basic science exist. But the notion of causal idleness and its connection with the question of whether or not natural signs fit into a scientific worldview is worth further remark.

By causal idleness, as applied to a category of properties, I mean the characteristic of being such that whatever can be explained by the invocation of any of those properties (or, more precisely, their exemplifications) can just as well or better be explained otherwise. Explanation, in this context, means lawful explanation (of which so-called "causal" explanations are a subset). If both a dualism of properties and psychophysiological parallelism are true, as I believe them to be, then whatever can be explained — behavior, physiological states, social phenomena, other mental states — by anyone's mental state can be explained just as well or better by the brain or other physiological states that "parallel" through laws of coexistence those mental states. (By 'can' I mean, of course, that the laws are such that those explanations are "there" to be discovered.) Natural signs are mental properties, and while their invocation is reasonable in common explanations of behavior (as is 'She reversed her steps in suddenly remembering that she needed to stop at the grocery store'), one may reasonably also believe that all such behaviors admit as well of full, purely physiological explanations. Thus, if it is part of the scientific worldview to believe that everything that occurs admits of purely physical explanation — and I believe that it is — then the theory of natural signs, provided that it is coupled with a parallelistic view of the connection of mental with physical properties, is entirely consistent with that critical component.

I submit then that it is *not* part of the scientific worldview to believe that only physical properties exist, that is, to be an absolute materialist. Indeed, insofar as that worldview requires us to be, broadly speaking, *empiricist* in deciding what exists, we should be prepared to accept as existing whatever we do or seem to come across in our experience provided that there are no compelling reasons to believe otherwise (as with ghosts and gods). And because mental properties that are unknown to physics are among the things that we come across in our experience and because there are no compelling reasons to deny their existence, we should accept them as existing and be uninhibited in recognizing among them those that are natural signs.

THE NATURE OF THE ISSUE

What are the new theorists really up to? Are their "theories" really about the same phenomenon as those of the Fregeans and the neo-Fregeans? When the new theorists argue, both abstractly and by example, that it is often the case that when a person refers to someone or something, that person has no description or other content in mind that uniquely picks out the person or thing referred to, they take entirely for granted that, in such a situation, one can still truly say that the person "succeeded" in referring. Indeed, in general, it is customary to assume (and not only among the new theorists) that with respect to reference, a person either "succeeds" in referring or "fails" to refer in any particular case of what I suppose would have to be "trying" to refer, and that is all there is to it.

But is the assumption correct? Or rather, what is the nature of the assumption and how does it shape the new theorists' accounts of reference?

Suppose one starts instead with the idea suggested earlier that while granting that a person often does not have in mind a uniquely determining description of anything, to the extent that that is so one is simply not referring to any particular person or thing alone. If all that one has in mind is something that might be put into words as 'that old Greek philosopher' when asked whom he or she means by 'Socrates' (and ignoring the fact that with these two notions together one might get a successful definite description), why shouldn't we say that that person has only *to a certain extent* referred to Socrates in that while that person has, as it were, conceived a relatively small class of which Socrates is a member, he or she has not really picked him out uniquely?

The answer that many philosophers, including the new theorists, would give to that question is, I believe, that *we* know whom the speaker is talking about and, in any case, we would *say* that the person has referred to Socrates unless some other very special circumstances are known also to obtain (such as that the speaker believes that ancient Greece was a myth or that a philosopher is a kind of plant). So, assuming the conditions are "normal," has the speaker *really* referred to Socrates, after all?

What I want to suggest is that the answer to this question is not very interesting. Or, more precisely, it is of no philosophical importance once one sees clearly that to answer it one way or the other is to do no more than either to *report* on what one takes to be the linguistic habits of certain communities or else to *stipulate* how the word 'refer' is to be used. The important philosophical question is, rather, what is the nature of aboutness in its primary sense—the sense in which if there were no aboutness of that kind, there would be no reference and no "semantics" at all? The rest really *is* just linguistic anthropology or stipulation. Let us explore this idea in more detail.

If one were to attempt to set out in a relatively uncontroversial way what facts obtain in a situation in which we *say* that a person has, or might have, referred to someone or something, we might come up with something like this: that person is conscious and probably is in *some state of mind* that is somehow relevant to his or her having referred to one person or thing instead of at least some other persons or things or nothing at all; that person and more particularly the speech act by which he or she was said to have referred stand in certain *causal connections* to the person or thing to which he or she was said to have referred; and this person's speech act took place in a certain *context* which may include the rules of the language, the particular histories of speaker and listeners, and anything else. States of mind, causal connections, contexts: these seem to be the "materials" out of which contemporary philosophers of language would forge their "theories" of reference.

But many of these "theories" are not theories at all. When Putnam tells us, at great length, that a brain in a vat cannot really refer at all to most of the things that it (the brain) is "thinking about" because the usual causal connections do not obtain and no matter what the nature of the brain's conscious states, what really are we being told except how the word 'refer' *does* or *ought* to lay on the world?[12] It is certainly not a theory about how the extralinguistic reality *is*. Of course, the ruminations of the new theorists *start* from a certain account of how the world is in an interesting respect; namely, in insisting that many if not all states of consciousness fail to contain contents adequate to pick out a particular person or thing. That is a genuine theory about a philosophically interesting part of the world. The theory may be false, or at least vastly overdrawn, but it is not a piece of "concept analysis" so much as a piece of *phenomenological* analysis. But having convinced themselves of this theory, the new theorists feel called upon to deliver an account of what reference in language "really" is, given that is does not consist, presumably, in the having of certain states of consciousness while uttering certain words. And so we are told about causal connections and contexts.

One can labor as one will with trying to specify accurately the external conditions that must obtain in order for it to be the case that, *as we speak*, someone has "succeeded" in referring to someone or something. This is essentially a matter of behaviorist anthropological linguistics, for once one clearly separates the two questions of (1) What are the external conditions that must obtain for it to be the case that, as we speak, someone has "succeeded" in referring? from (2) What is the nature of that kind of state of consciousness that is the "presupposition" for anyone to have referred, in thought or language? One comes to see, first, that the new theorists have been largely confused in trying to have a "theory" of reference that would somehow at the same "level" combine external features such as causal conditions and context with internal features such as contents of consciousness; and, second, that whatever the new theorists say about the alleged paucity of states of consciousness with respect to traditional theories of reference, this is largely irrelevant to what they should really be about. One new theorist, and perhaps so far the only one, who seems to have arrived at much the same conclusions is Howard Wettstein, and a closer examination of his journey will further advance my argument.

THE WETTSTEIN CASE

In a series of papers over the last few years, Howard Wettstein has increasingly separated some kind of intellectual enterprise said to involve the "semantics" of language and deriving from the new theory of reference from what he takes to be the Fregean project of understanding the "structure" of thought (albeit, at least in Frege's own case, through the study of language). And although, in at least one crucial respect, Wettstein is not in accord with most of the new theorists, a brief survey of his papers will be instructive with respect both to my quasi-historical prediction about the future of the new theories and my systematic claims about reference.

One theme that has not changed in Wettstein's thinking is his emphasis on what is *asserted* or *communicated* in contrast to what is *thought* when a person is said to have referred in speech to someone or something. His first published paper, "Can What Is Asserted Be A Sentence?"[13] while more or less assuming the existence of propositions, something he comes later to question, argues that sentences are *not* what we assert while implicitly assuming that the "content" of what is asserted depends on the public meaning of one's words and not on one's individual thoughts.

In "Proper Names and Referential Opacity,"[14] the emphasis on communication in thinking about reference remains strong while at the same time Wettstein begins his defense of what is one hallmark of the new theory—the account of singular reference. This defense continues in his third paper "Indexical Reference and Propositional Content" in which he undertakes to "defend an account of indexical expressions which sides with Mill against Frege with regard to its model of singular reference."[15] And in rejecting any Fregean-type account of reference, Wettstein again sounds the theme that while a person may make a "complete and determinate" reference to something or a "successful" reference to something in uttering certain words, what goes on in the speaker's mind may be quite incomplete and indeterminate. So reference cannot be wholly determined by the speaker's conscious state.

Yet again, in "Demonstrative Reference and Definite Descriptions," we are told that "Russell's theory [of reference] fails as an account of *what is communicated*."[16] And in this paper, following an attack on Russell's theory when descriptions have *either* a "referential" or an "attributive" use, Wettstein begins to separate himself from most of the other new theorists by maintaining that it is *context* and not *causal connection* that supplies the additional elements for "determinate" reference, given that thought contents are not sufficient. In his next paper, "The Semantic Significance of the Referential-Attributive Distinction," Wettstein again invokes context as the crucial additional element while still retaining the assumption that in many cases in which no uniquely specifying description is operating and thus no uniquely specifying thought involved, nevertheless "determinate references are made and determinate propositions [are] asserted."[17]

In a short paper, "Did the Greeks Really Worship Zeus?"[18] Wettstein addresses the ancient problem of reference to non-existents, while in "How to Bridge the Gap Between Meaning and Reference" he distinguishes *three* distinct accounts of reference—the *causal* theory, the *intentional* theory, and the *context* theory.[19] Advocates of causal and context theories, by locating some or all of what I just called the "elements" of reference outside states of consciousness, tend to agree with Wittgenstein that "an individualistic or agent-centered picture of language and thought is inadequate and needs to be replaced or at least supplemented by a picture that sees language as a social institution."[20] This emphasis on the "social" aspect of reference becomes more and more pronounced as Wettstein begins to doubt that the new theorists and the Fregeans are even trying to answer the same questions.

This, indeed, is the main theme of "Has Semantics Rested on a Mistake?" in which Wettstein proposes, after arguing that neither "linguistic meanings" nor anything else will account adequately for the "cognitive significance" of certain utterances within the resources of the new theorists, "that we make a more radical break with Frege's outlook. The new theorist should reject Frege's adequacy condition outright."[21] (Frege's adequacy condition is that the correct account of reference must explain how identity sentences with proper names can be both true and informative.) And in language that I also believe gets at the heart of the matter, Wettstein tells us that "Frege, unlike the new theorist, was not concerned—at least not primarily concerned—with what we might call the *anthropology* of those institutional arrangements which constitute natural language, the uncovering of the semantic rules that govern our linguistic practices."[22] Even if the new theorists cannot answer the questions that Frege raised about reference, Wettstein wants to maintain that "there is no reason to suppose, in general, if we successfully uncover the institutionalized conventions governing the references of our terms, we will have captured the ways in which speakers think about their referents."[23] Thus, too, "An account of linguistic meaning is no longer to be seen as an account of anything like what the competent speaker understands by his terms, but rather as an account of the practices he has mastered."[24]

In his most recently published paper (as of this writing), "Cognitive Significance Without Cognitive Content," Wettstein further develops this idea of the new theorists as engaged in an almost altogether different enterprise from that of the Fregeans while arguing that the latter are not, however, merely doing something different but are wrong or confused in many particulars, whereas the former can, after all, give an adequate account of the cognitive significance of some utterances without appeal to anything mental. As for the purposes of the new theorist, now conceived as anthropologists, "the aim of the anthropological semanticist is not, after all, to solve Frege's problems"[25] for "Reference . . . has little to do with the head of the speaker."[26] And it is appropriate to this clarified conception of his enterprise that Wettstein will no longer have any use for propositions: "a truly social and naturalistic conception will want to do without propositions"[27] for it is no longer a question of the thoughts of the person but of "the practices he has mastered."

This brief sketch hardly begins to indicate the richness and subtlety of much of Wettstein's writing, nor does it make clear that most of his detailed arguments are directed not at Fregeans but rather at other new theorists. Its primary value in the larger scheme of things, as my review has tried to show, is the emergence of the conception of the enterprise of the new theorists as an *anthropological* one that has everything to do with externally observable behavior of human beings and little or nothing to do with what goes on in their minds. This, in my judgment, is exactly as it should be. But, at the same time, I believe that Wettstein's admirable journey has not reached its end, and that certain confusions hinder its completion; and so I shall now argue.

In one sense what I want to argue is that as the role of consciousness is an ever-retreating one in the anthropological enterprise that the new theorists are engaged in, so will the notion of reference, with which their challenge to the Fregeans began, itself begin to recede. This is a partly predictive, partly analytic claim. As to the latter, the idea is that if Wettstein and the other new theorists were to carry through fully on their enterprise as anthropological and as treating language (I now pointedly do not say "reference") as "social" and "naturalistic" (where 'naturalistic' apparently means something like: ignoring consciousness, something profoundly "unnaturalistic" in another sense), it would come to be seen that while the *word* or, better, the *sound* (or *mark*) 'reference' is part of the anthropologist's data because it is a sound that is produced by certain humans, reference itself, at least as preanalytically conceived as *some* kind of connection between a person and something else, will have disappeared from the scene.

To put the notion a bit more precisely: The student of observable human behavior will not find anything reasonably called reference: there is no relation in "nature" (in *their* sense) that connects words with things. The reason is that, strictly speaking, *there are no words in "nature"*! There are human organisms behaving in certain ways including making certain sounds. To be sure, the anthropologist of such behavior may also discover that those sounds are produced under certain causal conditions and in certain contexts, and one *could* say that when one of these organisms does produce a certain sound or sequence of sounds under a certain causal condition or context that that organism has "referred" to something. Perhaps the reason for saying that would be that some other organisms of that species sometimes make certain sounds that include the sound 'refer' in the "same" situation. (We cannot, of course, if we are strict behavioral anthropologists, say that those other organisms were *talking about* the first one.)

Now, despite what may sound almost like a parody of what a strict behaviorist anthropologist (where 'behaviorist' means here: really ignoring the realm of the mental and relying only on what is strictly observed) of human soundmaking should say about the subject matter, I have no objection in principle to proceeding in that way. If one is going to approach the subject of human behavior, including "linguistic" behavior, scientifically—that is, by allowing only the observable and what can in appropriate ways be understood through the observable but excluding the mental—this is the approach one should take. That is what it would really be to look at "language" from a "social" or "naturalistic" viewpoint. And I, for one, do not doubt the possibility or the value of such inquiry.

But Wettstein and the new theorists want to have it both ways: on the one hand, they reject, or tend to reject, the role of consciousness and the intentional connection in understanding philosophically what, at root, it is for a person to refer to something and instead look increasingly to discovering the external conditions under which we *say* that a person has referred to something. Brushing aside the important fact that such an enterprise should be a purely empirical and inductive one, I observe that, on the other hand, the new theorists also still wish to preserve the notion of reference in their cogitations in something like its original, relevant sense of *aboutness*. Otherwise, there is little point, if any at all, in continuing to say that they are giving accounts of reference. Let Wettstein and the other new theorists say very clearly (1) whether or not, if a certain population of humans were suddenly to become devoid of consciousness altogether but continued to behave as before, they would be sometimes *referring* to people and things; and (2) if not, why not. In short, is there really any such thing as *semantics* for the "anthropological semanticist"?

CONCLUDING REMARKS

Wettstein prefaces his "Cognitive Significance Without Cognitive Content" with a passage from Percy Walker's "The Delta Factor" about how an intelligent Martian without language would regard human speech; and while Wettstein a couple of pages later says that "Making the anthropological semanticist a Martian—that is, one who is not a participant in our, or perhaps any, linguistic practices—raises its own problems that, for the present, I would rather avoid,"[28] he clearly regards the thrust of the passage approvingly. Here is most of it:

> Imagine how it must appear to the Martian making his first visit to earth. Let us suppose that he too is an intelligent being whose intelligence has, however, evolved without the mediation of language, but rather, say, through the development of ESP. . . . What is the first thing he notices about earthlings? That they are forever making mouthy little sounds—clicks, hisses, howls, hoots, explosions, squeaks—some of which sounds *name* things in the world and are uttered in short sequences which *say* something about these things and events in the world.
>
> Instead of starting out with such large, vexing subjects as soul, mind, ideas, consciousness, why not set forth with language, which no one denies, and see how far it takes us.[29]

Is the *first* thing the Martian would notice about humans that they make sounds "some of which sounds *name* things in the world and are uttered in short sequences which *say* something about these things and events in the world"? Is it even the second or the third thing the Martian would notice? Indeed, would the Martian *ever* notice this thing? I have already suggested that, in the strict sense, there is nothing in what is observed that is the *naming* of things by sounds or the *saying* of things by sequences of sounds; there are just the sounds and their sequences. But would the Martian eventually *deduce* or otherwise reasonably *conclude* that, as we might now put it, these sounds have a semantics; and if so, on what basis would the conclusion be reached? Why would the Martian ever suppose that there is anything "semantical" going on at all?

The Martian has no language; the Martian observes only the outward behavior of soundmaking by the humans. Surely the only way the Martian could come to conclude that there is something "semantical" going on would require it first to have come to conclude that the soundmaking of these humans is part of a *language*, that is, an instrument for purposeful communication among themselves. Although it is not completely clear how the Martian would arrive at *that* conclusion, it seems clear that only *if* that happens will the Martian ever arrive at the further or more specific notion that there is anything "semantical" involved, that is, at some notion of *aboutness*. But where will the Martian's notion of aboutness have ever come from in the first place? Not from its own language, for it has none. The obvious answer is that it gets it, if it has it at all, from the intentionality of its own thoughts, and nowhere else. And if our intelligent alien does conclude that we humans are speaking a language and not just making sounds, it will naturally understand this phenomenon as one in which the meanings of the sounds are derived somehow from the intentionality of the thoughts of which those sounds are somehow the expression.

One "hears" someone *refer* to something not by hearing sounds or knowing the causal conditions that led to producing the sounds or taking notice of the context in which the sounds are produced but by taking the sounds as expressive of the speaker's actual or possible intentional state. In everyday life we all know that very well and could not possibly believe otherwise.

Notes

1. Laird Addis, *Natural Signs: A Theory of Intentionality* (Philadelphia: 1989) and "Natural Signs," *The Review of Metaphysics* 36 (March 1983).

2. William of Ockham, *Philosophical Writings*, edited and translated by P. Boehner (London: 1957), 47.

3. In the forthcoming book on natural signs, I argue in the fifth chapter that the intentional connection actually holds only when its object actually exists. But this is a complication that can be ignored here.

4. I restrict my discussion to these cases. I believe that Russell's acquaintance/description distinction, which is smudged or denied by the new theorists and others in their accounts of singular reference, well accounts for the obvious phenomenological difference between *perceiving* someone or something and all other modes of awareness of persons and things. This is another reason for believing that there is no such thing as "singular" reference to particular persons and things that are not present.

5. Another account is that of Searle, who would locate the "missing" intentional content elsewhere in the mind—in what he calls the Background and the Network. Part of the reason I cannot follow him in this is that I do not share his view that beliefs and other *dispositional* mental states are literally intentional states. For more detailed discussion of Searle's views on this matter, see the fifth chapter of my forthcoming book. For Searle's account of the Background and the Network, see John Searle, *Intentionality: An Essay in the Philosophy of Mind* (Cambridge: 1984), 141-59 and 65-71.

6. In the fifth chapter of the forthcoming book, I make a detailed argument why it is *ontologically* impossible to think of a particular except by way of description. The basic idea is that a particular, as contrasted with some properties and conceived as independent of the properties that it happens to exemplify, is only numerically different from some or all other particulars, and so is not recognizable or thinkable as such.

7. Michael Devitt, *Realism and Truth* (Oxford: 1984), 83.

8. Ibid., 83.
9. Hilary Putnam, *Reason, Truth and History* (Cambridge: 1981), 3.
10. For details, see Laird Addis, "Behaviorism and the Philosophy of the Act," *Noûs* 16 (September 1982).
11. Even some descriptive relations are at least initially recalcitrant to treatment as purely external relations. Some examples are: *being-darker-than* as in the fact that red is darker than pink and *being-higher-in-pitch-by-a-major-third* as in *e* is a major third higher than *c*. For what is probably the best treatment of these kinds of cases and thus for the argument that all descriptive relations are external, see Gustav Bergmann, "Synthetic A Priori," published in his *Logic and Reality* (Madison, Wisc.: 1967).
12. Hilary Putnam, *Reason, Truth and History*, 1-21.
13. Howard K. Wettstein, "Can What Is Asserted Be a Sentence?" *Philosophical Review* 85 (April 1976).
14. Howard K. Wettstein, "Proper Names and Propositional Opacity," *Midwest Studies in Philosophy* 2 (1977).
15. Howard K. Wettstein, "Indexical Reference and Propositional Content," *Philosophical Studies* 36 (July 1979): 91.
16. Howard K. Wettstein, "Demonstrative Reference and Definite Descriptions," *Philosophical Studies* 40 (September 1981): 247.
17. Howard Wettstein, "The Semantic Significance of the Referential-Attributive Distinction," *Philosophical Studies* 44 (September 1983): 189.
18. Howard Wettstein, "Did the Greeks Really Worship Zeus?" *Synthese* 60 (September 1984).
19. Howard K. Wettstein, "How to Bridge the Gap Between Meaning and Reference," *Synthese* 58 (January 1984): 64.
20. Ibid., 65.
21. Howard Wettstein, "Has Semantics Rested On a Mistake?" *Journal of Philosophy* 83 (April 1986): 200.
22. Ibid., 200.
23. Ibid., 201.
24. Ibid., 204.
25. Howard Wettstein, "Cognitive Significance without Cognitive Content," *Mind* 97 (January 1988): 5.
26. Ibid., 5.
27. Ibid., 14.
28. Ibid., 3.
29. Walker Percy, "The Delta Factor" in *The Message in the Bottle* (New York: 1954) as quoted by Wettstein, ibid., 1.

References

Addis, Laird. "Behaviorism and the Philosophy of the Act." *Noûs* 16 (September 1982): 399-420.
Addis, Laird. "Natural Signs." *The Review of Metaphysics* 36 (March 1983): 543-68.
Addis, Laird, *Natural Signs: A Theory of Intentionality*. Philadelphia, 1989.
Bergmann, Gustav. *Logic and Reality*. Madison, Wisconsin, 1967.
Devitt, Michael. *Realism and Truth*. Oxford, 1984.
Percy, Walker. *The Message in the Bottle*. New York, 1954.
Putnam, Hilary. *Reason, Truth and History*. Cambridge, 1981.
Searle, John. *Intentionality: An Essay in the Philosophy of Mind*. Cambridge, 1984.
Wettstein, Howard. "Can What Is Asserted Be a Sentence?," *Philosophical Review* 85 (April 1976): 196-207.
Wettstein, Howard. "Proper Names and Propositional Opacity," *Midwest Studies in Philosophy* 2 (1977): 187-90.

Wettstein, Howard. "Indexical Reference and Propositional Content," *Philosophical Studies* 36 (July 1979): 91-100.
Wettstein, Howard. "Demonstrative Reference and Definite Descriptions," *Philosophical Studies* 40 (September 1981): 241-57.
Wettstein, Howard. "The Semantic Significance of the Referential-Attributive Distinction," *Philosophical Studies* 44 (September 1983): 187-96.
Wettstein, Howard. "How to Bridge the Gap Between Meaning and Reference," *Synthese* 58 (January 1984): 63-84.
Wettstein, Howard. "Did the Greeks Really Worship Zeus?" *Synthese* 60 (September 1984): 439-49.
Wettstein, Howard. "Has Semantics Rested On a Mistake?" *The Journal of Philosophy* 83 (April 1986): 185-209.
Wettstein, Howard. "Cognitive Significance without Cognitive Content," *Mind* 97 (January 1988): 1-28.
William of Ockham. *Philosophical Writings*. Edited and translated by P. Boehner. London, 1957.

What Water Is or Back to Thales
AVRUM STROLL

I

The theory of direct reference embodies at least three mistakes: first, that there is such a thing as direct reference; second, that proper names are directly referential whereas definite descriptions are not; and third, that natural kind terms are directly referential. As interesting and important as the first two claims are, I will not have space to discuss them here.[1] Instead, this paper will be devoted to exploring the contention that natural kind terms are directly referential. I will not only show that this assertion is false, but I will also give an account of the factors that have impelled some philosophers into espousing such a view. The deepest of these, I will argue, is an obsessive concern with so-called identity sentences.

II

Hilary Putnam and Saul Kripke are, of course, the two most famous exponents of the view that natural kind terms are directly referential. In frequent cross-references to one another, they indicate that their views are virtually identical; and this seems to me to be correct. Let us concentrate on Putnam's version of the theory.[2] His account, stemming from his Twin Earth examples, is so well known that no extensive exposition of it is necessary here. The theory of direct reference he proposes is designed to undermine a certain "classical" doctrine whose author he does not name, but which very much resembles the famous view advanced by Frege in *"Über Sinn und Bedeutung"*. According to Putnam, this theory asserts that every descriptive term in a natural language expresses a sense (intension); that to understand what such a term means is to grasp its sense or intension; and that sameness of intension determines sameness of extension. It is thus the sense of a term that determines or fixes its reference. Accordingly, in referring to a certain natural kind, say water, one does so indirectly, via the intermediation of the sense expressed by the term "water."

Putnam also indicates that, according to this theory, the sense or intension of any natural kind term is a defining set of concepts that refer to the gross, or what Kripke calls the "phenomenological,"[3] features of the natural kind in question. In the case of "water" for instance, the definition, hard to state precisely, would be something like: "Water is the transparent, tasteless, odorless, liquid which constitutes rain, oceans and lakes, and which can freeze into ice and boil into steam." Being odorless, tasteless, etc., constitute the set of concepts one grasps in understanding the meaning (sense, intension) of the term "water." The point which Putnam wishes to emphasize is that the concepts comprising the intension are taken by the theory to refer to properties of water that are readily observable (hence Kripke's term "phenomenological") as distinct from those that determine its chemical composition. These latter are underlying and are not gross in the way that the fluidity and transparency of water are.

Indeed, that water was composed of a particular combination of hydrogen and oxygen was discovered comparatively recently, as the result of sophisticated scientific experiments conducted between 1830 and 1865, and therefore was a fact not known to most native speakers of English until much later. The classical theory is thus taken to imply that long before anything resembling modern chemistry was developed, human beings learned what water was in terms of its phenomenological or gross properties; and it is also taken to imply that as far back as we can trace the development of the English language, the word "water" was understood by native speakers to mean the liquid exhibiting these phenomenological features.

Putnam's argument against this theory begins with the stipulation, basic to the Twin Earth scenario, that the gross properties of the liquids that are respectively called "water" in these twin worlds are identical, so that they could not be distinguished from one another in terms of appearance, texture, weight, behavior, etc. Given that stipulation, the Twin Earth examples then go on to show: (1) that Earthling and Twin Earthling can be in the same psychological state in the sense that both are grasping the same intension, namely that "water" means the liquid having the phenomenological properties mentioned in the above definition; (2) that in fact the extension of "water" is a liquid that is H_2O on Earth and XYZ (where XYZ is not identical with H_2O) on Twin Earth, i.e., that the liquids referred to by the same term are different substances; (3) that "water" therefore means different things in these two contexts; (4) and hence, that the common concept or definition that Earthling and Twin Earthling were grasping was not what "water" means; (5) and, finally, what "water" means is its extension, so that "water" is directly referential, referring without intermediation to its extension which is H_2O.

Putnam concludes from these premises that the classical theory is wrong in two ways. First, since both Earthling and Twin Earthling were grasping the same intension, it follows that intension does not determine extension. For as the Twin Earth scenario shows, the term "water" determined two different extensions. And second, and even deeper, the theory was clearly wrong in holding that "water" meant the liquid having certain phenomenological properties. What "water" meant had nothing to do with any such Fregean sense or intension but was wholly determined by what water is; and this in turn was determined by the chemical composition of water. Thus, even those native speakers of English who learned and used the language before the nineteenth century were mistaken in thinking that "water" meant *the* liquid that exhibited certain gross properties, for the Twin Earth narrative indicates that *two* different liquids exhibited exactly those same properties.

This is a compelling analysis, now almost universally accepted by philosophers of language. But it is wrong, and it can be shown to be so by definitive counterexamples.

III

Let us distinguish between two issues: what the term "water" means and what water is. In this paper I will focus mainly on the latter question, but eventually will want to make a few comments about the former. The issues are obviously distinct: one of them is about words, the other about a nonlinguistic constituent of the world. Thales seems to have been interested in questions of the latter sort rather than those of the former. Putnam and Kripke frequently assimilate them, no doubt because they presuppose that the debate about what "water" means will be settled once it is determined what water is. It can be disputed whether the relationship is that close; but I shall not challenge them on that point. What I shall argue is that Kripke and Putnam are wrong in their account of what water is, and hence in their account of what "water" means.

So what do they take water to be? Here, for example, is a typical quotation from Kripke:

> . . . I want to go on to the more general case, which I mentioned in the last lecture, of some identities between terms for substances, and also the properties of substances and natural kinds. Philosophers have, as I've said, been very interested in statements expressing theoretical identifications; among them, that light is a stream of photons, that water is H_2O, that lightning is an electrical discharge, that gold is the element with the atomic number 79. (116)

Putnam's view is indistinguishable from Kripke's. As he puts it:

> Once we have discovered that water (in the actual world) is H_2O, *nothing counts as a possible world in which water isn't H_2O.* (130)

I think both Kripke and Putnam would agree that the expression, *water is H_2O*, exactly captures what they intend. Moreover, both of them take this locution to be an identity sentence, so that the word "is" means "is identical with." Let us simplify what they intend by using the formula: "Water = H_2O." I do not think that anything substantive in the theory is affected by this notational simplification. There is just no doubt that they mean that water is identical with H_2O.

But if that is so, the theory is unacceptable as the following counterexample will show.

(i): "Water = H_2O"
(ii): "Ice = H_2O"
(iii): Therefore, "Water = Ice."

The conclusion follows as an instance of the valid formula that if $A = B$, and $B = C$, therefore $A = C$. But since the conclusion of the argument is false at least one of its premises must be false (in fact both are). That the conclusion is false is obvious. Clearly, water is not identical with ice. If I ask you to put some ice in my glass I am not asking you to put water in my glass. Water is a liquid and ice is not; water is transparent and ice is not. Indeed, water and ice stand in a virtually unique relationship to one another. Nearly all other liquid substances have solids that are more dense than they are. But at 4 degrees C., water is more dense than ice and therefore ice will float on water. Ice could not in truth, and perhaps not even meaningfully, be said to float on water if ice and water were identical. Neither can ice and steam be phases of water, i.e., subsets of water, because something cannot be ice (a cold solid) and warm (a liquid) at the same time.

For analogous reasons, it is also false that steam is identical with water even though the chemical composition of steam is also H_2O. But if Putnam believes that water is identical with H_2O, then he would also have to subscribe to the belief that ice is identical with steam, since both ice and steam have the same chemical composition. That they do have the same chemical composition is a fact that can be confirmed by asking any chemist.

What is the import of such counterexamples for the Putnam-Kripke theory? Since patently water is not identical with ice, and since both water and ice have the same chemical composition, it follows *that the difference between them cannot be accounted for in terms of their chemical composition.* The difference will have to be explained in terms other than those referring to their common microcomposition—indeed, as I have indicated, in terms of their gross physical differences. And in order to do that, we shall have to employ the locutions that ordinary, nonscientific human folk have used for this purpose since time immemorial. It is the gross properties denoted by those locutions that allow us to make the distinction; these tell us that when water freezes it becomes ice; that ice is invariably cold but that water is not, and that water is transparent whereas ice is not. None of these is an underlying chemical component of water in the way that H_2O is. Yet they not only serve to allow us to distinguish water from ice, *they are the only means we have for doing so.* It follows that water is not identical with H_2O, that ice is not identical with H_2O, and that water is not identical with ice. All this is consistent with maintaining what is true, namely that the chemical composition of water is H_2O. For that statement which speaks about the *composition* of water *is not an identity sentence.*

Putnam-Kripke's basic mistake is to think that it is; or putting the point in the material mode of speech, we can say that their error is to have inferred from the fact that water is a substance composed of two parts of hydrogen and one of oxygen that it is identical with the union of those components. But as the previous argument shows, this is a sheer mistake, having such paradoxical consequences as that steam and ice, and water and ice, are identical.

Their idea that one can state what a natural kind is in terms of a simple identity sentence is not an uncommon error; indeed it permeates the literature on direct reference, and we can find it in other authors as well.[4] It arises, at least in part, from a failure to make certain distinctions that are crucial in understanding the science involved. Here is what Putnam says:

> Suppose, now, that I have not yet discovered what the important physical properties of water are (in the actual world)—i.e., I don't yet know that water is H_2O. I may have ways of *recognizing* water that are successful (of course, I may make a small number of mistakes that I won't be able to detect until a later stage in our scientific development), but not know the microstructure of water. If I agree that a liquid with the superficial properties of "water" but a different microstructure *isn't really water*, then my ways of recognizing water cannot be regarded as an analytical specification of what *it is to be* water. (129)

We can contrast what Putnam says with what chemists tell us about water. But first note that in the preceding passage Putnam asserts that water is H_2O and that it is to be identified with its "microstructure," implying with this last remark that H_2O is the microstructure of water. Further, what we have been calling the "gross" properties of water, Putnam calls "the superficial properties" of water. But scientists would deny both that the microstructure of water is H_2O and that the gross properties, which they also call the "physical" properties, of water are superficial. If they were superficial in Putnam's sense any chemist would tell you that you could not distinguish steam from ice.

In contrast with Putnam, scientists distinguish between the gross or physical properties (its fluidity and transparency, say) of a substance such as water and its chemical properties, such as its disposition to produce rust when, in the presence of air, it comes in contact with iron. Its properties, whether gross or chemical, are to be distinguished from its chemical *structure*. The term "structure" is used to speak both about the internal spatial arrangements of atoms within a molecule and about the internal spatial arrangements of the molecules within a substance. If one is speaking about a molecule of water, then the microstructure of that molecule would be the particular (and characteristic) arrangement of the hydrogen and oxygen atoms within the molecule. If one is speaking about a natural kind[5] such as pure water, the microstructure of the substance will be certain characteristic spatial relationships between its molecules. In the case of steam, this is a virtually random set of relationships; in the case of water, the arrangement is complex, characterized by much molecular movement and tumbling; in the case of ice, the molecular arrangement is regular and crystalline.

Putnam's term "microstructure" blurs these distinctions and leads to serious confusions. The basic point is that there is not a one-to-one correspondence between the physical, chemical, or gross properties of water and its chemical components. Thus, water, ice, and steam all have the same chemical components. Each is composed of molecules containing two atoms of hydrogen and one of oxygen. Yet their gross properties are different, ice being rigid and water not. The example is directly relevant to the point we have been making above. Ice, water, and steam are all identical in chemical composition, but their physical properties are distinct. If each of them were identical with its chemical composition, then each would be identical with the other and then by Leibniz's Law each of them would have identical gross properties. Since they clearly do not, it follows that none of them is identical with its chemical components (or indeed, with its "microstructure" as Putnam uses that term). One cannot therefore distinguish between them in terms of their chemical composition. It follows that Putnam is wrong in holding that water *is identical* with H_2O, and indeed, that natural kinds in general are to be identified with their chemical composition. His mistake stems, as I have indicated, from not distinguishing the propositions, *water is identical with H_2O* and *water is composed of H_2O* from one another. The "is" in "water is H_2O" is not the "is" of identity but the "is" of composition.[6]

One can make the same point by adopting a technique made famous by Kripke. Kripke will ask "Can you imagine a situation in which a liquid can have all the properties usually associated with water, such as being transparent, non-viscous, etc., and yet not be composed of H_2O?" Since the Twin Earth narrative gives one good grounds for saying "yes," both Putnam and Kripke would argue that water cannot be identified with the liquid having those phenomenological properties. Both infer therefore that water must be the single liquid composed of H_2O. But this is a non sequitur as my counterexample shows. Can one, we now ask, imagine something composed of H_2O which is not water? Of course, we answer: ice and steam. (And these are real cases, unlike the Twin Earth examples.) That shows by an argument parallel to that of Kripke and Putnam that water cannot be identified with its compositional constituents. But if water is not identical with a substance having those phenomenological properties, as Putnam and Kripke claim, or with a substance that is identical with H_2O, as I claim, then what can it be?

IV

To this question we have an answer. In giving that answer, we shall find it helpful to begin by considering two theses that Kripke advances in this connection. First, as an earlier quotation establishes, he states that "water is H_2O," "light is a stream of photons," and "lightning is an electrical discharge" are identity statements.

Second, he holds that a natural kind is determined by (is to be identified with) its *internal* structure. He writes:

> Even though we don't *know* the internal structure of tigers, we suppose—and let us suppose that we are right—that tigers form a certain species or natural kind. We then can imagine that there should be a creature which, though having all the external appearance of tigers, differs from them internally enough that we should say that it is not the same kind of thing. We can imagine it without knowing anything about this internal structure—what this internal structure is. We can say in advance that we use the term 'tiger' to designate a species, and that anything not of this species, even though it looks like a tiger, is not in fact a tiger. (120–121)

These two passages raise some issues we have already examined, but some we have not. A consideration of these will help us with the question of what water is. First, by the examples he cites, Kripke suggests (though he does not explicitly assert) that there is a distinction to be drawn between the internal and the external features of a natural kind. But is this true? If lightning is a natural kind, and is identical with an electrical discharge, then which features are internal and which external? Shall we consider the color of a bolt of lightning to be external; but external to what? Surely not to the electrical discharge, for presumably the color just is that discharge. Second, he claims that a natural kind is to be identified with its internal rather than with its external features. But we have already shown this thesis to be incorrect in the cases of ice and water. Third, Kripke avers that the internal features of a natural kind are to be identified with its internal *structure*. Do we know that every natural kind has an internal structure? Kripke insists that this must be so, even if we do not know what that structure is. Surely, this is *a priori* stipulation masking itself under the guise of scientific philosophy.

But as unconvincing as the above claims are, the Kripke-Putnam insistence upon drawing an *exclusive* distinction between the external and internal features of a natural kind in order to lay the groundwork for the claim that it is the internal features that determine the kind in question is even less justifiable. That is, it is assumed (rather than argued for) by Putnam and Kripke that if a natural kind like water has both internal and external features, one cannot identify the natural kind with features of *both* sorts. That is the whole thrust of Putnam's Twin Earth arguments and their Kripkean congeners. Their strategy is designed to force us to choose between competing alternatives: between the phenomenological and the microstructural. But there is simply no reason to do so. A correct account of what water is will mention *not only its phenomenological features but also those that are not readily observable*.

There is thus a double mistake in their approach. First, they assume that one can give an accurate account of what water is in terms of a simple identity sentence, and second, they infer, via a factitious distinction between supposedly competing alternatives, that water is to be identified with only one of those, namely, its internal microstructure. In giving a correct account of what water is, I reject both their assumption and their inference. Instead, I submit that in order to understand what water is we need an extensive characterization that is open textured. I will not attempt to give a full characterization here; it would require too much space. But I will now offer a shorter version of such a description; I give this to illustrate the points that the characterization is complex, that it cannot be reduced to a simple identity sentence, and that it will refer both to features that are readily observable and to features that are not.

> Water is a substance. That substance has various observable features: it is liquid, transparent, collects in pools, etc. (The "etc." informs the reader that in a fuller description other items would be added to that set of features). In its pure state, it is odorless, tasteless, colorless, and possesses a high degree of fluidity. In oceans, lakes, etc. it is generally found in an impure state, containing minerals, mud, and other substances. Pure water is composed of molecules each of which contains two parts of hydrogen and one part of oxygen. The microstructure of water is complex, because its molecules are in a highly active state that causes tumbling and other rapid movements. When water is cooled to the temperature of zero degrees Celsius it freezes, forming ice, and when heated to 100 degrees C. it boils, forming steam. It has the peculiar property that when near its freezing point, it becomes more dense than ice so that ice can float on it. Its molecular *composition* does not change during these processes but its *microstructure* does. (One can explain these scientific points at much greater length.) Water is and can be used for various purposes, such as (and here a lengthy list would follow).

That complex statement describes accurately, though not completely, what water is. It will be noted that it is not a simple identity statement of the kind that the Putnam-Kripke approach requires, and in particular that it does not *identify* water with any particular feature, whether gross or nongross.

V

What has all this to do with the theory of direct reference? That theory, as I mentioned earlier, is a theory about language, especially about the meaning and referential uses of certain categories of words, and not primarily a theory about the constituents of the world *à la* Thales. But because its proponents maintain that natural kind terms directly refer to so-called microstructures in the world, they believe that it is necessary to give an account of such structures in order to articulate and defend the theory. Hence, the attempt to explain what water is via its putative microstructure. In particular, as we noted, Putnam and Kripke suppose that a good reason for believing that the word "water" means H_2O is that water is identical with H_2O. But since, as we have demonstrated, their supposition is false, it is not a good reason for believing that "water" means H_2O.

But there is more to the theory than we have indicated so far. Taken as a linguistic thesis, it makes another important claim. It holds that one can explain what "water" means by a technique similar to that which used to be called an "ostensive definition." An ostensive definition is thought to be a paradigm of direct reference. It gives the meaning of a word by directly correlating the word with its referent. The technique rests upon the familiar principle that one can explain what "water" means by indicating what water is. One will point to a sample of H_2O while uttering the word "water." It is believed that an auditor will come to understand what "water" means via this procedure, which is sometimes referred to as an "initial baptism." I will now show that one cannot come to understand what "water" means in this way, and, further, that it would not enable an auditor to distinguish between the supposedly diverse meanings of "water" on Earth and Twin Earth.

The direct reference account implies that the process is similar to the following case. Suppose we take a small child to a zoo for the first time, and point out various animals the infant has never seen before. We point and say "That is an aardvark," "that is a tiger," etc. In this way, the child comes to understand what "aardvark" and "tiger" mean.

Here is Putnam's account of how one explains what "water" means:

> Let W1 and W2 be two possible worlds in which I exist and in which this glass exists and in which I am giving a meaning explanation by pointing to this glass and saying 'This is water.' Let us suppose that in W1 the glass is full of H_2O. . . . (127)

To whom is Putnam giving this explanation? Presumably his auditor is not a foreigner since Putnam uses English in communicating with that person. Is the individual a very young child, someone who does not know what "water" means? Let us assume so, since all normal adults, and virtually all older children, already know what "water" means, and therefore do not need an initial baptism. Yet as we shall see, the power of the example does not depend upon the auditor's being a child; we shall show that similar difficulties will also arise for an adult. But by beginning in this way we can delineate the central issues more perspicuously. Let us therefore assume that Putnam is trying to explain what "water" means to a young child. Then, would his explanation be a good one? Could such an infant come to understand that "water" means H_2O via the process Putnam describes?

A profound difficulty with this account is that if H_2O is the microstructure of water as Putnam claims, how would the child know what Putnam is pointing at? Surely, with the naked eye the child cannot see the microstructure of water. So what will the child be looking at? Putnam states that he is pointing to a glass, and saying: "This is water." Why shouldn't the child take Putnam to mean "This glass is water?" After all, that is the most obvious interpretation of what he said. So how does his listener come to understand that Putnam intends to refer to the liquid in the glass rather than to the glass? Perhaps Putnam should have put a finger in the liquid, stirred it a bit, and then said: "This is water." But then maybe the child will have understood him to mean that his finger is water. How can he get the child to know that he means the liquid?

Let us suppose that somehow Putnam does succeed in getting the child to attend to the liquid in the glass. Then will the child be seeing the microstructure of water? Of course not. What that person will be looking at is a liquid with certain observable features. So how could Putnam's explanation teach the child that "water" does not mean the liquid having those overt characteristics, but instead means H_2O?

Clearly, it could not. One would need a more elaborate set of instructions than Putnam provides in order to get the child to believe that "water" means a certain sort of microstructure. Those instructions, if they are to get off the ground at all, will have to include the locutions "H_2O" and "microstructure." But then how could Putnam get a young native speaker who does not know what "water" means to understand, especially by an ostensive process, what "H_2O" and "microstructure" mean? Indeed, where could one find a young child who could understand Putnam's sentence, "This is water," and yet not know what "water" means? Note also that nowhere in this process does Putnam talk explicitly about the word "water." Instead, his effort is directed to getting the child to recognize that what is in the glass is water. Even if the effort were successful, how would it help explain what a word means? Surely, we need some additional explanatory procedures to go from talk about water to talk about the meaning of a word.

As I mentioned earlier, the difficulties I have described would exist if the person being given such a meaning explanation were an adult. Such a person looking at a sample of what is called "water" on earth could not distinguish it from a sample of what is called "water" on Twin Earth, since both specimens would have exactly the same phenomenological properties. For Putnam to explain that one sample consists of H_2O, whereas the other consists of XYZ, would amount to distinguishing them via definite descriptions. That is, Putnam would have to say something like "what is called 'water' on Earth is *the same stuff* as this sample here (pointing to the liquid in a glass), and by 'same stuff', I mean that it is composed of H_2O."

That is just what he does say, as the following quotation makes clear:

> Then the theory we have been presenting may be summarized by saying that an entity *x*, in an arbitrary possible world, is *water* if and only if it bears the relation *same* (construed as a cross-world relation) to the stuff *we* call "water" in the actual world. (129)

Accordingly, his meaning explanation would no longer involve just directly referential terms, but would identify water through the intermediation of a description—"the stuff that like this sample is composed of H_2O." So, the direct reference account would not work for an adult either, since that adult could not directly observe the underlying chemical components of the stuff that Putnam is pointing at.

The scenario becomes increasingly implausible as one explores it. It also fails, for example, to distinguish cases where one is being introduced to items that are unfamiliar, like aardvarks and tigers, from those cases where the items are very familiar, such as water and human beings.

VI

I will now propose an alternative to Putnam's account. Suppose we wish to explain to a child what the word "water" means. How do we in fact go about it? We can exclude the direct reference myths that we do this by an initial baptism—by showing a child a glass of water and saying: "This is water" or by telling a child that what we now call "water" in the twentieth century is H_2O.

The notions of *explaining*, *understanding*, and *meaning* are connected elements in an ongoing instructional process designed to promote communication between human beings. Meanings play a crucial role in this process. They are the links that tie the chain of communication together. They allow thoughts to be encoded in sentences and transmitted to others; they allow the thoughts of others to be understood. In teaching an infant its native language, including what words mean, we do not begin with definitions, ostensive or otherwise. We train children to obey commands and to follow orders, such as "Don't spill the water," "Bring me a glass of water," "There is too much water in the glass," and so on.

As Wittgenstein writes:

> Children do not learn that books exist, that armchairs exist, etc. etc., — they learn to fetch books, sit in armchairs, etc.[7]

These kinds of training procedures initiate a child into a community united by common linguistic practices. Their effect is to provide modes of explanation that are not totally explicit but which through a cumulative, developmental process eventually endow a child with the understanding of what words mean.

The outcome of the process is that the young child in an effort to communicate his thoughts to others, and to understand theirs, learns to use the word "water" in a way which is consonant with community practice. The child learns, that is, to apply the word to a liquid having certain phenomenological properties; and beyond that, to use the word in a variety of other ways, as an active verb, for instance.

This learning process extends through time. At first a child may only understand "water" to mean a fluid that is tasteless and colorless. Later, he may learn that this fluid which is colorless in a glass takes on a bluish hue in thick layers, that mud and salts dissolve in it, and yet that the word "water" is still applied to it. He may also discover that when sufficiently cold it is transformed into a different substance which he is taught to call "ice." How should one describe these supplemental pieces of information? Are they additions to the meaning of "water"? Let us not try to decide the matter here. What is clear is that such additional pieces of information allow for fuller communication between the child and others. The important point is that at this level of education, all the components of the meaning of a word like "water" that a child grasps are phenomenological, i.e., they consist of such concepts as *being liquid, being fluid, being transparent, being odorless*. Meaning thus arises as a function of what the child observes and experiences. And what he observes are the gross properties of water. As his education proceeds, he may eventually come to learn (though not by seeing) that water is composed of H_2O. Shall we say, as Putnam and Kripke insist, that the child only knows what "water" means at the very end of this process—i.e., when he learns that water is composed of H_2O? Why should we? We do not and we should not.

If Putnam and Kripke were right no native speakers of English before 1800 could have known what "water" meant. But if so, they could not have communicated with one another; they could not have sensibly given or obeyed such commands as "Don't spill the water" and "Bring me a glass of water." But since they did communicate with one another in saying these things, and without knowing anything about the molecular structure of water, it follows that they did know what "water" meant, and accordingly that the theory advanced by Putnam and Kripke is mistaken.

These early training procedures do not make use of the techniques of direct reference. They do not rely upon ostensive definitions and they do not initially teach a child that water is composed of H_2O. Instead, they teach a child what "water" means by reference to what the child observes, viz., to the phenomenological features of water.

The direct reference doctrine cannot account for the developmental process I have described, or for the role that the phenomenological features of water play in determining the meaning of "water," or for the historical fact that early speakers of English in using the word "water" obviously communicated with one another. These thus comprise decisive reasons for rejecting it.

VII

But now it might be objected: You have described how we *explain* the meaning of a particular word. But that is different from telling us what the word means. What does "water" mean in English? Indeed, how do we decide what any word means?

We begin our answer by noting that we are speaking about individual words rather than about phrases, sentences, or longer units of language such as paragraphs or chapters. Unlike some of these longer units, words are the kind of linguistic entities to which the question "What does x mean?" singularly applies. Indeed, they are paradigms of the linguistic units about which we can ask that question. *In general* we cannot sensibly ask that question about a whole sentence, though we can *sometimes* ask it—say, if one is trying to translate a sentence from a foreign language into English. One can then ask of the sentence itself, "What does it mean?" The answer will consist in translating it into a synonymous English sentence. But we do not normally ask what a sentence means, though of course we might be asking what somebody means in using the particular sentence he does. In contrast, even native speakers frequently ask what an English word means.

Fortunately, we have a decision procedure which allows us to answer questions about the meanings of words; namely, we can look up their meanings in a dictionary. For any word in common use, a good dictionary will give us its meaning (in contrast, we cannot look up the meaning of a sentence or a paragraph in a dictionary). When we do this in the cases of "aardvark," "tiger," and "water," the results are very interesting.

Here is what *The American College Dictionary* gives as the meaning of "aardvark."

A large, nocturnal, burrowing mammal of Africa, subsisting largely on termites, and having a long, extensile tongue, claws, and conspicuously long ears. There is only one genus, *Orycteropus*, constituting a separate order, *Tubulidentata*.

And here is what it gives for "tiger."

A large, carnivorous feline, of Asia, tawny-colored, striped with black, ranging in several races from India and the Malay Peninsula to Siberia.

Four other dictionaries I have consulted give similar definitions. *Webster's Third New International Dictionary* (p. 2392) says:

Tiger: A large Asiatic carnivorous mammal having a tawny coat transversely striped with black, a long untufted tail that is ringed with black, underparts that are mostly white, and no mane, being typically larger than the lion with a total length, usu. of 9 to 10 feet but sometimes of more than 12 feet, living usu. on the ground, feeding mostly on larger mammals (as cattle), in some cases including man, and ranging from Persia across Asia to the Malay peninsula, Sumatra, and Java, and northward to southern Siberia and Manchuria.

You will note that in none of these definitions is anything said about the microstructure, DNA, or the internal structure of any of these natural kinds. Instead, the emphasis is upon the phenomenological characteristics: in the case of a tiger, its having a tawny coat, black stripes, no mane, underparts that are mostly white, and so forth.

What the word "tiger" means, then, is the animal having those particular features. Kripke is wrong in thinking that the meaning of "tiger" has anything to do with the "internal structure" of tigers.

Now Kripke might respond to this by saying that there are animals we call "tigers" that do not fit the above description—albino tigers, three-legged tigers, two-headed tigers, and so forth. And he would argue that what determines all of them to be tigers is their identical genetic make-up. But this is a sheer mistake. People do not call albino tigers "tigers" because of their genetic make-up, which in fact almost nobody knows anything about. Such aberrant animals are called "tigers" because experience, based upon observed properties, makes it plain that we can expect such deviations from the norm. That is, persons observing tigers over lengthy periods of time will note that some of them are of a slightly different color than others, are striped in different patterns, and indeed vary in all sorts of ways from prototypical tigers. Experience teaches us that there is a spectrum of such features, an extreme example of which is an unstriped tiger such as an albino. It is still thus the observable features that are decisive in determining whether something is to be called "tiger" or not, and not the underlying structure of tigers. The case is thus parallel to that of "water."

The instance of tigers is interesting for another reason. It gives us good grounds for suggesting that in general overt considerations, including the functions that certain natural kinds serve, are decisive in overriding microfeatures in determining what a word means. The common noun "table" (not a natural kind word, of course) is applied to objects made of glass, steel, wood, plastic, and other materials. The microstructures of tables will vary depending on the material of which the table is made. Yet, function determines whether we subsume objects having such diverse microstructures under the rubric "table." So here is a case in which objects with different microstructures are assigned to the same category. Now it is easy to extend the point to natural kind terms. Consider the following modification of the Twin Earth scenario by way of illustration.

Suppose that for centuries now there has been considerable interaction between Earth and Twin Earth. Persons have been flying between these planets for eons, and for some time now planes leaving Earth have been stocking up on what Earthlings call "water," and which they use for drinking, washing, cooking, and other purposes. Planes returning from Twin Earth have been stocking up on what Twin Earthlings call "water," and this liquid is used for the same set of purposes on the return trip. But let us suppose that nobody before 1989 had performed a chemical analysis on the fluids they respectively call "water" on the two planets, but that in 1989 that was done. It was then determined that the liquid on Earth was composed of H_2O and that the liquid on Twin Earth was composed of XYZ. Would the persons moving between the planets stop calling one of the fluids "water"? I doubt it. I think they would say that water is composed of different ingredients, depending on where it is found, or perhaps they would say it comes in at least two different forms, like jade. They would thus treat the word "water" in the way we now treat the word "table." Function would override microcomposition in such a case. The example shows that there are plausible alternatives to Kripke's contention that the microcomposition of a substance is always decisive with respect to what we call that substance. With the sorts of modifications I have mentioned, similar comments apply to albino tigers.[8]

VIII

Still, there are differences between the case of "water" and the cases of "tiger" and "aardvark." Unlike those nouns, "water" is defined by all good modern dictionaries both in terms of the phenomenological features of water *and* the chemical composition of water. *The American College Dictionary* says:

> Water. n. The liquid which is a more or less impure state constitutes rain, oceans, lakes, rivers, etc. and which in a pure state is a transparent, odorless, tasteless liquid, a compound of hydrogen and oxygen, H_2O, freezing at 32 F or 0 C., and boiling at 212 F or 100 C. It contains 11.188 percent hydrogen and 88.8812 percent oxygen, by weight.

The emphasis in this definition is upon the phenomenological features of water. But water is also said to be a compound of hydrogen and oxygen, H_2O. In mentioning that water is composed of hydrogen and oxygen, the dictionary, to be sure, does not state that water is identical with H_2O, as Putnam and Kripke contend. Yet its reference to the chemical components transcends the merely phenomenological.

Since I am arguing that dictionaries give us the meaning of words, it would seem that I must be committed to the view that it is part of the meaning of "water" that the composition of water is H_2O, and therefore that Kripke and Putnam are at least partially right. But am I committed to such a view? The matter is complex.

Dictionaries written before 1830 do not mention H_2O at all in defining "water"—see Thomas Sheridan's *A General Dictionary of the English Language* of 1780, and Samuel Johnson's *A Dictionary of the English Language*, 9th ed., 1805, for example.

Given the difference between such early modern and contemporary lexical definitions, we have at least five different options for describing what "water" now means. Some of these support Kripke and Putnam, though most do not. We can say: (1) that the meaning of "water" changed after 1860; (2) that English speakers before 1860 did not know what the word "water" meant since they did not know that water was composed of H_2O; (3) that meaning is a matter of degree, the full meaning of "water" having been arrived at only after 1860; (4) that we should abandon the notion that it is dictionaries that give us the meaning of words; or, (5) that dictionaries give us *the* meaning of "water" in terms of the phenomenological characteristics of water, and also give us certain supplementary pieces of information about water that are not part of its meaning: the references to its chemical properties being such additional pieces of information. I reject (2) for reasons already stated, and (4) on methodological grounds, i.e., it seems clear to me that dictionaries do give us the meanings of words.

I am unable to decide categorically between (1), (3) and (5), though I entertain (1) with considerable reluctance, because I have the hard intuition that English speakers in the eighteenth century meant by "water" exactly what we mean today. But I am unable to mount a compelling defense of this intuition. For reasons explained earlier, I am attracted to (3) but with reservations over how to distinguish different degrees of meaning. Thus, if I had to, I would probably defend (5). This proposition has the merit that it assimilates "water" to "tiger" and "aardvark," thus giving us a uniform account of the meaning of natural kind terms. That is, it allows one to claim that what all natural kind terms mean is determined by the phenomenological features of the natural kinds they denote, and accordingly that the references to H_2O, etc., are not strictly part of the meaning of "water." But I will not argue firmly for that position here.

What is really clear to me is that water is not identical with H_2O, that "water" does not mean H_2O, and that early speakers of English knew what the word "water" meant. Since the Putnam-Kripke theory of direct reference, as it applies to natural kind terms, asserts or implies the negation of each of these propositions it is to be rejected for the reasons adduced earlier in this paper.

Notes

1. Still, a few words about each mistake to illustrate the sorts of objections I would have developed with more space. Consider the issue of whether there is such a thing as direct reference at all. There may well be such, but if so, it would not resemble that which the tradition has so described. According to the tradition, or more specifically to some of its variants, direct reference is to be identified with picking out, or tagging, or naming, or identifying, or denoting, or baptizing something. These I believe are different sorts of activities from one another, but those differences are not connected with error-making propensities. That is, there is nothing wrong with the contention that a person can pick out, identify, or name something. These are things we do all the time. But it is a mistake to assert that one can pick out (identify, tag etc.) something *directly*. That is quite a different claim. I believe I can show convincingly that "directly" in such a use fails to mark out any contrast. What would one have to do to identify something *indirectly*? My view is that there is no such defensible contrast. There are other objections to the view. When we identify someone or something, we always identify that person or thing *as* something or other (e.g., as the guilty person). To specify what someone is being identified as requires the use of a description, so the reference is not direct in the sense that the theory mandates.

With respect to the second mistake, that proper names are directly referential whereas definite descriptions are not, I ask you to consider the sentence: "The floor of Santa Maria in Cosmedin dates from the twelfth century." I am making two references in using this sentence, one about a certain Roman basilica which I name, the other about its floor. It is paradoxical to hold that one of these references is less direct than the other. Why do I use a description to refer to the floor? The answer is that the floor, *like most things we refer to*, has no name. That is why we employ descriptions. But in so doing, we are not referring to the floor *indirectly*.

2. Hilary Putnam, "Meaning and Reference," *The Journal of Philosophy*, 70 (1973): 699–711. (Also reprinted in *Naming, Necessity and Natural Kinds*, edited by S. P. Schwartz, (Ithaca, N.Y., 1977), 119–32. All page references in the text are to Schwartz.

3. Saul A. Kripke, *Naming and Necessity* (Cambridge, Mass., 1980), 118. All page references in the text are to this edition.

4. Here, for instance, is what J. J. C. Smart says: "Consider lightning. Modern physical science tells us that lightning is a certain kind of electrical discharge due to ionization of clouds of water vapor in the atmosphere. This, it is now believed, is what the true nature of lightning is. Note that there are not two things: a flash of lightning and an electrical discharge. There is one thing, a flash of lightning, which is described scientifically as an electrical discharge to the earth from a cloud of ionized water molecules." "Sensations and Brain Processes," in *The Philosophy of Mind*, edited by V. C. Chappell (Englewood Cliffs, N.J., 1962), 163-64.

5. Throughout this paper I do not challenge the assumptions that there are natural kinds and that we have good criteria for distinguishing natural kinds from non-natural kinds, such as chairs. But I think they could be challenged. Paul M. Churchland has indeed done so in his "Conceptual Progress and Word/World Relations: In Search of the Essence of Natural Kinds," *Canadian Journal of Philosophy* 15 (no. 1, 1985): 1-17.

6. A number of writers have emphasized the distinction, e.g., John Pollock in *Knowledge and Justification*, 158, and Nathan Salmon in *Reference and Essence*, 225.

7. Ludwig Wittgenstein, *On Certainty* (London, 1969), 62e, entry 476.

8. I am especially indebted to A. P. Martinich for his incisive analysis of and suggestions about the arguments in this section. I also wish to thank Rod Jenks, Paolo Dau, Paul M. Churchland, and Warren Dow for their help with this paper.

Belief and the Identity of Reference
KEITH S. DONNELLAN

What has sometimes been called the "new theory of reference," although it is not that new anymore, faced from the beginning a couple of embarrassing problems. One has to do with existence, which I will not address here. The other has to do with propositional attitudes, or, more precisely, reports of propositional attitudes, reports about beliefs, desires, and other mental states which involve propositions. Saul Kripke in his paper, "A Puzzle About Belief,"[1] has proposed a radical way of dealing with this second problem.

I believe Kripke's paper may be a breakthrough for anyone who thinks, as I do, that the new theory of reference is essentially correct. I think, however, that the paper does not quite justify the title. Kripke makes use of a nest of principles having to do with our treatment of the believer's linguistic avowals of belief. I am inclined to protest that the puzzle really is a puzzle about *belief*, about the psychological state itself, which at best manifests itself in one guise as a derivable consequence of such principles. My protest, however, is in no way a rejection of Kripke's general strategy for dealing with the problem posed for the new theory of reference; indeed it is in its unveiling of the strategy that his paper represents, for me at least, a breakthrough.

I

The details of the new theory of reference are well known by now. But let me emphasize a few general points which will concern us here. The theory can be divided into a negative and a positive aspect (with the latter having variations which will not concern us).

The negative aspect is that classical theories about how singular terms must function are wrong. Indexicals, such as "I," "here," "now," and proper names, "Paris," "John Stuart Mill" are paradigms of singular terms. Definite descriptions, such as "the capital of France," "the most famous utilitarian," etc., are also singular terms. On the classical theory there is no great difference between the two. On the new theory of reference there is a big gulf. But here let us just look at proper names.

Classical theories about the reference of proper names hold that the users of a name must in some way have access to criteria, in the end necessary and sufficient conditions, for the correct application of the name—else, they might say, how could the name really refer to anything?

The new theory of reference by various examples and arguments has shown, I believe, that the classical theory is mistaken. I can, to use my own example, succeed in referring to "Thales" when I say, "Thales held that all is water," even though the stock of properties I could come up with which someone would have to have to be "Thales" would be either insufficient to pick out any particular person or, worse, might just happen to fit some wanderer in the agara. And similar sorts of objections can be made, I believe, to any variants on the classical view, even current sophisticated ones using modal techniques.

The positive side of the theory can be simply stated: proper names have no semantic function other than to refer to their bearers. In this the theory echoes Bertrand Russell's account of what he called "names" in "the proper strict logical sense of the word."[2] The vital difference, of course, is that the kind of names for which Russell suggested this account form such a restricted set—names of items in immediate experience and possibly of universals—that many have doubted that such names even exist. The new theory of reference holds, on the other hand, that mundane everyday proper names directly refer to their bearers without the mediation of sense, meaning, or anything of the kind.

It is perhaps possible to hold that the new theory of reference is correct on the negative side, that it succeeds in its attack on classical reference theory, while not embracing the positive side, that is, while denying that ordinary proper names directly refer in this unadorned manner. For this reason I will call the positive side, following current usage, the "direct reference theory."[3]

The problem facing the direct reference theory is by now well known. If proper names have no other semantic role but to refer, then it appears that if two proper names refer to the same individual then a principle of substitution is warranted, a principle that says that substitution of one name for the other will not only preserve truth value but also the proposition expressed. And this gives rise to apparently fatal difficulties when the substitutions are made in propositional attitude contexts. In the well-worn example, the ancient Babylonians had two names for what in fact is a single planet. As it appeared as the last heavenly body before dawn they called it "Phosphorus" and as it appeared as the first in the evening they called it "Hesperus," not realizing that a single object was involved. It seems straightforward to imagine that they believed that Phosphorus was the god of light, while not believing this about Hesperus. But since the two names in fact refer to the same object, the direct reference theory seems, via substitution, to give the unpalatable result that the ancient

Babylonians both believed Phosphorus to be the god of light and did not believe that Phosphorus is the god of light.

To make matters worse, theories about proper names such as that of Russell seem to have no problems dealing with these cases. The names "Hesperus" and "Phosphorus," it would be said, abbreviate different definite descriptions and so different propositions are expressed by "Phosphorus is the god of light" and "Hesperus is the god of light." The Babylonians in the imagined example believe the first and do not believe the second and there is no contradiction.

II

Philosophers who are persuaded by the attack on the classical view of reference and who then move to a direct reference theory have sometimes attempted to get out of their difficulties with propositional attitudes, such as believing, by attempting some new analysis of reports of these attitudes.

It is tempting to try to find something which does not amount to a Fregean sense or to meaning which nevertheless does the job of distinguishing when it is true that, e.g., an ancient astronomer believed that Hesperus is Hesperus from when it is true that the same astronomer believed that Phosphorus is Hesperus.

With indexicals, as opposed to proper names, this strategy may have a hope of succeeding. David Kaplan's notion of the character of an indexical such as "I" or "here" or "tomorrow" associates with the indexical a semantical rule for assigning to it a referent which is nevertheless not to be equated with a sense or meaning as in classical theories.[4] Suppose someone thinks "I am handsome" while merely ruminating on his virtues and the same person, gazing at himself in a mirror without realizing that the image is of himself, thinks "He is not handsome." On the view of demonstratives and indexicals which makes them directly referential, the proposition involved seems identical in the two episodes. But the threatened paradox of a person both believing a proposition and believing its negation at the same time may be forestalled by the fact that in the one case the person expresses the proposition to himself employing the indexical "I" which makes its contribution to the expression of the proposition via its "character," a character which, of course, is not functioning when he expresses the same proposition using the demonstrative "he." The notion of "character" may have the potential for short-circuiting the paradoxes which constitute the problem for the direct reference theory. But, unfortunately, proper names have nothing associated with them which plays the role of "character" for indexicals. So that when we are dealing with the possible contradictory beliefs one may have when they are expressed by two *names* for the same thing, we cannot look to this sort of remedy.

The attempt to disarm the paradoxes in the case of proper names by an analysis of statements ascribing beliefs which seems to me to come closest to succeeding is that made by Nathan Salmon in his book *Frege's Puzzle*.[5] Belief is treated as a three-termed relation among a believer, a proposition, and a "guise" under which the proposition is believed. The guise plays the role of the mode of presentation under which the proposition is believed, but it is no part of the content of the proposition believed. The upshot of Salmon's analysis is that in the Hesperus/Phosphorus story, the ancient Babylonians believed that Phosphorus was the first star of the morning, but under a certain guise. One can say without contradiction that they also did not believe that Hesperus was the first star of the morning, if that means that there is a guise under which they did not believe the proposition. But if it means that it is simply false that they believed the proposition, that under no guise do they believe it, a contradiction, of course, would result. In the story, as we have it, however, it simply is not true that the Babylonians were in this situation. They do believe that Hesperus is the first star of the morning, however much they may deny this when it is put to them using the name "Hesperus."

Salmon is willing to admit that our raw intuitions do not go along with this, that we are inclined to say that in the story, it is simply false that the ancient Babylonians believed that Hesperus is the first star of the morning. These intuitions and others (e.g., that contrary to the Salmon analysis, it is simply false that the ancient Babylonians believed that Hesperus is Phosphorus and certainly false that they believed that Hesperus is not Hesperus) Salmon needs to explain away. I find the necessity for this sort of explanation a somewhat heavy burden for the theory to bear, given that intuitions are usually the bottom line in philosophical argumentation.[6] Still, *if* the analysis *is* correct, the problem raised by Hesperus/Phosphorus-like cases for the direct reference view would be gotten over.

III

In "A Puzzle About Belief," Kripke's remedy is radically different. He proposes no new analysis of sentences ascribing beliefs or other propositional attitudes, nor novel ways in which we might enjoy something like Frege's "modes of presentation" without erecting them into senses.

Instead the problem is to be, as the title of his paper suggests, a puzzle about *belief* (and other propositional attitudes). A puzzle, thus, that all theories of reference are saddled with. Or so one might conclude.

I think that Kripke may have shown us, we who want to defend the new theory of reference, the way to go. But I am more dubious that he has shown us that there is a puzzle about *belief*.

Let us first see what Kripke's argument is, because there can be some misconceptions about it.

In developing the puzzle about belief Kripke uses three principles: the *disquotational principle*, the *reverse disquotational principle*, as I shall call it, and the *principle of translation*:

Disquotation:

BELIEF AND THE IDENTITY OF REFERENCE 279

If a normal speaker of *[L]*, on reflection, sincerely assents to '*p*', then he believes that *p*.[7]

(There are a number of qualifications, as Kripke points out, which would need to be made if the principle is to be made fully acceptable.)

Reverse Disquotation:

If a normal speaker of *[L]* believes that *p*, then he will be disposed to "sincere reflective assent to '*p*'."

(Kripke proposes a "strengthened 'biconditional' form of the disquotational principle"[8] which I have here separated into its two directions.)

Translation:

If a sentence of one language expresses a truth in that language, then any translation of it into any other language also expresses a truth (in that other language).[9]

All three principles have some initial plausibility, especially the principle of translation. (The first, the principle of disquotation, however, which purports to connect the propositional attitude, belief, with verbal behavior would certainly give some philosophers some pause.)

By developing a couple of ingenious examples of what could happen in the ordinary way of things, Kripke appeals to our intuitions about when we would say that someone believed, disbelieved, or had no belief to argue that with these three principles at hand we can develop the very same paradoxical results which the direct theory of reference is supposed to founder upon. From just the principle of disquotation and translation and some not extraordinary background circumstances, and without any theory of reference involved at all, one can, Kripke argues, arrive at the same paradoxical result that the new theory of reference has been charged with.

A fast reading of Kripke's paper might give one the impression that the argument is that there are some very plausible principles about language which do not involve a principle of substitution nor any theory of reference and which together can yield the same paradoxical result which opponents charge the direct reference theory with. So, it is a sort of standoff.

I believe that that is not Kripke's argument and there is good reason why it should not be. If that were the argument, a lot would depend upon how plausible his two principles are as compared to the argument that the new theory of reference forces on us the validity of substitution with its apparently paradoxical consequences.

Instead, what Kripke argues is that opponents of direct reference presuppose, in their argument, at least the disquotational principle and, in applying their argument to particular examples, the other two principles as well.

But where in their argument do the presuppositions come in? They come in at the very point where, using any particular example, the argument appeals to our intuitions about belief states. The problem for the direct reference theory comes to this: On the direct reference theory proper names such as 'Cicero' and 'Tully' seem to make the same semantic contribution; they both do no more than to pick out a referent and in this case the same referent. So, as Kripke asks, on behalf of the opponents, "How, then, can anyone believe that Cicero was bald, yet doubt or disbelieve that Tully was?" if the direct reference theory is correct. But *of course we all know*, it seems, that someone certainly can be in just such a state.

It is just here—in the seemingly innocuous appeal to what we all know to be possible—that the ancient Babylonians, to shift the example, might well have believed that Hesperus was on certain dates the first star of the evening while doubting that Phosphorus was—that the presupposition of Kripke's principles is supposed to enter.

The problem posed for the direct reference theory appeals to our intuitions that a certain psychological state, a certain belief state is possible—a state which the direct reference view seems to rule out. "Why," Kripke asks, "do we think that anyone *can* believe that Cicero was bald, but fail to believe that Tully was?" "Well," he says, "a normal English speaker, Jones, can sincerely assent to 'Cicero was bald' but not to 'Tully was bald'."[10]

Kripke then says,

> Let us make explicit the *disquotational principle* presupposed here, connecting sincere assent and belief.[11]

He then gives the principle: "If a normal English speaker, on reflection, sincerely assents to '*p*', then he believes that *p*."

Kripke's argument, then, seems to be this. The opponents of the direct reference theory maintain that it licenses a principle of substitution in ascriptions of belief that would make it seem impossible for it to be true that someone, e.g., believes Cicero to be bald but fails to believe that Tully is bald, given their identity. The opponents make this out to be an objectionable result by appealing to our intuitions that someone can be in just such a state. But these intuitions of ours depend upon our acceptance of the three principles, the two disquotation principles and the translation principle. These principles are principles of our practice in ascribing belief states and our intuitions about what belief states are possible depends upon accepting them. So in appealing to our intuitions, the opponents of the direct reference view are tacitly accepting these principles.

But, and this is the kicker, the same paradox upon which the direct reference theory is supposed to founder can be derived from just those principles alone, without any theory of reference being assumed at all.

In other words, quite independently of any theory of reference we might adopt there is a paradox which can be derived from principles we use in ascribing beliefs to people. And those who pose the objection to the direct reference theory must implicitly rely upon these principles. (That is why Kripke's argument does more than simply claim to be able to derive the paradox from another source.) The principles, of course, result in paradox only in certain cases—the very cases which are used to attack the direct reference view. This, if I am correct, is why Kripke thinks we are dealing with a puzzle about belief, not a problem with the direct reference theory itself.

IV

This is an ingenious solution to what seemed at times to be an intractable problem for the theory of reference some of us hold near and dear. As I have said, I think Kripke's approach may well be a breakthrough. But I have some worries about the actual argument.

If I am correct about the structure of Kripke's argument, everything depends upon whether we *do* presuppose his three principles in our intuitions about puzzle cases—the Cicero/Tully and Phosphorus/Hesperus sort of examples. If our intuitions are not necessarily based on these principles, then the fact that one can derive the same paradox from the principles that critics of the direct reference theory purport to derive from it will give us only the weaker conclusion that the paradox is not the peculiar burden of the direct reference view.

So, my worry about Kripke's reliance on these principles comes down to questioning whether our intuitions which the critics of direct reference theory trade upon *do* in fact involve a use of the principles.

Well, let us take one of the two well-known cases. In the Hesperus/Phospherus case we are, for example, asked to agree that of course the ancient Babylonians might have believed that Phosphorus is the first star of the morning and also disbelieved that Hesperus is—even though their names in fact referred to the same star. Let us suppose that our intuitions are in entire agreement with this. In what way do our intuitions involve Kripke's three principles?

Let us look at the disquotational principle. To paraphrase Kripke, "Why do we think that an ancient Babylonian can believe that Phosphorus is the first star of the morning, but fail to believe that Hesperus is?" Is it really that we are assuming some such principle as that "If a normal Babylonian speaker, on reflection, sincerely assents to, in Babylonian, 'The first star of the morning is Phosphorus', then he believes that the first star of the morning is Phosphorus"? And also assuming the principle, "If a Babylonian assents to 'The first star of the morning is not Hesperus' then he believes that the first star in the evening is not Hesperus"?

Insofar as we have the intuition that the ancient Babylonians could have believed that Phosphorus is the first star of the morning and at the same time believed that Hesperus is not, although the same star is the object of both beliefs, I very much doubt that we make use of the principle of disquotation.

It is no doubt very plausible that in our ascriptions of beliefs to each other we often make use of the disquotation principle or something like it.

Perhaps we do assume that what we take to be sincere assenting to a sentence is *prima facia*, at least, proof that the assentor believes what the sentence expresses.

In fact if the principle is hedged around enough, disquotation may have the status of a truism. If it is in the end a truism, then, of course, it is entailed by anything whatsoever and so entailed by our intuition about the ancient Babylonians. But the question, I believe, is whether our intuition depends upon the principle of disquotation. And I hesitate to say that it does. It certainly is not that I have known some ancient Babylonians who have confided in me their assents and dissents in these matters. That is, I do not think that insofar as I have an intuition about the possible belief states of the ancient Babylonians that it involves making use of the principle of disquotation.

I think rather that the source of our intuition lies in reflections about belief itself, not about a principle about assent. I think we suppose that a person, an ancient Babylonian, for example, might confront an object, a planet, in two sets of circumstances, sets of circumstances that for one reason or another do not allow the person to recognize that one and the same object is involved. And in such a hypothetical case we can see that a person may believe about that object that it has a certain property, say, of being the first star in the evening, when he is in certain circumstances, such as gazing at a familiar sight in early evening, while at the same time believing that another familiar object viewed in the morning is never the first star in the evening, even though the two objects are in fact the same.

This sort of explanation of our intuitions, has nothing to do with *expressions* of belief, it has to do with the psychological state of belief itself. It seems, then, to make no use of the disquotational principle (nor of the other two principles).

Look at the reverse disquotational principle: (paraphrasing) If a normal Babylonian speaker who is not reticent believes that Hesperus is the first star of the evening, then he will be disposed to sincere reflective assent to (here we have to substitute something in the Babylonian language) "Hesperus is the first star of the evening."

Surely, I would like to say, our intuitions about what could have been the case about Babylonian beliefs does not depend upon our assuming this principle.[12]

The principle of translation, that if a sentence of one language expresses a truth in that language, then any translation of it into any other language also expresses a truth, seems to me to be also susceptible to degenerating into a truism. But in any case the explanation I have given of our intuitions about the Babylonians makes no use of it as far as I can see. I can understand and appreciate the appeal to intuitions about the Babylonians' beliefs without having any knowledge about what the Babylonian sentences mean.

Let me sum up. Insofar as we have intuitions about a hypothetical case such as that of the ancient Babylonians, they are based upon judgments about what it is possible for someone to believe or disbelieve in such a situation and not upon Kripke's principles about sentences which *express* beliefs or upon a principle about translation from one language to another. The intuition, that is, has nothing to do with language.

We must be careful here. We have not shown yet that an intractable paradox or puzzle results from our judgments about what it is possible to believe or not believe. We have at best shown that the critics of direct reference theory in appealing to our intuitions need not be making any use of certain principles from which a paradox or puzzle can be derived.

It may be also that the only reasons we have for ascribing beliefs or other propositional attitudes to people have to do in the end with their assent or dissent from propositions expressed in language. But that is another matter, another theory to be assessed. I am willing, for example, to ascribe long-term beliefs to animals who lack language altogether and to find it possible to imagine one of them in a Hesperus/Phosphorus-like situation. Perhaps my dog, who has always, I would avow, believed me to be trustworthy, when seeing me one day dressed in some outlandish costume begins to shake and growl showing that she does not believe me trustworthy. If I dress up this way often enough with similar consequences, I am inclined to ascribe the belief in my trustworthiness still—she has no fear of me dressed in my usual garb—as well as the disbelief, and to explain this for a start by assuming that she does not realize that she is dealing with the same person. Perhaps for theoretical reasons I should stop anthropomorphizing animals in this blatant way. But my intuitions about the possibility of such a belief situation depends upon no assumptions about linguistic expressions of belief.

V

We can, however, begin to generate a puzzle or paradox merely from our intuitions about what it is possible to believe. In the well-known example Kripke imagines a French-speaking person, Pierre, who while in Paris, speaking French, comes to believe what he would express in French as *"Londres est jolie."* Later he moves to London, lives in a pretty awful neighborhood, learns English, and then sincerely expresses a belief in English by saying "London is not pretty." But in his French moments, as we might put it, he still assents to *"Londres est jolie."* Pierre does not connect the city he heard about and longed for in France and the city he knows from living in it.

Here is Kripke's first conclusion about the Pierre example:

Now (using the *strengthened* disquotational principle), we can derive a contradiction, not merely in Pierre's judgments, but in our own. For on the basis of his behavior as an English speaker, we concluded that he does *not* believe that London is pretty.... But on the basis of his behavior as a *French* speaker, we must conclude that he *does* believe that London is pretty.[13]

I might put my worry about the argument as saying that the puzzle we feel really has nothing to do with *language* or with languages at all. We can, it seems, construct the paradox without appealing to principles about expressions of belief. Let us tell the story in this way: Pierre, whatever language he may speak, has heard of a city which he believes to be pretty. His thoughts are about that city — how can he get there, for instance. Then he lands up in the very city his thoughts have been about, not knowing it, of course. He hates that city and believes it to be as ugly as a city can be, not realizing that it is in fact the city he has often thought about. Suppose this city in fact to be London.

I surely want to say that at one time Pierre believed London to be pretty. And, in fact, if the last part of the little story were omitted, the part about his visit to London, I would suppose it quite appropriate to say that unless something changes his mind, he continues to believe this. On the other hand if only the last part of the story were given, only the part about his reaction to the squalor of the city he visits, I would want to say that he does not believe London to be pretty. And, unless this represents a change of mind, I would be happy to say that he never believed this.

But the story has two parts and one can make them seem, at least, to clash in a puzzling and even paradoxical way. Kripke, I think, pinpoints one source of paradox when he says, "It seems undeniable that Pierre *once* believed that London is pretty — at least before he learned English . . . if any Frenchman who was both ignorant of English and never visited London believed that London is pretty, Pierre did."[14] "Should we say," he argues, "that Pierre, now that he lives in London and speaks English, no longer believes that London is pretty? Well, unquestionably Pierre *once* believed that London is pretty. So we would be forced to say that Pierre has *changed his mind, has given up his previous belief.*"[15] And he rightly points out that nothing shows that such an event has taken place.

The paradox arises because each part of the story of Pierre, taken separately and as exhausting what is relevant, would warrant opposing, contradictory, conclusions. In an important sense the two parts of the story are independent of each other — Pierre might never have visited London while retaining his treasured thoughts about the pretty English city; Pierre might never have had those thoughts while being unfortunate enough to make his sojourn in London's nasty precincts. And this independence of the two makes it seem impossible that the presence of one part of the story should have any effect on the consequences normally to be drawn from the other by itself. Kripke, I think, illustrates this stance when he says:

> Nor does it have any plausibility to suppose, because of his latter situation *after* he learns English, that Pierre should *retroactively* be judged *never* to have believed that London is pretty. To allow such *ex post facto* legislation would, as long as the future is uncertain, endanger our attribution of belief to *all* monolingual Frenchmen. We would be forced to say that Marie, a monolingual who firmly and sincerely asserts, "Londres

est jolie," may or may not believe that London is pretty depending upon the *later* vicissitudes of her career . . . [16]

Kripke makes his point with several allusions to the linguistic situation. But it could have been made about my version of Pierre's plight which is silent about those matters. If Pierre never made the journey to London we should be happy to attribute a certain belief to him. How can we deny it to him because he later made the journey? To do so, it would seem, would put in doubt the ascription of the belief to anyone now whose future perambulations and attitudes is uncertain. But yet Pierre's journey to London and his reaction to his stay there *by itself* would seem to license our saying that he does not believe London to be pretty. And so a puzzling — indeed paradoxical seeming — situation is created by reflections on the state of belief itself.

VI

I have tried to generate the paradox about belief in a way which should give it a familiar ring. In fact it begins to look very much like certain puzzles about identity. The ship of Thesseus paradox or the more recent puzzles about split brain and brain transfer cases come to mind.

Perhaps we can see this if we characterize these puzzles in general terms and interpolate the Pierre situation as an illustration.

We have, in the general case, two states of affairs, call them *A* and *B*, which are independent of each other in the way just illustrated in the Pierre example. We are then invited to agree that if one state of affairs, say *A*, had existed alone without *B* then a certain proposition *P* would have been true. (In the main example, if Pierre had stayed in Paris, never learned English, then it would have been true — given the assumptions of the example — that he believed that London is beautiful.

Next we are challenged to say how the existence of the second state of affairs, *B*, could have any bearing on the truth value of *P*. How could Pierre's sojourn in London affect the truth value of the proposition that he believes London to be beautiful? After all, it is a quite independent state of affairs.

Nevertheless, in the general case, the existence of *B* does cast doubt on the truth of *P*. (One of the things puzzles and paradoxes about identity should teach us is that the existence of the seemingly utterly independent event *can* make a difference.) We are left with a puzzle, a paradox.[17]

VII

I have tried to argue that a puzzle about belief can be generated without presupposing the principles given us in Kripke's paper. And I suggest that the puzzle is of a kind with the hoary ship of Theseus puzzle and the newer ones involving personal identity. In doing this I have in a way absolved the critics of the direct reference theory of necessarily assuming these principles. But the puzzle seems to me to be reinstated at the level of the concept of belief itself.

If so, then Kripke's strategy in defense of the direct reference theory can be once again followed. The puzzle is a puzzle no matter what theory of the reference of proper names one has and it cannot be in and of itself a devastating objection that a particular theory seems to generate the puzzle in contexts of ascriptions of belief.

If what I have said is correct the puzzle about belief is a part of our very concept of belief in much the same way as the puzzle about split brains and the puzzle about the ship of Theseus is a very part of our concept of identity. Of course, there may be ways of defusing the puzzle, just as there have been attempts to do this with the puzzles about identity. So, for example, arguing that belief essentially involves a mode of presentation may remove what would then be only an apparent conflict between the two parts to the story of Pierre. But this will be a theory about the nature of belief. How it would be mirrored in ascriptions of belief will then be a question and there is no reason, I think, to suppose that the direct reference theory could not accommodate such a theory nor reason to suppose that its main alternative, a Russell-Frege view, has a better shot. Indeed, on the first score Salmon's analysis is at least very plausible and on the second Kripke in the paper we have been concerned with shows that the Russell-Frege view at least has grave difficulties with the puzzle about belief.[18]

There is, however, an important objection which might be raised about the attempt to locate the puzzle in the very concept of belief. A central strategy of mine has been to describe the puzzle cases in general terms, in particular to describe them without the use of names for the object in question. But, it might be said, if we *do* describe the cases with names, our intuitions do not, in fact, lead to a puzzle or paradox. If we imagine the Babylonians, without realizing it, to have named the same heavenly body "Hesperus" and, at another time, "Phosphorus," we have no conflict, no obvious paradox in holding that, for example, they believed that Phosphorus was the first star of the morning, that they disbelieved or even that it is false that they believed Hesperus to have this property. In a similar fashion, if we allow ourselves a marriage of French and English, we find no conflict in holding that Pierre believes Londres is pretty but does not believe that London is pretty. This seems to me to be true and it is a raw datum that must be accounted for in the end. But that there is no puzzle lurking here is, I think, wrong.

Kripke says, "This is the puzzle: Does Pierre or does he not believe that London is pretty?" adding "I know of no answer to *this* question."[19] And this *is* the puzzle which remains. Kripke's question is couched in English and uses the English name for London. But if one translates his article into another language, other than French, one should use here the name for London associated with that language, a name with which, we can add to this story, Pierre is utterly unfamiliar. There is a way of hearing the question, "Does Pierre believe London to be pretty?" in the context of Kripke's story about Pierre to which I think we may want to say "No, he does not." But whatever the analysis is of that reading of the question, that is not the reading to give to

Kripke's challenging question. This becomes clearer if we use the Hesperus/Phosphorus story. Those names are supposedly Babylonian names and bound to the story. But we, of course, have a name for the heavenly body central to that story, the name "Venus." And we get the analogue, I think, of Kripke's question if we ask, for example, "Did the Babylonians believe or did they not believe that *Venus* is the first star of the morning?" And I want to say, echoing Kripke, "I know of no answer to *this* question."[20]

Notes

1. Saul Kripke, "A Puzzle about Belief," in *Meaning and Use*, edited by Avishai Margalit (Dordrecht, 1979), 239-83.
2. The expression is used in Lecture II of "The Philosophy of Logical Atomism" (1918), reprinted in *Logic and Knowledge*, edited by Robert C. Marsh (London, 1956), 201. The doctrine, of course, occurs in many places in Russell's writings.
3. I believe the expression is due to David Kaplan.
4. I am not attributing this "resolution" of the problem to Kaplan.
5. Nathan Salmon, *Frege's Puzzle* (Cambridge, 1986).
6. And there is another consideration which bothers me, namely what to say about the beliefs of the ancient Babylonians when expressed using our name for the heavenly body involved, "Venus." It seems that on Salmon's view the answers are clear-cut in the end: They believed, for example, that Venus is not identical to Phosphorus (because they believed that Hesperus [= Venus] is not identical to Phosphorus) and they believed that Venus is identical to Phosphorus (because they believed that Phosphorus [= Venus] is identical to Phosphorus.) But I find it very dubious that any such beliefs expressed by using the name "Venus" can be attributed to the ancient Babylonians. I am not satisfied, then, that Salmon's analysis is correct, although my reasons for feeling this are less than absolutely conclusive.
7. Kripke, "Puzzle about Belief," 248-249.
8. Ibid., 249.
9. Ibid., 250.
10. Ibid., 248. Emphasis added.
11. Ibid.
12. Again, hedged around with qualifications, the principle may be a truism. But that does not mean that the principle is used in generating our intuition. Once again, of course, a truism being a truism is entailed by anything at all, and so entailed by our intuitions, whatever they may be.
13. Kripke, "Puzzle about Belief," 258.
14. Ibid., 256.
15. Ibid., original emphasis.
16. Ibid., 256.
17. In many instances, the troubling second state of affairs admits of degrees along the dimensions of quantity or duration. And when it does, whether we find the situation puzzling or paradoxical can depend upon the answer to the question, how much or how long?

Replacing only a few planks of the ship of Theseus and with these and a lot of new material building a duplicate will probably not generate a puzzle about whether the repaired boat or its duplicate is identical to the original ship of Theseus. But replacing 90 percent of the planks and constructing the duplicate from these and only a small number of additional planks lands us in apparent paradox.

The same thing happens, I believe, in the puzzle about belief. And perhaps this adds some confirmation to the position that the structure of the argument which generates it is akin to the one we find in the ship of Theseus story.

Imagine that Pierre, instead of residing in London for some time, as in Kripke's example, merely passes through. Perhaps his plane on a flight to Marseilles is diverted because of weather to Heathrow. The bus, we can suppose, which busses the passengers to a hotel passes through the worst quarters of London. Pierre is told that this is London but fails to make the connection with his beloved Londres. The next morning he remarks to fellow passengers as they return to the airport "London is certainly not beautiful." (Most of the other passengers are English speaking and Pierre has some command of the language).

I think this little episode in Pierre's life would not call into question the belief he expresses by saying *"Londres est jolie"* nor should we hesitate to report his belief in English by saying that Pierre believes London to be pretty.

18. See Kripke, "Puzzle about Belief," 260ff.

19. Ibid., 259.

20. Does the Frege-Russell give us a solution to this problem? No. Kripke argues this persuasively, as I have mentioned. In the context of the present discussion another strong reason for believing this is that on the Frege-Russell view we *ought* to be able to answer questions about whether the Babylonians believed that Venus has certain properties. To stick to Russell's version of the view, our name "Venus" is really a concealed definite description and we can surely have reason to suppose that the Babylonians did or did not believe that something satisfying that description possesses this or that property. But in fact we do not really know what to say in the cases where the Babylonians believed, e.g., Phosphorus to have a property, but had no such belief about whether Hesperus does. Even worse, given that if "Venus" were for us a concealed definite description the description would probably make use of concepts the Babylonians lacked or concepts which they would not have thought applied to either Hesperus or Phosphorus, the answer we might well be forced to give on the Russell-Frege view would seem clearly wrong. We would probably be forced to say that they did not believe that Venus is the first star in the morning. Or even that they believed Venus definitely not to be the first star of the morning.

Contradictory Belief and Cognitive Access
JOSEPH I. OWENS

In his celebrated paper, "A Puzzle about Belief," Saul Kripke tells the tale of Pierre.[1] Relying on what appear to be noncontroversial principles governing belief ascription, he tells a story which seemingly forces us to regard Pierre as both believing that London is pretty and that London is not pretty. This is problematical in that Pierre is by hypothesis a paradigm of rationality; he is, Kripke stipulates, one who would never let contradictory beliefs pass. What then are we to say of Pierre? To deny him either of the contradictory beliefs seems to violate clear criteria of belief attribution, or at least the received view of that practice, but, Kripke argues, neither can we ascribe both beliefs to him; to do so is to violate his assumed rationality. Kripke writes:

> Does Pierre, or does he not, believe that London is pretty? It is clear that our normal criteria for the attribution of belief lead, when applied to *this* question, to paradoxes and contradictions. . . . As in the case of the logical paradoxes, the present puzzle presents us with a problem for customarily accepted principles . . . [2]

Even though Kripke himself defends no particular resolution of the puzzle, he certainly seems to think that the puzzle can be solved only by abandoning some of the customary principles which led us to attribute contradictory beliefs to Pierre; to attribute inconsistent beliefs to this paradigm of rationality would be, he claims, intolerable.[3] In this paper I defend a different line, arguing that the puzzle should be solved, not by abandoning any of the principles that led us to attribute contradictory beliefs to Pierre, but rather by abandoning the supposition that a perfectly rational individual could never subscribe to contradiction. The issues here are too many and too complex to receive a thorough discussion; some important issues are not discussed at all, while others receive only a very terse treatment.[4] In section I I outline the puzzle, and in II I urge my own resolution, arguing that a more adequate understanding of the principles governing belief ascription reveals rationality to be fully compatible with subscription to contradictory beliefs. There is, however, a widespread conception of belief content, which clearly is antagonistic to the solution proposed in II, and thus III and IV are taken up with an examination of this idea, which I label the 'Cartesian conception of cognitive content'; this conception is, I argue, without value. The only notion of belief content that plays any role in our ordinary belief attributions is the one I envoke in II, and on *that* conception holding contradictory beliefs is entirely compatible with rationality. Indeed this paper is as much an investigation of, and an attack on, this alternative notion of content as it is a resolution of Kripke's puzzle.

I. THE PUZZLE

Pierre, we suppose, is perfectly rational; he is fluent in French, but without a word of English. He has, however, heard of London, though only as *'Londres'*; he has seen photographs of London, and so on. He thinks of it as a pretty place, and is disposed to assent to:

(a) *Londres est jolie.*

He is transported to London where he lives in a dingy quarter of that city. He acquires English from his new acquaintances and learns that the city he now lives in is called 'London'. All this without ever learning that the city he now lives in is the one he formerly called *'Londres'*. He now sincerely says:

(b) London is not pretty. (without withdrawing assent to (a)).

And he is not at all inclined to assent to:

(c) London is pretty.

There seems to be nothing inconsistent in this story, no reason to think that this sequence of events is an impossible one. Nevertheless this story casts doubt on the coherence of the following principles, ones we ordinarily employ in ascribing beliefs:

(W.D.) Weak Disquotation: If a normal English speaker, on reflection, sincerely and knowingly assents to ⌜P⌝, then he believes that P. (The sentences that replace '*P*' in this principle are not to contain indexical or other devices which might induce *content* variation from context to context.)[5]

(F) A principle analogous to (W.D.) can be formulated in any natural language for that language; in particular, such a principle may be fashioned in French for French.[6]

(T) If a sentence of one language expresses a truth in that language, then a translation of it into any other language expresses a truth in that language (again with a restriction on the use of indexicals, etc.).[7]

These principles are intuitive. It is hard to see how anyone could reasonably dissent from (W.D.), suitably qualified; it seems to be part of our customary understanding of what is involved in sincerely assenting to a sentence one understands. Kripke goes so far as to say that (W.D.) appears to be a self-evident truth; and if (W.D.) has this stature, can (F) have anything less? As for (T): it appears to be little more than a truism about correct translation. Self-evident or not, these same principles give rise to apparent paradox when applied to Pierre.

From the fact that Pierre is disposed to assent to *(a)* we get (by [F], the French version of [W.D.]):

Pierre croit que Londres est jolie.

And from this sentence and the translation principle (T) we get (1):

(1) Pierre believes that London is pretty.

From Pierre's disposition to assent to (b) (given [W.D.]) we get (2):

(2) Pierre believes that London is not pretty.

How can this be since Pierre is by hypothesis perfectly rational? If holding contradictory beliefs does not merit the charge of irrationality, what does? It looks then as though Kripke is fully warranted in his suggestion that "our normal criteria for the attribution of belief lead, when applied to this question, to paradoxes and contradictions . . . (the) puzzle presents us with a problem for customarily accepted principles. . . . "

The problem, once again, is simply put: some principle of (W.D.) seems to figure in our ordinary practice, but once one admits this one has no option but to attribute contradictory beliefs to Pierre, despite his presumed rationality; and this surely casts a dark shadow on the coherence of the practice. Responses to the puzzle fall into three categories: (1) One might take the puzzle to demonstrate genuine incoherence in our practice. This is a desperate and unattractive move, and I shall ignore it. (2) One might, more plausibly, attempt to block the puzzle by rejecting the one principle that is crucial in its derivation — (W.D.), and indeed a number of authors have responded to the puzzle by denying that any principle of disquotation figures in our practice.[8] (3) The third option is to allow that our practice is as Kripke suggests it is (i.e., to allow that it embodies [W.D.]), but to deny that this in any way casts doubt on the coherence of the practice. One who takes this route attempts to resolve the puzzle, not by blocking the attribution of contradictory beliefs to Pierre, but rather by explaining how a fully rational person might subscribe to contradictory beliefs.

In one way or another most published responses have been of the second variety; they have focused on undermining our reasons for attributing one or other of the beliefs to Pierre. In this paper, however, I want to pursue the third strategy. Kripke is, I think, correct in emphasizing the intuitive character of (W.D.).[9] The principle, it should be remembered, is quite weak, and it is not to be confused with any behaviorist principle of the kind:

(B) x believes that P if and only if x is disposed to assent to $\ulcorner P \urcorner$.

No, (W.D.) is not biconditional in form and it is not behavioristic in spirit; it is hedged all around with nonbehavioral qualifiers: the subject must be sincere, reflective, etc. When so qualified (W.D.) is difficult to fault. The competent speaker who is disposed to assent to $\ulcorner P \urcorner$ is disposed to sincerely assert *that P* (for simplicity we restrict ourselves to English), and once one grants this much it is difficult to deny the corresponding belief ascription. This, of course, hardly constitutes a conclusive argument for (W.D.), but rather than attempting any further justification, I will simply assume, with Kripke, that it does appear to be part of our practice. My goal is to show that this practice is not incoherent, that the story Kripke tells us does not force us to suppose that "our normal criteria for attribution of belief lead . . . to paradoxes and contradictions."

From a metalinguistic perspective, our goal is simply to demonstrate the consistency of the ascriptions, 'Pierre believes that London is pretty', and 'Pierre believes that London is not pretty', with Pierre's presumed rationality. If there is no genuine inconsistency here then there is no puzzle.[10]

II. THE RESOLUTION OF THE PUZZLE

The resolution I propose is essentially a simple one; indeed, the main difficulty lies in defending it from the charge of being simple-minded rather than merely simple. The resolution is as follows: A subject may rationally subscribe to contradictory beliefs for the simple reason that more than rationality may be needed to discern the contradiction. On the traditional conception the epistemology of contradiction is quite different from that of mere inconsistency. It is generally conceded that detecting mere inconsistency in one's beliefs may be difficult, and it would be extreme to suppose that such inconsistency always constituted a threat to the subject's rationality. Contradictions, however, are another matter; they are supposed to stand naked in front of the "inner eye," detectable by rational introspection alone. The inadequacies of this picture are, of course, all too evident, but, in particular, it fails to do justice to the subtle ways in which our practice is sensitive to contextual features. In a nutshell, the appropriateness of belief ascriptions (sentences of the form $\ulcorner x$ believes that $P \urcorner$) and the contents of the beliefs so ascribed, is determined, among other things, by a variety of contextual factors — factors pertaining to the subject's physical and social environment — and ignorance of these same factors (rather than any lack of rationality) may blind a subject to the contradictory character of his own beliefs. To see that this is indeed the case it is helpful to explicitly attend to features of our practice hitherto implicit in our talk of disquotation. I confine my attention to four such features. Each is an intuitive element in the practice; each is essential to the story Kripke tells; and proper appreciation of them undermines the tendency to think of rationality as being incompatible with subscription to contradictory beliefs, thereby resolving our puzzlement. I shall briefly characterize the four features. Each one could be refined in various ways, but the result would be to clutter what is intended to be a simple solution.

(A) One and the same *content*, thought, or proposition may be expressed by different sentences. I use the notion content in a rough-and-ready intuitive way, as that which is ascribed in indirect ascriptions of assertion and belief, as that which is preserved in adequate translation. We shall have more to say of this notion later, but for now it should be clear that some such intuition is central to the puzzle. We need, for example, to suppose that the sentences 'London is pretty' and *'Londres est jolie'* express the same content (in some sense of content) if we are to derive the paradoxical result.

(B) The content of a given expression S in public language L is in part determined by a variety of public factors: by prevailing linguistic conventions, by environmental context, and by historical chains. I shall not attempt to complete this list; it would no doubt contain a potpourri of elements. Such factors may play a role in determining whether or not two linguistic expressions S_1 and S_2 have the *same* content; more specifically, they may play a role in determining whether or not a sentence S_1 of language L_1 is an appropriate translation of S_2 in L_2. Not only is this the case for sentences construed simply as sentences of a language, but similar considerations hold for *individual utterances*; contextual factors may be crucial in determining whether or not two utterances S_1 and S_2 agree in content. Thus, it is essential to the story Kripke tells that Pierre's two terms 'London' and *'Londres'* are linked in some manner or other to the same physical entity, the city of London (orthographic features are simply not enough). In the absence of some such agreement in origin, we would not be justified in treating *his* French and English *utterances* (or the thoughts they serve to express) as contradictory.[11]

(C) A speaker may qualify as a competent user of a given term R even if he is not fully cognizant of *all* the factors governing the employment of that term. Again, more pertinent to the puzzle at hand, one may qualify as a competent user of two coreferential expressions R_1 and R_2 even though one is not aware that they are coreferential — that their respective causal chains are such as to make them co-designative. This too is clearly necessary to the puzzle: we have to assume that Pierre passes as a competent user of both 'London' and *'Londres'* even though he is ignorant of their coreferentiality.

(D) Finally, there is, of course, the principle of (W.D.) itself. A speaker who qualifies as a competent employer of a sentence $\ulcorner S \urcorner$, and who sincerely and reflectively assents to $\ulcorner S \urcorner$ is said to believe that S (all appropriately restricted to the language at hand). Furthermore, the result of applying disquotation to an utterance of a subject is a sentence in a public language and is to be construed and translated as a sentence of that language; in particular, in translating the *indirect report* (the result of applying disquotation) one is governed by the relevant conventions, and *not* by any desire to capture all the peculiarities of the *individual's* usage. Thus, for example, we start with Pierre's assent to *'Londres est jolie'*; we apply disquotation to obtain, *'Pierre croit que Londres est jolie'*, and *this* we then translate as 'Pierre believes that London is pretty'. We do this even though *we* know that Pierre does *not* use 'London' and *'Londres'* interchangeably. There is no need to reemphasize the importance of this intuition in the development of the puzzle.

While each of these intuitions plays a role in generating the puzzle, and while they are individually intuitive, one should be under no misapprehension as to their joint impact. Taken together, they provide for a strikingly *anti-Cartesian* perspective: they entail for example, that one with intimate knowledge of the workings of a language may be in a better position to determine whether a given speaker entertains and expresses the same thought or belief on different occasions than the speaker herself. They provide the ingredients for a simple, but profoundly anti-Cartesian solution to the problem posed by Pierre. We are warranted in attributing contradictory beliefs because our practice embodies principles such as (A)-(D), and appreciation of these principles serves to explain how rationality is compatible with holding contradictory beliefs. Indeed I am inclined to view Kripke's story as being not so much a puzzle as an *illustration of how* an individual might rationally come to hold contradictory beliefs. Pierre has acquired two names, 'London' and *'Londres'*, which happen to be codesignative; he uses them to refer to the same city, though he is not aware of himself as doing so. He fails to recognize himself as using these terms coreferentially for the simple reason that his doing so is, in part, due to something outside his head, something he is unaware of—the contextual factors linking the two names to the same physical city. This much is relatively uncontroversial; but a similar story may be told about content. Pierre uses the two sentences, *'Londres est jolie'* and 'London is pretty', to frame and express the same thought. Once again, the sameness of the thought expressed is, in part, a function of various contextual features, and Pierre's ignorance of these features blinds him to this fact. Sameness of thought, like sameness of reference, is in part a function of factors outside the head, and the one need be no more open to introspective access than the other. Just as ignorance of the fact that one is using coreferential names need not undermine the claim that one is using them to refer to the same thing, so ignorance of the fact that one is using two sentences with the same content need not undermine the judgment that one is using them to express the same thought. There is, of course, a wide spectrum of cases. A subject's mistaken beliefs about the meaning of a sentence *may* be such as to undermine the intuitive interpretation (Consider: 'Mary is a physician', uttered by a speaker who consistently interchanges the terms 'physician' and 'physicist'). The important point is that ignorance of contextual factors *need not* undermine ordinary belief ascriptions, and in those interesting cases in which it does not it can play the different role of explaining how the subject rationally subscribes to contradictory beliefs. This is how it is with Pierre.

To put it very simply: in interpreting Pierre's utterances, and attributing beliefs to him, *we* take account of contextual factors of which Pierre is ignorant. The interpreter, aware of the synonymy of 'London' and *'Londres'*, properly construes his utterances, 'London is not pretty', and *'Londres est jolie'*, as expressing contradictory claims, and assigns him contradictory beliefs. But Pierre, of course, is in no position to make the same assessment. Pierre uses the sentences *'Londres est jolie'* and 'London is pretty' to fashion and express the same thought but, given his lack of information regarding the relationship between the terms 'London' and *'Londres'*, this sameness is not something he is in a position to recognize.

In a sense this is all there is to it. To simply insist that a fully rational person *must* be able to discern the contradictory character of his beliefs is, I think, tantamount to Descartes' insistence that a fully rational person must be able to discern any conceptual confusion that might reside in his beliefs; it arises from a failure to grasp the anti-Cartesian character of the principles implicit in our disquotation-guided practice—principles which play a central role in the genesis of the puzzle.[12] These principles serve to "define" or at least delimit a non-Cartesian notion of belief, and to the extent that we operate with them we ought to abandon the conception of ourselves as having some simple introspective way of discerning contradictions among our beliefs. If, on the other hand, we abandon these principles in favor of some different conception of belief then we simply lose the puzzle.

III. AN INITIAL RESPONSE

It is tempting to stop at this point, and perhaps one should, but to do so is to invite the inevitable response that the proposed solution is indeed simpleminded, that it is vitiated by our neglect of the rudimentary distinction between what a *speaker* means or expresses by a sentence and what a sentence means *as* a sentence of a public language (speaker or cognitive-meaning versus sentence-meaning).[13] Of course, our imagined objector agrees, the meaning of a sentence-in-a-language *is* a function of public conventions, and hence in *this* sense of meaning a speaker may express and subscribe to contradictory propositions without being guilty of any irrationality. But, he insists, this is not the sense of meaning or content that is relevant here. Our concern is with cognitive content, with the *contents of the beliefs* that Pierre attempts to express in the language, and not with the conventional meaning of his utterances. And while it is plausible to suppose that conventional and contextual factors play a role in determining the contents of his utterances when construed as sentences of a public language, it is a very different matter to suppose that such factors play a similar role in determining the contents of the beliefs he attempts to express via these sentences. The conventions of the public language play a role in enabling us to express and communicate such beliefs, but they do not play any role in determining the contents of the beliefs expressed; their content is determined independently of any such conventional and contextual factors. Hence one cannot save Pierre's rationality by supposing that the contradictory character of his *beliefs* (as opposed to his utterances) is hidden from him by his ignorance of the fact that *'Londres'* and 'London' are "synonymous." Thus, it is claimed, the solution fails to address the real issues at stake. Moreover, our objector is likely to add, once you make this commonplace distinction the real solution to the puzzle is close at hand: Pierre, it is true, assents to two sentences which *as* sentences of English and French are contradictory, but Pierre is not guilty of irrationality because he *uses* these same sentences to express noncontradictory beliefs—*he means* something different by 'London is pretty' and *'Londres est jolie'*.

This is a familiar story, and one with strong initial attraction. But alluring though it is, it should, I contend, be rejected as embodying a fundamentally misconceived picture of the mental. In section IV I will examine in some detail the concept of cognitive content presupposed by this kind of response; popular or not, it should be abandoned as incoherent. But first some initial reasons for being dissatisfied with this easy response to the story told in II. It is, I think, evident that this kind of response is, by itself, inadequate; it is at very best only a partial response.

(a) In the first place this line of response fails to give due weight to principles (A) through (D). To the extent that we operate with these principles we clearly *do* take contextual factors into account in *ascribing belief*, as Kripke's story vividly illustrates. Hence one cannot simply appeal to cognitive content and leave it at that. One must *either* provide good reason for rejecting some of (A)-(D), and hence good reason for rejecting the account of conventional belief *ascription* defended in II; *or* one must undertake the unenviable task of arguing that our practice of ascribing beliefs is a poor guide to the content of the states thereby ascribed. One who takes this latter option needs to argue that our belief ascribing practice is systematically misleading in cases like Pierre's. He needs to defend the improbable claim that Pierre does not really have one belief with the content that London is pretty and another one with the content that London is not pretty, *even though* the ascriptions 'Pierre believes that London is pretty' and 'Pierre believes that London is not pretty' *are both true* (remember that the theorist who takes this second approach *accepts* our account of the conventional belief ascribing *practice*, and so accepts the ascription of contradictory beliefs to Pierre). Prospects for both alternatives are bleak: examples such as Kripke's clearly attest to the context sensitivity of our practice, thereby reinforcing the story told in II, while the second strategy seems to be strikingly counterintuitive.[14]

(b) Second, in taking this line on belief-content—assuming that it, unlike sentence-content, is independent of such contextual factors—one flies in the face of a variety of apparent counterexamples. The familiar Twin-Earth examples of Hilary Putnam, Tyler Burge, and others indicate that *mental* or cognitive *content is* a function of various contextual factors, linguistic and otherwise. To consider just the one celebrated example: Twin-Earth, we suppose, is pretty much a replica of Earth, with the exception that on Twin-Earth there is no water (H_2O), but rather a water look-alike, XYZ. Now consider two physical replicas, Alf and Alf*. They both sincerely utter, "Water is clear," thereby expressing their respective beliefs. If Burge's treatment of such examples is at all accurate, they not only utter sentences which differ in content (as sentences of their respective linguistic communities), but in doing so they thereby express different *beliefs*. And this difference is not the result of any internal physical difference, but is rather the result of contextual differences, physical and *conventional*.[15] Once again, the contents of attitudes and hence the relationships that obtain between them seem to turn on contextual factors.

IV. CARTESIAN CONTENT

However, this speaker-meaning/sentence-meaning distinction is a deep-seated one, and unless we can provide direct and compelling reasons for rejecting our objector's notion of cognitive content we will continue to be tempted by the thought that the puzzle is best solved by *some* form of that distinction. In this section, I propose to provide just such reasons, and this calls for an extended discussion of cognitive content. In subsection (A) I offer some additional characterization of the notion presupposed by our objector's line of response, and then, in subsection (B), I argue that the notion is ill conceived — that nothing can fill the role our objector assigns to "cognitive content."

(A) The nature of cognitive content

It is important to note at the outset that insisting on retaining a distinction between sentence-meaning and speaker-meaning does not in and of itself provide a response to the account offered in II. That account is perfectly compatible with retaining such a distinction wherever it is clearly called for. To consider just a few examples: nothing we have said tells against the possibility of a speaker using public language sentences in an intentionally idiosyncratic fashion (as some kind of code, for example). In *such* cases one interprets in the light of the speaker's atypical communicative intentions rather than mechanically employing disquotation. Likewise, nothing we have said tells against the supposition that different tokenings of an indexical sentence (e.g., 'I am in pain') might be said to express different thoughts or different cognitive contents, even though the tokens need not be said to differ in *"linguistic meaning."*[16] These and other similar distinctions are quite compatible with the conception of belief advanced above. Our ordinary *conventions* allow for *such* distinctions between what a speaker means by a given sentence and what that sentence means as a sentence of a language. It is *not* the intuitive sentence-meaning/speaker-meaning distinction that is called into question by our account, but the particular construal of speaker-meaning or cognitive content as being independent of contextual factors. This notion of cognitive content is crucial to the entire debate and it is this that should be abandoned.

Talk of cognitive content, of course, crops up in all kinds of theoretical contexts (in psychology, in semantics, in linguistics, in epistemology, and in metaphysics) and it would be simple-minded in the extreme to suppose that different theorists all construe the notion unambiguously—they do not. Cognitive content, however, is typically supposed to satisfy something like the following three rough conditions, (a)–(c). In any case, I argue, *our objector* must be employing a notion which is intended to satisfy such conditions, at least, the crucial ones, (b) and (c).

(a) First there is the "big picture" in which cognitive content finds its natural home; this is the familiar picture of language learning and communication, one in which linguistic content is derivative, a function of a more primitive content, cognitive content. On this model a speaker uses natural language sentences to communicate her beliefs, her cognitive contents. Each utterance is taken to inherit its content from the speaker's specific communicative intentions, encoding the belief she is attempting to communicate—this is its "speaker meaning." If in a given linguistic community a sentence S_i is the conventional expression of cognitive content C_i, then C_i is said to constitute the "linguistic meaning" of S_i. To learn the language is to learn which sentence S_i encodes which content C_i.

(b) Cognitive content is taken to satisfy the following stringent epistemic requirement: whenever a speaker uses two sentences to express the *same cognitive content* (the same belief), then that speaker's ability to recognize himself *as* expressing the same cognitive content cannot be thought of as being contingent upon his having information which is not necessary for rationality or competency in the language. Certainly a speaker may be mistaken in selecting sentences that poorly reveal what he is attempting to convey, but if he is attempting to convey the same thought-content by sentences S_1 and S_2 then his ability to recognize himself as doing *this* cannot be contingent upon his having information about contingent features of his world, about such things as whether or not there is H_2O rather than XYZ out there; nor can it be contingent upon his awareness of the subtleties of our linguistic conventions, subtleties which are not revealed to rational introspection, and knowledge of which is not required for competence.[17]

(c) In the third place this notion of cognitive content is intended to be semantically relevant; belief ascriptions are supposed to be ascriptions of such contents, and hence these contents are supposed to figure in the semantic analysis of such ascriptions. The traditional picture is very roughly this: each natural language sentence S_i is assigned a specific *cognitive content* as *one* of its "semantic values," and this particular range of semantic values is then employed in evaluating sentences of the form, ⌜x believes that S_i⌝. In the simplest and most familiar version of the story such a sentence is deemed true if and only if x has the appropriate relationship (the 'believing relationship', whatever that is) to the appropriate semantic value, i.e., to the cognitive content assigned S_i.

Recent years have seen various complex developments in this well-worn path; in particular, many have argued that the truth conditions of sentences of the form ⌜x believes that S⌝ should be construed as more complex functions of cognitive content plus various other factors, while still others have leaned towards justification rather than truth conditions. I shall not try for any precise statement of this semantic requirement. I intend to be imposing only a very weak constraint when I claim that cognitive contents must play a semantic role: these cognitive contents must be supposed to play *some* objective role in fashioning the truth conditions for sentences of the form ⌜x believes that S. Or, more generally still, these cognitive contents must be construed as objective semantic values (correlated with expressions of the language) to be employed in the evaluation of such belief ascriptions (perhaps of a non-truth-functional kind). What is important is that cognitive contents be objectively correlated with sentences of the language so that we can pose questions of the form: ⌜Do sentences S_1 and S_2 agree or disagree in cognitive content?⌝ 'Do sentences ⌜x believes that P⌝ and ⌜x believes that $P*$⌝ attribute the same or different cognitive contents to x?' Cognitive contents are not to be regarded as obscure theoretical constructs unrelated to our linguistic practice. They are correlated with, and ascribed by, sentences of the form ⌜x believes that P⌝, and so we are entitled to employ intuitions regarding the "application conditions" of such sentences in determining the identity conditions for cognitive contents.

These conditions are undoubtedly vague, but this is of no real concern since the characterization is intended to be vague enough to capture what is common to a variety of more specific proposals. Though I am not familiar with any account in which cognitive content is *explicitly* stipulated to satisfy conditions (a)–(c), such conditions are I think an integral part of a familiar, widely shared picture—the "big picture" alluded to in (a).[18] A full and adequate treatment of these conditions would take us far too far afield, and I shall confine my attention to the claim that our objector must be employing a notion which is intended to satisfy (b) and (c), limiting myself to a few very general comments on (a). This is sufficient for my purposes, since the primary objection I lodge against this notion of content (in section B) is that no notion of content can satisfy the epistemic requirement (b) and be semantically relevant after the manner suggested in (c). In what follows I shall speak of this conception of cognitive content as the Cartesian conception of cognitive content; I shall speak of (b) as the Cartesian epistemic requirement, and of (c) as the semantic requirement. Though my discussion will focus on resolving the puzzle at hand, I invite the reader to keep the wider implications in mind: if no notion of content is such as to satisfy both the epistemic and semantic requirements then much contemporary work in the semantics of intentional ascriptions is fundamentally misguided, for much of that work may fruitfully be viewed as searching for a *semantic* value which is individuated in such a way as to satisfy the Cartesian *epistemic* requirement.[19]

The Cartesian requirement, (b), characterizes the way in which a subject is alleged to have peculiar access to sameness and difference of cognitive content. The subject's ability to discern such agreement and disagreement cannot be supposed to be dependent upon his having access to information about the physical details of his environment or about the details of the conventions which govern his language. Some such principle is clearly presupposed in much contemporary work in philosophy of language and mind. But, more important for our purposes, this kind of Cartesian principle is crucial in any attempt to reject the solution of section II by appealing to cognitive content. For that solution turned on the claim that lack of knowledge of certain factors not necessary for rationality or competence blocked Pierre's ability to recognize himself as entertaining and expressing the same content by '*Londres est jolie,*' and 'London is pretty.' Our objector's response was to deny that a subject's ability to detect sameness and difference of *cognitive content* could be in any way conditional upon his having *that* kind of knowledge. Whatever may be the case about other kinds of content, our objector's notion of cognitive content is presumed to satisfy an epistemic requirement such as (b); the solution proposed in II is open to any theorist who rejects (b) as a constraint upon cognitive content. To reject (b) as a constraint on cognitive content is to allow for the possibility that a fully rational and competent speaker might entertain, express, and subscribe to a given cognitive content and its negation simply because he is not in a position to recognize the sameness of content in the two cases.

But while (b) is the heart of the matter it does not in and of itself constitute a response to our position; it has to be taken as part of a larger package such as (a)–(c). Once again, I am assuming that (a) is not controversial in this context; it is difficult to conceive of anyone appealing to cognitive content except in the context of the broad picture painted in (a), a picture that is near and dear to the heart of many in both philosophy and psychology. But it is important to recognize that our objector must suppose that the cognitive content which he stipulatively introduces as satisfying (b) also satisfies a requirement such as (c). Simply put, our objector must suppose that our ordinary conventional belief ascriptions are ascriptions of such content. This is so because of the character of the problem at hand and the nature of the solution under attack. The problem after all was this: on the one hand disquotation seems to play a central role in our conventional practice (and it is implicitly appealed to by Frege and subsequent theorists), while on the other hand the example of Pierre clearly demonstrates that any practice which incorporates disquotation will be one which underwrites attributing contradictory beliefs to a fully rational subject; and this, Kripke claims, is intolerable. The puzzle is a puzzle about our practice and the kinds of content ascribed therein. We have attempted to resolve *this puzzle* by reflecting on the conventions that govern our ascriptions. Assuming that the practice does incorporate disquotation, we have argued that a genuine appreciation of other elements in the conventional practice undermines Kripke's intuition that *such conventional* ascriptions of contradictory beliefs are incompatible with the subject's presumed rationality.

The point, in a nutshell, is this: *The intuition that the ascription of contradictory beliefs to a subject is incompatible with that subject's assumed rationality rests on the presupposition that such ascriptions serve to attribute contents which are such as to satisfy (b)*, and our argument then is that this presupposition is mistaken. *The convention-governed ascriptions do not assign contents which are such to satisfy (b)*. Conventional assignments of content to a subject x are sensitive to factors which x need not be aware of, and hence the conventions legitimize ascribing content in such a way as to violate (b). Rationality, it seems, *is* compatible with entertaining beliefs with contradictory contents (since more than rationality may be needed to detect such contradictions). *The practice which incorporates disquotation is thus shown to be perfectly coherent*. In response to this our objector introduces a notion of cognitive content which is intended to satisfy (b). Clearly this will constitute a response to my argument only if we suppose in addition that it is the task of ordinary attitude ascriptions — those of the form ⌜x believes that P⌝ — to assign such content. *Our concern is only with the contents these conventional ascriptions ascribe*, and they apparently serve to ascribe contents which violate the epistemic requirement (b). This is all I need for the solution proposed in II, and it is *this* our objector must respond to. This point is particularly evident when one views the problem from the *metalinguistic* perspective as the problem of demonstrating the consistency of the contradictory belief *ascriptions* with the subject's presumed rationality.[20]

I think it fair to conclude then that the proponent of cognitive content must construe those cognitive contents which Pierre is supposed to examine for contradiction as satisfying both the epistemic requirement and the semantic requirement. In the next section I will argue that this notion of content must be abandoned for the simple reason that nothing satisfies this twin requirement.

(B) Reasons for abandoning the Cartesian conception of content

In this section I will offer two extended arguments against the Cartesian conception of cognitive content, but first a negative note of an *ad hominem* character. For a full-blooded Cartesian, one who accepts the Cartesian dualistic metaphysics, the Cartesian epistemic requirement is an integral part of the larger picture; mental states are, on this conception, nonphysical; they are just the kind of thing one might expect to have special access to; they have their content as a "primitive mental property," and the subject has direct, unmediated access to this primitive property. Today, however, this is not a popular metaphysics, and in particular it is not accepted by most contemporary proponents of cognitive content, who, for various reasons, tend to reject any conception of content as some kind of a *primitive* property. The popular line is to suppose that the content of a state is determined or fixed by this or that nonpsychological property of the state, by functional role, by the state's nomological covariance with environmental features, or by something else of this sort.[21] Such theorists are, I think, occupying a very inhospitable middle ground, trying to retain the epistemic Cartesian requirement — that picture of ourselves as having some kind of immediate access to sameness and difference of psychological state — while at the same time abandoning the Cartesian metaphysics in favor of some more popular physicalistic picture of content determination. Suppose, for example, that the contents of states S_i and S_j were determined by the elaborate functional roles of these states, then surely it would be nothing short of miraculous if pure "rational introspection" were sufficient to ascertain the character of these functional roles and thereby decide the issue as to whether or not such states agree or disagree in content. In short, there seems to be no good reason for retaining the Cartesian epistemological picture enshrined in (b) once we have abandoned the Cartesian metaphysics.

I turn now to the first of our two extended arguments against this notion of cognitive content, and its alleged ability to resolve the puzzle Kripke hands us. In this argument I focus on showing that this notion of content does *not* provide for an *intuitive* solution to the puzzle, while the next argument challenges the very coherence of the notion. The proponent of cognitive content purports to resolve the puzzle in a relatively straightforward and intuitive way, to resolve it as one resolves more commonplace puzzles by distinguishing between the contents of Pierre's beliefs, his cognitive contents, and the conventional contents of the sentences he selects in his efforts to communicate those beliefs. Pierre's rationality, he claims, may be saved by simply recognizing that Pierre does not have *beliefs* with the contradictory contents that London is pretty and that London is not pretty, despite his disposition to sincerely assent to 'Londres est jolie', and to 'London is not pretty'. At least one of these sentences misrepresents Pierre's cognitive content. The attraction of this appeal to cognitive content is, I argue, an attraction derived from the mistaken supposition that *this* appeal to cognitive content is of a kind with ordinary intuitive appeals to cognitive or belief content. This appeal to cognitive content to save Pierre's rationality is, I claim, strikingly different from these other perfectly legitimate appeals to cognitive content, in that in this case the appeal is not, as our objector would have us believe, to some intuitive distinction but rather to a very peculiar notion of belief *content*, one which lacks any independent or intuitive motivation. Once this appeal is seen for what it really is, and no longer allowed to parade as simply an instance of a commonplace strategy, we shall, I think, find it to be an appeal without any attraction.

This objector rejects our crucial move: he denies that knowledge of contextual factors may be relevant when it comes to determining sameness and difference in one's own beliefs; such information, he claims, is not relevant for the simple reason that, contrary to the story told in II, genuine cognitive or belief content is not a function of contextual factors. In opting for this context independent construal of cognitive content our objector opts for a constraint of the following kind:

(L): In attributing *cognitive* content to a subject S one must not suppose that the subject is in a state (e.g., a belief state) with *cognitive content that-P* if there is a possible world W_i which satisfies the following conditions: (i) in W_i the subject S and its proximate environment are physically replicated, and (ii) in W_i the subject is not in a (belief) state with the content *that-P*.

Our objector is clearly committed to some such principle, for if he were to allow that physically identical subjects could differ in cognitive content simply *because* of remote differences in their worlds (not physically reflected in their proximate environment) he would, in effect, be treating cognitive content as sensitive to contextual factors.[22] And if one is to suppose that sameness and difference in cognitive content might be contingent upon such contextual factors, perhaps quite remote, then, magic aside, we must surely allow that the subject's ability to determine *such sameness and difference* might likewise be contingent upon his awareness of these same contextual factors. But this is to violate (b).

The Cartesian requirement requires us then to individuate and assign cognitive content in such a way as to satisfy (L), and the implications of this are extremely odd, weighing heavily against this notion of content. First, this constraint commits one to a Russellian conception of content—the rejection of singular content with the possible exception of states whose content is about oneself or about items in one's immediate consciousness. In particular, on this approach, it is a mistake to suppose that any subject S *could* have a belief whose *cognitive content* is appropriately captured by a singular sentence of the form ⌜*Fa*⌝, where ⌜*a*⌝ is a proper name for some subject other than S (and *a* is not itself an item in S's consciousness), and ⌜*F*⌝ is any predicate. Let Alf be our subject and Fred McFizz his close associate. Regardless as to their intimacy, it will not, on this account, be possible for Alf to have a belief whose *cognitive* content is, say, that Fred McFizz is boring. Alf cannot have such a cognitive content since there will always be a possible world W_i in which Alf is physically just as he is, experiencing the same sounds, etc., but which lacks Fred, though it does contain a physical doppelganger of Fred (also called 'Fred McFizz'). In W_i, Alf's physical situation is just as it is in the actual world, but in that world he does not have a belief with the cognitive content that Fred McFizz is boring (where *we* are using the name 'Fred McFizz' in the 'sense' in which it was used, in English, to characterize Alf's original belief). Hence, given *L*, we must deny this cognitive content to Alf in the actual world.[23] If we are to abide by the Cartesian requirement we must deny such very ordinary contents not only to Alf but to each one of us. And a similar story can be told for other singular terms, including such indexicals as 'you', 'she', etc. While we might *use* such terms to characterize and attribute beliefs, there remains a strict sense in which the *real cognitive content* of what one believes can never be, for example, that Fred is tall, that *you* are here, and so on. Indeed the problems extend far beyond singular contents. "Natural kind" cognitive contents, for example, are also out; it is an easy matter to conceive of examples analogous to the one just considered in which natural kind terms such as 'tiger' figure in place of singular terms. This Cartesian notion of cognitive content is then a far remove from *any* common sense conception of psychological content, and, indeed, it bears all the marks of philosophical invention.

It should be evident now that the strategy of those theorists who wish to retain the Cartesian requirement and to resolve the puzzle by appealing to cognitive content is not what it appeared at first glance. Such theorists appeared to be relying on the intuitive distinction between the content of one's beliefs and the conventional contents of the sentences one selects to express them. This distinction *is* intuitive and it is intuitively employed in many instances to explain how a rational individual might assent to strikingly inconsistent *sentences*. Consider Jones, for example, who sincerely assents to both 'Mary is a doctor' and 'Mary is not a physician'. Jones, like Pierre, looks to be guilty of holding beliefs which are so clearly inconsistent as to threaten his rationality. This threat is quickly dispelled, and Jones's behavior rationalized once one realizes that Jones has confused and interchanged the English words 'physician' and 'physicist'. The belief (content) Jones was trying to express by the second of these sentences was not that Mary is not a physician, but rather that she is not a physicist. Jones's assent to inconsistent sentences reveals no radical inconsistency in his beliefs, and he is guilty of no irrationality. The idea that we can save Pierre's rationality by appealing to cognitive content is attractive because we tend to think that in doing so we are saving Pierre's rationality in pretty much the same way as we saved Jones's rationality. But in fact the two cases are quite different, and the appeal to cognitive contents in Pierre's case is not at all like the superficially similar appeal in Jones's case. In Jones's case we point to something about the *individual* which justifies us in distinguishing between the content of his beliefs and the contents of the sentences he assents to — his mistaken beliefs about the language. We allow, of course, that Jones *could* have had the belief that Mary is not a physician, and indeed would have expressed that very belief by the sentence 'Mary is a not a physician' had he understood that sentence and sincerely asserted it. Now if this were the strategy of our proponent of cognitive content I would have no quibble with it; if one *could* save Pierre's rationality in *this* way, while retaining the Cartesian requirement, then this would be the way to do it (remember there is simply no need to go this way if you abandon the Cartesian requirement). But it is now clear that the similarity of the appeal to cognitive content in these two cases is both superficial and deceptive; the defender of Cartesian content does not save Pierre's rationality by any intuitive distinction comparable to the one employed in the service of Jones's rationality. Were this defender of Cartesian content using the kind of intuitive distinction used to save Jones's rationality, he should be prepared to point to some serious failing on Pierre's part, and, more important, he should be ready to allow that *Pierre would express the cognitive content that London is pretty* by the sentence *'Londres est jolie'* were the failing removed, were he not confused, etc. But this is something the defender of cognitive content simply cannot do. Cognitive contents must satisfy the Cartesian requirement (b). No *London*-contents satisfy this requirement, and they are accordingly not the kind of cognitive content Pierre can have, much less express. He saves Pierre's rationality *not* by distinguishing between the contents of Pierre's sentences and his beliefs as we did in the case of Jones, but rather by *sharply limiting the kinds of things that can be belief contents* for Pierre or anyone else. He does not save Pierre's rationality, as we have saved Jones's, by pointing to some fact about Pierre which explains why it is improper in *this* case to suppose that Pierre really believes that London is pretty; rather, relying upon highly suspect philosophical principles (in particular the Cartesian requirement), he invokes a notion of belief and belief content which is such as to make it impossible for *anyone* to believe that London is pretty, or for that matter that London is not pretty. To save Pierre the embarrassment of holding the contradictory beliefs that London is pretty and that London is not pretty, this theorist evokes a notion of belief (content) that renders all such singular belief impossible. This surely is too much; we are being asked to abandon intuitive and central elements in our ordinary conception, and all for the sake of a certain dubious philosophical principle — the Cartesian epistemic requirement (b). Better to retain the commonplace, and abandon any appeal to a notion of content meant to satisfy (b).[24]

My second argument contests the very coherence of the Cartesian conception, rather than its ability to solve the puzzle. I begin this argument with a few uncontroversial metaphilosophical remarks about philosophical investigation into intentional contexts.[25] The proponent of the Cartesian conception of cognitive content is, I argue, unable to do justice to certain obvious features of that investigation. I will concentrate on four simple features of the investigation, features which are, I claim, incompatible with the Cartesian conception of cognitive content as satisfying both the epistemic requirement (b) and the semantic requirement (c).

(I) Theoretical investigation of intentional contexts has, from its Fregean inception, been marked by controversy and disagreement; it is consequently an area of study *in* which little can be said with total confidence. From a metaphilosophical perspective, however, certain points are beyond debate. The first of which is that *there does exist substantial disagreement* among sophisticated and experienced theorists regarding the identity conditions of beliefs; they disagree as to what conditions, if any, must be satisfied by sentences ⌜S_i⌝ and ⌜S_j⌝ if they are to express the same belief (or, more generally, theorists differ as to what conditions must be satisfied if these sentences are to agree in the relevant semantical value). Compare, by way of example, the different positions of Burge and Kripke on the following questions:

(A) Is the belief that Mary is a doctor the same belief as the belief that Mary is a physician?

(B) Do the English sentences 'Mary is a doctor', and 'Mary is a physician' express the same belief?

Burge, I am supposing, would respond negatively to both questions, while Kripke apparently would opt for a positive response in both cases.[26] Our first point then is simply this: competent speakers of the language do disagree, even after prolonged reflection, on questions such as (A) and (B). I shall assume that this simple point is *not* a matter of debate.

(II) The second point is, I think, equally nontendentious, although it is easy to confuse it with a more controversial claim. It is that the English sentences, 'Mary is a doctor' and 'Mary is a physician' respectively serve to express the belief(s) that Mary is a doctor and that Mary is a physician. This is intended simply as a remark about a *surface* phenomenon, and as such it is hardly an issue of controversy. If we wish to speak of sentences of a language as expressing beliefs, as indeed we do, then surely we want to suppose that the belief expressed by 'Mary is a doctor' is simply the belief that Mary is a doctor. This fact surely lies behind our willingness to see questions (A) and (B) as "equivalent" even though one is explicitly metaphysical in character while the other is metalinguistic. As I said above, my concern is simply with the surface phenomenon; it is not with the interpretation and theoretical understanding of that phenomenon. Theorists certainly do disagree regarding the theoretical characterization of the belief expressed by a sentence such as 'Mary is a doctor' (the belief that Mary is a doctor), some opting for possible world accounts, others for variations on the Fregean approach, and still others for more syntactic characterizations. I have no desire to enter into *that* fray. My concern once again is with a much more modest claim; regardless as to how we carry out the subsequent analysis, we surely want to suppose that the belief expressed by 'Mary is a doctor' is the belief that Mary is a doctor. I should also caution that I am not supposing that every speaker uses the sentence 'Mary is a doctor' to express the belief that Mary is a doctor; we clearly want to allow that individuals may, on occasion, use this sentence to express some quite different belief. My claim is only that the belief conventionally expressed by 'Mary is a doctor' is the belief that Mary is a doctor, and *as such* the claim surely verges on the banal.[27]

(III) The third triviality concerns the kinds of considerations that are taken into account in our efforts to resolve questions such as (A) and (B). Every party to the debate agrees that information about the details of our linguistic practice is relevant in deciding questions such as (A) and (B), and this information is often of a decidedly arcane sort. In attempting to resolve such questions it is considered proper, indeed necessary, to take into account (linguistic) intuitions regarding such things as multiply embedded contexts (Mates), unusual cases of disquotation and translation (Kripke), speakers who fail to have a complete grasp of the concepts they employ (Burge), and the list goes on. Such reflection exposes us to features of our practice that we were previously unaware of and it thereby helps resolve questions such as (A) and (B). There is then general agreement among investigators that such arcane considerations are relevant in deciding questions such as (A) or (B), and I see no reason to think that we are all mistaken in this; such considerations seem to be relevant. (If they are not, it is time to abandon the entire game.)

Information regarding some of these more obscure features of our practice is, of course, just the kind of information that is not meant to be relevant when my concern is with the question "Do *I* use the sentences 'Mary is a doctor' and 'Mary is a physician' to express the same or different beliefs or cognitive contents?" Given the Cartesian epistemic principle, this latter question is meant to be decidable without reliance on such esoteric information. The idea that I might fail to recognize myself as using $\ulcorner S_1 \urcorner$ and $\ulcorner S_2 \urcorner$ to express the same cognitive content because I have not given sufficient time to the study of Twin Earth examples is the very kind of thing the Cartesian requirement is meant to exclude. But this in itself appears to pose no problem for the defender of the Cartesian conception. He can rightly insist that the kinds of consideration which are relevant in deciding the abstract semantic issue—relevant when it comes to assigning semantic values to natural language sentences $\ulcorner S_1 \urcorner$, $\ulcorner S_2 \urcorner$, etc.—are not relevant when determining sameness and difference in *one's own* cognitive contents. In the first kind of case our concern is with sentences of a natural language, with what they conventionally express, more generally with the conditions under which they agree in various semantic values; and in carrying out this inquiry *any* information about the conventions might be relevant. But in the second kind of case our concern is with the question 'Do *I* use the sentences $\ulcorner S_i \urcorner$ and $\ulcorner S_j \urcorner$ to express the same or different beliefs?' and we have been given no reason to think that these same abstract considerations are relevant in deciding questions of this latter kind. So far, then, no apparent problem for the proponent of Cartesian content. Problems do arise, however, when we make one more assumption (IV).

(IV) Burge and Kripke both use the sentences 'Mary is a doctor' and 'Mary is a physician' to express, respectively, the beliefs that Mary is a doctor and that Mary is a physician, and each one recognizes himself as doing so. I think that (IV) is fairly obviously true. Burge and Kripke are both highly proficient in the language; they both use, and intend to use, these sentences in the usual way, and each certainly thinks of himself as using these very simple English sentences to express the correlated belief.[28] But let me leave off any defense of (IV) for a moment so as to indicate the problem it poses for the defender of the Cartesian conception.

Having assumed (IV) we must conclude that Burge and Kripke both use the sentence 'Mary is a doctor' to express the same belief (the belief that Mary is a doctor), and that they both use the sentence 'Mary is a physician' to express the same belief (the belief that Mary is a physician). Burge, who thinks that these sentences express different beliefs in English, clearly thinks that *he uses them to express different beliefs* (two beliefs rather than one). Kripke, on the other hand, apparently thinks of himself as using these sentences to express the same belief, since he, unlike Burge, thinks that the belief that Mary is a physician is the same belief as the belief that Mary is a doctor. Clearly something has to give. If they both express the belief that Mary is a doctor by 'Mary is a doctor', and they both express the belief that Mary is a physician by 'Mary is a physician', then either they *both* express the same belief by these two sentences, or they *both* express different beliefs by them. Despite their strong convictions, it cannot be true that one of them expresses the same belief by the two sentences while the other expresses different beliefs by the same two sentences. At least one of them is wrong in his judgment that he is using the two sentences to express the same or different beliefs. How are they, or we, to decide this issue? The injunction 'introspect' is here clearly as worthless as Descartes' injunction to think clearly and distinctly. Rather than introspection providing the magic key, (IV) suggests a very different kind of strategy. Since they each use the sentence 'Mary is a doctor' to express the belief that Mary is a doctor, and they each use the sentence 'Mary is a physician' to express the belief that Mary is a physician, and they know that they do so, then the issue as to whether or not *they use* these sentences to express the same or different beliefs will be resolved once we answer the question: 'Is the belief that Mary is a doctor the same or different than the belief that Mary is a physician?'

If there are good reasons for thinking that the belief that Mary is a doctor is the same as the belief that Mary is a physician, then these will be equally good reasons for thinking that Kripke is correct in his judgment that *he uses* the two sentences to express the same belief; and these will be good reasons for thinking that Burge is incorrect when he judges himself to be expressing different beliefs by these two sentences. Similarly, reasons for thinking that the belief that Mary is a doctor is a different belief from the belief that Mary is a physician will be equally good reasons for thinking that Burge is right and Kripke wrong; they will be reasons for thinking that Burge's judgment that he uses the sentences to express different beliefs is correct, and for thinking that Kripke's judgment that *he uses* the sentences to express the same belief is incorrect. But we have just seen that the kinds of considerations which are relevant in determining whether or not the belief that Mary is a doctor is the same or different from the belief that Mary is a physician are considerations about details of our linguistic practice, details which are often of a very obscure and abstract character. Hence it would seem that once we have (IV) on hand (given [I], [II], and [III]), we have no option but to recognize that these kinds of considerations about detailed features of our practice are relevant when it comes to answering the question "Do I or do I not express the same belief content by 'Mary is a doctor' and by 'Mary is a physician'?" But this is an intolerable situation for the defender of the Cartesian conception. These kinds of considerations are, on his account, paradigmatic of what should not be relevant when it comes to answering this question. It would seem then we have no option but to abandon the Cartesian conception of content or at least one of (I), (II), (III), or (IV). I shall assume that (I)–(III) are not at issue – they seem to be obviously true – and thus the defender of the

Cartesian picture must reject (IV). Indeed I think the stock response to this kind of argument would turn on a rejection of (IV). Which shall it be then, (IV) or the Cartesian picture of access?

I myself think (IV) is about as evidently true as anything is in this area, and that the previous argument should be accepted as telling against the Cartesian conception, but rather than offering any direct defense of (IV) I will show that the rejection of (IV) is, surprisingly, of no help to the defender of Cartesian content. Such a one is still unable to do justice to the obvious facts.

If one rejects (IV) then one inherits a very different picture of the ongoing investigation into intentional contexts. Some issues are untouched however. Even if one rejects (IV) there is still no reason to doubt that theorists such as Burge and Kripke (pick your own actors) disagree on a variety of questions, nor is there any doubt but that they and others think of a certain kind of philosophical inquiry as being pertinent to resolving *these* questions. In particular, they have conflicting intuitions about the conditions under which *English sentences* may be said to conventionally express or attribute the same belief, and they and other theorists agree that wide-ranging theoretical considerations are relevant in resolving *these* differences. They also "differ" in that Burge thinks of *himself* as expressing different beliefs by the sentences 'Mary is a doctor' and 'Mary is a physician', while Kripke thinks of himself as using these sentences to express the same belief. As I said this much seems to be beyond doubt, and to be part of *any reasonable* picture. But in my appeal to (IV) I have cast this latter "difference" as being in effect a disagreement as to whether the sentences 'Mary is a doctor' and 'Mary is a physician' express the same or different beliefs (as a disagreement about the identity conditions of beliefs). I have used (IV) to argue that whatever bears on the abstract semantic or metaphysical issue is also relevant when it comes to determining sameness and difference in one's own beliefs. This is the move the defender of the Cartesian picture is now tempted to reject.

Having abandoned (IV) one can no longer assume that Kripke and Burge both use the sentence 'Mary is a doctor' to express the belief that Mary is a doctor, or that they both use the sentence 'Mary is a physician' to express the belief that Mary is a physician. And, thus, even though abstract semantic investigation may be relevant in determining whether the belief that Mary is a doctor is or is not identical with the belief that Mary is a physician, there is, on this approach, no reason to think that it provides the investigators with any new insight into sameness and difference *among their own beliefs*. This theorist attempts to limit the investigation to questions of the form: Do sentences ⌜S_1⌝ and ⌜S_2⌝ conventionally express the same or different beliefs?

I myself have little sympathy for this conception of the philosophical project; it does, I think, ignore crucial, normative elements in our practice, elements that are reflected in our reliance on disquotation. Here, however, I am content to argue that the Cartesian picture of content cannot be saved by abandoning (IV) for the simple reason that this resulting conception of the philosophical inquiry is equally inhospitable to the Cartesian requirement. On this, as on any reasonable conception of the inquiry, we are to suppose that abstract theoretical considerations are relevant in determining whether two *sentences* ⌜S_1⌝ and ⌜S_2⌝ *conventionally* express the same or different cognitive contents, the same or different beliefs. Suppose now that such considerations reveal Burge to be wrong in his claim that 'Mary is a doctor' and 'Mary is a physician' conventionally express different beliefs (a similar story may, of course, be told if they go in favor of Burge and reveal Kripke to be wrong). Prior to this result Burge certainly believed:

(a) that he expressed the belief that S_1 by ⌜S_1⌝, and the belief that S_2 by ⌜S_2⌝ (where ⌜S_1⌝ and ⌜S_2⌝ abbreviate the two sentences), and

(b) that the beliefs he expressed by ⌜S_1⌝ and ⌜S_2⌝ were different beliefs.

Given that the theoretical investigation reveals the belief that S_1 to be the same as the belief that S_2, he has to abandon (a) or (b). He has to abandon one of his second order beliefs about his own beliefs. Once again something has to give.

He can retain his initial conviction that he used the sentences ⌜S_1⌝ and ⌜S_2⌝ respectively to express the beliefs that S_1 and S_2, i.e., he can retain (a). But then he must, in the light of this theoretical result, abandon the belief that he uses these two sentences to express different beliefs. To take this option, however, is to abandon the Cartesian requirement; it is to allow abstract theoretical considerations a role in determining sameness and difference in one's own beliefs — the very thing the Cartesian picture was directed towards outlawing.

The defender of the Cartesian picture has no option then but to suppose that the proper response for one such as Burge, is to abandon (a) in the light of the unwelcome result that the belief that S_1 is identical to the belief that S_2. Rather than simply modifying his beliefs about sameness and difference among his beliefs, he should abandon his conviction that he really used ⌜S_1⌝ and ⌜S_2⌝ to express the beliefs that S_1 and that S_2. In taking this option, the only one left to him, the Cartesian is forced to recognize that abstract theoretical considerations are relevant when a speaker attempts to determine what exact beliefs *he* expresses by sentences ⌜S_1⌝ and ⌜S_2⌝ (not just what beliefs are conventionally expressed by ⌜S_1⌝ and ⌜S_2⌝). There is, I think, little need to emphasize the point that it is going to be very difficult indeed to reconcile this position with the claim that these same considerations are not relevant when a speaker is concerned with determining sameness and difference among the beliefs he expresses by sentences ⌜S_1⌝, ⌜S_2⌝, etc. If theoretical considerations are relevant in deciding what beliefs *I express* by ⌜S_1⌝ and ⌜S_2⌝ then surely they must be equally relevant in deciding whether or not I express the same or different beliefs by ⌜S_1⌝ and ⌜S_2⌝. If, for example, such considerations may lead me to abandon the belief that I expressed the belief that S_1 by ⌜S_1⌝ then clearly they may lead me to abandon the belief that I expressed the same belief by ⌜S_1⌝ and ⌜S_2⌝. The conviction that I expressed the same belief by these sentences rested on the now admittedly false belief that I expressed the belief that S_1 by $\ulcorner S_2 \urcorner$. It seems then that regardless as to whether or not one accepts (IV) one cannot hang on to the Cartesian conception of cognitive content. At least one cannot do so and retain the very plausible intuitions enshrined in (I), (II), and (III). We have to abandon the Cartesian conception or one of (I)–(III), and in the absence of any philosophical commitment to Cartesian content the choice seems clear: abandon the Cartesian conception as worthless.[29]

To conclude this long discussion of cognitive content. If one is to resolve Kripke's puzzle by appealing to cognitive content then that appeal must be to contents which are supposed to satisfy *both* the Cartesian epistemic requirement and the semantic requirement. Contrary to first impressions, this kind of strategy rests not on any intuitive speaker-meaning/sentence-meaning distinction, but rather on a counterintuitive 'Russellian' conception of psychological content. Moreover, such appeals are doomed from the outset. Once we undertake the task of constructing a semantics for the intentional ascriptions and allocate cognitive contents an objective semantical role (treat them as semantical "values" to be employed in our analysis of natural language sentences) then one has to allow abstract theoretical considerations a role in determining whether or not one expresses the same or different contents by sentences $\ulcorner S_1 \urcorner$ and $\ulcorner S_2 \urcorner$. But this is incompatible with the epistemic requirement. Despite its strong initial appeal the Cartesian notion of cognitive content embodies inconsistent elements; there simply are no such contents and the solution defended in section II retains its status as the obvious solution: A fully rational subject may subscribe to contradictory beliefs for the simple reason that *belief contents* are, in part, a function of contextual factors, and so recognition of sameness and difference among such contents may require much more than mere rationality.[30]

Notes

My thanks to seminar participants at the University of Minnesota, and a special debt of gratitude to my colleagues H. E. Mason and C. A. Anderson.

1. Saul Kripke, "A Puzzle about Belief," in *Meaning and Use*, edited by A. Margalit (Dordrecht: 1979), 239–83 (Subsequent references to 'Kripke' are to this essay).
2. Kripke, 259.
3. Kripke, 257. On the one hand Kripke argues that disquotation is intuitive, and, in particular, that there is no reason to withhold either of the contradictory beliefs (255-257); while on the other hand he claims that attributing these contradictory beliefs to Pierre seems to give rise to "insuperable difficulties" (259).
4. Some of the issues not discussed at all or only touched on: Are coreferential names generally interchangeable *salve veritate* in belief contexts? (Surely not!) What special treatment, if any, should be afforded multiply embedded belief sentences? What are the criteria that figure in everyday rationality evaluations? What is the relevance of the solution I propose in this paper to other problems, as, for example, that posed by Kripke in *Wittgenstein on Rules and Private language* (Cambridge: 1982)? And, finally, I have had to restrict my discussion of one very important issue—the problem of blocking the strengthened paradox—to a couple of notes (see notes 10 and

30). Though Kripke's paper has received widespread attention, obvious considerations have forced me to ignore alternative accounts.

5. Kripke elaborates on and defends this principle in 249ff.

6. See Kripke, 250.

7. Ibid., 250.

8. See, for example, D. E. Over, "On Kripke's Puzzle," *Mind* 92 (1983), and Ruth Barcan Marcus, "A Proposed Solution to a Puzzle about Belief," in *Midwest Studies in Philosophy* 6, edited by P. A. French, T. E. Uehling, and H. K. Wettstein (Minneapolis: 1981).

9. See 256 ff. in which Kripke argues in favor of ascribing the contradictory beliefs to Pierre in accordance with (W.D.).

10. A comprehensive response actually requires something more than this, for there is a second set of principles which seemingly inherits all the plausibility of (W.D.), (F), and (T), but which is such as to lead *us* into contradiction, into saying of Pierre that he both believes that London is pretty and does not believe that London is pretty. I discuss this issue in note 30.

11. I do not mean to suggest that coreferentiality is enough for interchangeability in belief contexts; the names 'London' and *'Londres'* are not only coreferential, they translate each other. I use the "coreference" terminology merely for convenience.

12. Further support can be drawn from a variety of very ordinary considerations relating to "conceptual confusion." A subject may be said to *use* the term 'whale', for example, in fashioning and expressing his beliefs even though he thinks it applies to a certain kind of fish rather than mammals. The beliefs, and not merely the utterances, of such a one are said to be conceptually confused. This confusion *in his beliefs*, however, is not taken to undermine his rationality (though it is not quite an ordinary empirical mistake), for it is perceived as arising from the public conventions governing the terms 'whale' and 'fish', and he is simply not fully aware of these same conventions. Just as lack of knowledge about one's language can blind one to the existence of conceptual confusion in one's innermost beliefs, so too it can blind one to relations of sameness and difference among these beliefs.

13. See, for example, H. P. Grice's classic, "Meaning," *Philosophical Review*, no. 3 (1957), 378-88.

14. I discuss one particular variant of the second strategy in note 24.

15. Such Twin-Earth cases are discussed by H. Putnam, "The Meaning of 'Meaning'," in Putnam's *Philosophical Papers 2: Mind, Language, and Reality* (Cambridge: 1975), and by T. Burge, "Other Bodies," in *Thought and Object*, edited by A. Woodfield (New York: 1982). The role of conventions is highlighted in Burge's original and influential paper, "Individualism and the Mental," in *Midwest Studies in Philosophy* 4, edited by P. A. French, T. E. Uehling, and H. K. Wettstein (Minneapolis: 1979).

16. See, for example, David Kaplan's treatment of such sentences in "Dthat," in *Syntax and Semantics*, vol. 9, edited by P. Cole (New York: 1978). I do not wish to endorse any particular psychological reading of the semantic distinctions Kaplan draws in this paper.

17. Actually the received view is even more "Cartesian" than this: a fully rational subject is supposedly able to determine sameness and difference in belief contents independent of *any* knowledge of the world, including *any* knowledge of the language she operates in. I shall ignore this in what follows; the weaker formulation, (b), is adequate for my purposes.

18. The "Big Picture" has been articulated and defended by a variety of theorists, perhaps most vividly by J. Fodor in his *The Language of Thought* (New York: 1975).

19. So, for example, the recognition that "Fregean propositions" do not satisfy (b) led to the search for a new, more finely individuated kind of semantic value, one designed to satisfy (b); perhaps the most popular suggestion was that cognitive content

should be construed as being akin to "character" (a semantic value introduced by Kaplan to represent what is common to different tokenings of a sentence containing indexicals). See, for example, J. Perry, "The Problem of the Essential Indexical," *Noûs* 13 (1979): 3-21. Again, see note 24.

20. This project is not to be confused with David Lewis's project in his paper, "What Puzzling Pierre does not Believe," *The Australasian Journal of Philosophy* 59 (1981): 283-89. In that paper Lewis argued for the consistency of the three claims: 'Pierre believes that London is pretty'; 'Pierre believes that London is not pretty'; and 'Pierre is not inconsistent'. This has the appearance of an impossible task.

21. See, for example, the account offered by H. Field in "Mental Representation," *Erkenntnis* 13 (1978): 9-61; and that offered by J. Fodor in "Semantics, Wisconsin Style," *Synthese* 59 (1984): 1-20.

22. This principle L is a kind of *psychophysical supervenience* principle: no difference in cognitive content without some physical difference in the subject. Various kinds of supervenience principles are discussed by J. Kim in "Concepts of Supervenience," *Philosophical and Phenomenological Research* 45 (1984): 153-76; and psychophysical supervenience, in particular, is discussed by him in, "Psychophysical Supervenience," *Philosophical Studies* 41 (1982): 51-70. My own view is that we have good reason to reject any strong principle of psychophysical supervenience, and I argue for this in "In Defense of a Different Doppelganger," *Philosophical Review* 96 (1987): 521-54. In particular, I argue that we have no reason to suppose that there is a notion of content, commonsensical or theoretical, which is such as to be invariant across Twin Earths, etc., that any such notion of "narrow content" is empty.

23. I think it evident that the two Alfs have different beliefs—they differ in truth value, etc. But in case one is seduced by the fact that they both fashion their beliefs using the same expressions (especially the same name). Consider the following example: Pierre, who resides in Paris, sincerely says: "Paris est jolie." We say, in English, that he believes that Paris is pretty. In W_i Pierre's experiences are qualitatively the same as they are in the actual world. In particular, he experiences his native city in the same way in both worlds: he only experiences certain local regions of it; those regions are qualitatively the same, and in both cases the city is called 'Paris' by its natives (including Pierre). However, we stipulate that this city in W_i is not the Paris we were talking of in the original case; the two cities are very different once one goes beyond the districts familiar to Pierre. In W_i the city called 'Paris' by the "Fwench" speakers of W_i is called 'Pharis' by the "English" speakers of W_i. In this case, I think, there is little or no inclination to say of Pierre in W_i that he believes that Paris is pretty. His belief is not about Paris, and there is not reason to suppose that the "Fwench" name 'Paris' (as used in W_i) should be translated into English as 'Paris', no good reason to think the English sentence 'Pierre believes that Paris is pretty' is true of him.

24. The defender of cognitive content is likely to complain that I am badly misrepresenting him, that he is not in the business of rejecting any of the familiar platitudes about what we can and cannot believe, and that my entire argument rests on a simplistic construal of belief ascriptions, one he does not share. The objection goes like this: the argument just given rests on the claim that Alf has different cognitive contents in W_i and in the actual world. This is supposed to follow from the fact that the sentence 'Alf believes that Fred is boring' is true in the actual world but not in W_i. Our imagined objector rejects this inference as resting on a simplistic semantics. The inference is plausible only if one supposes that the truth value of the ascription ⌜S believes that P⌝ is a function of the subject S, the believing relation, and the cognitive content ascribed by ⌜P⌝. But, he claims, this is not his semantics: it is not his intention to model cognitive content on some kind of Fregean propositional content, which was, of course, explicitly designed to provide for such a simple semantics. If one abandons this element in the Fregean model and construes the truth value of belief ascriptions as a

function of the subject S, the believing relation, cognitive content, *and context*, then the crucial inference in my argument is undermined; one can no longer infer that Alf has different cognitive contents in W_i and the actual world from the fact that the ascription true of him here—'believes that Fred is boring'—is not true of him in W_i. The difference in context warrants different ascriptions even though there is no difference in cognitive contents. It is now commonplace to compare sentences which ascribe beliefs to sentences which contain indexicals. One construes the propositional content of indexical sentences as a function of meaning (character) plus contextual factors and one should in like fashion construe the propositional content (the truth conditions) of belief ascriptions as a function of subject, cognitive content *and context*. S believes that P if and only if S has the believing relationship to the appropriate *cognitive content*, and the context is of a certain kind (e.g., it contains water rather than XYZ). On this model the differences between the actual world and W_i do not support the claim that Alf has a different cognitive content in the two worlds. Variations on this kind of account may be found in J. Perry, "Problem of the Essential Indexical," and in C. McGinn, "The Structure of Content," in *Thought and Object* edited by A. Woodfield (New York: 1982). This objection demands a much more extended response than I can possibly give it here. But the following points are noteworthy.

(i) It is one thing to talk of cognitive content, but it is another thing to justify that talk, to show that *any notion of content satisfies* the Cartesian requirements (or indeed satisfies the supervenience requirement). I have argued elsewhere that no notion of content satisfies the supervenience requirement (see note 22), and if content cannot be made to conform to this requirement it can hardly be made to conform to the Cartesian requirement. The second extended argument in the text is also meant to tell against the coherence of any such notion, see, e.g., notes 27 and 28.

(ii) It is true that one may usefully distinguish between two notions of "content" in developing a semantics for sentences containing indexicals, but this provides no support for the thought that this distinction may usefully be applied across the board, to sentences which have no indexical features at all. After all, this distinction was meant to capture what is distinctive of sentences containing indexicals.

(iii) The theorist who opts for this account—treating propositional content as a function of cognitive content plus context—accepts the primary component of my response: he accepts my claim that Pierre's rationality is compatible with his believing that London is pretty and his believing that London is not pretty. At the metalinguistic level, he agrees that ascribing contradictory beliefs to a subject is compatible with the assumption that the subject is perfectly rational. This really is the core of the solution.

In addition, once one grants that rationality is compatible with holding contradictory *beliefs*, then it is very difficult to see what the motivation is for thinking there should be some *further* kind of content which is such that rationality requires of us that we not tolerate any contradictions therein.

(iv) Finally, this reply is not relevant to the main point of the argument above; the point of that argument was to disabuse ourselves of the idea that this puzzle could be solved by some straightforward appeal to the intuitive distinction between belief content and the conventional content of the believer's words (while retaining the Cartesian epistemic requirement); the defender of Cartesian content "solves" the puzzle not by any such intuitive distinction but rather by appealing to a very odd conception of belief content. And this point is simply not touched by this reply.

25. For uniformity I speak throughout of 'intentional contexts' even though in some instances 'intensional contexts' would be the more appropriate expression.

26. See Burge, "Belief and Synonymy," *Journal of Philosophy* 75 (1978): 119-38; Kripke's intuitions are evident in notes 23 and 45 to "A Puzzle about Belief."

27. Actually, I do not need anything quite this strong. I can make my case so long as we assume that the sentences 'Mary is a doctor' and 'Mary is a physician' are each

correlated with (conventionally express) specific cognitive contents C_1 and C_2—perhaps of some "narrow" kind (see note 28). Nevertheless it is intuitive to suppose that these sentences do express the particular beliefs that Mary is a doctor and that Mary is a physician, and I shall continue to make this assumption (largely for expository purposes).

28. Those who quibble as to whether the sentences 'Mary is a doctor' and 'Mary is a physician' really do express the beliefs that Mary is a doctor and that Mary is a physician (see notes 24 and 27) may rewrite (IV) as follows:

(IV*) Burge and Kripke both use the sentences, 'Mary is a doctor' and 'Mary is a physician' to express, respectively, the cognitive contents C_1 and C_2 (whatever these may be—narrow or what have you), and each one recognizes himself as doing so.

The purist should then alter the subsequent discussion in obvious ways so as to reflect this change in (IV); he should, e.g., replace occurrences of 'to express the same belief' by 'to express the same cognitive contents'. Having done this, the argument will be substantially the same as the one actually provided, though it will no longer depend upon any simply acceptance of (II).

29. It should be clear now why I went to such length, in section (A), in arguing that our objector's notion of cognitive content was intended to satisfy two very different requirements, one epistemic and the other semantic. We need both of these to make this argument. The supposition that there is a notion of sense that satisfies the twin requirements is, I think, a supposition that is more seriously misguided than, e.g., the supposition that there is a single item which is both the object of belief and the bearer of truth or falsity (one of the many objections lodged against Fregean senses).

30. At this point a brief word on dissent, or the lack of a disposition to assent to a sentence ⌜P⌝. The problem is that assent and dissent seem to be on a par; if sincere reflective assent to ⌜P⌝ is supposed to warrant attributing the belief that P, then surely sincere reflective dissent from ⌜P⌝ (or the lack of any disposition to assent to ⌜P⌝) should be taken to warrant the denial of that belief. But if this is so, then our reasons for accepting weak disquotation should be equally good reasons for accepting a principle of strong disquotation, i.e., a principle of the following sort: *x* believes that *P if and only if x* is disposed to assent to ⌜P⌝ (with the usual restrictions on understanding, etc.). This principle, however, is intolerable: it leads *us* into contradiction, into saying of Pierre that he both believes and does not believe that London is pretty. Any solution which retains weak disquotation, as mine does, must somehow justify this unequal treatment of assent and dissent; it must undermine the appearance of symmetry between assent and dissent. Space prohibits any full discussion of this issue, but let me note the key ingredients in the anti-Cartesian response. Consider the following two principles:

(S) If *x*, a fully competent and rational speaker, is sincerely disposed to assent to ⌜P⌝, then *x* is disposed to assert that *P* (assuming, with Kripke, that *x* is not in any way incapacitated, etc.).

(T) If *x*, a fully competent and rational speaker, is sincerely disposed to dissent from ⌜P⌝ (or lacks the disposition to assent to ⌜P⌝), then what speaker lacks the disposition to assert that *P*.

These principles have very different standing: (S) appears to be something of a conceptual truth, while (T) appears to be false. If anything is clear in all of this, it is that Pierre is disposed to assert that London is pretty even though he lacks the disposition to assent to 'London is pretty'. We are now in a position to appreciate the different status assigned dispositions to assent and dispositions to dissent. A subject's sincere disposition to assent to ⌜P⌝ justifies attributing a disposition to assert that *P* (by *S*), and this, in turn, justifies attributing the belief that *P*. On the other hand, the falsity of (T) undermines any attempt to similarly link the disposition to dissent from ⌜P⌝ to the lack of the corresponding belief. We have what we need to justify our unequal treatment of strong and weak disquotation.

This paper was all but completed when Nathan Salmon's exciting and provocative study, *Frege's Puzzle*, appeared (Cambridge, 1986). He discusses the problem posed by Pierre, and there are some similarities in our accounts: in particular we both see the puzzle as turning on a certain conception of cognitive access to sameness and difference in cognitive content; and we both urge the rejection of the Cartesian position. The differences, however, are perhaps greater: the reasons we give for rejecting the Cartesian picture are very different, and we extract very different lessons from this rejection; unlike him, I do not think the rejection of the Cartesian picture lends any support to direct reference theorists in their quest to defend interchanging coreferential proper names in belief contexts (even if it does undermine some arguments against interchange).

How I Say What You Think

MARK RICHARD

Mutt and Jeff agree on what sentences Odile accepts. They agree about her dispositions to behavior. They agree on just about everything which seems relevant to the question, does Odile believe that Twain is dead?

They don't agree on the answer. When Mutt was asked, it was because someone wanted to know whether Odile would list Twain under dead Americans. Mutt knew she accepted 'Twain is dead' and thus said 'yes'. Jeff was asked by someone who couldn't understand why Odile, who's pointing to Twain's picture, wants to meet him. Doesn't she realize that Twain is dead? Jeff knew she rejected 'he's dead'. He answered that, no, Odile didn't believe that Twain was dead.

What are we to make of this? This paper investigates a way of saying that they're both right. Not because

(1) Odile believes that Twain is dead

is syntactically ambiguous. Not because there is a semantic ambiguity in the sentence. At least, (1) is not semantically ambiguous in the way that, say,

(2) Odile dropped Marie Bernard

is.

I propose that 'believes' and other verbs of propositional attitude are indexical. The truth of (1) varies across Mutt's and Jeff's contexts. There is not a change in reference in expressions other than 'believes', nor any change in Odile. And in some important sense 'believes' remains constant in meaning. If we accept all this then we will say that 'believes' is an indexical.

© 1989 by Mark Richard.

What varies across contexts that is relevant to the interpretation of 'believes'? I think that it's what counts as an acceptable translation of the sentences (in a *very* broad sense of 'sentence') Odile accepts; what varies is what functions are acceptable translation or correlation functions. (1) is true in a context iff its content sentence is an acceptable translation of some sentence Odile accepts. In Mutt's context, we may suppose, there are no substantive restrictions on translation at work: If Odile accepts ⌜*a* is dead⌝ for some name *a* of Twain, that makes (1) true, since 'Twain is dead' here translates any such sentence. In Jeff's context, something more stringent is required. Perhaps it's required that Odile accept ⌜I am pointing at *a*⌝ before 'Twain' can translate *a*.

I sketch some of the details of this view in section I. The claim that attitude ascription involves translation will remind *cognoscenti* of Church's objections to Carnap's and other translational accounts of such sentences. In section II, I turn to consider how the view fares in the face of some Church-style objections. Section III discusses Kripke's Pierre-London and Peter-Paderewski cases. I conclude with a discussion of some broadly logical issues.

I

I'm going to make a somewhat controversial assumption: that belief and the other attitudes are had in virtue of relations to sentence-like entities, whose constituents determine (relative to a context) Russellian referents. That is, when I have a belief, I'm related to a "sentence" which typically contains things which function like natural language proper names and demonstratives (in determining an individual), predicates (in determining properties or relations), as well as constituents which have the semantic roles of natural language connectives, quantifiers, and so on.

In fact, for simplicity, I am going to assume that attitudes like belief are realized by relations to natural language sentences. The account I'll give could get by with a *considerably* weaker assumption than this — for one thing, the mediators of belief needn't be sentences of a natural language. But I'll leave a discussion and defense of this assumption for another occasion.[1]

I thus assume a picture of the attitudes much like that assumed by many contemporary Russellians, who see belief as a relation to a Russellian entity, a relation mediated by relations to sentences or sentence-like entities.[2] I think this picture is a good first approximation to the truth about belief. But I am now unsatisfied with the account of belief *ascription* which the Russellian offers, on which 'Odile believes that Twain is dead' and 'Odile believes that Clemens is dead' must agree in truth value, since their 'that'-clauses name the same Russellian proposition.

What shall we offer in its place? Consider the example of Hammurabi, who reputedly believed that Hesperus was Hesperus, but not that Hesperus was Phosphorus. If we allow ourselves to talk about belief blackboards and such, we can describe what the relevant facts are: There are two possible mediators of Hammurabi's belief—pretend that they are

(1) $H = H$

and

(2) $H = P$.

Here, 'H' is doing duty for the Babylonian word canonically translated 'Hesperus'; 'P', for that canonically translated 'Phosphorus', and '$=$' goes proxy for a Babylonian identity predicate. Hammurabi, presumably, had (1) written on his blackboard, but not (2). It is this fact, or one like it, that someone who utters

(3) Hammurabi believes that Hesperus is Hesperus; but

(4) Hammurabi doesn't believe that Hesperus is Phosphorus

is trying to get across. The question is, how do (3) and (4) get this across?

In some way or other, in uttering (3) and (4) the speaker uses 'Hesperus' to represent 'H', 'Phosphorus' to represent 'P' and 'is' to represent '$=$'. And thus, the 'that'-clause 'that Hesperus is Hesperus' represents (1), while the 'that'-clause 'that Hesperus is Phosphorus' represents (2). (3) is true just in case what its t-clause represents is on Hammurabi's belief blackboard; likewise for (4). Since what (3)'s 'that'-clause represents is on the board, while what (4)'s represents isn't, (3) is true while (4) is not.

It will be said, perhaps, that this is correct, but that it leaves unanswered the most important question: How does 'Hesperus' come to represent 'H'?

A popular answer is that 'Hesperus' and 'H' have the same or similar nonreferential, cognitive content: they have the same or similar Fregean senses or conceptual roles (for the speaker and Hammurabi, respectively).

I've argued elsewhere that this sort of answer is untenable.[3] It is untenable because the sense (conceptual role, etc.) of a sentence will, on any reasonable account, vary intersubjectively. Here's a hint of the sort of problems which arise because of intersubjective variation. Observe that it's obvious that, if x can use sentence S to express a belief, and I can use S without altering the references of its expressions, then I can use S to ascribe to x the belief she expresses with S. If, for example, Odile can express a belief about Twain with 'Twain is dead', then I could echo her words, and use 'Odile believes that Twain is dead' to ascribe a belief to her.

Now this is so, even if Odile and I associate wildly divergent senses with the sentence 'Twain is dead'. Odile needn't *grasp* my sense for the sentence, for my ascription to be true. And what's more, when I echo someone's words to ascribe belief or assertion to them, I never seem to worry about identity or similarity of sense between their words and mine.

These facts refute Frege's account of attitude ascription. He held that in 'Odile thinks that Twain is dead', the 'that'-clause names a sense, my sense for

'Twain is dead'; the sentence as a whole says that Odile believes the sense named. But as we saw, the ascription may be true even though Odile doesn't believe my sense for 'Twain is dead'.

We were wondering how 'Hesperus' in 'Ham believes that Hesperus is Hesperus' comes to represent one or another of the expressions in Ham's belief mediators. If we reject Fregean and allied accounts of attitude ascription, we will agree that the right answer to the question is *not*: 'Hesperus' has for us the same sense, or cognitive role, as '*H*' for Hammurabi. Is, perhaps, the fact that one of the expressions conventionally translates the other relevant here?

Well, of course it's relevant. But it is also something which is an accidental feature of the example. Recall the case of Mutt, Jeff, and Odile. Jeff is asked if Odile believes that Twain is dead. His inquisitor wonders whether Odile, pointing at Twain's picture, realizes that Twain's dead. Jeff knows that she does not accept 'that one is dead'; he says 'Odile doesn't believe that Twain is dead'. Jeff's use of 'Twain' represents Odile's use of 'he' or 'that one'. So t can represent t' without t being a conventional translation of t', or vice versa.

In this case there doesn't seem to be any interesting connection—beyond sameness of Russellian referent—between Jeff's use of 'Twain' and the part of Odile's belief mediator it represents. Beyond the identity of Russellian interpretation of 'Twain' and 'that one', there doesn't seem to be anything about the content of 'Twain'—in an intuitive sense of 'content'—which makes it an apt representative of Odile's use of 'that one'. The two needn't have the same cognitive content; neither need the one be a translation, in some meaty sense of 'translation', of the other, etc.

The idea that there is something intrinsic to the content of Jeff's sentence, which would make it represent one but not another of the mediators of Odile's belief, is a mistake. 'Twain' can in principle represent any name, demonstrative or indexical, which Odile uses to refer to Twain. Of course, given contextual factors, there may be something which makes 'Twain' a more apt representative of 'that one' than other expressions the speaker might have used. Given the context of Jeff's remark, it's clear to all—that is, to Jeff and the inquisitor—that what's at issue is whether or not Odile accepts 'that one [Odile points at the picture] is dead'. Given that the question the inquisitor asked was 'Doesn't she realize that Twain's dead?' it is quite appropriate to use 'Twain' as a representative of 'that one'.

The right answer to the question—How does e in

Odile believes that . . . e. . . .

come to represent some expression (or class thereof) in Odile's belief mediators?—seems to go something like this. The interests and intentions of a speaker (and, to some extent his audience) determine how expressions in a 'that'-clause may be and are used to represent mediators of belief. Sometimes, for example, the speaker and audience are focusing on a specific name or term or other way of representing something. This is what is going on in the case of

Mutt and Jeff. This produces a restriction on what the expressions in a 'that'-clause can represent. In Mutt's case, a restriction like—use 'Twain' to represent 'Twain'—is operative. In Jeff's, something like—'Twain' is to represent only terms Odile associates with her current perceptual experience of Twain('s picture)— is operative.

Of course, in some situations we are not focusing on how someone thinks about the objects and properties about which they have beliefs. In some contexts, as the Russellian is fond of pointing out, we just don't care about the how of Odile's belief—that is, about the sentences whose acceptance constitute her beliefs—but only the Russellian what. In these situations there's no restriction operative on what 'Twain' may represent—as long as it represents a name of Twain.

Let's see if we can parley these remarks into an account of the overall semantics of belief ascription. Perhaps the most straightforward way to proceed makes use of hybrids which come from fusing sentences and Russellian referents. Think of a sentence as being a set-theoretic entity. Identify, for example, 'Twain is dead' with

(4) <'is dead', 'Twain'>.

A pure Russellian can identify the proposition a sentence expresses (in a context) with the result of replacing the expressions in a sentence with their Russellian referents. In the case of (4), this yields

(5) <being dead, Twain>.[4]

Consider what we get if we pair off the constituents of a sentence with their Russellian interpretations. If we do this with (4), for example, we get

(6) <<'is dead', being dead>, <'Twain', Twain>>.

Such hybrids are not Russellian propositions. They are not Fregean thoughts. They are fusions of things which represent—in this case, the expressions in a 'that'-clause—with their Russellian interpretations. Perhaps we should give them a new name, since they are somewhat different from run of the mill propositions. Since they are obtained by annotating the matrix provided by a sentence with the Russellian interpretations of its parts, we call them RAMs, for Russellian Annotated Matrices.

In general, one gets RAMs by fusing English sentences and Russellian referents, German sentences and such referents, indeed, from fusing arbitrary things which could be words or representations with Russellian referents. Take an arbitrary set of objects which could play the roles of parts of a language or system of representations. Pair off these "vocabulary" items with the parts of a Russellian proposition, and you have a RAM. The RAM represents, in a somewhat crude way, what it is for a sentence made out of the "vocabulary" to express the proposition.

Think now of the believer. She accepts various sentences, each of which has a Russellian interpretation. Just as we can fuse the content sentence of a t-clause with its Russellian interpretation, mating (4) and (5) to get (6), so can we do this to each of the mediators of the believer's belief. If we do this for all of the mediators of her beliefs, we end up with a set of RAMs. This set encodes all of the facts about the believer which are relevant to the truth and falsity of belief ascriptions to her. Let's call this set the believer's representational system, or RS.

When we ascribe an attitude, using, say

(7) Odile believes that Twain is dead

we seem to be saying something about the believer's RS, and not something simply about the collection of Russellian propositions believed. The remarks we made above suggest that what we are doing is saying (roughly) that the RAM our 'that'-clause determines represents one of the believer's RAMs.

For our RAM to represent one of the believer's RAMs, it seems necessary (but not always sufficient) that our RAM be related to the believer's in a certain straightforward way. Putting the matter crudely, the necessary condition is that, stripped of their linguistic parts, the two RAMs amount to the same Russellian proposition.

Let's not rest with a crude statement of the condition. Call the pairs of things in RAMs, consisting of a vocabulary item and an interpretation, annotations. So <'Twain', Twain> is an annotation, <'he', Twain> is an annotation, <'is dead', being dead> is an annotation, and so forth.

Say that a correlation is a rule (a function) which maps annotations to annotations and preserves reference: that is, if a correlation takes $<a,b>$ to $<a',b'>$, then b is b'. It's often convenient to speak as if correlations just mapped expressions to expressions, leaving the fact that annotations contain references as understood. Thus, for example, I'll sometimes say things like such and such a correlation takes 'Twain' to 'Clemens' and 'Clemens' to 'Clemens'.

Take a RAM p, and a correlation f (assume f is defined for all the annotations in p). Consider what we get if we systematically replace what's in p with its image under f. For example, if we begin with the RAM p determined by

Hesperus is Phosphorus

and use the correlation

f: 'Hesperus' → 'H'; 'Phosphorus' → 'P'; 'is' → '='

we obtain the RAM — call it q — determined by

$H = P$.

When p, q, and f are related in this way — q comes from p via the correlation f — I say that p represents q under f.

The relation I mentioned above, the one that is necessary for the truth of a belief ascription

Odile believes that *S*

is that the RAM determined by the 'that'-clause represent, under some correlation or another, a RAM in Odile's RS. So, for example, our old friend

(7) Odile believes that Twain is dead

is true only if the RAM determined by the 'that'-clause

(6) <<'is dead', being dead>, <'Twain', Twain>>

represents, under some correlation, a RAM in Odile's RS. As I remarked above, this is roughly equivalent to what the Russellian thinks to be necessary and sufficient for the truth of (6).

But we don't think it to be *sufficient* for the truth of a use of (7). As remarked above, sometimes we impose restrictions on the way an expression can be used to represent parts of the mediators of someone's belief. Some contexts contain restrictions on the functions we may use to correlate our RAM (the one determined by the 'that'-clause in an attitude ascription) and the RAMs in the subject's RS. When Mutt uttered (7), it was understood that 'Twain' was to represent 'Twain' and nothing else. So in evaluating Mutt's claim for truth, we are restricted in what correlations we can use. We can only use ones which map 'Twain' to 'Twain'. What Mutt said was true provided that his RAM ((6) above) represents one of Odile's RAMs under a 'Twain' to 'Twain' correlation.

A context, then, provides a collection of restrictions on correlations. We can think of each restriction provided by a context as containing three things: A person u, an annotation a, and a collection of annotations S. For example, Mutt's context provides the restriction

Odile; <'Twain', Twain>; {<'Twain', Twain>}

A restriction involving u, a, and S tells us that, in evaluating an ascription of attitude to u, we are restricted to using correlations which map a to something in S. Mutt's restriction, for example, tells us that in evaluating an ascription to Odile, we are restricted to using correlations which map 'Twain' to 'Twain'.

Our remarks above may now be codified as follows: Taken in a context, call it c, an ascription of the form of

a believes that *S*

is true if and only if the RAM determined (in c) by *S* represents a RAM in the representational system of what *a* names (in c), under a correlation which obeys all the restrictions operative in c. Or, a bit more loosely: the ascription is true iff the RAM *that S* represents one of *a*'s RAMs, given the context's restrictions on correlations.[5]

It should be tolerably clear how this proposal works in the case of Mutt, Jeff, and Odile. In the case of Hammurabi, too, matters seem relatively straightforward. Suppose we have heard the story of the ancient Babylonians, and say that Hammurabi believes that Hesperus is Hesperus, but not that Hesperus is Phosphorus. Given our focus on the way Hammurabi thought about the planets, it is natural to suppose that we are operating under the restrictions

> Ham; <'Hesperus', Hesperus>; {<the Babylonian word which 'Hesperus' conventionally translates, Venus>}
>
> Ham; <'Phosphorus', Phosphorus>; {<the Babylonian word which 'Phosphorus' conventionally translates, Venus>}.

We can abbreviate here, and represent the restrictions thus:

> Ham: 'Hesperus' → the Babylonian it conventionally translates
>
> Ham: 'Phosphorus' → the Babylonian it conventionally translates.

Given these restrictions, as well as the noncontroversial assumptions— 'Hesperus' conventionally translates 'H', and not 'P'; 'Phosphorus' conventionally translates 'P', and not 'H'; the facts about what Ham accepted as given at the beginning of this section—it is clear that the RAM determined by 'Hesperus is Hesperus' represents one of Ham's RAMs, relative to the context's restrictions, but that determined by 'Hesperus is Phosphorus' does not. If we are ascribing belief to Hammurabi, the latter RAM

> <<'is', Identity>, <<'Hesperus', Venus>, <'Phosphorus', Venus>>>

can, given the restrictions, *only* represent a RAM of the form

> <<e, Identity>, <<'H', Venus>, <'P', Venus>>>

where H and P are fixed as above. (Since there are no restrictions on 'is', e can be any piece of vocabulary). Since such a RAM is clearly not in Hammurabi's RS, the claim that he believes that Hesperus is Phosphorus is false.

Isn't this a sort of closet Fregeanism, with expressions in 'that'-clauses doing duty for the senses of expressions for those to whom we ascribe attitudes? I don't want to quibble about the epithet (or honorific, depending on your perspective) 'Fregean'. If you're willing to accept this account, and it makes you feel better about things to call it Fregean, by all means do so. But we have wandered quite far from any *traditional* sort of Fregeanism. For example, as I observed above, this view abandons the Fregean view, that attitude ascription involves a match of nonreferential, cognitive content between a t-clause and some state of, or sentence accepted by, the subject of the ascription. Whether or not Mutt and Odile associate similar ways of thinking of Twain with their uses of 'Twain' is wholly irrelevant to the question, "Does, or could, Mutt use 'Twain' to represent Odile's uses of 'Twain'?" In fact, one can comfortably hold the sort of view I am urging and insist that in general, interpersonal comparisons of a sentence's sense or cognitive role cannot be made. One could say, for instance, that such comparisons presuppose an isomorphism of the subjective probability functions users associate with their sentences, a sort of isomorphism which, practically speaking, is never to be found.

Furthermore, there is nothing in this view which suggests that associated with a use of an expression, as a matter of the expression's meaning or otherwise, is a descriptive condition which determines the expression's reference. This view does not retain even the shade of the idea that sense determines reference.

It is also worth comparing the way this and Fregean views treat quantification into attitude ascriptions. For Fregeans, quantification into an attitude ascription, as in

(8) There's an x such that Odile believes that x is dead

involves implicit quantification over senses, with (8) being glossed as

For some x and s: s is a sense which presents x and Odile believes ^{s}s is dead^s,

the "s"'s here being "sense quotes." The view I've glossed allows a straightforward, objectual treatment of quantification in. Relative to an assignment v to the variables, the sentence 'x is dead', 'x' a variable, determines the RAM

<<'is dead', being dead>, <'x', v ('x')>>.

For example, if v('x') is Twain, then 'x is dead' determines the RAM

<<'is dead', being dead>, <'x', Twain>>.

This can represent one of Odile's RAMs just as well as the RAM that Twain is dead. So quantification in is treated quite straightforwardly, with (8) true just in case 'Odile believes that x is dead' is true for some assignment to 'x'.[6]

It would be misleading to say that the view of attitude ascriptions I am sketching has nothing in common with Fregean views. Like the Fregean, I see the truth of an attitude ascription as being sensitive to facts about the way an individual represents objects and properties. But I reject the mechanism the Fregean proposes to explain this sensitivity. I also would prefer to be committed to as "thin" an account of ways of thinking as possible. I am somewhat dubious of the significance of comparisons of nonreferential content across speakers, and am trying to offer an account which avoids them. In fact, so far I've said nothing that commits us to a very interesting notion of *intra*personal identity of nonreferential content, between different expressions or "modes of thought."

My account also has a good deal in common with Russellian accounts of attitude ascription. It rejects the idea that senses or nonreferential, cognitive "contents" like conceptual roles are apt semantic values for 'that'-clauses. It is compatible with views about reference—for example, that names and demonstratives are directly referential—which partially motivate Russellianism. My view honors the intuitive evidence for Russellianism—for example, that the truth of an attitude ascription is often unaffected by substituting one directly referential expression for another which names the same thing. It gives a natural, objectual account of quantifying in. But unlike Russellianism, this account is consistent with the idea that, for example, someone might know that Clark Kent is Clark Kent, but not know that Clark Kent is Superman.

II

On my view, a 'that'-clause of English names something quite different from its natural translation into German. 'that Twain is dead' names something in which the expression 'is dead' occurs; its German translation, *'dass Twain tot ist'* names something in which the German expression *'ist tot'* occurs. You might anticipate that this would make English belief ascriptions and their natural German translations diverge in truth conditions in an objectionable way.

This, in essence, was Church's complaint against Carnap.[7] I do not think that any version of this objection has force against the account I've given. Consider first

(1) Odile believes that Twain is dead

and its German translation

(1′) *Odile glaubt, dass Twain tot ist.*

If a sentence has indexical elements, we can speak of its truth conditions only relative to a particular context or use. We are treating 'believes' as an indexical, and would give its German translation *'glaubt'* a perfectly parallel treatment. So both (1) and (1′) can be assigned truth conditions only relative to a context.

Now, there are a number of worries you might have about the way in which truth conditions are assigned to uses of (1) and (1′) on this theory. For example, you might complain that a use of (1) in one context and a use of (1′) in some other context could have different truth conditions. And this, you might say, is unacceptable, (1) and (1′) being translations of one another.

Of course (1) and (1′) can be used so that they have different truth conditions. But this is no objection: One of the *motivations* for this view, you will recall, is that sentence (1) *itself* can be used in such a way that it says different things in different contexts. One reason for adopting the view is that a sentence like (1) is used some, but not all, of the time to say something quite specific about the how of Odile's belief. The same is true of (1′). So the observation that (1) and (1′) might be used to say different things is not an objection to the theory.

For another thing, you might worry that no use of (1) can have precisely the truth conditions of a use of (1′). *If* this were true it would be a serious objection.

However, consider 'believes' and *'glaubt'*. There is no reason that they can't have exactly the same meaning. (To use Kaplan's terminology: They have the same character.) The verbs' common meaning is something which given a contextually supplied "translation manual" (i.e., a set of restrictions) pairs off people and RAMs: Person P is paired with a RAM R, provided R represents, under the manual, a RAM that P has in his RS. Of course, the manuals the English verb is given are usually different from those the German verb gets. So in context the verbs typically have different contents. But this is consistent with their having the same meaning. (The situation is to *some* extent parallel to that of 'I' and '*ich*' – in contexts they may refer to different things; the two still have the same meaning.)

Thus it is perfectly possible for uses of (1) and (1′) to have the same truth conditions. (I suppose truth conditions to be sets of worlds.) If (1) is used in a context in which no restrictions are operative, then (speaking roughly) (1) says that Odile accepts some sentence of the form $D(t)$, where D refers to being dead, and t refers to Twain. Used in a context without restrictions, (1′) says exactly the same thing.

Even when restrictions are operative, (1) and (1′) may have the same truth conditions. For example, suppose (1) is used in a context c in which the restrictions require that 'is dead' be mapped to 'is dead' (and no other restriction is operative). A use of (1′) in a context in which just the restriction Map 'ist tot' to 'is dead' is operative will be one in which (1′) is assigned the same truth conditions as is (1) in c.

Here is another issue raised by Church's objections to Carnap's account of attitude ascriptions. Church himself noted that his objection to Carnap was really only forceful for the case of iterated attitude ascriptions like

(2) John believes that Hammurabi believes that Hes is hot

and their natural translations into foreign languages.[8]

What will we assign a 'that'-clause in which 'believes' occurs, like 'that Hammurabi believes that Hes is hot'? What we need to know is whether, in constructing a RAM for this, we pair off 'believes' with its meaning (the rule for getting from context to content) or with its content in a particular context. It's clear that for most indexicals we should pair the indexical off with its content. Thus, for example, in a context where I am speaking, the 'that'-clause in

(3) Peter believes that I am fat

should name the RAM

(3′) <<'is fat', being fat>, <'I', mark richard>>.

The exception to this rule is the verbs of attitude. In constructing the RAM that Hammurabi believes that Hes is hot, 'believes' is paired with its (context-independent) meaning. We also think of the RAMs in the believer's representational system, which correspond to sentences in which 'believes' occurs, as being constructed out of the meaning of 'believes', not out of its content in the believer's context.

If we proceed in this way, there's nothing particularly puzzling about iterations of 'believes'. Consider, for example, (2) and its natural German translation. The only difference between what the English

that Hammurabi believes that Hes is hot

names and what its natural German translation names is in the vocabulary items in the RAMs. There's no difference in the semantic values paired with the vocabulary.

So what we will say here will be exactly parallel with what we would say about (1) and (1'). For example, suppose that we use (2) in a context without restrictions. Suppose further that John accepts the sentence 'Hammurabi believes that Hes is hot'. Then what we say is true. It's easy to work out that a use of the natural German translation of (2) (*'John glaubt, dass Hammurabi glaubt, dass Hes heiss ist'*, or something of the sort), used in a context with no restrictions, will be true in the same circumstance. In fact, it will have the same truth conditions.

A last, related objection. Ali Kazmi pointed out to me that on my view, a sentence like 'Odile believes that Cologne is large' and its translation into a foreign language (say, *'Odile glaubt, dass Köln gross ist'*) may differ in truth value taken relative to one context. For the context may provide restrictions which deal only with English vocabulary, not with foreign language vocabulary. Kazmi suggested that this was a problem.

If it is a problem, it is because of the truth of a principle like:

(I) If a sentence type S of one language is naturally and correctly translated by a sentence type T of a second language, then there is no context relative to which S and T do not have the same truth values.

I doubt that (I) is true. As I understand it, there is a sort of animal, the woodchuck, for which English has two expressions ('woodchuck' and 'groundhog'), where French has but one (*'la marmotte'*). The French *'Louis croit que Chuck est une marmotte'* is thus correctly and naturally translated by both 'Louis believes that Chuck is a woodchuck' and 'Louis believes that Chuck is a groundhog'. But presumably, the latter two sentences can diverge in truth value relative to some context. So the French and a natural and correct translation thereof will diverge in truth value relative to some context.

III

I want to discuss Kripke's puzzle about belief, both in its version involving Pierre, 'London', and *'Londres'*, and that involving Peter and 'Paderewski'. I assume familiarity with the case of Pierre. Kripke writes "This is the puzzle: Does Pierre, or does he not, believe that London is pretty?" Kripke argues successively that

(1) Pierre believes that London is pretty

is (or at least seems) true (focusing, of course, on Pierre's "French beliefs"); that

(2) Pierre believes that London is not pretty

is (or at least seems) true (focusing now on Pierre's "English beliefs"); but that they can't both be true, because Pierre, a leading logician, "would *never* let contradictory beliefs pass. And surely anyone, leading logician or no, is in principle in a position to notice and correct contradictory beliefs if he has them."[9]

What counts as a solution to the puzzle? Certainly, all else being equal, we want to preserve as much of our pre-theoretic intuitions about sentences (1) and (2) as possible. This suggests that in the ideal, a solution to the puzzle will provide a way of saying that both sentences are true—that is, the uses Kripke makes of them, when he ascribes truth to them, are true uses; and yet (1) and (2) together can't be true, for more or less the very reason Kripke gives.

One nice thing about the view I've been sketching is that it does allow us to say something like this. One way in which restrictions on correlations should come to be operative is this: If the speaker is focusing on how someone expresses his beliefs, thinks that his audience is so focusing (and thinks his audience thinks he knows that they are so focusing), then the appropriate restrictions tend to come into play. So when Kripke begins walking us through the puzzle, focusing on Pierre's French beliefs, we might expect the restriction

(3) 'London' → *'Londres'*

to be operative. This will make (1) true. Then Kripke asks us to focus on Pierre's English language beliefs. The old restriction is no longer operative, and a new one

(4) 'London' → 'London'

comes into play. So (2) is true. Then Kripke asks us, in effect, to answer the question: Can (1) and (2) be true together? And he observes that they seem to imply that Pierre is in some sense irrational.

And this is quite correct. Any natural way of evaluating (1) and (2) in the context of one conversation will use a single correlation function. It would be unnatural to adopt a completely new correlation each time we reascribe belief (or desire or another attitude) to an individual within the course of a single discourse.[10] So any natural way of evaluating the conjunction of (1) and (2) makes it false.[11] And it is false for just the reason Kripke suggests: It suggests that Pierre is irrational, accepting some sentence and its negation. It is (roughly) in this sense that anyone with contradictory beliefs is in a position to recognize such and correct it.

The case of Peter and 'Paderewski' may appear to present something of a problem for my view. The case seems like that of Pierre and 'London'-*'Londres'*: Peter hears one day of a famous musician, Paderewski, and thinks to himself 'Paderewski had musical talent'. He hears on some other day of a Polish statesman, Paderewski. Thinking that politicians are poor musicians, he thinks to himself 'Paderewski did not have musical talent'. We have, Kripke urges, exactly the same sort of puzzle about

(5) Peter believes that Paderewski had musical talent

(6) Peter believes that Paderewski did not have musical talent

as we did concerning the Pierre sentences.

I suggested that on any natural reading of the Pierre sentences they wouldn't be true in the same context. It would seem that I can't say this sort of thing about this case. For here there seems to be but one sentence (type), that of

Paderewski had musical talent

one such that Peter accepts both it and its negation. So it seems that no matter what restrictions are operative, if (5) is true, so is (6). So, it appears, I have to treat like cases (Pierre and Peter) in unlike ways.

I do not think I do. I could say that the expression 'Paderewski' in Peter's spoken dialect is ambiguous: appearances to the contrary, Peter does not accept some natural language sentence and its negation. I think this somewhat *ad hoc*, so I will try to get by without saying it.

Let's go back to the picture of belief that we are working with. Think of the believer as having sentence tokens written inside of his head, on a blackboard next to the pineal gland. Think of his representational system, the set of RAMs we quantify over in giving truth conditions for attitude ascriptions, as being determined somehow by what's written on the blackboard.

Up to now, I have been pretending that the way the blackboard determined the RAMs was as follows. Suppose a token of 'Twain is dead' is on Odile's blackboard. Then a RAM that looks thus:

<<'is dead', being dead>, <'Twain', Twain>>

is in Odile's RS. Here, the quoted items are the types of the relevant tokens. On this picture, we would have in the case of Peter a RAM and its negation in Peter's representational system. (I haven't defined a negation-of operation for RAMs, but it's obvious, I think, how to go about it.)

I want now to distinguish between the sentence tokens on the blackboard and representations. I think of the sentences on the believer's blackboard as determining representations; in constructing RAMs to put in the believer's RS, we form them from the representations which the sentences on the blackboard determine. Instead of putting *expression* and referent in the RAM, we pair the *representation* determined by the expression with the expression's referent.

To return to the example above: If Odile tokens 'Twain is dead', then her RS contains the RAM

HOW I SAY WHAT YOU THINK 331

<<R1, being dead>, <R2, Twain>>

where R1 and R2 are the representations determined by her tokens of 'is dead' and 'Twain', respectively.

We could identify representations with sets of tokens on the blackboard. Then we have only the problem of saying when two inscriptions on the blackboard determine the same representation. I won't give a full blown theory about this. But I think such a theory is possible, and I think its broad outlines are fairly clear.

As I see it, there will be two sorts of conditions which together will be necessary and sufficient for two tokens to determine the same representation. Intuitively, the two sorts of conditions are what we could call "outside" and "inside" conditions. The outside conditions will be broadly causal in nature. If we have two proper name tokens written on the blackboard, for example, they will have to be residues of the same causal or historical chain (and thus refer to the same thing) in order to satisfy the outside condition. I take it that this will result, if we make the outside condition (in the case of proper name tokens) that two proper name tokens determine the same representation if and only if they are tokens of the same name (type). Let us do this. Observe that this rules out, for example, 'Hesperus' and 'Phosphorus' determining the same representation.

The interior condition should be a "recognition" condition. Let me speak rather intuitively about this. Usually, when we hear someone talking about someone, we think we know who is being talked about. We *hear* someone say 'Reagan is going to bomb Nicaragua', and assume that it's Reagan the president who is being discussed, not the Regan the animal rights philosopher. When this happens, we somehow "file" the token of 'Reagan' we are hearing with certain other tokens ("presidential tokens") on our blackboard, and segregate if from others. In such a case, the new token of 'Reagan' has the interior relation to the presidential tokens. Our segregating the new token with the older ones is a sort of "recognition." Suppose that it was the president that was being talked about, and that outside conditions were satisfied. Then, with both outside and inside conditions satisfied, the new token of 'Reagan' and the older presidential tokens will all determine the same representation.[12]

I haven't given a theory of representations here, of course. At the least, before I have even the vague outlines of a theory, I need to talk about demonstratives and sensuous experiences. It's a lacuna, but for now I have to live with it.

In the case of Peter, we have a token of 'Paderewski has talent' on one place on the blackboard, a token 'Paderewski has no talent' somewhere else. It is quite clear, I hope, that on any way of spelling them out, the interior conditions will not be satisfied with respect to the two tokens of 'Paderewski'. So they determine different representations.

This means that, in principle, we can treat the Paderewski case just as we treated the case of Pierre.

IV

I close by mentioning some issues of a broadly logical nature. First of all, we can introduce propositional quantifiers and variables, letting them range over the class of all RAMs. These are treated as one would expect, with

For all p: a believes p → b believes p

being true just in case any assignment of a RAM to 'p' makes the matrix sentence true.

A second issue is that of RAMs and truth bearers. Traditional Russellian propositions are both the objects of attitudes and the bearers of truth. Many RAMs are indistinguishable, *qua* truth bearers, from such. The RAM of 'Hesperus is hot', for example, is more or less the Russellian proposition that Hesperus is hot with some extra material in it, material we can ignore for the purposes of assigning truth conditions.

But RAMs corresponding to sentences in which belief predicates occur are in a certain sense incomplete. For these RAMs contain the (context constant) meaning of 'believes', not one of its contextually varying contents. If we appoint RAMs to the office of official bearers of truth, then we will have some truth bearers—e.g., that Odile believes that Twain is dead—which are true in some contexts and false in others.

This means I'm committed to either (a) contextual variation in the truth value of the bearers of truth, or (b) uses of a sentence like 'It's true that Odile believes that Twain is dead' ascribing a property not to the RAM that Odile believes that Twain is dead, but to a supplemented RAM, a pair consisting of the RAM and the restrictions operative in the context of use.

There's nothing objectionable *per se* about either (a) or (b). There is, after all, a long tradition which sees the object of belief as changing truth value across contexts. Some have wanted to say, for example, that the proposition that Reagan is president is true now, but—patience—won't always be true. I happen to disagree that the objects of belief change truth value in response to change of time. But just because objects of belief don't change truth value in response to some contextual variations doesn't mean that they don't respond to others. And there is evidence that certain objects of belief have their truth value relativized, in one way or another, to context. When Mutt and Jeff say 'Odile thinks that Twain is dead', we agree that, within the confines of their respective conversations, one may speak truly, the other falsely. But they both believe that Odile believes that Twain is dead. So it looks as if one thing, their common belief, is true at one place, false at another.

In any case, we evaluate beliefs for truth, as well as tie the truth of beliefs to the truth of the sentences which express them. So we should give some account of how truth and RAMs are related. A natural way to do this is as follows. Let us say that a supplemented RAM is a pair consisting of a regular RAM and a set of restrictions. Note that a sentence taken in a context determines a unique supplemented RAM: pair the RAM the sentence determines with the contextual restrictions.

A supplemented RAM will determine truth conditions, and thus a truth value at the actual world, in a straightforward way. If the RAM corresponds to a sentence with no belief operator, the supplemented RAM has the truth conditions of the corresponding Russellian proposition. If the RAM corresponds to a sentence with a belief operator, one uses the set of restrictions in the supplemented RAM to turn the meaning of the 'believes' operator into a content, and then assigns truth conditions in the way suggested by the truth definition for belief ascriptions.

We can thus introduce a predicate 'is true' which combines with 'that'-terms to form sentences. ⌜That S is true⌝ is itself true in a context c iff the supplemented RAM consisting of the RAM named by ⌜that S⌝ in c and the set of restrictions in c is true. The predicate behaves nicely enough. We have such intuitively satisfying results as the validity of the argument schema:

For all p: a believes $p \to p$ is true

a believes that S

Thus, that S is true.[13]

Finally, I'll say something about reference to, and individuation of, propositions. We ought to treat ⌜that S⌝ and ⌜the proposition that S⌝ in the same way. So let terms of the latter form name what those of the former do.

People will object that this cuts propositions far too finely. I can't answer every objection to the fineness of the cut here, so I'll address only the one I think most serious.

Objection: Surely the sentences 'snow is white' and 'la neige est blanche' say the same thing, a thing which Odile believes. So there's something, p, such that Odile believes p, 'snow is white' says p, and 'la neige est blanche' says p. You have to deny this, because you say that the proposition that snow is white is distinct from that named by 'que la neige est blanche'.

Response: Well, this depends upon the exact semantics of 'say' as it is used in " 'snow is white' says that snow is white," doesn't it?

Note, in working up to an account of this use of 'says', that it does not make sense to assess what a sentence says, unless we imagine the sentence taken relative to some context or other. After all, 'London is pretty' says one thing at noon (that London is pretty then), and quite another at six o'clock.

Suppose we take a sentence relative to a context c. The sentence will determine a RAM p in the context. We can ask whether p represents, relative to the restrictions of the context, various other RAMs. Call the set of RAMs so represented p's profile in the context. (Strictly, the profile of a RAM is a function from worlds to pairs of an individual and a RAM, since restrictions are keyed to individuals.) Then we might say that

"S" in context d says that T

is true in a context c iff the profile in c of the RAM determined by T in c is identical with the profile in d of the RAM determined by S in d.

If we suppose that we are working in a context in which no restrictions are operative, and that 'la neige est blanche' and 'snow is white' are to be taken relative to that context, then it will be true that 'snow is white' says (in the context) that snow is white, and 'la neige est blanche' (in the context) says that snow is white. And so it will be true (assuming Odile's beliefs are rightly arranged) that there's a p such that Odile believes p, 'snow is white' says p, and 'la neige est blanche' says p.[14]

Notes

1. I defend this assumption in chapter 1 of *Propositional Attitudes* (Cambridge, forthcoming).
2. Such a view is strongly suggested, for example, by some passages in Kaplan's "Demonstratives," in *Themes From Kaplan* edited by Almog, Perry, and Wettstein (Oxford, 1988). Nathan Salmon invokes a more general notion, that of being acquainted with a proposition under a *guise* or *way of apprehending* such. (See *Frege's Puzzle* [Cambridge, Mass., 1986].) Salmon's guises are sententially structured at least to the extent of having parts corresponding to constituents of the proposition: "The means by which one is acquainted with a singular proposition includes as a part the means by which one is familiar with the individual constituent(s) of the proposition" (108).
3. I have argued for this in "Taking the Fregean Seriously," in *Philosophical Analysis: A Defense by Example*, edited by David Austin (Dordrecht, 1988). See also chapter 2 of *Propositional Attitudes*. Kripke also notes this problem: see Kripke's "A Puzzle about Belief," in *Meaning and Use*, edited by A. Margalit (Dordrecht, 1979).
4. I ignore, here and elsewhere, complications introduced by tense.

The identification of Russellian propositions (and RAMs) with interpreted sentence structures must of course be made with some care. The structures cannot invariably be surface structures, if only because of the existence of idioms. So I assume some assignment of "logical forms" to sentences, which will yield Russellian propositions when their linguistic constituents are replaced with interpretations.

5. It is probably not obvious what the semantic value of the verb 'believes' is supposed to be. Simplifying somewhat: 'Believes' and its ilk are to be treated as indexicals. They have a constant meaning, or, to use Kaplan's term, character; their interpretation, or content, varies from context to context. The character of 'believes' is a rule which, given a collection of restrictions, returns an appropriate intension. Since 'believes' looks at a person and a RAM—it acts as a dyadic predicate which joins a term like 'Odile' with something that names a RAM, like 'that Twain is dead'—appropriate intensions for 'believes' will be functions from pairs, of individuals and RAMs, to sets of worlds. Write

$Rep(p,q,f)$

for 'p represents q under f'. Write

$Obey\ (r,f,u)$

for 'f obeys all the restrictions in r which are relevant to u'. (A restriction $<x,a,S>$ is revelant to u iff $x=u$; f obeys the restriction if $f(a)$ is in S.) Then, if r is the collection of restrictions operative in c, 'believes' takes as value in c the function which maps $<u,p>$ to the set X of worlds such that w is in X iff, at w, u has a RAM in her RS such that, for some f, Obey (r,f,u) and $Rep(p,q,f)$.

The simplification here is that of making 'believes' two-placed. In *Propositional Attitudes*, the proposal of this paper is given an alternative development, in which the verb is made three-place, with the extra argument place one for correlations. This allows the nicest formalization of the treatment of Kripke's puzzles which is given in section III of this paper. The resulting system retains the virtues of the system of this paper — e.g., it avoids Church-style objections and allows the sorts of generalizations discussed in section IV.

6. I assume that a context cannot provide restrictions on how free variables are treated by correlations. This is necessary (and sufficient) to validate arguments like

Odile thinks that Twain is dead.
Thus, for some x, Odile thinks that x is dead.

I think this account of quantification in escapes the objections which Scott Soames made to the account I proposed in "Quantification and Leibniz' Law" (*The Philosophical Review* 96, 1987). Soames' objections are in his "Substitutivity" in *On Being and Saying*, edited by J. J. Thompson (Cambridge, Mass., 1987).

7. "On Carnap's Analysis of Statements of Assertion and Belief," *Analysis* 10 (1950).

8. Ascriptions like (2) raise the following problem. Consider an ascription like (2) in the context of a pure Russellian account. The Russellian assigns a relation to 'believes' and a structured entity to the 'that'-clause. The assignment to the 'that'-clause contains the semantic values of the expressions in the 'that'-clause. So if the 'that'-clause contains 'believes' — as it does in (2) — we have the relation assigned to the main verb — the belief relation — trying to relate something which contains that very relation. Besides sounding like the opening of a book by Kierkegaard, this is more or less like a function taking itself as an argument, something which on the normal set-theoretic understanding of a function is impossible.

I have investigated what happens, in a system like the one I have been sketching, if we stratify the belief predicate, more or less in the way Tarski stratified the truth predicate, by introducing a series of languages. (This requires that RAMs come in levels, as well.) I have found nothing untoward in the system, save that it requires fragmenting 'believes' (as Tarski's approach, adapted to natural language, would require fragmenting 'true'.)

I am aware that many people object to this way of treating 'true' in natural languages. I believe that other treatments of 'believes' would also work here — in particular, I think that modeling propositions and the semantic values of expressions like 'believes' in a set theory like that of Peter Aczel's, in which sets can be members of themselves, would mesh quite well with the approach I am sketching, and would yield a more satisfactory treatment of 'believes'. (See Aczel's *Nonwellfounded Sets*, CSLI Lecture Notes, no. 14, [Stanford, Calif., 1988].) But at present I have not fully investigated this.

In the text, I suppress all reference to this complication. This paper is about the way expressions — in particular, singular terms and garden variety predicates — function within the scope of attitude verbs. It is not about the semantical paradoxes or paradoxes like the knower. While the latter are of course important, I think it is fair to ignore them in discussing the current problems. One insoluble problem at a time, please.

In section IV, when I discuss the introduction of a truth predicate, I again ignore the fact that some method to forestall paradox is needed. Again, I have investigated a series of languages approach here, each with a truth predicate for the languages below, in the context of implementing the proposal of this paper. Other than objections to the levels approach, which are not relevant to the issues this paper is concerned with, I do not see any problems with the resulting system.

9. "A puzzle about Belief," 257.

10. Conversational principles ("Don't be confusing") alone dictate this much. Furthermore, only if we assume that sets of ascriptions are to be so interpreted does the widespread belief—that explanations of action in terms of beliefs and desires are at least candidates for true explanations—even make sense. For example, the claims

Randi thought that if there were waving, Ann would smile

Randi wished that Ann smile

evaluated together, instead of separately, are true only if (roughly speaking) part of Randi's overall text (the family of sets of sentences believed-true, wished-true, and so on) looked thus:

Belief: $W \to Sa$; Desire: Sa

where W, s, and a are expressions determining the set of worlds in which there's waving, the property of smiling, and Ann, respectively. But it is plausible to think that this being true is a reason for thinking that Randi waved. So the explanation which goes 'Randi waved, because he thought that if there were waving, Ann would smile, and he wanted Ann to smile' can plausibly be said, in a very straightforward sense, to be a genuine explanation. If, on the other hand, we switch correlations in midstream, then the truth of the belief and desire ascriptions gives us no reason to think that Randi will wave.

The fact that on this view we can make sense of the *idea* that action could be explained by attitude ascription is surely a strong reason to prefer this approach to Russellianism. For on Russellian grounds the truth of the premises of a belief-desire explanation give one *absolutely no reason whatsoever* to think its conclusion true.

It is not trivial to systematically assign truth conditions to complex sentences (i.e., ones containing truth functional and temporal operators, as well as quantifiers), once we allow that sentences of the form *he believes that S, and he believes that T* can have truth conditions on which they imply that *that S* and *that T* represent RAMs under a single correlation, especially if we want to preserve the validity of classical logical principles. I try to characterize one way of assigning truth conditions, while preserving classical logic, in chapter 4 of *Propositional Attitudes*.

11. I do have to say that there is a way of interpreting the conjunction of (2) and (3) so that it is true. If we are in a context in which no restrictions are operative, and we interpret the ascriptions singly, and not jointly, then both (2) and (3) will be true. I don't think that this is a disaster. First of all, as I argued above, this is a very unnatural way to evaluate multiple ascriptions. So, I think, I may fairly say that the account I've been presenting leads us to expect that there will be at best a weak inclination among speakers to say that (2) and (3) are both true, if they are presented together. And this is what we do seem to find.

And we do have *some* inclination to say that in the case of Pierre that both are true. Most of us are inclined to reason as follows: Well, (2) *is* true. And, gosh, (3) *is* true. (Notice one does this by evaluating (2) and (3) individually.) So I guess (gulp) their conjunction is true.

12. I assume that all the old presidential tokens are tokens which refer to Reagan the president. Incidentally, I take the interior, "recognition," condition to be such that terms which do not name the same thing may satisfy it. For example, suppose I hear 'Reagan will bomb Nicaragua', and see someone point at a man and say 'he is president'. If I "group" 'Reagan' and 'he' together (I take the same person to be spoken of and ostended), the terms satisfy the interior condition, even if the man pointed at was not Reagan.

I should say here that, while none of what I say can be attributed to David Kaplan, much of it is influenced by various remarks he has made about identity of words, recognition, and other matters.

13. I suppose consequence to be defined as follows: Sentence A is a consequence of a set S of sentences (in a model M, relative to a context c thereof) iff for any w in the model, if w is in the intension of each member S, taken relative to c, then w is in the intension of A, taken relative to c. (Intuitively, this amounts to: A is a consequence of S iff, taken in any context, what S's members say jointly entails what A says.) Logical consequence is a relation between sets of sentence types defined by the obvious generalization of the above.

14. I assume, of course, that 'la neige' is a syntactical unit.

I am indebted to Ed Gettier for a discussion of an earlier draft of this paper, as well as for conversations over the years on the topics of this paper. David Austin, Jody Azzouni, Harold Levin, Graeme Forbes, and Ali Kazmi made helpful editorial and philosophical comments on versions of the paper, for which I thank them as well. I acknowledge a general debt to Richard Grandy, who tried many years ago to convince me that attitude ascription had something to do with translation.

You Can Say *That* Again

ERNEST LEPORE AND BARRY LOEWER

It has been two decades since the publication of Davidson's twin papers, "Truth and Meaning" (1967) and "On Saying That" (1968). The first proposed that a Tarskian truth theory for a language L can be (the heart of) a theory of meaning for L. The second proposed a radically novel approach, the paratactic account, to the logical form of indirect discourse. The two proposals are related in a number of ways. The paratactic account claims to show how to construct a truth theory for languages containing indirect discourse and propositional attitude reports. The truth theoretic account of meaning provides motivation and support for the paratactic account. And, somewhat surprisingly, the paratactic account provides a way to get around an objection that many have seen as fatal to Davidson's truth theoretic account of meaning. Indeed, the proposals are so interconnected, that if one fails, it is likely that the other cannot be successfully defended. Our primary aim in this paper is to motivate the paratactic account and defend it from certain widely known criticisms. Along the way, we will spell out various connections between the paratactic account and the truth theoretic account of meaning, and explain how the former can be used to support the latter.

I

One aim of a theory of meaning for a language L is to specify information concerning L, which, if someone possessed it, would enable him to interpret utterances of speakers of L. But what is it to interpret another's utterances? To answer this question, consider two people, one understands Italian, the other does not. Suppose both hear Andrea utter *"Il gatto siede dietro al forno."* Each may know that Andrea's utterance is an assertion and that it is true.[1] But only the one who understands Italian, other things being equal, will be justified in believing the cat sits behind the oven on the basis of hearing

Andrea. What semantic information would justify this belief? The inevitable answer is this: *Andrea's utterance is true only if the cat sits behind the oven.* The following reasoning makes this explicit:

1. Andrea's utterance *"Il gatto siede dietro al forno"* is true.
2. Andrea's utterance is true *only if* the cat sits behind the oven.
3. So, the cat sits behind the oven.

Furthermore, the information that:

2′. Andrea's utterance is true *if* the cat sits behind the oven

can justify Andrea's uttering *"Il gatto siede dietro al forno,"* supposing that Andrea wants to produce an utterance which is true if a cat sits behind an oven.[2]

An Italian speaker is also in a position to learn from utterances something about the beliefs of Italian speakers, in our example, that Andrea believes that the cat sits behind the oven. Knowledge of truth conditions can play a role in this justification as well:

4. Andrea believes that his utterance of *"Il gatto siede dietro al forno"* is true.
5. Andrea believes that his utterance is true iff the cat sits behind the oven.
6. So, Andrea believes that the cat sits behind the oven.

(4) is based on the presumption of sincerity. (6) does not logically follow from (4) and (5) (unlike the first inference, where (1) and (2) imply (3)). But in this case it is overwhelmingly plausible that (6) is true, given (4) and (5). Why else would Andrea have made the utterance? These observations provide straightforward support for the truism that understanding a language involves knowledge of truth conditions.

A truth theory for a language L assigns to the infinitely many possible utterances of L truth conditions based (in part) on the syntax of the sentences uttered, and thus systematizes the truth conditions of the sentences of L. The information embodied in such a theory, as we just saw, provides justifications for (certain of) the beliefs that a competent language speaker can acquire upon hearing the assertive utterances of speakers of L. It also provides (partial) justifications for some of his own utterances. A truth theory for L will also specify a great deal of other information concerning L, information concerning relations among the truth conditions of sentences of L (for example, logical relations) and information concerning reference relations. But our interest here is in a truth theory's role as a systemization of the truth conditions for utterances of L.

It seems to us uncontroversial that speakers of a language know the truth conditions of sentences of their language. But whether speakers actually know a truth theory and whether such knowledge (or even knowledge of truth conditions) is causally involved in the production and understanding of utterances are psychological questions we do not intend to address here. Our conception of truth conditional semantics emphasizes its *epistemological* rather than its psychological role. It is clear that a speaker of Italian will be in a position to acquire and be justified in acquiring a great many beliefs about the world and about the mental states of his fellow speakers in virtue of his understanding Italian. A semantic theory of Italian, in our view, should systematize information which a speaker possesses and which justifies the beliefs acquired in the ways we outlined.

A competent speaker of Italian will also be in a position to acquire from his belief that Andrea assertively uttered *"Il gatto siede dietro al forno"* the belief that Andrea said that the cat sits behind the oven. The justifying inference might look like this:

7. Andrea assertively utters *"Il gatto siede dietro al forno."*
8. [Some premise stating semantic information.]
9. So, Andrea said that the cat sits behind the oven.

What should premise (8) be? It is clear that *"'Il gatto siede dietro al forno'* is true iff the cat sits behind the oven" is too weak. Supposing the cat sits behind the oven, then *"Il gatto siede dietro al forno"* is true iff snow is white. This certainly does not justify the conclusion that Andrea said that snow is white. And even knowing that *Andrea* knows his utterance is true iff the cat sits behind the oven, or that this is common knowledge among all the speakers of Italian, will not suffice. The "obvious" missing premise that would suffice is that Andrea's utterance *means that* the cat sits behind the oven. But, of course, one main point of "Truth and Meaning" is to replace the view that a theory of meaning for *L* entails sentences of the form "*S* means that *p*" (*M*-sentences) with the view that it entails sentences of the form "*S* is true iff *p*" (*T*-sentences). Davidson made this claim because:

(i) He thought that, due to the intensionality of "means that," the logical machinery involved in proving correct *M*-sentences would certainly prove vastly more complex, and might ultimately prove unobtainable, and
(ii) He thought that a theory which issues in *T*-sentences will accomplish what we can rightfully expect from a theory of meaning.

We do not want to discuss Davidson's doubts about theories issuing in *M*-sentences here.[3] But Davidson was mistaken in the second claim, since as we have just noted a truth theory falls short in that it fails to justify beliefs concerning what is said. This does not seem to be a minor failing, since knowing that *A* said that *p* on the basis of his uttering *S* is central to understanding *S*. So, defenders of truth theoretic approaches to meaning are left with the problem of discovering a way of representing information which can justify conclusions concerning what is said compatible with the truth theoretic approach. As we will show, the paratactic account, somewhat unexpectedly, provides an end run around this problem.[4]

Our strategy for explaining the paratactic account is to describe a population P which speaks a language L for which we stipulate that the account is correct. Let us suppose that L is a first-order language containing names (of people, places, things, times, and [utterances of] sentences of L) and predicates. Among these predicates are three two-place predicates: $U(a,u)$, $S(u,u^*)$, $SS(u,u^*)$. The first relates a person to an utterance, the second and third relate one utterance to another. (We will explain them later.) L also contains indexicals, tenses, and demonstratives. We will suppose that the sentences of L have truth conditions and that the speakers of L all know the same truth theory. This will enable, for example, one member of P to learn from another that snow is white when he hears him assertively utter "Snow is white," assuming, of course, that he believes the utterance is true. The presence of indexicals and demonstratives in L enables speakers of L to use a single sentence to convey different information. The information conveyed depends on the utterance's context in systematic ways. For example, an utterance of "I am hungry" is true iff the speaker of the utterance is hungry at the time of the utterance. The presence of indexicals, demonstratives, and tenses causes certain complications in the form of T-sentences. Suppose that one member of P, Arabella, hears another, Barbarella, assertively utter "I am hungry." Then Arabella could reason as follows:

10. Barbarella's utterance of "I am hungry " is true.
11. (u) (x) (if u is an utterance of "I am hungry" by x, then u is true iff x is hungry)
12. So, Barbarella is hungry.

The truth condition associated with utterances of the syntactic type "I am hungry" is a generalization. Someone who knows it is in a position to employ information she possesses concerning the utterance to draw conclusions about who is hungry. If Arabella did not know that the utterance was made by Barbarella, but, say, that it was made by that woman over there, then she would not be justified in concluding that Barbarella is hungry, but she would be justified in concluding that the woman over there is hungry. Minimally, she will always be justified in the belief that whoever made the utterance is hungry. The truth conditions for a sentence containing a demonstrative are also generalizations:

13. (u) (x) (if u is an utterance of "That is F," in which "that" demonstrates x, then u is true iff x is F)

A truth theory for languages which contain indexicals and demonstratives will imply for each sentence type S of L, a theorem of the form:

(T^*) (u) (c) (if u is an utterance of S in context c, then u is true in L iff $p(f(c),g(c),....))$,

where "f," "g," etc., are functions which assign to a context certain of its features, for example, the speaker of c, the time of c, and so on. A point worth noting is that the metalanguage in which a truth theory for an indexical language like L is constructed may itself contain indexicals and demonstratives. In that case, we can represent in the metalanguage an inference from:

14. Arabella's utterance of "I am hungry" is true.
15. She is hungry, demonstrating Barbarella.

We will not construct a theory for L, but we will assume that the speakers of L all know the *same* truth theory for L. This knowledge will enable a speaker of L to obtain information from the utterances of other speakers of L, information not necessarily obtainable by those who do not understand L.

Speakers of L have various ways of referring to sentences and utterances, including corner quotes, definite descriptions, names, but an especially convenient means is to refer demonstratively. Demonstrative reference to utterances is convenient, since one can produce an utterance and then demonstrate it. The predicates "$U(a,u)$" and "$S(u,u^*)$" work as follows:

"$U(a,u)$" is true of a person $\underline{a}$ and utterance u iff a is the utterer of $\underline{u}$.

"$S(u,u^*)$" is true of utterances u and u^* iff u and u^* are utterances of the same sentence.

Suppose Arabella assertively utters:

16. (Eu) $(U(\text{Barbarella},u)$ & $S(u,\text{that}))$ [Snow is white.]

Her utterance of (16) consists of two utterances, an asserted utterance, and an utterance demonstrated by this asserted utterance. (The demonstrated utterance is of the bracketed sentence in (16).) The first utterance is true just in case Barbarella made an utterance of the same sentence-type as the second utterance.

Utterances like (16) potentially carry a great deal of information which can be unlocked by someone who knows a truth theory for L. The first part of (16) has generalized truth conditions (17):

17. (v) (c) (if v is an utterance of "(Eu) $(U(\text{Barbarella},u)$ & $S(u,\text{that}))$," then v is true in c iff Barbarella made an utterance which is of the same sentence-type as $d(c)$,

where "$d(c)$" is the utterance demonstrated in context c. If Cinderella believes that Arabella's utterance is true and knows its truth conditions, then she will be licensed to conclude that Barbarella made an utterance of "Snow is white." The soundness of the inference requires Cinderella to recognize that the demonstrated utterance is of "Snow is white" but, since such an utterance has *just* been produced and since she is a speaker of L, we may assume that her phonological and syntactic knowledge warrants this belief. Although it is conventional in L that the demonstrated utterance is, other things being equal, not an assertion, Cinderella may be in a position to extract information from it.

Suppose that she believes that Barbarella, as well as Arabella, is reliable. She could then reason as follows:

18. (Eu) $(U(\text{Barbarella},u)$ & $S(u,\text{that}))$ [from previous inference]
19. $U(\text{Barbarella},u^*)$ & $S(u^*,\text{that})$ [by existential generalization]
20. u^* is true. [Barbarella's reliability]
21. That is true. [Utterances of the same non-indexical sentences have the same truth value]
22. "Snow is white" is true. [That is an utterance of "Snow is white"]
23. "Snow is white" is true iff snow is white. [from the truth theory]
24. So, snow is white.

Observe the role played by Arabella's having produced and then demonstrated an utterance in this inference. The demonstrated utterance "stands in" for Barbarella's utterance, so she can apply her semantic knowledge to it and learn from it, for example, that snow is white.

It should be clear that (16) plays a role similar to a direct discourse report in English. L also contains a device similar to English *indirect* discourse. Such a device is needed for at least the following reason. We saw that Cinderella could conclude from Barbarella's reliability and the truth conditions for the second part of (16) that snow is white. Her reasoning involved the assumption that if $S(u,u^*)$ and u is true, then u^* is also true. But generally this is false. Utterances of the same sentence, for example, "I am hungry," obviously may differ in truth value. On the other hand, utterances of sentences of different syntactic types can agree in import; that is, in the information which someone who understands the utterances can obtain in virtue of his understanding. When Barbarella utters "I am hungry," Arabella can produce an utterance with the same import by uttering "She is hungry," demonstrating Barbarella. We will say that utterances which agree in import *samesay* each other. In L the samesaying relation is expressed by "$SS(u,u^*)$." So, Arabella utters:

25. (Eu) $(U(\text{Barbarella},u)$ & $SS(u,\text{that}))$ [She is hungry.] [demonstrating Barbarella]

In asserting the first half (25), Arabella is asserting that Barbarella produced an utterance which samesays the utterance of the bracketed sentence in (25). Cinderella can use her knowledge of the truth conditions of each utterance that together compose an utterance of (25) to conclude, in accordance with patterns of inference now familiar, that:

(i) Barbarella made an utterance which samesays that, demonstrating the second part of (an utterance of) (25), and
(ii) Barbarella is hungry.

The question naturally arises of when two utterances samesay each other. We can begin to answer this by considering the point of reports like (25). In uttering the demonstrated utterance in (25), Arabella is attempting to convey to Cinderella some of the information which would have been conveyed to her had she heard and understood Barbarella's utterance. For Arabella's report to be correct it need not convey all the information contained in Barbarella's utterance—that is probably impossible—but it is usually required that it convey the information that could be extracted in virtue of knowing the truth conditions of the utterance and certain of the features of contexts of the two utterances, for example, the utterer, time of utterance, demonstrata, and so forth. In saying this we are not providing necessary and sufficient conditions for $SS(u,u^*)$, but merely giving an initial explanation of the relation. We will suppose that the practices of indirect reporting in L suffice to (approximately) fix the extension of $SS(u,u^*)$ for utterances of L. But it may prove impossible to explicate this relation in other terms or even provide an axiomatized theory of it. We will return to these points later.

Competent speakers of L know a correct truth theory for L, know that speakers of L know the truth theory, and grasp the samesaying relation sufficiently well to know generally whether $SS(u,u^*)$. Is this knowledge sufficient to account for L speakers' understanding L? We previously saw that knowledge of a truth theory (and even knowledge that the truth theory is common knowledge among a certain population) falls short in capturing one central aspect of linguistic competence. We saw that A's knowing a truth theory for L does not license inferences from B assertively uttered u to B said that p, for example, from "B assertively uttered 'Snow is white'" to "B said that snow is white." But speakers of L do possess information that licenses that inference from "B uttered u" to "$(Eu)(U(B,u)$ & $SS(u,\text{that}))$." For example, suppose A knows that B assertively uttered "I am hungry." Then knowing that this utterance samesays her own utterance, should she make one, of "B is hungry" (or her thought of "B is hungry") justifies her in concluding that $(Eu)(U(B,u)$ & $SS(u,\text{that}))$, where the demonstratum is an utterance (or thought) of "B is hungry."[5] *If*:

26. $(Eu)(U(\text{Barbarella},u)$ & $SS(u,\text{that}))$. [She is hungry.]

is a correct paraphrase of:

27. Barbarella said that she is hungry.

then we have solved the problem of how to complete the inference from "A assertively uttered S" to "A said that p" within a truth theoretic account of meaning.

The "if" above is, of course, a big one. The way (26) functions in L is similar to the way (27) functions in English. However, there are numerous objections to the paratactic account—the claim that (26) is a correct paraphrase of (27)—that have been voiced. We turn next to a consideration of the most important of these.

II

Semantic theory for some fragment of natural language has two aims. One is the construction of a truth theory for the fragment. The other is the systemization of logical properties of, and relations among, sentences of this fragment. These two aims are related and commonly thought to be simultaneously satisfiable by paraphrasing the sentences of the fragment into a formal notation for which truth and truth-in-a-model are definable. Propositional attitude attributions, and specifically indirect discourse, have long been known to possess features which frustrate the construction of satisfactory theories of truth and implication. Perhaps the most discussed feature is the apparent failure of the principle of substitutivity of identity:

From $t = t'$ and $\phi(t)$, where "t" and "t'" are singular terms and the wff $\phi(t')$ is obtained from the wff $0(t)$ by replacing an occurrence of t by t'.

Thus, the inference from (28)–(29) to (30) is an apparent instance of substitutivity of identity but is invalid:

28. Galileo said that the earth moves.
29. The earth = the third planet from the sun.
30. So, Galileo said that the third planet from the sun moves.

One kind of response to this problem is to deny that the inference is really an instance of substitutivity of identity. Frege claims that the reference of a singular term depends on whether it occurs in a propositional attitude context (Frege 1892, 57). In (29), "the earth" refers to the earth, but in (28) it refers to the sense of "the earth." Quine's view is that singular terms in propositional attitude contexts do not refer at all. Thus, "the earth" is no more a meaningful component of (28) than "cat" is of "concatenation" (1960, chap. 6). These accounts "explain" the failure of substitutivity of identity by claiming that the semantic value of an expression in a propositional attitude context differs from its ordinary semantic value. The cost of this approach is a loss of *semantic innocence* (Davidson 1968, 108). The semantically innocent believe that occurrences of the same word in and out of propositional attitude contexts possess the same meaning. Surrendering semantic innocence makes it difficult to understand how is it that one can learn from an utterance of "Barbarella said that the cat sits behind the oven" that the cat sits behind the oven?[6]

One of the most striking features of the paratactic account is that while it is similar to the Fregean and Quinean accounts in denying that the inference from (28)–(29) to (30) involves a genuine failure of substitutivity, it, unlike them, preserves semantic innocence. Explaining how this works will require us to add to our discussion in section I of the logic of first-order languages with demonstratives and indexicals. We will suppose that our language contains subscripted demonstratives: "$that_1$," "$that_2$," etc. The truth value of the utterance of a sentence with demonstratives and/or indexicals depends both on the sentence uttered and on the context of utterance. A context is specified by an n-tuple of features of a possible utterance or sequence of utterances, for example <a possible world, speaker of utterance, location of speaker, time of utterance, {a sequence of items to serve as demonstrata}, ... >. We assume that indexicals and demonstratives are logical constants constrained so that "*I*" is always assigned the speaker, "that$_n$" is assigned the nth demonstratum. We also assume that contexts are constrained so that the utterer is located at the place and time in the world of the context. "*S*, therefore, *S**" is valid iff there is no context and no assignment of interpretations to the nonlogical vocabulary in *S* and *S**, which makes *S* true and *S** false. On this account, "I am *F* and I am *G*, therefore, I am *F*" is valid and so is "I am here now."

Let us see how this account applies to the paratactic paraphrases of indirect discourse sentences. According to the paratactic account, the first-order paraphrase of (28) is (31):

28. Galileo said that the earth moves.
31. $(Eu)(U(\text{Galileo},u)$ & $SS(u,\text{that}))$ [The earth moves.]

The paraphrase consists of two sentences. According to the account, a typical utterance of (28) is an assertion equivalent in import (and purport) to the first sentence in (31). Since (31) contains a demonstrative, it is not true or false except relative to a context. A typical utterance of (31) creates a context relative to which "that" refers to an utterance of the bracketed sentence. It is obvious that according to our account of validity, (31) implies "Galileo said something," that is, "$(Eu)(Eu^*)$ $(U(\text{Galileo},u)$ & $SS(u,u^*))$," since relative to any context in which (31) is true, "that" refers to something which samesays Galileo's utterance (contra Arnauld 1976, 289).

According to the paratactic account, the paraphrase of (28)–(30) is (31)–(33) respectively:

31. $(Eu)(U(\text{Galileo},u)$ & $SS(u,\text{that}))$ [The earth moves.]
32. The earth = the third planet from the sun.
33. So, $(Eu)(U(\text{Galileo},u)$ & $SS(u,\text{that}))$ [The third planet from the sun moves.]>

Since there are contexts in which the occurrences of "that" in (31) and (33) refer to different individuals (strictly speaking, in *L* they must have different subscripts), this inference is invalid. It is also clear that the inference is not an instance of substitutivity of identity, since the singular terms "the earth" and "the third planet from the sun" do not even occur in (31) and (33). The expressions that occur in the demonstrated utterances possess their usual semantic values—their usual truth conditions—and so the account is semantically innocent. (It is just this feature that allows someone who knows the truth conditions for both "Galileo said that" and "The earth moves" to infer from an utterance of (31) and Galileo's truthfulness that the earth moves.)

Despite these important virtues, the paratactic account has not won anything like general acceptance. The literature is replete with objections to the account. But in view of how beautifully the paratactic account works in *L* to enable the speakers of *L* to fulfill the functions of indirect discourse, it seems to us to be worthwhile, though perhaps heroic and quixotic, to see to what extent the account as an account of *English* indirect discourse can be defended from these objections. Though it would be impossible to review and respond to every criticism in the literature, we have identified a few serious kinds of objections. Almost all the criticisms can be separated into three sorts: (a) it is too strong, (b) it is too weak, and (c) it fails to generalize, for example, to other propositional attitudinal ascriptions and *de re* constructions. In this paper we address all these with the exception of how to extend the account to *de re* attributions.[7]

It has seemed to a number of commentators that (28) is *about* Galileo and perhaps an utterance of his, but *not* about an English utterance, while its purported paraphrase (31) is about an English utterance. We doubt that intuitions concerning what a sentence is about should carry much weight by themselves in deciding the correctness of paraphrases. However, the objection would be a good one if it could be shown that because of this difference (31) implies or in some way requires the existence of something whose existence is not required by the truth of (28). The worry is that (31) does imply or require the existence of an English utterance while (28) does not. Let us see if this is correct.

While it may seem that (31) implies "There exist English utterances," in fact it does not. Given our characterization of implication for a language with demonstratives, (31) does not *imply* the existence of any utterance other than Galileo's. On that account, recall, S implies S^* iff there is no context and no interpretation of the nonlogical vocabulary relative to which S is true and S^* is false. (31) is true relative to a context C iff there is an utterance made by Galileo which bears the samesay relation to the referent of "that" in C. Consider a domain containing a single utterance u^* such that $U(Galileo, u^*)$ and $SS(u^*, u^*)$ and the context C relative to which "that" refers to u^*. Relative to that context, (31) is true and "(Eu) (Ex) $(U(x,u)$ & $u \neq u^*)$" is false. So, (31) does not imply the existence of any utterance other than an utterance by Galileo.

Even though (31) does not imply "There exist English utterances," still, according to the paratactic account, an utterance of (28) makes reference to an English utterance. Some authors think that a consequence of this is that the paratactic paraphrase of (34) is false, even though (34) is true (Lycan 1973, 139; Blackburn 1975, 184; Bigelow 1980, 17). If this charge were correct, then it would seem to show that (28) and (31) are not equivalent. But the charge is incorrect. The paratactic paraphrase of (34) is (35):

34. It is possible that Galileo said that the earth moves even though no English utterance ever existed.
35. $(Ex)($ $(x = $ that$)$ & $P(U(Galileo,u)$ & $SS(u,x)$ & $(y) - $ English $(y)))$ [The earth moves.]>

In possible world semantics, (35) is true relative to a context in which the demonstratum of "that" is an utterance u^* of the "The earth moves" iff there is some possible world w and utterance v made by Galileo in w and u^* samesays v in w and there are no English utterances in w. If the truth of $SS(v,u^*)$ in w required that u^* exist in w and be an English utterance, then (35) would be false. But neither of these seem to be the case. In particular, we see nothing wrong with supposing that $SS(v,u^*)$ may be true at w even though v and u^* do not exist in the same world. Within the context of possible world semantics, it is not unusual to appeal to similarity relations across worlds, for example, the counterpart relation, which relates individuals in different worlds. Samesaying is such a relation.

There is another objection to the paratactic account based on the fact that an utterance of (28) makes reference to an English utterance due to Brian Loar (reported in Schiffer 1987a, 131-133). Call an occurrence of a singular term in a sentence *primary* iff it is not properly contained within the occurrence of another singular term, for example, "George" is not primary in "George's car is red." Loar claims that principle (*P*) is true:

(*P*) If the occurrence of *t* in "*A* said that . . . *t* . . . " is primary and refers to *x*, then that sentence is true only if *A* referred to *x*.

For example, suppose that Arabella utters "The president is funny" and Barbarella reports her by saying "Arabella said that Ronald Reagan is funny." According to (*P*), Barbarella's report can be true only if Arabella referred to Ronald Reagan in making her utterance. If Barbarella said "Arabella said that the star of *Bedtime for Bonzo* is funny," then her utterance still meets the test since *"Bedtime for Bonzo"* has secondary occurrence.

Loar (see also Burge 1986, 193-194; Blackburn 1975, 184) observes that the paratactic account results in a violation of (*P*). According to (*P*), a problem is created for the paratactic account by (utterances of) sentences like (36):

36. Laplace said that Galileo said that the earth moves.

An utterance of (36) may be true even though Laplace never referred to an utterance of English. But the paratactic paraphrase of (36) is (37):

37. (Eu) (U(Laplace,u) & $SS(u,$that)) [Galileo said that the earth moves.]

According to (*P*), if (37) is a correct report, then Laplace must have referred to the referent of the second occurrence of "that," since it has primary reference. But its referent is an English utterance of "The earth moves" and it is certain that Laplace never referred to this utterance. Since (36) may be true even though Laplace never referred to an utterance of English, it follows, according to Loar, that the paratactic account must be mistaken. In short, Loar, noticing that on the paratactic account an utterance of (36) is about an English utterance, asks how Laplace could have said that, since he never referred to an English utterance? We are not impressed. (*P*) does not seem to us to be generally true and in the case of iterated indirect discourse reports we can easily see how the paratactic account not only violates the principle but motivates its violation.

Here is an example of an apparent counterexample of (P). Barbarella utters "I want a car like that," pointing at a Saab 900. Arabella correctly reports "Barbarella said that she wants a car like that," pointing at a different Saab 900. Barbarella did not refer to the car which is the demonstratum of Arabella's second "that." A defender of (P) might reply that the occurrence of "that" is really a secondary occurrence by claiming that the above sentence is really expressing "I want a car of the same type as that." "The same type as that" has primary occurrence. But this paraphrase is itself controversial — it cannot be this easy to establish that types exist — and so is unsuitable as part of a defense of a principle designed to establish the failure of the paratactic account. In any case, we can show how the paratactic account *motivates* a violation of (P).

Recall that in L the point of Arabella's indirectly quoting Barbarella to Cinderella was for Arabella to produce an utterance which would convey to Cinderella what Barbarella's utterance would have conveyed to her had she been in a position to hear and understand it. Now suppose that Arabella, a speaker of L, attempts to conform to (P) when reporting what Laplace said. We assume that Laplace speaks a version of French for which the paratactic account is correct. Suppose that Laplace uttered *Galilei dit que.* [*La terre bouge.*]" If Arabella wants to report what Laplace said while conforming to (P), she needs to say "Laplace said that. [Galileo said that]," where the demonstratum of the second "that" must be the very same utterance Laplace demonstrated. Not only is this likely to be very inconvenient — Laplace's utterance is long gone — but if her audience does not understand Laplace's utterances, that is, does not know their truth conditions, then the point of indirect discourse is lost. If instead Arabella demonstrates not Laplace's utterance but an utterance of her own which samesays Laplace's utterance, then her audience (which we assume understands her utterances) will be in a position to learn that if Galileo spoke the truth, the earth moves. If we are right, then Laplace's utterance of *"Galilei dit que la terre bouge"* and Arabella's utterance of "Galileo said that the earth moves" samesay each other even though they refer to different utterances. We see no problem with this. So, although it is true that on the paratactic account an utterance of (28) will be about an English utterance, we have seen that this entails neither that this sentence logically implies the existence of English utterances nor the falsity of the modal (34). And while the paratactic account does lead to a violation of (P), that principle is not always true and in the case of indirect discourse, it is justifiably violable.

A second kind of objection is that the paratactic paraphrase of an indirect discourse statement is logically weaker than the paraphrased statement (Arnauld 1976, 289–291; Platts 1979, 123; Burge 1986, 203; Schiffer 1987a,

134–137). For example, each of the following has been claimed to be logically valid:

> 38. Galileo said that Osiander and Bellarmine are wrong.
> 39. So, Galileo said that Bellarmine and Osiander are wrong.
> 40. Galileo said that the earth moves.
> 41. So, Galileo said that the earth moves.
> 42. Galileo said that the earth moves.
> 43. The earth moves.
> 44. So, Galileo said something true.
> 45. Galileo said that the earth moves.
> 46. Everything Galileo said is true.
> 47. So, the earth moves.

Each of these inferences appears to be valid, yet their paratactic paraphrases are not valid. The inference from (38) to (39) fails, since there are contexts relative to which the two occurrences of "that" refer to different utterances. (The occurrences of "that" will be paraphrased by "that$_i$," and "that$_k$," $i \neq k$, since their actual demonstrata differ.) For exactly the same reason (40) does not imply (41).

Before concluding that this shows the paratactic account is hopeless, let us note that this feature of the account is sometimes an advantage, especially when compared with competing accounts. According to these, "*A* says that *p*" relates a person and a proposition—the proposition expressed by "*p*." These accounts differ in what they count as a proposition: a class of possible worlds, a Fregean thought, a structured entity, for example <individual, a property>. Consider each of the following inferences:

> 48. Galileo said that the earth moves.
> 49. So, Galileo said that the earth moves and (*p* or -*p*).
> 50. Galileo said that bachelors are unmarried males.
> 51. So, Galileo said that bachelors are bachelors.
> 52. Galileo said that Cicero = Cicero.
> 53. Galileo said that Cicero = Tully.>

Each of the propositionalist accounts just mentioned validates one of these inferences, but each seems invalid. Defenders of propositionalist accounts have devoted a considerable amount of effort attempting to persuade their readers (and themselves?) that the inference each one claims to be valid really is valid (Hintikka 1969; Stalnaker 1984; Salmon 1986). But their defenses seem to us to be lame. It is difficult to believe, for example, despite her protestations to the contrary, that Lois Lane believes that Superman is Clark Kent (see Schiffer 1987b). The paratactic paraphrases of each of the above inferences are, of course, invalid for exactly the same reason that the inference from (38)-(39) is invalid. But pointing to the faults of other accounts does not show that the paratactic account is correct about the inferences with which we began this discussion.

We begin by talking about the paratactic paraphrase of the arguments (42)-(44) and (54)-(56) respectively (see Davidson 1969, 50-52):

54. $(Eu)(U(Galileo,u)$ & $SS(u,that_1))$ [The earth moves.]
55. The earth moves.
56. So, $(Eu)(U(Galileo,u)$ & true$(u))$

It is obvious that (54)-(56) is invalid. However, if we add to this argument premise (57), the argument is valid:

57. That$_1$ is true iff the earth moves.

The additional premise (57) expresses a truth known to anyone who knows that "that$_1$" refers to an inscription of "The earth moves" and who understands this inscription. Of course, any English speaker who examines this argument will know this. So, the paratactic account has a ready explanation for why the argument (54)-(56) appears valid to an English speaker even though it is an enthymeme. A perfectly similar account can be given of the argument (42)-(44).

An explanation can also be given of the apparent validity—apparently, that is, according to the paratactic account—of the inferences (38)-(39) and (40)-(41). The missing premises in the first of these inferences are:

58. $SS(that_1,that_2)$
59. $(u)\ (u')\ ((True(u)$ & $SS(u,u')) \rightarrow SS(u,u'))$[8]

Premise (58) will be known by anyone who knows that that$_1$ is of "Osiander and Bellarmine are wrong" and that that$_2$ is of "Bellarmine and Osiander are wrong" and understands English. Recall that someone who understands English is able to recognize when an utterance of one sentence samesays an utterance of another sentence. So, according to the paratactic account these two inferences are not valid, but they can be turned into valid inferences by adding premises known to any English speaker who attends to them.

The fact that the inferences (42)-(44) and (45)-(47) are not valid according to the paratactic account suggests a slightly different objection. As we have seen, it is on the paratactic account logically possible for someone, for example, to know that Galileo said that the earth moves without understanding what Galileo said. This follows since on the truth theoretic account of meaning what Galileo said includes knowing the truth conditions of what Galileo said. The fact that speakers of English who hear someone utter "Galileo said that the earth moves" and believe the utterance true will understand what Galileo said only partially answers this objection. It must be admitted that on the paratactic account A may know that B said that p without understanding what B said. But is this so obviously a bad consequence? Think of A, who mistakenly enters a room in which a physicist is lecturing and hears the lecturer utter "We conducted three tests of Bell's inequalities." *B* asks *A* what the physicist said and *A* replies "He said that he and his colleagues conducted three tests of Bell's inequalities—but I must admit I did not understand what he said since I have no idea what Bell's inequalities are." There seems to us to be nothing preventing all of *A*'s utterances from being true, contrary to the assumption that underlies the objection.[9]

A third kind of objection to the paratactic account concerns whether it can be extended to propositional attitude reports other than "says that," to *de re* attributions, and to interrogative constructions ("*A* said who the Prime Minister is"). There are formidable problems to be confronted in developing such extensions and we have by no means solved them all. However, we do think that the situation is considerably more promising than it is commonly thought. Here we will confine ourselves to showing how the paratactic account can be extended to propositional attitude reports.

The natural extension of the paratactic account to belief reports is to paraphrase, for example, (60) as (61):

60. Galileo believes that the earth moves.
61. Galileo believes that. [The earth moves.]

According to the account, "believes that" relates a person to an utterance, so that (61) is true just in case Galileo bears this relation to the demonstrated utterance of "The earth moves." Schiffer thinks that this account cannot be correct (see also, Haack 1971, 360-61; Leeds 1979, 51; Bigelow 1980, 17). Schiffer writes:

> The representation of the saying—that relation as ["$(Eu)(U(\text{Galileo},u)$ & $SS(u,\text{that}))$"] is plausible because if "Galileo said something" is true, then there can be no barrier to inferring "$(Eu)S(\text{Galileo},u)$" for there is always Galileo's own utterance to be an utterance to which he stands in the saying-relation as portrayed in ["$(Eu)(U(\text{Galileo},u)$ & $SS(u,\text{that}))$"]. But if "Galileo believed something" is true, then there *is* a barrier to inferring "$(Eu)B(\text{Galileo},u)$;" namely, that there may not be any actual utterance that gives the content of Galileo's belief. . . . Believing could be represented as a relation to actual utterances only if one could be assured that for every belief there was some actual utterance that gave the content of that belief; but of course one cannot be so assured. (1987a, 126-27)

Schiffer thinks that the only revision open to the paratactic account is to declare that belief relates a person, not to an utterance, but to an utterance-kind, and this revision undermines Davidson's extensionalism. But Schiffer is mistaken. There is a viable alternative.

It is relatively uncontroversial that someone believes that *p* just in case he is in a token (brain) state which has the content that *p*. Let $B(a,s)$ be the relation that holds between an individual *a* and a token state, for example, an event of neuron firings, which is a belief state of a.[10] The full paratactic account of (60) is (62), and (63) is paraphrased by (64):

62. (Es) (B(Galileo,s) & SS(s,that)) [The earth moves.]
63. Galileo believes something.
64. (Es)B(Galileo,s)

(64) does not entail that there exist any actual utterance which samesays s. Our account assumes that belief states and utterances can samesay each other. We think this is untendentious.

It seems possible to extend this account to other kinds of propositional attitudes. (65) is paraphrased as (66):

65. Galileo desires that the earth moves.
66. (Es)(D(Galileo,s) & SS(s,that)) [The earth moves.],

where $d(a,s)$ holds of a person and a token state of desire. Sentences like (67) seem to create problems for this approach (Higginbotham 1986, 39), since they do not contain "that" and the complement of "wants" is not a sentence. But we tentatively suggest that it be paraphrased by (68):

67. Galileo wants the earth to move.
68. (Es)(W(Galileo,s) & SS(u,that)) [the earth to move]

This paraphrase assumes that the content of Galileo's mental state is the same as the content of the demonstrated utterance of "the earth to move."

Of course, even if it is granted that our replies to the various objections help deflect them, one still might wonder why it would not be better to have an account which completely avoids them? That is, wouldn't it be better to have an account which entails Galileo's utterance is true iff the earth moves, and given that it is true that the earth moves and Galileo said that the earth moves, then Galileo said something true *without the help of all the additional premises*, and which did not have utterances of "Galileo said that the earth moves" being about an English utterance, and so on? And in fact aren't such theories readily available, namely, the Fregean theory, for example, which claims that sentences in indirect discourse (or other propositional attitude sentences) express a relation between a person and (not an utterance but) a *proposition*. On such an account (28) is true iff (69):

28. Galileo said that the earth moves.
69. (Ep) (p = the proposition that the earth moves and Galileo says p)

On Frege's view, the words on the right of "that" refer to their usual senses. So, the sentence says something like this: Galileo said the thought composed of such and such senses in such and such ways. The reasons propositions seem so well suited to be the relata of propositional attitudes is that, first, they are abstract entities, so that (69) does not entail the existence of any utterance of an utterer of (28), and second, they have the truth conditions essentially, so that (69) together with "It is true that the earth moves" entail that "Galileo said something true."

We have shown that none of the objections to the paratactic account we have considered is fatal to it. The account, like other accounts (Russell's theory of descriptions, possible world accounts of subjunctive conditionals, Davidson's account of action and event sentences), has consequences which seem surprising to our intuitions. But we think we have shown that the account is sufficiently explanatory of our practices of indirect discourse and attitude reports to be counted as plausible, more plausible than its propositionalist rivals.[11] If the paratactic account is correct, then, as we have shown, it provides a way of overcoming what has been a vexing problem for truth theoretic accounts of meaning, the problem of specifying what someone says in uttering u.[12]

Notes

1. Evidence for an utterance being an assertion and for a particular utterance being true need not be semantic. For example, one might know that certain sentential forms and tones of voice indicate assertion and that a particular person's assertions in certain circumstances are generally true without knowing what his assertions mean.

2. Andrea may have various reasons for wanting to produce an utterance which is true if the cat sits behind the oven. One is that he wants his audience to acquire the belief that the cat sits behind the oven and he believes that his producing an utterance which is true if the cat sits behind the oven is likely to accomplish this. The reasonableness of the latter belief may involve his believing that the audience believes *"Il gatto siede dietro al forno"* is true iff the cat sits behind the oven.

3. See our "Idle Meaning," forthcoming.

4. There are two problems concerning truth theoretic proposals that sometimes are conflated. There are truth theories for L which entail T-sentences where S and *"p"* differ in meaning. In fact, any (interesting) truth theory will have this feature. The second problem is that *"S is true iff p"* does not *say* that S means that p. Davidson tried to remedy the first problem by requiring that truth theories meet certain empirical constraints on the theory of interpretation and the second by adding that an interpreter must know not just that S is true iff p, but that *"S is true iff p"* is entailed by a theory meeting those constraints. We argue in "What Davidson Should Have Said," forthcoming, that Davidson's remedies are inadequate.

5. Arabella's thought that $(Eu)(U(\text{Barbarella},u) \ \& \ SS(u,\text{that}))$ [She is hungry.] will be true as well and for the same reason, if we suppose that the thought itself has a paratactic structure; that is, contains a demonstrative element referring to the thought that she is hungry. We are indebted to Stephen Schiffer and Ernest Sosa for helping us get clear about this.

6. Davidson's main objection to the Fregean and Quinean accounts is that it does not seem possible to construct finitely axiomatized truth theories for them, since they contain infinitely many primitive predicates. Davidson also mentions that these accounts are not semantically innocent. These two points are related, since it is the proliferation of words and their meanings which blocks finite axiomatization. But even if it were possible, as it seems to be for the Fregean theory, to produce a finitely axiomatized truth theory, the loss of semantic innocence would still be objectionable, since we would have no explanation of how someone is warranted in concluding that the cat sits behind the oven from an utterance of "Barbarella said that the cat sits behind the oven." See our "Idle Meaning," forthcoming.

7. We show how to extend the paratactic account to *de re* attributions in "Idle Meaning."

8. A qualification on premise (59) is needed for utterances of sentences which do not contain context sensitive features.

9. The intelligibility of *A*'s remarks suggest that the relation between knowing what someone said and understanding what he said is one of conversational implicature.

10. This relation may have a functional characterization and the state may possess syntactic properties, but we are not assuming either.

11. In our "Idle Meaning," we actually discuss propositional accounts and show that in addition to the problem we discussed in this paper, namely, that these accounts countenance inferences intuitively invalid as valid, there are other even more serious problems with these accounts.

12. Earlier drafts of this paper were read at the Universities of Bologna, Milan, Minnesota, Siena, Modena, Pisa, Venice, and at the Conference on Information Based Semantic Theories in Tepotzlan, Mexico. We would like to thank all those who have helped us improve this paper, in particular, John Biro, Andrea Bonomi, Michael Hand, James Higginbotham, Paolo Leonardi, Ernesto Napoli, Eva Picardi, Stephen Schiffer, and the graduate students in LePore's philosophy of language seminar, spring 1988.

References

Arnauld, B. Richard. 1976. "Sentences, Utterance, and Samesayer." *Nous* 10: 283-304.
Bigelow, J. 1980. "Believing in Sentences." *Australasian Journal of Philosophy* 58: 11-18.
Blackburn, Simon. 1975. "The Identity of Propositions." In *Meaning, Reference, and Necessity*, edited by S. Blackburn, 182-205. Cambridge.
Burge, Tyler. 1986. "On Davidson's 'Saying That'." In *Truth and Interpretation*, edited by Ernest LePore, 190-210. Oxford.
Davidson, Donald. 1967. "Truth and Meaning." In *Truth and Interpretation* (1984), 17-36. Oxford.
Davidson, Donald. 1968. "On Saying That." In *Truth and Interpretation* (1984), 93-108. Oxford.
Davidson, Donald. 1969. "True to the Facts." In *Truth and Interpretation* (1984), 37-54. Oxford.
Frege, Gottlob. 1892. "On Sense and Reference." In *Translations from the Philosophical Writings of Gottlob Frege* (1952), edited by P. T. Geach and M. Black, 56-78. Oxford.
Haack, R. J. 1971. "On Davidson's Paratactic Theory of Oblique Contexts." *Nous* 5: 351-61.
Higginbotham, James. 1986. "Davidson's Program in Semantics." In *Truth and Interpretation*, edited by Ernest LePore, 29-48. Oxford.
Hintikka, J. 1969. "Semantics for Propositional Attitudes." In *Models for Modalities*. Dordrecht.
Leeds, Stephen. 1979. "Church's Translation Argument." *Canadian Journal of Philosophy* 9: 43-51.
LePore, Ernest, and Barry Loewer. Forthcoming. "What Davidson Should Have Said."
LePore, Ernest, and Barry Loewer. Forthcoming. "Idle Meaning."
Lycan, William. 1973. "Davidson on Saying That." *Analysis* 33: 138-39.
Platts, Mark. 1979. *Ways of Meaning*. London.
Quine, W. V. O. 1960. *Word and Object*. Cambridge, Mass.
Salmon, N. 1986. *Frege's Puzzle*. Cambridge, Mass.
Schiffer, Stephen. 1987a. *Remnants of Meaning*, Cambridge, Mass.

Schiffer, Stephen. 1987b. "The 'Fido'-Fido Theory of Belief." In *Philosophical Perspectives I*, edited by James Tomberlin, 455-80. Atascadero, Calif.
Stalnaker, R. 1984. *Inquiry*. Cambridge, Mass.

Might

JONATHAN WILWERDING

Some philosophers have thought that cats might turn out to be robots. Perhaps the best-known example of this is Hilary Putnam. In his essay "Is Semantics Possible?" Putnam wanted to prove that the meanings of natural kind terms are not given by "analytic definitions." One of his arguments begins with the premise that cats might turn out to be robots controlled by Martians. So, Putnam at least, and anyone who accepts his argument, has a commitment to the claim that cats might turn out to be robots.

In the years since *Naming and Necessity*,[1] some philosophers also have wanted to say that, if cats are animals, then, necessarily, they are animals. Kripke believes this, and others have followed him in so believing. Indeed, it is not uncommon for philosophers to maintain something stronger than this conditional. Cats are animals, after all. So, for someone who believes the conditional, it makes sense simply to think that cats necessarily are animals.

Apart from theoretically ambitious arguments like those of Putnam and Kripke, it is attractive, finally, to say that we know that cats are animals. Let me not try to locate the source of the attraction; I will just assume that we do know that cats are animals and not, say, robots.

I would like to ask whether we can maintain all of these doctrines:

(i) Cats might turn out to be robots.
(ii) Necessarily, cats are animals.
(iii) We know that cats are animals and not robots.

In asking this my primary interest rests with (i), and with uses of 'might' which, like Putnam's, seem to be epistemic. I would like to be able to say in what sense cats might be robots. I do care as well about (ii) and (iii). But I care about them chiefly because I want to know whether some epistemic sense of 'might' would let us retain these claims while still insisting that cats might turn out to be robots. There is a second question that concerns me as well.

Philosophers often think about what (epistemically) might be true. They use such claims in order to prove philosophical doctrines. On occasion, these doctrines are not themselves epistemological. Putnam's argument is one case where this happens. His results are about language or metaphysics (depending on the version of the argument).

Sometimes the doctrines are epistemological. Cartesian skeptical arguments, for example, provide a case in which epistemic uses of 'might' appear in arguments about knowledge. We want to say that we know that there is an external world. At the same time, it is hard to resist the thought that we might be dreaming, or that we might be victims of a deceiver. And it is hard to say why this thought would not undermine some of our claims to know about objects outside of us.

The general point is that epistemic uses of 'might' figure in philosophical arguments, and it bears asking how premises of this kind prove what they appear to prove. In the present essay, I take up this question as it arises for Putnam. I assume that his argument about cats proves what he set out to prove; my objective is to find a construction of the argument which vindicates this assumption. But, if we want to see Putnam vindicated, we need to gain some understanding of the epistemic sense of 'might'. That is what I attempt here.

I

Philosophers often have said that natural kinds have essential properties. One traditional commitment of this view is that we can characterize any kind by appeal to a class of properties. So, if cats comprise a natural kind, there is a set of properties, $F_O \ldots F_n$, such that

(i) $(x) : x$ is a cat if and only if $F_O(x)$ & ... & $F_n(x)$:.

This is a doctrine about the metaphysics of kinds. We can construct a parallel doctrine about, not kinds, but the reference of natural kind terms. We can do this in two ways, depending on whether we want to define the name for the kind, or the predicate corresponding to it. One might illustrate the latter as follows:

(ii) The extension of "is a cat" is the set all xs such that $F_O(x)$ & ... & $F_n(x)$

These claims, of course, are too weak. If cats represent a natural kind, we do not want to say merely that there is a class of properties, $F_O \ldots F_n$, for which (i) is true. We want to say that (i) is necessarily true. Essential properties, traditionally, are properties that characterize kinds as a matter of necessity.

What determines the class of properties that are essential to a kind? This may seem like a bad question, but important philosophical doctrines represent themselves as answers to it. Positivism, for example, implies that (i) and (ii) are analytic, and so truths by convention. For positivists, what determines the class of properties essential to a kind is the meaning of the natural kind term, and, consequently, our decisions about the use of words.

This view about how kinds get "defined" is vulnerable to a counterexample that Putnam gives in "Is Semantics Possible?"[2] This is the example whose main thesis, for my purposes, is that cats might turn out to be robots. In the essay, the immediate target of Putnam's attack is Positivism. He offers several counterexamples to the doctrine that "analytic definitions" determine the identities of kinds and the reference of kind terms. The argument about cats begins this way:

> If cats turn out to be robots remotely controlled from Mars, we will still call them 'cats' :and: not only will we still call them 'cats', they are cats.

The antecedent and consequent of this conditional are stated in the simple future and the present respectively. But I assume that Putnam had in mind something like the following counterfactual:

> If cats were to turn out to be robots remotely controlled from Mars, we would still call them 'cats' :and: they would still be cats.

It is difficult to see how Putnam could get what he wants from this premise without supposing that cats might turn out to be robots. So, it seems as though we should outline the argument as follows:

(1) Cats might turn out to be robots.
(2) If cats were to turn out to be robots, we would still call them 'cats' :and: they would still be cats.
(3) It could happen that our analytic definition did not determine the reference of a kind term and did not determine the identity of the kind.

This locates the claim that cats might turn out to be robots. But why ought we think that 'might' has an epistemic sense in (1)?

The best way to see this is to examine alternative readings of 'might'. A first alternative would regard the occurrence of 'might' in (1) as the operator "it is metaphysically possible that." On this reading, premise (1) says that it is metaphysically possible for cats to turn out to be robots. To many, this will seem a simple falsehood. Kripke, in particular, will be inclined to say that, necessarily, cats are animals. If this is right, of course, then it is not metaphysically possible that cats are robots.

There is a second reason not to see (1) as a claim about metaphysical possibility. The reason here is methodological. Putnam's argument seems to work; it has seemed this way even to some who believe that cats necessarily are animals. When we try to explain how the argument works, then we ought, at least, to begin with constructions that are not needlessly alienating. In the beginning, we should seek not to disaffect people who share Kripke's views about natural kinds. But we would disaffect them immediately, if our construction of Putnam's first premise were that it is metaphysically possible for cats to be robots.

Could we read (1) as the premise: it is logically possible for cats to be robots? We cannot, I think, if this would mean only that 'Cats are robots' is not a first order contradiction. Positivism does not entail that 'Cats are robots' is a contradiction, so Putnam could get nothing from a premise like this.

We can generate a first order contradiction, if (i) there are analytic definitions of the form

$(x) (K(x)$ iff. $F_0(x)$ & ... & $F_n(x))$

and (ii) it is part of the analytic definition of 'cat' that cats are not robots. We can get a contradiction from first order logic and the analytic definition of 'cat', that is, if both (i) and (ii) are true. This point suggests two ways of interpreting someone who says that 'Cats are robots' is not a contradiction. We might see this, first, as the assertion that (i) is false: there are no analytic definitions of the above kind. If there were no such definitions, 'Cats are robots' would not be a contradiction. In that event, it would be logically possible for cats to be robots.

This strategy would not give a useable sense in which it is logically possible for cats to be robots. In "Is Semantics Possible?" Putnam wants to conclude that natural kind terms do not have analytic definitions of the relevant form. For this reason he cannot deny (i) without begging the question.

The second strategy is simply to deny that our analytic definitions of 'cat' and 'robot' alone entail that cats are not robots. In that case, 'Cats are robots' would not yield a contradiction; hence, a second way in which it might be thought logically possible for cats to be robots.

This too is useless for Putnam's purposes. Putnam wants to show that there could be a case in which a name referred to a kind even though the kind lacked some property occurring in our analytic definition. So, he must not begin by assuming that our analytic definitions leave it open whether cats are robots.

There is another, perhaps simpler, way in which to put this point about logical possibility. According to the most common conception of logical possibility, it is logically possible that Q just in case Q is not a logical falsehood. On this conception, it is logically possible that cats are robots: "Cats are robots" is not logically false. If 'might' in Putnam's premise were the 'might' of logical possibility, the premise would be true. Still, this would be a bad reading of the premise, since it is impossible to get from it what Putnam does get.

We could introduce a notion of "analytic possibility" as follows: it is analytically possible that Q just in case it is not analytic that not-Q. Could the premise "Cats might be robots" claim that it is analytically possible for cats to be robots? It could not, I think. Suppose that it is analytically possible for cats to be robots. By the definition of analytic possibility, this is just to say that "Cats are not robots" is not analytic. Can Putnam begin with this premise?

If it were analytic that cats are animals, and that no animal is a robot, then it would be analytic cats are not robots. Now, either the positivist would agree that these are analytic truths, or he would not. In the first case Putnam's premise would beg the question, if it were the premise that "Cats are robots" is an analytic possibility. If the positivist were not to agree that the relevant truths are analytic, then Putnam's argument cannot show that our analytic definitions do not determine the reference of our kind terms.

II

It is not altogether easy, then, to say that 'might' in Putnam's premise is the 'might' either of metaphysical or of logical possibility. This makes it reasonable at least to consider the idea that Putnam's use of 'might' is epistemic. If we do suppose this, what is the force of saying that cats might be robots? Twenty years ago, and longer, epistemic logicians tried to give definitions of epistemic possibility. The simplest of these is:

It is epistemically possible that Q iff. it is not known that not-Q.

Is this of any help to us, when we set out to find a sense in which cats might be robots?

It is not. On the above conception, it is epistemically possible that cats are robots only if we do not know that cats are not robots. But surely we do know this, so it would not be epistemically possible for cats to be robots. The above conception, consequently, would not give us what we want.

There are other familiar interpretations of epistemic uses of 'might':

(i) it is not certain that cats are not robots,
(ii) it is not *a priori* that cats are not robots.

What do we mean when we say that we are "certain" that such and such? I think that this notion of certainty is no clearer than the one that I want to explain. So, it seems to me that (i) does not much illuminate the epistemic sense of 'might'.

I am not any more optimistic about (ii). The immediate suggestion here is that, when we say that cats might be robots, or might "turn out to be," we mean to say that it is not *a priori* that they are not robots. Here is a generalized statement of the suggestion:

It might be that Q just in case it is not *a priori* that not-Q

Let me set aside worries about whether anything really is *a priori*. Even then this general claim does not seem true. The obvious counterexamples here come from logic and mathematics. Since I elect not to worry about a prioricity itself, I suppose that truths of logic and mathematics are *a priori*. One sometimes thinks, of what is not in fact a theorem, that it (epistemically) might be theorem. I am inclined to say that we are sometimes correct when we think such things. We can be correct, even though in such cases it would be *a priori* that the relevant proposition was false. If this is right, then there are cases in which "It might be that Q" is true, and where it is *a priori* that not-Q.

In offering this as an objection against (ii), I assume that the sense of 'might' in Putnam's premise is the same as the sense one would use in mathematics and logic. Someone could therefore mute the objection by casting this assumption away. I do not have much to say about this move, except that it seems like unwise method to begin by supposing that our uses of 'might' are equivocal. If there were arguments for this, of course, that would be a different matter.

III

What are we thinking when we think that cats might be robots? It is attractive to say that we are thinking something like this: We could have the evidence that we do even though cats were robots. There are other natural expressions of either this idea or others that resemble it. One might instead say: it does not follow from our evidence that cats are not robots; or, our evidence is compatible with its being true that cats are robots; or, finally, that we can imagine having the evidence that we do and yet discovering that cats are robots. It is not madness to see a single theme in these expressions. Let me identify this theme with my first way of putting it: we could have the evidence that we do even though cats were robots.

In what sense of 'could' is it true that we could have our actual evidence even though cats were robots? One view is that the occurrence of 'could' here is the 'could' of metaphysical possibility. If this were right, Putnam's premise would say that it is metaphysically possible for us to have the evidence that we do even though cats were robots. This is close to the view that Kripke describes in *Naming and Necessity*. In place of the claim that cats might be robots, Kripke considers

This table might have been made of ice,

said of a table that is actually made of wood. His example is in the past tense, while Putnam's is in the present. In order not to oscillate between tenses, let me consider an altered version of Kripke's example:

This table might be made of ice.

Here is a construction of the example which would parallel the one that I have just given for Putnam's premise:

It is metaphysically possible for us to have the evidence that we do regarding the table and for the table to be ice nevertheless.

In fact, Kripke would not accept either this construction, or the earlier one for Putnam's premise. The second entails that it is metaphysically possible for cats to be robots; the first entails that it is possible for the table to be ice. But it would be Kripke's view that, since cats are animals, necessarily they are animals and not robots. In the same way, since the table actually is wood, necessarily it is wood.

Can we escape this problem while saving our leading idea about epistemic uses of 'might'? Kripke thinks that we can do this:

> What, then, does the intuition that the table might have turned out to have been made of ice or of anything else, that it might even have turned out not to be made of molecules, amount to? I think that it means simply that there might have been *a table* looking and feeling just like this one and placed in the very position in the room, which was in fact made of ice. In other words, I (or some conscious being) could have been *qualitatively in the same epistemic situation* that in fact obtains, I could have the same sensory evidence that I in fact have, about *a table* which was made of ice. The situation is thus akin to the one which inspired the counterpart theorists; when I speak of the possibility of the table turning out to be made of various things, I am speaking loosely. *This* table itself could not have had an origin different from the one it in fact had, but in a situation qualitatively identical to this one with respect to all the evidence I had in advance, the room could have contained *a table made of ice* in place of this one.[3]

The strategy that Kripke describes here exploits the idea of hypothetical tables which look like the actual table but are not identical with it. Let me refer to these as epistemic counterparts of the actual table. Pursuant to Kripke's view one would replace my first reading of Putnam's premise as follows:

(i) It is metaphysically possible for us to be qualitatively in our actual epistemic situation and the epistemic counterparts of cats be robots.

Kripke's example, of course, we could reread in the same way:

(ii) It is metaphysically possible for us to be qualitatively in our actual epistemic situation regarding the table and the epistemic counterpart of this table be made of ice.

I will have repeated occasion to refer to this general way of seeing epistemic uses of 'might'. On such occasions, I will sometimes refer to it as the counterpart strategy.

From (i) we cannot infer that it is metaphysically possible for cats to be robots. Neither does (ii) imply that it is possible for the table to be made of ice. So, the appeal to counterparts does solve the immediate problem. It remains to ask whether the counterpart strategy gives a generally correct account of claims in which 'might' is used epistemically.

To some it will seem obvious that it cannot. In its rough, intuitive form, the complaint is this. One wants to say that

This table might be ice

says of this table that it might be ice; it does not say, of an epistemic counterpart that it might be ice. There is more than one criticism embedded in this remark. Let me try to separate them. The first is that, when we say "This table might be ice," we say something about the actual table. A second, related thought is that the actual table is the logical subject of what we say. At first, it might appear that Kripke's view is hostile to these thoughts.

I believe this appearance is an illusion. According to Kripke, we do say something about the actual table. In particular, we say, of the actual table, that there (metaphysically) could be another object made of ice that looked, etc., just like it. Moreover, when we state Kripke's view this way, it is clear that he can allow the actual table to remain the logical subject of what we say.

A second objection is suggested by the thought that we say of the actual table that it might be ice. The worry here is that our use of 'might' attaches, in the first instance, to the actual table. In Kripke's account this may seem not to happen; there it is only a counterpart that counterfactually is ice.

The blueprint of Kripke's strategy is to understand epistemic uses of 'might' by appeal to the metaphysical use of 'might' and two epistemic relations. In the relevant use, this table might be ice if and only if it is metaphysically possible for us to be in our actual epistemic situation where an epistemic counterpart of the table is ice. In the way Kripke intends, the epistemic possibility of the table being made of ice attached via an epistemic counterpart to the table itself. To complain about this mode of attachment is just to reject Kripke's strategy without argument.

Finally, there is a worry that, when we say "This table might be ice," it does not seem as though we say anything about epistemic counterparts of the table. Indeed, it is clear that someone could believe that the table might be ice, even though he or she lacked the very concept of an epistemic counterpart.

There are two things to say about this complaint. First, it is not obvious that we have no concept of epistemic counterparts. Of course, only a philosopher would attach these words to the idea. But, roughly speaking, epistemic counterparts are just hypothetical things that might cause us the experiences that actual objects cause. And, surely, it is not very unusual for a person to think of such things.

But suppose I admit that we do not ordinarily think Kripke's analysis, when we make epistemic use of 'might'. Again, I do not have very much to say about this, except that it is not a problem peculiar to Kripke's view. This is just an instance of what is sometimes called the paradox of analysis. In saying this, of course, I do not mean to dismiss the problem. But neither am I able to address it here.

While I do not believe that these first complaints are any trouble for Kripke, his view is still beset by hard questions. Consider Kripke's example once again. The passage from *Naming and Necessity* suggests this reading of it:

It is metaphysically possible for us (or someone) to have qualitatively the evidence that we do regarding this table, and an epistemic counterpart of the table be ice.

Suppose that our actual evidence regarding the table resides in our having seen it in a lecture hall on many occasions. Imagine that the table is at the back of a lecture hall that we often visit, and that, later, thinking about the many times when we have seen the table, we think 'That table might be made of ice'. Now consider a hypothetical situation. In this situation, we also see a table at the back of the lecture hall, one that looks exactly like the actual table. But let the hypothetical situation differ from the actual one in two ways: (i) the hypothetical table is ice, and (ii) in the hypothetical case, we have very nearly but not exactly the experiences caused by the actual table. Suppose that, hypothetically, when we do see the ice table, it looks just as the actual table looks, but we see it fewer times.

Does reflection on this hypothetical case incline us to say, actually, that the table might be made of ice? Surely it does, so the hypothetical case, in some sense, entails the actual truth of 'That table might be ice'. But it is not a case in which we have qualitatively the evidence that we actually do, since we have fewer experiences of the table. So, the hypothetical case entails that the table might be ice, but does not entail Kripke's putative analysis of this claim.

Examples like this suggest that Kripke's formulation of the counterpart strategy is not correct. But they represent no crushing defeat of the leading idea behind it. In what remains of this essay, I want to put *Naming and Necessity* aside, and to ask whether this leading idea could usefully be developed. In particular, I want to explore possible formulations of it, and to ask whether these tell us anything about epistemic uses of 'might'.

For this purpose, I begin with a general statement of the strategy. Recall Kripke's example

This table might be ice,

and its proposed analysis:

It is metaphysically possible for us to be qualitatively in our actual epistemic situation and for an epistemic counterpart of this table to be ice.

Two relations are prominent here: (i) being qualitatively in our actual epistemic situation, and (ii) being an epistemic counterpart of the table. In order to give a clear statement of the counterpart strategy, it is necessary to explain these relations. This is where I concentrate my efforts for the rest of the essay.

Two constraints guide this discussion. First, a statement of the counterpart strategy should give a sense in which cats might be robots, and should let us explain why this claim shows what it does. Second, formulations of the counterpart strategy, and therefore of the two relations, will be correct to the extent that they explain our reactions to examples in which epistemic uses of 'might' occur. My immediate plan is to examine intuitions of this kind, and to seek formulations that accommodate them.

I begin with an example about the Hope diamond. In my discussion of Kripke, I imagined a case in which we have often seen a table at the back of a lecture hall. Later, thinking back on these occasions, we say 'That table might be ice'. Let this be the actual situation once again. What would convince us to say that the table might be ice?

Think about a hypothetical case in which the table we see looks exactly like the actual table, but is made of ice. Let this be a case in which we have qualitatively exactly the sense experiences caused by the actual table, but imagine that their cause is an ice table. Apart from this assumption, let the hypothetical world differ from the non-hypothetical one in only one other way: suppose that we do not have any of the experiences actually caused by the Hope diamond.

The hypothetical case is one where (i) experiences actually caused by the table are caused by an ice table, (ii) we have all of our actual experiences, qualitatively speaking, (iii) except those actually caused by the Hope diamond. Is this a case that would incline us actually to say "That table might be ice"? Surely, it would. After all, it is a hypothetical case where all evidence relevant to the table is preserved; what is lost seems irrelevant, and what looks exactly like the actual table is ice.

This intuition shows that there are cases which entail "That table might be ice," even though our hypothetical experiences differ from our actual ones. The counterpart strategy is meant at least to give the truth conditions of claims in which 'might' is used epistemically. If this were done correctly, the counterpart-strategic analysis would follow from the same hypothetical cases that entail "That table might be ice." So this ought to happen with the present example.

How are we to make it happen? Recall the counterpart-strategic interpretation:

> It is metaphysically possible for us to be qualitatively in our actual epistemic situation and for the epistemic counterparts of that table nevertheless to be ice.

One of our problems is to state the relation "being qualitatively in the same epistemic situation." We might have thought at first that someone could be qualitatively in our epistemic situation only if he or she had experiences qualitatively identical to each of our actual experiences. In other words, we might have thought that such a person must have had an experiential history qualitatively identical to our own. The example seems to show that this is wrong.

In fact, our formulation of the counterpart strategy should not require even that we have the same experiences regarding the table. Think about a hypothetical case, once again, where there is an ice table in the lecture room. Suppose that this table looks exactly like the actual one: whenever we look at it, it looks just as the actual table looks in the corresponding non-hypothetical observation. But imagine that we look at the table one or two times fewer. This is just the case I considered in connection with Kripke. Is it a case that inclines us to say, of the actual table, 'That (this) table might be ice'?

It is, I think, and several consequences follow here. First, in order to be in our epistemic situation, it is not necessary that we (or someone) have exactly the experiences that we do regarding the table. Second, since the lost experiences, in the hypothetical case, are experiences of the table, it is also not necessary that one have all experiences that are actually experiences of the table. Third, in the hypothetical case, the ice table is a counterpart of the actual table, even though (i) it does not cause exactly those experiences that the actual table causes, and (ii) we do not have the same experiences of it that we have of the actual table. So we should reject the corresponding necessary conditions on being an epistemic counterpart. Finally, the hypothetical ice table need not cause us to have exactly the experiences that are in fact our best, most trustworthy, observations of the table. Causing exactly these experiences, therefore, is also not a necessary condition on the counterpart relation.

In order for someone to be in our epistemic situation and for there to be an epistemic counterpart of the table, it is necessary that he or she have enough of our actual experiences. We can easily describe hypothetical cases in which we have very few of the experiences actually caused by the table. And we can stipulate that, hypothetically, there is an ice table that causes some, though very few, of our actual table experiences. In general, these cases would not incline us to say "This table might be ice."

Something similar seems true for epistemic counterparts. There are hypothetical cases, for example, where we see a different ice table each time we enter the lecture room. This would not prevent us from having experiences qualitatively like the ones that are caused by the actual table. But I think this case would not satisfy the truth conditions of "That table might be ice." Within the counterpart strategy, the right explanation for this is simply that the hypothetical case contains no epistemic counterpart. No single object causes enough of the right experiences.

In order to be in our epistemic situation one must have enough of our actual experiences; and, in order to be an epistemic counterpart of the actual table, a hypothetical table must cause enough of the experiences caused by the table. What counts as enough? In this essay, I will not attempt a general treatment of this question. But we can say something about what it is to have enough of our actual experience: having enough is not always simply a matter of having a certain number of our actual experiences. Think about a case in which we have actually seen the table many times. But suppose that all but a very few of these observations have been fleeting, incautious, and at a distance. Suppose that we have looked at the table closely and carefully only once, or only a few times. Now think about a hypothetical case where an ice table causes all, but only, the experiences arising from our careful looks at the table. Could this case incline us to say that the actual table might be ice?

Once more, I assume that it could, even though the hypothetical case could be one where (i) we have very few of our actual experiences, and, (ii) the putative counterpart causes very little of what the table actually causes. What seems important, in this case, is not the number of experiences caused by the counterpart, but rather which of our actual experiences it causes.

Thus far I have talked only about necessary conditions on the relations "being qualitatively in the same epistemic situation" and "being an epistemic counterpart." I turn now to conditions sufficient for these relations.

In order to be in our epistemic situation, is it sufficient to have qualitatively exactly the sense experiences that we actually have regarding the table? Similarly, in a hypothetical case, if an object causes exactly the experiences that the table causes, does it follow that the object is an epistemic counterpart of the table?

Let me try to address this by way of another example. This example begins in the way that the first ones did. To start with, we imagine actually visiting a lecture room many times and seeing a table there. It still remains to say what would incline us to think that the table might be ice? Now consider a hypothetical case. Suppose that, in this situation, we have qualitatively exactly the experiences that we actually do regarding the table. And let the cause of these be an object made of ice. What distinguishes this case is an assumption about ourselves. In particular, we suppose that our own sensory mechanisms are not at all as they actually are, and that this is why an object made of ice could cause the relevant experiences. In the hypothetical case, ice of a certain shape naturally looks to us as wooden tables actually look.

So, in the hypothetical case, we have exactly the right experiences, qualitatively speaking, and the right experiences are all caused by an object that is made of ice. Would this incline us to say, of the actual table, "This table might be ice"?

Reactions to this example are less strong than reactions to the other cases that I have introduced. Still, I would not be inclined to say that the table might be ice. When I say "That table might be ice," in ordinary cases, I am saying that the evidence I possess, arising by way of my senses constituted as they are, is compatible with the table being ice. Exotic cases, in which my senses are utterly different, strike me as irrelevant.

If this intuition is right, then the hypothetical case should not entail the counterpart-strategic analysis. So, either the hypothetical case is not one where we are in our actual situation, or it is not one in which there is an epistemic counterpart.

One might have thought that "That table might be ice" is true as long as some conscious being could have experiences qualitatively like our own, even though the relevant experiences were caused by an ice table. Kripke's own remarks represent this view. But cases in which our constitution is altered suggest that this condition is too weak. When we wonder whether the table might be ice, it is relevant to think about hypothetical situations only if their agents are like us in the right ways.

IV

It really is too early to try stating the two relations that figure in the counterpart strategy. But I think this would be a good way in which to consolidate our gains. When we do try to state these relations, our chief task is to decide what intuitions to accommodate. As I mentioned earlier, there is a further constraint: we want, if possible, not only to explain the above cases, but also to get a formulation of the counterpart strategy which makes it true that cats might be robots.

Let me try to say what it is to be an epistemic counterpart, and what it is to be in our actual epistemic situation. I begin by trying to give formulations that are consistent with what I take to be our reactions to the examples that I have discussed.

Here is a first version of the two relations:

(i) x is in qualitatively our actual epistemic situation iff. (a) x has enough of the experiences that constitute our evidence for thinking that the table is not ice, and (b) x has sensory mechanisms like ours.

(ii) x is an epistemic counterpart of the actual table iff. (a) x causes us (or someone) to have enough of the experiences that the table actually causes, and (b) it causes them by way of sensory mechanisms like ours.

(i) and (ii) explain our intuitions about epistemic uses of 'might', as far as we have seen them. Still, there are formulations which depart sharply from (i) and (ii). Consider a last case. Imagine a case in which we have none of our actual experiences regarding the table. Imagine that there is an ice table, and that we have as good experiential reason to say that it is not ice as we do for saying that the actual table is not ice.

I think this case would convince us to say, non-hypothetically, that the table might be ice. But when we consider this example, we have not imagined a case that places someone in our actual epistemic situation. Neither is the ice table that we imagine an epistemic counterpart of the actual table. What are we to say about this?

I think we ought to say that the example is not relevant to the question "What is it to be in our epistemic situation, and what is it to be an epistemic counterpart?" This is not to say that it is irrelevant simpliciter; it bears explaining why the example is not ultimately embarrassing to the counterpart strategy. Still, I think the explanation need not reform (i) and (ii) above. We may say, instead, that there are cases that convince us to say "That table might be ice," but which force no revision in the formulation of the counterpart strategy.

Why should we not treat some of my other examples in the same way? We can give a very restrictive formulation of the counterpart strategy: someone would be in our epistemic situation only if he or she had exactly our experiences regarding the table. Epistemic counterparts would cause all of the experiences that the table actually causes. Our reactions to cases appear to run against this view. But why could we not say that our reactions are only about what convinces us, not about what it is to be in our epistemic situation, or what it is to be an epistemic counterpart?

This restrictive view associates epistemic uses of 'might' with exact sameness of sense experience. In the liberal view of (i) and (ii), what is held constant between individuals in qualitatively the same epistemic situation? It is plausible that what is held constant here is something like one's justification. We have a reason for thinking that the table is not ice or that cats are not robots. In cases where we have seen a table many times, maybe our justification, in some sense, is not affected by the loss of a few experiences. As long as what is lost does not represent an entire kind of evidence, or close to it, maybe we can say that our reason or justification does not change. Perhaps a liberal conception of 'might' could be tied to this view of justification.

It is difficult to give here an overall assessment of the counterpart strategy. My discussion has focused almost entirely on a single case, so any assessment is in danger of overstating things. Nevertheless, (i) and (ii) encourage the thought that we could account for our intuitions about 'might' without giving up the leading idea of the counterpart strategy.

This fact may encourage as well the thought that the counterpart strategy give a sense in which cats might be robots. I do not believe that this is unreasonable, exactly, but I resist this extension of our results here. There are, after all, salient differences between the case in which we are saying "That table might be ice" and saying that cats might be robots. In all of my cases here, for example, putative counterparts of the actual table were other inanimate objects. We have entertained only counterparts whose ontological category was the same as the actual object. But, in hypothetical cases relevant to Putnam's premise, putative counterparts of cats would be robots. What is more, I have not asked how to state the counterpart strategy for examples where natural kinds, not individuals, are in question. Maybe these differences, and others, will come to nothing. But I would not like to suppose this in advance.

In the end, what has all of this shown about epistemic uses of 'might'? Three points are important here. First, the counterpart strategy handles in a natural way at least the cases that I have described. This must count as some recommendation for it. Second, within the counterpart strategy there are two conceptions of the epistemic 'might' to consider. The first is associated with sameness of sense experience, the second with something like sameness of justification. I doubt that anyone would want to hold the first of these, but the second hardly counts as an articulated theory about the epistemic sense of 'might'. Finally, one example here suggested that epistemic uses of 'might', perhaps including Putnam's, are tied to our actual constitution. This connects such uses to our actual situation in a way that one might not have expected.[4]

Notes

1. Saul Kripke, *Naming and Necessity* (Cambridge, Mass., 1980).
2. Hilary Putnam, "Is Semantics Possible?" in Putnam's *Philosophical Papers 2: Mind, Language, and Reality* (Cambridge, 1975).
3. Kripke, *Naming and Necessity*, 142.
4. For helpful comments on this paper I am grateful to W. D. Hart, Alan Nelson, and David Sachs. I am especially indebted to Joseph Almog, Tyler Burge, and Keith Donnellan. It would please me to think that their influence is evident here. I also have a special debt to Andrew Hsu for conversations on these and other matters.

Quantified Modal Logic and the Plural *De Re*

PHILLIP BRICKER

Quantified modal logic has proven itself a useful tool for the formalization of modal discourse. It has its limitations to be sure: many ordinary modal idioms must be artificially restructured if they are to be expressed within a language whose only modal operators are the box and the diamond; other modal idioms cannot be expressed within such a language at all. Nonetheless, quantified modal logic has enjoyed considerable success in uncovering and explaining ambiguities in modal sentences and fallacies in modal reasoning.

A prime example of this success is the now standard analysis of the distinction between modality *de dicto* and modality *de re*. The analysis has been applied first and foremost to modal sentences containing definite descriptions. Such sentences are often ambiguous between an interpretation *de dicto*, according to which a modal property is attributed to a proposition (or, on some views, a sentence), and an interpretation *de re*, according to which a modal property is attributed to an individual. When these sentences are translated into the language of quantified modal logic, the *de dicto/de re* ambiguity turns out to involve an ambiguity of scope. If the definite description is within the scope of the modal operator, then the operator attaches to a complete sentence, and the resulting sentence is *de dicto*. If the definite description is outside the scope of the modal operator, then the operator attaches to a predicate to form a modal predicate, and the resulting sentence is *de re*. Quantified modal logic has the resources to clarify and disambiguate English modal sentences containing definite descriptions.

In this paper, I explore to what extent the analysis in terms of scope can be applied to modal sentences containing denoting phrases other than definite descriptions, phrases such as 'some *F*' and 'every *F*'.[1] I will focus upon categorical modal sentences of the following two forms:

372

QUANTIFIED MODAL LOGIC AND THE PLURAL *DE RE* 373

(◇A) Every *F* might be *G*.

(□I) Some *F* must be *G*.

These sentences, I will argue, have a threefold ambiguity. In addition to the familiar readings *de dicto* and *de re*, there is a third reading on which they are examples of the *plural de re*: they attribute a modal property to the *F*s plurally in a way that cannot in general be reduced to an attribution of modal properties to the individual *F*s. The plural *de re* readings of (◇A) and (□I) cannot be captured simply by varying the scope of an individual quantifier. Indeed, there is an ambiguity associated with the general term '*F*' that cannot be analyzed at all within standard quantified modal logic.[2]

I will consider three basic strategies for extending standard quantified modal logic so as to provide analyses for the sentences in question. On the first strategy, all denoting phrases have a rigid/nonrigid ambiguity parallelling the ambiguity some have proposed for definite descriptions and formalized using Kaplan's 'dthat' operator. I will argue that, although there is some plausibility to the ambiguity posited, the first strategy fails to provide a general solution because it cannot provide adequate translations for sentences involving iterated modality. On the second and third strategies, the ambiguity associated with the denoting phrase is again a matter of scope: in this case, the scope of the general term '*F*'. The second strategy introduces new operators that serve to represent the scope of a general term by indexing it, implicitly or explicitly, to distant modal operators; the third strategy represents scope by appropriately relocating the general term, and then introduces either quantifiers over sets or Boolos's plural quantifiers to solve a resulting problem of cross-reference. I will argue that only the third strategy with plural quantifiers can provide an adequate formalization of modal discourse within the framework of quantified modal logic.

I

I will make use of two principles in evaluating proposals for formalizing modal discourse. Let *S* be an English sentence to be formalized, and let *T(S)* be its translation into the formal language. The first principle requires that *T(S)*, when interpreted, provide a correct semantic analysis of *S* in at least the following minimal sense: *For any possible context of utterance, if S has a determinate truth value in that context, then T(S) has the same truth value as S in that context.*[3]

The first principle applies to formalization in general. What further requirements should be imposed will depend upon the goals of the particular project of formalization at hand. Such goals might include, for example, any of the following: (1) exploring the expressive power of a particular logical framework; (2) developing a perspicuous logical regimentation of English; (3) showing that English is free of certain unwanted ontological commitments; (4) modeling the psychological processes by which a language user comprehends

English. The first- and second-mentioned goals are relevant to the present project of formalization; especially, exploring the expressive power of the framework of quantified modal logic. It is essential to this framework that the concepts of possibility and necessity be expressed by means of propositional operators that do not use the full resources of quantification over possible worlds. Thus, for the project at hand, there is a second principle that proposals must satisfy: *The formal language must not contain the equivalent of full variable-binding operators ranging over possible worlds.* A *full* variable-binding operator has the power to bind a variable occurring at any position syntactically within its scope. Although the notion of equivalence in question is difficult to make precise, standard quantified modal logic itself clearly satisfies the principle: when sentences of quantified modal logic are translated in the usual way into first-order world theory, the box and the diamond become quantifiers that are constrained by the rule: world variables must be bound by the nearest possible quantifier (unless they occur in an argument-place of the accessibility predicate). For this reason, a box or a diamond, unlike a full variable-binding operator, always has its influence disrupted by the presence of another box or diamond within its scope. The principle does restrict, however, the ways in which standard quantified modal logic can be extended for purposes of formalizing English modal sentences.

What about the ontological goal of showing that English modal discourse lacks a realist commitment to possible worlds and *possibilia*? Formalization within quantified modal logic has less to offer the nonrealist, I think, than has sometimes been supposed. I will touch upon this question briefly at the end of the paper.

II

I turn now to the formalization of particular English sentences. It will be useful to begin by illustrating a method for applying the analysis in terms of scope to modal sentences containing definite descriptions. Consider the following familiar example:

(1) The President is necessarily a U.S. citizen.

The source of ambiguity in (1) is immediately apparent if one applies Russell's analysis of definite descriptions. On Russell's analysis, there are two ways of eliminating the definite description in (1): the description can be taken to have either narrow scope or wide scope.[4] As a result, there are the following two possible translations into quantified modal logic (using the obvious abbreviations):

(2) $\Box(\exists x)((y)(Py \leftrightarrow y=x) \ \& \ Cx)$.

(3) $(\exists x)((y)(Py \leftrightarrow y=x) \ \& \ \Box Cx)$.

In (2), the box attaches to a complete sentence; (2) is therefore *de dicto*. So interpreted (1) is presumably true: it asserts that at every accessible possible

QUANTIFIED MODAL LOGIC AND THE PLURAL *DE RE* 375

world the President at that world is a U.S. citizen, and this will be true as long as only worlds that conform to the U.S. Constitution are considered accessible. In (3), the box attaches only to the predicate '*Cx*'; (3) is therefore *de re*. So interpreted (1) is presumably false: it asserts of the person who is in fact President, Ronald Reagan, that he has the modal property of being necessarily a U.S. citizen. Reagan lacks that property because his parents might have renounced their citizenship and left the country before he was born. Thus, sentences of quantified modal logic can be provided that succeed in capturing the two possible readings of (1), and that show the difference in readings to be a matter of scope.[5]

The explanation of ambiguity in terms of scope has also been applied to modal sentences containing denoting phrases other than definite descriptions. For example, as has often been noted, the difference between uses of 'any' and 'every' can sometimes be explained by the rule that the former takes the wider of two available scopes whereas the latter takes the narrower scope.[6] Thus, suppose that a lottery is to take place in which various numbers are to be chosen, and compare (4) with (5):

(4) Any number less than a hundred might be chosen.

(5) Every number less than a hundred might be chosen.

(4) asserts of each number less than a hundred that it has a certain modal property: the property of possibly being chosen. The quantifier is outside the scope of the modal operator and the sentence is *de re*:[7]

(6) $(x)(Nx \rightarrow \Diamond Cx)$. ($Nx = x$ is a number less than a hundred.)

(5), on the other hand, is ambiguous. On one reading it is equivalent to (4) and analyzed as (6). On another reading, it asserts that it is possible for a certain proposition to be true: the proposition that every number less than a hundred is chosen. The quantifier is within the scope of the modal operator and the sentence is *de dicto*:

(7) $\Diamond(x)(Nx \rightarrow Cx)$.

In this example, then, the difference between 'any' in (4) and 'every' in (5) can be accounted for in terms of quantifier scope in sentences of quantified modal logic.[8]

Distinctions of quantifier scope can also be used to resolve ambiguities involving the denoting phrase 'some *F*'. Thus,

(8) Some number less than a hundred must be chosen

is ambiguous between the *de re* assertion

(9) $(\exists x)(Nx \ \& \ \Box Cx)$,

which would be true if the lottery were rigged to ensure that, say, the number seventeen be the chosen number, and the *de dicto* assertion

(10) $\Box(\exists x)(Nx \ \& \ Cx)$,

which would be true if only ninety-nine tickets were sold, numbered consecutively from one. The explanation of the ambiguity involving 'some F' in terms of quantifier scope exactly parallels the explanation of the ambiguity involving 'every F'. In the case of 'some F', however, English provides no alternative denoting phrase that serves to force either the narrow scope or the wide scope interpretation.[9]

III

So far, so good. But when one considers sentences of the form ($\Diamond$A) and ($\Box$I) that have readings that are *plurally de re*, the standard analysis in terms of scope breaks down. A modal proposition is *plurally*, as opposed to *individually*, *de re* if it involves the assertion or denial of a joint possibility for two or more individuals. A plurally *de re* proposition is not in general reducible to a combination of individually *de re* propositions; for example, given the possibility that a is F and the possibility that b is F, nothing in general follows about the joint possibility that both a and b are F.[10]

I turn now to an example where the difference between 'any F' and 'every F' cannot be attributed simply to the scope of an individual quantifier. Suppose that a drawing for prizes is about to occur. Three of the people who entered the drawing — Tom, Dick, and Harry — are gathered together in a room awaiting the results. Compare the following two assertions:

(11) Any person in the room might win a prize.

(12) Every person in the room might win a prize.

(11) asserts that each person in the room has the modal property, *possibly wins a prize*. It can be translated by the standard *de re*:

(13) $(x)(Rx \rightarrow \Diamond Wx)$. ($Rx = x$ is a person in the room.)

(12), on the other hand, is ambiguous. Like (5), the standard *de re* and *de dicto* formulas provide possible readings. Unlike (5), however, (12) has a third — plurally *de re* — reading which, I will argue, is not equivalent to either of the other two. This reading can be expressed in a preliminary way as follows: (12) asserts of the people who are actually in the room — in this case, Tom, Dick, and Harry — that it might be the case that all of them win a prize.

Assume throughout what follows that (12) is to be interpreted according to the plurally *de re* reading just given. There is no problem finding a plurally *de re* sentence of modal logic (enhanced with proper names) that is guaranteed to have the same truth value as (12) for all contexts of utterance in which Tom, Dick, and Harry are the people in the room:

(14) $\Diamond(Wt \ \& \ Wd \ \& \ Wh)$.

QUANTIFIED MODAL LOGIC AND THE PLURAL *DE RE* 377

But (14), of course, fails to provide an analysis of (12); it does not have the same truth value as (12) for every context of utterance.[11] How, then, can (12) be analyzed as a sentence of quantified modal logic?

I argue first that (12) cannot be analyzed as the standard *de re* (13). For suppose that when (12) is uttered Tom, Dick, and Harry are in the room, and suppose that according to the rules of the drawing only one person can win a prize. Then (14), and so (12), is false, since there is no accessible world at which all three of them win a prize (allowing only worlds that satisfy the rules of the drawing to be accessible). But (13) is true. In the context in question, (13) has the same truth value as the individually *de re*

(15) ◇*Wt* & ◇*Wd* & ◇*Wh*;

and (15) is true as long as Tom, Dick, and Harry each have a chance to win. So (13) cannot provide an analysis of (12).

If the difference between (11) and (12) were simply a matter of the scope of the universal quantifier, then (12) could be translated by the *de dicto*:

(16) ◇(*x*)(*Rx* → *Wx*).

But (16) fares no better than (13) as an analysis of (12). Since in (16) the predicate '*Rx*' is within the scope of the diamond, the truth value of (16), unlike (12), will depend upon who is in the room at worlds other than the actual world. This allows there to be cases where (12) and (16) diverge in truth value. Suppose again that according to the rules of the drawing only one person can win a prize, thus making (12) false. But (16) is true. (16) asserts that the proposition *every person in the room wins a prize* is a possible proposition, and so true at some possible world. Consider a world at which Tom is the only person in the room, and at which Tom wins the prize. Such a world is possible assuming only that being in the room is a contingent property of Dick and Harry, and that Tom has a chance to win a prize (irrespective of who is in the room). Moreover, the proposition *every person in the room wins a prize* is true at this world. So (16), unlike (12), is true, and (16) cannot provide an analysis of (12). I conclude, then, that the *de dicto/de re*, narrow scope/wide scope distinction is unable by itself to capture all the possible readings of sentences of the form (◇A) 'Every *F* might be *G*'.[12]

The difficulty in formalizing (12) within quantified modal logic afflicts other modal constructions involving other denoting phrases. Thus, suppose that the following sentence of the form (□I) 'Some *F* must be *G*' is uttered in the same circumstances as (12) above:

(17) Some person in the room must win a prize.

Both the *de re* (18) and the *de dicto* (19) provide possible readings of (17):

(18) (∃*x*)(*Rx* & □*Wx*).

(19) □(∃*x*)(*Rx* & *Wx*).

But (17) also has a plural *de re* reading that is captured neither by (18) nor by (19). On this reading, (17) asserts of the people actually in the room—in this case, Tom, Dick, and Harry—that it must be the case that at least one of them wins a prize. To see that neither (18) nor (19) can capture this reading, suppose that the drawing has been rigged by removing all tickets belonging to entrants other than Tom, Dick, or Harry. In this case, (17) is true, but (18) and (19) are false (under the natural accessibility assignment). (18) is false because there is no particular person who is guaranteed to win a prize: it could be either Tom, Dick, or Harry. (19) is false because being in the room is, I suppose, a contingent property of Tom, Dick, and Harry, and irrelevant to the selection of a winner.[13]

How widespread is the plural *de re* phenomenon exhibited by (12) and (17)? For one thing, it is not restricted to the logician's favorite denoting phrases: 'every F' and 'some F'. The threefold ambiguity in the following examples should now be readily apparent to the reader:

(20) Most students from out-of-state must live off-campus.

(21) Exactly five students in my class can win a fellowship.

Moreover, the phenomenon occurs not only in connection with modal operators, but in connection with temporal operators as well. The ambiguity in (22) gives rise to the same difficulty in formalization as do the modal examples:

(22) Every book in the store was on sale.[14]

Indeed, the phenomenon can also be recognized in connection with propositional attitude constructions such as:

(23) Ralph believes someone in the house committed the murder.[15]

For each of these examples, the usual *de dicto/de re*, narrow scope/wide scope distinction can be used to analyze two possible readings, but a third, plural *de re* reading remains unanalyzed.

IV

I turn now from illustration to diagnosis. In what follows, I will focus upon the two schemas ($\Diamond$A) and ($\Box$I) interpreted in the plural *de re* way illustrated above. Why were the ordinary *de re* and *de dicto* analyses unable to provide translations for ($\Diamond$A) and ($\Box$I)? Consider ($\Box$I): 'Some F must be G'. On the *de re* analysis, the existential quantifier is outside the scope of the box, and the box attaches to the predicate 'Gx'. On this analysis, ($\Box$I) would assert that one and the same individual has the property expressed by 'G' at every possible world. This, we have seen, misconstrues the plurally *de re* ($\Box$I) (unless there is only one F), because ($\Box$I) is compatible with the property expressed by 'G' being had by different individuals at different worlds. On the *de dicto* analysis, the quantifier occurs within the scope of the box. This forces the

QUANTIFIED MODAL LOGIC AND THE PLURAL *DE RE* 379

predicate '*Fx*' also to occur within the scope of the box, for '*Fx*' must occur within the scope of the quantifier that binds its free variable. Since '*Fx*' occurs within the scope of the box, which individuals are *F* at nonactual worlds is relevant to the truth value of the *de dicto* analysis. And that, we have seen, also misconstrues the plurally *de re* (□I), since it is only which individuals are *F* at the actual world that is relevant to its truth value. A correct analysis of (□I), it seems, must have the predicate '*Fx*' governed by the existential quantifier, but not governed by the box that governs the existential quantifier. No sentence of standard quantified modal logic can do that.[16]

In what follows, I will consider three basic strategies for extending quantified modal logic so as to provide formalizations for (◇A) and (□I). The first strategy focuses upon the fact that only the actual *F*s, not the otherworldly *F*s, are relevant to the truth value of (◇A) and (□I). According to this strategy, the analyses need to have an *actuality operator* prefixed to the predicate '*Fx*' in order to ensure that only the individuals that are actually *F* will be considered, even when '*Fx*' occurs within the scope of a modal operator. As a first step, then, let us add to the two modal operators of standard quantified modal logic an actuality operator, 'A', to be interpreted as follows ('φ' stands for a formula of the object language that may or may not contain free variables; *f* is an assignment of individuals, actual or possible, to the variables of the object language):

'Aφ' is true at world *w* on assignment *f* if and only if 'φ' is true at the actual world on assignment *f*.[17]

With the actuality operator at hand, (□I) can be formalized by:

(24) □(∃x)(A*Fx* & *Gx*).

It is instructive to compare the truth conditions of (24) with the truth conditions of the failed *de dicto* analysis

(25) □(∃x)(*Fx* & *Gx*).

(25) is true just in case, at all worlds *w*, there exists an individual at *w* that is *F at w* and *G* at *w*; (24) is true just in case, at all worlds *w*, there exists an individual at *w* that is *F at the actual world* and *G* at *w*. (24) can accomplish what (25) could not because the actuality operator provides the means by which the predicate '*Fx*' can be syntactically within the scope of a modal operator, but semantically unaffected by its presence.

Simply prefixing the actuality operator to the predicate '*Fx*', however, cannot be trusted by itself to give a correct analysis of sentences of the form (◇A) or (□I) unless one makes the implausible assumption that the same individuals exist at every possible world. Let us first consider the problem with respect to (◇A) 'Every *F* might be *G*', whose translation using the actuality operator alone would be:

(26) ◇(x)(A*Fx* → *Gx*).

Suppose that (◊A) is false, that is, that there is no possible world at which all the actual Fs are G.[18] (26) might nonetheless be true. For suppose further that at some world one of the actual Fs is not G because it fails to exist at the world, although all the other actual Fs exist and are G at the world. At this world, all the individuals that exist *at the world* and that are F at the actual world are G. So (26) is true, and (26) does not adequately translate (◊A).

The problem with (26) is easily diagnosed. The predicate '*Fx*' has been freed from the tyranny of the diamond, but the universal quantifier remains enslaved. On the standard interpretation of the quantifiers — the *inner* interpretation — the quantifier in (26) ranges only over the individuals that exist at the world at which the quantification is being evaluated. If one of the actual Fs does not exist at this world, then the quantifier will not range widely enough to capture the sense of (◊A). This suggests that we try adding to the inner quantifiers of standard quantified modal logic *outer* quantifiers: quantifiers that range over the entire universe of *possibilia*. Using '<x>' and '<∃x>' for the outer quantifiers, (◊A) can be translated by:

(27) ◊<x>(AFx → Gx).

For the case considered above, (27), unlike (26), will be false as required: the subformula '<x>(AFx → Gx)' is false at a world at which an actual F fails to be G by failing to exist at the world.[19]

But if inner quantifiers sometimes fail to range widely enough, outer quantifiers sometimes have the opposite defect of ranging too widely. To see this, consider the translation of (□I) that results from the joint use of the outer quantifier and the actuality operator:

(28) □<∃x>(AFx & Gx).

(28) need not correctly capture (□I) in cases where other worlds contain individuals that do not exist at the actual world. Thus, suppose that (□I) is false, that is, that there are worlds at which none of the actual Fs are G. (28) might nonetheless be true. For suppose further that at every such world there exists a G that is F at the actual world without existing at the actual world. ('F' might be a compound, negative general term, such as 'person not in the room'.) Such individuals are irrelevant to the truth value of (□I); but since they lie within the range of the quantifier in (28), they satisfy the subformula 'AFx & Gx', and so make (28) true. In an extreme case, (28) could be true even though there were no Fs existing at the actual world. But surely (□I), as it would ordinarily be understood, has existential import and implies the sentence '(∃x)Fx'. It follows that (28) does not provide a correct analysis of (□I).

If the first strategy is to succeed, then, it needs to introduce, not outer quantifiers, but rather what might be called *actuality* quantifiers: quantifiers that range over all and only the individuals that exist at the actual world even when occurring within the scope of a modal operator.[20] Using '[∃x]' and '[x]' as the actuality quantifiers, the first strategy provides as the final translations for (◊A) and (□I):

QUANTIFIED MODAL LOGIC AND THE PLURAL *DE RE*   381

(29) ◇[x](A*Fx* → *Gx*).

(30) □[∃x](A*Fx* & *Gx*).

The problems associated with earlier attempts to translate (◇A) and (□I) no longer arise; in particular, (30) has existential import like (□I) and unlike (28). Moreover, (29) and (30), like (◇A) and (□I), are not equivalent to either of the standard *de dicto* or *de re* sentences that can be formulated in standard quantified modal logic: the additional apparatus plays an essential role.

This strategy for handling the denoting phrases 'every *F*' and 'some *F*' can be generalized in a natural way beyond (◇A) and (□I). Consider any sentence having one of the forms:

(31) *O*(every *F* is *G*).

(32) *O*(some *F* is *G*).

where '*O*' stands for a simple or compound modal propositional operator. For each such sentence, the strategy posits an ambiguity in the denoting phrase 'every *F*' or 'some *F*'. On one reading, the denoting phrase is contextually analyzed by way of an ordinary inner quantifier; on the other reading, by way of an actuality quantifier with an actuality operator. Note, for comparison, that the strategy posits a similar ambiguity in the denoting phrase 'the *F*'. Thus (33) can be analyzed (using Russell's theory) as either (34) or (35):

(33) *O*(the *F* is *G*).

(34) *O*(∃x)((y)(*Fy* ↔ x=y) & *Gx*).

(35) *O*[∃x]([y](A*Fy* ↔ x=y) & *Gx*).

When analyzed as (35), the denoting phrase 'the *F*' functions as if it had Kaplan's dthat-operator prefixed to it, at least in cases where there is one and only one *F*. Indeed, the ambiguity here posited for 'every *F*' and 'some *F*' can be seen as a natural generalization of the purported ambiguity in 'the *F*' captured by 'dthat the *F*'.[21]

On the strategy being considered, one would expect an ambiguity to be present even in the simple categorical sentences 'Every *F* is *G*' and 'Some *F* is *G*', that is, even in the case where the operator '*O*' in (31) and (32) has been dropped. For, in this case, the two readings of (31) may diverge in truth value at other possible worlds, as may the two readings of (32); and on most accounts, this is sufficient for divergence in meaning. But since the readings cannot diverge in truth value at the actual world, it is difficult to find evidence for or against the presence of an ambiguity in English. Both readings have, in effect, been put forward. The possible-worlds literature standardly uses inner quantifiers to give the truth conditions of simple categorical sentences. But writers of logic texts over the years have frequently opted, perhaps unwittingly, for an actuality interpretation of the quantifiers. Whenever it is said that 'Every *F* is *G*' is equivalent in meaning to a (perhaps infinitary) conjunction and that

'Some *F* is *G*' is equivalent to a (perhaps infinitary) disjunction, and that in a (finite) universe in which all individuals had names, the quantifiers would be dispensable (except as a convenient abbreviation), the actuality interpretation is tacitly being endorsed.[22] That the strategy being considered allows for a possible ambiguity in simple categorical sentences counts, if anything, in its favor.

But when one turns to cases involving iterated modality, the strategy being considered is inadequate to the task at hand. For example, consider the sentence that results from prefixing a possibility operator to (17):

(36) It might have been the case that some person in the room had to win.

Interpret (36) as asserting that the plurally *de re* (17) might have been true. Suppose again that Tom, Dick, and Harry were actually in the room. Suppose further that Heckle and Jeckle have entered the drawing, that the lottery might have been rigged so as to ensure that either Heckle or Jeckle win a prize by removing all tickets belonging to entrants other than Heckle or Jeckle, and that this is the only way the drawing might have been rigged. Finally, suppose that Heckle and Jeckle might have been in the room instead of Tom, Dick, and Harry, but that being in the room has nothing to do with whether or not the drawing is rigged. (36) is true in the situation just described, but all of the available translations of (36) are false, and so fail to capture the intended interpretation. Let me quickly run through the options. Suppose first that (36) is taken to be of the form (32) with '*O*' standing in for '$\Diamond\Box$'.[23] Then there are two translations available:

(37) $\Diamond\Box(\exists x)(Rx \,\&\, Wx)$.

(38) $\Diamond\Box[\exists x](\mathbf{A}Rx \,\&\, Wx)$.

According to (37), it might have been the case that the drawing was rigged so as to guarantee that a room-dweller win a prize. By assumption, this is false, since the only way the drawing might have been rigged was so as to guarantee that either Heckle or Jeckle win; and guaranteeing that either Heckle or Jeckle win does not guarantee that a room-dweller win because Heckle and Jeckle might not have been in the room. According to (38), it might have been the case that the drawing was rigged so as to guarantee that Tom, Dick, or Harry win a prize, which, by assumption, is false. Nor can the reading under which (36) is true be captured by giving the existential quantifier wide or intermediate scope. Varying the scope of the actuality quantifier in (38) has no effect upon truth conditions. Varying the scope of the quantifier in (37) results in the following two readings:

(39) $(\exists x)(Rx \,\&\, \Diamond\Box Wx)$.

(40) $\Diamond(\exists x)(Rx \,\&\, \Box Wx)$.

QUANTIFIED MODAL LOGIC AND THE PLURAL *DE RE* 383

Neither (39) nor (40) captures the sense in which (36) involves the plural *de re*. The wide scope reading, (39), asserts that either Tom, Dick, or Harry is such that the drawing might have been rigged so as to guarantee that he win. The intermediate scope reading, (40), asserts that there might have been some person in the room such that the drawing was rigged so as to guarantee that that person win. Both of these are false because, by assumption, it was not possible to rig the drawing so as to guarantee that any one person win, only that of two people, one of them win. In sum, (36) is true when interpreted as saying that the plurally *de re* proposition (17) might have been the case; but no sentence of quantified modal logic, even when enhanced with actuality quantifiers and an actuality operator, can capture that interpretation.

It should now be clear why the first strategy cannot handle sentences involving iterated modality. In evaluating the truth value of a sentence like (36) there is a double shift away from the actual world, one shift for each modal operator. We have seen that if a translation of (36) is to capture the sense in which it involves the plural *de re*, the existential quantifier—and so the predicate 'Rx'—must be within the scope of the box. In standard quantified modal logic, if the predicate 'Rx' is within the scope of the box (as in (37)), then the people in the room *at doubly shifted worlds* will be relevant to the evaluation of truth value. In the extended modal logic with actuality quantifiers and an actuality operator, it is possible to have the predicate 'Rx' within the box (as in (38)) and yet to have the people in the room *at the actual world* be relevant to the evaluation of truth value. But since the actuality apparatus always takes us all the way back to the actual world, we still lack the means to construct a sentence of quantified modal logic that would make the people in the room *at singly shifted worlds* relevant to the evaluation of truth value, and so we are unable to provide a translation for the reading of (36) on which it is true. The first strategy fails to provide a general solution to the problem of analyzing the use of denoting phrases to express the plural *de re*; for a general solution must be able to handle not only simple examples of the plural *de re* such as ($\Diamond$A) and ($\Box$I), but also an example such as (36) in which the plural *de re* is embedded within a modal context.

V

We need a fresh diagnosis of the failure of standard quantified modal logic to capture the plural *de re*, one that will generalize to cases involving iterated modality. Consider again the denoting phrase 'some F' or 'every F' as it occurs within a (perhaps iterated) modal context. As we have seen, there are often two sorts of ambiguity associated with the denoting phrase, only one of which can be analyzed in terms of quantifier scope. The second sort of ambiguity was analyzed in the previous section as, in effect, a rigid/nonrigid ambiguity: when interpreted rigidly, the denoting phrase serves to pick out the actual Fs, and rigidly refers to them at all worlds throughout the process of evaluation; when interpreted nonrigidly, the denoting phrase refers to whatever is *F* at the world at which the evaluation is taking place. Positing a two-way, rigid/nonrigid ambiguity, however, could not handle the multiple ambiguity associated with assertions of iterated modality. On the strategy now to be considered, the second sort of ambiguity involves, like the first, an ambiguity in scope: the scope of the general term '*F*'. To illustrate what is meant by the "scope" of the general term, return once more to (36). We have seen that (36) has three distinct readings depending upon whether the people in the room at the actual world, at singly shifted worlds, or at doubly shifted worlds are relevant to the evaluation of truth value. For these three readings, I say that the term 'person in the room' has, respectively, wide scope, intermediate scope, or narrow scope. Normally, the way to give the term 'person in the room' the appropriate scope is to place the predicate '*Rx*', respectively, outside the diamond, between the diamond and the box, or within the box. But in standard quantified modal logic, the appropriate placement cannot always be had because the predicate '*Rx*' cannot take wider scope than the quantifier that binds its variable. Thus, on the new diagnosis, the crucial limitation of standard quantified modal logic is that it does not provide the means by which the scope of a predicate can vary independently of the scope of the quantifier that governs it.

How might standard quantified modal logic be extended so as to provide for such independence? As a first method, we might try introducing two new operators, ↓ and ↑, which can be used in tandem to give a selected predicate any available scope.[24] If the predicate is governed by the ↓-operator, it need not have narrow scope, but may instead have whatever scope is indicated by the placement of the ↑-operator. To illustrate, consider again (36). Standard quantified modal logic was constrained to give the predicate '*Rx*' narrow scope if the quantifier was given narrow scope, resulting in the mistranslation:

(37) $\Diamond\Box(\exists x)(Rx \ \& \ Wx)$.

Our two new operators allow the predicate '*Rx*' to be syntactically within the scope of the box, although semantically tied to the diamond:

(41) $\Diamond\uparrow\Box(\exists x)(\downarrow Rx \ \& \ Wx)$.

By placing a '↓' in front of '*Rx*' and a '↑' after the '◇', the predicate '*Rx*' is given intermediate scope, thus making the people in the room at singly shifted worlds relevant, as desired.

However, (41) fails as a translation of (36) because the quantifier wrongly ranges over the individuals inhabiting doubly shifted worlds. On a correct translation of (36), the *domain* of the quantifier has intermediate, not narrow, scope. This suggests relocating the '↓' as follows:

(42) $\Diamond\uparrow\Box\downarrow(\exists x)(Rx \ \& \ Wx)$.

Out of the frying pan and into the fire! In (42), the predicate '*Wx*' is wrongly given intermediate, instead of narrow, scope. Using the operators ↓ and ↑ by themselves cannot succeed in capturing the sense of (36).[25]

QUANTIFIED MODAL LOGIC AND THE PLURAL *DE RE* 385

Even supposing that the problem of assigning scope to quantifier domains could be separately solved (for example, by partial use of the method of indexing introduced below), there is a more general objection. The ↓- and ↑-operators provide some freedom in representing the scope of predicates, but not enough. Although any given predicate can be assigned any available scope, it is not the case that any two or more given predicates can independently be assigned any available combination of scopes. Suppose we have a sentence with n predicates, each of which has m available scopes. Then there are m^n possible assignments of scope, each of which may correspond to a distinct proposition with distinct truth conditions. But only a fraction of these propositions can be expressed using the ↓- and ↑-operators. Thus, countless sentences will have readings involving the plural *de re* that cannot be formalized within the extension of quantified modal logic that adds only the operators ↓ and ↑.[26]

We need to extend quantified modal logic in a way that provides for complete independence in the assignment of scope to predicates (and quantifier domains). This suggests a second method, what I call the method of indexing. We can index predicates *directly* to modal operators to indicate the desired scope. Let us use the letters 'w' and 'v' (with or without subscripts) as indices, placing them as superscripts after an operator and as subscripts after a predicate. Then, the predicate 'Rx' in (37) can be given intermediate scope as follows:

(43) $\Diamond^w \Box (\exists x) R_w x \ \& \ Wx)$.

To capture the sense of (36), however, we must index the quantifier '$(\exists x)$' to the diamond as well so that it will appropriately range over the individuals inhabiting singly shifted worlds:

(44) $\Diamond^w \Box (\exists x)_w (R_w x \ \& \ Wx)$.

In (44), although the quantifier has narrow scope, the *domain* of the quantifier has intermediate scope. This notion of scope can be applied not only to predicates and quantifier domains, but also to modal operators: the box in (44) has a suppressed index binding it to the diamond, since we are interested in who wins at worlds *accessible to singly shifted worlds*, not at worlds accessible to the actual world—and these may differ if the logic is not S5. In general, predicates, quantifier domains, and modal operators that are to have the narrowest possible scope can be seen as being indexed to the operator immediately governing them, but with their indices suppressed. Restoring the suppressed indices in (44) gives:

(45) $\Diamond^w \Box_w^v (\exists x)_w (R_w x \ \& \ W_v x)$.

Finally, for the case where a predicate, quantifier domain, or modal operator is to be given wide scope, the symbol '@' for the actual world can be used as the index. Thus, (45) is equivalent to:

(46) $\Diamond_@^w \Box_w^v (\exists x)_w (R_w x \ \& \ W_v x)$.

Applying the method of indexing to the plurally *de re* readings of ($\Diamond$A) and ($\Box$I), we have, with all suppressed indices restored, respectively:

(47) $\Diamond_@^w (x)_@ (F_@ x \rightarrow G_w x)$.

(48) $\Diamond_@^w (\exists x)_@ (F_@ x \ \& \ G_w x)$.

The method of indexing, it is clear, provides the resources to formalize the plurally *de re* readings of modal sentences, even those involving multiply iterated modality.[28]

The method of indexing is powerful. But if the goal is to formalize English modal discourse within the framework of quantified modal logic, then the method is a cheat. The "indices" are nothing but variables ranging over possible worlds; the "indexed" modal operators are full variable-binding operators — namely (variably) restricted quantifiers over possible worlds. To see this, note that sentences (46) through (48) can be transformed into sentences of first-order world theory by making the following notational substitutions (where vRw iff v is accessible from w, and xIw iff x exists at w):

'Fwx'	for	'$F_w x$'
'$(v)(vRw \rightarrow \_\_\_)$'	for	'$\Box_w^v \_\_\_$'
'$(\exists v)(vRw \ \& \ \_\_\_)$'	for	'$\Diamond_w^v \_\_\_$'
'$(x)(xIw \rightarrow \_\_\_)$'	for	'$(x)_w \_\_\_$'
'$(\exists x)(xIw \ \& \ \_\_\_)$'	for	'$(\exists x)_w \_\_\_$'

Applying these substitutions to (47) and (48) results in the following formalizations of ($\Diamond$A) and ($\Box$I) within first-order world theory:

(49) $(\exists w)(wR@ \ \& \ (x)(xI@ \rightarrow (F@x \rightarrow Gwx)))$.

(50) $(w)(wR@ \rightarrow (\exists x)(xI@ \ \& \ (F@x \rightarrow Gwx)))$.

The method of indexing is a notationally deviant way of formalizing modal sentences within first-order world theory. As such, it does nothing to help accomplish the present goal, explicated in section I, of formalizing modal sentences within the framework of quantified modal logic.[29]

VI

Let us turn, then, to a third strategy for formalizing modal examples of the plural *de re*. As seen above, we need to extend quantified modal logic so as to allow the scope of a predicate to vary independently of the scope of the quantifier that governs it. In the previous section, we considered extensions to quantified modal logic that represented the scope of a predicate not, as is customary, by its syntactic placement, but by means of exotic modal opera-

QUANTIFIED MODAL LOGIC AND THE PLURAL *DE RE*

tors. In this section, I consider the other tack: representing the scope of a predicate by syntactic relocation. Thus, consider the plurally *de re* ($\Diamond$A). It can be paraphrased in a way that locates the general term 'F' outside the scope of the modal operator: The Fs are such that, possibly, all of them are G. But translation of this paraphrase into quantified modal logic is blocked because there is no way to capture the pronoun 'them' as it refers back plurally to the Fs. This suggests that the deficiency in standard quantified modal logic resides no in its modal apparatus, but in its apparatus for expressing plurality.

One solution, familiar from other contexts, is to systematically replace plural reference by singular reference to sets. That will turn, for example, the above paraphrase of ($\Diamond$A) into: The set of Fs is such that, possibly, all of its members are G. And this can straightforwardly be formalized if we add to standard quantified modal logic first-order quantifiers ranging over sets. Before turning to particular formalizations, however, we need to say how modal sentences with quantifiers over sets are to be interpreted. The interpretation of such sentences will depend upon our choice of modal set theory, that is, upon decisions about the modal properties of sets.[30] Different decisions are possible, but the most natural, I think, are these:

(A1) *Contingency of set existence.* A set exists at a world if and only if all of its members exist at the world.

(A2) *Necessity of set membership.* If an entity is a member of a set at some world, then it is a member of that set at every world — including worlds at which either the entity or the set does not exist.

(A3) *Transworld criterion of identity.* A set existing at one world is identical with a set existing at another world if and only if they have the same members.

We are now in a position to provide translations of the plurally *de re* readings of ($\Diamond$A) and ($\Box$I). Suppose we add to quantified modal logic first-order variables 's' and 't' (with or without subscripts) ranging over sets. Consider the following translation of ($\Diamond$A):

(51) $(\exists s)((y)(y \epsilon s \leftrightarrow Fy) \,\&\, \Diamond{<}x{>}(x\epsilon s \rightarrow Gx))$.

It is clear that (51) is *de re*, although the *res* in question is a set rather than an individual: it asserts of the *set* of Fs that all of its members might be G. It is perhaps not surprising that one way to express the plural *de re* is to make assertions that are *de re* sets. Note that (51) contains an outer quantifier '$<x>$' for reasons similar to those given in discussing (26) above; for if there is a world at which some actual Fs fail to exist and the rest of the actual Fs are G, then the version of (51) with an inner quantifier comes out true, although ($\Diamond$A) as intended may be false.[31]

Applying the same technique to ($\Box$I) results in the translation

(52) $(\exists s)((y)(y \epsilon s \leftrightarrow Fy) \,\&\, \Box{<}\exists x{>}(x\epsilon s \,\&\, Gx))$.

(52) asserts of the set of Fs that at least one of its members must be G. Note that there is no danger in (52), as there was with (28), that the outer quantifier will range too widely: the use of an inner quantifier '(y)' together with the restriction on the outer quantifier given by '$x\epsilon s$' ensure that only the actual Fs will be relevant to the evaluation of truth value. Note further that (52) has existential import as required. Finally, note that the assertion that ($\Diamond A$) or ($\Box I$) is possible or necessary, such as the once problematic (36), can be translated, as would be expected, simply by prefixing a diamond or a box to (51) or (52).

Can the addition of quantifiers over sets (together with outer quantifiers) match the expressive power of the method of indexing without introducing the equivalent of variable-binding operators ranging over possible worlds? Indexed predicates can always be eliminated using quantified set variables in accordance with the following schema (where 'O' is '$\Box$' or '$\Diamond$' or absent if the index is '@'):

$$O^w(...F_w x...) = O^w(<\exists s>(<y>(y\epsilon s \leftrightarrow Fy) \& (...x\epsilon s ...))).$$

(Note that outer quantifiers are needed for the general case to ensure that the set picked out contains all the possible individuals that are F at the world in question, whether or not they exist at the world.) Indexed inner quantifiers can always be replaced by outer quantifiers restricted by an indexed existence predicate; and then the indexed existence predicate can be eliminated as above. This results in the following schema for replacing the indexed universal quantifier:

$$O^w(...(x)_w(\underline{})...) =$$
$$O^w(<\exists s>(<y>(y\epsilon s \leftrightarrow Ey) \& (...<x>(x\epsilon s \rightarrow (\underline{})) ...))),$$

and similarly for the indexed existential quantifier. (The existence predicate, 'Ey', is definable by '$(\exists x)x=y$'.) Superscripts may be dropped from modal operators as soon as all subscripts have been dropped to which they were previously tied. Applying the above schemata to (47) and (48) results in sentences longer than, but logically equivalent to, (51) and (52). If the underlying modal logic is S5, then sentences with subscripted modal operators are equivalent to their unsubscripted counterparts interpreted as having their subscripts suppressed; so subscripts on modal operators can simply be dropped. But if the underlying logic is not S5, subscripts on modal operators cannot always be eliminated. For example, quantification over sets can do nothing to help formalize 'Necessarily, something exists that might not have existed' when it is given the following reading using indexed operators: $\Box_@^w(\exists x)_w \Diamond_@^v \sim E_v x$. Thus, the addition of quantifiers over sets cannot quite match the power of indexing—that is, of full quantification over possible worlds. But the cases in which it falls short have nothing to do with the plural *de re*.

The use of sets to formalize the plural *de re* is on the right track, I think; but a serious problem remains. There are sentences of the form ($\Diamond A$) and

QUANTIFIED MODAL LOGIC AND THE PLURAL *DE RE* 389

(□I) for which the formalizations given above, (51) and (52), fail even to get the truth value right. Whenever there are "too many" *F*s for them to form a set, (51) and (52) come out false; but the corresponding English sentences might well be true. For example, consider the plurally *de re* reading of

(53) Every impure set might fail to exist,

where a set is impure if one of its members, or its member's members, . . . , is not a set. Assuming that there is a world at which all the actually existing nonsets fail to exist, (53) is true. But the formalization of (53) given by (51) is false, since there exists no set whose members are all and only the impure sets. In general, quantified modal logic with quantifiers over sets cannot be trusted to translate a plurally *de re* sentence containing the general term '*F*' unless the *F*s form a set at every world.[32]

Although (51) and (52) give the wrong truth value only in the special case where there is no set of *F*s, this failure is symptomatic, I think, of a more general problem. Even when the *F*s do form a set, the plurally *de re* (◇A) and (□I) make no reference to this set. For it is clear that (53), which is of the form (◇A), makes no reference to a set of all impure sets. Assuming that all plurally *de re* sentences of the form (◇A) are to be translated alike, it follows that no translation of (◇A) should make reference to a set of *F*s, whether or not such a set exists. We need a means for referring plurally to the *F*s that makes no mention of the set of *F*s.

To find such a means, we need look no further than our native language: English. Return to the paraphrase of (◇A) given above by: The *F*s are such that, possibly, all of them are *G*. This in turn can be paraphrased: There are some things such that each of them is *F* and each *F* is one of them and, possibly, all of them are *G*. English already contains just the device we need for referring plurally to the *F*s without mentioning the set of *F*s: the *plural quantifier* 'there are some things such that . . . they (them) . . . '.[33] I thus propose that we add the plural quantifier to quantified modal logic, and use plural quantification instead of quantification over sets to formalize the plural *de re*. If the plural quantifier is represented by means of a second-order existential quantifier, '(∃X)', then (◇A) and (□I) can be formalized, respectively, by:

(54) (∃X)((y)(Xy ↔ Fy) & ◇<x>(Xx → Gx)).

(55) (∃X)((y)(Xy ↔ Fy) & □<∃x> (Xx & Gx)).[34]

(More generally, in the translation schema above, '<∃s>' can be replaced throughout by '<∃X>', and '*x*ϵ*s*' by '*Xx*'.) It is important to realize that the quantifier '(∃X)' in (54) and (55) ranges neither over sets, nor classes, nor properties; it ranges in an irreducibly plural way over the *F*s themselves. Truth conditions for sentences of quantified modal logic with plural quantifiers can be given within a metalanguage that itself partakes of plural quantifiers; and that is enough, since plural quantification, being part of English, is antecedently understood.[35] To demand that such truth conditions be given without using plural quantifiers is no more legitimate here than it would be to demand that truth conditions for individual quantifiers be given without using individual quantifiers, or that truth conditions for propositional connectives be given without using propositional connectives.

When plural quantifiers are used to formalize the plural *de re*, the problem associated with quantifiers over sets no longer arise. If every general term 'F' of an English sentence is such that the Fs form a set at every world, then the formalization using plural quantifiers will have the same truth value at every world as the corresponding formalization using quantifiers over sets. In particular, (51) and (54) agree in truth value if there is a set of Fs; as do (52) and (55). So plural quantifiers do at least as well as quantifiers over sets in capturing the truth conditions of plurally *de re* English sentences. If anything, plural quantifiers are to be preferred even in this case because they avoid the irrelevant reference to sets. In cases such as (53) where the Fs fail to form a set, only plural quantifiers succeed in capturing the truth conditions. I thus conclude that quantified modal logic with plural quantifiers provides the best solution to the problem of formalizing the plural *de re* within the framework of quantified modal logic.

VII

I turn in conclusion to the metaphysical implications of the foregoing, or the lack of them. I have argued that denoting phrases in modal sentences sometimes require a plurally *de re* interpretation that eludes standard quantified modal logic, but that such sentences can be formalized within the framework of quantified modal logic if plural quantifiers are permitted. Thus, the full power of quantification over possible worlds, or its equivalent, is not needed to capture the plural *de re*. Does it follow that plurally *de re* sentences such as (◇A) and (□I) do not involve an ontological commitment to possible worlds? I recommend caution in drawing metaphysical consequences from results in philosophical logic. For one thing, the translations of (◇A) and (□I) contain outer quantifiers, and it is hard to see what ontological gain can be had from trading quantifiers over possible worlds for quantifiers over *possibilia*.[36] But there is a more central concern. On what grounds is it claimed that sentences formalizable within quantified modal logic are free of ontological commitment to possible worlds? Quinean criteria of ontological commitment that look to the values of the variables can only be applied to sentences couched within first-order predicate logic, lest variables be hidden within nonstandard operators. All satisfactory translations of modal sentences into first-order logic contain variables ostensibly taking possible worlds as values. Granted, the translations do not require full quantification over worlds, but only the limited sort of quantification that results from placing certain syntactical constraints on variable binding. These constraints are interesting, I think, from a logical point of view. But I fail to see why they should carry any ontological significance. Indeed, modal operators in S5 correspond to quantifiers that are permitted to use only a single world variable; surely, the use of one world variable carries the same ontological weight as the use of denumerably many. Thus, on Quinean criteria, quantified modal logic has the same *prima facie* commitment to worlds as first-order world theory. This is not an argument for realism about possible worlds, but an attempt to shift the ontological dispute out of philosophical logic and into the metaphysical arena. The appropriate question is: What is a world? And, in particular: Can worlds be constructed out of entities acceptable to the nonrealist? Formalizing English within quantified modal logic will not shed much light on these questions.

Notes

1. I use 'F' and 'G' as schematic letters replaceable by simple or compound English general terms; single quotes should be read as quasi-quotes, where appropriate. I use 'denoting phrase' without prejudice towards any theory as to how, or whether, such phrases denote.
2. For definiteness, by 'standard quantified modal logic' I will mean the language and semantical treatment in Saul Kripke's "Semantical Considerations on Modal Logic," reprinted in *Reference and Modality* edited by Leonard Linsky (Oxford, 1971), 63–73. I assume that quantifiers range only over individuals (concrete or abstract), not over sets.
3. Of course, one generally requires also that $T(S)$ in some sense capture the logical form of S; but it will not be necessary to appeal to such a requirement in what follows.
4. For Russell's theory, see his *Introduction to Mathematical Philosophy* (London, 1919), 167–80. Russell speaks of primary and secondary occurrences of a description instead of wide and narrow scope, respectively. Russell's theory is applied to the modal case in Arthur Smullyan, "Modality and Description," *Journal of Symbolic Logic* 13 (1948): 31–37.
5. An alternative analysis takes (1) to involve a primitive description operator. See, for example, Jaakko Hintikka, "Semantics for Propositional Attitudes," reprinted in *Reference and Modality*, 145–67. Thomason and Stalnaker use a description operator and a device for forming complex predicates to analyze (1) in "Modality and Reference," *Noûs* 2 (1968): 359–72. All these methods agree in attributing the ambiguity in (1) to a distinction of scope.
6. There is a discussion of various nonmodal examples in Quine, *Word and Object* (Cambridge, Mass., 1960), 138–41. Thomason and Stalnaker explicitly apply the rule to a modal example in "Modality and Reference," 361.
7. On this extended (though now standard) use of *de re*, the individual or individuals to whom the modal property is attributed need not be individually named or described. This allows the classification of sentences as *de dicto* or *de re* to be exhaustive for standard quantified modal logic. For a precise explication of an exhaustive *de dicto/de re* distinction, both syntactic and model theoretic, see Kit Fine, "Model Theory for Modal Logic Part I: the *De Re/De Dicto* Distinction," *Journal of Philosophical Logic* 7 (1978): 125–56.
8. It should be noted, however, that sometimes the role of 'every' in 'every *F*' is to signal that the *F*s are to be taken collectively rather than distributively, and the main predicate interpreted accordingly. Thus, although the sentence 'I can say any English word is less than a minute' can be formalized by giving a universal quantifier wide scope, the sentence 'I can say every English word in less than a minute', on the reading that makes it false, cannot be formalized by giving a universal quantifier narrow scope because the predicate 'is said in less than a minute' is to be applied, not to individual

English words, but to English words taken altogether. In the examples discussed below, all predicates are to be taken distributively.

9. Russell distinguishes between 'some F' and 'an F', giving the former wide scope and the latter narrow scope. Perhaps English exhibits some tendency in this direction; but, in contrast to 'any F', each of these denoting phrases can take either scope. Russell's account is in *Principles of Mathematics* (New York, 1903), 58-60.

10. An exact analysis of the plural *de re* is beyond the scope of this paper. It requires the problematic—though, I think, genuine—distinction between qualitative and nonqualitative properties. Thus, even '$\Diamond Ga$' is plurally *de re* if 'Gx' is equivalent to the nonqualitative 'Fx & Fb'. The plural *de re* has been discussed in connection with counterpart theory in Allen Hazen, "Counterpart-Theoretic Semantics for Modal Logic," *Journal of Philosophy* 76 (1979): 319-38; and David Lewis, *On the Plurality of Worlds* (Oxford, 1986), 232-34. A full account requires the consideration of *ordered* pluralities, that is, *sequences* of individuals.

11. In standard quantified modal logic without names, the sentence '$(\exists x)(\exists y)(\exists z)(x \neq y\ \&\ y \neq z\ \&\ Rx\ \&\ Ry\ \&\ Rz\ \&\ \Diamond(Wx\ \&\ Wy\ \&\ Wz))$' has the same truth value as (12) for all contexts in which there are three people in the room; but, again, this does not provide an analysis of (12).

12. It should now be apparent why (5), unlike (12), does not possess a reading that cannot be captured by the standard *de dicto* and *de re* formulas. The property *being a number less than a hundred*, unlike the property *being in the room*, applies necessarily to whatever has it.

13. Note, in contrast, that for sentences of the form ($\Box$A) 'Every F must be G' and ($\Diamond$I) 'Some F might be G', the plurally *de re* reading is equivalent to the ordinary *de re* reading. This is due in essence to the distributivity of the box over conjunction and the diamond over disjunction.

14. Temporal examples of the plural *de re* were noticed by Hans Kamp and Frank Vlach; but neither provides an adequate general solution to the problem of formalization. On Vlach's solution, see n. 24 and n. 25 below.

15. Belief sentences such as (23) give rise to further ambiguities having to do with the issue of actual vs. imaginary objects of thought. For this reason, and others, I think it best to use modal (or temporal) examples to isolate the phenomenon here in question. But what I say about the modal case, it should be apparent, can be applied to the propositional attitude case as well.

16. That neither ($\Box$I) nor ($\Diamond$A) can be expressed by any sentence of standard quantified modal logic follows (for S5) from a result of Harold Hodes; see Theorem 13 of "Some Theorems on the Expressive Limitations of Modal Languages," *Journal of Philosophical Logic* 13 (1984): 13-26. A more general result can be derived from the proof of Theorem 6 in Hans Kamp, "Formal Properties of 'Now'," *Theoria* 37 (1971): 227-73.

17. Only sentences uttered at the actual world are here considered; otherwise 'the actual world' should be replaced by 'the world of the utterance' making the actuality operator overtly indexical like 'now'. An indexical actuality operator was introduced by David Lewis in "Anselm and Actuality," *Noûs* 4 (1970): 175-88; see also Allen Hazen, "Expressive Completeness in Modal Language," *Journal of Philosophical Logic* 5 (1976): 25-46. Kamp, "Formal Properties of 'Now'," uses the 'now'-operator to formalize a temporal example of the plural *de re*.

18. By 'the actual Fs', I mean the individuals that are F at the actual world *and* exist at the actual world. The second clause is not redundant: the Kripkean semantics here presupposed allows that an individual be F at the actual world without existing at the actual world (both for simple and complex 'F'). Taking the alternative approach, however, would affect what follows only in detail.

19. For other examples of the expressive power conferred by the joint use of outer quantifiers and an actuality operator, see Allen Hazen, "Expressive Completeness in Modal Language." The inner and outer quantifiers are often called *actualist* and *possibilist* quantifiers, respectively, but I prefer to reserve the term 'actualist' for the quantifiers to be introduced below.

20. Alternatively, an actuality *predicate* can be introduced, and the actuality quantifier defined as a restricted outer quantifier.

21. For the logic of 'dthat', see David Kaplan's "Dthat" and "The Logic of Demonstratives" in *Contemporary Perspectives in the Philosophy of Language* edited by Peter French et al. (Minneapolis, 1977), 383-400, 401-14.

22. For example, see W. V. Quine, *Methods of Logic*, 3d. ed. (Cambridge, Mass., 1972), 140. But note that Quine (and others) take 'Some F is G' to be equivalent to '(Fa & Ga) ∨ (Fb & Gb) ∨ ...' (where 'a', 'b',... are all the actual individuals), which is equivalent to using the actuality quantifier without prefixing the actuality operator to 'Fx'—a most implausible hybrid. To get the second reading above, 'Some F is G' should be taken to be equivalent to 'Ga ∨ Gb ∨ ...' (where 'a', 'b', ... are all the actual Fs).

23. For the case at hand, the diamond and the box may be tied to different accessibility relations. This should be made notationally evident, but I will not bother since it affects nothing that follows.

24. Frank Vlach used the ↓- and ↑-operators to formalize an example of the plural *de re* involving iterated tenses. A semantics for these operators can be given by the method of "double indexing," that is, by assigning truth values relative to ordered pairs of worlds rather than single worlds. See Frank Vlach, "'Now' and 'Then': A Formal Study in the Logic of Tense and Anaphora," doctoral dissertation (UCLA, 1973); and David Lewis, *Counterfactuals* (Oxford, 1973), 62-64.

25. Vlach focuses upon an example that involves an analog of (◇A) rather than (□I), and formalizes it by using ↓and ↑together with *outer* quantifiers. But as we saw in connection with (27) above, outer quantifiers range too widely to capture sentences like (36) that involve (□I).

26. If an example is wanted, consider "It might have been the case that someone in the room who lost had to win" uttered in the same circumstances as (36). (Assume also that Heckle and Jeckle actually lost.) For the reading on which this is true, the predicates 'person in the room', 'person who lost', and 'person who wins' are inside the '□' and have intermediate, wide, and narrow scope, respectively—a combination that cannot be had using only ↓and ↑.

27. If 'F' or 'G' is complex rather than atomic, then each atomic predicate, quantifier, and modal operator within 'F' or 'G' is to be appropriately subscripted.

28. The method of indexing used here is similar to that introduced in Christopher Peacocke, "Necessity and Truth Theories," *Journal of Philosophical Logic* 7 (1978): 473-500, but with the following difference: Peacocke introduces indexed operators, 'A_i', to tie the evaluation of predicates, quantifiers, and operators within their scope to a previous modal operator with index 'i'; I directly index atomic predicates, quantifiers, and operators to previous modal operators. The two methods are equivalent if nesting of the indexed operators 'A_i' is permitted (with precedence given to the innermost competing operator). Indexed operators (with nesting) are used extensively by Graeme Forbes in *The Metaphysics of Modality* (Oxford, 1985).

29. I here disagree with Forbes, when he denies that the indexed operators "are really nothing but devices for disguised quantification over worlds" on the grounds that "each successive step in introducing the operators was motivated by the production of an *English* sentence which required . . . the operator introduced at that step" *Metaphysics of Modality*, (93-94). But, first, Forbes has not shown that the English sentences he gives *require* the use of indexed operators; indeed, some of them can be

handled by the method to be introduced below. And, second, if some English sentences do require indexed operators, why not conclude, in light of the above equivalences, that some English sentences involve disguised quantification over worlds?

30. For developments of modal set theory, see Kit Fine, "First-Order Modal Theories] — Sets," *Noûs* 15 (1981): 177-205, and Graeme Forbes, *Metaphysics of Modality*, 96-131.

31. Michael Jubien suggested '$(\exists s)(y)(y \in s \leftrightarrow Fy)$ & $\Diamond((\exists t)t = s$ & $(x)(x \in s \rightarrow Gx))$' as a translation of $(\Diamond A)$. This avoids outer quantifiers and captures an intuition that worlds at which the set of actual Fs fails to exist are to be ignored. But such worlds cannot always be ignored, as is seen by considering the plurally *de re* sense of 'Everyone in the room might fail to exist'. I prefer to provide uniform translations for all sentences of the form $(\Diamond A)$, and to ignore worlds, when appropriate, by restricting the accessibility relation.

32. One might be tempted to replace quantifiers over sets with quantifiers over classes, thus allowing the initial quantifiers in (51) and (52) to range over proper classes as well as sets. But that would be a mistake. For one thing, embarrassing questions will arise when the Fs are themselves proper classes, and so do not even form a class. More importantly, proper classes are dubious entities, and I for one do not believe in them. Yet, clearly, I can believe that (53) is true without inconsistency.

33. George Boolos has championed the use of plural quantifiers in a series of recent articles. See especially "To Be Is To Be a Value of a Variable (or To Be Some Values of Some Variables)," *Journal of Philosophy* 81 (1984): 430-49.

34. In the case where there are no Fs, we want (54) and (55) to agree in truth value with (51) and (52); so in this case the second-order quantifier '$(\exists X)$' cannot be read as 'there are some things such that'. This minor mismatch between the formal language and English is no more problematic here, however, than it is with the individual quantifiers. An exact scheme for translating second-order sentences, such as (54) and (55), into English can be found in Boolos, "To Be is To Be a Value of a Variable."

35. Or so it seems to me. Critics maintain that plural quantifiers in English can only be understood if interpreted as ranging over sets (or classes, or collections of some sort). They will have to make do with the previous proposal that uses quantifiers over sets to formalize the plural *de re*. They will also have to explain away the intuition that (53) is true and has the same logical form as other plurally *de re* examples of $(\Diamond A)$. For a critical view of plural quantifiers, see Michael D. Resnick, "Second-order Logic Still Wild," *Journal of Philosophy* 85 (1988): 57-74.

36. Perhaps outer quantifiers can be defined in terms unobjectionable to the nonrealist. Conditions on the eliminability of the outer quantifier are given in Fine, "First-Order Modal Theories," 192-93.

A Vagueness Paradox and Its Solution[1]
FELICIA ACKERMAN

William Alston has said that

> It is characteristic of vague terms that there is no precise boundary between areas of clear application or nonapplication and areas of indeterminacy of application, any more than there are sharp boundaries between application and nonapplication. This is not surprising. It would be absurd to have the term 'city' sharpened to the point at which the area of indeterminacy of application is bounded precisely at, for example, 25,000 inhabitants and 40,000 inhabitants, without going farther and making a sharp boundary between application and nonapplication, that is, removing the area of indeterminacy altogether[2]

where a term is vague if and only if "there are cases in which there is no definite answer as to whether the term applies."[3] I will argue that this view leads to a paradox, and I will offer a solution. As the above quoted passage indicates, Alston holds that vague terms do have areas of clear application and nonapplication, as well as areas of indeterminacy. This contrasts with the view of Peter Unger[4] that such vague expressions are logically inconsistent and hence have no areas of application at all. The paradox that concerns me here arises within the framework of Alston's view that vague terms do have areas of application, and I will offer a solution that presupposes this framework without discussing Unger's views further in this paper.

The paradox goes as follows. Alston seems right in saying that vague terms have no precise boundary between areas of clear application or nonapplication, on the one hand, and areas of indeterminacy of application, on the other. This can be seen most easily by considering cases of degree vagueness where small increments in the degree of the quality in question can be easily imagined for hypothetical cases, such as with the terms 'middle-aged' or 'tall'.

Just as it seems impossible in fact to specify a precise boundary between being clearly middle-aged and being clearly not middle-aged, it seems in fact equally impossible to specify a precise boundary between being clearly middle-aged and being in the indeterminate area for middle-agedness. The paradox is that an argument can be given to show that there *must* be a precise boundary between being clearly middle-aged and being in the indeterminate area (and between being clearly non-middle-aged and being in the indeterminate area). This argument goes as follows. If there is the *slightest* unclarity about whether a given age falls within the category of "clearly middle-aged" or in the indeterminate area, then it follows that this age must fall in the indeterminate area, since unclarity about clarity is itself a form of unclarity. And in any given case, there will be a completely clear answer whether the slightest unclarity exists, because if it is not completely clear that there is complete clarity, it follows that there is not complete clarity. Thus, there must be a sharp cut-off point between areas of clear application (or clear nonapplication) and areas of indeterminate application. But if there is, what is it? No sharp cut-off point seems forthcoming as a plausible candidate, hence the paradox.

Now for some possible replies. First, it might be argued that I am conflating the metaphysical issue of whether there is a clear answer whether the term applies with the epistemic issue of whether the user has any doubts whether the term applies. But this reply would fail because the nature of vagueness is such that the meaning of a given vague term requires its indeterminacy of application in certain cases, so an epistemically full understanding of that term would require understanding that it is indeterminate. As Alston says, "It is not that we have not succeeded in finding the answer [to the question of whether a 41-year-old man is middle-aged]; there is no answer. This shows that the situation is due to an aspect of the meaning of the term, rather than to the current state of our knowledge."[5]

A more promising approach to the paradox is to look at what happens when we try out actual cases on people. I have done this with students in my philosophy of language course, by starting with an age (45) at which they agree that an American in the 1980s would be absolutely clearly middle-aged[6] (i.e., that the term 'middle-aged' would apply without the slightest unclarity) and working my way up or down by asking if the hypothetical person would still count as absolutely clearly middle-aged at 46½, 47, 48 . . . , 44½, 44 . . . etc. This exercise yields several interesting results.

First of all, while students agree unanimously over central cases, such as being middle-aged at 45, there is much less consensus over peripheral cases, such as being middle-aged at 37 or 58. Thus, it seems reasonable to say these students' concepts of middle-agedness differ somewhat at the boundaries while being centrally similar enough to allow for easy communication. Second, even if the responses of only one student are considered, the answers turn out to be unstable at what are taken to be the boundaries. For example, a student who, when the test cases begin with age 45, says Smith would be "absolutely clearly middle-aged" at 45 may keep on saying Smith would be absolutely clearly middle-aged until we get down to 39, and then start having doubts. But I have found that such a student will subsequently start having doubts about some of the supposedly "absolutely clear" steps he has already taken. Thus, a student who applies "absolutely clearly middle-aged" all the way down from 45 to 39 but not to 38 and 11 months virtually always reverses himself for a while when asked to retrace his steps; for example, he denies that he still thinks Smith would be "absolutely clearly middle-aged" at 39 after all. Does this mean such a student's boundary for "absolutely clearly middle-aged" has changed at t_2 when he reverses himself from what it was a few minutes previously at t_1 when he said being 39 made one absolutely clearly middle-aged? Probably not, since it seems reasonable to suppose that at the very moment t_1 when the student was calling 39-year-old Smith absolutely clearly middle-aged, the following counterfactual was true: *if* the student had been asked the questions he was in fact asked at and shortly before t_2, he would not have said the 39-year-old Smith was absolutely clearly middle-aged. The point is that answers given at the boundaries seem to depend partly on how the question is asked, e.g., on whether we start with 45 and work downward or start with 39 and work upward.

The solution to the paradox seems to be this. At any given moment of interrogation, there will be, as there must be, a sharp cut-off point between perfectly clear and indeterminate cases, since, as I have mentioned, any unclarity about clarity is itself a form of unclarity. But Alston's remarks quoted at the beginning of this paper reflect the insight that there is no *general and stable* sharp boundary between being clearly middle-aged and being in an area of indeterminate application. On my view, this is because the sharp cut-off answer that applies in a given case will vary not only with different members of a given linguistic community, not only with one person over time, but even with one person at a given time relative to how the question is phrased and what questions have immediately preceded it. Rather than saying one's concepts associated with such vague terms are in a continuing state of flux, however, it seems more reasonable and more parsimonious to say it is the nature of these vague concepts to be dependably such as to permit such flexibility.

Notes

1. This paper was completed while I was a fellow at the Center for Advanced Study in the Behavioral Sciences, as well as a fellow of the National Endowment for the Humanities. The support provided by the NEH (#FC-10060-85) and the Andrew W. Mellon Foundation is gratefully acknowledged. I also thank James Van Cleve for discussing the material in this paper with me.
2. William P. Alston, *Philosophy of Language* (Englewood Cliffs, N.J., 1964), 95.
3. Ibid., 84.
4. See Peter Unger, "Why There Are No People," *Midwest Studies in Philosophy* 4, (Minneapolis, Minn., 1979), 177–222.
5. Alston, *Philosophy of Language*, 85.

6. The qualification about time and place is necessary because 'middle-aged' has a relative quality. For example, in the times when the average life expectancy was 40 years, a 45-year-old person would not have counted as middle-aged. All discussion of middle-agedness in this paper should be taken as qualified this way.

Geometrical Semantics for Spatial Prepositions*
COLLEEN CRANGLE AND PATRICK SUPPES

Among the most frequently used words in English are simple prepositions alike *in* or *on* whose basic meaning is spatial in character. What we propose in this article is a classification of the kinds of geometry that underlie the basic meaning of various spatial prepositions. The distinctions among geometries underlying these prepositions has not, as far as we can tell, been previously noted in the literature of linguistics and philosophy. In fact, in spite of the spate of articles in the last decade or so on locative expressions, spatial prepositions, and the like, detailed attention to the kinds of geometry needed to give a semantic analysis of the various locative expressions does not seem to have been previously attempted.

For example, consider the work of Cresswell (1978) which gives an interesting analysis of points of view, meaning spatial points of view, that are implicit in understanding the meaning of such words as *come, go, left, right,* and *behind*, to use his initial list. Cresswell goes far beyond what we attempt here in that he gives a formal semantics in terms of the categorical semantics he has written about extensively. But while we do not formalize the semantics we outline, in contrast with Cresswell we distinguish between spatial prepositions requiring a point of view and those that do not and we place this distinction, along with others, in a geometrical framework. For example, if someone says *The book you want is to the left of the dictionary* we all immediately understand that a point of view is involved. On the other hand, we are just as firmly convinced, without argument, that in many uses of language we describe the world in terms of the relations between objects and possibly other phenomena, without any attention to an implicit point of view on the part of the speaker or writer. It would seem absurd in most contexts to say that the pencil is on the table from my point of view but not from yours. Thus the ordinary primitive or basic meaning of *on* is in terms of a geometry that does not assume a point of view. However, the preposition *on* assumes a physical orientation of verticality that is missing, for example, from three-dimensional Euclidean geometry. We can rightly claim that in many contexts the basic or primitive meaning of the preposition *in* does not assume any such orientation and can be given a perfectly reasonable account in terms of a weaker geometry, as when a child says *The penny is in the piggy bank*.

Still other kinds of geometrical considerations enter when processes or events are talked about. For example, when we talk about the location of processes it is appropriate to think of the underlying geometry as being four-dimensional space-time, as we shall illustrate later. Perhaps the most interesting point is that these different underlying geometries used to formulate the appropriate geometrical semantics for spatial prepositions reflect the different ways in which we talk about the world in a spatial sense.

We emphasize that in no sense do we think that purely geometrical analysis can provide a satisfactory account of the meaning of spatial prepositions. The uses are too many and varied and the ways in which language is used too flexible to sanction any simple geometrical account as being wholly adequate. There are at least three major reservations that need to be made. First of all, even prepositions that seem mainly spatial depend also on additional assumptions about the physical world. For example, in the use of the common preposition *on* there is a familiar notion of support that is physical rather than geometrical in character. In the next section we characterize *on* in purely geometrical terms but this does not mean we think that characterization is complete. We only mean to catch in the definition given the geometrical aspects of the meaning.

Second, even if we bring in commonsense physics, the context of use is an even more important aspect of meaning that prohibits any simple account of the semantics of the prepositions we consider. In other publications we have emphasized, from our standpoint, the importance of context in fixing the meaning of words, phrases, and sentences (Crangle and Suppes 1987). Everyone who has thought about these matters is aware of the importance of context, so that we shall not say more on this point until our later detailed discussion of several examples. The brevity of what we say here is not in any sense meant to decrease the essential and salient role of context in fixing the meaning of locative expressions.

Third, even the purely geometrical interpretation is not straightforward. The geometry of ordinary objects and of talk about these objects is not the pristine and precise geometry of Euclid and his mathematical successors. What we have to say in the next section builds upon Euclid but this is just because we do not have an adequate alternative foundation. There is in the use of spatial language an inherent vagueness intrinsic to the geometry itself that we will not characterize satisfactorily in a formal way. When someone says *The pencil is near the book* we are not able to define a precise geometrical semantics to *near* that will deliver the appropriate truth conditions. Even when we take in the context of objects, we will still be faced with difficulties in saying what the exact meaning is. This is just one of many different kinds of examples. It is important to emphasize this class of examples, however, because they show that even within the framework of purely geometrical considerations we cannot hope to achieve the kind of result familiar in the formal analysis of the semantics of geometrical theories in the standard mathematical sense.

These many different reservations do not mean we consider it impossible to make any distinctions. Our insistence on different types of geometry underlying the basic meaning of different spatial prepositions is evidence to the contrary. However, there is one general philosophical remark we would like to make about the situation. Everyone who writes about language in any detail rapidly becomes impressed with the bewildering complexity and subtlety of actual language use. What we want to emphasize is that this is not a peculiar characteristic of language but is characteristic of all natural phenomena. The simplest sorts of physical phenomena exhibit the same kind of bewildering complexity and subtlety. We think that our understanding of physics is better than our understanding of language, from the standpoint of systematic analysis, more because of the successful isolation over a long period of time of a few salient cases that are simple: two bodies in planetary motion, a free-falling body, the pendulum of a clock, and so forth. But if we just walk out and look at some physical phenomenon occurring as a breeze sweeps across a patch of dust and leaves, we are no more able to account for the details of the motion of the objects than we are of the kinds of linguistic examples we can as easily generate. Of course, physics is a more developed science than linguistics, and the philosophy of physics reflects this long development in comparison with the philosophy of language. On the other hand, we think that the similarities regarding problems of complexity are much more important than the differences. The case of language is not at all unique but is typical for the analysis of any natural phenomenon. We can no more give a really satisfactory foundational account of physical phenomena than we can of linguistic phenomena. What we hope to do in both cases is to be lucky enough to find some salient distinctions in ways of looking at the phenomena that advance our understanding a modest amount. It is this viewpoint that has characterized what we have tried to do in this article.

Current work on the spatial locatives is characterized in large part by the recognition that both geometrical and physical notions are needed for an analysis of the locatives, but without any detailed exposition of those notions being given. Bennett (1975), for instance, provides a componential analysis in which the components (or "semantic markers" as they are sometimes called) include the concepts of interior, surface, anterior (the space in front of something), and posterior (the space behind something). For example, the concept of interior is thought to be part of the meaning of the prepositions *in, into,* and *through* but not, say, *behind*. Perhaps precisely because Bennett's emphasis is the relationships holding between words, not the relationship, as he puts it, between words and the world, he provides no analysis of any of the geometrical notions that he uses. Components or concepts such as interior and surface function as unanalyzed wholes. These he uses along with notions such as source, path, and goal supplied by his framework of case grammars to explicate various semantic notions. In our view, this level of abstraction from geometrical details precludes adequate accounts of the locatives in English. Their meaning is too intricately tied up with geometrical and physical facts about the world. Bennett's own brief discussion of the following two sentences supports this view even though he fails to incorporate such facts in his analysis. Consider the sentences (a) *Judy fell over the cliff* and (b) *Judy fell over the curb*. The word *over* works differently in the two sentences. An informal paraphrase of the first is *Judy fell downwards from the edge of the cliff*, a reading that results because we take Judy to be considerably smaller than the cliff. A paraphrase of the second is *Judy fell as a result of a collision with the curb*, a reading that results because we take Judy to be somewhat larger than the curb. However, if 'Judy' names a giant in (a) and a creature the size of an ant in (b), the readings are reversed.

A more recent study of the prepositions in English is found in Herskovits (1986). Herskovits proposes various geometric idealizations, and adaptations of these idealizations, that are thought to underlie the many different uses of a preposition. Her work is worth particular mention here in that it acknowledges the extent to which context intrudes into the interpretation of a locative expression. However, like Bennett, Herskovits does not make explicit the various geometrical notions such as interior, outline, contiguous, and at-the-back that appear in her analysis. They are consequently left unanalyzed and as a result no unifying geometrical or computational framework is provided.

A work that must be mentioned in relation to ours is that of Talmy (1983). Talmy recognizes many of the basic geometrical distinctions we do but fails to organize these distinctions along their natural geometrical lines. Instead he proposes four "imaging systems" a speaker is thought to use in forming spatial expressions and he proposes various spatial schemata the expressions are thought to represent. These schemata are said to be built up from rudimentary spatial elements such as points, lines, and planes. We find ourselves in serious disagreement with Talmy's approach and trace this disagreement to the absence of a coherent geometrical framework in his work. This absence, we believe, is responsible for contradictions we note in his work. Talmy explicitly rejects the properties of metric spaces, claiming rather that a central role be assigned to qualitative or topological concepts in the analysis of spatial expressions. But his own careful discussion of specific prepositions is replete with references to properties such as length and breadth, and relations such as parallelism and longer than, all of which require at least an affine not merely a topological space. In addition, it is abundantly clear that we usually need a metric for any adequate analysis of spatial expressions. We will in fact show in this article that, far from eliminating Euclidean geometry as Talmy seems to suggest, a more productive strategy is to strengthen it in various ways. One of the ways in which it should be strengthened is with a theory of geometrical figures so that we do not always have to take as primitives points in space but can rather express basic spatial relations in terms of figures and their parts. This possibility seems to be what Talmy is driving at when he talks about abstracting from specifics such as the magnitude of points, lines, and planes and focusing rather on topological properties such as distinguishability of parts or "partiteness." Talmy's work, rich as it is in subtle examples, shows more clearly than any other the need for an organizing classification of the geometry that underlies spatial expressions. We make a start on this task in this article.

SOME RELEVANT GEOMETRIES

We have entitled our semantic analysis of spatial locatives *geometrical semantics* to emphasize that we use throughout in the set of models admitted strong geometrical assumptions that go beyond ordinary set-theoretical semantics. It is our conviction that in the use of language to describe events, actions, or situations in space and time the largest piece of unfinished business is the spelling out of the geometrical and physical assumptions that are implicit in the semantics of ordinary talk. There is an implicit mistaken view in much general semantic analysis by philosophers and linguists that it is adequate to give a purely set-theoretical framework that does not go beyond the axioms of general set theory. In our view, in contrast, the real task is to analyze the implicit assumptions of a spatial or temporal nature.

Much work must be done before a satisfactory theory of geometry and physics implicit in ordinary language is put in a satisfactory form. What we do in this article is modest in scope, but even with this limitation some geometrical distinctions that seem essential to distinguishing among spatial locatives can be made. Roughly speaking, the idea of our classification is to begin with affine geometry, to which the concept of parallel lines is central, but for which there is no concept of perpendicular lines or a natural metric, and then to strengthen it in various ways to give a satisfactory account of the implicit geometrical semantics behind the understood meaning of a particular spatial locative. In brief terms, some locatives can be given a reasonably satisfactory semantical underpinning just in terms of affine or Euclidean space. Others require that Euclidean geometry be strengthened to an oriented geometry with a preferred vertical direction. Notice that in most ordinary talk we have an agreed-upon direction of vertical up and down, but no preferred horizontal direction. The horizontal direction is fixed by the introduction of restricted projective geometry and the concept of a station point for a perspective point of view. We restrict the projective geometry to the projective geometry of the plane because most of the points of view in the use of spatial locatives can be so restricted. We also consider the geometry that is intrinsic to individual bodies in terms of an orientation. For example, an object may have at least one axis of symmetry, and also in terms of use a designated front and back, top and bottom, and so on. We end our proposed classification by considering some prepositions that are topologically invariant.

In our discussion of these geometrical distinctions and concepts, we will take an informal route but provide enough technical detail to make clear how a more formal development can be given. There is one aspect of the geometrical developments that is not really satisfactory. Just because of its familiar and well-developed character we have begun with the standard conception of geometry in terms of a basic set of points. It is clear that the geometry underlying ordinary language is intrinsically of a different character, being deeply intermixed with physics. The natural primitive elements are not points but physical objects, as well as fluids and gases. There is not a well-developed foundation in these terms and we are not able to begin where we would really like to. It is a matter for research not yet undertaken to provide a foundation of geometry more closely matching the use of concepts in ordinary language. (For review of the earlier literature, see Suppes 1972).

Affine geometry. We shall consider affine geometry as given by the usual primitives of a set A of points and the ternary relation B of betweenness between points. (This is actually ordered affine geometry.) For a recent development, see Suppes et al. (in press). We shall assume all the standard geometrical relations that can be developed that are familiar for affine geometry. As already noted, the key concept is that of two lines being parallel. A good example of a spatial locative for which a fairly good account can be given just in terms of affine geometry is the preposition *in*. Thus, for the analysis of the sentence *The pencil is in the box* where P is the set of points constituting the pencil and B the set of points constituting the box, one might give as a simple set-theoretical analysis that P is a subset of B. Of course this is a mistake because the box itself does not include the inside open space. We are especially thinking here, as an example, of a box without a top. On the other hand, the right geometrical notion is to take the convex closure of B, that is, the set of all points lying on any segment connecting any two points in B. Then, when we say that the pencil is in the box we can express this geometrically by saying that P is contained in the convex closure of B. Notice that orientation enters into our judgment of whether or not the pencil will stay in the box, as we move the box about, but no concept of orientation is needed for our judgment of whether or not the pencil is in the box.

We also note immediately that for many cases of usage some adjustment to this condition has to be made. Consider, for example, the sentence *The flowers are in the vase*. As ordinarily understood, the flowers are not in the convex closure of the vase but only the lower part of the stems of the flowers is in the convex closure of the vase. A similar example is *The bat is in his hand*. In a thorough and detailed analysis we would need to separate those cases of *in* which are covered in a straightforward way by the convex closure of the container from those that require more subtle constraints.

A second obvious example suitable for affine geometry is just the preposition *between*, based as it is on the primitive relation of betweenness. The sentence *Mary is sitting between José and Maria* does not imply exact linearity of seating arrangement, but would ordinarily be assumed to be approximately so.

Euclidean geometry. The best-known modern axiomatization of Euclidean geometry, at least among philosophers, is that of Tarski (1959). To the primitives of affine geometry he adds the standard relation ≈ of congruence for line segments—technically formulated for quadruples of points. An example fitting clearly within Euclidean, and not merely affine, geometry is the spatial locative *near*. Thus, consider the sentence *The pencil is near the box*. We can introduce a metric d for Euclidean distance, and there are of course here several alternatives. It seems to us there is no single metrical relation that expresses nearness but several that may be considered satisfactory. The simplest in concept we feel is one that says simply that the minimum distance between the box and the pencil is less than some ϵ, say ϵ_1, which at the least is a function of the size of the two objects. We may express this relation as follows:

$$0 < \min_{p \in P, b \in B} d(p,b) < \epsilon_1(P,B).$$

A very different ϵ is needed to express nearness when the objects are quite different in size, as in *Philadelphia is near New York, but Pittsburgh is not*. It is worth noting that it is not clear that we want the negation of nearness to be simply the change in inequality. We might want to think of it in terms of something stronger, that is, having a second ϵ, ϵ_2 that is greater than ϵ_1. Thus, in that case we would formulate the underlying relation for the sentence *The pencil is not near the box* by the metrical relation:

$$\min_{p \in P, b \in B} d(p,b) \geq \epsilon_2(P,B).$$

It is even doubtful that a deterministic relation should be used. There is a long tradition in psychology, supported by a variety of empirical studies, that such threshold phenomena, exemplified by the meaning of *nearness*, should be represented by a probability distribution. Following this lead we would need to replace the metric $d(p,b)$ by a probabilistic metric.

The geometry of oriented physical space. To give a geometrical semantics for such simple spatial locatives as *on*, we need to move from Euclidean space to physical space, where what we mean by physical space in the present context is something quite restricted, namely, the addition of a preferred direction *up* and its converse *down*. Obviously, in ordinary experience the sense of up comes from gravitational pull. We can introduce it purely geometrically by introducing two distinguished points, α and β, with the understanding that α is vertically above β. Our restricted physical space is then based upon the quintuple $(A, B, \approx, \alpha, \beta)$. We are then in a position to define various standard intuitive notions of vertical and horizontal: A line or line segment is *vertical* if and only if it is parallel to $\alpha\beta$. Correspondingly, a line or line segment is *horizontal* if and only if it is perpendicular to a line that is parallel to $\alpha\beta$. (Note that in these definitions when we talk about a segment being perpendicular we of course have in mind the extension of the segment to the full line.) Next we can define a Euclidean plane as horizontal if and only if it is perpendicular to $\alpha\beta$. In this restricted physical space we have the obvious theorem: *Any point lies on a unique horizontal plane.* For a given point *a* we designate the unique horizontal plane *H(a)*. Notice that without introducing a point of view, i.e., station point, we have no natural orientation in a horizontal plane. We have in restricted physical space just the natural orientation of up and down or, more abstractly, the natural orientation of verticality. Using the concepts introduced, we can characterize the spatial relation *higher than*. Point *a* is higher than point *b* if and only it $a = \alpha$ and $b = \beta$, or either segment $a\alpha$ does not intersect *H(b)* or segment $b\beta$ does not intersect *H(a)*. We can now define the spatial locative *above* for points. Point *a* is above point *b* if and only if *a* is higher than *b* and the segment *ab* is approximately vertical. It is apparent that we can replace *approximately* by a metrical formulation in terms of a small angular disparity from the vertical, but no real gain in clarity would result. We use this same concept of approximate in defining *above* for bodies. There are three natural cases. Body *A* is above body *B* if and only if

(i) If *A* and *B* have approximately the same horizontal profile, then every point of *B* has some point of *A* above it,
(ii) if *A* has a larger horizontal profile than *B*, then every point of *B* has some point of *A* above it,
(iii) if *A* has a smaller horizontal profile than *B*, then every point of *A* is above some point of *B*.

Using now *above* we can define the simple geometrical sense of the spatial locative *on*.

A is on *B* if and only if (i) *A* and *B* have a boundary in common and (ii) every interior element of *A* is above some interior element of *B*.

On is an important case about which we need to say more. It is so widely used that it has many subtle aspects. For example, if a book is on the table in the sense just defined, and a second book is on this book in the sense just defined, we still are inclined to say that the second book is on the table, even though the definition just given is not satisfied because the second book and the table do not have a boundary in common. One way to solve this is to recognize that *on* as defined is ordinarily intransitive and to extend *on* to the relative product about four or five times. The number of elements is not very definite, but in most cases we would not use *on* when the number of intermediate elements exceeded four or five. Moreover, there are other still more subtle matters. The table is on the floor, we can all agree, but we are not inclined to apply transitive closure to say, therefore, that the book that is on the table is also on the floor. What blocks this simple closure where the same number of objects are involved, as in the case of saying that the second book on top of the first book is also on the table? We think that the main "change of pace" in concepts involved as we move from the table to the floor is that the boundary contact between the table and the floor is very limited, as opposed to the extensive flat contact between the book and the table. So this very limited contact breaks the use of the transitive closure. Another different kind of consideration is the relative size of the table and the book. We ordinarily apply *on* as the relative product of several elements only until we reach a sizable stable object like a table. We do not go further. It would be a Lewis Carroll-type joke to go on and say, *Indeed the table is on the floor but the floor is on the ground, so the book is on the ground.* By this point we get something that seems very counterintuitive. We do think that the relative size of the objects is as important as the minimal boundary contact between the table and the floor. We do not attempt a systematic analysis of these features in this article.

Projective geometry. We do not begin from scratch, as we might, in developing projective geometry, for in ordinary language and ordinary experience we commingle completely three-dimensional physical space and a perspective point of view. The topic of perspective itself is complicated and has a long history. We assume for this discussion the standard geometrical theory of perspective. A distinction is often introduced between "artist's perspective" and "geometrical perspective." In the former case, the artist attempts to draw the object as he sees it projected on the spherical surface of the retina of his eye, while geometrical perspective is very much what we see in a photograph, that is, projection onto a plane. Fortunately, except in wide angles of vision, the difference between the two is scarcely noticeable. What we have termed "artist's perspective" can also be given a geometrical treatment, but it is more complicated than that of projection onto a plane. Also, as already mentioned, for simplicity of formulation and because it covers most standard cases, we assume that the perspective point of view operates only in a horizontal plane, and not in any inclined plane. It is a standard psychological experiment, for example, in studying visual perception to have the viewer assume a horizontal position and to view perspective in the vertical plane. But this is not standard in most of ordinary experience, so that the restriction we impose is a natural one even if in no sense it is meant to cover all the cases that do occur. (For a good psychological analysis of the perception of vertical and horizontal distances in ordinary outdoor settings, see Higashiyama and Ueyama 1988.)

In the standard language of perspective the viewer is said to be at a *station point* and the projection takes place from that point. The station point is also often called the *point of view*. A fascinating thing about spatial locatives is that many which we think of initially in terms of three-dimensional physical space have a second interpretation in terms of relative position in the horizontal plane. For instance, in the case of *above* we have the following definition that covers the usage we have encountered in high school students' descriptions of place settings at a dinner table: A is *above* B (in the horizontal plane) if and only if A is further, in the same direction, from the station point than B. Two examples from our writing samples are *the cup above the plate* and *the glass above the knife*.[1] In the same spirit we can characterize the locative *in front of*: A is in front of B if and only if A is closer, in the same direction, to the station point than B. Among the familiar spatial locatives perhaps the ones most purely perspectival in nature are *to the left of* and *to the right of*, which need no further definition. But even in these apparently simple cases, complications lie close at hand. We ordinarily think of *to the left of* as denoting an ordering relation among objects seen from a particular point of view. However, when the occasion demands, we make a substantive out of the leftmost part of the field of view, as in *Hand me the book on the left*. The sense of spatial order from a point of view is still present but now not necessarily among given objects.

Geometries that include figures and shapes with orienting axes. Even when bodies are located in three-dimensional space with no sense of direction intrinsic to the space we still assign orienting axes and other geometrical distinctions to them. It is important to recognize that these distinctions are intrinsic to the body and remain with the body no matter what the body's overall orientation is in physical space. In ordinary talk, for example, the top of the table remains the top of the table even if the table is sitting upside down on the floor. There is a whole language about this intrinsic orientation of bodies and there are also many cases of spatial locatives that involve the use of a body's intrinsic orientation. For example, the instruction *Stand in front of the house* will in many instances be understood to refer to the side of the house where the main entrance is, the side that typically faces the street. This understanding of *in front of* would prevail no matter where the participants in the conversation were located. The object's intrinsic orientation predominates. There are times when such an understanding of *in front of* may be overridden, however, especially when — unlike the above example — the reference object is smaller than the located object. In these cases a prevailing point of view may predominate. Consider the expression *in front of the chair*. A chair typically has an intrinsic front and back, yet despite this the command *Stand in front of the chair* will generally receive two competing interpretations, one in which the person stands at the chair's own front, the other in which he or she stands on this side of the chair relative to some station point. (For a good analysis of how complicated the geometry of a chair is, see Strang 1982).

Geometry of classical space-time. For verbs of process or action, or for prepositional phrases locating events, it is often necessary to go beyond static three-dimensional physical space to four-dimensional space-time to provide the proper setting for their semantic analysis. Corresponding to oriented physical space, we use a four-dimensional affine space, and the sets of points simultaneous with any point is a three-dimensional physical space in the sense defined above.

It will perhaps be helpful to be more explicit about the primitive concepts. The four-dimensional space *(A,B)*, where *B* is the ternary relation of betweenness is affine. Note that the four-dimensional space-time is not Euclidean, for in classical space-time there is no comparison possible of the spatial distance between two points and the temporal distance between them. But the classical space-time is affine, i.e., the notion of being parallel is meaningful as well as the notion of linearity, both of which are definable in terms of betweenness. Now let a be any space-time point. Then $[a]$ is the set of all points simultaneous with a. For each point a the subspace $([a], B, \approx, \alpha_a, \beta_a)$ is a three-dimensional oriented physical space, as defined above.

Let us now look at some uses of spatial prepositions for which such space-time geometry is appropriate. *She was hurt in an auto accident.* This sentence implies a clear sense of spatial location, but what is also essential is the sequence of events occurring there. In many other uses of *in* with verbs of process or action, the prepositional phrase locates the action, even if a strict sense of containment between objects does not hold. *She peeled apples in the kitchen. He walked in the park. She wrote her essay in her bedroom.* In these three sentences we can give a strict geometrical sense of location for the process, actions, or events, but our original geometrical scheme must be enlarged to space-time. Convex closure of the kitchen in a certain space-time region will contain the space-time process of peeling the apples, but now spatial points are replaced by four-dimensional space-time points.

A way of seeing that space-time, not merely space, is required is to ask for the satisfiability or truth conditions of the kinds of sentences just considered. A mere point or region in space is not enough to confirm that an appropriate process took place, such as walking or peeling apples; a space-time region is required. Casually, we often think of evaluating the satisfaction of such commands just in terms of results, but obviously for full confirmation of the appropriate process taking place, examination only of end results is not enough.

Some sentences make the process aspect even more prominent, as in the following examples.

Go to the store, but walk in the shade.

Run under the bridge.

Walk back and forth in front of the entrance.

Watch the ball roll on the table.

The relatively unsatisfactory state of the current semantic analysis of process verbs is perhaps partly due to their involving a rich framework of concepts, of which we have sketched only the geometrical space-time part. The semantical analysis of these examples is rather complex. For this reason, various levels of abstraction are needed. In planning an action we often ignore the temporal aspects and consider only the spatial features. For example, in going to the store we may think only of the route in terms of a spatial map. The more detailed examples of actions of getting and putting considered later make such an abstraction.

Topology. We have reserved for last our discussion of spatial prepositions invariant under any homeomorphism, i.e., any continuous transformation, because of the much greater generality of topological concepts. All of the geometries considered up to this point assume at least affine space, which in many ways is part of the implicit background of most ordinary talk. Moreover, in the experience of a young child learning language, and its way around the world as well, topological, affine, metric, Euclidean, and projective notions are not nicely separated, but intermingled from the beginning.

All the same, as part of the geometrical analysis that is the focus of this article, it is germane to ask which common spatial prepositions are, in at least some of their uses, purely topological in character. The obvious example is the use of *in* to express enclosure in a two- or three-dimensional region. *The horse is in the south pasture* would ordinarily mean the horse was contained by a continuous fence in a certain two-dimensional region. *The button is in the box with a white lid* would ordinarily mean the button was enclosed by the continuous surface of the box. The same purely topological analysis does not hold for an object inside a box without a lid, the case discussed earlier. Notice that the ordinary language user surely shifts between these two kinds of enclosure without consciously noting it.

A less common example, but nicely illustrative of a topological concept, is found in the use of the compound preposition *over and under*. *In tying a knot, one piece of rope must go over and under the other*. Similar examples work for knitting and weaving. The familiar complex prepositional phrase *in contact with* expresses the topological concept of contiguity, and its negation, separation.

The metal is in contact with the wood at this point.

The difficulty is that the first gear is not in contact with the second.

A more prominent place for topology in linguistic analysis has been argued for by Thom (1970, 1973a, 1973b). In (1973a) especially he argues for a geometrical interpretation of language generally, and particularly of the traditional grammatical categories of noun, verb, and adjective, but these considerations go beyond the scope of this article. The idea most relevant here is set forth in the 1970 article. Thom proposes that the topological classification of structures, especially their geometrical points of singularity, be used to interpret the semantics of sentences describing various actions or events, e.g., *John throws a stone*, but in its present tentative development the classification does not seem to bear at all directly on the semantics of spatial prepositions.

Problem of context. No doubt exceptions to our proposed geometrical definitions of various spatial locatives have already occurred to the reader. The reason, we think, is obvious. Except for the most straightforward cases, the meaning of a spatial locative is only finally determined by the context of use. Consider again the case of *in*, for which we have already noted some difficulties of applying in an unrestricted manner our definition in terms of convex closure. (i) *She is in Italy*. How do we think about the convex closure of a country? (ii) *I saw joy in her countenance*. Even though visual appearance, as a way of expressing emotion, is the issue, we do not seem to have in the phrase *in her countenance* a literal geometrical use of *in*. (iii) *The infec-*

tion is in his arm. Here the geometrical sense of containment is kept, but a phenomenon rather than an object is contained in the arm, and so the definition of being a subset of the convex closure of the arm does not work. (iv) *Your daughter is sitting in the dirt.* In this case a geometrical relation is denoted, but not in terms of the basic meaning of *in.* (v) *The prisoner is in chains.* Again a geometrical relation is denoted but one more complicated than containment in the convex closure of an object.

The general sense of *in* is found in all these examples, but a correct and accurate semantic analysis must depend on many particular contextual features. Furthermore, these contextual features include the immediately adjacent words, the prior discourse, the perceptual scene in front of the speaker, writer, listener, or reader, etc. What applies to *in* applies to the other spatial locatives as well, as far as context is concerned. We touch briefly on some of these problems of context in the detailed examples that follow, and we return to the topic in our concluding remarks.

We conclude this section with a table showing the geometrical distinctions we have drawn and examples of prepositional use that fall in each category. Several of the examples will be discussed in detail in the next section.

TABLE 1

Kinds of geometry and examples of prepositional use.

Topology	*The pencil is in the box.* (box closed) *One piece of rope goes over and under the other.*
Affine geometry	*The pencil is in the box.* (box open) *Mary is sitting between José and María.*
Euclidean geometry	*The pencil is near the box.*
The geometry of oriented physical space	*The book is on the table. Adjust the lamp over the table.*
Projective geometry	*The post office is over the hill. The cup is to the left of the plate.*
Geometries that include figures and shapes with orienting axes	*The dog is in front of the house.*
Geometry of classical space-time	*She peeled apples in the kitchen.*

SOME DETAILED EXAMPLES

In this section we discuss two pairs of examples. The first pair uses the locative *near*, which was discussed earlier. Our aim is to delve a little deeper into the semantics of *near* and to place our inquiry within a specific semantic enterprise, that of instructable robots. As we have done in other articles, we ask what would be required for a robot to interpret commands addressed it in a natural language such as English. The second pair of examples uses the locative *over*. Here our aim is to show how an interesting problem posed by Cresswell can be solved within the geometrical framework we propose. For both pairs of examples, we also take a look at some aspects of the interaction between syntax and semantics.

These examples bring out an important geometrical feature of spatial prepositions. There is, as in other aspects of geometry, a contrast between a general property, e.g., being the bisector of a given line segment, and the particular procedure or process by which the property is generated or verified. This distinction, which, within the history of geometry, comes to the distinction between theorems and constructions, was already important and the subject of much discussion in ancient Greek geometry. Here the distinction is evident in the contrast between our earlier general analysis of the preposition *near* and the two procedures for *near* given below which arise from the contrasting actions of getting and putting.

Much of our preceding discussion has contained expressions that describe static locations — *The red book is next to the blue book, Find the pencil in the drawer, He chopped onions at the sink*. In contrast, prepositions are often used in expressions that describe a change of location — *The dog went under the table, Put the red book on the blue book, Go around the table*. This distinction is a familiar one in studies of the prepositions in English but the change-of-location cases tend to be neglected. We will examine both kinds of prepositional usage in our first pair of examples.

The robot we feature in our discussion consists of a manipulator (somewhat approximating the human arm in its shape and form) equipped with a simple gripper. For our remarks on spatial expressions, the only details of robot control and operation we need to introduce are the following. (For further details and a more extended discussion of the specific problems involved in natural-language communication with a robot, see Suppes and Crangle [1988] and Crangle [1989].) The robot system has several primitive actions: *open-gripper, close-gripper, move-gripper-to-region, gripper-back, gripper-up, move-gripper-direction-distance*, and so on. From these primitive actions we build up higher-level basic actions. Three examples are PUT, GET, and LOCATE. We describe each briefly.

> The PUT action takes two arguments: *item* and *region*. As suggested by these labels, the first argument specifies what is to be placed by the manipulator and the second specifies where it is to be placed. The region must be a horizontal surface. Note that we have a target *region*, not point, because natural-language spatial expressions very seldom refer to specific points in space. Consider the expressions *on the floor, under the canopy, near the door*, for instance. These expressions do not on their

GEOMETRICAL SEMANTICS FOR SPATIAL PREPOSITIONS 413

own specify any one point but rather a region within which any one point could be selected.

The GET action takes one argument, *item*, which specifies the item that must be located and grasped.

The LOCATE action takes one argument, *item*, which specifies the item whose position must be determined.

A few further remarks are needed on the PUT and GET actions. The PUT action checks that the item specified by its first argument is already in the gripper. If it is not, the GET action is performed. The gripper is then moved to a point immediately above the nearest point of the target region. The gripper is then opened and moved back, thus allowing the item in its grasp to come to rest on the surface.

The GET action uses the LOCATE action to locate the item specified by its argument, moves the gripper to that item, opens the gripper, positions it in the appropriate grasp configuration for that object (a book, a cup, and a fork will each need to be grasped differently, for instance), closes the gripper and then moves the gripper up some small distance with the item firmly in its grasp.

Now consider the following pair of English commands addressed to this robot:

Put the knife near the plate.

Get the knife near the plate.

In the first command, the expression *near the plate* describes the target region for the robot's placement of the knife. In the second command, the expression *near the plate* describes a spatial restriction that helps the robot select the knife it must get. In rough terms, the robot's interpretation of the commands is PUT(the-knife, near-the-plate) and GET(the-knife-that-is-near-the-plate).

We have of course chosen the basic robot actions PUT and GET precisely for the verbs *put* and *get* of our examples. These verbs are not analyzed further in our discussion but we emphasize that it is possible and indeed necessary to do so in general. The reason we adopt this level of analysis is that our interest here is in the locative *near* and the semantic constraints it is subject to in the context of the actions of putting and getting.

We will use square braces to show denotations; [*get*] therefore indicates the denotation of the word *get*. We write GET(*item*) and PUT(*item, region*) for the two robot actions that are the denotations of the verbs *get* and *put*. Further, we have [*the plate*] = S, the set of all plates in the physical environment, and [*the knife*] = K, the set of all knives in the physical environment.

The question of interest now is what is the denotation of *near*? We answer the question by asking what it needs to be for the interpretation of the *get*-command and the *put*-command. For the *get*-command, the denotation of *the knife near the plate* must be some $k \in K$ such that for some particular $s \in$

S the minimum distance between k and s is less than some ϵ. (This description follows from our earlier discussion of *near*.) We define a function g_{near} of two arguments to select this element. Intuitively, the function ensures that some minimal distance ϵ exists between pairs of plates and knives if the one item in the pair is said to be near the other. When the phrase refers unambiguously in the given physical environment at the time the phrase is used, only one pair satisfies the requirement. It is the knife in that pair that is selected as the denotation of *the knife near the plate*. The denotation of *the knife near the plate* will thus be $g_{\text{near}}([\textit{the knife}], [\textit{the plate}])$ where

$$g_{\text{near}}(K,S) = \{k : 0 < D(s,k) < \epsilon \text{ and } s \in S \text{ and } k \in K\}.$$

We define D in terms of the metric d given in our earlier discussion of the word *near*. That is, the distance D between two bodies s and k is the minimum distance d between the points s_i of s and k_j of k.

$$D(s,k) = \min_{s_i \in s, k_j \in k} d(s_i, k_j) .$$

(Keep in mind that S is the set of plates, K the set of knives, and s and k are individual plates and knives.) As before, we assume that ϵ is at the least a function of the size of the two bodies s and k. Note that the phrase *the knife near the plate* is most likely to refer unambiguously if only one plate had already been selected as the denotation of *the plate*. Often, this condition does indeed hold; either there is only one plate in the environment or a particular plate is already established as the focus of attention at the time the phrase is used. It is important to note too, however, that we do not want to define g_{near} in terms of some one particular reference object (i.e., some one plate in this case) under the assumption that there is always a unique reference object. There might be several plates and several knives but only one knife that is near a plate. The function g_{near} must be defined over sets.

Turning now to the *put*-command, the denotation of *near the plate* must be some region defined with respect to the geometry of the plate. We define a function f_{near} for this purpose. Then $[\textit{near the plate}] = f_{\text{near}}([\textit{the plate}])$ where the value of the function f_{near} is the region bordering the plate uniformly in the plane of the flat surface holding the plate, with the border being in width no more than the radius of the plate. Note that the size of the region is directly related to the size of the plate. Were we to take into account plates other than round ones—square and oval plates are not unusual—we would redescribe the computation to take shape into account. The function f_{near} takes a set as its argument. This set contains just one element when the prepositional noun phrase refers unambiguously at the time it is used.

We now give tree diagrams for the interpretation of our two commands. An interpretation tree is generated from a grammar that has been extended by appending to each production rule at most one semantic function. This function stipulates how a node in the tree obtains its denotation from the denotations of its daughter nodes. In our trees, the category symbols at the nodes are VP for verb phrase, V for verb, NP for noun phrase, N for noun, DA for

GEOMETRICAL SEMANTICS FOR SPATIAL PREPOSITIONS

definite article, Nom for nominal, and Adv for adverbial. $Prep_D$ stands for preposition of distance, the preposition appearing in the *get*-command, and $Prep_R$ for preposition of region, the preposition in the *put*-command. To the right of the colon at each node in the tree we show the denotation at the node.

The grammar fragment needed to generate the two interpretation trees is as follows. We use the subscripted capitals U_1, U_2 for sets of objects (all objects in a set are of the same kind), and the mnemonics *it* and *reg* for single-element sets of objects and single-element sets of two-dimensional regions respectively. Note that the semantic functions associated with the two verb-phrase rules and the two preposition rules use the operation of function application.

Production Rule	*Semantic Function*
VP → V Nom Adv	[VP] = [V] ([Nom],[Adv])
VP → V NP	[VP] = [V] ([NP])
Nom → DA N	[NOM] = [N]
NP → Nom_1 $Prep_D$ Nom_2	[NP] = $[Prep_D]$ ($[Nom_1]$,$[Nom_2]$)
Adv → $Prep_R$ Nom	[Adv] = $[Prep_R]$ ([Nom])
V → get	[V] = GET(*it*)
V → put	[V] = PUT(*it, reg*)
$Prep_D$ → near	$[Prep_D]$ = g_{near} (U_1, U_2)
$Prep_R$ → near	$[Prep_R]$ = f_{near} (U_1)
N → knife	[N] = K = the set of knives
N → plate	[N] = S = the set of plates
DA → the	

Get the knife near the plate

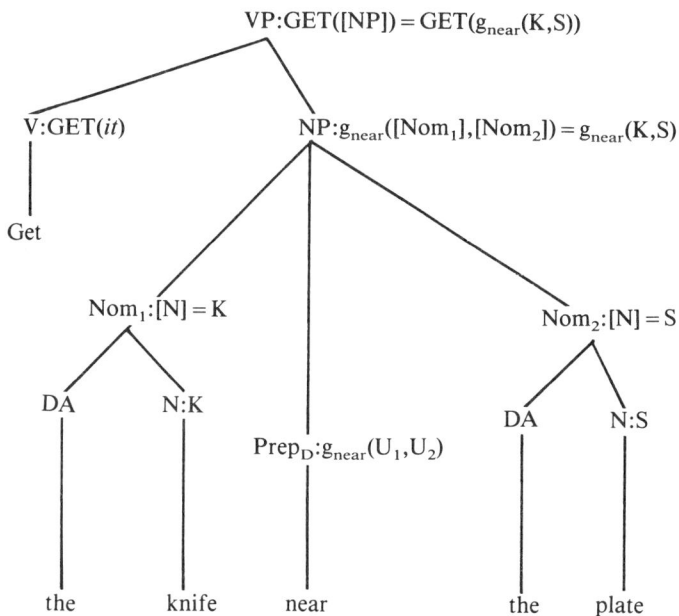

Put the knife near the plate

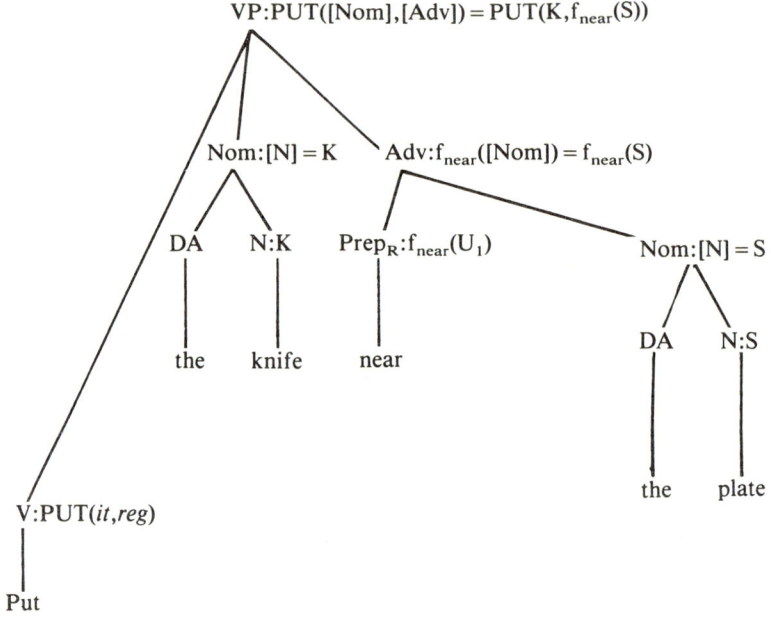

We make one final set of remarks on the preposition *near* in the command *Put the knife near the plate*. Although we have shown the denotation of *near* to be a function of one argument, [*the plate*], there is good reason to think that it should in fact be a function of both [*the plate*] and [*the knife*], for we ordinarily think that the size, shape, and, particularly, orienting axes of the object to be placed have something to do with correct placement near the reference object. A geometry that includes figures and shapes with orienting axes would therefore be required, not merely Euclidean geometry.

We now consider another pair of English expressions. This time they are both simple noun phrases but ones that pose an interesting problem. Our concern in this discussion is to make explicit just a few of the many contextual factors that come into play to help specify the appropriate interpretation of the English. We emphasize that the contextual details come into play at the lexical level, that is, at the level of the individual locatives. We emphasize this point because appeals to context are not new within the philosophy of language but the more usual assumption is that contextual factors operate at the sentence level. Our assumption is that they intrude at the lexical level. The example we use here is the word *over*. What is particularly interesting about this word is that an adequate account of its use, even in the restricted cases we consider, requires a geometrical framework like the one we have given in this article.

At first glance, several different uses of *over* seem hard to reconcile. In *the lamp over the table* we see a lamp hanging vertically above some portion of the table. And in *the axe over his head* we see an axe held in place vertically above someone's neck. However, in *the post office over the hill* we see the post office on the other side of the hill relative to some reference point roughly in the same horizontal plane. The simple notion of vertically above is not at work here but, at least in part, the notion of horizontally across and to the other side of. In geometrical terms, the basic idea is that of a point of view (or station point) in the horizontal plane and a body whose far side relative to the station point defines a point along the line of projection.

It is useful at this stage to introduce Cresswell's discussion of the word *over* because he ends his discussion with this puzzle—how to reconcile the two uses of *over*—that we believe can be solved. We emphasize that it is worth reconciling the two uses not because we expect there to be some one overarching notion of *over* that should prevail but because there are cases, and our pair of noun phrases presents such a case, where the surface structure of the *over*-expression does not indicate which use of *over* is intended. For our interpretation trees, therefore, we require there to be the one denotation of *over* that suffices for both uses.

Cresswell suggests that for many prepositions (he discusses *across, through, along, around, beyond, past, behind,* and *over*) the basic semantical idea is that of a hypothetical journey which an observer would have to make to be 'where the action is' as he puts it. With *over*, however, Cresswell feels forced to distinguish between a journey and a non-journey sense of the word, a prime example for him of a non-journey sense being *the lamp over the table*. But in fact it is possible to reconcile the two uses of the word if the primacy of *verticality* is acknowledged. In terms of Cresswell's journeys, the journey involved in the interpretation of *the lamp over the table* would start at the table, proceed in the direction vertically up, and finish at the lamp. The journey involved in the interpretation of *the post office over the hill* would start on one side of the hill and move vertically up then horizontally across to the other side of the hill. It is important not to neglect the vertical component of this journey because the journey is not through the hill but up to some higher point and then to the other side. The reference object in these cases typically forms some barrier which must be traversed without being penetrated.

In terms of our geometrical distinctions, these remarks point out that *over* must be interpreted within oriented physical space, not simple Euclidean geometry, and in fact that principles of projective geometry may also have to be used. The puzzle that *over* then presents is the choice between the simple relation *vertically above the reference object* and the compound relation *vertically up from a station point and horizontally across to the other side of the reference object*, which may be expressed as the choice between the geometry of oriented physical space and projective geometry. We will use h_1 for the first, simple relation and h_2 for the second. h_1 will in fact be a function of two arguments, the reference object and the located object, and h_2 will be a function of three arguments, the reference object, the located object, and the station point.

The choice between h_1 and h_2 can be resolved by taking into account more of the context than Cresswell did. Consider the idea, now standard within many studies of the locatives, that for expressions of the form *the x <locative> the y*, it is generally the case that *y* is large relative to *x* and less mobile than *x*. The idea has commonsense appeal in that if *y* is to be used to locate *x*, its greater size and relative fixity would increase the likelihood of its own location being known beforehand. In the case of *over*, when this condition holds, the natural reading of *x over y* is one in which *x* is *vertically up from some station point and horizontally across to the other side of y*, our relation h_2. If the condition does not hold — that is, *x* and *y* are of the same general size and exhibit similar degrees of fixity — *over* is more naturally interpreted using the simple relation of *vertically above*, our relation h_1. Returning to our earlier examples, in *the axe over his head* we have two objects of similar size and degree of fixity, whereas in *the post office over the hill* the reference object is larger than the located object. And in other examples, *the dog over the road*, for instance, the reference object is considerably less mobile than the located object.

In our previous pair of examples, the commands to a robot, we saw how factors such as size and shape of the reference object came into play to specify the appropriate interpretation of *near*. The function f_{near} computed a region the dimensions of which depended on the size and shape of the plate that was specified as its argument. And the function g_{near} computed a distance relation that was defined in terms of the size of both the reference and located objects. Here we have similar contextual factors at work to select the appropriate geometrical computation for *over* — whether the simple one of vertically above the reference object or the more complex one of vertically up from a station point and horizontally across to the other side of the reference object. It is important to note that there are no clues in the surface structure of the two expressions as to which geometrical computation is appropriate. Both are simple noun phrases consisting of a preposition flanked on either side by a nominal. Another point to note is that the station point is itself often fixed by the wider context. The appropriate response to the command *Go to the house over the river* will depend on where the speaker and hearer are and what reference location — the speaker's or the hearer's or some other point altogether — is established in the conversation. Often the command itself will specify that information, as in *Go to the house over the river from you* or *Go to the house over the river from Sue's cabin*.

In the interpretation trees for *the lamp over the table* and *the post office over the hill*, we therefore show the denotation of *over* to be the following function of three arguments: $H_{over}(R_1, L_1, v)$ where R_1 is a structure including the set of objects one of which is intended to function as the reference object,

GEOMETRICAL SEMANTICS FOR SPATIAL PREPOSITIONS 419

L_1 is a structure whose set of objects has the property that one of them is to be located, and v is a contextually determined point of view.

The value of the function H_{over} is one of the two functions h_1 and h_2 depending on its arguments R_1 and L_1. Two comments are needed. First, the third argument, v, must still be included because it will, as pointed out above, sometimes be set in the language itself, as in *the post office over the hill from you*. Second, we need structures not ordinary sets because structures can extensionally represent properties of the objects. The properties we are interested in are those already mentioned, namely, size and relative mobility.

$$H_{over}(R_1,L_1,v) = \begin{cases} h_1(R_1,L_1) & \text{if } R_1\text{-type objects and } L_1\text{-type objects are of the same general size and degree of fixity} \\ h_2(R_1,L_1,v) & \text{if } R_1\text{-type objects are much larger than } L_1\text{-type objects or much less mobile} \end{cases}$$

The denotations of *the lamp over the table* and *the post office over the hill* are thus $h_1([the\ table], [the\ lamp])$ and $h_2([the\ hill], [the\ post\ office],v)$ respectively. As with the functions f_{near} and g_{near}, h_1 and h_2 must be defined in terms of sets of objects. These sets will in many instances be single-element sets.

We introduce the category $Prep_O$ for the preposition *over*. We regard *post office* as a compound noun and give it the category N without further comment. We add to the grammar fragment given earlier the following rules.

Production Rule	*Semantic Function*
NP → Nom$_1$ Prep$_O$ Nom$_2$	[NP] = [Prep $_O$] ([Nom$_2$],[Nom$_1$],v)
Prep$_O$ → over	[Prep$_O$] = $H_{over}(R_1,L_1,v)$
N → lamp	[N] = J = the set of lamps
N → table	[N] = T = the set of tables
N → post office	[N] = Q = the set of post offices
N → hill	[N] = W = the set of hills

Here are the two interpretation trees. At the top of each tree we show the result of applying the H_{over} function to its arguments.

the lamp over the table

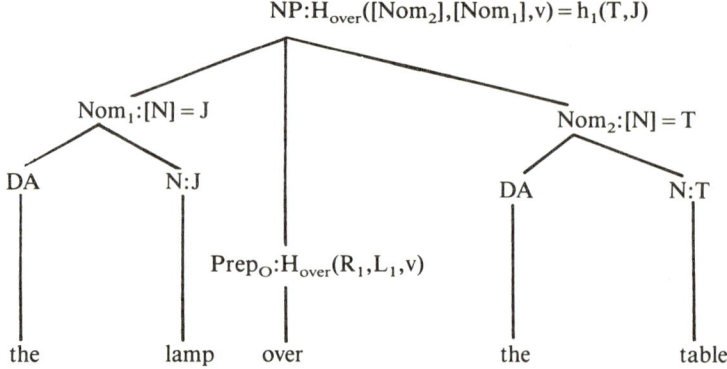

the post office over the hill

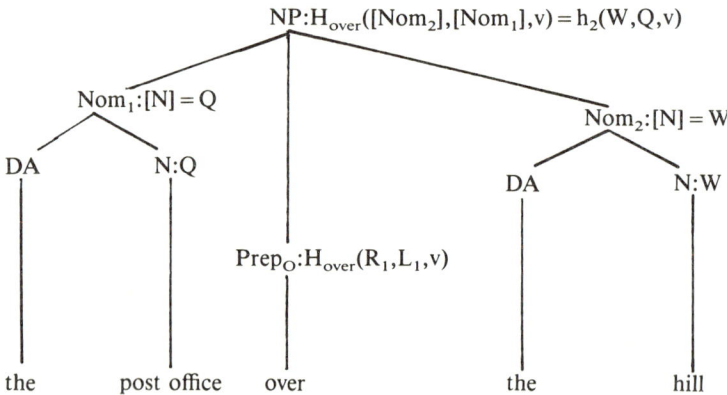

CONCLUDING REMARKS

Although this article is full of detailed comments and suggestions, it is far from offering a worked-out semantic theory of spatial prepositions. Much additional work is needed to complete the geometrical analysis begun. Moreover, here, as in related papers we have written, we are sensitive to the importance of context, the theory of which is only in the early stages of development.

One important aspect of context we have not utilized here, but hope to in the future, is the introduction of naive physics, i.e., the physics of ordinary experience (Hayes 1978, 1985). Physics, compared to geometry, is the study of context. *This ball will not roll into the pocket because it is blocked by the red ball.* The pure spatial geometry of the ball is untouched by context. The dynamics of its motion is completely determined by it.

The full meaning of many spatial prepositions requires physics as well as geometry. We have already noted that many uses of *on* imply a physical notion of support. In *John ran into the tree and hurt his head*, the meaning of *into* is closer to the physical concept of impact than the geometrical concept of enclosure, as in *Mary ran into the house*. But more extended analysis of the necessary physical concepts we must leave for another occasion.

Notes

*The authors acknowledge the support of the Spencer Foundation in the work described in the article.
1. The writing samples we refer to were collected as part of a study sponsored by the Spencer Foundation on the writing of high school students in the San Francisco Bay Area, 1986-88.

References

Bennett, D. C. 1975. *Spatial and Temporal Uses of English Prepositions: An Essay in Stratificational Semantics.* London.
Crangle, C., and P. Suppes. 1987. Context-fixing semantics for instructable robots. *International Journal of Man-Machine Studies* 27:371-400.
Crangle, C. 1989. On saying 'stop' to a robot. *Language and Communication* 9(1).
Cresswell, M. J. 1978. Prepositions and points of view. *Linguistics and Philosophy* 2:1-41.
Hayes, P. J. 1978. The naive physics manifesto. In *Expert Systems in the Microelectronic Age*, edited by D. Michie, 262-70. Edinburgh.
Hayes, P. J. 1985. The second naive physics manifesto. In *Formal Theories of the Commonsense World*, edited by J. Hobbs and R. Moore, 1-36. Norwood, N.J.
Herskovits, A. 1986. *Language and Spatial Cognition.* New York.
Higashiyama, A., and E. Ueyama. 1988. The perception of vertical and horizontal distances in outdoor settings. *Perception & Psychophysics* 44(2):151-56.
Strang, G. 1982. The width of a chair. *The American Mathematical Monthly* 89:529-34.
Suppes, P. 1972. Some open problems in the philosophy of space and time. *Synthese* 24:298-316.
Suppes, P., and C. Crangle. 1988. Context fixing semantics for the language of action. In *Human Agency: Language, Duty, and Value*, edited by J. Dancy, J. Moravcsik, and C. Taylor. Stanford, Calif.
Suppes, P., D. H. Krantz, R. D. Luce, and A. Tversky. In press. *Foundations of Measurement*, Vol. II: *Geometrical, Threshold and Probabilistic Representations.* New York.
Talmy, L. 1983. How language structures space. In *Spatial Orientation: Theory, Research, and Application*, edited by H. L. Pick, Jr., and L. P. Acredolo, 225-82. New York.
Tarski, A. 1959. What is elementary geometry? In *The Axiomatic Method, with Special Reference to Geometry and Physics*, edited by L. Henkin, P. Suppes, and A. Tarski, 16-29. Amsterdam.

Thom, R. 1970. Topologie et linguistique. In *Essays on Topology and Related Topics (Memoires dedicated to Georges de Rham)*, edited by A. Haefliger and R. Narasimhan, 226-48. New York.

Thom, R. 1973a. Langage et catastrophes: Eléments pour une sémantique topologique. In *Dynamical Systems*, edited by M. Peixoto, 619-54. New York.

Thom, R., 1973b. Sur la typologie des langues naturelles essai d'interprétation psycholinguistique. In *The Formal Analysis of Natural Languages. Proceedings of the First International Conference*, edited by M. Gross, M. Halle, and M.-P. Schützenberger, 233-48. Paris.

Contributors

Felicia Ackerman, Department of Philosophy, Brown University
Laird Addis, Department of Philosophy, University of Iowa
Alan Berger, Department of Philosophy, Brandeis University
Simon Blackburn, Pembroke College, Oxford University
Phillip Bricker, Department of Philosophy, Yale University
Hector-Neri Castañeda, Department of Philosophy, Indiana University
Michael Devitt, Department of Philosophy, University of Maryland
Keith Donnellan, Department of Philosophy, University of California, Los Angeles
Graeme Forbes, Department of Philosophy, Tulane University
Igal Kvart, Philosophy Department, Hebrew University
Ernest LePore, Department of Philosophy, Rutgers University
Barry Loewer, Department of Philosophy, Rutgers University
Genoveva Marti, Department of Philosophy, University of Washington
Julius Moravcsik, Department of Philosophy, Stanford University
Joseph Owens, Department of Philosophy, University of Minnesota
Christopher Peacocke, Magdalen College, Oxford University
Mark Richard, Department of Philosophy, Tufts University
Avrum Stroll, Department of Philosophy, University of California, San Diego
Patrick Suppes, Department of Philosophy, Stanford University
Jonathan Wilwerding, Department of Philosophy, University College London
Crispin Wright, Department of Philosophy, University of Michigan
Andrzej Zabludowski, Department of Philosophy, University of New Mexico

Peter A. French is Lennox Distinguished Professor of Philosophy at Trinity University in San Antonio, Texas. He has taught at the University of Minnesota, Morris, and has served as Distinguished Research Professor in the Center for the Study of Values at the University of Delaware. His books include *The Scope of Morality* (1980), *Ethics in Government* (1982), and *Collective and Corporate Responsibility* (1980). He has published numerous articles in the philosophical journals. **Theodore E. Uehling, Jr.**, is professor of philosophy at the University of Minnesota, Morris. He is the author of *The Notion of Form in Kant's Critique of Aesthetic Judgment* and articles on the philosophy of Kant. **Howard K. Wettstein** is professor of philosophy at the University of California, Riverside. He has taught at the University of Notre Dame and the University of Minnesota, Morris, and has served as a visiting associate professor of philosophy at the University of Iowa and Stanford University. He is the author of *Has Semantics Rested on a Mistake? and Other Essays* (Stanford University Press, forthcoming).